VISUAL WEB DATABASE INTERACTIVE COURSE

GUNNIT S. KHURANA, SATWANT S. GADHOK

WAITE GROUP PRESS™

A Division of

Sams Publishing

Corte Madera, CA

PUBLISHER • Mitchell Waite
ASSOCIATE PUBLISHER • Charles Drucker

ACQUISITIONS MANAGER • Susan Walton

EDITORIAL DIRECTOR • John Crudo
PROJECT EDITOR • Andrea Rosenberg
CONTENT EDITOR • Russ Jacobs
TECHNICAL EDITOR • Amy Sticksel
COPY EDITOR • Deirdre Greene/Creative Solutions

PRODUCTION DIRECTOR • Julianne Ososke
PRODUCTION MANAGER • Cecile Kaufman
PRODUCTION EDITORS • Cameron Carey, Brice Gosnell
COVER DESIGNER • Sestina Quarequio
DESIGNER • Karen Johnston
COVER ILLUSTRATION • Robert Dougherty
CHAPTER OPENER ILLUSTRATION • ©Stephen Hunt/Image Bank
PRODUCTION • Rick Bond, Jena Brandt, Chris Livengood, Andrew Stone
INDEXER • Cheryl A. Jackson

Printed in the United States of America
97 98 99 • 10 9 8 7 6 5 4 3 2 1

Library of Congress Cataloging-in-Publication Data
    Khurana, Gunnit S., 1969-
        Visual Basic Web Database interactive course / Gunnit S. Khurana.
            p.   cm.
        Includes index.
        ISBN 1-57169-097-2
        1. Client/server computing.   2. World Wide Web (Information
    retrieval system) 3. Micrrosoft Visual BASIC. 4. Database
    management. I. Title.
    QA76.9.C55K49 1997   97-19465
        005.75 ' 8--dc21   CIP

www.waite.com/ezone
eZone Guided Tour

The Interactive Course title in your hands provides you with an unprecedented training system. *Visual Basic Web Database Interactive Course* is everything you're used to from Waite Group Press: thorough, hands-on coverage of this important, cutting-edge programming language. There is far more, however, to the Interactive Course than the pages you are now holding. Using your Internet connection, you also get access to the eZone where you'll find dedicated services designed to assist you through the book and make sure you really understand the subject.

FREE TUTORS, TESTING, CERTIFICATION, AND RESOURCES

The eZone provides a host of services and resources designed to help you work through this book. If you get hung up with a particular lesson, all you have to do is ask an online mentor, a live expert in the subject you're studying. A mailing list lets you exchange ideas and hints with others taking the same course. A resource page links you to the hottest related Web sites, and a monthly newsletter keeps you up to date with eZone enhancements and industry developments. Figure 1 shows the page.

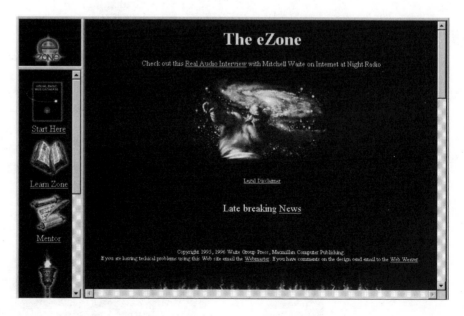

Figure 1
The eZone home page...a whole new way to learn

You'll also be able to work toward a certificate of completion. You can take lesson quizzes online, receive an immediate grade, and track your progress through the course. The chapters are available online, too, so that you can refer to them when you need to. Once you've finished the course with a passing grade, you can print a personalized certificate of completion, suitable for framing.

Best of all, there's no additional cost for all of these services. They are included in the price of the book. Once you journey into the eZone, you'll never want to go back to traditional book learning.

EXPLORING THE EZONE

You'll find the eZone on the World Wide Web. Fire up your Web browser and enter the following site:

`http://www.waite.com/ezone`

From there, click the eZone icon and you're on your way.

NOTE

If your browser does not support frames, or if you prefer frameless pages, click the *No Frames* link insteadof the eZone icon. Your browser must also support "cookies." Interactive Course titles that come with a CD-ROM include a copy of Microsoft's Internet Explorer browser (version 3.01), which supports frames and cookie technology. These books include an appendix to help you with browser installation, setup, and operation.

Navigating the eZone

When you enter the eZone, the eZone home page, shown in Figure 1, appears. As you can see in Figure 2, the screen is divided into three frames. The eZone icon in the

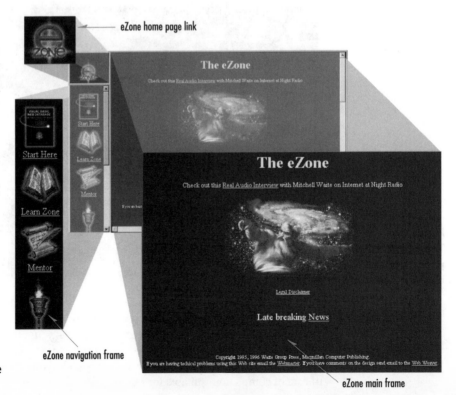

Figure 2
There are three frames in the eZone

top-left frame is always visible. This icon is a link back to the eZone home page. No matter where you are, you can always find your way home by clicking this icon. Beneath the eZone icon is a navigation frame containing several icons. Each of these icons links to an area of the eZone. You'll learn about each of these areas as you read through this guide.

The largest frame on the page is the main frame. This is where you'll find the information. Scroll down this frame and you'll see text-based links to the eZone areas. Keep going and you'll find the latest eZone news and information, updated regularly. Be sure to check out this information each time you enter the eZone.

Start Here

Click the *Start Here* icon in the navigation frame. This takes you to the Getting Started page where you'll find different sets of instructions. Your options are:

```
I am a GUEST and visiting the EZONE.
I HAVE the EZONE BOOK and I am ready to start the course.
I want to BUY an EZONE COURSE and get my Book.
```

Clicking on these options provides instructions for how to sign on as a guest, register for a course for which you have a book, or sign up for a course and order the corresponding book.

In the next couple of pages, you'll see how to explore the eZone as a guest, register yourself, enroll in a course, and take advantage of the many service areas provided at no additional charge.

Signing on as a Guest

On your first visit to the eZone, consider signing on as a guest, even if you have a book and are eager to get started. Signing on as guest lets you roam the eZone and familiarize yourself with its various areas and features before setting any options. You can view the first chapter of any available course and take the quizzes for that chapter (although Guests' scores aren't saved).

You can ask support questions, view the latest news, and even view the FAQs for a course. Until you register, you can't ask the mentors any questions, sign up for the eZone newsletter, or access the resource links page, but there's still plenty of stuff to check out as a Guest.

To explore the eZone as a Guest, click the *Learn* icon in the navigation frame or on the word *Learn* at the bottom of the main frame. The first time you do this, the Registration Page appears. As a Guest, you can ignore this form.

Just click the *Guest* link, and the Course Matrix appears. From here, you can navigate the eZone in the same manner as registered course members. Remember, however, that access for Guests is limited.

THE INITIATION ZONE

Once you're comfortable navigating the eZone, we know you'll be eager to start learning and taking advantage of this cutting-edge training system.

The first thing you have to do is create an entry for yourself in the eZone records by registering. Click the Initiation icon in the navigation frame or on the Initiate link at the bottom of the main frame, and you move into the *Initiate Zone*, shown in Figure 3.

Click here to begin
eZone registration

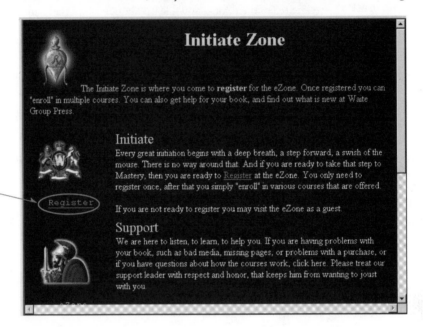

Figure 3
Go to the Initiate
Zone to start your
training

The Initiate Zone contains three options: *Initiate (Register)*, *Support*, and *Announcements and What's New*. Use the *Support* option to report difficulties you are having with your Interactive Course material and services: problems with the book or CD-ROM, trouble getting eZone to work, whatever you need. This is not, however, where you'll ask questions related to the course content. Answering those questions is the mentor's job. The *Announcements and What's New* option lets you quickly find out about the latest additions and deletions at the eZone. It also contains information about upcoming courses.

Initiate (Register)

But what you want right now is the *Initiate (Register)* option. Click the *Register* link and a registration form appears.

NOTE

You don't need a book to register in the eZone; in fact, you can pre-register and order an Interactive Course title while you're online. When your copy arrives, you'll already have a recognized password and ID, so that you can enroll immediately in your course of choice.

You need to fill out the registration form completely. Click inside each text box, then type in the appropriate information; pressing the TAB key cycles you through these text fields. In addition to a little information about yourself, you'll need to enter the following:

`Requested User ID` — Type the name you'd like to use online.

`Password (5-8 Characters)` — Type the password you'd like to use online.

`Password (Verify)` — Retype your selected password, to be sure it's properly recorded.

Once you've supplied all the information, click the *Register* button to submit the form to the eZone's data banks. A confirming message lets you know that you've successfully registered. Registration is important. If you don't register, you can't take advantage of the full power of the eZone.

Entering the eZone as a Registered User

Once you've registered, you'll use your unique ID and password to enter the eZone. Next time you enter the eZone, you need only click the *Learn Zone* icon in the navigation frame or the *Learn* link in the main frame. A simple two-line form pops up, allowing you to type in the user ID and password you created when you registered.

THE LEARN ZONE

Now that you're registered, it's time to get down to business. Much of the course work is done in the Learn Zone, shown in Figure 4. To get here, click the *Learn* icon in the navigation frame.

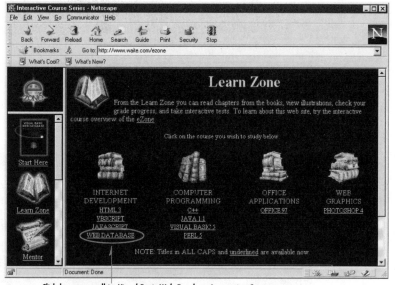

Figure 4
Use the Course Matrix in the Learn Zone to select courses

Click here to enroll in *Visual Basic Web Database Interactive Course*

The Course Matrix

When you enter the Learn Zone, you'll see lists of courses and certification programs. This is called the Course Matrix, and it provides a way to select the various eZone cours-es. Under each discipline—such as Internet Development, Computer Programming, Office

Applications, or Web Graphics—are a list of core courses. To select the *Visual Basic Web Database Interactive Course* using this Course Matrix, click on Web Database (the titles in underlined white letters are currently available). In a moment, a three-columned Chapters Grid appears.

Verification

The first time you select a specific course, you must enroll. You'll need a copy of the book to do so. You will be asked to provide a specific word from the book. This verifies that you have the proper book for the selected course. The verification process uses the familiar page-line-word formula; in other words, you'll need to look and enter a word from a specified line of text on a specified page of your book. Click your mouse in the text box and type the specified word to verify that you have the course book.

Passing Percentage

You can also set a minimum passing percentage for your course. This determines what percentage of test questions you need to answer correctly in order to pass the course. The percentage is preset at 70%, but you can select 50%, 60%, 70%, 80%, 90%, or 100%.

To set a minimum passing percentage, click the text box for this option to see a list of choices, then click the option you prefer. Once you've typed in the correct word and set the desired passing percentage, click the *Verify* button to enroll in the course. The Chapters Grid appears.

The Chapters Grid

The Chapters Grid, like the one featured in Figure 5, lets you select topics and quizzes for your course, while keeping track of your progress.

Click here to go back to the Course Matrix

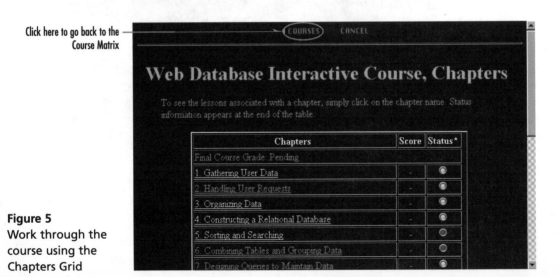

Figure 5
Work through the course using the Chapters Grid

The Chapters column lists the chapters of the book; clicking on a chapter lets you view and select its lessons. The middle column, Score, shows your current grade for the chapter (as a percentage). The Status column uses a colored indicator to let you know with a glance whether you've passed (green), failed (red), are still working through (yellow), or have not yet started (gray) a particular chapter.

Click a chapter, and the Lessons Grid appears for that chapter. (Remember, only Chapter 1 is enabled for Guests.)

The Lessons Grid

As you take the course, the Lessons Grid (Figure 6) tracks your performance within each chapter. You can use it to read a chapter lesson or take a lesson quiz.

Click here to go back to the Chapter Grid

Click here to go back to the Course Matrix

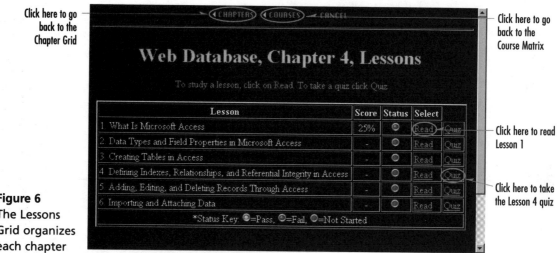

Click here to read Lesson 1

Click here to take the Lesson 4 quiz

Figure 6
The Lessons Grid organizes each chapter

To read a lesson, click the *Read* link in the Select column. To take a quiz, click the *Quiz* link in the Select column. The LEDs in the Status column show whether you've passed (green), failed (red), or not yet started (gray) each quiz. A percentage grade appears for each completed quiz in the Score column.

Most likely, you'll achieve the best results if you read through the lessons, then take the quiz. If you prefer, however, you can jump directly to the corresponding quiz, without reading through the lesson.

Testing

Each quiz is a multiple-choice questionnaire. In some courses, there is only one answer to each question, but other courses allow more than one answer. Read the instructions for your course so you know how the quizzes work.

Taking Quizzes

To answer a quiz question, click the checkbox next to the answer you want to choose. When you've answered all the questions, click the *Grade My Choices* button. Your quiz is corrected and your score shown. To record your score, click either the *Lessons* or *Chapters* link at the top of the main frame.

CAUTION
Do not use your browser's Back button after taking a quiz. If you use the Back button instead of the Lessons or Chapters link, your score will not be recorded.

Midterm and Final Exams

The Interactive Course includes midterm and final examinations. The midterm covers the first half of the book, while the final is comprehensive. These exams follow the same multiple-choice format as the quizzes. Because they cover more, however, they're somewhat longer. Once you have successfully passed all the quizzes, as well as the midterm and final exams, you'll be eligible to download a certificate of completion from Waite Group Press.

MENTOR ZONE

In the Mentor Zone, shown in Figure 7, you can review FAQs (Frequently Asked Questions) for each chapter. You can also ask a question of a live expert, called a mentor, who is standing by to assist you. The mentor is familiar with the book, an expert in the subject, and can provide you with a specific answer to your content-related question, usually

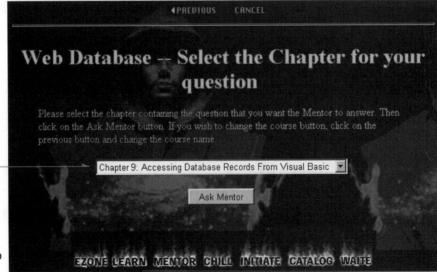

Click on this pull-down menu to see a list of chapters. Click on the chapter to which your question relates.

Figure 7
Get personalized help in the Mentor Zone

within one business day. You can get to this area by clicking on the *Mentor* icon in the navigation frame.

Just the FAQs

When you ask a mentor a question, you're first shown a set of FAQs. Be sure to read through the list. Since you have a limited number of questions you may ask, you'll want to use your questions carefully. Chances are that an answer to your question has already been posted, in which case you can get an answer without having to ask it yourself. In any event, you may learn about an issue you hadn't even considered.

If the FAQ list does not contain the answer you need, you'll want to submit your own question to the mentor.

Ask Your Mentor

eZone students may ask ten questions of their course mentor. This limit ensures that mentors will have the opportunity to answer all readers' questions. Questions must be directly related to chapter material. If you ask unrelated or inappropriate questions, you won't get an answer; however, the question will still be deducted from your allotment.

If the FAQ doesn't provide you with an answer to your question, click the button labeled *Ask Mentor*. The first time you contact the mentor, the rules and conditions for the mentor questions are provided. After reading these, click the *Accept* button to continue. In a moment, a form like the one shown in Figure 8 appears.

This form specifies the course, the chapter, and other information pertinent to your question. The mentor emails the answer to your question directly to you, but keep in mind that Mentor Zone questions must be *directly* related to the chapter subject matter.

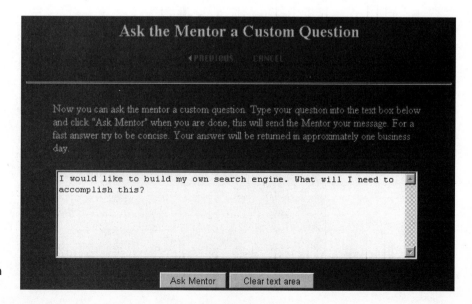

Figure 8
Use this form to send your question to your mentor

More Assistance

Keep in mind that there are other sources of assistance in the eZone, too. If you are experiencing technical problems with the book or CD-ROM, you'll want to contact the Webmaster; you'll find a link on the eZone's main page. If you want to discuss related issues, such as developments and applications, check out the newsgroups available in the Chill Zone. There are other ways to discuss issues with real people, as you'll discover, when you visit the eZone.

CHILL ZONE

Think of the Chill Zone as your student lounge, a place where students hang out and discuss their classes. But the Chill Zone does a student lounge one better—it's also a library chock full of information. It's a place where you can interact with others reading the same book and find expert resources to assist you as you develop and use your new skills. Perhaps the coolest thing about the Chill Zone is that its options are all included with the cost of your book.

To get into the Chill Zone, click the Chill Zone icon in the navigation frame. Once there, you can click three Chill Zone options:

Discussion List—You can subscribe (or unsubscribe) to a dedicated newsgroup centered on your book.

Newsletter—Select this option to subscribe (or unsubscribe) to the quarterly eZone newsletter.

Resources—These are links to Web sites, tools, and other useful materials related to the course subject.

To select a Chill Zone option, click the link and follow the on-screen instructions.

THE EZONE AWAITS

As you have seen from this tour, this Interactive Course book is a lot more than the pages before you. It's a full-blown, personalized training system—including textbook, testing, guidance, certification, and support—that you can pick up and work through at your own pace and at your own convenience.

Don't settle for just a book when you can get a whole education. Thanks to this comprehensive package, you're ready to log on and learn in the eZone.

Dedication

I would like to dedicate this book to my parents, Balbir and Amrita Khurana; to my wife's parents, Balbir and Harbans Chilana; and to my host family, Wayne and Verla Roelle for all their love, encouragement, and support.

— Gunnit S. Khurana

To my wonderful wife, Taranjot; and our lovely daughters, Arshveen and Ishrat.

— Satwant S. Gadhok

About the Authors

Gunnit S. Khurana has an M.S. in Computer Science from the University of Nebraska at Lincoln. He has been involved with publishing databases on the Web since the standardization of the Common Gateway Interface (CGI). Initially, he worked with the World Wide Web servers and CGI programs in the UNIX environment but quickly realized that it was not the easiest way to develop database-oriented Web sites. Being an expert Microsoft Access programmer, he saw great benefits in Windows- and Windows NT–based World Wide Web Servers that supported Windows CGI, and he employed that combination to rapidly develop various database-oriented applications for the Web. Gunnit is also the main author of *Web Database Construction Kit*, another Waite Group Press book that deals with Web database application programming. He can be reached at `gunnit@cssnet.com`.

Satwant S. Gadhok is an electrical engineer with rich experience in the Indian power industry. He lives in New Delhi, India and is presently working as a senior manager for National Thermal Power Corporation, India's largest power utility. A prolific writer with wide ranging interests, Satwant is also a technology buff. He has a keen interest in the latest Internet and Web technologies and likes to keep pace with state-of-the-art developments.

Acknowledgments

We wish to thank Andrea Rosenberg for coordinating and overseeing this project to its successful completion. We are grateful to Russ Jacobs for pointing out the grammatical "kinks" in the initial drafts and to Amy Sticksel for doing such a thorough technical review of this book. Our special gratitude to Aseem Chandra for helping and guiding us through the JavaScript-related portions of this book. Also, many thanks to Dan Scherf, Cameron Carey, and the rest of the staff involved with the production of this book. On the home front, we wish to extend our sincere appreciation to Amit, Navtej Pal, Arshdeep, and Raman for their constant encouragement and support.

Table of Contents

Contents

Part I *Fundamentals of Web Interaction*

CHAPTER 1 Gathering User-Data: HTML Forms and Queries 1

PART II Fundamentals of Database and Query Design

CHAPTER 3 Organizing Data: Tables and Relationships

PART III Fundamentals of Web Database Application Development

CHAPTER 8 Creating Windows CGI Applications: The Visual Basic Framework

PART IV *Fundamentals of Web-Database Publishing and Maintenance*

CHAPTER 10 Presenting Information: Web Database Publishing .475

CHAPTER 13 Using Client-Side Scripting Languages: JavaScript and VBScript

INTRODUCTION

With the 21st century just around the corner, millennium watchers are knocking each other over, trying to put an accurate spin on the future. But the future, or at least its most important underpinning, is already here. The world as we knew it has changed irrevocably, thanks to the Internet and the World Wide Web. The bleeding-edge technologists amongst us are endlessly chasing 3D animation, real-time video, stereo sound, virtual reality, long-distance telephony, video conferencing, and so on, and crying until hoarse telling us how "cool" these technologies are. While we acknowledge the hype, we remind ourselves of another side of the story. By the year 2000, over a billion people will use the Net representing trillions of dollars in electronic commerce, and we cannot but exclaim, "Wow, what a great medium for database publishing."

The appeal of platform-independence, the vast reaches of the Internet, and the ever-increasing popularity of electronic publishing are all ample reasons to justify the inevitable marriage of the Web with the current database technology. The only problem is that anyone contemplating this marriage is easily baffled by the plethora of different marriage ceremonies being advertised on the market.

WHAT THIS BOOK IS ABOUT

There is no doubt that all these Web-database unification ceremonies posess some alluring attraction—some claim swiftness, some portray elegance, while others just charm developers with their simplicity. One such popular ceremony that utilizes the Microsoft Access database management system, Windows Common Gateway Interface, and Visual Basic programming has appealed to a lot of developers because it provides a balanced blend of all these attractions.

Visual Basic Web Database Interactive Course is all about the ins and outs of this ceremony. This book exposes the inherent beauty of the Web, describes the powerful character of Microsoft Access, and provides the reader with the thrill and adventure of Web-database application development using Visual Basic. The whole experience is made more meaningful and practical through a ready-to-use Web event calendar application that is consistently developed all through the book from the ground up. Every concept explained in this book eventually finds its place in this application.

WHOM THIS BOOK IS FOR

Visual Basic Web Database Interactive Course is meant for any serious Web site developer who understands the upcoming trend of interactive Web applications that either use a database for efficient data-storage and retrieval mechanism or act as a cost-effective front-end to existing databases. Visual Basic and Access programmers interested in learning how to use the existing database technology with the Web to produce fully functional Web applications will find this book extremly helpful. Even those with minimal programming experience can benefit from this book, due to its exhaustive coverage of the subject matter. While very little is assumed in terms of database construction or CGI programming, a basic understanding of HTML is helpful.

Finally, *Visual Basic Web Database Interactive Course* includes an automatic membership into the Waite Group Press eZone Web site, which allows you to interact with the printed pages, take online quizzes, ask questions of a mentor, find resources, and more. The eZone is actually a Web database application—one that you can design yourself after following the techniques described in this book.

HOW THIS BOOK IS ORGANIZED

This book is organized into four distinct parts comprising thirteen chapters and two appendixes.

Part I – Fundamentals of Web Interaction

Part I of the book explains how data input/output occurs over the Web. It describes the different elements of the Web and how they fit into the Web's client-server architecture. Even if you are familiar with the Web model, we recommend that you go through this part, as many key concepts, which are used throughout the book, are described here.

Chapter 1: Gathering User-Data: HTML Forms and Queries

Most Web-database applications are interactive and thus require user-input. This chapter focuses on methods available for gathering data from the user over the Web. It explains the structure of all Web requests, the role of the extra- path and query-string portion of a URL, and the various HTML-based user-interface controls that you can use for designing Web data entry forms.

Chapter 2: Handling User Requests: Static and Dynamic Response

This chapter explains how a Web server responds to a user request, how it passes data to external applications using Standard and Windows CGI, and how external applications return their response to the requesting user via the Web server.

Part II – Fundamentals of Database and Query Design

Part II of the book deals with the design and development of relational databases and different types of SQL-based queries. First, the basic database design principles such as table normalization and referential integrity are presented using the example of an event calendar database; then, a practical implementation of that database is shown using Microsoft Access.

Chapter 3: Organizing Data: Tables and Relationships

This chapter deals with the principles of database construction and data integrity. It describes the method of data storage need analysis, discusses the various data types, and looks into the data validation requirements. Ultimately, this chapter explains the steps involved in database normalization and in identifying referential constraints and other database integrity rules. Practical issues such as multi-user environment and data security are also covered.

Chapter 4: Constructing a Relational Database: The Microsoft Access Way

This chapter provides a step-by-step tutorial on how, using the Microsoft Access database management system, to actually build the calendar database we conceptually designed in Chapter 3. It then shows how you can use Access's intuitive user interface to insert and manipulate data in that database. Data access from other types of desktop and client-server databases is also discussed.

Chapter 5: Sorting and Searching: Simple Select Queries

This chapter explains how Microsoft Access's powerful query design interface can be used to construct queries and filters for sorting and searching data and for creating calculated fields. Concepts are illustrated using numerous examples. A full lesson is devoted to parameterized queries, which prove extremely useful in Web-database application development.

Chapter 6: Combining Tables and Grouping Data: Joins and Total Queries

This chapter talks about multiple-table queries, table joins, and the use of aggregate functions to group data and calculate counts and totals. It also covers query performance issues and some advanced data analysis techniques that utilize union queries, nested queries, and subqueries.

Chapter 7: Designing Queries to Maintain Data: Action Queries

This chapter shows the use of Action queries to update, append, or delete records from a database table and then presents some of their typical applications with relation to the calendar database.

Part III – Fundamentals of Web-Database Application Development

Part III of the book explains the general steps involved in creating a Web-database application in Visual Basic. In particular, you will learn about the Visual Basic CGI framework (the CGI32.BAS module), the data access object (DAO) model of Visual Basic, and how to integrate these two components in a Visual Basic project to create and debug a Web-database application.

Chapter 8: Creating Windows CGI Applications: The Visual Basic Framework

This chapter explains how to use the publicly available CGI32.BAS library module to quickly create Windows CGI programs in Visual Basic. Step-by-step instructions for Visual Basic project setup, user-data processing, CGI output generation, and program troubleshooting are given.

Chapter 9: Accessing Database Records from Visual Basic: Data Access Objects

This chapter explains the recordset and other data access objects (DAO) provided in Visual Basic (Professional and Enterprise edition) and shows how Windows-CGI programs can use these objects to search and display records of one or more database tables.

Part IV – Fundamentals of Web-Database Publishing and Maintenance

Part IV of the book shows how to present and manipulate database information over the Web. Practical issues such as static and dynamic publishing, data validation, user-level security, and multi-user editing are all discussed using a common example of a Web-based event calendar application. Finally, this part also teaches how to use JavaScript and VBScript client-side scripting languages to enhance any Web-database application.

Chapter 10: Presenting Information: Web Database Publishing

This chapter discusses the different approaches you can consider when creating a Web publication from a database and presents techniques for implementing them. In particular, you will learn about the differences between data browsing and data searching, how to use the Web Publishing Wizard of Access for static publishing, how to present information as a series of linked pages and in the drill-down fashion, how to group and format database information, and how to program field-based search capability in a Web-database application.

Chapter 11: Populating Tables: Web-Based Data Entry

Most Web database applications require that the database be kept up to date in order to be useful. The widespread availability of Web browsers and the data input support of HTML make the Web a perfect medium for accepting new information to be stored in a database. However, the stateless nature of the Web poses some difficulties when the database is made up of many related tables. This chapter looks at these difficulties and presents commonly used techniques of overcoming them.

Chapter 12: Creating a Data Entry Wizard: Advanced Data Entry and Maintenance

This chapter shows how you can use and implement the concept of a data entry wizard to create an interface for populating and maintaining multiple database tables. It also describes standard session-building techniques using hidden fields and persistent cookies, which play an important role in the wizard implemention.

Chapter 13: Using Client-Side Scripting Languages: JavaScript and VBScript

This chapter describes how to use JavaScript and VBScript client-side scripting languages for enhancing a Web-database application in terms of both performance and flexibility.

Appendix A: Quiz and Excercise Answers

Each chapter in this book contains quiz questions, whose answers are provided in Appendix A.

Appendix B: Internet Explorer 3: A Field Guide

This appendix shows you how to master Internet Explorer.

ABOUT THE CD-ROM

The CD-ROM accompanying this book contains the Web-based event-calendar application, HTML documents and forms, and all the Microsoft Access databases and Visual Basic projects described in the book. The following "Installation" section provides detailed instructions on how to install these projects and what system requirements are needed to run these projects.

Some of the software included on the bundled CD-ROM, including A-XOrion and Internet Assistant for Microsoft Access, are shareware, provided for your evaluation. If you find any of the shareware products useful, you are requested to register it as discussed in its documentation and/or in the About screen of the application. Waite Group Press has not paid the registration fee for this service.

INSTALLATION

Visual Basic Web Database Interactive Course is a hands-on guide that deals with creating database applications with Microsoft Access and Visual Basic using the communication model of the World Wide Web. Like many application development books, this book describes the concepts through a functional practical application (the Web-based event calendar), numerous small examples, and step-by-step instructions. Although the Web communication model is one of the main topics of this book, you do not have to be connected to the World Wide Web in order to run this application or any of these examples. In fact, you can examine this application and all the examples in the privacy of your own PC by installing a Web server that supports a special standard called *Windows CGI*.

WebSite from O'Reilly & Associates is one such popular Web server that fully supports Windows CGI. It even provides a Visual Basic library module and various debugging options for designing applications that use Windows CGI. All the examples and applications described in this book (and provided on the accompanying CD-ROM) have been implemented and tested using this server. If you do not already have a copy of this server, then you can download its fully functional unlimited time evaluation version (WebSite version 1.1e or later) from O'Reilly's download site:

`http://software.ora.com/download`

The next two sections describe how to install the WebSite server and the examples and exercises covered in the book. The last section covers the configuration parameters of the WebSite server that are relevant to our subject. However, before you proceed, check out the following URL for the latest information and updates related to this book:

`http://www.cssnet.com/wdbic`

While other popular Web servers such as Alibaba, Folkweb, and Netscape also support the Windows-CGI standard, we highly recommend that you run the book examples with the WebSite server. This way all the figures will match those presented in this book, the examples will work exactly as described, and you will not encounter any unexpected difficulties caused by the personality variations of other Web servers. After you are comfortable with the Web-database concepts, you can then easily port the book examples to run with any Windows-CGI compatible Web server of your choice. In most cases, this porting process requires no other step than moving the files to a different directory.

INSTALLING THE WEBSITE SERVER

The WebSite Web server is a 32-bit multithreaded server designed to run on Windows 95 and Windows NT systems. It is a robust and efficient server capable of delivering over 100,000 transactions per hour on a single CPU Pentium through a full T-1 connection. Its developer, Robert Denny, is known for his prompt technical support over the Usenet newsgroup `comp.infosystems.www.servers.ms-windows` as well as over a dedicated mailing list whose subscription information is available at `http://www.ora.com/archives/website-talk/`.

The following steps describe how to install and test the downloadable version of the WebSite server. You may skip these steps if this downloadable version (or any higher version of this server) is already installed on your system in the `C:\WEBSITE` directory (which is the server's default installation directory) and proceed to the next section that explains how to install the book examples.

Step 1: Complete the Prerequisites

The following requirements must be met to install and run the WebSite server:

Hardware

The hardware requirements are as follows:

- 80486 or higher microprocessor; Pentium recommended

- 16MB RAM; 32MB recommended

- 10MB free hard disk space

- CD-ROM drive (local or accessible through your local area network)

Software and Connectivity

The software and connectivity requirements are as follows:

- Windows 95 (or later) or Windows NT (version 3.51 or higher) with long filenames enabled

- TCP/IP protocol stack installed and running (even if your PC is not connected to any TCP/IP network)

Tools And Utilities

To follow the examples and exercises described in this book, you also need the following application development tools and programs:

- A WWW client such as Netscape (version 3.0 or higher) or Internet Explorer (version 3.0 or higher) that supports HTML tables, JavaScript, Magic Cookies, and other HTML 3 extensions

- Visual Basic (version 5.0 or higher) development environment (32-bit Professional version)

- Microsoft Access 97 (or later version)

Step 2: Setting Up WebSite

The downloadable version of WebSite 1.1e is provided as a zip file. You must first extract all the files packaged in this zip file into a temporary directory (using an unzipping program such as Winzip or Pkunzip) using the directory structure stored in the zip file. This action should create a subdirectory named `WS_SETUP` (containing all the extracted files) under the specified temporary directory. The following steps describe how to install the WebSite server from these extracted files:

1. Start the WebSite Setup Wizard by executing the file named `WS11E.EXE` which resides in the `WS_SETUP` directory.

   The Setup program asks if you want to install the WebSite server.

2. Press Yes to confirm the installation process.

   The program starts the InstallShield Wizard and displays the Welcome screen as shown in Figure I-1.

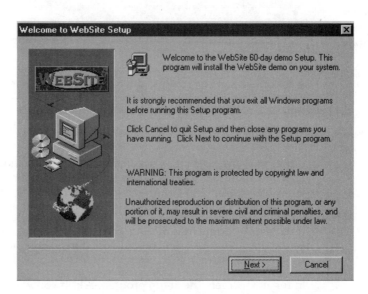

Figure I-1
First screen of
WebSite Setup
Wizard

3. Click on the Next button to proceed with the installation.

   The Setup program displays the license agreement.

4. Read through the agreement, and click on the Yes button to proceed with the rest of the setup. The Setup program then asks for the location of the installation directory. It shows `C:\WEBSITE` as the default directory.

5. Click on the Next button to select the default value for the installation directory.

6. The Setup program then asks for the path of the document root directory and the filename pattern of the index documents, as shown in Figure I-2. It gives `C:\WEBSITE\HTDOCS` and `INDEX.*` as the default values for these fields. Select the default options by clicking on the Next button.

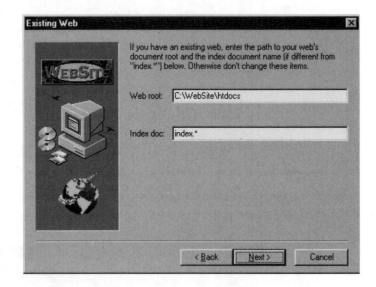

Figure I-2
Setup program asking for Web root and index document information

A document *root directory* is the directory that is mapped to the first slash of a URL path. So, when the Web server gets a request for the following URL:

`http://YourServerName/`

it tries to deliver the index document located in the document root directory. If you chose the default values for the document root directory and the index document, then the server will try to deliver the first file matching the file path `C:\WEBSITE\HTDOCS\INDEX.*` to the requesting client.

If the index document is missing, then the server returns a directory index of the document root directory (unless the directory index option is turned off for this directory).

7. In the next screen, the Setup program asks if you want to start the server manually or automatically. Since you will need to run the server to follow this book, we recommend you select the Automatic option and then click on the Next button.

The Setup program then asks for your machine's Internet name.

Specify the fully qualified domain name of your machine for the Internet name field, and click on the Next button. A *fully qualified domain name* is a unique name that identifies your computer on the Internet. It is listed in the format *hostname.domainname*. If your PC does not have a fully qualified domain name yet, then specify localhost for the Internet name in the setup. You can always change this setting later from the Server Admin utility, as explained in the next section.

8. As the last installation option, Setup asks for your email address as shown in Figure I-3. Specify your Internet email address in the email address field, and click on the Next button.

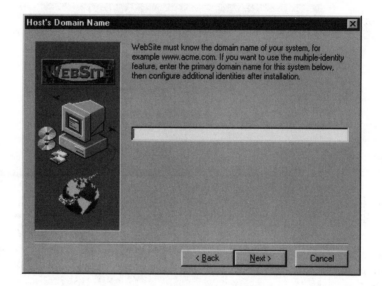

Figure I-3
Setup program asking for the administrator's email address

The setup then installs the WebSite server (HTTPD32.EXE) and all related files and subdirectories into the C:\WEBSITE directory. After the installation is complete, the setup program gives you the option of displaying the Readme file and automatically launching your Web server. We recommend that you go through the contents of the Readme file and launch the server at this point by clicking on the Finish button.

The Setup program creates a program group named WebSite 1.1, which contains icons that you can click on to launch the WebSite server, Server Admin utility (labeled Server Properties) and other programs that are included in the WebSite evaluation package.

Step 3: Testing the WebSite Server

To test whether the server is functioning correctly, start the WebSite server on your PC (if it is not already running) and specify the following location on your Web client:

`http://Your_PCs_Internet_Name/`

You can use `localhost` for *Your_PCs_Internet_Name* if your PC does not have an assigned Internet name.

If everything is installed correctly, you should see the home page (`C:\WEBSITE\HTDOCS\INDEX.HTML-SSI`) returned by your WebSite server as shown in Figure I-4.

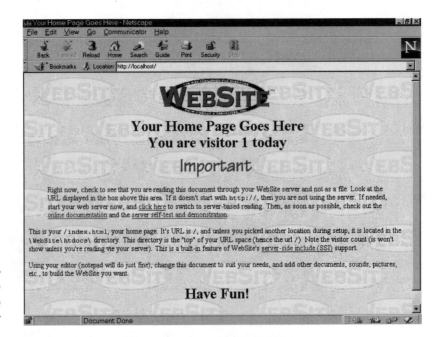

Figure I-4
Initial home page
of your WebSite
server

If you do not see a home page, try the following:

1. **Check whether the TCP/IP stack is installed on your computer by viewing the Network settings from your control panel.**

If you are able to connect to other servers through your Web client, then your TCP/IP stack is configured properly.

2. **Check whether the Web server is running. Press** ALT-TAB **to display the icons of each program running, and then tab through each icon to locate the Web server. If the Web server is not running, try restarting it from the WebSite group.**

3. View the file `C:\WEBSITE\LOGS\ERROR.LOG` by using the Notepad application. It may give some hints on why the server may not be starting.

4. Reinstall WebSite by repeating the instructions listed in the previous section, "Setting Up WebSite."

5. Post an article to the WebSite's mailing list at

`http://www.ora.com/maillist/archives/website-talk/`

6. Post an article on the Internet in the Usenet newsgroup:

`comp.infosystems.www.servers.ms-windows`

or consult WebSite's on-line tech support at

`http://software.ora.com/techsupport/`

Hopefully, some kind soul will help you bring up your home page.

7. If all else fails, purchase the commercial version of WebSite from `http://website.ora.com` and get technical support.

Step 4: Demonstrating the Server Features

From the home page shown in Figure I-4, click on the "server self-test and demonstration" link. Your browser now displays a document (see Figure I-5) that demonstrates the various features of the WebSite server described earlier in this chapter. At this point, you can go through the links on this page and familiarize yourself with the server's features.

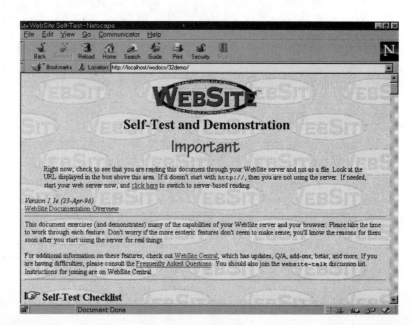

Figure I-5
WebSite server's
self-test page

Finally, if your computer is connected to the Internet, you can also check the link pointing to WebSite Central, (`http://website.ora.com/`) for the latest news, technical support, and other related information about WebSite.

INSTALLING THE BOOK EXAMPLES

The accompanying CD-ROM also contains the Web-based event-calendar application, HTML documents and forms, and all the Microsoft Access databases and Visual Basic projects described in this book. The following steps describe how to install these examples on your C drive so that you can run them with the WebSite server as per the instructions given in each chapter. (The CD-ROM drive is assumed to be your D drive.)

1. Run the executable file `D:\WSETUP.EXE` to start the setup wizard.

   The setup wizard displays its welcome screen as shown in Figure I-6.

Figure I-6
The setup wizard
displaying the
welcome screen

2. Press the Next button.

   The setup wizard asks for the destination directory and shows `C:\WEBSITE` as the default option. (See Figure I-7.)

3. Select the default option by pressing the Next button. (Note that many initial examples in this book assume that the WebSite server and these examples are installed in the `C:\WEBSITE` directory.)

   The setup wizard now asks you to select the components that you want it to install. It gives you three options as shown in Figure I-8.

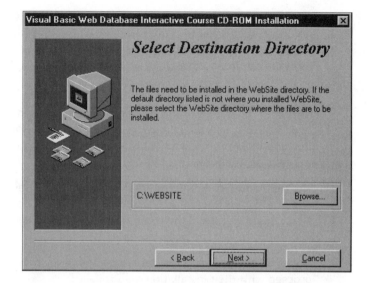

Figure I-7
The setup wizard
displaying the
installation
directory selection
screen

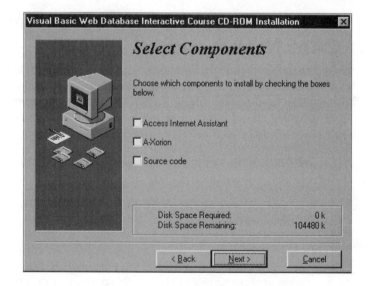

Figure I-8
The setup wizard
displaying the
component
selection screen

The first two options (Access Internet Assistant and A-XOrion) refer to two third-party products that help in linking Access databases to the Web.

The Access Internet Assistant is a simple utility that allows you to create static Web pages based on the data from an Access 95 database. This utility was incorporated into Access 97 as part of its Publishing to the Web wizard and is discussed in detail in Chapter 10, "Presenting Information: Web Database Publishing."

The second product, A-XOrion, is a PC Web database server (evaluation version) that allows you to create dynamic Web pages without much programming. It uses many concepts discussed in this book, and the explanation of its usage can be found at

`http://www.clark.net/infouser/endidc.htm`

Note that the details of this product are not discussed in this book since the book's focus is on Visual Basic–based Web-database solutions. We suggest that you look into this product after you have read through the first eight chapters of this book.

The third and last option installs the sample databases and Web applications discussed in this book. If you are short on hard disk space, it is sufficient to select this option from the component selection screen of the setup wizard in order to follow the book examples.

4. Once you have selected the desired components, press the Next button to proceed with their installation.

RUNNING THE SAMPLE EVENT CALENDAR APPLICATION

After performing the previous steps, test whether everything was installed correctly by running the sample event calendar application that is explained below. This application allows users to list, search, and add events over the Web and is used as an example to illustrate most of the concepts discussed within this book:

1. Ensure that you have Visual Basic (Professional version 5.0 or later) and Microsoft Access 97 (or later version) installed on your system.

2. Start your WebSite server if it is not already running.

3. Run the event calendar application by entering the following location in your Web browser:

`http://localhost/wdbic/calendar/index.htm`

Your Web client should display the main menu of the event calendar application as shown in Figure I-9. At this point, you may click on the given hyperlinks to see how each feature works.

UNINSTALLING THE BOOK EXAMPLES

If you need to uninstall the book examples from your hard drive, simply delete the `C:\WEBSITE\HTDOCS\WDBIC` and `C:\WEBSITE\CGI-WIN\WDBIC` subdirectories.

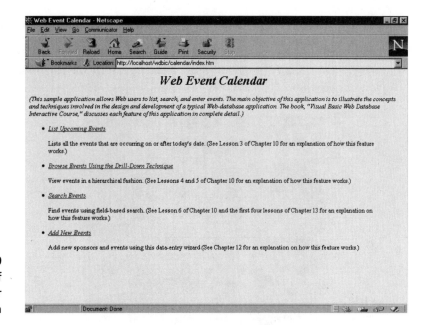

Figure I-9
The main menu of
the event calendar
application

ADMINISTERING WEBSITE

The Server Admin utility included with the WebSite server contains nine sections that can be configured for administering the server. Table I-1 lists these sections and their purposes.

Table I-1 List of sections in the Server Admin utility

Section	Purpose
General	Setting the basic information about the WebSite server
Identity	Configuring multiple Web identities
Mapping	Establishing document, CGI, and other mappings
Dir Listings	Configuring automatic directory indexes
Users	Configuring user names, passwords, and group assignments
Access Control	Securing a URL path by users, groups, IP addresses, and host names
Logging	Specifying the path and name of log files and setting server tracing options
CGI	Fine-tuning the CGI process

Only those sections and parameters of the Server Admin utility that are important in creating database applications for your Web site are reviewed. You can refer to the on-line help provided with the Server Admin utility for details on the configuration settings not discussed in this section.

To launch the Server Admin utility, double-click on the Server Properties icon in the WebSite 1.1 program group. It should display the parameters in the General section as shown in Figure I-10.

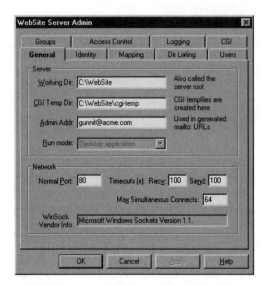

Figure I-10
The General section of the Server Admin utility

General Section Parameters

The general section parameters help dictate the basic functionality of the WebSite server.

Working Dir

The working directory is the directory relative to which all other file and directory paths in the Server Admin utility can be defined. It is also called the server root directory. By default, the working directory is the same as the WebSite's installation directory (`C:\WEBSITE`).

CGI Temp Dir

The WebSite server uses the `C:\WEBSITE\CGI-TEMP` directory to store all the temporary files created during a Windows CGI session. The role of this directory is discussed in Lesson 4 of Chapter 2, "Handling User Requests: Static and Dynamic Response."

Admin Addr

This field holds the email address of the WebSite server administrator. This email address is automatically shown by the server to a Web user if the server encounters any error in processing that user's request.

Run Mode

This option is enabled if WebSite is running on a Windows NT platform. It has three choices:

● Desktop application

● System service with icon

● System service without icon

Normal Port

This option makes the WebSite server listen on the TCP port shown in this field. The default value is set to 80, which is the port used by a client when no port number is specifically listed in the requested URL. If you want to specify any other value besides 80 for the TCP port, then we recommend you use a value greater than 1024. The port numbers below 1024 are used for other standard Internet services such as FTP, Gopher, and Telnet.

One reason for using a different TCP port number is to prevent general-public access to your server, since most outside users will not know which port number your server is listening on. This does not prevent any user from connecting to your server, it just reduces the chances of a random Web user accessing your Web site. For complete security, you will need to use the WebSite server's access control feature.

Recv and Send Timeouts

Again, these are standard settings that generally should be left as they are. You may increase the timeouts to 60 seconds if your server is running on a slow PPP/SLIP connection.

Maximum Simultaneous Connects

This parameter limits the number of simultaneous connections that the server will accept. You use this to guarantee a minimum speed for each active connection. This is most important for slower lines (56K and below). You can click on this section's Help button to list the recommended values for different line speeds.

Hold Connections Open For Re-use

This parameter informs the server to keep a connection alive so that a Web browser can request documents in the same connection.

WinSock Vendor Info

This option shows all the WinSock-compliant TCP/IP stacks detected on your computer. This setting is for information only and cannot be changed.

Mapping Section Parameters

The mapping section parameters control how the server interprets the incoming URL requests and the types of files it serves. Click on the Mapping tab in the Server Admin utility to display its mapping section. (See Figure I-11.)

Figure I-11
The Mapping
section of the
Server Admin
utility

The mapping section lets you specify seven types of mappings using the following elements of the section:

● A List Selector box that lets you select the mapping you want to work with.

● A rectangular window, called the *mapping window,* that displays the object pairs participating in the currently selected mapping.

● Two input fields through which you specify the objects that need to be mapped.

● Command buttons to add, change, or remove a mapping between objects.

Next, we discuss the purpose of each type of mapping, except Directory Icon mapping (since it is not relevant to the subject of this book), and show how to associate objects through them.

Document Mapping

A document mapping is created between a URL path (or a portion of a URL path) and a physical directory location on your system.

A URL path is the information specified after the server name (or IP address) in a URL. For example, a URL path for the URL

```
http://Your_Server_Name/server/support/logcycle.txt
```

is

```
/server/support/logcycle.txt
```

As a standard rule, your server considers a URL path to be the file path relative to the document root directory (`C:\WEBSITE\HTDOCS`). So, for the URL in the previous example, your WebSite server will try to fetch the file:

`C:\WEBSITE\HTDOCS\SERVER\SUPPORT\LOGCYCLE.TXT`

The document mapping lets you overwrite this default URL path to a directory path associated with your own mapping. Let's say you want the server to return the icon file `C:\WEBSITE\SUPPORT\LOGCYCLE.TXT` for the URL listed in the previous example. You can tell the WebSite server that any time it encounters a URL path beginning with `/server/support/`, it should start from the directory `C:\WEBSITE\SUPPORT\` by creating a document mapping. Refer to Figure I-12 and use the following the steps to create this document mapping.

Figure I-12
Creating a document mapping

1. Click on the option labeled "Document Mapping" in the List Selector box, if that option is not already selected.

2. Click on the input field labeled "Document URL Root" and type "/server/support/" in the field.

3. Click on the input field labeled "Directory (full or server-relative)"; type "C:\WEBSITE\SUPPORT\" in the field.

4. Click on the Add button to add this document mapping.

5. Click on the OK button to close the Server Admin utility.

If your Web server was running when you closed the Server Admin utility, it will beep after a few seconds indicating that it has accepted the new configuration settings. You do not need to shut down the server and restart it.

To test whether the document mapping you added is correct and active:

1. **Start the WebSite server, if it is not already running.**

2. **From your Web client, specify the following URL:**

`http://localhost/server/support/logcycle.txt`

Your browser should display the contents of the `LOGCYCLE.TXT` file residing in the `C:\WEBSITE\SUPPORT\` directory.

Absolute and Relative Directory Paths

In a document mapping, you can specify an absolute path for the directory location or a path relative to the server working directory (`C:\WEBSITE\`). If you refer to Figure I-12, you will see that the URL path `/` is mapped to `C:\WEBSITE\HTDOCS\`, which indicates an absolute directory path. You can achieve the same result by mapping the URL path `/` to `HTDOCS\` (and not `\HTDOCS\`). The absence of the first backslash tells the server that it is a relative path.

How the Server Determines Which Mapping to Apply

If there are many mappings that may match a URL path, the server uses the mapping matching the longest portion of the URL path. For example, if you have the following two document mappings:

```
/users/ <==> C:\USERS\
/users/bob <==> C:\USERS\ROBERT\
```

and you specify the URL path `/users/bob/picture.gif`, the server will try to retrieve the file `C:\USERS\ROBERT\PICTURE.GIF`.

Changing the Document Root Directory

You can assign a different directory as the document root directory by changing the mapping for the URL path `/` as described next:

1. **Click on the mapping of `/` in the mapping window.**

2. **Specify the new document directory (in a relative or absolute path) in the Directory field.**

3. **Click on the Replace button and then the OK button.**

Serving Documents Residing on Many Computers

You can use document mapping to serve documents residing on other computers through one URL hierarchy. For example, if your colleagues want to serve their home pages through your server but enjoy the flexibility of maintaining the pages from their computer, you can share their home page directories from your computer and map them to a URL path hierarchy as shown in the following example:

```
/home/jim/  <==>  \\JIMMY\C\WWW\
/home/mary/ <==>  \\MARRY_PC\C\WEBDOCS\
```

Redirect Mapping

Redirect mapping lets you reassign a URL to another URL (possibly leading to another Web server). When your WebSite server receives a request for a redirected URL, it tells the browser to go to the new URL. The user generally is unaware that this redirection has taken place.

You can use redirection mapping if some of your documents become inaccessible due to a network-connection or hard-disk failure, and you want to temporarily redirect the URLs leading to those documents to a URL that explains the current problem. By default, WebSite does not carry any redirect mappings.

CGI Mapping

WebSite allows three types of CGI mappings: Windows, Standard, and DOS. These CGI mappings let you map a URL path to the location of a CGI directory. A CGI directory contains programs and scripts that the server should execute if it encounters a URL containing the CGI-mapped URL path.

Purpose of CGI Mapping

The normal role of the WebSite server is to deliver document files (whether text or images) to the Web browser. However, your server is also capable of executing external programs and delivering their output to the Web client using the CGI.

To distinguish between executable programs and regular document files, the server requires that these programs be present in their own directories. By default, the following subdirectories of the working directory are assigned for the three types of executable programs:

- **CGI-WIN for Windows programs, assigned to URL path** /cgi-win/

- **CGI-BIN for scripts based on a scripting language such as PERL, assigned to URL paths** /cgi-bin/ **and** /cgi-shl/

- **CGI-DOS for DOS programs, assigned to URL path** /cgi-dos/

As an example, if your server receives the following URL request:

```
http://Your_Server_Name/cgi-win/cgitest.exe
```

it executes the Windows program C:\WEBSITE\CGI-WIN\CGITEST.EXE and returns the output of this program to the browser. On the other hand, if the CGITEST.EXE program file resides in the C:\WEBSITE\CGI-WIN\HTDOCS directory and the following URL is requested:

```
http://Your_Server_Name/cgitest.exe
```

the server simply delivers the executable code of this program to the Web client.

You can apply a special content type mapping, as explained in the "Content Type Mapping" section to make the server execute the **CGITEST.EXE** file even when it is residing in the **HTDOCS** directory.

Creating a CGI Mapping

To create a CGI mapping:

1. Select the CGI mapping type from the List Selector box.

2. Follow the steps described in the "Document Mapping" section to associate a URL path to a CGI directory location.

When you mark a directory as a CGI-type directory, the server automatically considers its subdirectories as part of that CGI-type mapping.

Content Type Mapping

A content type mapping associates a file extension to a content type. A content type classifies a document and is defined using the MIME (Multipurpose Internet Mail Extensions) format. A MIME format contains a main type and a subtype, separated by a forward slash (/). For example, a plain text document generally has a MIME content type of **text/plain**, whereas an HTML document is classified with a MIME content type of **text/html**.

Purpose of Content Types

When a Web client requests a document from your WebSite server, the server not only sends that document file, but also passes the content type of that document. The server is able to determine the content type based on that document's file extension and the content type mappings. The Web client uses the content type supplied by the server to appropriately display that document.

If the Web client is not programmed to handle a particular content type by itself, it checks its configuration settings to see if the user has configured an external application for that content type. If no application is configured to handle that content type, then the Web client takes some default action, such as giving the user an option to save that file.

If the server cannot match a file extension of a document to any content type mapping, it does not send any content type information with that document. It is up to the Web client as to how it should handle a document with no attached content type information. Also, if a server is sending the output of a CGI program, then it is the responsibility of that program to provide the content type of the output.

Adding A New Content Type

By default, the WebSite server includes the content type mappings for almost 50 types of file extensions. Figure I-13 shows some of the predefined content type mappings.

Even though the default mappings are sufficient to classify most types of documents served over the Web, there are times when you may have to add a new content type mapping. Let's say your friend brings you a number of *.DAT files, claiming that they are HTML-formatted data files, and wants you to publish them through your Web site. The easiest way to correctly present these files to Web clients is if you map the .DAT extension to the content type text/html as follows:

Figure I-13
Content type
mappings

1. Run the Server Admin utility, and click on the Mapping tab.

2. Click on the Content Types option in the List Selector box.

3. Click on the File Extension (Class) input field, and type .dat in the field.

4. Click on the MIME Content Type input field, and type text/html in the field.

5. Click on the Add button to add this content type mapping.

6. Click on the OK button to close the Server Admin utility and apply the new settings.

CGI Programs and Content Types

As described earlier in the "CGI Mappings" section, the WebSite server determines whether a file is a CGI program by checking if that file resides in a CGI directory. This also means that if you place a regular document file in a CGI directory, the server assumes that file to be a CGI program. To keep CGI programs and regular documents in the same directory and maintain their proper identities, the WebSite server provides three special content types:

- `wwwserver/wincgi` for Windows CGI programs

- `wwwserver/shellcgi` for standard shell scripts

- `wwwserver/doscgi` for DOS-based CGI programs

You can map special file extensions to these content types and keep the CGI programs with those file extensions in a non-CGI directory. For example, if you create a content type mapping between `.WIN` and `wwwserver/wincgi` and design a Windows-CGI application named `TEST.WIN`, the server always tries to run this application regardless of which directory this file resides under.

Logging Section Parameters

The parameters in the logging section control the type of information you want the server to log during its operation. These parameters are further consolidated into subsections in the Server Admin utility. To display the logging section of the Server Admin utility as shown in Figure I-14.

Figure I-14
Logging section of the Web Server Admin utility

1. Run the Server Admin utility.

2. Using the navigation buttons next to the tabs, scroll to the Logging tab.

3. Click on the Logging tab to display the Logging section.

   The subsections of the Logging section are described next.

Log File Paths

This section lets you specify the file paths of the three logs maintained by the server:

- *Access log*, which records the completed requests made to the server and their corresponding response codes, is by default kept in the file ACCESS.LOG.

- *Server log*, which traces the information generated by the options marked in the Tracing Options subsection, is by default kept in the file SERVER.LOG.

- *Error log*, which logs the errors that occurred while processing requests, is by default maintained in the file ERROR.LOG.

If you do not specify a directory path for these log files, the WebSite server stores them in the C:\WEBSITE\LOGS\ directory. If you delete a log file, the server automatically creates a new log file the next time it is started. The server also clears the server log each time it starts.

Client Hostname Lookup

By default, the WebSite server records the IP address of the requesting clients in its access log. If you check the Enable DNS Reverse Lookup option, the server tries to determine the fully qualified domain name of the client and store that name instead of the client's IP address. Be careful when setting this option as the reverse lookup can decrease the server performance.

Tracing Options

The tracing options dictate what information the server provides in the server log. You can enable the appropriate tracing options to troubleshoot your server if it appears to function incorrectly. Brief descriptions of the tracing options are provided next:

- HTTP Protocol—The server traces incoming requests, translation of URL to file paths, and the request action. The HTTP protocol is described in Chapter 1, "Gathering User-Data: HTML Forms and Queries," and Chapter 2, "Handling User Requests: Static and Dynamic Response."

- Dump Sent Data—This option produces a hex/ASCII dump of all data sent by the server to the client. This and the HTTP protocol option together can help detect the cause of any problem between a client and your server.

- Image Maps—This option traces the operation of the imagemapping process, including the location coordinates sent by the client when the user clicked an imagemap, and the result returned by the server.

- API/CGI Execution—This option records the server's handling of all CGI programs, including the command line used to launch the program, and the server's processing of the results that come back from the CGI program. Lesson 6, "Troubleshooting Windows-CGI Programming Errors," of Chapter 9, "Accessing Database Records From Visual Basic: Data Access Objects," shows how to use this tracing option for debugging Windows CGI applications.

● Access Control—This option traces the actions taken by the server for access control, showing access control path searching, user authentication requirements, IP address filtering, and host name filtering.

● Authentication—This option traces all attempts at user name and password validation.

● Control Threads, Service Threads, Network I/O, and Network Buffering— These options provide traces of threads and network input/output. These options are mainly used by the technical support staff for diagnosing server performance and other operational and network-related problems.

This concludes our discussion on the server installation and administration issues. Note that other Web servers also support similar configuration parameters although the user interfaces of their administration utilities are different. Also, we would like to remind you to check out the following URL for the latest information and updates related to this book:

http://www.cssnet.com/wdbic

Fundamentals of Web Interaction

PART I

CHAPTER 1

GATHERING USER-DATA: HTML FORMS AND QUERIES

Most Web database applications are interactive and thus require user input. This chapter focuses on methods available for gathering data from the user over the Web. It explains the structure of all Web requests, the role of the extra path and query string portions of a URL, and the various HTML-based user interface controls that you can use for designing Web data entry forms. In this chapter, you will learn about:

- The Web communication model

- Characteristics of HTTP (Hypertext Transfer Protocol)

- The format of the GET- and POST-type Web requests

- The role of the extra path and query string portions of a URL path

- `<FORM>` ... `</FORM>`, `<INPUT>`, `<TEXTAREA>` ... `</TEXTAREA>`, `<SELECT>` ... `</SELECT>`, and `<OPTION>` tags of HTML

- URL and multipart encoding schemes

- `CGITEST32.EXE` and `FORMINP.EXE` Windows CGI utilities

1

THE WEB COMMUNICATION MODEL

The World Wide Web works on a simple communication model consisting of a set of two main elements—Web clients and Web servers. In this *client-server* model, a Web client (a Web browser in most cases) first initiates a connection with the desired Web server and then sends a *precomposed* request that the Web server is expected to understand. The Web server receives the incoming request and responds by transferring the appropriate information.

The roles of the Web client and the Web server are clearly defined. Although the Web client is responsible for generating the request, it is up to the Web server to gather the requested information. The Web client interprets or displays the response returned by the Web server. The Web server helps the Web client in this final step by supplying some data about the type of information being returned as part of its response. Figure 1-1 illustrates how this client-server interaction takes place.

This lesson outlines the role of the three protocols (TCP/IP, HTTP, and HTML) involved in the Web communication model, explains how the concept of a Universal Resource Locator (URL) helps uniquely identify each and every information resource on the Web, and describes the `GET` and `POST` request methods that Web clients commonly use to create a Web request.

Web Communication Protocols

As shown in Figure 1-1, the data transfer between a Web client and a Web server occurs using three communication protocols: TCP/IP, HTTP, and HTML. Each protocol operates at its own independent level.

Figure 1-1
The Web communication model

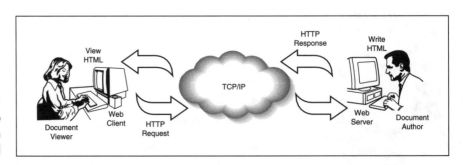

TCP/IP

Transmission Control Protocol/Internet Protocol (TCP/IP) is the protocol followed by all computers connected to the Internet and is responsible for accurately transporting any data between any two computers on the Internet.

HTTP

Hypertext Transfer Protocol (HTTP) is the standard that a Web client and a Web server use to speak to each other. By using the concept of a standard document addressing method called the *universal resource locator* (explained in the next section), HTTP promotes minimal transaction between the server and the client to achieve maximum communication efficiency. The main features that characterize HTTP are

- In one connection, a client can request only a certain number of documents from the server. This maximum limit is generally a configurable parameter of the Web server as well as the Web client.

- Either party can close the connection. Although the server automatically closes the connection after the request is completed, the client has the option to terminate the connection anytime during the document transfer.

- HTTP is a *stateless* protocol. Every transaction between the client and the server is assumed to be independent of other transactions.

- HTTP is a message-based protocol that follows the *object-oriented* paradigm. In this paradigm, the list of messages can be easily extended for newer versions of HTTP or to design customized information retrieval systems based on this protocol.

HTML

Hypertext Markup Language (HTML) is a standard usually followed by the document author to provide information that can be presented by the Web client in a manner most suitable to the reader. HTML not only supports the capability of displaying text, pictures, and hyperlinks on the same page but also provides a powerful mechanism for collecting user data. Its simplicity, extensibility, and widespread applicability have made HTML the language of choice not just for document publishing but for creating interactive Web applications. Many tools and user-friendly editors now exist to facilitate Web page creation, making the process of writing HTML code easier than ever.

Although HTML and HTTP are designed to work on independent levels, HTML does imbibe a few personality traits that directly reflect its close relationship with HTTP. Among these inherited traits, the two prominent ones are its use of URLs for specifying hyperlinks and support for the various request methods allowed by HTTP.

Universal Resource Locator

The *Universal Resource Locator* (URL) is a text string that uniquely identifies an information resource. In other words, it defines the address of the data being sought. A URL is constructed using the following syntax:

```
protocol://host[:port]/URL_path
```

An example of a URL is

```
http://www.mcp.com:80/waite/newbooks/search?keyword=web
```

In a URL, the protocol entry (`http`) defines the communication method needed to access the document. Some other examples of this protocol entry are `ftp` (File Transfer Protocol), `file` (for file residing on a local machine), `telnet` (for a telnet session), `https` (http protocol channeled through secure socket layer), `mailto` (for Internet mail), and `news` (for Usenet news).

The host entry (`www.mcp.com`) specifies a legal Internet host domain name or IP address in dotted-decimal form. The port entry (`80`) lists the TCP port to use for establishing the connection. This entry is optional if the host Web server is listening for client requests on TCP port 80 (which is the case most of the time). The URL_path entry (`/waite/newbooks/search?keyword=web`) indicates the location of the requested information on the host server. The server uses its standard set of rules (described in Chapter 2, Lesson 1) to determine how to retrieve the actual information based on the specified URL_path entry.

HTTP Request Methods

As part of the object-oriented model, HTTP provides many different methods of defining a Web request. `GET` and `POST` are the two most commonly used methods and are supported by almost all Web browsers and Web servers currently on the market.

GET *Method*

The `GET` method is the simplest and the fastest method for sending a Web request. In its shortest form, a request using the `GET` method need contain only the method name, the URL path, and a new line (`<NL>`) character:

```
GET URL_Path <NL>
```

A fully formed `GET` request can also include the protocol version and various header fields (containing information about the client or the request itself), as shown in the following example:

```
GET /waite/newbooks/search?keyword=web HTTP/1.0
Accept:text/*; image/jpeg
Host: www.mcp.com:80
If-Modified-Since: Friday, 15-Aug-97 02:12:28 GMT
User-Agent: Mozilla/3.0Gold (Win95; I)
<NL>
```

In this example, **HTTP/1.0** is the protocol version and **Accept**, **Host**, **If-Modified-Since**, and **User-Agent** are four HTTP header fields that are passed along with this **GET** request. Note that the actual HTTP request does not attach the host or the port entry of a URL with the URL path but supplies this information through an optional **host** header field.

POST *Method*

The **POST** method allows an HTTP request to carry supplemental data along with the URL path and the header fields, as shown in the following example:

```
POST /cgi-win/wdbic/test/test.exe HTTP/1.0
<NL>
Accept:text/*; image/jpeg
Host: localhost
If-Modified-Since: Friday, 15-Aug-97 02:12:28 GMT
User-Agent: Mozilla/3.0Gold (Win95; I)
Content-type: application/x-www-form-urlencoded
Content-length: 11
<NL>
keyword=web
```

The **content-type** and **content-length** header fields describe the format and size of the supplemental data. This additional data is generally used by the information resource being requested, which is normally an executable program (**/cgi-win/wdbic/test/test.exe** in the above example). It is up to the Web server and the executable program to work out the details of exchanging that data after it has been received by the Web server. The *Common Gateway Interface* (CGI), which you will study in Chapter 2, "Handling User Requests: Static and Dynamic Response," is one prominent standard supported by most Web servers for making the data available to the requested executable script or program.

Web Browser and Request Methods

Web browsers use the **GET** method to request information unless another request method is specifically indicated. In particular, the following events always cause Web browsers to send a **GET**-type request:

● Whenever a user clicks on a hyperlink created using the anchor HTML tag, as shown below:

   `<A HREF="URL">Linked Item</A>`

● Whenever a user types a URL in the browser's location window.

● Whenever a user submits an HTML form whose METHOD attribute is set to "GET" or is absent from that form's <FORM> tag, as shown below:

   `<FORM ACTION="URL" METHOD="GET">` or `<FORM ACTION="URL">`

You can make a browser send a **POST**-type request only through an HTML form and by setting the **METHOD** attribute of that form's **<FORM>** tag to **"POST"**, as shown below:

`<FORM ACTION="URL" METHOD="POST">`

Which Request Method to Use?

As you can see, the question of whether to use a GET or a POST method arises only when you are specifying a <FORM> element in an HTML document. As a rule of thumb, a GET-type request is considered appropriate when the size of the request is small. For large data transfers, a POST request method is recommended. Besides, some CGIs such as Windows CGI perform additional decoding on the data sent through the POST request to ease the CGI application development process. This neat feature of Windows CGI is explained further in Chapter 2, "Handling User Requests: Static and Dynamic Response."

Lesson Summary

In this lesson, you learned how different elements of the Web function and how Web requests are sent using the GET and POST methods. Looking at the format of these two request methods, you may think that the POST method is the only way to attach other data along with the location of the information resource. Well, appearances can be deceptive: As you will see in the next lesson, you can embed any type of custom information in the URL path itself and have the browser send that information to the Web server (and thereby to the requested CGI program) using the GET request.

1. What is the role of a Web client?
   a. Make requests to Web servers.
   b. Create the requested information.
   c. Interpret or display information in an appropriate manner.
   d. Communicate with other Web clients.

2. Which of the following entries cannot be specified in a URL?
   a. Location information
   b. Protocol information
   c. Host and port information
   d. Request method

3. Which of the following actions does HTTP not support?
   a. Automatically passing data between multiple Web transactions
   b. Sending more than one document in one connection
   c. Using URLs for identifying information resources
   d. Using a new set of messages for its newer versions

4. Which of the following information must *always* be included in a Web request?
   a. Request method
   b. URL path
   c. Host information
   d. Header fields

5. In which of the following cases can you make a browser generate a **POST**-type request?
    a. Hyperlinks listed in an HTML document
    b. Typing a URL in a browser's location window
    c. HTML forms
    d. None of the above

EXERCISE 1

Complexity: Easy
1. Design a simple **GET** request for requesting the document **/index.html** hosted by the Web server named **www.doc.com**.

Complexity: Moderate
2. Design a **POST** request containing the following information:

    URL path: /cgi-win/cgitest.exe/form

    HTTP version: 1.1
    Accept header field: text/*; image/jpeg
    Host header field: www.doc.com
    If-Modified-Since header field: Monday, 18-Aug-97 00:00:00 GMT
    User-Agent header field: Mozilla/3.0Gold (Win95; I)
    Content-type header field: text/plain
    Supplemental data: Hello, are you there?

The answers to lab exercises are provided in the HTML-formatted file named **LABANSWERS.HTM** residing in the root directory of the accompanying CD-ROM.

USING THE EXTRA PATH AND QUERY STRING FOR PASSING DATA

As described in Lesson 1, a **GET** request includes a URL_Path entry and some optional header fields that are automatically created by the Web browser when sending the request. The only portion you control in a **GET** request is the URL_Path entry itself. Although it is true that the main purpose of the URL_Path entry is to indicate the location of the requested information resource, that is not the only purpose. Actually, a URL path can consist of the following three sections:

● **Location path**, which gives the whereabouts of the information resource

● **Extra path**, which is the supplemental path information specified after the location path

● **Query string**, which is the data that follows the question mark symbol (?) in the URL_Path entry

An example of a URL path containing all these sections is given below:

`/cgi-win/calendar/viewevents.exe/marketing/sales?fromdate=10/1/97&todate=12/31/97`

In this example, `/cgi-win/calendar/viewevents.exe` is the location path, `/marketing/sales` is the extra path, and `fromdate=10/1/96&todate=12/31/96` is the query string portion of the URL_Path entry. Although the Web server uses the location path to determine the requested information resource (in this case, a Windows CGI program named `VIEWEVENTS.EXE` residing in the `C:\WEBSITE\CGI-WIN\CALENDAR` directory), the extra path and the query string portions are used by the information resource itself to qualify the request further. For instance, in this example, the `VIEWEVENTS.EXE` program (which, let's say, is designed for listing existing calendar events) may use the location path to locate the appropriate calendar file and then use the date range specified in the query string as a filter criteria for selecting the desired events.

How Location Path, Extra Path, and Query String Are Identified

Identifying the query string from a URL_Path entry is easy. Find the first question mark (?) symbol in that entry and mark all the text following that symbol as the query string. Distinguishing the extra path from the location path is not always that simple because extra paths do not have any predefined delimiting characters to separate them. In fact, their separation is really dependent on the rules followed by the Web server that receives the URL_Path entry. To clarify this point, let us take another look at the URL path we studied in the previous section:

`/cgi-win/calendar/viewevents.exe/marketing/sales?fromdate=10/1/97&todate=12/31/97`

When this URL path is received by the WebSite server, it sees that this path starts with `/cgi-win/` (which has a special meaning to this server, as explained in Chapter 2, Lesson 2) and treats this path as a request for a Windows-CGI-based executable program. It keeps parsing this path until it locates the executable file, which in this case happens to be the `VIEWEVENTS.EXE` program. This server treats anything listed after the name of the executable file and before the question mark symbol as the extra path information. A different Web server that does not have any special significance for `/cgi-win/` may consider the complete `/cgi-win/calendar/viewevents.exe/marketing/sales` portion as the location path, especially if this server is able to identify a directory hierarchy to match that location path, as shown in Figure 1-2.

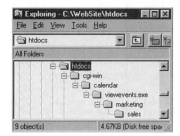

Figure 1-2
Directory hierarchy matching a location path

Application of the Extra Path Information

Originally, the concept of the extra path was conceived to allow CGI application developers the ability to pass supplemental path information to their CGI programs. Most Web servers automatically convert this extra path information into an equivalent physical path using standard mapping rules and then supply this converted path to the CGI program in addition to passing the extra path information. This feature of a Web server is explained in Chapter 2, "Handling User Requests: Static and Dynamic Response."

An Example of Using an Extra Path for Passing Path Information

The event calendar example discussed in the previous two sections illustrates how the extra path portion is used for its originally conceived role. In this example, the WebSite server will first convert the **/marketing/sales** extra path into its equivalent physical path **C:\WEBSITE\HTDOCS\MARKETING\SALES** (assuming the server is using its default mapping configurations) and then pass both the extra path and the physical path information to the **VIEWEVENTS.EXE** CGI program. The **VIEWEVENTS.EXE** program can then use the calendar database file located under the **C:\WEBSITE\HTDOCS\MARKETING\SALES** directory as the data source for its response. If the **VIEWEVENTS.EXE** program is executed in lieu of the following URL path:

```
/cgi-win/calendar/viewevents.exe/marketing/advertizing?fromdate=10/1/97&todate=12/31/97
```

then this program can return the requested events from the calendar database residing in the **C:\WEBSITE\HTDOCS\MARKETING\ADVERTIZING** directory.

Using an Extra Path for Passing Parameters

Many CGI developers have started using the extra path section for passing predefined parameters that have nothing to do with any path information. A typical example of this case is when you have to specify the desired task to a multifunctional CGI program, as illustrated by the following URL_Path entries:

```
/cgi-win/calendar/calendar.exe/viewentries?fromdate=10/1/97&todate=12/31/97
/cgi-win/calendar/calendar.exe/getevententryform
```

Here, a multipurpose CGI program named **CALENDAR.EXE** can perform different functions based on the task (**viewentries** or **getevententryform**) specified in the extra path section of the URL path. Note that the Web server still translates the extra path to its equivalent physical path in both these cases; the CGI program may consider it irrelevant information and simply ignore it.

Application of the Query String Section

The query string section of a URL path is available for providing any type of supplemental data with a **GET** request. In fact, if you are not using the extra path section for its original purpose (and thus the translated physical path information is not important), you can eliminate the need for this section for data passing by using the query string section instead. The following URL_Path entries illustrate this point:

```
/cgi-win/calendar/calendar.exe?task=viewentries&fromdate=10/1/97&todate=12/31/97
/cgi-win/calendar/calendar.exe?task=getevententryform
```

Although there are no conceptual limitations on the kind or amount of data you can send through the query string section (except the physical limits dictated by the Web browser, Web server, and/or their operating environment), there are some restrictions on how you send the data. In particular, you cannot list spaces and many other special characters directly on the query string portion (or on any other part of the URL path). These "forbidden" characters can be sent only using reliable encoding schemes, as explained in Lesson 6 of this chapter.

Lesson Summary

In this lesson, you saw how you can attach any data in a URL path through its extra path and the query string sections. Sometimes this data has to be encoded to propagate special characters. The query string is the data listed after the question mark symbol; the determination of the extra path is dependent on the rules followed by the Web server. The extra path section is mainly used for providing supplementary path information, although it can also be used for passing non-path-related information such as script parameters.

One issue closely related to data passing is data collection. How does a user know what parameters a CGI program requires? For example, if you want to view the calendar of events for November 1997, you need to know the exact syntax for passing the date range. The **VIEWEVENTS.EXE** program may not work as desired if you make the following request:

```
/cgi-win/calendar/viewevents.exe/marketing/sales?startdate=10/1/97&enddate=12/31/97
```

where you use **startdate** and **enddate** (instead of the expected **fromdate** and **todate**) to name the date range parameters.

The important thing to realize from this example is that as a Web application developer, you need to consider not only the aspects of how to pass data through a Web request, but also how to help a user provide that data. Fortunately, the user interface controls supported by HTML forms ease this data collection task, and are the topics of the next four lessons.

1. What sections of a URL path can you use to pass supplemental data?
   a. Location path
   b. Extra path
   c. Query string
   d. All of the above

2. What is the extra path information in the following URL according to the WebSite server running under its default configuration?

   `/cgi-win/cgitest32.exe/form?name=test`

   a. `cgitest32.exe`
   b. `form`
   c. `/form`
   d. `name=test`

3. In which case can you not substitute the extra path section with the query string section for passing data?
   a. Specifying what task to perform to a multipurpose CGI program
   b. Supplying parameters for performing a data query
   c. Providing additional path information that is dependent on the Web server's current configurations
   d. All of the above

4. What is the query string in the following URL?

   `/cgi-shl/mail.sh?1+2`

   a. `3`
   b. `1+2`
   c. `?1+2`
   d. `mail.sh?1+2`

5. Which of the following URL paths are valid?
   a. `/abc/abc?abc abc`
   b. `/?abc`
   c. `?abc`
   d. `/abc/abc.exe/abc`

Complexity: Easy

1. Identify the three logical sections of the following URL path (assuming the rules followed by the WebSite server):

```
/cgi-win/marketing/sales/query.exe/sales/data?username=john+pass-
word=z123+5
```

Complexity: Moderate

2. List four possible ways you can pass the following data through a URL path containing the location **/cgi-win/test.exe**.

```
Task: addrecord
ID: com
Description: Commercial
```

You may include methods where the parameter names (**Task, ID, Description**) can be implicitly assumed.

ADDING A USER INTERFACE

A computer application is effective only when it appears intuitive and friendly to its users. The same holds for an interactive Web application, except the challenge is bigger because often you don't know the users who might be using your application. Most computer application developers achieve the desired intuitiveness and friendliness by using the various user interface objects at their disposal. In the same manner, you can also provide data entry screens employing the variety of input controls supported by HTML (see Figure 1-3) to produce an effective front end for your Web application.

This lesson describes the steps required to create a data entry form using raw HTML code and how to verify the functionality of that form.

You can also use an HTML editor to create HTML forms (without having to master the HTML syntax). Although HTML editors do speed up the form-designing process, it is worthwhile to gain reasonable familiarity down to the HTML level of how these forms are created. In our experience, we have found that the user interfaces of these editors can sometimes become too restrictive and it is faster to review and modify the HTML code directly to achieve the desired form functionality.

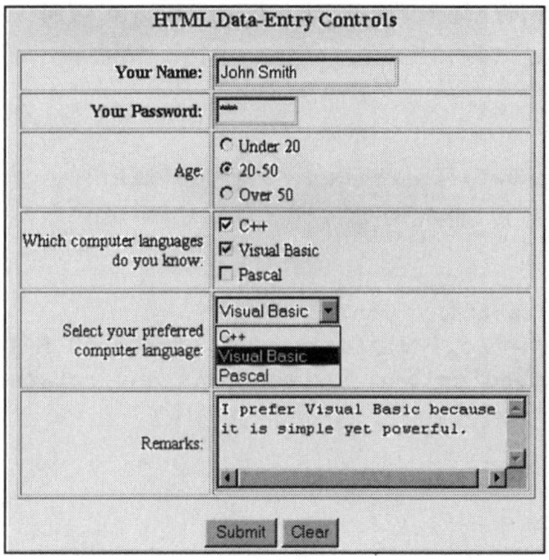

Figure 1-3
Various data entry
controls supported
by HTML

Creating an HTML Form

To design any data entry screen for your Web application, you need to go through the following steps:

1. Create an HTML form within your HTML document.

2. Write the HTML-formatted text for adding labels, images, and other pertinent data entry instructions.

3. Embed the desired data entry controls at the appropriate positions within the scope of the HTML form.

4. Add a Submit button and a Reset button to your form.

Let's examine these steps further by creating the data entry form shown in Figure 1-3.

1. Start by designing a regular HTML document, as shown below:

```
<HTML>
<HEAD>
  <TITLE>HTML Data-Entry Controls</TITLE>
</HEAD>
<BODY>
<CENTER>
  <H3>HTML Data-Entry Controls</H3>
</CENTER>
</BODY>
</HTML>
```

2. Next, insert an HTML form at the appropriate position within this document using the `<FORM...> ... </FORM>` tag pair:

```
<HTML>
<HEAD>
  <TITLE>HTML Data-Entry Controls</TITLE>
</HEAD>
<BODY>
<CENTER>
  <H3>HTML Data-Entry Controls</H3>
  <FORM ACTION="/cgi-win/cgitest32.exe/form" METHOD="POST">
      <!-- Embed data-entry controls and related HTML text in this⇐
section -->
  </FORM>
</CENTER>
</BODY>
</HTML>
```

The ACTION attribute of the `<FORM>` tag indicates the location (URL) of the information resource to which the form data will be sent, which in this case is a CGI-WIN program named CGITEST32.EXE. The functionality of this program is discussed later in this lesson. The METHOD attribute, whose value can be either GET or POST, specifies the HTTP request method the browser should use to send the Web request containing the form data.

3. The data entry screen of Figure 1-3 displays the labels aligned with their respective data entry controls. This formatting technique is commonly used to create informative and visually appealing user interfaces. To create this alignment effect, use the rows and columns of an HTML table within your form, as shown below:

```
<FORM ACTION="/cgi-win/cgitest32.exe/form" METHOD="POST">
      <!-- Embed data-entry controls and related HTML text in this⇐
section -->
  <TABLE BORDER>
      <TR>
          <TD ALIGN=RIGHT><B>Your Name: </B></TD>
          <TD> <!-- Add a text box here --> </TD>
      </TR>
      <TR>
          <TD ALIGN=Right><B>Your Password: </B></TD>
          <TD> <!-- Add a password type text box of size 8 here --><⇐
</TD>
      </TR>
      <!-- Add more rows for other fields -->
  </TABLE>
  </FORM>
```

4. Next, add the appropriate data entry controls using the `<INPUT>`, `<TEXTAREA...>` ... `</TEXTAREA>`, or `<SELECT...>` ... `</SELECT>` HTML tags at their designated positions (here, indicated by the bold-faced text):

```
<FORM ACTION="/cgi-win/cgitest32.exe/form" METHOD="POST">
  <!-- Embed data-entry controls and related HTML text in this⇐
section -->
  <TABLE BORDER>
      <TR>
         <TD ALIGN=RIGHT><B>Your Name: </B></TD>
         <TD> <INPUT NAME="YourName"> </TD>
      </TR>
      <TR>
         <TD ALIGN=Right><B>Your Password: </B></TD>
         <TD> <INPUT NAME="Password" TYPE="PASSWORD" SIZE=8> </TD>
      </TR>
      <!-- Add more rows for other fields -->
   </TABLE>
   </FORM>
```

The exact role and syntax of these tags is discussed in the next three lessons.

5. Finally, add a Submit button and a Reset button at the end of your form (after the table but before the `</FORM>` tag), as shown below:

```
</TABLE><BR>
<INPUT NAME="SUBMIT" TYPE="SUBMIT" VALUE="Submit">
<INPUT NAME="RESET" TYPE="RESET" Value="Clear">
</FORM>
```

Listing 1-1 contains the complete HTML source of the data entry screen shown in Figure 1-3.

Listing 1-1 HTML source of the data entry screen shown in Figure 1-3

```
<HTML>
<HEAD>
  <TITLE>HTML Data-Entry Controls</TITLE>
</HEAD>
<BODY>
<CENTER>
  <H3>HTML Data-Entry Controls</H3>
  <FORM ACTION="/cgi-win/cgitest32.exe/form" METHOD="POST">
    <!-- Embed data-entry controls and related HTML text in this section -->
    <TABLE BORDER>
      <TR>
         <TD ALIGN=RIGHT><B>Your Name: </B></TD>
         <TD> <INPUT NAME="YourName"></TD>
      </TR>
      <TR>
         <TD ALIGN=Right><B>Your Password: </B></TD>
```

continued on next page

continued from previous page

```
                <TD> <INPUT NAME="Password" TYPE="PASSWORD" SIZE=8></TD>
            </TR>
            <TR>
                <TD ALIGN=RIGHT>Age: </TD>
                <TD><INPUT NAME="Age" TYPE="RADIO" VALUE="<20">Under 20 <BR>
                    <INPUT NAME="Age" TYPE="RADIO" VALUE="20-50" CHECKED>20-50 <BR>
                    <INPUT NAME="Age" TYPE="RADIO" VALUE="50+">Over 50
                </TD>
            </TR>
            <TR>
                <TD ALIGN=Right>Which computer languages <BR> do you know: </TD>
                <TD><INPUT NAME="C++" TYPE="CHECKBOX">C++<BR>
                    <INPUT NAME="VB" TYPE="CHECKBOX">Visual Basic<BR>
                    <INPUT NAME="Pascal" TYPE="CHECKBOX">Pascal
                </TD>
            </TR>
            <TR>
                <TD ALIGN=RIGHT>Select your preferred <BR> computer language: </TD>
                <TD><SELECT NAME="Preferred Language">
                    <OPTION>C++
                    <OPTION>Visual Basic
                    <OPTION>Pascal
                </SELECT>
                <BR><BR><BR><BR>      <! To create some blank space >
                </TD>
            </TR>
            <TR>
                <TD ALIGN=RIGHT>Remarks: </TD>
                <TD><TEXTAREA NAME="Remarks" ROWS=3 COLS=30></TEXTAREA></TD>
            </TR>
        </TABLE><BR>
        <INPUT NAME="SUBMIT" TYPE="SUBMIT" VALUE="Submit">
        <INPUT NAME="RESET" TYPE="RESET" Value="Clear">
    </FORM>
</CENTER>
</BODY>
</HTML>
```

Things to Remember When Creating HTML Forms

⬤ If you do not specify the METHOD attribute in the <FORM> tag, the GET method is assumed as the default.

⬤ The <FORM> tag can also accept another optional attribute named ENCTYPE, which specifies the encoding scheme a browser should use to encode form data before sending it to the Web server. In the absence of this attribute, the browser sends data using a scheme called *URL encoding*. Lesson 6 provides more information on how this encoding scheme works.

- You can use the <PRE> ... </PRE> tags for aligning labels and controls in case you want to support older browsers that cannot handle HTML tables.

- You can create multiple forms in the same HTML document, as shown below:

```
<HTML>
  <HEAD>
    <TITLE>Multiple forms</TITLE>
  </HEAD>
  <BODY>
    <!-- Here is form 1 -->
    <FORM ACTION=...>
        <!-- Data-entry controls and associated labels of this form⇐
go here -->
    </FORM>
<!-- Here is form 2 -->
    <FORM ACTION=...>
        <!-- Data-entry controls and associated labels of this form⇐
go here -->
    </FORM>
  </BODY>
</HTML>
```

- You cannot send the form data to multiple destinations.

- You can embed extra path information in the URL listed in the ACTION attribute of the <FORM> tag. However, specifying a query string with that URL when using the GET request method for the form is not recommended because it causes inconsistent behavior among different browsers. For example, in the following case:

```
<FORM ACTION="/cgi-win/cgitest32.exe/form?id=5" METHOD="GET">
```

some browsers (including Netscape) ignore the query string portion (id=5) when sending the form data, whereas others (such as Microsoft Internet Explorer) attach this query string data with the rest of the form data. (Lesson 6 covers the details of how browsers send form data.)

Testing the User Interface

Although you design the user interface with the intention of using it with your Web application, you first create that application to test your interface. It is possible (and fairly easy) to verify the proper functionality of any HTML form by using a general purpose CGI application that simply echoes the data sent through that form. The **CGITEST32.EXE** program, which comes with the WebSite server, is an example of such a general purpose CGI application. By setting the **ACTION** attribute of any HTML form to **/cgi-win/cgitest32.exe/form**, you can view the data the browser sends when you fill out that form and press the Submit button.

Let's examine this testing technique with the HTML form shown in Listing 1-1. However, before you proceed, make sure that you have installed the WebSite server and the book examples per the instructions given in the Installation section of the "Introduction."

1. Start your WebSite server if it is not already running.

2. Load our example HTML form in your Web browser by specifying the following URL:

   `http://localhost/wdbic/chap01/lesson3/example1.htm`

3. Fill out this form as follows:

   ```
                Your Name: John Smith
            Your Password: abc (although it will appear as a string
   of asterisks)
                      Age: 20-50
   Known Computer Languages: C++ and Visual Basic
        Preferred Language: Visual Basic
                  Remarks: I prefer Visual Basic because
                           it is simple yet powerful.
   ```

4. Press the Submit button.

   The `CGITEST32.EXE` program echoes the data it received from this form, as shown in Figure 1-4.

The information presented by the `CGITEST32.EXE` program provides a good overview of how form data is sent. We will analyze this echoed data in more detail when we examine the function of the various HTML data entry controls in the remainder of this chapter.

Lesson Summary

This lesson introduced you to the basic steps required to create an HTML form, which is normally used for collecting information in a user-friendly and organized fashion. The fact that you can test the functionality of these forms without actually having to create the corresponding CGI application first gives you a lot of flexibility. On a large-scale Web application development project involving a team of people, this flexibility can help in the delegation of tasks: One subteam could be designing and testing the data entry screens while the other subteam is programming the CGI application.

1. What is *essential* to make an interactive Web application intuitive and easy to use?
   a. Making it look pretty
   b. Providing appropriate data entry screens
   c. Eliminating some of the functionality to keep it simple
   d. All of the above

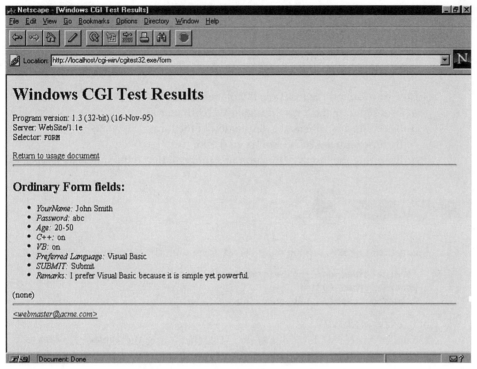

Figure 1-4
Response of the CGITEST32.EXE program

2. Which of the following elements can you include in an HTML form?
   a. HTML-formatted text and images
   b. HTML-based data entry controls
   c. Another HTML form
   d. Submit and Reset buttons

3. Which of the following attributes belongs to a `<FORM>` tag?
   a. `INPUT`
   b. `ACTION`
   c. `ENCTYPE`
   d. `METHOD`

4. What do you specify in the **ACTION** attribute of an HTML form?
   a. Data encoding scheme
   b. Request method
   c. Name of the HTML form
   d. Destination URL

5. How can you test the functionality of an HTML form?
   a. By examining the form through a Web browser
   b. By setting any URL as the destination of the form
   c. By reviewing the HTML source of the form
   d. By setting the form's destination to a program that echoes the data it receives

Complexity: Easy

1. Create the **<FORM...>** tag of an HTML form with the following characteristics:

   Form destination: `/cgi-win/marketing/sales/query.exe/sales/data`
   Request type: POST
   Encoding scheme: URL encoding

Complexity: Moderate

2. Convert the HTML form of Listing 1-1 so that it uses the **<PRE> ... </PRE>** tags for alignment instead of tables and then test this form. Do you notice any change in the functionality of the form by making this change?

TEXT CONTROLS

HTML provides the **<INPUT>**, **<TEXTAREA...> ... </TEXTAREA>**, and **<SELECT...> ... </SELECT>** tags to create different types of user interface objects. These objects are also referred to as data entry controls because they regulate how users supply their data. Table 1-1 provides a summary of all the data entry controls you can create in HTML.

Table 1-1 Data entry controls provided by HTML

Control	Construction Syntax
Single-line text box	`<INPUT TYPE="TEXT" NAME=...>`
Multiline text box	`<TEXTAREA NAME=...> ... </TEXTAREA>`
Password box	`<INPUT TYPE="PASSWORD" NAME=...>`
Radio button	`<INPUT TYPE="RADIO" NAME=...>`

Control	Construction Syntax
Checkbox	`<INPUT TYPE="CHECKBOX" NAME=...>`
Drop-down list box	`<SELECT SIZE=1 NAME=...> ... </SELECT>`
Scrollable list box	`<SELECT SIZE=n NAME=...> ... </SELECT>` *(n>1)*
Multiselect list box	`<SELECT MULTIPLE NAME=...> ... </SELECT>`
Submit button	`<INPUT TYPE="SUBMIT" NAME=...>`
Reset button	`<INPUT TYPE="RESET" NAME=...>`
Area-sensitive image	`<INPUT TYPE="IMG" NAME=...>`
Hidden text box	`<INPUT TYPE="HIDDEN" NAME=...>`
File	`<INPUT TYPE="FILE" NAME=...>`

Among all the HTML-based data entry controls, *text controls* enforce the least amount of restraint because they allow a user to enter any text data. Text controls come in the following varieties (see Figure 1-5):

● Single-line text box

● Password box

● Hidden text box

● Multiple-line text box

This lesson reviews the functionality and attributes of these different types of text controls and how the browser passes the data entered through these controls to the Web server.

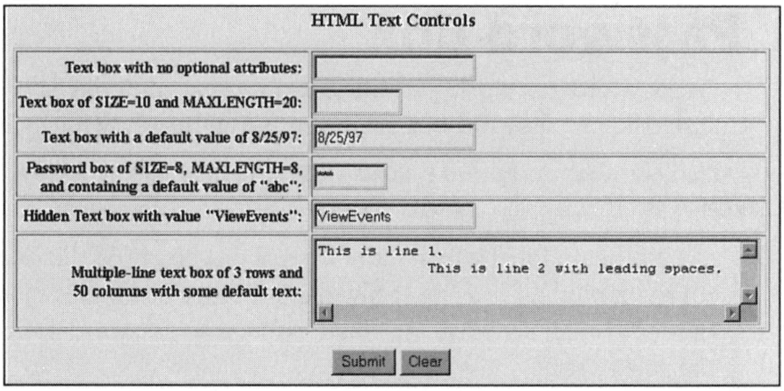

Figure 1-5
Text controls

Single-Line Text Box

A single-line text box is the most widely used control because it accepts any character input from the user without taking too much physical space on the form. It is created using the following syntax:

```
<INPUT NAME="ControlName" [TYPE="TEXT" SIZE=width MAXLENGTH=n VALUE="DefaultValue"]>
```

Note that the **NAME** attribute is the only essential parameter needed with the **<INPUT>** tag to create a text box. The browser sends the value of this **NAME** attribute along with the data entered by the user in that text when the user submits the form. All other attributes are optional. If you do list the **TYPE** attribute with the **<INPUT>** tag, then it must be specified as **"TEXT"** to create a text box.

The SIZE and MAXLENGTH Attributes

The **SIZE** attribute specifies the visible width of the text box on the form, whereas the **MAXLENGTH** attribute indicates the number of characters that text box can accept. The value of the **MAXLENGTH** attribute can be greater than the value of the **SIZE** attribute, in which case the text box will scroll appropriately. (If **MAXLENGTH** is greater than **SIZE**, the data the user enters scrolls to the right until the number of characters entered equals the value of **MAXLENGTH**.) If the **MAXLENGTH** attribute is absent, then a user can enter any number of characters in that text box.

The VALUE Attribute

You can supply a default value to a text box through the **VALUE** attribute. When a user receives the HTML form from the Web server or clicks the Reset button, the Web browser automatically fills in the default value for each text box when displaying that form. If the user does not overwrite that default value, then that value is sent to the server as the data entered for that text box. If the **VALUE** attribute is missing, then the default value of "" is assumed by the browser.

Password Box

A password box works just like a text box except it displays all inputted characters as asterisks. A password box is created using the following syntax:

```
<INPUT NAME="ControlName" TYPE="PASSWORD" [SIZE=width MAXLENGTH=n
VALUE="DefaultValue"]>
```

All the optional attributes of a password box hold the same meaning as in the case of a text box. As you can easily guess, a password box is mainly used when you want a user to enter sensitive information (such as passwords!) that other users should not be able to see.

Although a password box hides the information on a user's screen, the data entered in this box is not implicitly protected (using an encryption method) when the browser sends it to the server, which receives that data just like the rest of the form data.

Hidden Text Box

A hidden text box is not displayed on the form and thus cannot be used to input user data. Its value is generally set by the form developer using the following syntax:

```
<INPUT NAME="ControlName" TYPE="HIDDEN" VALUE="HiddenValue">
```

Hidden text boxes are mainly used for the purpose of passing script parameters or embedding state information within a form, as shown in the following examples:

```
<INPUT NAME="Task" TYPE="Hidden" VALUE="ViewEvents">
<INPUT NAME="SessionID" TYPE="HIDDEN" VALUE="2501">
```

We shall expand on this the role of hidden text boxes in Chapter 12, "Creating A Data Entry Wizard: Advanced Data Entry and Maintenance," Lesson 3.

Multiple-Line Text Box

As the name suggests, a multiple-line text box allows a user to enter one or more lines of any character data (in contrast to a single-line text box, which restricts a user to only one line). You generally use it to collect memo data such as notes or user comments. The syntax for creating a multiple-line text box is as follows:

```
<TEXTAREA NAME="ControlName" [ROWS=nrows COLS=ncols]>Default text</TEXTAREA>
```

The optional **ROWS** and **COLS** attributes dictate the physical width and height of the multiple-line text box. You can fill it with the default text by listing that text within the **<TEXTAREA>...</TEXTAREA>** tag pair.

File Control

The latest version of HTML includes a special file-type text control (**<INPUT TYPE="FILE" NAME=...>**) that allows users to enter a valid file name. This tag is mainly used when there is a need to upload files; not all browsers currently support it. A detailed explanation of this tag is beyond the scope of this book. However, you can experiment with it by loading the following URL in Netscape:

```
http://localhost/cgi-win/uploader.exe
```

Examples of Text Controls

Figure 1-5 displays an HTML form containing the three types of text controls supported by HTML. Listing 1-2 presents the HTML source of this form. Based on the syntax of these controls, you can easily determine the characteristics of each control present in this HTML form and then verify that each control abides by those characteristics by loading the form using the following URL:

```
http://localhost/wdbic/chap01/lesson4/example1.htm
```

and then entering sample data in each control.

Listing 1-2 HTML source of the HTML page shown in Figure 1-5

```
<HTML>
<HEAD>
  <TITLE>HTML Text Controls</TITLE>
</HEAD>
<BODY>
<CENTER>
  <H3>HTML Text Controls</H3>
  <FORM ACTION="/cgi-win/cgitest32.exe/form" METHOD="POST">
    <!-- Embed data-entry controls and related HTML text in this section -->
    <TABLE BORDER>
      <TR>
        <TD ALIGN=RIGHT><B>Text box with no optional attributes: </B></TD>
        <TD> <INPUT NAME="TextBox1"></TD>
      </TR>
      <TR>
        <TD ALIGN=Right><B>Text box of SIZE=10 and MAXLENGTH=20: </B></TD>
        <TD> <INPUT NAME="TextBox2" SIZE=10 MAXLENGTH=20></TD>
      </TR>
      <TR>
        <TD ALIGN=Right><B>Text box with a default value of 8/25/97: </B></TD>
        <TD> <INPUT NAME="TextBox3" VALUE="8/25/97"></TD>
      </TR>
      <TR>
        <TD ALIGN=Right>
          <B>Password box of SIZE=8, MAXLENGTH=8, <BR>
          and containing a default value of "abc": </B>
        </TD>
        <TD> <INPUT NAME="PasswordBox1" TYPE="PASSWORD" SIZE=8 MAXLENGTH=8⇐
VALUE="abc"</TD>
      </TR>
      <TR>
        <TD ALIGN=Right><B>Hidden Text box with value "ViewEvents": </B></TD>
        <TD> <INPUT NAME="HiddenTextBox1" VALUE="ViewEvents"></TD>
      </TR>
      <TR>
        <TD ALIGN=RIGHT>
          <B>Multiple-line text box of 3 rows and <BR>
            50 columns with some default text: </B>
        </TD>
        <TD><TEXTAREA NAME="Multiple-Line TextBox1" ROWS=3 COLS=50>This is line 1.
          This is line 2 with leading spaces.
            </TEXTAREA>
        </TD>
      </TR>
    </TABLE><BR>
    <INPUT NAME="SUBMIT" TYPE="SUBMIT" VALUE="Submit">
    <INPUT NAME="RESET" TYPE="RESET" Value="Clear">
  </FORM>
</CENTER>
</BODY>
</HTML>
```

How the Data from the Text Controls Is Sent to the Web Server

When a user submits a form containing text controls, the Web browser sends the data entered in these controls in the form of name=value pairs, where the name corresponds to the value of the **NAME** attribute of a text control, and the value is data held by that control when the form was submitted. As an example, if you type **abc** in the first text box of the HTML form shown in Figure 1-5, the browser will include **textbox1=abc** in the data it sends to the Web server. The exact format used by a Web browser to send the name=value pair corresponding to each form control is discussed in Lesson 6.

If a text control is empty when a form is submitted, then a name=pair is sent, where the name corresponds to the value of the **NAME** tag of that control.

Lesson Summary

This lesson focused on the different types of text controls you can use in HTML forms to accept user input. The text box control (created using the **<INPUT TYPE="TEXT" ...>** syntax) is the most common type of text control and is used to accept one line of input. The password box control (created using the **<INPUT TYPE="PASSWORD" ...>** syntax) works similar to the regular text box control except it displays all inputted characters as asterisks. The hidden text box (also called a *hidden field*) is a special type of text control whose value is generally set by the form developer; it is used for embedding state information between multiple Web transactions. Each type of text control supports additional attributes to characterize its functionality further.

Although you can add certain input constraints to these text controls, you cannot make the browser enforce any data validation rules on them. For example, there is nothing that prevents a user from entering an invalid date in a text box labeled **Birth Date**. The latest version of HTML (3.2 or higher) does allow you to specify data-specific constraints on text boxes (for example, you can tell a text box to accept only valid dates), but it will take a while before all browsers fully adhere to these standards. On the other hand, if you want to restrict user input to the data values you provide, you have plenty of options, as shown in the next two lessons.

1. What does the **SIZE** attribute of a single-line text box indicate?
    a. The font size of the characters displayed in that text box
    b. The physical width of the text box
    c. The number of characters the text box can accept
    d. None of the above

2. Which of the following text controls can you create with the **\<INPUT\>** tag?
   a. A single-line text box
   b. A password box
   c. A hidden text box
   d. A multiple-line text box

3. Which attributes are common to all types of text controls?
   a. **NAME**
   b. **TYPE**
   c. **SIZE**
   d. **VALUE**

4. Which of the following statements about a hidden text box are correct?
   a. A user cannot change its value.
   b. Its data is displayed using asterisks.
   c. It is used for holding script parameters or state information.
   d. Its value is not sent when the form is submitted.

5. How do you set the default value in a multiple-line text box?
   a. Through the **VALUE** attribute of an **\<INPUT\>** tag
   b. Through the **VALUE** attribute of the **\<TEXTAREA\>** tag
   c. By listing it within the **\<TEXTAREA\> ... \</TEXTAREA\>** tag pair
   d. The default value cannot be set in a multiple-line text box.

Complexity: Easy

1. List the syntax for creating the following text controls:

   a. A 15-character-wide text box named **Your Country** that can accept up to 30 characters and has a default value of **USA**.

   b. A 10-character-wide password box named **Password** that accepts up to 10 characters.

   c. A hidden text box named **StartDate** holding the value **12/1/97**.

   d. A 40×3 multiple-line text box named **Notes** containing the following default text:

   ```
   -- Enter your notes here --
   You can add any number of lines.
   ```

Complexity: Easy

2. Create an HTML form containing the text controls listed in the previous exercise and test that form with different values.

RADIO CONTROLS, CHECKBOXES, AND SELECTION LISTS

Unlike text controls, radio controls, checkboxes, and selection lists limit the user's choice to predefined data values. These controls are applied when you want to ensure that the input data follows a consistent format.

By themselves, a radio control and a checkbox behave in the same manner—they both let you select an option. It is how these controls act in their respective *groups* that distinguishes them from each other. A collection of radio controls, when grouped together (as explained in the next section), becomes a single logical object where a user can select only one of these controls at a time. On the other hand, checkboxes (whether grouped or not) act as independent toggle switches and can be used to simulate a user interface object where you can select multiple choices, as shown in Figure 1-6.

A selection list can show a list of choices for an input field either as a drop-down list or as a scrollable window in which one subset of choices is displayed at a time. You can design a selection list to accept one selection (similar to a group of radio controls) or to accept multiple selections (similar to checkboxes with the same name), as shown in Figure 1-7.

The URL of the HTML form shown in Figure 1-7 is as follows:

```
http://localhost/wdbic/chap01/lesson5/example2.htm
```

The main advantage of using a selection list over a group of radio controls is that a selection list requires less space to present the choices on the form. You can easily add more choices to an existing selection list without increasing the physical size of your form.

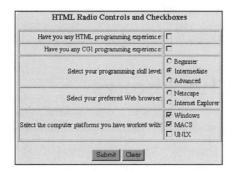

Figure 1-6
Radio Controls and
Checkboxes

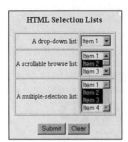

Figure 1-7
Selection lists

Creating and Grouping Radio Controls

A radio control (sometimes also called a *radio button*) is created using the following syntax:

```
<INPUT NAME="ControlName" TYPE="RADIO" [VALUE="ReturnValue" CHECKED]>
```

Like any data entry control, the **NAME** attribute identifies a particular radio control. The **VALUE** attribute defines the data that a browser should associate with that radio control when it is selected. This is an optional attribute, and if it is absent from the **<INPUT>** tag, the browser associates a default value of **on** with that control. The **CHECKED** attribute, if present, tells the browser to show the control as selected by default.

Multiple radio controls can be associated together to form a logical *option group* by assigning the same name to each control. For example, the question asking the programming skill level in the data entry screen shown in Figure 1-6 is formed using the following HTML code:

```
<TD ALIGN=RIGHT>Select your programming skill level:</TD>
<TD>
   <INPUT NAME="SkillLevel" TYPE="RADIO" VALUE="Beginner">Beginner<BR>
   <INPUT NAME="SkillLevel" TYPE="RADIO" VALUE="Intermediate" CHECKED>Intermediate<BR>
   <INPUT NAME="SkillLevel" TYPE="RADIO" VALUE="Advanced">Advanced<BR>
</TD>
```

Because all three radio controls have the same name, the browser allows you to select only one radio control. If you click on the radio control labeled **Advanced**, the browser will automatically deselect the radio control labeled **Intermediate** (which was selected by default).

Creating Checkboxes

A checkbox, which provides a natural way for seeking a yes/no type answer, is created just like a radio control except that the **TYPE** attribute is set to **CHECKBOX**.

```
<INPUT NAME="ControlName" TYPE="CHECKBOX" [VALUE="ReturnValue" CHECKED]>
```

Unlike radio controls, checkboxes do not behave any differently in a collection than they do individually, although you can simulate a *many-to-many* selection group by putting a bunch of checkboxes next to each other, as shown below:

```
<TD ALIGN=RIGHT>Select the computer platforms you have worked with:</TD>
<TD>
   <INPUT NAME="Platform" TYPE="CHECKBOX" VALUE="W" CHECKED>Windows<BR>
   <INPUT NAME="Platform" TYPE="CHECKBOX" VALUE="M" CHECKED>MACS<BR>
   <INPUT NAME="Platform" TYPE="CHECKBOX" VALUE="U">UNIX<BR>
</TD>
```

Defining a Selection List

A selection list is defined through the **<SELECT>** ... **</SELECT>** tag pair, as shown below:

```
<SELECT NAME=ControlName [SIZE=n MULTIPLE]>
   <OPTION [VALUE="ReturnValue1" SELECTED]>Item Description 1
   <OPTION [VALUE="ReturnValue2" SELECTED]>Item Description 2
   <!-- List more options using the OPTION tag here -->
</SELECT>
```

The **NAME** attribute of the **<SELECT>** tag describes the name of the input control represented by the selection list. The **SIZE** attribute specifies how many items are visible in the selection list at a time. It is an optional attribute, and in its absence, a default size of 1 is assumed. The presence of the **MULTIPLE** attribute allows a user to select many items at once from a selection list.

The **<OPTION>** tag delineates each item in the selection list. The item description that follows this tag is shown in the selection list, whereas the data specified in the **VALUE** attribute is returned to the server if that item is selected. In the absence of the **VALUE** attribute, the selected item's description is itself returned to the server.

The **SELECTED** attribute, if present for an option, informs the browser to preselect that item when it displays the form. You can set this attribute on more than one item in a multiple-selection list. To see all these list-related tags and attributes in action, refer to Listing 1-3, which shows how the three selection lists displayed in Figure 1-7 have been created.

Listing 1-3 HTML source of the selection lists shown in Figure 1-7

```
<HTML>
<HEAD>
   <TITLE>HTML Selection Lists</TITLE>
</HEAD>
<BODY>
<CENTER>
   <H3>HTML Selection Lists</H3>
   <FORM ACTION="/cgi-win/cgitest32.exe/form" METHOD="POST">
     <TABLE BORDER>
       <TR>
          <TD ALIGN=Right>A drop-down list:</TD>
          <TD>
             <SELECT NAME="List1">
```

continued on next page

continued from previous page

```
                <OPTION>Item 1
                <OPTION>Item 2
                <OPTION>Item 3
            </SELECT>
        </TD>
    </TR>
    <TR>
        <TD ALIGN=Right>A scrollable browse list:</TD>
        <TD>
            <SELECT NAME="List2" SIZE=3>
                <OPTION VALUE="1">Item 1
                <OPTION VALUE="2" SELECTED>Item 2
                <OPTION VALUE="3">Item 3
                <OPTION VALUE="4">Item 4
            </SELECT>
        </TD>
    </TR>
    <TR>
        <TD ALIGN=Right>A multiple-selection list:</TD>
        <TD>
            <SELECT NAME="List3" SIZE=4 MULTIPLE>
                <OPTION VALUE="1">Item 1
                <OPTION VALUE="2" SELECTED>Item 2
                <OPTION VALUE="3" SELECTED>Item 3
                <OPTION VALUE="4">Item 4
            </SELECT>
        </TD>
    </TR>
    </TABLE><BR>
    <INPUT NAME="SUBMIT" TYPE="SUBMIT" VALUE="Submit">
    <INPUT NAME="RESET" TYPE="RESET" Value="Clear">
    </FORM>
</CENTER>
</BODY>
</HTML>
```

For your reference, the code in Listing 1-3 is also provided in the file **EXAMPLE2.HTM**
residing in the **C:\WEBSITE\HTDOCS\WDBIC\CHAP01\LESSON5** directory.

How the Data from the Radio Controls and Checkboxes Is Sent

When a user submits a form containing radio controls and checkboxes, the browser
sends the value of only the selected controls in the form of name=value pairs. No data
is sent for radio controls or checkboxes that are not selected. Compare this with the
text controls, where a name=value pair is always sent regardless of whether or not a text
control contains any data.

The following experiment illustrates how data passing works in the case of radio controls and checkboxes:

1. Ensure that your WebSite server is running.

2. Load the HTML form shown in Figure 1-6 in your browser using the following URL:

   `http://localhost/wdbic/chap01/lesson5/example1.htm`

3. Select the radio control that says `Have you any HTML experience?` and leave everything else in its default state.

4. Press the Submit button.

5. The `CGITEST32.EXE` program echoes the name=value pairs it received from this form submission, as shown in Figure 1-8.

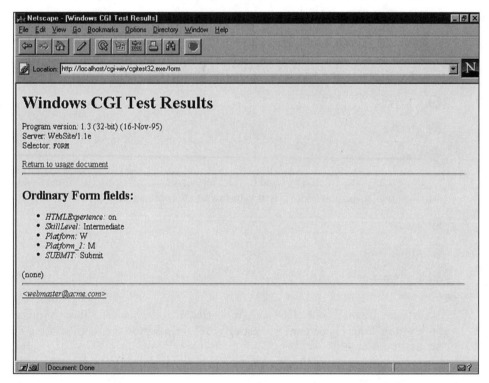

Figure 1-8
Data representing the selected radio controls and checkboxes

Observe in Figure 1-8 that no data (not even the name) appears for the checkboxes and radio controls that were unchecked. Also, in the case of the two selected checkboxes with the same name (`Platform`), the following two name=value pairs were received by the `CGITEST32.EXE` program:

```
Platform: W
Platform_1: M
```

As you will see in the next lesson, the Web browser actually sends these two pairs as `Platform=W&Platform=M`. The Windows CGI standard causes the Web server to add an incremental numeric index with every name that is repeated. Chapter 2, "Handling User Requests: Static and Dynamic Response," covers this behavior of Windows CGI in more detail.

How the Data from the Selection Lists Is Sent

A name=value pair is sent for every item selected in a selection list. As an example, if you select Item 1, Item 2, and Item 3 from the multiple selection list shown in Figure 1-7, then the following data pairs will be sent for that list:

- ● `List3=1`

- ● `List3=2`

- ● `List3=3`

These data pairs, when translated by the Web server according to the Windows CGI standard, will appear as follows to a Windows CGI application:

- ● `List3=1`

- ● `List3_1=2`

- ● `List3_2=3`

No data pair is sent if none of the items is selected in a selection list, although you can prevent this from happening by creating a default selection for that list using the `SELECTED` attribute.

Lesson Summary

Radio controls, checkboxes, and selection lists limit the range of user data to discrete values. A key thing to note is that the option you display next to a radio or checkbox control or in a selection list does not have to be the data that gets transmitted when that option is selected. This feature proves extremely useful when you are accepting data for adding records into a normalized database, in which codes representing the option (instead of the actual option description) may have to be stored as part of the record. (Database design and normalization concepts are discussed in Chapter 3, "Organizing Data: Tables and Relationships.")

Finally, remember that the browser does not send any information related with a radio control or checkbox or an item of a selection list that was not selected when the form was submitted. This also means that if you have an option group of radio controls and none is selected, no data will be sent for that option group. If you want to ensure that an option is always selected, whether in an option group or in a selection list, simply make an option the default selection.

1. What is the main function of radio controls?
   a. To allow a user to enter any data
   b. To select one option from multiple choices
   c. To select multiple options from a list of choices
   d. None of the above

2. In which of the following cases can you use selection lists in place of checkboxes or radio controls?
   a. To display available options using different formats
   b. To gather a yes/no answer
   c. To select one option from multiple choices
   d. To select multiple options from a list of choices

3. What information does the browser send for the following checkbox control when it is not selected?

   ```
   <INPUT NAME="Checkbox1" TYPE="CHECKBOX" VALUE="True">
   ```

   a. It does not send any information.
   b. It sends a **"Checkbox1="** name=value pair.
   c. It sends a **"Checkbox1=False"** name=value pair.
   d. It sends a **"Checkbox1=True"** name=value pair.

4. Which of the following attributes are required with the **<INPUT>** tag to create a checkbox or a radio control?
   a. **NAME**
   b. **TYPE**
   c. **VALUE**
   d. All of the above

5. How many name=value pairs will be sent if three items are selected in a multiple selection list?

    a. None

    b. 1

    c. 3

    d. Same as the total number of items in that list

Complexity: Easy

1. List the syntax for creating the following controls with their appropriate labels:

    a. A checkbox named **Married** that returns a **Yes** value when it is selected.

    b. A radio control option group named **Marital Status** containing the following options and their return values:

```
Single     (Return Value: 1)
Married     (Return Value: 2)
Divorced    (Return Value: 1)
```

    c. A drop-down list named **Marital Status** containing the above options with the **Married** option set as the default selection.

Complexity: Easy

2. Create an HTML form that asks the following questions:

    a. Are you employed?

    b. If yes, what is the nature of your job?

```
Computer Programming
Accounting
Marketing
Other
```

    c. If you selected "other" in the previous question, please explain further.

    d. What are your main hobbies?

```
None
Gardening
Sports
Travel
```

You may use any names and default values for your controls.

FORM SUBMISSION TECHNIQUES AND DATA ENCODING SCHEMES

Every form requires some mechanism that allows a user to submit the form data to the Web server. Until now, you have been using a Submit button for this purpose, which is created using the following syntax:

```
<INPUT NAME="ButtonName" TYPE="SUBMIT" [VALUE="ButtonValue"]>
```

The *ButtonValue* listed in the **VALUE** attribute acts as the button caption. Also, if you observe the data passed by the Web browser in lieu of pressing the Submit button (for example, see Figure 1-7), you will notice that the browser includes a name=value pair for the Submit button itself. This fact comes in very handy when you want to provide multiple Submit buttons on your form and then have your CGI program process the form data based on what button the user presses to submit the form.

Using Multiple Submit Buttons on a Form

You can use multiple copies of the **<INPUT TYPE="SUBMIT" ...>** tag to list any number of Submit buttons on your form, as shown in Figure 1-9.

Listing 1-4 lists the HTML source of the notification form shown in Figure 1-9. (For your reference, the code in this listing is also provided in the file named **EXAMPLE1. HTM** residing in the **C:\WEBSITE\HTDOCS\WDBIC\CHAP01\LESSON6** directory.)

Figure 1-9
A form with multiple Submit buttons

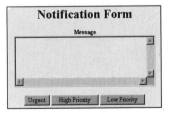

Listing 1-4 HTML source of the notification form shown in Figure 1-9

```
<HTML>
<HEAD>
  <TITLE>Notification Form</TITLE>
</HEAD>
<BODY>
  <CENTER>
  <H1>Notification Form</H1><P>
  <FORM METHOD=POST ACTION="/cgi-win/cgitest32.exe/form">
    <B>Message</B><BR>
    <TEXTAREA NAME="Message" ROWS=5 COLS=40></TEXTAREA><BR><BR>
    <INPUT NAME="SUBMIT" TYPE="SUBMIT" VALUE="Urgent">
    <INPUT NAME="SUBMIT" TYPE="SUBMIT" VALUE="High Priority">
    <INPUT NAME="SUBMIT" TYPE="SUBMIT" VALUE="Low Priority">
  </FORM>
</BODY>
</HTML>
```

As an example, if you type a message and use the High Priority button to send your message, the specified CGI program will receive `SUBMIT=High Priority` as the name=value pair for that button. The program can then use that information to process the received message appropriately.

Using an Image to Submit a Form

HTML also allows you to use an image to act as a Submit button, an approach often used to help in the layout of a form to enhance its visual effects. The syntax for creating such image buttons is as follows:

```
<INPUT NAME="ButtonName" TYPE="IMAGE" SRC="ImageURL">
```

Figure 1-10 shows the modified notification form that uses an image as a Submit button. (For your reference, the code in this listing is also provided in the file named `EXAMPLE2.HTM` residing in the `C:\WEBSITE\HTDOCS\WDBIC\CHAP01\LESSON6` directory.) Listing 1-5 shows the HTML source of this modified notification form.

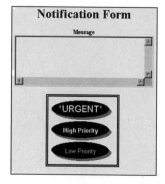

Figure 1-10
A form where an image is used as a Submit button

Listing 1-5 HTML source of the notification form shown in Figure 1-10

```
<HTML>
<HEAD>
  <TITLE>Notification Form</TITLE>
</HEAD>
<BODY>
  <CENTER>
  <H1>Notification Form</H1><P>
  <FORM METHOD=POST ACTION="/cgi-win/cgitest32.exe/form">
    <B>Message</B><BR>
    <TEXTAREA NAME="Message" ROWS=5 COLS=40></TEXTAREA><BR><BR>
    <INPUT NAME="SUBMIT" TYPE="IMAGE" SRC="btnimg.gif">
  </FORM>
</BODY>
</HTML>
```

Note that there is only one image (`btnimg.gif`) representing all three priority buttons. How can the CGI program determine the priority level of the received message in this situation? The answer lies in the type of data the browser sends for this image, which happens to be the horizontal and vertical coordinates of the point on which the user clicks this image. This coordinate set is passed to the Web server as the following two name=value pairs:

```
Submit.x = x_coordinate_value
Submit.y = y_coordinate_value
```

The CGI program can inspect these coordinates to identify which button the user pressed, sort of like processing an image map.

You can also use a separate image for each button instead of one image representing all three buttons. By giving separate names to each image (for example, `submit1`, `submit2`, and `submit3`), you can determine the priority level by inspecting the name of the image used for submitting the form.

Data Encoding Schemes

By now, you know that a Web browser sends both the name and the data associated for all the data entry controls present on a form except in the case of unselected radio controls, checkboxes, or selection list items. The actual format the browser uses to transmit this data depends on the encoding scheme specified in the **ENCTYPE** attribute of the **<FORM>** tag.

The most widely accepted encoding scheme in use today is called the *URL encoding scheme*, which is specified as follows:

```
<FORM ACTION="URL" METHOD="RequestMethod" ENCTYPE="application/x-www-form-urlencoded">
```

The **ENCTYPE** attribute is an optional attribute, and if it is not included in the **<FORM>** tag, the browser automatically applies the URL encoding scheme to send the data.

Characteristics of the URL Encoding Scheme

The URL encoding scheme packages data from all fields into a single text string using the following name=value pair format:

```
name1=value1&name2=value2&name3=value3...
```

During this URL encoding process, the spaces (in either the field name or the data) are converted into plus signs (+). The plus sign and other special symbols--such as ampersand (&), equal sign (=), quote ("), percentage sign (%), and most other nonalphanumeric characters—are translated as **%xx**, where **xx** denotes the hexadecimal representation of their ASCII code. For VB enthusiasts, who understand an algorithm better when it is presented in the form of actual code, Listing 1-6 presents a Visual Basic function that illustrates how the URL encoding translation process works.

Listing 1-6 The URLEncode Visual Basic function

```
'==================================================================
' Function URLEncode(DataString As String)
' Purpose: Returns the URLEncoding of the input parameter: DataString
' Assumption: Everything non-alphanumeric and not belonging to the
'             set [@*-.] is a special character
'==================================================================
'
Public Function URLEncode(DataString As String) As String
   Dim EncodedValue As String, i As Long
   Dim Char As String
Dim EncodedChar As String, Encode As Integer
   Dim HexValue As Integer
   Dim DataValue As String

   EncodedValue = ""                     'Initialize encoded value to an empty string
   For i = 1 To Len(DataString)          'For each character of this datastring
     Char = Mid$(DataString, i, 1)       'Get the ith character
     Encode = True                       'Start by assuming that the character is to be encoded
     If Char >= "0" And Char <= "9" Then Encode = False    'If character is a digit⇐
then do not encode
     If Char >= "A" And Char <= "Z" Then Encode = False    'If character is a letter
If Char >= "a" And Char <= "z" Then Encode = False     'then do not encode
     If InStr("@*-_.", Char) > 0 Then Encode = False       'If character belongs to ⇐
the set (@,*,-,.) then do not encode
       If Encode Then                    'If charcter is marked for encoding then
         If Char = " " Then              'if character is a space
           EncodedChar = "+"             'then encode it as a + character
```

```
        Else                          'otherwise
          HexValue = Hex(Asc(Char))    'Get the ascii value of the character in hex format
          If Len(HexValue) = 1 Then HexValue = "0" & HexValue    'Pad this hex format
with a 0 to make it 2 digits
          EncodedChar = "%" & HexValue  'Finally, attach an & sign to the 2-digit hex value
        End If
      Else                            'If character is not marked for encoding
        EncodedChar = Char               'then set the encoded char to the original character
      End If
      EncodedValue = EncodedValue & EncodedChar                'Append the character to⇐
the current encoded value
    Next
    URLEncode = EncodedValue               'Return the encoded value as the function's result
End Function
```

As an example, `URLEncode("Webs 'R Us")` would produce `"Webs+%27R+Us"` as the function's return value.

Viewing URL Encoded Data

For your convenience, we have provided a Windows-CGI utility called `FORMINP.EXE` residing in the `C:\WEBSITE\CGI-WIN\WDBIC\FORMAPPS` directory whose objective is to return any data it receives in its original encoded form. To use this utility, set the `ACTION` attribute of the HTML form as follows:

```
ACTION="/cgi-win/wdbic/formapps/forminp.exe"
```

As an example, the following URL points to the HTML form shown in Figure 1-11:

```
http://localhost/wdbic/chap01/lesson6/example3.htm
```

The actual HTML source of this form is identical to the source shown in Listing 1-2 except that the `ACTION` attribute of this form calls for the `FORMINP.EXE` utility instead of the `CGITEST32.EXE` utility. If you submit this form in its default, the `FORMINP.EXE` returns the URL encoded string, as shown in Figure 1-12. (Note that the figure does not show the complete string.)

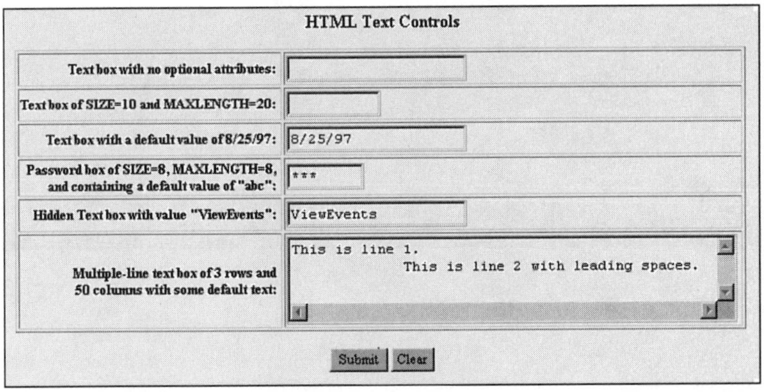

Figure 1-11
An HTML form using the FORMINP.EXE utility

Multipart Encoding Scheme

The multipart encoding scheme is another data encoding scheme that does not require translation of special characters while sending form data. This scheme is mainly used for uploading files through HTML forms and is specified by setting the **ENCTYPE** attribute of the **<FORM>** tag as follows:

```
ENCTYPE="multipart/form-data"
```

Under the multipart encoding scheme, the browser selects a boundary string that does not occur in any part of the form data. This boundary string selection is sometimes done using random text-generation algorithms. Each field of the form is sent in the order in which it occurs in the form, as a part of the multipart stream. Each part identifies the field name and is labeled with an appropriate content type if the media type of the data is known (for example, inferred from the file extension or operating system typing information).

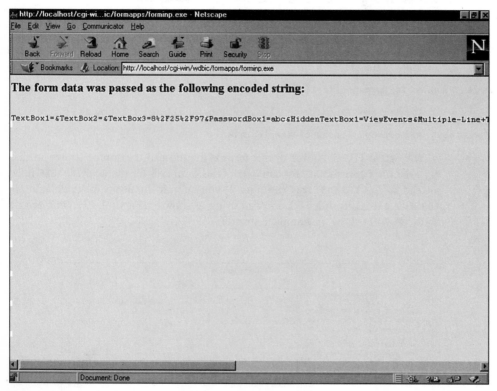

Figure 1-12
URL encoded data presented by the FORMINP.EXE utility

As an example, the HTML form represented by the following URL is constructed similar to the one shown in Figure 1-11 except that it has **ENCTYPE** set to `multipart/form-data`.

`http://localhost/wdbic/chap01/lesson6/example4.htm`

When you submit this form (in its default state) using the Netscape browser, the **FORMINP.EXE** utility outputs the received multipart encoded data, as shown in Figure 1-13.

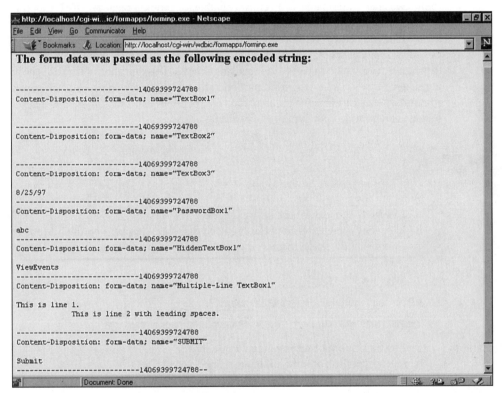

Figure 1-13
Multipart encoded data presented by the FORMINP.EXE utility

Lesson Summary

This lesson discussed how a Submit button or a submit image is not meant for just submitting a form but can also be used for passing data. Whereas the browser sends one name=value pair in the case of a Submit button, it passes two name=value pairs for a submit image, which represents the (x,y) coordinate of the point at which the image is clicked.

After the discussion of the form submission techniques, the focus of this lesson moved to the two encoding schemes currently available for sending data. The URL encoding scheme, which lists the name=value pairs as a connected string, is the default encoding scheme applied by Web browsers to send form data. The only negative aspect of this scheme is that spaces and many other special characters have to be translated into their hex representation as part of the encoding process. This limitation of the URL encoding scheme is resolved by the multipart encoding scheme, which uses the concept of a boundary string to separate different data components. The only problem is that this scheme is new and is not supported by all browsers yet.

1. What are the roles of the **VALUE** attribute in the case of a Submit button?
   a. To specify the text for the button caption
   b. To specify the URL of the bitmap image that should appear on the button
   c. To indicate the value that a browser should send when a user presses that Submit button
   d. All of the above

2. What does the following `<INPUT>` tag do?

   ```
   <INPUT NAME="btnQuery" TYPE="IMAGE" SRC="submit.gif">
   ```

   a. Creates a Submit button named `btnQuery`
   b. Sets a hyperlink around an image named `submit.gif`
   c. Creates a data entry control named `btnQuery` that accepts images instead of text data, with `submit.gif` being the default image
   d. Makes the `submit.gif` image act as a Submit button

3. How many name=value pairs are sent if an HTML form contains one Submit button and one submit image and a user clicks on the submit image?
   a. None
   b. 1
   c. 2
   d. 3

4. Which of the following characteristics apply to the URL encoding scheme?
   a. The data is encrypted.
   b. The data is packaged into a single text string that does not contain any spaces.
   c. Each space in the data is represented with a plus symbol (+).
   d. Most nonalphanumeric characters are translated into their hexadecimal representation using the **%xx** format.

5. What are the main advantages of the multipart encoding scheme over the URL encoding scheme?
   a. The multipart encoding scheme compresses data, whereas the URL encoding scheme does not.
   b. The multipart encoding scheme does not require any translation of original data.
   c. You can send the content type of the data in the multipart encoding scheme.
   d. You can conceptually send any type and any amount of data with the multipart encoding scheme but you cannot do this with the URL encoding scheme.

Complexity: Easy
1. Encode the following name=value pairs using the URL encoding scheme:

```
Name=John Smith
Address 1=123 'C' Street
Address 2=
City=Oakland
State=CA
```

Complexity: Advanced
2. Write a Visual Basic function named **URLDecode** that decodes the data encoded by the **URLEncode** function shown in Listing 1-6.

CHAPTER SUMMARY

This chapter discussed techniques for collecting and passing information from Web users. Knowledge of these techniques is essential for designing the appropriate front end of any Web application. Here is a recap of the salient points covered in this chapter:

● The Web follows a client-server model in which Web clients and Web servers interact through requests and responses using the protocol called HTTP.

● HTTP is a message-based but stateless communication protocol and supports many methods of sending a Web request, among which GET and POST are the most widely supported. The fact that it is stateless poses some interesting issues for developers of Web database applications, as you will see later in this book.

● Both GET and POST request methods accept a URL path and several optional header fields, but only the POST method allows a separate section in the Web request to attach additional data.

● You can also attach data in a GET request through the extra path and query string sections of a URL path, although you cannot directly list spaces and many other special characters in these sections.

● To collect data from users, you use HTML forms created using the <FORM ...> ... </FORM> tag pair.

● HTML supports several types of data entry objects, such as text controls, radio controls, checkboxes, and selection lists.

● Text controls can accept any text data. You can use them for single-line input fields, passwords, or comments.

● You can use hidden fields to embed parameters or state information within an HTML form.

● Radio controls allow you to create option groups in which you can select one of many available options.

● You use checkboxes for accepting a yes/no answer.

● Selection lists allow you to gather one or more choices from a user without taking a lot of screen space.

● Data from text controls and selected radio controls, checkboxes, and selection list items is passed using a name=value format.

● You can use multiple Submit buttons for your HTML form. The value associated with the Submit button used to submit is sent along with the rest of the form data as another name=value pair.

● An image can also be used to submit. In this case, two name=value pairs representing the (x,y) coordinates of the point at which the user clicked the image accompany as part of the form data.

● You can use the CGITEST32.EXE CGI utility to test the functionality of any HTML form.

- The URL encoding scheme and the multipart encoding scheme are the two methods of packaging form data. The URL encoding scheme is the most commonly used and is supported by all browsers.

- You can use the FORMINP.EXE CGI utility to echo the form data in its encoded form.

Most of the topics presented in this chapter are related to the functionality of a Web client and how you use that functionality to obtain user input and send that input to an executable program, which we sometimes also refer to as a CGI application. What is the nature of this executable program? Why is it called a CGI application? What role does a Web server play in passing data between the Web client and this CGI application? You will uncover these mysteries in the next chapter.

HANDLING USER REQUESTS: STATIC AND DYNAMIC RESPONSE

This chapter covers how a Web server responds to a user request, how it passes data to external applications using standard and Windows CGI, and how external applications return their response to the requesting user via the Web server. In particular, you will learn about

- The file server and the gateway functions of a Web server

- MIME types

- Document, content, and CGI mapping

- Environment variables in standard CGI

- Temporary files created under Windows CGI

- Differences between standard CGI and Windows CGI

● Format of an HTTP response

● Redirecting a URL

● Getting authenticating information from a Web user

ROLE OF THE WEB SERVER

A Web server is essentially a computer program that listens for incoming Web requests and returns appropriate responses that usually contain the information requested. The Web server can take the information from a static file or have it generated on the fly.

Serving Static Documents

In its primary role, a Web server acts like an efficient read-only file server that can send complete files residing in its domain to the requesting Web clients. The server identifies the file being requested by translating the URL path included in a Web request to a physical file path using a procedure called *document mapping* (discussed later in this lesson). Figure 2-1 shows the Web server in its basic file-serving role.

Acting as a Gateway to External Programs

Although delivering static files is the principal responsibility of any Web server, what makes Web servers so unique from other types of file servers (such as FTP and Gopher servers) is their ability to position themselves as a gateway between a Web client and an external program. In this gateway role, a Web server passes information

Figure 2-1
The Web server as a read-only file server

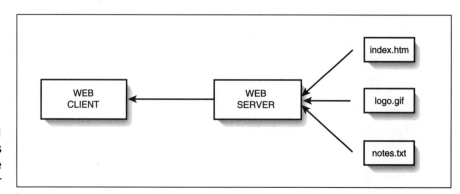

attached with the HTTP request to the specified external program and then delivers the response from that program to the requesting client. Figure 2-2 depicts the Web server in its role as a gateway to other programs.

An established standard known as the Common Gateway Interface (CGI) defines how a Web server and any external program should interact when the server is acting as a gateway. Like HTTP, which dictates how a Web server and a Web client should interact, the CGI is a simple, efficient, platform-independent communication standard. However, unlike HTTP, this interface has several different flavors; the two popular ones are

- Standard CGI

- Windows CGI

The *standard CGI* is actually the CGI specification originally developed by the World Wide Web (WWW) consortium and is widely used on UNIX platforms. However, it was found that due to the limitations of popular programming environments such as Visual Basic 3.0 and the idiosyncrasies of the 16-bit Windows operating system, Windows programs adhering to this specification could not be designed. As a result, a variation of the standard CGI called the *Windows CGI* was established to allow developers to create Windows programs for their Web applications.

Fortunately, the 32-bit Windows operating systems (Windows 95 and Windows NT) and their programming environments such as Visual Basic 5.0 have eliminated the limitations that originally prevented the creation of Windows applications using the standard CGI. However, this does not mean that Windows CGI is history. In fact, the simplicity and inherent debugging facilities of Windows CGI make it a popular standard for rapidly developing powerful Web applications. Lesson 3 describes the standard CGI specification; Lessons 4 and 5 cover the Windows CGI specification and highlight the main differences between the two standards.

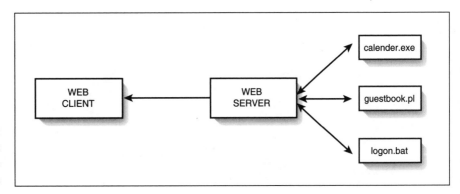

Figure 2-2
The Web server as a gateway to external programs

An Extendible Program

In addition to supporting the various CGI specifications, many Web servers have started providing their own application programming interfaces (server APIs) for creating Web applications. With server APIs, developers can extend the functionality of the Web server itself to create Web applications that perform better than their equivalent CGI versions. Server APIs do have their drawbacks. They tend to be platform and server dependent (each server sets its own standard) and are thus not as universal as CGI standards. In addition, it is generally a lot harder to design and debug Web applications using server APIs. A detailed discussion of the various server APIs currently on the market is beyond the scope of this book. We recommend that you go through your server's manuals for more information on this subject.

Document Mapping

Document mapping defines the set of rules by which a Web server identifies the file corresponding to any URL path. These rules are specified by associating a URL path (or a starting portion of a URL path) to a physical directory location. Figure 2-3 shows the default document mapping of the WebSite server included with this book. The installation section of this book describes how to set these associations.

When a Web server receives a URL path from the incoming request, it uses the following algorithm to determine the appropriate file:

● Find the URL path from the document mapping list that most closely matches this requested URL path and get the associated directory path.

Figure 2-3
Default document
mapping of the
WebSite server

⬤ Append the unmatched portion of the URL path to this directory path. In case of a Windows platform, also convert the forward slashes (/) to backward slashes during this appending process.

⬤ If the resulting directory path leads to an individual file, then that file corresponds to the requested path.

⬤ If the resulting directory path leads to a physical directory, then the designated default file (generally one that matches `index.*`, such as `index.htm` or `index.html`) residing in that directory corresponds to the requested path.

As an example, let's say the WebSite server receives the following URL path:

`/wsdocs/demo/home.htm`

Based on the document mapping shown in Figure 2-3 and the URL translation algorithm given above, that server will try to fetch the following file:

`C:\WEBSITE\WSDOCS\DEMO\HOME.HTM`

At the minimum, an association for the URL path / must exist in the document mapping of a Web server for the server to translate any incoming URL path successfully. The directory mapped to the / path is also called the *document root directory* of a Web server.

Lesson Summary

In this lesson, you studied the two most important functions of a Web server—to disperse files and to act as a gateway between a Web client and any external program that follows one of the supported CGI specifications. The gateway capability of a Web server imparts a three-tiered architecture to the client-server model of the World Wide Web and is the key to developing interactive Web applications.

For a Web server to function properly as a gateway, the server must have the appropriate permissions to execute the requested CGI program. Furthermore, remember that the CGI program and the Web server run on the same computer. These two factors raise a big security concern, because a badly designed or misrepresented CGI program without appropriate security control can potentially cause many undesirable effects, such as crashing the system, deleting critical files, and divulging sensitive information. Before you put any CGI application into a production environment, test it thoroughly on a test server first and then move it to the production server after ensuring that the proper security controls are in place.

1. What is the primary role of a Web server?
   a. To talk to other Web servers
   b. To create the environment of distributed computing
   c. To disperse files within its domain
   d. To run other programs

2. What does a Web server do when it acts in the role of a gateway?
   a. It sends the requested file to the Web client.
   b. It executes the requested program.
   c. It passes data between the Web client and the requested program.
   d. It allows a Web client to talk directly to the requested program.

3. What is a Common Gateway Interface?
   a. Another name for HTTP
   b. A formal specification on how the interaction between a Web server and an external program should take place
   c. A formal specification on how the interaction between a Web client and an external program should take place
   d. A general notation for UNIX-based Perl scripts

4. What are the main characteristics of a server API?
   a. It is generally more efficient than a CGI.
   b. It works on all types of Web servers in the same fashion.
   c. It extends the capability of a Web server.
   d. It generally eases the Web application development process.

5. Which file will a Web server retrieve if it encounters the URL path `/icons/book.gif` and has the following associations in its document mapping?

```
/               --> C:\WEBSITE\HTDOCS\
/icons/         --> C:\WEBSITE\ICONS\
/icons/book/    --> C:\WEBSITE\BOOK\
```

   a. `C:\WEBSITE\HTDOCS\ICONS\BOOK.GIF`
   b. `C:\WEBSITE\BOOK\ICONS\BOOK.GIF`
   c. `C:\WEBSITE\BOOK\INDEX.GIF`
   d. `C:\WEBSITE\ICONS\BOOK.GIF`

Complexity: Easy

1. Write a document mapping rule that sets the document root directory of a Web server to `C:\WEB`.

Complexity: Moderate

2. Create the shortest set of document mapping rules that will make a Web server associate URL paths to the files as shown below:

```
/                      --> C:\HOME\INDEX.HTM
/logo.gif              --> C:\HOME\LOGO.GIF
/webdocs/index.htm     --> C:\HOME\WEBDOCS\INDEX.HTM
/help/                 --> C:\HOME\WEBDOCS\INDEX.HTM
```

MIME TYPES, CONTENT MAPPING, AND CGI MAPPING

Besides serving the requested document, a Web server is also responsible for sending information about the document itself. The requesting Web client uses this additional information to display or process the data sent by the Web server. Two questions originate in this context. How does a server determine this supplementary information and what method does it use to specify this information to the Web client? The answers come from the use of MIME types and content mapping.

MIME Types

MIME, which stands for *Multipurpose Internet Mail Extensions*, is a technical specification originally developed for Internet mail to exchange different types of documents. Due to its inherent flexibility and growing popularity, the MIME standard was adopted by the WWW consortium as the means to identify the type of information a Web server sends to a Web client.

Under the general MIME specifications, the information about any data content is specified using a *type/subtype* pair. This pair is also referred to as a *media type*. The **type** attribute, which identifies the general category of a data content, must be one of the following seven predefined MIME types:

● Text: Used to describe text of various types, including plain text, HTML, and PostScript.

● Multipart: Denotes that a message contains multiple sections with potentially more than one MIME type.

● Message: Used for various types of messages, including messages that refer to other messages for elements of their bodies.

● Application: Used for miscellaneous data types.

● `Image`: Applied in the case of graphics files, such as GIF or JPEG.

● `Audio`: Used for audio formats such as *Sun u-law* (`.AU`) or Microsoft Windows (`.WAV`) files.

● `Video`: Used for video formats such as QuickTime, MPEG, or Microsoft Video files.

The **subtype** attribute is used to indicate the exact format of the data content. Like the approved MIME types, several subtypes have already been standardized. However, you can define your own subtypes for local use or experimental purposes as long as they contain **x-** as a prefix. Some examples of commonly used type/subtype pairs are given in Table 2-1.

Table 2-1 Examples of commonly used media types

Media Type	Used For
`text/plain`	Plain text documents
`text/html`	HTML-formatted documents
`image/gif`	GIF image
`image/jpeg`	JPEG image
`audio/basic`	Basic audio data (`.au` files)
`audio/wav`	WAV-formatted sound data
`audio/x-midi`	MIDI-formatted sound data
`video/quicktime`	QuickTime video file
`video/mpeg`	MPEG-formatted video
`application/octet-stream`	Any 8-bit data
`application/x-java-class`	Java applet
`application/msword`	Microsoft Word document

Content Mapping

Content mapping lists the association between a file extension and a media type, as shown in Figure 2-4.

When a Web server is ready to send a requested file, it looks at that file's extension (the section of the file name listed after the dot) and determines its designated media type from the content mapping list. The server then passes the media type in its response through a header field named **Content-type**. Lesson 5 describes the exact format of a Web server's response and the various header fields that can be included in that response.

As an example of content mapping, if a Web user requests a file using the following URL path:

`/marketing/salesdata.zip`

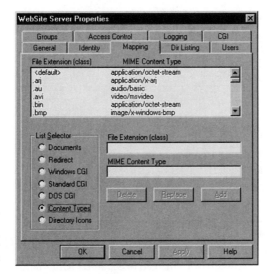

Figure 2-4
Content mapping
section of the
WebSite server

and the `.zip` file extension is associated with the media type `application/x-zip-compressed` in the content mapping of the Web server, then the server sends the `Content-type` header field as follows:

```
Content-type: application/x-zip-compressed
```

The Web browser, upon receiving this header field, checks its own action mapping table (that the Web user controls) to determine how the data of the media type `application/x-zip-compressed` is to be handled. For instance, if the action requires the client to save that data, then the client may prompt the Web user for the appropriate file name for saving that data. Figure 2-5 shows an action mapping table of the Netscape 3.0 browser (under Options, General Preferences).

Figure 2-5
Action mapping
table of the
Netscape 3.0
browser

CGI Mapping

Lesson 1 described how a Web server can act either as a file server or as a gateway to other programs. The question that remains is how does the server know when to send a file and when to execute it? For example, if you make a request containing the following URL path:

`/web/calendar.exe`

should the Web server send the file named **calendar.exe** or execute it and then send the results generated by this program? The answer lies in a concept called *CGI mapping*, which a Web server uses to resolve this question. CGI mapping works similarly to document mapping. You map URL paths to their appropriate directory location, except that the server treats these directories as CGI directories containing programs that should be executed instead of served. For instance, say you want the server to execute the **calendar.exe** file residing in the **C:\WEB** directory when a user requests the **/web/calendar.exe** URL path. In that case, you will go to the CGI mapping section of the server's configuration (instead of the document mapping section) and associate **/web/** with the **C:\WEB** directory path.

Web servers such as WebSite support multiple CGI standards. So when you are establishing CGI mapping in these servers, you need to make sure that you pick the appropriate CGI mapping section. For example, if you want to specify a directory mapping for Windows CGI programs in a WebSite server, select the Windows CGI option in its configuration utility, as shown in Figure 2-6.

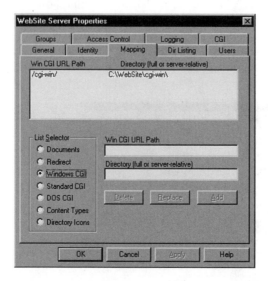

Figure 2-6
Windows CGI mapping section of the WebSite server

As you can see Figure 2-6, the `/cgi-win/` URL path is mapped to the `C:\WEBSITE\CGI-WIN\` physical path. This means that the server should consider the `C:\WEBSITE\CGI-WIN` directory and all its subdirectories as Windows CGI directories. So, if you have a Windows CGI application (say `GUESTBOOK.EXE`), then you must place that application under this directory hierarchy. If you want to place it under a different directory (say `C:\BIN\`) and have it accessed using the URL path `/bin/` (for example, `/bin/guestbook.exe`), then you need to create another Windows CGI mapping, as shown below:

```
/bin/   --> C:\BIN\
```

Lesson Summary

This lesson described how you can customize the behavior of a Web server using its content mapping and the CGI mapping configuration options. The content mapping establishes the association between a file extension and its corresponding MIME types. The server uses this mapping to send the correct value for the `Content-type` header field, which the browser uses to interpret the response appropriately. The MIME types, which are formatted as a type/subtype pair, follow an established convention; refer to the following URL for a complete list of standardized MIME types:

```
ftp://ftp.isi.edu/in-notes/iana/assignments/media-types
```

CGI mapping allows you to mark certain directories as CGI directories, in which you keep your CGI programs. If an incoming URL path maps to a file residing in a CGI directory, then the server executes that file instead of delivering it. This implies that you cannot keep regular files and CGI programs in the same directory (although the WebSite server provides a workaround for this, as indicated in the following tip). Remember that when specifying CGI mapping, it is important that you select the appropriate CGI option. For example, you cannot add a Perl script based on the standard CGI to a directory that has been mapped under Windows CGI.

To keep a Windows CGI program in a regular document directory, change its file extension to `.wcgi`. In the case of a standard CGI program, change its file extension to `.scgi`. This workaround is generally not recommended due to a higher security risk: Anyone who has access to a document directory can potentially run CGI programs. If you want to disable this workaround, delete the associations for these file extensions in your server's content mapping section.

Now that you have examined the relationship between a Web server and an external program, it is time to look into the nitty-gritty of the CGI specification. The next lesson describes the original CGI specification, which I have also been referring to as standard CGI.

QUIZ 2

1. What is the purpose of the MIME standard?
   a. To exchange different types of documents through Internet mail
   b. To send different types of documents on the Web
   c. To compress different types of documents
   d. To encrypt different types of documents

2. Which of the following MIME types adheres to the acceptable MIME convention?
   a. `html/text`
   b. `image/y-jpeg`
   c. `application/x-winhelp`
   d. `multipart/mixed`

3. How does a Web server determine the format of a document?
   a. Using document mapping
   b. Using content mapping
   c. Using CGI mapping
   d. By examining the contents of the document

4. What role does CGI mapping play in the Web server's operation?
   a. It allows you to mark a URL path as a CGI path.
   b. It allows a CGI program and a regular document to reside in the same directory.
   c. It associates a URL path with a physical directory location that holds the CGI programs.
   d. All of the above.

5. How will the Web server react to the URL path `/cgisrc/test.bat` if the server has the following mapping configurations?

```
Document Mapping
/                --> C:\WEBSITE\HTDOCS\

Content Mapping
.bat          --> application/x-script-batch
.exe          --> application/octet-stream

CGI Mapping
/cgibin/   --> C:\WEBSITE\CGIBIN\
```

   a. It will execute the `test.bat` file residing in the `C:\WEBSITE\HTDOCS\CGISRC` directory.
   b. It will send the contents of the `test.bat` file residing in the `C:\WEBSITE\HTDOCS\CGISRC` directory.
   c. It will execute the `test.bat` file residing in the `C:\WEBSITE\CGIBIN` directory.
   d. It will send the value `application/x-script-batch` for the `Content-type` header field.

EXERCISE 2

Complexity: Easy

1. List the standard MIME types used for the following types of files:

```
HTML documents
Windows Executable (.exe) Files
Postscript documents
Rich text documents
```

Complexity: Easy

2. Create a set of document, content, and CGI mapping rules that will make a Web server respond to URL paths as shown below:

```
/readme.doc              --> Return the file C:\DOCROOT\INDEX.HTM
with content type text/plain.
/cgisrc/test.bas         --> Return the file C:\CGISRC\TEST.BAS with
content type application/x-basic
/wincgi/test.exe         --> Execute the file C:\CGI-WIN\TEST.EXE
```

LESSON 3

THE STANDARD CGI

A CGI defines how a Web server and the external program (also called a CGI program) communicate with each other. Specifically, this interface provides answers to the following five questions:

1. How is the information transferred between the Web server and a CGI program?

2. What information is supplied by the Web server to a CGI program?

3. What format is used by the Web server to supply the information?

4. What information can be returned by a CGI program?

5. What format is used by a CGI program to return the information?

The standard CGI is a specification originally developed to answer these questions. It is designed so that developers can write external programs using a wide variety of programming tools (for example, C++, Perl). By using a memory-based data-passing mechanism (described in the next lesson), the standard CGI allows a Web server to communicate with multiple CGI programs (or multiple instances of the same CGI program) concurrently. In other words, a Web server can process multiple standard CGI-based requests at the same time.

How Data Is Passed in Standard CGI

As explained in Chapter 1, "Gathering User-Data: HTML Forms and Queries," a fully formed Web request includes a URL path and some header fields. The URL path has the location and optional extra path and query string information. If the request is sent using a **POST** method, then that request can also include supplemental data at the end. If the incoming request calls for the services of an external program based on standard CGI, then the Web server executes the CGI program as an independent process and passes all the data contained in the request to that process. In addition, the server provides some information about its current state. The CGI program reads the data from its environment and input channel (**STDIN**) established by the server for that program, processes the request based on that data, and then returns the response to the output channel (**STDOUT**) established by the server.

The Web server uses two methods to send all relevant information to a CGI process:

● Environment variables

● Standard input stream (STDIN)

The environment variables are like global variables attached to a CGI process that last only until that process is terminated. The standard input stream is like a sequential read-only file available to a CGI process, except that all the data resides in memory. The standard output stream, which the CGI program uses to communicate its response, is like a memory-mapped sequential write-only file. Most operating systems and programming tools that allow the creation of text-based (console-mode) command-line programs support these data-passing methods, which is why standard CGI claims its universal appeal.

Figure 2-7 provides more clarification on how the communication takes place through standard CGI. In this figure, the Web server receives three concurrent Web requests (from three different Web clients), one asking for the services of the **FIND.EXE** standard CGI program, and the other two asking for the services of the **SEARCH.PL** Perl script (which is also assumed to be based on standard CGI). The server executes the requested programs (two instances of the same program in case of the **SEARCH.PL** Perl script) and passes the data it receives from the incoming requests to these program instances via their standard input channels. The server then expects the response from these instances via their standard output channels and eventually forwards those responses to the waiting clients.

The following list summarizes the different types of information the server delivers to the CGI program and which of the two methods it uses to send each type of information, per the standard CGI specifications:

● The dissected URL path (as environment variables)

● The state of the server (as environment variables)

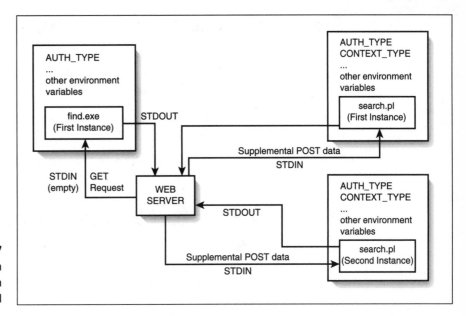

Figure 2-7
Communication
methods used in
standard CGI

- The header fields included in the request (as environment variables)
- The supplemental data attached with a POST request (fed through the standard input stream of the CGI program)

Path-Related Environment Variables

The Web server sets the following path-related environment variables based on the incoming URL path and its own document mapping rules:

- SCRIPT_NAME: Contains the location portion of a URL path.
- PATH_INFO: Contains the extra path portion of a URL path.
- PATH_TRANSLATED: Holds the physical path equivalent of the extra path information based on the server's document mapping.
- QUERY_STRING: Contains the query string portion of a URL path.

As an example, if the incoming request includes the following URL path:

```
/cgi-bin/search.pl/sales?keyword=web
```

then the server may set the above four path-related environment variables as follows:

```
SCRIPT_NAME: /cgi-bin/search.pl
PATH_INFO: /sales
PATH_TRANSLATED: C:\WEBSITE\HTDOCS\SALES
QUERY_STRING: keyword=web
```

Server-Related Environment Variables

The following environment variables provide information about the server itself:

- GATEWAY_INTERFACE: Provides the version number of the CGI specification used by the server. For example, CGI/1.1.

- SERVER_NAME: Gives the fully qualified domain name of the Web server as set in the server's configuration.

- SERVER_SOFTWARE: Indicates the name and version of the Web server software.

Request-Related Environment Variables

Several environment variables are created based on the header fields that accompany the CGI request. In addition, the Web server sets environment variables corresponding to the method and the HTTP version used by the client to make the request. The commonly used environment variables in this category are listed below:

- AUTH_TYPE: Specifies the type of authentication a client used to send the request. For example, BASIC.

- CONTENT_LENGTH: Indicates the length (in bytes) of the supplemental data attached with a POST request. For example, 124. Note that this variable may be blank or zero in the case of a GET request.

- CONTENT_TYPE: Holds the MIME type of the supplemental data attached with a POST request. For example, application/x-www-form-urlencoded.

- HTTP_ACCEPT: Provides a comma-delimited list of MIME types acceptable to the Web client. For example, text/html, image/gif, image/jpeg.

- HTTP_KEEP_ALIVE: If present, this variable indicates if the Web client requested the reuse of the connection for future use.

- HTTP_REFERRER: Holds the URL of the document that referred the user to the requested CGI program. For example, http://www.acme.com/directory.htm.

- HTTP_USER_AGENT: Lists the information on the requesting Web client, which generally contains the product code name, the version, and the operating platform for which the client software is designed. For example, Mozilla/3.0Gold (Win95; I).

- REMOTE_ADDR: Provides the IP address of the computer on which the client making the request is running. Note that if the client is going through a proxy server, then this holds the IP address of that proxy server. For example, 199.1.166.171.

- REMOTE_HOST: Lists the fully qualified domain name of the computer on which the client making the request is running. This information is not always available, because all computers connected to the Web do not have a fully qualified domain name. Moreover, some Web servers, including WebSite, require that a special option be set in their configuration to provide this information. For example, www.acme.com.

- REMOTE_USER: If AUTH_TYPE is set, this variable contains the user name provided by the user and validated by the server. For example, john.

- REQUEST_METHOD: Lists the method the client used to make the CGI request. For example, POST.

- SERVER_PORT: Indicates the TCP port on which the request came. For example, 80.

- SERVER_PROTOCOL: Indicates the name and version of the information protocol used by the Web client to make the CGI request. For example, HTTP/1.0.

Note that many new environment variables are added to the CGI specification as the HTTP protocol evolves. Refer to your server manual or consult the following URL for the latest request-related CGI environment variables:

```
http://www.w3.org/hypertext/WWW/CGI
```

Data in the Standard Input Stream

The supplemental data included in a POST request is supplied through the standard input stream (STDIN). The CONTENT_TYPE and the CONTENT_LENGTH environment variables reflect the format and size of this data. In case of a GET request, the standard input stream is empty and the user data comes via the QUERY_STRING variable. If your CGI program or script needs to access the user data, it should inspect the REQUEST_METHOD variable first to decide where to look for that data.

Lesson Summary

This lesson described how the standard CGI specification employs the concept of environment variables and a standard for transferring data from the server to each CGI process launched by that server. Because both these data-passing techniques are memory based, standard CGI communication is quite efficient. However, this efficiency comes at a small price, which you notice when you try to debug a program based on standard CGI independently.

To debug a standard CGI program quickly, say using the step-by-step debugging facilities included in your program development environment, you need to launch the CGI program directly (without involving the Web server). This means that you have to somehow first capture the environment the Web server creates when it launches that program and then re-create that environment before you launch that program through your debugger. Neither of these tasks is easy. It is hard to capture environment variables and standard input because they are both memory-bound entities that disappear when the process they are associated with terminates. Furthermore, although most debugging environments allow you to specify a file to act as standard input, the majority of them do not provide a built-in mechanism for creating environment variables. When developing large-scale Web applications, you will find that these debugging hindrances can become a big issue. On the other hand, Windows CGI eliminates these debugging limitations due to its use of files for data communication between the server and the external program. We will study the details of Windows CGI in the next lesson.

We also mentioned in this lesson that a CGI specification dictates not only how the server passes data to a CGI program but also how a CGI program should return its response to the server. We will examine this aspect of the equation with respect to both standard CGI and Windows CGI in Lesson 6.

1. Which of the following issues a CGI address?
   a. Data passed between a Web client and an external program
   b. Data passed between a Web server and an external program
   c. Information passed by the Web server to an external program
   d. Data returned by the external program to the Web server

2. What communication methods does the standard CGI use for transferring data from the Web server to an external program?
   a. Text files
   b. Dynamic Data Exchange (DDE)
   c. Environment variables
   d. Standard input/output streams

3. Which path-related environment variable depends on the current configuration of the Web server?
   a. `SCRIPT_NAME`
   b. `PATH_INFO`
   c. `PATH_TRANSLATED`
   d. `QUERY STRING`

4. Which environment variables contain the information related to the computer on which the Web client is running?
   a. `REMOTE_USER`
   b. `HTTP_USER_AGENT`

    c. `REMOTE_HOST`

    d. `REMOTE_ADDR`

5. Why is it difficult to debug Web applications based on standard CGI?

    a. Because it is hard to re-create the environment in which you can debug the CGI program without involving the Web server

    b. Because standard CGI programs must be programmed using sophisticated languages

    c. Because CGI programs are slower than regular programs

    d. All of the above

EXERCISE 3

Complexity: Moderate

1. List the values of the environment variables and the state of the standard input stream set by a Web server for the following standard CGI request. Assume that `C:\WEB` is the document root directory of the server. (Make reasonable guesses wherever you feel that complete information is not provided here.)

```
POST /cgi-bin/wdbic/search.exe/books/data HTTP/1.0
<NL>
Accept: text/*; image/jpeg
Host: localhost
If-Modified-Since: Friday, 15-Aug-97 02:12:28 GMT
User-Agent: Mozilla/3.0Gold (Win95; I)
Referrer: http://localhost/
Content-type: application/x-www-form-urlencoded
Content-length: 21
<NL>
keywords=web+database
```

Complexity: Moderate

2. Write an algorithm showing how you can correctly read all the data passed by the Web server using standard CGI.

THE WINDOWS COMMON GATEWAY INTERFACE

Windows CGI is a CGI specification designed by Robert Denny (the developer of the WebSite server) to facilitate CGI programming using graphical languages such as Visual Basic and Delphi that do not provide a direct mechanism to tap into the standard input/output streams. It closely follows the footsteps of standard CGI except it uses temporary files instead of memory-based environment variables and input/output streams to exchange data. The use of temporary files is clearly not the fastest way of communicating, but Windows CGI makes up for this deficiency in other areas, such as ease of debugging and automatic data decoding, as you will see later in this lesson.

How Data Is Passed in Windows CGI

Under Windows CGI, data communication occurs in the following sequence:

1. The Web server receives a client's request containing a URL path associated under Windows CGI mapping (refer to Lesson 2). This request is also termed a *Windows CGI request.*

2. The server locates the specified Windows CGI program using Windows CGI mapping. It then places the data to be passed to that program in a primary input file termed the *CGI profile* file (which generally ends with an .INI file extension). In certain cases (described later in this lesson), the server may create secondary input files for storing additional data. In such cases, the CGI profile file includes the file paths of all the secondary input files.

   The CGI profile file also contains the name and path of the file where the server expects the Windows CGI program to write its result. This file is termed the *CGI output* file (which generally ends with an .OUT file extension).

3. The Web server then executes the Windows CGI program, passing the location of the CGI profile file as its first command-line argument.

4. After executing the Windows CGI program, the server waits for the CGI program to terminate. While waiting, the server may process other regular or CGI requests.

5. The Windows CGI program reads the profile file whose location is specified in its first command-line argument and performs the necessary actions. The program may use the data included in the CGI profile file and any other associated secondary input files.

6. Before terminating, the CGI program writes its response to the CGI output file whose location is listed in the profile file.

7. Upon getting the termination signal, the Web server reads the CGI output file, determines if the output data needs any packaging, and sends the final data to the requesting client.

8. The Web server then deletes all the temporary files created during the processing of this request unless you disable this step in the server's configuration.

Figure 2-8 shows how the communication takes place in Windows CGI.

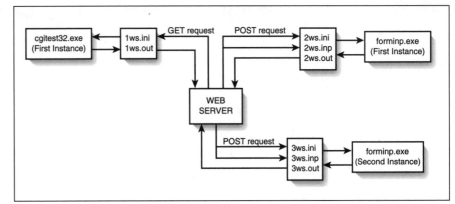

Figure 2-8
Communication
methods used in
Windows CGI

The CGI Profile File

The CGI profile file is a text file that mimics the structure of a regular Windows .INI file. It contains data organized under the following eight sections, some of which are optional:

- CGI
- System
- Form literal (optional)
- Form external (optional)
- Form huge (optional)
- Form file (optional)
- Accept
- Extra headers

The name of each section appears on its own line and is enclosed within square brackets ([]). The data appears as a name=value pair, and each pair is listed on a separate line. Figure 2-9 shows the contents of a sample CGI file.

The [CGI] Section

This section holds a name=value pair corresponding to each environment variable of standard CGI except for the **HTTP_ACCEPT** variable, which gets its own separate [Accept] section in Windows CGI. The name portion of this name=value pair does not exactly match the name of the standard CGI environment variable, but it is relatively easy to form the correlation. The value portion stays identical to the value found in the corresponding environment variable.

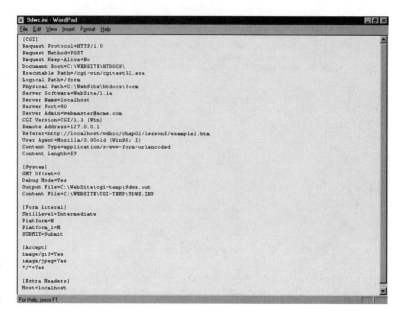

Figure 2-9
Format of a CGI
profile file

The [System] Section

This section contains parameters specific to Windows CGI:

- GMT Offset: This parameter specifies the number of seconds to be added to GMT time to reach local time.

- Debug Mode: This parameter indicates whether the CGI tracing option (explained in the next section) is enabled.

- Output File: This parameter refers to the name and path of the CGI output file in which the server expects to receive the CGI program's results.

- Content File: This parameter refers to the name and path of the CGI content file that contains the user data passed in the body of the POST-type Web request.

The [Form Literal], [Form External], [Form Huge], and [Form File] Sections

These sections contain information about the user data that accompanies a POST-type Web request. The next lesson explains these sections in complete detail.

The [Accept] Section

This section lists the information passed through the `Accept` header field of a Web request. The `Accept` header field contains data about all the Web client's acceptable content types in the following format:

```
Accept:  type/subtype [;parameters], type/subtype [;parameters]
```

The server writes each content type appearing in the preceding list on a separate line in the [Accept] section as a name=value pair. The type/subtype is listed in the name portion, and the parameters are set as the value of that pair. If there are no parameters supplied with the content type, then the server automatically assigns a `Yes` value.

As an example, if the following `Accept` header field is passed in an HTTP request:

```
Accept:  */*, text/html, text/plain; q=0.5, image/gif
```

The [Accept] section will contain the following lines:

```
[Accept]
*/*=Yes
text/html=Yes
text/plain=q=0.5
image/gif=Yes
```

The [Extra Headers] Section

This section contains the HTTP request header fields that do not have a CGI variable associated with them. As an example, the `Host` header field that some Web clients (such as Netscape) send to indicate the server's host name is listed in this section.

Do not confuse the `Host` header field with the `Remote Host` variable of the [CGI] section, although they both provide the fully qualified domain name of the Web server. The `Host` field is sent by the client based on the host name listed in the URL, whereas the value of the `Remote Host` variable is supplied by the Web server using Domain Name Server (DNS) lookup.

Identifying the Temporary CGI Files Under WebSite

The `CGITEST32.EXE` and `FORMINP.EXE` utilities discussed in Chapter 1 are Windows CGI programs. Whenever you send a request for these programs through an HTML form or as a direct URL, the server communicates with these programs using temporary files. The following steps describe how you can locate these temporary files in the case of the WebSite server:

1. Launch the `Server Admin` utility by selecting the Server Properties icon in the WebSite 1.1 program group.

   The `Server Admin` utility displays the general section, which lists the CGI temporary directory as `c:\WEBSITE\CGI-TEMP` (see Figure 2-10).

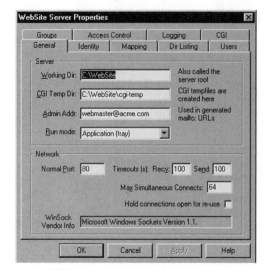

Figure 2-10
The General section
of the WebSite
Server Admin utility

2. Click on the Logging tab to display the Logging section.

3. Select the tracing option labeled API/CGI Execution, as shown in
   Figure 2-11.

4. Click on the OK button to close the Server Admin utility. Wait a few seconds
   for this configuration change to take effect.

5. Start your WebSite server if it is not already running.

Figure 2-11
The Logging
section of the
WebSite Server
Admin utility

6. Run your Web browser and enter the following URL in its Location window:

`http://localhost/cgi-win/cgitest32.exe/CGI`

This URL causes the WebSite server to execute the CGITEST32.EXE program.

7. After the browser shows the response to the preceding CGI request, go to an MS-DOS window and list the files matching the pattern *ws.* in the `c:\WEBSITE\CGI-TEMP\` directory by typing the following commands:

```
CD C:\WEBSITE\CGI-TEMP <ENTER>
DIR <ENTER>
```

The directory listing produces three files with the same first name but different file extensions, as shown in Figure 2-12. Note that you may see a different set of file names than the ones shown in the figure. This is because WebSite autoincrements the file name to ensure it is unique.

The files with the `.INI` and `.OUT` extensions are respectively the CGI profile file and the CGI output file created during this CGI interaction between the server and the **CGITEST32.EXE** program. You can view their contents in any text editor.

The directory listing also shows a file with an `.INP` extension. This is the *CGI content* file, and it holds any data attached with a **POST** request. Because in this demonstration you sent a **GET** request, this file appears as empty (file size is 0). The next lesson describes the format of the CGI content file in more detail.

Lesson Summary

This lesson discussed how Windows CGI works using temporary files as a means of communication between the Web server and an external program. Under this standard,

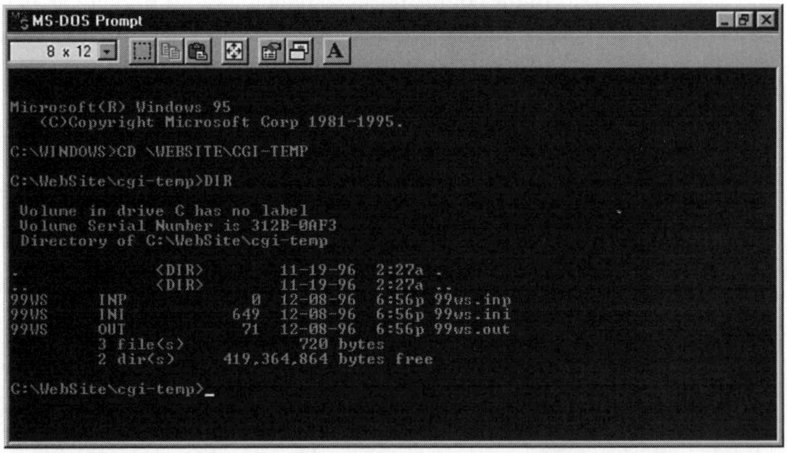

Figure 2-12
Temporary CGI files
created by the
WebSite server

the server stores most of the data in the CGI profile file and passes the name of that file to that program as a command-line argument. The server expects the results from the external program in the CGI output file whose location is listed in the [System] section of the CGI profile file.

The CGI profile file mimics the structure of a regular Windows .INI file and can contain a maximum of eight sections; the [CGI], [System], [Accept], and [Extra Headers] sections were covered in this lesson. The other four sections are devoted to the supplemental data passed through a POST request and are explained in the next lesson, where you will notice that, unlike standard CGI, Windows CGI requires a Web server to provide this supplemental data to the external program in both the original (encoded) as well as the decoded format.

1. How does Windows CGI differ from standard CGI?
   a. Windows CGI uses a different communication model.
   b. Windows CGI decodes the supplemental POST data, whereas standard CGI does not.
   c. Windows CGI variables and the corresponding standard CGI variables have different values.
   d. All of the above.

2. Which of the following statements are correct about the CGI profile file?
   a. This file is created every time a server executes a Windows CGI program.
   b. Its location is specified in the command-line argument of the Windows CGI program.
   c. This file mimics the structure of a regular Windows .INI file.
   d. This file contains a maximum of eight predefined sections.

3. Where is the location of the output file specified under Windows CGI?
   a. In the command-line argument of the executable program
   b. In the CGI profile file
   c. In the CGI content file
   d. As an environment variable

4. How does Windows CGI handle the data contained in the Accept header field of a Web request?
   a. By listing it as an Accept=fieldvalue pair under the [CGI] section of the CGI profile file.
   b. By listing it as an Accept=fieldvalue pair under the [Accept] section of the CGI profile file.
   c. By listing each type/subtype as a separate line under the [Accept] section.
   d. By putting it in a separate temporary input file whose name is listed in the [Accept] section.

5. According to the Windows CGI specifications, how should a Web server supply the request header field named **Cookie** containing the data **SessionID=5**?

   a. It should list it as **Cookie=SessionID=5** on a separate line under the [CGI] section.

   b. It should list it as a **SessionID=5** on a separate line under the [Extra Headers] section.

   c. It should create another section named [Cookie] and list **SessionID=5** as the only line under that section.

   d. It should list it as **Cookie=SessionID=5** on a separate line under the [Extra Headers] section.

Complexity: Moderate

1. List the contents of the CGI profile file that a Web server would create for the following Windows CGI request. Assume **C:\WEB** is the document root directory of the server and it picks the name **86ws.ini** for this file. (Make reasonable guesses wherever you feel that complete information is not provided here.)

```
GET /cgi-win/wdbic/search.exe/books/data HTTP/1.0
<NL>
Accept: text/*; image/jpeg
Host: localhost
If-Modified-Since: Friday, 15-Aug-97 02:12:28 GMT
User-Agent: Mozilla/3.0Gold (Win95; I)
Referrer: http://localhost/
```

Complexity: Moderate

2. Submit the following Windows CGI–based form (in its default state) to your WebSite server, and list the contents of all the temporary files created by the server due to this event:

```
http://localhost/wdbic/chap01/lesson4/example1.htm
```

WINDOWS CGI AND FORM DATA

In standard CGI, the Web server sends the supplemental data attached with a **POST**-type Web request through the standard input stream. In Windows CGI, the Web server puts this data in the CGI content (**.INP**) file and supplies the location of that file in the

[System] section of the CGI profile file. Furthermore, if this supplemental data is encoded using either the URL or multipart encoding scheme, the server also provides a decoded version of this data through the four form-related sections of the CGI profile file, as outlined below:

1. For each name=value pair occurring in the encoded data, the server decodes the value (replacing all the escape codes with the original characters as entered by the user) and lists each name=(decoded) value pair on a separate line under the [Form Literal] section of the CGI profile file.

2. If there are multiple pairs in the URL encoded string with the same name (for example, when a user selects more than one option for a multiple selection list), the server generates a regular name=(decoded) value line for the first pair. It appends an underscore (_) followed by a sequence number (starting with 1) to each subsequent occurrence of that key name.

3. If the decoded value string is more than 254 characters long and contains any control characters (for example, the sequence of line feed and carriage return characters that causes a new line in the data), the server puts the decoded value into an external temporary file. It then lists the following line under the [Form External] section of the CGI profile file:

   `name=pathname Length`

   where `name` represents the form field name, `pathname` is the path and name of the temporary file containing the decoded value string, and `Length` is the size in bytes of the decoded value.

4. If the raw value (before decoding) in a name=value pair is more than 65,535 bytes long, the server does no decoding. It marks the location and size of the value in the CGI content (`.INP`) file and lists the key name with these parameters under the [Form Huge] section of the CGI profile file as

   `formfieldname=offset Length`

   where `offset` is the offset from the beginning of the CGI content file at which the raw value for this field name appears and `Length` is the length in bytes of the raw value string.

5. If the form data contains any uploaded files, the server adds the following line for each file:

   `formfieldname=[pathname] length type encoding [filename]`

   where `pathname` is the path and name of the temporary file containing the uploaded file, `Length` is the size in bytes of the uploaded file, `type` is the content type of the uploaded file as sent by the client, encoding is the content encoding of the uploaded file, and filename is the original file name of the uploaded file.

Here is an example of how data appears in the four form-related sections of a CGI profile:

```
[Form Literal]
Title=Web Database Interactive Course
Keyword=Web
Keyword_1=Database
Keyword_2=Windows CGI

[Form External]
longfield=c:\website\cgi-temp\83ws.000 525
fieldwithlinebreaks=c:\website\cgi-temp\83ws.001 63

[Form Huge]
largefield=c:\website\cgi-tmp\83ws.002 512019

[Form File]
upl-file=[C:\WEBSITE\CGI-TEMP\83WS.003] 387 text/html binary
[C:\Internet\Netscape\Program\test.htm]
```

A Demonstration of How the Server Decodes Form Data Under Windows CGI

Let's look at a real example and examine the server-decoded data in the CGI profile and other related files by submitting an HTML form that contains the POST method in its <FORM> tag. Follow the steps given below:

1. Ensure that the API/CGI execution tracing configuration option of the WebSite server is enabled, as explained in Lesson 4.

2. Go to an MS-DOS prompt, and type the following commands to delete all the temporary CGI files currently existing in the c:\WEBSITE\CGI-TEMP directory:

```
CD C:\WEBSITE\CGI-TEMP <ENTER>
DEL *.* <ENTER>
```

You can also perform the above file deletion step via the Windows NT/Win 95 interface (the Explorer Window).

3. Start your WebSite server if it is not already running.

4. Specify the following URL from your browser to bring up the company entry form:

```
http://localhost/wdbic/chap02/lesson5/example1.htm
```

5. Fill in this form with the following information, and then click on the Submit button:

```
Your Name: John Smith
Your Password: abc
Age: 20-50
Known Computer Languages: C++ and Visual Basic
Preferred Language: Visual Basic
Remarks: I prefer Visual Basic because
         it is simple yet powerful.
```

6. Identify the files created in the c:\WEBSITE\CGI-TEMP directory. It should contain four files with the following file extensions:

```
.INI   --> CGI Profile File
.INP   --> CGI Content File
.OUT   --> CGI Output File
.000   --> CGI Secondary Input File
```

7. List the contents of the CGI profile (.INI) file from the Notepad application or any text editor, and scroll to the [Form Literal] section, as shown in Figure 2-13.

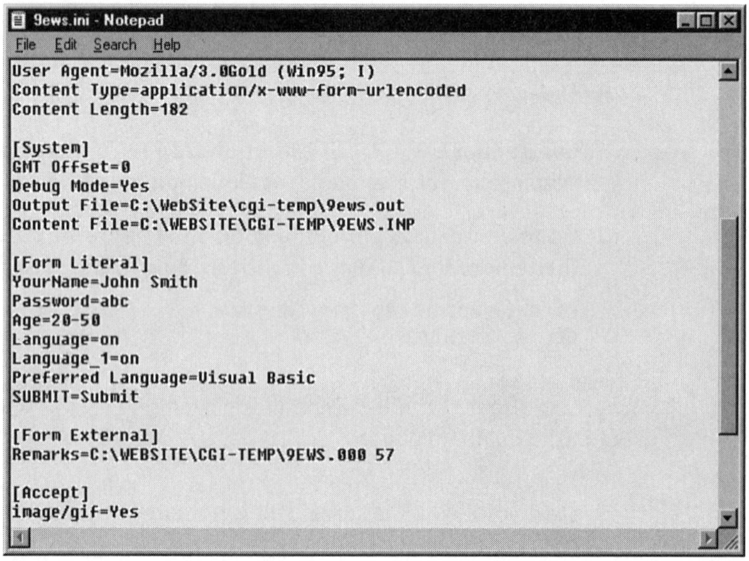

```
9ews.ini - Notepad
File  Edit  Search  Help
User Agent=Mozilla/3.0Gold (Win95; I)
Content Type=application/x-www-form-urlencoded
Content Length=182

[System]
GMT Offset=0
Debug Mode=Yes
Output File=C:\WebSite\cgi-temp\9ews.out
Content File=C:\WEBSITE\CGI-TEMP\9EWS.INP

[Form Literal]
YourName=John Smith
Password=abc
Age=20-50
Language=on
Language_1=on
Preferred Language=Visual Basic
SUBMIT=Submit

[Form External]
Remarks=C:\WEBSITE\CGI-TEMP\9EWS.000 57

[Accept]
image/gif=Yes
```

Figure 2-13
Form-related sections of the CGI profile file

Note that the WebSite server placed each field with one line of data (the way you entered in the form) under the [Form Literal] section. Because the Remarks field had two lines, the server placed it under the [Form External] section, associating it with the path and size of a secondary input file (with the .000 extension).

8. Examine the contents of the secondary input file listed in the [Form External] section in your text editor (see Figure 2-14).

9. Finally, if you inspect the CGI content (.INP) file in your text editor, it should contain the URL encoded string sent by the Web client, as shown in Figure 2-15.

The FORMINP.EXE utility that you used in Chapter 1 to display the encoded data of a submitted form simply returns the data contained in the CGI content file.

Lesson Summary

This lesson shows how Windows CGI goes one step further than standard CGI by providing data in both encoded and decoded form. This extra feature not only eases the CGI program development process but also helps in coordinating the front end (HTML forms) with the back end (CGI programs) of a Web application.

Another thing to note is that under Windows CGI, the server does not decode the data that comes through the query string. The reason is simple. Unlike the POST data, which has an associated Content-type header field, the server has no way of knowing how the data has been supplied through the query string. If your Web application requires that the data be sent through the query string, then it is up to your CGI

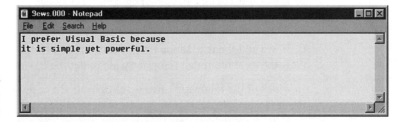

Figure 2-14
Contents of the
secondary input file

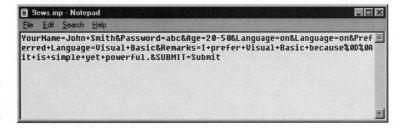

Figure 2-15
Contents of the CGI
input file

program to retrieve and interpret the value of the `Query String` variable in the [CGI] section of the CGI profile file.

In the next lesson, we shall focus on the format of a CGI response that the Web server expects from the CGI program. Interestingly, both the standard CGI and Windows CGI specifications publicize the same response format except for one difference. In standard CGI, the CGI program is required to return its response through its standard output stream, whereas in Windows CGI, the CGI program is expected to return its response through the designated CGI output file.

QUIZ 5

1. Which of the following strings in the encoded form data will cause a Web server to add the following two lines in the CGI profile file?

   ```
   Location=NY
   Location_1=CA
   ```

   a. `Location=NY&Location=CA`
   b. `LOCATION=NY&LOCATION=CA`
   c. `Location=NY&Location_1=CA`
   d. `Location=CA&Location=NY`

2. How will a Web server handle the following name=value pair of the URL encoded string?

   ```
   LocationType=Shopping+Mall
   ```

   a. It will add `LocationType=Shopping+Mall` under the [Form Literal] section.
   b. It will add `LocationType=Shopping Mall` under the [Form Literal] section.
   c. It will add `LocationType=Shopping Mall` under the [Form External] section.
   d. It will add the text `Shopping+Mall` in another temporary file and then specify the location of that temporary file under the [Form External] section.

3. In which of the following cases would a Web server put user data in a secondary input file?
   a. If the server encounters two or more name=value pairs having the same name portion.
   b. If the server encounters any hex-encoded character of the type `%xx` in the URL encoded string.
   c. If the value portion of a name=value pair contains a line break.
   d. If the value portion of a name=value pair exceeds 254 characters.

4. Under Windows CGI, what will a Web server do if it finds that the value portion exceeds 65,535 characters when it is decoding a name=value pair of a URL encoded string?

  a. It will decode the value portion, transfer that decoded data to a secondary input file, and then list the name of that file under the [Form External] section of the CGI profile file.

  b. It will decode the value portion, transfer that decoded data to a secondary input file, and then list the name of that file under the [Form Huge] section of the CGI profile file.

  c. It will transfer the value portion without decoding to a secondary input file and then list the name of that file under the [Form Huge] section of the CGI profile file.

  d. It will add a line under the [Form Huge] section indicating the size of the raw value portion and its starting position in the CGI content (`.INP`) file.

5. Under Windows CGI, what will a Web server do when it gets a `GET`-type CGI request with the following data in the query string portion of the URL path?

```
Title=Web+Database
```

  a. It will add `Title=Web+Database` on a separate line under the [Form Literal] section of the CGI profile file.

  b. It will add `Title=Web Database` on a separate line under the [Form Literal] section of the CGI profile file.

  c. It will add `Query String=Title=Web+Database` on a separate line under the [CGI] section of the CGI profile file.

  d. It will add `Query String=Title=Web Database` on a separate line under the [CGI] section of the CGI profile file.

EXERCISE 5

Complexity: Moderate

1. List the contents of the CGI profile file that a Web server would create for the following Windows CGI request. Assume `C:\WEB` is the document root directory of the server and it picks the name `86ws.ini` for this file. (Make reasonable guesses wherever you feel that complete information is not provided here.)

```
POST /cgi-win/wdbic/search.exe/books/data HTTP/1.0
<NL>
Accept: text/*; image/jpeg
Host: localhost
If-Modified-Since: Friday, 15-Aug-97 02:12:28 GMT
User-Agent: Mozilla/3.0Gold (Win95; I)
Referrer: http://localhost/
<NL>
Keyword=Web&Keyword=Database&SearchField=Title
```

Complexity: Moderate

2. Fill out each HTML form presented in Chapter 1 and examine the contents of all the temporary CGI files created by the WebSite server when you submit those forms.

CGI RESPONSE

Until now we have been discussing how a Web server passes data to an external program based on standard CGI and Windows CGI specifications. In this lesson, we will examine the other side of the equation and look at how these two CGI specifications require the external program to send its response back to the Web server. Luckily, both these specifications stick to the same response format in this regard. The differences between the two occur mainly in how the external program communicates its response to the Web server and when a Web server transmits that response to the requesting Web client.

Communicating the CGI Response

According to standard CGI, the external program should send its response through the standard output channel. It does not specifically lay out any direction on when a Web server should start responding to the client that made the CGI request, although most Web servers start transmitting data the moment the requested CGI program sends something through its standard output channel. Windows CGI, on the other hand, requires the external program to write the response into the CGI output file (whose location is specified in the CGI profile file). In addition, it directs the server to send the data contained in that output file only after that program has terminated. This second constraint of Windows CGI has both good and bad implications for a Windows CGI application developer.

The good implication comes from the fact that a Windows CGI program can have the flexibility to change or rewrite its output at any time. This flexibility is particularly helpful in case the program encounters an error condition during its execution and wants to send a properly formed error message instead of the partial output that it has already generated. The disadvantage of having the server not send any response till the CGI program terminates is that you cannot provide continuous feedback to the requesting user. Not only that, you cannot give an estimate on how long the CGI program will take to fulfill the request. It is therefore critical that all Windows CGI programs are designed to fulfill their tasks in a reasonable time; if the task is too big, the task should be broken into a chain of smaller tasks (such as breaking a large search result into a set of small linked pages). Chapter 11, "Populating Tables: Web-Based Data Entry," covers this technique in more detail.

If you want the flexibility of changing the output in a standard CGI program, you can have it write its output to a temporary file or a memory variable while it is executing and then output the final data held by that file or memory variable to the standard output channel just before the program terminates.

HTTP Response Format

To understand the format of a CGI program's response (which is same for both standard CGI and Windows CGI) fully, you should know the structure of an HTTP response, which is how a Web server communicates with a Web client. Any HTTP response must adhere to the following syntax:

ProtocolVersion StatusCode Reason NL *[Header]* *[NL Data]*

An example of a fully formed HTTP response is given below:

```
HTTP/1.0 200 OK
Server: WebSite 1.0
Date: Monday, 8-DEC-1997 10:10:00 GMT
Last-modified: Sunday, 8-DEC-1996 15:10:00 GMT
Content-encoding: Binary
Content-length: 123
Content-type: text/html

<HTML>
<HEAD>
<TITLE>HTTP Response Example</TITLE>
<BODY>
<H1>This is an example of an HTTP response.</H1>
</BODY>
</HTML>
```

HTTP Protocol Version and Status Codes

The *protocol version* (**HTTP/1.0**) in an HTTP response identifies the HTTP version being used by the server. The *status code* (**200**) following the protocol version is a three-digit integer describing the result of the request. The *reason string* (**OK**) is a brief description of the returned status code. The first digit of the status code characterizes the type of status being returned as follows:

- Informational (type 1xx)
- Successful (type 2xx)
- Redirection (type 3xx)
- Client error (type 4xx)
- Server error (type 5xx)

Some commonly used status codes with their explanations are listed in Table 2-2.

Table 2-2 Commonly used HTTP status codes

Status Code and Reason	Explanation
200 OK	The request has been fulfilled successfully.
204 No Content	The server has fulfilled the request, but does not have any information to send back. The client should stay in the same document view.
301 Moved Permanently	The requested resource has been assigned a new permanent URL specified in the Location header field (see Table 2-2). Any future reference to this resource should be done by use of that URL.
302 Moved Temporarily	The requested resource resides temporarily under a different URL. However, the client should continue to use the original URL for future requests.
304 Not Modified	The requested document has not been modified since the date specified in the If-Modified-Since field of the GET request. Date, Server, and Expires are the header fields passed with this response (see Table 2-3).
400 Bad Request	The request had bad syntax or was inherently impossible to satisfy.
401 Unauthorized	The request requires user authentication.
404 Not Found	The server has not found anything matching the requested URL path.
500 Server Error	The server was unable to fulfill a request due to an unexpected reason, such as an abnormal termination of an executable program.
502 Bad Gateway	The server needs to pass the request to another program or server that is not responding.
503 Service Unavailable	The server is temporarily overloaded and unable to handle the request.

HTTP Response Header Fields

The response header fields allow the server to pass additional information that cannot be covered in the status code, as well as indicate the structure of the attached data. Table 2-3 lists the header fields that commonly accompany an HTTP response.

Table 2-3 HTTP response header fields

Field	Used To
Location: *absoluteURL*	Define the exact location of the resource that was identified by Request-URL.
Server: *product*	Contain information about the software used by the server to handle the request.
WWW-authenticate: *challenge*	Specify the authentication scheme(s) and parameters applicable to Request-URL. Used with the 401(unauthorized) response messages to gather the necessary authentication information.
Last-modified: *HTTP-date*	Indicate the date and time at which the sender believes the resource was last modified.
Expires: *HTTP-date*	Represent the date and time at which the message originated.
Content-encoding: *encoding*	Indicate how the body message has been encoded.
Content-length: *number*	Specify the size in bytes of the data being transferred.
Content-length: *media-type*	Specify the MIME type of data being transferred.

CGI Response Types

A CGI program can generate a response in two ways: directly or indirectly. A *direct* response allows the CGI program to bypass the server and directly interact with the Web client that made the request. The Web server is involved only as a data transporting agent. The server does not modify the response in any way and assumes that the output of the CGI program is in an HTTP response format.

An *indirect* response from the CGI program requires additional processing from the server before it can be delivered to the Web client. Part of the processing is to package the output of the CGI program with additional header fields to make it a properly formed HTTP response.

A Web server inspects the first line of the CGI output file to determine the type of response being returned by a CGI program. If the first line starts with **HTTP/**, the server considers the response to be a direct response. The server recognizes an indirect response if the first line starts with any of the following header lines:

```
Content-type: type/subtype
Location: absolute or relative URL
URI: <value>
Status: code description
```

Let's look at an example of a direct response generated by a Windows CGI program. For this example, you will use a Windows CGI utility program called **CGIOUT.EXE**, whose only function is to send the contents of an external file as its output to the Web server. The CGI request to this program is made as follows:

```
http://localhost/cgi-win/wdbic/cgiout/cgiout.exe/file?filename
```

where ***filename*** refers to the name of the external file. The **CGIOUT.EXE** program assumes that this external file resides in the **C:\WEBSITE\WDBIC\CGIOUT** directory.

The **C:\WEBSITE\BOOK\CGIOUT** directory has a file called **DIRRESP.OUT** whose contents are shown in Figure 2-16. These contents represent an instance of a direct response.

You can see the effect of returning a direct response by making **CGIOUT.EXE** return the contents of the **DIRRESP.OUT** file as its output.

1. Ensure that your WebSite server is running.

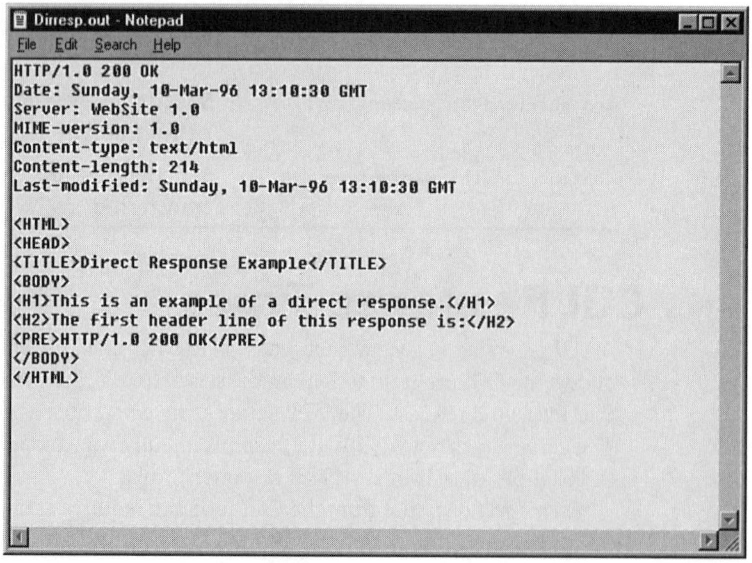

```
HTTP/1.0 200 OK
Date: Sunday, 10-Mar-96 13:10:30 GMT
Server: WebSite 1.0
MIME-version: 1.0
Content-type: text/html
Content-length: 214
Last-modified: Sunday, 10-Mar-96 13:10:30 GMT

<HTML>
<HEAD>
<TITLE>Direct Response Example</TITLE>
<BODY>
<H1>This is an example of a direct response.</H1>
<H2>The first header line of this response is:</H2>
<PRE>HTTP/1.0 200 OK</PRE>
</BODY>
</HTML>
```

Figure 2-16 A direct-response–type CGI output

2. Enter the following Windows CGI request from your browser:

`http://localhost/cgi-win/wdbic/cgiout/cgiout.exe/file?dirresp.out`

Figure 2-17 shows the response returned to the browser.

The browser displays a direct response like any other regular response. It has no way of knowing what part of this response the server created and what part was created by the CGI program.

When sending a direct response, a Windows CGI program has to generate all the necessary HTTP header fields. If new HTTP standards evolve, the CGI program will have to be updated to accommodate any changes deemed necessary for a smooth HTTP operation. Also, CGI programs are usually designed to return information independent of the HTTP being used to communicate that information. For these reasons, a CGI program is given the option to use an indirect response, where the Web server takes care of most of the HTTP formalities. The formats of the different types of indirect responses are explained in the following section.

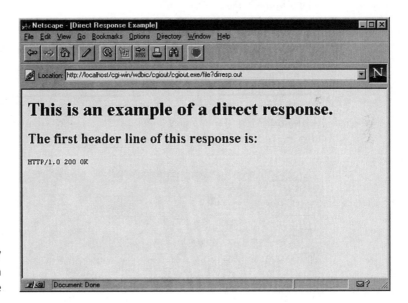

Figure 2-17
Browser showing a
direct response

Using the Content-type **Header**

One standard way of returning information through an indirect response is by listing a **Content-type** header line as the first line of the CGI output file. The syntax of this type of indirect response is as follows:

```
Content-type: type/subtype

<Data Starts from the third line>
```

where the *type/subtype* parameter in the **Content-type** header describes the MIME type of the data included in the output. The following steps demonstrate an example of an indirect response that uses a **Content-type** header line:

1. Ensure that your WebSite server is running.

2. Enter the following URL from your browser:

   ```
   http://localhost/cgi-win/wdbic/cgiout/cgiout.exe/file?ctypehtm.out
   ```

   The CGIOUT.EXE program returns the contents of the file CTYPEHTM.OUT (shown in Figure 2-18) as its output.

Figure 2-19 shows the browser displaying the information returned, indicating that the browser has appropriately treated this information as an HTML response.

A CGI program can attach binary data instead of text data in the body of the output when the MIME type listed in the **Content-type** header refers to a binary object. For example, if a CGI program is sending a binary GIF image, the **Content-type** should list **image/gif**, and the binary data representing the GIF image should start from the third line of the CGI output file.

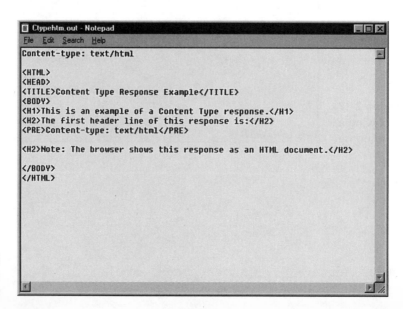

Figure 2-18
A Content-type
CGI output

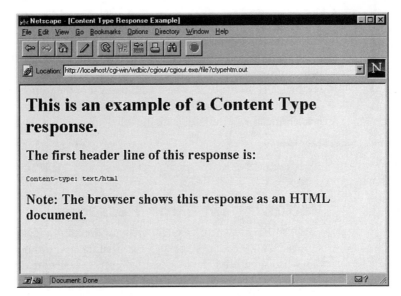

Figure 2-19
Browser showing a
`Content-type`
response

Redirecting to Another URL

Rather than generating the output itself, a CGI program can point to another information resource as its response by generating a `Location` or a `Universal Resource Identifier` (URI) header line as the first line of the CGI output. The syntax of these header lines is as follows:

```
Location: absolute or relative URL
URI: <absolute or relative URL>
```

When the Web server encounters either of the preceding header lines in the CGI output file, it returns a redirection status code with the specified URL to the client. The client then is responsible for fetching and displaying the contents of the new URL to the user.

As an example, the `REDIRCGI.OUT` file in the `C:\WEBSITE\CGI-WIN\WDBIC\CGIOUT\` directory contains the following redirection line (followed by a blank line):

```
Location: /cgi-win/wdbic/cgiout/cgiout.exe/file?ctypehtm.out
```

Test this redirection response by entering the following URL in your browser:

```
http://localhost/cgi-win/wdbic/cgiout/cgiout.exe/file?redircgi.out
```

The browser will display the text from the `CTYPEHTM.OUT` file as shown in Figure 2-19 because the redirection called for another request to the `CGIOUT.EXE` program with `CTYPEHTM.OUT` as the query string parameter.

Using Different Status Codes

When a CGI program returns a `Content-type` response to the Web server, the server assumes that the CGI program has successfully handled the request. Hence, while delivering the response to the client, the server automatically sends a **200 OK** message for the HTTP status header field with the rest of the response.

However, if the CGI program needs to send a different status code, it may add a **Status** header line in its response using the following syntax:

```
Status: code description
```

where *code* and *description* represent the standard HTTP status code and reason phrase, respectively.

Returning an Error Message

Consider the case where a CGI program cannot fulfill a request due to insufficient data supplied with the request. Chances are that the user did not provide all the information when submitting the request. However, the client may not have delivered all the data successfully. In either case, the CGI program can return a **400 Bad Request** status header with the error message as follows:

```
Status: 400 Bad Request
Content-type: text/html

<HTML>
<TITLE>Bad Request</TITLE>
<BODY>
<H1>400 Bad Request</H1>
<H4>The request cannot be fulfilled since all required data was not supplied.</H4>
</BODY>
</HTML>
```

This sample response is also included in the file named **stat400.out**. You can enter the following URL from your browser to see the effect of this response on your browser:

```
http://localhost/cgi-win/wdbic/cgiout/cgiout.exe/file?stat400.out
```

Returning a No Content Message

If a CGI program does not have any information to send back to the requesting client, it should send a **204 No Content** status message as its response to indicate that it has completed the request. On receiving this status code, the browser stays in its current document view. You can enter the following URL from your browser to test whether your browser correctly responds to a **204** status code:

```
http://localhost/cgi-win/wdbic/cgiout/cgiout.exe/file?stat204.out
```

Asking for User Authentication

For certain status codes, it may be necessary to provide additional information through the header fields. In these situations, you have to set the status code and the header fields using a direct CGI response. A typical example would be when you want to authenticate the user by asking the browser to prompt for the user name and password. This is done by setting the response status code to **401**, as shown below:

```
HTTP/1.0 401 Unauthorized
WWW-authenticate: basic realm="cgitest"
```

The `realm` parameter can be anything you want and is displayed in the browser's user name/password dialog box. To test this user authentication example, enter the following URL from your browser:

```
http://localhost/cgi-win/wdbic/cgiout/cgiout.exe/file?stat401.out
```

Your browser will ask for a user name and password, as shown in Figure 2-20.

When you fill out the authentication dialog box and press the OK button, the browser again makes the same CGI request and passes the user name and password with that and all subsequent requests until it gets another response with status code **401**. The Web server supplies the user name and password information as environment variables under standard CGI and as name=value pairs in the [CGI] section of the CGI profile file under Windows CGI.

Note that some Web servers (including WebSite) will pass the password information to the CGI program only if the name of that program begins with the **$** character. To check this feature, examine the CGI profile created in the previous example and then compare it with the CGI profile file created when you enter the following URL:

```
http://localhost/cgi-win/wdbic/cgiout/$cgiout.exe/file?stat401.out
```

Lesson Summary

This lesson explained the various ways a CGI program can send its response to a Web server. The easiest and the most straightforward way is to start the response using a **Content-type** header in the standard output channel (in the case of standard CGI) or in the CGI output file (in the case of Windows CGI). To create a redirection, you can simply create a response that includes a **Location** or **URI** header with the destination URL. To specify a different status code, you can use a **Status** header. If you want full control of what gets sent to a Web client, then provide a fully formatted HTTP response as the output of your CGI program.

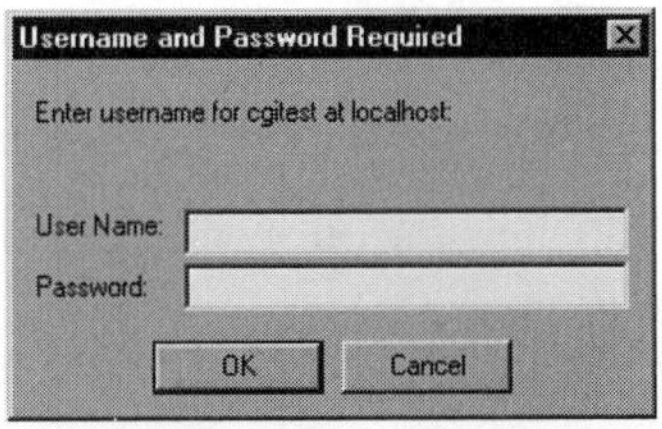

Figure 2-20
Browser asking for
user name and
password

1. Why should Windows CGI programs terminate in a reasonable time?
   a. Because they consume a lot of CPU time
   b. Because they consume a lot of system memory.
   c. Because they require a lot of temporary hard disk space
   d. Because the Web server will not send their output until they terminate

2. How does a Web server determine that it has to pad the CGI program's response to make it an HTTP response?
   a. If the first line of the CGI response begins with the text `HTTP/`
   b. If the first line of the CGI response begins with the text `Content-type`
   c. If the first line of the CGI response begins with the text `Location`
   d. If the first line of the CGI response begins with the text `Status`

3. Which status code is best suited to indicate that a CGI program cannot fulfill the task in a reasonable amount of time?
   a. `200`
   b. `404`
   c. `500`
   d. `503`

4. What is the simplest way of sending a stored GIF image file as your CGI program's response?
   a. Using an HTTP formatted direct response
   b. Using a `Content-type` header
   c. Using a `Location` header
   d. Using a `Status` header

5. What does the browser do when it encounters a `401` status code from the server?
   a. It prompts the user for a user name and password.
   b. It validates the user name and password before sending another request to the server.
   c. It sends the user name and password to the server with the original request.
   d. It first sends the user name to the server with the original request and then sends the password if gets `401` status code in the response.

Complexity: Easy
1. Write a fully formed HTTP response that temporarily redirects the browser to the following URL. Then do the same using an indirect CGI response.

```
http://www.acme.com/mainmenu.htm
```

Complexity: Easy

2. Determine how your server and browser handle the following cases:

a. The CGI response does not start with any of the expected header lines.

b. A blank line is not present between the header and the body of a CGI response.

CHAPTER SUMMARY

This chapter explained the role of a Web server and how it communicates with external programs using the two popular CGI specifications—standard CGI and Windows CGI. All the examples and applications described in this book are based on Windows CGI because it is simple to understand and easy to work with. Here is a recap of the salient points covered in this chapter:

- A Web server can play two roles—be a (read-only) file server and act as a gateway between a Web client and an external program.

- A Web server uses document mapping to determine the physical location of an information resource specified by a URL path.

- A Web server uses content mapping to identify the MIME type of the requested document from the file extension. If the request is for a CGI program, then the CGI response must include the `Content-type` header.

- A Web server determines whether the incoming request is a CGI request if a portion of the URL path is mapped in the server's CGI mapping.

- Under standard CGI, the server passes the data to the external program through environment variables and standard input and expects a response through the program's standard output.

- Under Windows CGI, the server passes the data through a temporary CGI profile (`.INI`) and other secondary input files. It expects a response in the CGI output file. The location of the CGI profile file is specified as a command-line argument of the external program, whereas the locations of all other temporary files are listed in the CGI profile file itself.

- Under Windows CGI, the server also provides supplemental data attached to a `POST` request in the decoded form.

- A CGI program can send its response either as a fully formed HTTP response or as an indirect response. In the later case, the server automatically pads the response with the necessary information before sending it to the client.

With this chapter, we conclude the discussion on how data is passed over the Web and how Web servers can communicate with external programs to send dynamically generated information. To create these on-the-fly pages, the source data must be organized and stored in a manner that makes it easy and quick to retrieve the desired information. This is where a relational database management system comes into the picture. So, in the next four chapters (Chapters 3 through 7), we move our focus from Web-related issues to designing relational databases and data queries.

Fundamentals of Database and Query Design

CHAPTER 3

ORGANIZING DATA: TABLES AND RELATIONSHIPS

This chapter deals with the principles of database construction and data integrity. It describes data storage need analysis, discusses the various data types, and looks into data validation requirements. This chapter explains the steps involved in database normalization and identifying referential constraints and other database integrity rules. Practical issues such as multiuser environments and data security are also covered. In particular, you will learn about:

- Steps involved in desiging a relational database

- The concept of a primary key

- Table relationships

- The process of table normalization

- The relevance of data validation, security, and data locking schemes

THE IMPORTANCE OF DATA ORGANIZATION

Most interactive Web applications can be classified into two broad categories, depending on how they use the widespread connectivity of the Web:

● Expert system

● Information exchange system

The *expert system* Web applications allow industry gurus to use their knowledge, experience, and techniques to provide interactive tools that help Web users make sound decisions or achieve desired results. Typical examples range from a simple Web mortgage calculator to advanced Web-based insurance and tax planners (see Figure 3-1). The common characteristic among most expert system applications is that the techniques and knowledge bases (for example, tax rules and tables) used by these applications are usually created and maintained by a responsible and often predetermined group of individuals.

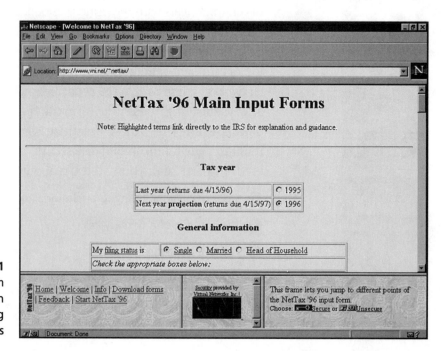

Figure 3-1
An expert system
Web application
for computing
taxes

The *information exchange system* Web applications use the Web as a matchmaker—users having information can connect with users in need of that information. Common examples that fall under this category include job listing systems, dating services, classified and want ads, and real estate listings (see Figure 3-2), event calendars, chat lines, and Web search engines. The common characteristic here is that the shared knowledge base in these applications is dynamically and regularly populated by the Web users themselves, using the Web interface elements discussed in Chapter 1, "Gathering User-Data: HTML Forms and Queries." Furthermore, these applications do not rely on the actual contents of the supplied information to determine how they operate. Mostly, they just use portions of those contents to help Web users find the relevant information.

The concept of information exchange has been in practical operation since before the idea of the World Wide Web was conceived—through Usenet newsgroups, Internet relay chats (IRCs), and bulletin board systems. The main advantage in using an interactive Web application for this purpose is that you can control or customize the exchange of information to any level.

Finally, you may also encounter Web applications that combine the elements of an expert system and an information exchange system to accomplish their overall objectives, as shown in Figure 3-3. Searchable Internet directories, in which users supply the URL information but experts rate and classify it, are a good example of such an application.

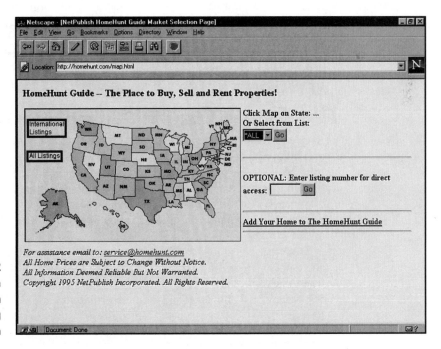

Figure 3-2
An information exchange system real estate listing application

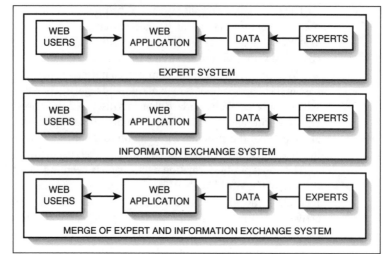

Figure 3-3
Characteristics of
Web applications
acting as an expert
system and an
information
exchange system

Note in Figure 3-3 that no matter how you classify them, most Web applications hover around the basic functionality of gathering, sharing, using, updating, and dispersing information. Hence, if you are planning to design such applications, you will have to tackle these core tasks in an efficient manner. To accomplish that, the first step is to identify the nature of the information your application will be dealing with, which is done by listing and reviewing its key objectives. We will demonstrate this step through a practical example of a Web-based event calendar application. We will review the main purpose of this application, determine its essential goals, and then examine those goals to extract the basic elements of information associated with this type of application.

The Event Calendar Application

A wide variety of events such as exhibitions, conferences, talk shows, performing arts, auctions, product demonstrations, and other festivities are taking place all the time all over the world. How often have you missed an important event that you really wished to attend but could not because timely information about that event was not available? Information at the touch of a button regarding all events that you desire to know about, not only in your neighborhood but in the entire global village, could make life so much easier.

From the sponsoring organization's perspective, being able to dispatch information about upcoming events to millions of viewers in every nook and corner of the world, many of whom could be potential visitors to these events, and yet not worry about expensive promotional campaigns and mounting communication charges seems too good to be true.

All this is entirely possible through a Web-based event calendar application that meets the following objectives:

● Allows Web users to view information on any event and its sponsor. The information displayed could provide an insight into the type of event and its venue, pertinent details about the sponsoring organization, and perhaps a hyperlink for seeking further information about the sponsor.

● Allows Web users to find events by date range, location, sponsor, or type of event. Such searches could help a user narrow down the events and identify potential events of interest. A quick snapshot of events of the day could also be generated.

● Allows multiple Web users to add new events to the calendar or edit existing events concurrently. Past events should automatically be removed.

● Generates various kinds of statistical information for the keen-minded to analyze whether dentists of the world hold more conferences or modern art exhibitions are the rage. Educational events tend to get concentrated in the region that boasts the most breakthroughs in frontier technologies. The outcomes of such analyses could be amazing.

It is easy to see from these objectives that the event calendar application must deal with the following two basic types of information:

● Events

● Sponsors

Going a step further, let's determine what kind of data is essential to describe these two entities.

Event Details

Information about an event could contain the following data:

● Type of event (category), which could include a brief description of the event and what it proposes to offer.

● Time frame of the event, which could include date and time.

● Location of the event, which could include details of the venue and the physical address in terms of street number, city, state, province, and country.

● Contact address, which could refer to the sponsor of that event.

Sponsor Details

A sponsor could be described with the following data:

- Name of the organization.

- Nature of the sponsor, which could include some details about the nature of the work of the sponsoring organization and its various activities.

- Some descriptive and contact information about the sponsor, such as phone number, email address, and a Web link.

- The various events organized by that sponsor.

You can see that even though the events and sponsors are two separate types of information, they depend on each other. What makes any organization a sponsor is the event(s) it organizes. Similarly, every event needs some information about its associated sponsor to describe that event fully.

Lesson Summary

In this lesson, you learned about the main characteristics of the expert system and information exchange system types of Web applications and their typical real-world examples. Although both these applications perform the same basic functions of gathering, sharing, using, updating, and dispersing information, their approach is different. Whereas the former has a lot of expert knowledge and experience built into the system as an information source, the latter primarily connects users in need of particular information with those who have it.

In this lesson, you were also introduced to the Web event calendar application, which helps in tracking information about various events and their sponsors on the Web for the benefit of all Web users. You saw an overview of the nature and various types of information this application has to deal with. How to organize this information consistently and efficiently is discussed in the next lesson.

1. Which of the following is an expert system type of Web application?
   a. Insurance planner
   b. Real estate listing
   c. Astrology-based future prediction system
   d. Job listing system

2. What kind of information can users view through the Web event calendar application described in this lesson?
   a. Any event
   b. Any sponsor of events
   c. Events and sponsors registered on the application
   d. Events held in the past

3. What is the first step in analyzing the information needed by a Web application?
   a. Design of the application
   b. Knowledge of the Web server
   c. Objectives of the application
   d. Getting information about users of the application

4. How does the event calendar application discussed in this lesson let users search for events?
   a. By date range
   b. By location
   c. By sponsor's name
   d. By events organized by the sponsor in the past

5. The event calendar application allows users to do which of the following?
   a. Add their events to the calendar.
   b. Edit their events on the calendar.
   c. Edit events of other sponsors on the calendar.
   d. Generate various statistical reports.

Complexity: Easy
1. Explore the World Wide Web and list the URLs of a pure expert system and a pure information exchange system type of Web application. Also list a Web site that shows characteristics of both systems.

Complexity: Moderate
2. List the objectives and the basic information entities of a typical Web-based job listing application.

WHAT IS A RELATIONAL DATABASE?

The Web-based expert systems or information exchange systems that you dealt with in Lesson 1 are essentially interactive front ends to repositories of organized information. Such information repositories are also called *databases*. Over the years, many approaches have been developed to create these databases, among which the relational model conceived in 1969 by E. F. Codd (then a researcher at IBM) has gained immense popularity because of its sheer consistency and efficiency.

A *relational database* is a collection of data or objects related to a particular topic or purpose. Whereas the *data* represents the information in the database, the *objects* help define the structure of that information and automate the data manipulation tasks. Some of the advantages of a relational database are

● Efficient data entry, data update, and deletion

● Efficient data retrieval, summarization, and reporting

● Easy to implement changes in database design

Components of a Relational Database—Tables, Records, and Fields

A relational database is composed of *tables*, which are used to represent "topics" in the real world. Each table has a two-dimensional layout where data is placed in a grid of *rows* and *columns*. A table row (also called a record) constitutes a set of related data items that collectively define one element of the topic denoted by that table. These data items are set in columns (also called *fields*), where each column individually represents a distinct part of each row.

Information pertaining to the event calendar application discussed in Lesson 1 conforms well to this row-column setup. As shown in Figure 3-4, you can organize and store all that information using just one big table (although you will see later that this is not the best approach).

Sponsorer	Contact	Event	DatesAndVenues
Florence Historical Association (Historical)	Mrs Florence (402) 333-2322 florence@florence.com http://www.florence.com/	Hiroshoma revisited Conference Second round table by war vetrans	12/23/1996 3.00PM-6.00PM Crown Plaza, 356 N 24 Street, Washington DC, VA-87646
American Association of Orthodontists (Dentist)	Beck Marcia J (607) 498- 5800 Marcia@aao.com http://www.aao.com	Laser surgery for dental care Conference Annual world conference organised by AAOO	01/05/97 8.00AM-6.00PM Bergan Mercy Hospital, 208 West Dodge Road, New York, NY-23456 01/09/97 9.00 AM-7.00PM Clark Hospital, 456 XYZ Street, Chicago, IL 34521
Aero International Limited (Aviation)	aero@aol.com http://ail.aero.com	Micro light aircraft show Exhibition 5th Asian micro light aircraft show	01/16/97-01/17/97 8.00AM Aero International Limited, Sunrise Bay Area, Hongkong
L&M Motor Car Industries	Jean P. Belmando Jean@lmm.com http://lmm.lorenzo.com	Falcon-"2zx" Unleashed Product launch Release of futuristic model ZX series sports car	01/01/97 10.00 A.M. Walter Heights, Toulene Bay Area, Nice, France-64267
Smith Microsystems Incorporated	Clara Jhonson 117- 406-4423	1st Level Testing Interviews Walk in interviews for software developers	12/23/97 8.00am-4.00pm Smith Microsystems Inc., 34,Oak View Industrial Area, Swindon,UK-32F416
Aero Management Institute (Aviation)	A.B.Deol abd@pmi.vsnl.net.in	AirShow-97 Exhibition Asian annual exhibition of aviation industry	09/07/97 10.00am-6.00pm Aero Management Institute, Noida, Uttar Pradesh, India-1100
Smith Microsystems, Inc.	Clara Jhonson 117- 406-4423	Access Classes Training Covers Microsoft Access database design and development, Query design, Visual Basic programming techniques.	12/23/97 8.00am-4.00pm Peter Kiewit Center, 45 Smith Street, Leeds, UK-26AW17

Figure 3-4
An event sponsor table

Fields and Data Types

In a relational database, information in a field must adhere to the same class of data, also called a *data type*. A data type establishes two things about a field:

● The amount of storage required to hold a field item

● The kind of values that field can accept

Table 3-1 lists the standard data types supported by most relational databases (although some database systems may use different names).

Table 3-1 Commonly used data types

Data Type	Description	Size
BOOLEAN	For yes/no type information	1 bit
BYTE	For small positive numbers	8 bits
SMALLINT	For small integers	16 bits
LONGINT	For large integers	32 bits
CURRENCY	For high-precision money amounts	64 bits
TIMESTAMP	For date and time	64 bits
REAL	For single-precision numbers	32 bits
FLOAT	For double-precision numbers	64 bits
VARCHAR	For small text data	1–255 bytes
LONGVARCHAR	For large text data	Data dependent
LONGBINARY	For images or OLE objects	Data dependent

When defining fields and assigning data types in a table, you should ask yourself the following questions:

Does Each Field Represent an Atomic Entity or Can It Be Broken into More Fields?

The definition of *atomic* depends on many factors, but as a general rule, if you feel that your application may need to manipulate or search portions of field data, then that field should be split into multiple fields representing the various portions of data. A common case occurs when you have to store a person's name. If you do not need to distinguish the first name from the last name, then one field (such as `ContactName`) may be sufficient. However, if you envision searching or sorting the table records by a person's last name, use two fields, one for the first name and one for the last name, to represent the data.

The location information is another good example. If you want to allow users to locate information by cities, states, and so on (as in the case of the event calendar application), you should divide the event location information into smaller fields representing these individual entities.

What Is the Nature of the Field and What Kind of Values Should a Field Accept?

Often you encounter data entities such as phone number, social security number, and postal codes that appear to be numeric by virtue of their name but usually do not require any numeric processing. They may even contain nonnumeric characters. For example, phone numbers can include (,), or – characters and postal codes of some countries can contain alpha characters. So unless you have other compelling reasons, it is best to keep these fields as text fields (VARCHAR data type).

What Is the Storage Capacity and the Data Range of a Field?

Pick the smallest-sized data type that can hold all data values for that field. For example, if you design a field to hold a person's age in years, a BYTE data type, which accepts only integer values from 0 to 255, is sufficient. However, if you want to store decimal information (for example, 5.25 years), a BYTE will not work. You will have to select the REAL data type for this field.

Defining the Structure of the Event Sponsor Table

Let's reexamine the event sponsor table of Figure 3-4. It lists all the pertinent information in separate fields but does not indicate their data type. Moreover, its fields clearly need refinement based on the points discussed above. Also note that some of the events shown in Figure 3-4 are either occurring on two dates or at two different locations or both. Table 3-2 presents one way of how you can redefine the structure of the original event sponsor table without losing any part of the currently displayed data.

Table 3-2 Data types of the fields of the event sponsor table

Field Name	Data Type
SponsorName	VARCHAR(100)
SponsorType	VARCHAR(50)
ContactName	VARCHAR(50)
Phone	VARCHAR(50)
Email	VARCHAR(255)
WebAddress	VARCHAR(255)
EventName	VARCHAR(100)

Field Name	Data Type
EventType	VARCHAR(50)
EventDescription	LONGVARCHAR
LocationName_1	VARCHAR(100)
Street_1	VARCHAR(50)
City_1	VARCHAR(50)
State_1	VARCHAR(50)
PostalCode_1	VARCHAR(50)
Country_1	VARCHAR(50)
EventDate_1	TIMESTAMP
StartTime_1	TIMESTAMP
EndTime_1	TIMESTAMP
LocationName_2	VARCHAR(100)
Street_2	VARCHAR(50)
City_2	VARCHAR(50)
State_2	VARCHAR(50)
PostalCode_2	VARCHAR(50)
Country_2	VARCHAR(50)
EventDate_2	TIMESTAMP
StartTime_2	TIMESTAMP
EndTime_2	TIMESTAMP

Creating Related Tables

Although one table is sufficient to hold all the data about the events and their sponsors, experience shows that large tables like these are difficult to work with. You would start getting into trouble if a sponsor organized more than one event or there was more than one sponsor for an event or an event was to be simultaneously organized at more than one location. In all these cases, information such as sponsor details is repeated for every event organized by that sponsor, which introduces the following data storage and manipulation problems:

⬤ Data redundancy and waste of disk storage space

⬤ Data inconsistency

⬤ Difficulties in propagating data changes

⬤ Inefficient processing of data

As an example, look at the two events sponsored by Smith Microsystems in Figure 3-4. In the first event record, the sponsor name is listed as "Smith Microsystems Incorporated," while the other record lists the name as "Smith Microsystems, Inc." This clearly indicates a discrepancy in the data. Say this company changes its Web address and wants to use that new address with all its events listed in the event sponsor table. In that case, someone will have to go through all the event records, carefully identify which ones belong to this company, and then make the change to all applicable records. Imagine doing that when the event sponsor table is populated with thousands of records!

These issues can be resolved if you split the event sponsor table into two tables (event table and sponsor table) and establish a mechanism of connecting them. This way, information pertaining to an event and its sponsor is stored in two separate tables and the necessity of duplicating one for the sake of the other is eliminated. The following procedure outlines the tasks involved in accomplishing this one-to-two table division process:

1. Move all the sponsor-related fields from Table 3-2 to a new table. Give an appropriate name to this table, such as tblSponsors.

2 Add a new field named SponsorID to the tblSponsors table. Assign it a data type of LONGINT. Table 3-3 depicts the final structure of tblSponsors table.

Table 3-3 The tblSponsors table structure

Field Name	Data Type
SponsorID	LONGINT
SponsorName	VARCHAR(100)
SponsorType	VARCHAR(50)
ContactName	VARCHAR(50)
Phone	VARCHAR(50)
Email	VARCHAR(255)
WebAddress	VARCHAR(255)

3. Move all the event related fields from Table 3-2 to a table named tblEvents.

4. Add the SponsorID field to the tblEvents table. This field and the SponsorID field of the tblSponsors table must have the same data type. Table 3-4 depicts the final structure of tblEvents table.

Table 3-4 The `tblEvents` table structure

Field Name	Data Type
EventName	VARCHAR(100)
SponsorID	LONGINT
EventType	VARCHAR(50)
EventDescription	LONGVARCHAR
LocationName_1	VARCHAR(100)
Street_1	VARCHAR(50)
City_1	VARCHAR(50)
State_1	VARCHAR(50)
PostalCode_1	VARCHAR(50)
Country_1	VARCHAR(50)
EventDate_1	TIMESTAMP
StartTime_1	TIMESTAMP
EndTime_1	TIMESTAMP
LocationName_2	VARCHAR(100)
Street_2	VARCHAR(50)
City_2	VARCHAR(50)
State_2	VARCHAR(50)
PostalCode_2	VARCHAR(50)
Country_2	VARCHAR(50)
EventDate_2	TIMESTAMP
StartTime_2	TIMESTAMP
EndTime_2	TIMESTAMP

5. Add one record for information pertaining to each sponsor in the
   `tblSponsors` table while assigning a unique value to the `SponsorID` field
   for each record (see Figure 3-5).

6. Add one record for each event in the `tblEvents` table. Set the `SponsorID`
   field in each event record to the `SponsorID` value of the event's sponsor
   (see Figure 3-6).

Figure 3-5
The `tblSponsors`
table

SponsorID	SponsorName	SponsorType	ContactName	Phone	Email	WebAddress
1	Florence Historical Association	Historical	Mrs Florence	(402) 333-2322	florence@florence.com	http://www.florence.com/
2	American Association of Orthodontists	Dentist	Beck Marcia J	(607) 498-5800	marcia@aao.com	http://www.aao.com
3	Aero International Limited	Aviation			aero@aol.com	http://ail.aero.com
4	L&M Motor Car Industries		Jean P. Belmando		Jean@lmm.com	http://lmm.lorenzo.com
5	Smith Microsystems Incorporated		Clara Jhonson	117- 406-4423		
6	Aero Management Institute	Aviation	A. B. Deol		abd@pmi.vsnl.net.in	

Figure 3-6
The `tblEvents`
table

EventName			SponsorID	EventType	EventDescription				
LocationName_1	Street_1	City_1	State_1	PostalCode_1	Country_1	EventDate_1	StartTime_1	EndTime_1	
LocationName_2	Street_2	City_2	State_2	PostalCode_2	Country_2	EventDate_2	StartTime_2	EndTime_2	
Hiroshima Revisited		1	Conference	Second round table by war vetrans					
Crown Plaza	356 N 24 Street	Washington D	Virginia	87646	USA	12/23/96	03:00 PM	06:00 PM	
Crown Plaza	356 N 24 Street	Washington D	Virginia	87646	USA	12/23/96	03:00 PM	06:00 PM	
Laser surgery for dental care		2	Conference	Annual world conference organised by AADD					
Bergan Mercy Hospital	208 West Dodge	New York	New York	23456	USA	1/5/96	08:00 AM	06:00 PM	
Bergan Mercy Hospital	208 West Dodge	New York	New York	23456	USA	1/5/96	08:00 AM	06:00 PM	
Micro light aircraft show		3	Exhibition	5th Asian micro light aircraft show					
Aero International Limited	Sunrise Bay Area	Hongkong	Hongkong		Hongkong	1/16/97	08:00 AM		
Aero International Limited	Sunrise Bay Area	Hongkong	Hongkong		Hongkong	1/16/97	08:00 AM		
Falcon-"2zx" Unleashed		4	Product launch	Release of futuristic model 2X series sports car					
Walter Heights	Toulene Bay Area	Nice	Nice		France	1/1/97	10:00 AM		
Walter Heights	Toulene Bay Area	Nice	Nice		France	1/1/97	10:00 AM		
1st Level Testing		5	Interviews	Walk in interviews for software developers					
Smith Microsystems Inc.	34, Oak View Ind	Swindon	Swindon	32F416	UK	12/23/97	08:00 AM	04:00 PM	
Smith Microsystems Inc.	34, Oak View Ind	Swindon	Swindon	32F416	UK	12/23/97	08:00 AM	04:00 PM	
Access Classes		5	Training	Covers Microsoft Access database design and development, Query d					
Peter Kiewit Center	45 Smith Street	Leeds	UK	26AW17	UK	12/23/97	10:00 AM	06:00 PM	
Peter Kiewit Center	45 Smith Street	Leeds	UK	26AW17	UK	12/23/97	10:00 AM	06:00 PM	
AirShow-97		6	Exhibition	Asian annual exhibition of aviation industry					
Aero Management Institut		Noida	Uttar Pradesh	110034	India	9/7/97	10:00 AM	06:00 PM	
Aero Management Institut		Noida	Uttar Pradesh	110034	India	9/7/97	10:00 AM	06:00 PM	

As you can see, a linking field called **SponsorID** provides the necessary data to connect the records between the event and sponsor tables. This field is also referred to as the *key field* of the two tables. In the sponsor table, where this field must be unique, it is called the *primary key*. In the **tblEvents** table, it is called the *foreign key* because it can contain duplicate values (in the case of two or more events from the same sponsor). A table can only have one primary key but any number of foreign keys (for linking with other tables).

Characteristics of a Primary Key

A primary key acts as a unique tag for addressing a record in a table. It not only plays an important role in linking two related tables but also helps in quickly locating a particular record. Even though you may not have an immediate need to link a particular table, it is considered good practice to establish a primary key for all the tables in your relational database.

You can specify one or more table fields to act as the table's primary key. Once a set of fields is made into a primary key, the data in those fields must adhere to the following two constraints:

● None of the primary key fields can have a Null value. A Null value in a field means that the field does not contain any data. (Note that a Null value is not the same as an empty string or a zero value. It means no data.)

● Together, all fields in the primary key must produce a unique value for each table record. (Note that individually, any of those fields can have duplicate values.)

How to Select a Primary Key

As a first step, you should try to create a primary key from one or more existing table fields. For example, if you are creating a table of book records, you may use the ISBN number field of each book for the primary key because it easily meets all the primary key requirements.

Sometimes, however, none of the table fields (individually or as a set) appears to be a good choice for a primary key. The sponsor table discussed above is one example. Instinctively, you may think that because sponsors generally have a distinct name, the `SponsorName` field is a good primary key candidate. This supposition may be true within in a limited area, but this certainly cannot be assumed in a global context. (Also, you may have database performance problems if you make a `varchar(100)` field a primary key!) Alternatively, you might consider using the `SponsorName` and the `WebAddress` fields together for the primary key. That would certainly establish uniqueness, but it would require every sponsor to have a Web site, which again is not a practical assumption.

In such situations, where the choice of one or more existing fields for a primary key is not obvious or practical, add a new field (such as `SponsorID`) to your table that serves as a primary key. Usually, this new field is set as a numeric field because it is easy to come up with a unique number sequence. Many database engines (including Access) support a special `AUTOINCREMENT` data type for such a field where the engine automatically assigns a unique numeric value to that field for every new record added to the table.

Lesson Summary

In this lesson you learned how a relational database is made up of tables, which consist of rows and columns (or records and fields). Information in a field has to adhere to the same category of data, called data types. While designing a table, ensure that each field identifies an atomic data item and ascertain appropriate data type and size for each field.

Although just one table can be used to represent all the information, you would be riddled with problems of data redundancy, waste of disk storage space, and data inconsistency, which may cause further difficulties in incorporating data changes. To overcome these problems, you should decompose a large table into two or more smaller tables and connect them by introducing a primary key in one table and a foreign key in the other. The primary key can be made up of one of more fields and it acts as a unique tag for addressing a record.

The technique of simplifying a large table into two smaller tables appears fairly intuitive because it is based on how information entities (such as sponsors and events) relate in the real world. Hence, if you identify such relationships beforehand, you can design appropriate tables right away. The next lesson looks into the types of relationships that can exist between two entities and how to represent them in a relational database.

1. What are the advantages of organizing information using a relational database?
   a. Efficient data entry, data update, and deletion
   b. Automatic data identification for data type
   c. Efficient data retrieval and reporting
   d. Easy implementation of changes in database design

2. What does a field in a relational database represent?
   a. A real-world topic
   b. A set of related data items
   c. One atomic element of a topic
   d. A table column

3. Which data type would be appropriate for a driver's license number?
   a. SMALLINT
   b. LONGINT
   c. VARCHAR
   d. REAL

4. Which data types can you use to represent sound data?
   a. LONGBINARY
   b. LONGVARCHAR
   c. REAL
   d. LONGINT

5. What would be an appropriate choice for the primary key in the tblEvents table?
   a. EventName
   b. EventName and EventType
   c. EventName and SponsorID
   d. A new LONGINT field named EventID

Complexity: Easy

1. Create one table named tblBookInfo to represent the following book-related information. List the field names, data types, and primary and foreign keys and assume you want the capability to search books based on the ISBN number, title, and author's last name.

   ● The ISBN number

   ● The title, editorial, number of pages, cover price, and subject category

● The name, email address, and Web address of the publisher

● The names and bibliographies of the authors (maximum three)

Complexity: Moderate

2. Simplify the `tblBookInfo` you created in the previous exercise so that the information about the publisher is not repeated with every book by that publisher.

LESSON 3

TABLE RELATIONSHIPS

In Lesson 2, you saw the potential benefits of splitting one large event sponsor table into two tables. In a way, this split helps model the natural relationship between sponsors and events more closely than the original table. Looking at this two-table design, you can easily gather that a sponsor is an entity that can offer one or more events.

When building a relational database, you should identify such natural relationships that occur between the various informational components you are trying to represent. Your database design is considered good if the tables closely portray these relationships. So, how do you identify and define these relationships in a database, especially when the relationships in the real world can be very complex? You do that by relating only two tables at a time. In doing so, you will find that only one of the following three types of relationships can occur between them:

● One-to-one

● One-to-many (also called many-to-one)

● Many-to-many

One-to-One Relationships

Two tables are related in a one-to-one relationship if, for every record in the first table, there is at most one related record in the second table. This type of relationship proves useful under the following cases:

● When portions of a table contain sensitive information and it may be necessary to split that table into two tables, one of which is subjected to higher security constraints.

⚫ When you observe that some fields of your table stay empty most of the time. For example, suppose you have a table that records payment information and most of the payment records in that table reflect checks for payment method. Only a handful of those records show a payment by credit card and have data in the credit card type, credit card number, and other credit-card–related fields. In such a situation, you may split the table into a basic payment table and a related credit card table, in which a record in the credit card table exists only for payment records that indicate credit card as their payment method.

Tables in a one-to-one relationship should always have the same structure for the primary key, which serves as their linking field, as shown in Figure 3-7.

One-To-Many Relationships

This relationship occurs most frequently in the real world and is also referred to as a *parent-child* relationship. Here, for every record in the first (*parent*) table, there can be zero, one, or many related records in the second (*child*) table, but for every row in the second (child) table, there is exactly one related row in the first (parent) table. It is easy to see that the sponsor and event tables created in Lesson 2 fall under this relationship because a sponsor can offer zero, one, or more than one event at any given time (see Figure 3-8).

Many-to-Many Relationships

Two tables have a many-to-many relationship when, for every record in the first table, there can be many records in the second table, and for every record in the second table, there can be many records in the first table. Many-to-many relationships do occur in the real world, although not as frequently as one-to-many relationships do. As an example, consider the accounts receivable section of any business. It can have one invoice be paid in multiple payments and have many invoices be paid by just one payment. If each invoice is stored in an invoice table and each payment is stored in a payment table, then the invoice these two tables depict is a many-to-many relationship.

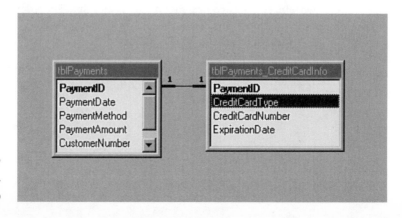

Figure 3-7
Tables in a one-to-one relationship

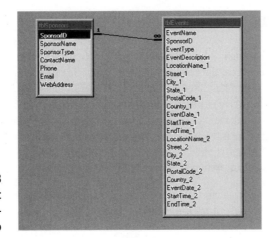

Figure 3-8
Sponsor and event
tables in a one-to-
many relationship

However, unlike the other two types of relationships, you cannot directly model this relationship in a relational database with just two tables. Instead, you establish this relationship by creating a *junction table* (say `tblInvoicesPayments`), which contains the primary key fields of the invoice and payment tables and individually participates in a one-to-many relationship with both these tables, as shown in Figure 3-9. Then every time you want to associate an invoice with a payment, you simply add a record containing the `InvoiceID` of that invoice and the `PaymentID` of that payment to the `tblInvoicesPayments` table.

You can add other fields to the junction table to store more information about the many-to-many relationship. For example, if you want to know how much of an invoice was paid by a particular payment, just add an `Amount` field to the `tblInvoicesPayments` table.

Figure 3-9
Tables in a one-to-
many relationship

Circular Relationships

A circular relationship is established when a table somehow ends up relating with itself. You can create a circular relationship with just one table by having its foreign key link to its own primary key. This arrangement is useful when you want to represent a hierarchical (or recursive) information structure. A genealogy database is a good example. Let's say this database has a person table containing one record for each individual in the genealogy tree and you want to store father-child information in that database. One way to handle that is to add another field named `FatherID` to that person table and relate it to its primary key (say `PersonID`), as shown in Figure 3-10.

Think of single-table circular relationships whenever you encounter a situation in which you have to represent an information element that is made up of other similar sub-elements.

Lesson Summary

In this lesson you learned about the importance of identifying natural relationships that may exist between various information components of a database and mapping them to one-to-one, one-to-many, or many-to-many type relationships that can exist between two tables.

A one-to-one relationship exists between two tables if, for every record in the first table, there can be at most one related record in the second record. One-to-many relationships occur where you see tables forming a parent-child paradigm, in which every record in the parent table can have zero, one, or many related records in the child table but a child record must link to only one parent record. Many-to-many relationships exist between two tables if several records of each table can relate with each other. Such relationships cannot be modeled directly and are simulated using additional junction tables. You can also create a circular relationship, in which a table ends up relating with itself. A single-table circular relationship is particularly helpful when you want to represent hierarchical information.

Figure 3-10
Representing
hierarchical
information using
circular relationship

Note that in this lesson we identified the sponsor and event table as forming a one-to-many relationship. In the real world, however, this is not how sponsors and events always relate because multiple sponsors can jointly offer an event. To handle this situation, you have two choices:

● Establish a many-to-many relationship between the two tables by creating a junction table.

● Redefine the meaning of sponsor to keep things the way they are.

For this application, we will stick to the second option, where we define a sponsor as the main organization that directs the event and acts as the contact for that event.

1. Under which of the following situations does a one-to-one relationship exist between two tables?
   a. Every record in the first table is related to many records in the second table.
   b. Many records in the first table are related to one record in the first table.
   c. For every record in the first table, there is at most one related record in the second table.
   d. Fields of a table are related to each other.

2. What kind of a relationship would exist between an order table and an order details table of a pizza delivery business?
   a. One-to-one relationship
   b. One-to-many relationship
   c. Many-to-many relationship
   d. Circular relationship

3. A patient is covered under many insurance plans. An insurance company covers many patients. What kind of relationship exists here?
   a. One-to-one
   b. One-to many
   c. Many-to-many
   d. None of the above

4. A circular relationship exists under which of the following circumstances?
   a. A number of tables are related to each other in a closed loop.
   b. A foreign key of one table links to the primary key of another table.
   c. A table contains foreign key fields of more than one table.
   d. A table has its foreign key link to its own primary key.

5. A junction table would normally hold which of the following fields?
   a. Primary key of one table and foreign key of another table to which it is supposed to relate
   b. Its own primary key and foreign keys from the tables to which it is going to relate.
   c. Primary keys of both the tables to which it is going to relate
   d. Any fields that provide more information about the relationship of the two tables to which it is supposed to relate

Complexity: Moderate

1. Assume that at any given time, more than 95% of the events listed in the **tblEvents** table (Table 3-4) occur at only one location and have no data in the fields for the second location. List the steps you can take to prevent waste of this storage space.

Complexity: Moderate

2. Identify the relationship between books and authors. How will you represent this relationship in a relational database?

NORMALIZING TABLES

Table normalization is a step-by-step process of simplifying the design of a database so that it acquires the optimum structure for modeling the real-world scenario represented by that database. This process works by refining each database table using a sequence of steps (also called *normal forms*) until it achieves its most optimum design (or the *highest normal form*).

Although texts have been written on the normalization theory describing several normalization rules, it is the first three normal forms that perform most of the optimization during this normalization process. The higher normal forms just act as fine-tuning elements but require a deeper understanding of the whole theory. With this in mind, we have limited this discussion to the first three normal forms.

First Normal Form

The first normal form dictates that all repeating columns in a table must be eliminated. In other words, if you are using table columns as arrays to represent multiple instances (or values) of a particular type of information, you should remove those columns from that table and create a new table containing the primary key of the original table and one instance of those columns.

Let's look at our Web calendar database to see if we can apply this rule to either of its two tables that we created at the end of Lesson 2. Clearly, the event table (refer to Table 3-4) contains two sets of `location` and `date` fields and does not follow the principle of the first normal form. So, to bring this table to the first normal form, we need to perform the following steps:

1. Delete the `location` and `date` fields from this table and establish a primary key for this table. Table 3-5 shows the new structure of the event table.

Table 3-5 The `tblEvents` table in the first normal form

Field Name	Data Type
EventID	LONGINT (primary key)
EventName	VARCHAR(100)
SponsorID	LONGINT
EventType	VARCHAR(50)
EventDescription	LONGVARCHAR

2. Create another table (`tblEventsLocations`) that contains the primary key field of the event table and one instance of the `location` and `date` fields, as shown in Table 3-6.

Table 3-6 The `tblEventsLocations` table

Field Name	Data Type
EventLocationID	LONGINT (Primary Key)
EventID	LONGINT (Foreign key)
LocationName	VARCHAR(100)
Street	VARCHAR(50)
City	VARCHAR(50)
State	VARCHAR(50)
PostalCode	VARCHAR(50)
Country	VARCHAR(50)
EventDate	TIMESTAMP
StartTime	TIMESTAMP
EndTime	TIMESTAMP

Figure 3-11 shows how the sample event data (shown in Figure 3-6) would appear in the `tblEvents` and `tblEventsLocations` tables.

Now let's examine the sponsor table in Table 3-3. At first glance, this table does not appear to have any arraylike columns. However, in the real-world environment, a sponsor can have different contact information for different events. To allow for this possibility, the `ContactName`, `Phone`, and `Email` fields can be moved to a separate related table called the `tblSponsorsContacts`, as shown in Table 3-7.

Table 3-7 The `tblSponsorsContacts` table structure

Field Name	Data Type
ContactID	LONGINT (Primary Key)
SponsorID	LONGINT (Foreign Key)
ContactName	VARCHAR(50)
Phone	VARCHAR(50)
Email	VARCHAR(255)

The new structure of the sponsor table is given in Table 3-8.

Table 3-8 The `tblSponsors` table in its first normal form

Field Name	Data Type
SponsorID	LONGINT
SponsorName	VARCHAR(100)
SponsorType	VARCHAR(50)
WebAddress	VARCHAR(255)

The separation of the contact information from the sponsor information requires us to modify the event table slightly because an event is related to its sponsor through the

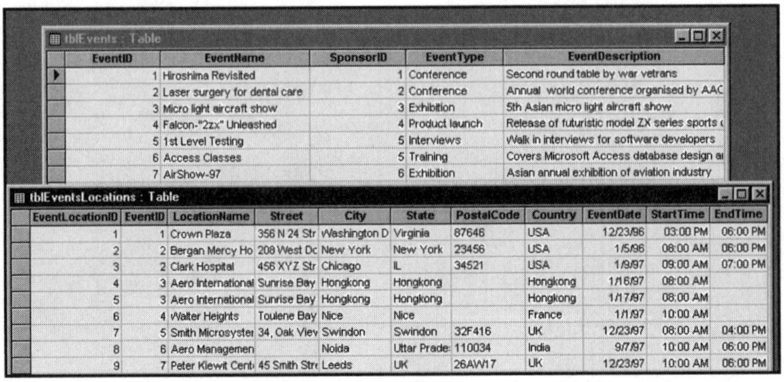

tblEvents : Table

EventID	EventName	SponsorID	EventType	EventDescription
1	Hiroshima Revisited	1	Conference	Second round table by war vetrans
2	Laser surgery for dental care	2	Conference	Annual world conference organised by AAC
3	Micro light aircraft show	3	Exhibition	5th Asian micro light aircraft show
4	Falcon-"2zx" Unleashed	4	Product launch	Release of futuristic model ZX series sports (
5	1st Level Testing	5	Interviews	Walk in interviews for software developers
6	Access Classes	5	Training	Covers Microsoft Access database design ai
7	AirShow-97	6	Exhibition	Asian annual exhibition of aviation industry

tblEventsLocations : Table

EventLocationID	EventID	LocationName	Street	City	State	PostalCode	Country	EventDate	StartTime	EndTime
1	1	Crown Plaza	356 N 24 Str	Washington D	Virginia	87646	USA	12/23/96	03:00 PM	06:00 PM
2	2	Bergan Mercy Ho	208 West Dc	New York	New York	23456	USA	1/5/96	08:00 AM	06:00 PM
3	2	Clark Hospital	456 XYZ Str	Chicago	IL	34521	USA	1/9/97	09:00 AM	07:00 PM
4	3	Aero International	Sunrise Bay	Hongkong	Hongkong		Hongkong	1/16/97	08:00 AM	
5	3	Aero International	Sunrise Bay	Hongkong	Hongkong		Hongkong	1/17/97	08:00 AM	
6	4	Walter Heights	Toulene Bay	Nice	Nice		France	1/1/97	10:00 AM	
7	5	Smith Microsyster	34, Oak Viev	Swindon	Swindon	32F416	UK	12/23/97	08:00 AM	04:00 PM
8	6	Aero Managemen		Noida	Uttar Prade:	110034	India	9/7/97	10:00 AM	06:00 PM
9	7	Peter Kiewit Cent	45 Smith Stre	Leeds	UK	26AW17	UK	12/23/97	10:00 AM	06:00 PM

Figure 3-11 The data view of the `tblEvents` and `tblEventsLocations` tables

contact. Hence, `tblEvents` should be linked with `tblSponsorsContacts` instead of `tblSponsors`, as shown in Table 3-9.

Table 3-9 The revised `tblEvents` table

Field Name	Data Type
EventID	LONGINT (primary key)
EventName	VARCHAR(100)
SponsorContactID	LONGINT (foreign key)
EventType	VARCHAR(50)
EventDescription	LONGVARCHAR

Figure 3-12 shows how the current tables of the Web calendar database are related to each other.

What Does the First Normal Form Achieve?

The first normal form strives to eliminate artificial physical constraints that do not exist in reality but may show up due to an improper table design. For example, when we designed the original event table in Lesson 2, we included two sets of `location` and `date` fields to allow for when an event occurs at two different locations or two different dates or both. We could have extended this set to allow for three or more events. But no matter how much you extend, there will always be an upper limit on how many locations or dates you can specify for an event. By separating the location and date from

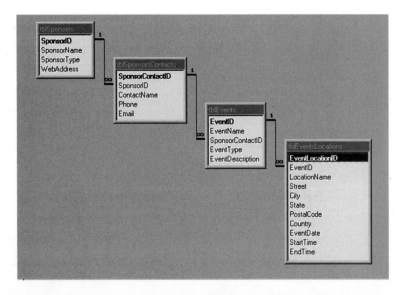

Figure 3-12
Relationships
among the tables
of the Web
calendar database

the event table as dictated by the first normal form, you avoid getting stuck with such upper limits. For each different location or date (or both) of an event, you simply add a record to the `tblEventsLocations` table and link that record back to the `tblEvents` table using the `EventID` field.

Second Normal Form

The second normal form requires that every nonkey field of a table be fully dependent on the primary key. Essentially, this means that a table should store data related to just one information topic, and that topic should be entirely described by its primary key. You already have seen an application of this rule when you decomposed the event sponsor table into an event table and a sponsor table in Lesson 2. However, the normalization process does not have to stop at that high level. Even the smaller tables (a result of first-level normalization) may require further decomposition according to this rule.

As an example, examine the `tblEventsLocations` table in Table 3-6. This table deals with the topic of event location and date, not the location itself. But some of its fields such as `Street`, `City`, `State`, `Zip`, and `Country` are dependent on `LocationName`; that is, if you change the location name of an event, the rest of the location-related fields will have to be changed appropriately. According to the rule of the second normal form, you need to separate the location fields from this table as follows:

1. Create a new table named `tblLocations`, as shown in Table 3-10.

Table 3-10 The `tblLocations` table

Field Name	Data Type
LocationID	LONGINT (Primary Key)
LocationName	VARCHAR(100)
Street	VARCHAR(50)
City	VARCHAR(50)
State	VARCHAR(50)
PostalCode	VARCHAR(50)
Country	VARCHAR(50)

2. Restructure the `tblEventsLocations` table, as shown in Table 3-11.

Table 3-11 The revised `tblEventsLocations` table

Field Name	Data Type
EventLocationID	LONGINT (Primary Key)
EventID	LONGINT (Foreign Key to tblEvents)
LocationID	LONGINT (Foreign Key to tblLocations)

Field Name	Data Type
EventDate	TIMESTAMP
StartTime	TIMESTAMP
EndTime	TIMESTAMP

Figure 3-13 shows how sample data will get distributed between the `tblEventsLocations` and `tblLocations` tables.

Figure 3-14 shows the relationships between all the tables currently in the Web calendar database. Note that `tblEventLocations` now appears as a junction table that establishes a many-to-many relationship between `tblEvents` and `tblLocations`.

Figure 3-13
Data view of the
`tblLocations` and
`tblEventsLoca-
tions` tables

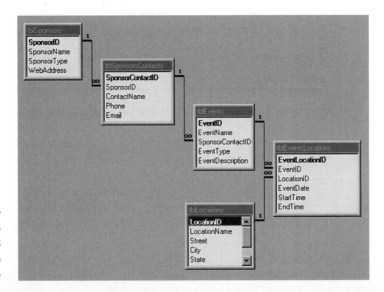

Figure 3-14
Relationships
among the tables
of the Web
calendar database

Third Normal Form

The third normal form extends the philosophy of the second normal form on a field level. It seeks to eliminate any individual table fields not dependent on the primary key. In other words, it promotes the idea of using *lookup tables* for data consistency and storage efficiency within a field.

As an example, consider the `EventType` field of our `tblEvents` table. This field helps categorize event records into general groups such as conferences and exhibitions, which can then be used to quickly find appropriate events. Now, if you decide that you want to change the event type `exhibition` to `presentation`, you have to make that change in all the event records that have `exhibition` as their event type. This implies that the data in the `EventType` field does not associate with just one record, which further indicates that you should use a lookup table for this field, as described in the following steps:

1. Create a new table named `tblEventsTypes_Lkp`, as shown in Table 3-12.

Table 3-12 The `tblEventsTypes` table

Field Name	Data Type
ID	BYTE (primary key)
Description	VARCHAR(50)

2. Restructure `tblEvents`, as shown in Table 3-13.

Table 3-13 The `tblEvents` table in its third normal form

Field Name	Data Type
EventID	LONGINT (primary key)
EventName	VARCHAR(100)
SponsorContactID	LONGINT (foreign key to tblSponsorsContacts)
EventTypeID	BYTE (foreign key to tblEventsTypes)
EventDescription	LONGVARCHAR

Figure 3-15 shows how these two tables form a one-to-many relationship between each other.

Based on the rule of the third normal form, you can also create the lookup tables for the fields listed in Table 3-14.

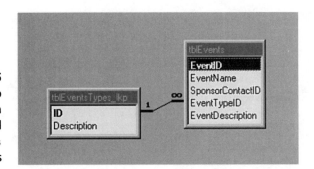

Figure 3-15
Relationship
between
`tblEvents` and
`tblEventsTypes`
`_lkp` tables

Table 3-14 The lookup tables

Field Name	Table	Lookup Table	Key Field Size
SponsorType	tblSponsors	tblSponsorsTypes_lkp	BYTE
City	tblLocations	tblLocationsCities_lkp	INTEGER
States	tblLocations	tblLocationsStates_lkp	INTEGER
Countries	tblLocations	tblLocationsCountries_lkp	BYTE

When defining lookup tables, you should consider the following points:

● Use an appropriate size for the primary key field of the lookup table. For example, it is hard to imagine a large number of different event types so a BYTE-sized numeric field should suffice as a primary key of the `tblEventTypes_lkp` table.

● Use the same structure and field names (such as `ID` and `Description`) for as many lookup tables as possible. This way you can design reusable code for handling lookup tables in your database application.

● A lookup table can be either static, where the lookup values are predefined (for example, `tblLocationsCountries_lkp`), or dynamic, where a user may add a new lookup value on the fly (for example, `tblEventsTypes_lkp`).

Figure 3-16 shows the final set of tables in the Web calendar database after completing the normalization process.

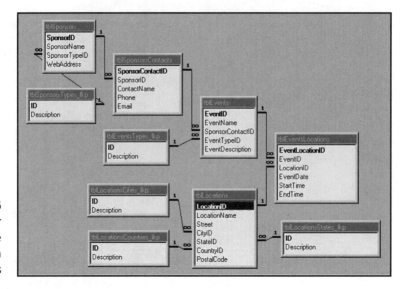

Figure 3-16
Web calendar
database after the
normalization
process

Lesson Summary

This lesson explains the techniques of simplifying the design of a database so that it achieves optimum structure through a step-by-step process called table normalization. A sequence of steps called the normal forms is followed to achieve the above objective.

The first normal form requires all column values to be atomic and all repeating columns in a table to be eliminated. This is achieved by moving all such columns to another table that contains the primary key of the original table. The second normal form requires that every nonkey field be fully dependent on its table's primary key. Thus each table should store data related to just one information topic and that topic should be entirely described by its primary key. The third normal form brings out the idea of using lookup tables for eliminating any individual table fields not dependent on the primary key. This form also discourages using fields that otherwise can be computed from other fields. For example, if you want to track how much time an event will take, you should dynamically compute that from the **StartTime** and **EndTime** fields (using a query, as explained in Chapter 5, "Sorting and Searching: Simple Select Queries"), rather than storing it in another field.

1. Which of the following objectives is achieved through table normalization?
    a. Identify the primary keys of each table.
    b. Optimize structure of the database.
    c. Establish tables that describe only one entity.
    d. All of the above.

2. What should you do to the database structure of Figure 3-16 if you want to allow multiple contacts for a particular event? Assume that most events will not have more than five contacts.
   a. Make no changes.
   b. Create five sets of `ContactID` fields (`ContactID_1`, `ContactID_2`, and so on) in the `tblEvents` table.
   c. Remove the `ContactID` field from the `tblEvents` table.
   d. Create another table named `tblEventsContacts` containing only the `EventID` and `ContactID` fields.

3. Which forms of normalization help in maintaining data consistency?
   a. First normal form
   b. Second normal form
   c. Third normal form
   d. All of the above

4. What should you do to the database structure of Figure 3-16 to store directions on how to reach a particular event?
   a. Add a `LONGVARCHAR` field named `Directions` to the `tblEvents` table.
   b. Add a `LONGVARCHAR` field named `Directions` to the `tblLocations` table.
   c. Add a `LONGVARCHAR` field named `Directions` to the `tblEventsLocations` table.
   d. Add a `DirectionID` field in the `tblEvents` table. Then create another lookup table named `tblEventsDirections` containing the fields `ID` and `Description` and link the `ID` field of this table to the `DirectionID` field of the `tblEvents` table.

5. Why do all the lookup tables in Figure 3-16 have the same names for their fields?
   a. It is a requirement of the third normal form.
   b. It helps in designing reusable code to handle lookup tables.
   c. To indicate that they all have the same type of information.
   d. None of the above.

Complexity: Moderate

1. Let's say you want to keep the sponsor's location in the Web calendar database. List the steps needed to change the database structure of Figure 3-16 to store this information.

Complexity: Advanced

2. Refer to the first exercise in Lesson 2, and create a normalized book database showing all the table structures and their relationships.

DATA VALIDATION AND FIELD PROPERTIES

Once you have designed the structure of your database, it is important to ensure that the data it holds is as accurate and complete as possible. This is usually done by validating the data before it finds its place in the database. Overall, your data validation process should help meet the following objectives.

Maintaining Accurate Information

Any unintentional mistakes while entering data should be immediately pointed out and corrected if possible. For example, warnings could be issued for invalid dates, phone numbers without area codes, and inappropriate email and Web address formats. Many database packages have some of these safeguards (for example, error messages for out-of-range dates, such as February 30) built right in.

Allowing Meaningful Information

The adage of garbage in, garbage out applies very well to databases. Just as a person's age cannot be a negative integer, nor can a social security number have alpha characters. Such absurdities should be prevented at all levels.

Ensuring Data Consistency

When data is entered by multiple users, data inconsistency can easily creep in. For example, one user may specify California as CA, whereas another may type the full state name. This can create difficulties for users searching for events in that state because the search process may not be able make the correlation between CA and California.

Levels of Data Validation

You can perform the data validation process at the following hierarchical levels based on the scope of data errors:

- Field level
- Record level
- Table level
- Database level

Validating Data at Field Level

Here the validation rules are applied to individual fields. An obvious example is when you test each primary key field against a Null value. Some other rules that can be applied at this level are enumerated below.

● For certain fields (besides the primary key) the presence of valid data is a must. For example, in our sponsor table, it does not make sense to store a sponsor record without any data in the SponsorName field.

● A field can be expected to fall under a reasonable range. For example, the date of a future event may be validated against the date on which the information about that event is being entered.

● Allow only certain types of characters in a particular field. For example, you may want a phone number field to accept only numbers and some special characters such as (,), or –.

● Data in certain fields may have to meet a certain length requirement. For example, a social security number should be between 9 (without any dashes) and 11 (with dashes) characters.

Validating Data at Record Level

Sometimes independently validating individual fields is not enough and you have to apply rules that involve multiple fields or at a record level. For example, if an event end time is specified, then it must be later than the event start time.

Validating Data at Table Level

Table-level data validation involves rules that look for data consistency between records of a same table. A common case of this is when you check the value of the primary key of a new record against existing records to test for uniqueness.

Validating Data at Database Level

Although the objective of carrying out field, record, or table level validation is to store good and sensible information, you have to perform additional checks when you divide the information into related tables. For example, in the event and the sponsor table created in Lesson 2, the event record and its corresponding sponsor record must correlate. This correlation can be adversely affected if you change the value of the SponsorID field in the sponsor table and do not propagate that change in the event table or delete a sponsor record while related events are in the event table. To avoid such situations, establish the referential integrity rule on your database, which says that no table of the database should contain unmatched foreign key values. This essentially means that:

● A row may with a reference to the parent table may not be added to the child table unless the referenced record exists in the parent table.

● If the primary key value of the parent table changes or a record in the parent table is deleted, the rows in the child table must not be left "orphaned."

The referential integrity can be maintained using the following three options:

● *Forbid*: Simply disallow changes that may disturb the referential integrity.

● *Cascade*: Propagate any change to the primary key of the parent table to the foreign key of the associated records in the child table. Similarly, on deletion of a record in the parent table, delete the corresponding records in the child table.

● *Nullify*: When deleting a parent record, set the foreign key value of the corresponding child records to Null.

Besides maintaining referential integrity, you may have to enforce other database-specific integrity rules that may be required by your application. These rules are also called *business rules*. For example, in the Web calendar database, you may want to ensure that for every event record in the tblEvents table, there is at least one corresponding record in the tblEventsLocations table; otherwise, you will end up having an event with no location and date information.

When to Validate Data?

Data can be validated either by the user interface accepting the data or by the database engine that actually stores the data (see Figure 3-17), depending on the choice and features of your database management system. This also depends on the rules of the shop in which your are working.

As a recommended practice, you should always enforce data validation rules through your database management system. This way the system's engine will faithfully enforce those rules and automatically ensure the integrity of the database no matter which user interface you use to accept the data. The only limitation is that most database systems cannot support all types or levels of data validation. Furthermore, they may not provide the appropriate error trapping and reporting mechanisms. In such cases, you need to check for data errors at the data input stage itself.

Some shops prefer to enforce data validation rules programmatically rather that letting the database management system handle them due to performance considerations.

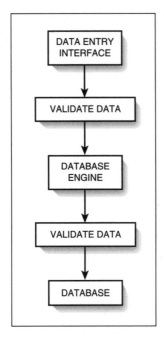

Figure 3-17
Data validation
stages

Lesson Summary

Data validation has to be an integral part of the database design to ensure accuracy, consistency, and meaningful information in the database. Data validation can be carried out from the field level to the database level, depending on the nature of the database and the scope of errors that may creep in. This lesson explains how data validation can be carried out at each hierarchical level.

The choice of data validation by the user interface accepting data or the database system engine depends on the features and capabilities of the database system. Even though enforcement of validation rules through database management is a preferred practice, limitations of the system have to be borne in mind and taken care of at the data input stage.

1. Which of the following objectives can be met by the data validation process?
   a. Maintain accurate information.
   b. Automate the process of information gathering.
   c. Process the information.
   d. Ensure data consistency.

2. At what stage should data validation be performed?
   a. Data processing stage
   b. Report generation stage
   c. Data entry stage
   d. Information gathering stage

3. Which level of data validation will you have to perform if you want to ensure that every contact has either an email address or a phone number or both?
   a. Field level
   b. Record level
   c. Table level
   d. Database level

4. Which level of data validation will you have to perform if you want to ensure that a valid start time is specified for every event?
   a. Field level
   b. Record level
   c. Table level
   d. Database level

5. How will you ensure that no one changes an event type if one or more event records of that type exist in the database?
   a. By using a forbid-type referential integrity
   b. By using a nullify-type referential integrity
   c. By using a cascade-type referential integrity
   d. By creating a business rule

Complexity: Easy

1. List three field-level validation rules that would be applicable to the **tblEventsLocations** table given in Table 3-11. NOTE: The "required field" rule is considered as one type.

Complexity: Moderate

2. List five different types of validation rules and their levels that would be applicable to a book database. At least one rule belonging to each level must be specified.

SECURITY AND MULTIUSER ISSUES

Any database design would be incomplete without considering the necessary security controls on the information the database will hold, especially in an environment in which multiple users are expected to work with that database. Furthermore, if you want to allow these users to manipulate data concurrently (which is a standard feature expected of most Web applications), you need to plan for the appropriate locking strategies to avoid potential data clashes. This lesson looks at the various issues related to data security in a multiuser environment and how they affect database design in general.

Securing Your Database

Security may have to be built into your database for performing any of the following operations:

- Viewing data

- Adding new data

- Updating existing data

Establishing Security to View Data

This becomes necessary if all the information in your database is not meant for global consumption. Essentially, you have to discern from among your users who can view data and what part of it they can view. For example, you may want to restrict access to certain tables of your application to those who have database administration rights. A typical case is when you have an accounting database and you need to ensure that only a chosen few top executives of the organization have access to sensitive information such as the salary details of the employees. In regard to Web applications used for commercial purpose, you may want to use different security levels for members and nonmembers.

Establishing Security to Add and Update Data

You may have to restrict users to certain portions of the database for adding or updating data. For example, in the Web calendar application, you may want only sponsors who have been registered by your customer service staff to add their events to the calendar. A limit may also be set on the number of events a sponsor can list at a time on that sponsor's subscription level. Furthermore, you need to prevent one sponsor from meddling with the records of other sponsors. In other words, you need to set up a suitable security mechanism to identify who can interact with your application's database and what tables or records they can manipulate.

Methods of Establishing Security

There are two ways of implementing the security issues discussed above:

● Use the security model built into your database engine.

● Build the security as part of your application.

Most relational database systems have some security provisions built in by which you can define your users and assign them various permissions and privileges. Although using this built-in security capability has the advantages of speed and ease of administration, this approach proves helpful usually in an environment in which the users are known and limited in number.

When you have to deal with a large and unspecified number of users who can be added on the fly, it is best to implement security at the part of your application where you have the flexibility to exercise any amount or type of security control. Application-level security can be enforced at the *user* level or *group* level or both.

At the user level, you associate permissions to database information with individual users. A good example is when you allow an event record to be edited only by the contact person who originally added that record to the Web calendar application. If you allow any contact person of a sponsor to edit any event record of that sponsor, you will be dealing with group-level security. In addition, you may consider classifying users or groups into incremental security levels and use those levels to determine the nature of tasks users can perform on different database objects. This would be needed in case you want to restrict contact persons with low security level to edit only their event records and not their sponsor records.

Whichever approach you adopt to implement security, you have to identify your users first. This is done by having the users authenticate themselves by supplying a user name and password (or in some cases just the password) that either you assign to them before they start using the application or they assign themselves when they first use the application. It all depends on the nature and objective of the application.

For our Web calendar application, we will use a simple group-level security where any new sponsor can assign its own user name and password and any contact person of that sponsor can access and edit its information. To store these user names and passwords, we will need to add two fields to the tblSponsors table, as shown in Table 3-15.

Table 3-15 tblSponsors with username and password fields

Field Name	Data Type
SponsorID	LONGINT
SponsorName	VARCHAR(100)

Field Name	Data Type
SponsorTypeID	BYTE (Foreign key to tblSponsorsTypes_lkp)
WebAddress	VARCHAR(255)
UserName	VARCHAR(20)
Password	VARCHAR(20)

Resolving Multiuser Issues

When exposing your database in a multiuser environment as in the case of the Web calendar application, in which many users may be simultaneously adding or editing events, you need to address the following two issues:

● Ensure that the primary key stays unique when multiple users concurrently add records to a table.

● Ensure that data conflicts occurring due to multiple users concurrently editing the same record are properly resolved.

Maintaining a Unique Primary Key

Keeping the primary key unique depends on how you have defined that key. For example, in the case of a book table in which the ISBN number is set as the primary key, you do not have to do much. Every book has a unique ISBN number, thereby ensuring the uniqueness of the primary key. The problem arises when you use additional fields such as SponsorID or EventID to act as a primary key. How do you guarantee that each user adding the record will provide a unique value for such fields? There are two ways to handle this situation:

● Use the AUTOINCREMENT data type for these fields, in which case the database engine automatically assigns a unique value to the primary key field of each new record added to the database.

● Have your application generate a unique value for the primary key field before it asks the database engine to add the record to the database.

The AUTOINCREMENT data type approach is certainly superior, but it imposes three constraints:

● Your database engine must support this data type.

● Four bytes (in some case even 8 bytes) are used by the primary key field.

● You generally do not have much control over how the database engine ensures uniqueness.

The second approach, in which you generate the primary key values yourself, requires significantly more programming effort because you not only have to find a new value but also must implement appropriate data locking schemes (described later) to ensure the uniqueness of this value. However, this approach gives you more flexibility and you can work with small-sized (such as `BYTE` and `SMALLINT` type) primary keys. This is discussed further in Chapter 11, "Populating Tables: Web-Based Data Entry."

Locking Schemes

You resolve data conflicts in a multiuser environment by ensuring that only one user has control of a particular data record at any moment. This is accomplished by establishing one of the following locking schemes, depending on the features and requirements of your application:

- *Optimistic locking*: Here you lock a record only when the record is being saved but not during the editing process. This allows multiple users to edit the same record concurrently and whoever saves the record last has the final say.

- *Pessimistic locking*: Here you lock up the currently edited record as soon as the user begins to edit a record and unlock it only when that user either saves the changes or decides to cancel editing that record. Only one user is allowed to edit a particular record at a time, although different users can edit different records.

- *Table locking*: Here you lock a complete table and no other user is allowed to edit any record of that table until you free that lock. This scheme is used only when you want to do batch updates.

Although most database management systems provide a lot of built-in support for these data locking schemes, they are all based on a connection-based multiuser environment in which all users interacting with the database must maintain active connections. For example, they use the loss of a connection as an indication that a user is no longer editing the record and the lock established by that user can be removed. Unfortunately, the inherent nature of the Web, in which the user editing the record does not keep an active connection with the database application, renders the built-in locking provisions practically ineffective. You essentially have to implement the locking functionality in your Web application itself; we describe one common method of doing that in Chapter 11.

Lesson Summary

Building appropriate security measures in most database designs is of paramount importance; in a multiuser environment, it is an absolute must. This lesson explains the need to secure your database to control who can view data, add new data, and update existing data. To incorporate the necessary security features, you can either use the inherent security model built into your database engine or develop your own custom model in which you store user names and passwords as part of your database. See Chapter 12,

"Creating a Data Entry Wizard: Advanced Data Entry and Maintenance," for more on this.

In the event of multiple users concurrently manipulating your database, you need to ensure that the primary key of each database table remains unique. Similarly, you have to consider data conflicts that can occur when multiple users edit the same record simultaneously and properly resolve them using appropriate data locking schemes, depending on the requirements of your application. Although most database engines provide built-in support for various locking schemes, you cannot use them for Web-based database applications due to the way the Web model works. Instead, you have to develop your own data conflict resolving and locking strategies, as explained in Chapter 11.

1. In a hospital, what kind of security would a pharmacist generally have regarding a patient's prescription?
   a. View a prescription
   b. Add a prescription
   c. Change the prescription
   d. Delete a prescription

2. In an online ordering system, what actions should a potential customer be able to do?
   a. View product information
   b. Add products to the product table
   c. Change the product code of an existing product
   d. Add products to the shopping basket table

3. In the Web calendar application, where will you store the user name and password information if you want to allow contacts to change only their own event records?
   a. In the `tblSponsors` table
   b. In the `tblSponsorsContacts` table
   c. In the `tblEvents` table
   d. In the `tblEventsLocations` table

4. Which of the following methods should be preferred to ensure a unique primary key for the sponsor table in the Web calendar database?
   a. Allow the sponsor to specify the `SponsorID` along with the rest of the information.
   b. Use the `AUTOINCREMENT` data type for the `SponsorID` field.
   c. Let the Web calendar application provide a default `SponsorID` when it supplies a blank sponsor entry form to the new sponsor.
   d. Let the Web calendar application generate a `SponsorID` when it is ready to store the information entered by the new sponsor.

5. Which of the following schemes locks data at the record level?
   a. Optimistic locking
   b. Pessimistic locking
   c. Table locking
   d. Password locking

Complexity: Moderate

1. How will you structure the Web calendar database if you want to enforce the following security constraints?

   ● A contact should be able to edit only the event records that he or she has added.

   ● Only the primary contact of a sponsor can add other contacts for that sponsor.

   ● Any contact with a superpassword can change or delete any event record of his or her sponsor.

Complexity: Difficult

2. Let's say you want to allow only one contact to edit the sponsor information at any given time in the Web calendar application. What kind of locking scheme is required? List a way and the necessary changes you will have to make to your database structure to implement this scheme.

CHAPTER SUMMARY

This chapter explained the general structure of most Web applications and how they all need to store and retrieve information. A relational database provides an intuitive model for organizing such information. You represent each individual information topic as a table in that database, which further consists of fields and records. Database tables can be related by creating linking fields. To ensure data consistency and prevent the waste of storage space, you should always strive to optimize the structure of your database. This is generally done by identifying the relationships that exist between tables and following a table simplification process called table normalization.

When designing your database, you should also enumerate what kind of validation rules apply to your database. Furthermore, if your database is meant to be used in a multiuser environment, you may need to modify your database design to help in the implementation of data security and record-locking schemes.

Here is a recap of the salient points in this chapter:

- Information is a key component of most Web applications, and it is vital that this information is properly organized.

- The first step in organizing information is to determine the objectives of your application and identify the main information entities your application will be dealing with.

- The second step is to represent each information entity as a database table. Each table should have an appropriate primary key and each field should represent an atomic item.

- The third step is to simplify each table using the rules of normalization and establish appropriate relationships.

- The fourth step is to identify the data validation requirements.

- The final step is to review your current structure and make appropriate changes (generally adding extra fields) to allow for other factors such as security and data locking.

- The first rule of normalization requires that you move repeating groups of fields from the parent table to another child table.

- The second rule of normalization requires that each table should represent only one topic by ensuring that all fields of a table are completely dependent on the primary key.

- The third rule of normalization promotes the idea of creating lookup tables for fields whose values must stay consistent between records.

- Data validation can be performed at field, record, table, or database level. At field level you check for null data, valid data ranges, and the like. At record level, your validation rule involves multiple fields. When you compare a record against other records (such as checking for duplicate values), you do a table-level validation. At database level, you test data values of one table against another and establish referential integrity rules.

- For attaining maximum control, flexibility, and portability, you can implement security through your Web application rather then depending on the security functionality of any database management system.

- Under the Web model, the data locking features provided by most database management systems become unusable. Often, you need to implement alternate locking strategies to get around the data conflict problem that can arise in a multiuser environment.

In this chapter, you also saw how to design a relational database for the Web calendar application. Now, it is time to construct a real database based on this design. For this, we will use Microsoft Access, which is a user-friendly database management system that fully supports all the principles of a relational database.

CHAPTER 4

CONSTRUCTING A RELATIONAL DATABASE: THE MICROSOFT ACCESS WAY

This chapter provides a step-by-step tutorial on how to build the calendar database you conceptually designed in Chapter 3, "Organizing Data: Tables and Relationships," using the Microsoft Access database management system. It then shows how you can use Access's intuitive user interface to insert and manipulate data in that database. Data access from other types of desktop and client-server databases is also discussed. In particular, you will learn about

- Features and architecture of Access

- How to create an Access database

- Data types and field properties supported by Access and how to use them to define tables

- How to specify validation rules

- How to create relationships and enforce referential integrity between Access tables

⬤ How to populate and manipulate data in an Access database

⬤ How to use the import and link wizards of Access

WHAT IS MICROSOFT ACCESS?

To construct a relational database, you usually employ a high-level software called a *relational database management system* (RDBMS), which provides a consistent and efficient way of implementing database-intrinsic operations. Depending on where these operations are processed, an RDBMS can be classified as a client-server or a file-based system. This lesson explains the key differences between these two classifications and then describes the features and architecture of Microsoft Access 97, which is an extremely popular and powerful file-based RDBMS.

Client-Server RDBMS

A *client-server RDBMS* uses a dedicated database server that provides database access and management services to any requesting client program. The client does not have direct access to the database. It can send requests to the server using only the protocols and communication methods supported by that server. All data processing occurs at the server end; only the results are returned to the client. The client can of course further manipulate those results to complete its task. Figure 4-1 shows the basic model followed by a client-server RDBMS.

File-Based RDBMS

In a *file-based RDBMS*, a database is stored as one or more regular files that are kept on a user's local hard drive (in the case of a single user environment) or on a shared file server (in case of a multiuser environment). To perform any database operation, each user runs a copy of the RDBMS on his or her own desktop machine and issues instructions through that system's user interface. Based on those instructions, the database engine of that RDBMS then directly accesses and manipulates the shared data files. To improve performance, the engine normally maintains its own cache of physical pages from the file residing on the file server and sends the updated physical pages back to the file server over the network as needed. Figure 4-2 shows the basic model followed by a file-based RDBMS.

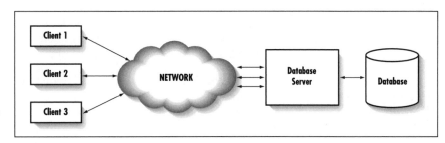

Figure 4-1
Client-server
RDBMS model

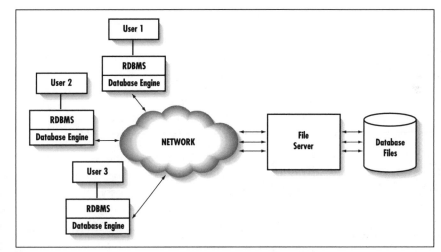

Figure 4-2
File-based RDBMS
model

Where Does Microsoft Access Fit into the Picture?

Microsoft Access is a feature-rich, multiuser, user-friendly, file-based RDBMS. In addition, it can act as a powerful client in a client-server RDBMS environment. This versatility makes Access stand out among other file-based RDBMSs available in the market today. Some of the key features of Access 97 are

● Access supports all attributes of a relational model, such as primary keys, relationships, and referential integrity, as you will see in the next three lessons.

● By itself, Access is a graphical and interactive environment, though it includes strong macro and programming capabilities to automate data processing tasks.

● Due to its object-oriented architecture, Access can be used as a front end to another ODBC-compliant client-server database such as Oracle, Sybase, or Microsoft SQL server. Lesson 6 provides some insight on how this is done.

● Access follows the SQL (Structured Query Language) standard for querying and manipulating data, although you hardly need to learn the SQL syntax due to its intuitive query design interface. Chapters 5 "Sorting and Searching: Simple Select Queries," 6, "Combining Tables and Grouping Data: Joins and Total Queries," and 7, "Designing Queries to Maintain Data: Action Queries," cover this intuitive query design aspect of Access in more detail.

● Access is based on a sophisticated database engine called the JET (Joint Engine Technology), which incorporates state-of-the-art technologies to deliver high performance.

● With Access, you can import or link to data from various data sources, including HTML documents. These data sources could even reside on an FTP or HTTP server. See Lesson 6 for more details.

● The `Hyperlink` data type (described in the next lesson) allows you to insert hyperlink addresses into your tables. You can also publish your data to a static or dynamic HTML page for easy integration of your Access objects into a Web site. (The dynamic HTML generation feature works only with Microsoft's Internet Information Server and is not covered in this book.)

● Microsoft has sold millions of copies of Access worldwide and its latest versions clearly reflect Microsoft's vision for the future. In addition, comprehensive and up-to-date technical support on all Access-related issues is available from Microsoft's Web site at `www.microsoft.com`.

Simply put, Access has the right mix of features for occasional users as well as full-time developers. It also compliments the Visual Basic development environment; together, Access and VB are a powerful and attractive combination for designing Web-database applications. You will see this combination at work when you develop the Web event calendar application later in the book.

The Access Architecture

In the Access framework, shown in Figure 4-3, users specify their database operations either through Access's user interface tools or by building programs using macros and Access Basic. These components in turn interact with the JET database engine by making calls to its dynamic link libraries (DLLs). The code in these DLLs then directly accesses and manipulates the database files.

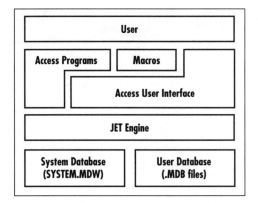

Figure 4-3
Conceptual
framework of
Access architecture

Every time you use Access (and thus start the JET database engine), it looks to a special database called the system database, which contains information about the users and their associated passwords. By default, this database is stored as a file named `SYSTEM.MDW` residing in the directory where Access is installed. All regular Access user databases are stored in files that have a `.MDB` file extension.

Access uses an advanced and distributed model for handling database security. Unless you are familiar with all the security aspects of Access, we suggest that you use the default security (no security) mode Access when following this book.

The Access User Interface

The main user interface of Access, shown in Figure 4-4, consists of a menu bar, a toolbar, a status bar, and a database container that presents the user with the following six kinds of objects:

● Table, which you use to create and populate database tables

● Query, which you use to define any query and view its results

● Form, which you use to design customized data entry forms

● Report, which you use to produce custom layouts for presenting data

● Macro, which you use to automate the user interface tasks

● Module, which you use to write Access Basic code

All objects that you create for your database (such as table definitions, queries, and report designs) are stored in one `.MDB` file. In addition, that file holds the data contained in the tables unless the tables are linked from another database, as explained in Lesson 6. The tab buttons attached to the database container allow you to list and select the stored objects, whereas the menu and toolbars allow you to perform applicable database creation and management operations.

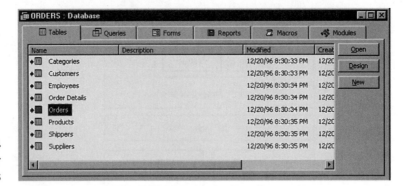

Figure 4-4
The main user
interface of Access

Opening a Sample Database in Access

When you install Microsoft Access, it includes a sample database named **NORTHWIND.MDB** that contains the sales data for a fictitious company called Northwind Traders. By viewing the tables, queries, and other objects included in this database, you can learn how the different features of Microsoft Access can be used to create a functional database. The following steps describe how to open this database in Microsoft Access:

1. Start Microsoft Access.

   Access displays the opening dialog box, as shown in Figure 4-5.

2. Select the Open an Existing Database option if it is not already selected and then click on the OK button.

   Access displays the Open dialog box.

Figure 4-5
The opening dialog
box

3. In this dialog box, use the Look In box to locate the `Samples` folder. This folder is usually in the `Program Files\Microsoft Office\Office` folder.

4. Double-click on the `Samples` folder.

   The Open dialog box will display all the sample databases, as shown in Figure 4-6.

If you are unable to locate these sample databases, chances are they were not installed when you installed Microsoft Access. To install these databases, rerun the Setup program for Microsoft Access and select Sample Databases from the installation options.

5. Double-click on the Northwind database to open it.

   Access shows Northwind's logo screen.

6. Click on the OK button on this logo screen to display the database container (refer to Figure 4-4).

7. Click on the Show Me option to bring up the help file that gives you an overview of the Northwind database and demonstrates its main features.

Getting Help in Access

Microsoft Access comes with extensive online documentation provided in the form of help files. To get more information on any topic, do any one of the following:

⬤ Select the Help option from the menu bar.

⬤ Press [F1].

⬤ Click on the clip-shaped (and cute) online assistant.

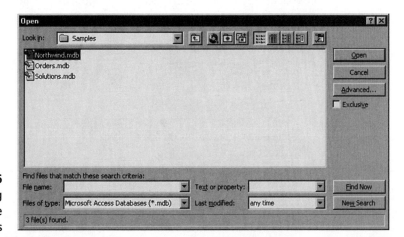

Figure 4-6
The Open dialog box showing the sample databases

Lesson Summary

Relational database management systems are categorized as client-server or file-based systems depending on whether the database-intrinsic functions are performed on a dedicated server or at the client end. Microsoft Access is a powerful file-based RDBMS that also has the versatility to act as a database client in a client-server environment. Access is easy to use and is based on a sound and modern relational database architecture with enough capabilities and expandability to take you to the 21st century.

In this lesson, you were given a conceptual overview of Access architecture and the various objects the Access user interface provides. You also saw how to open the sample Northwind database, which is generally the recommended starting point for learning about the various features of Access. We urge you to spend time exploring this database before moving on to the next lesson, where we show how to create a new database and discuss the data types and the various field properties supported by Access.

1. Which of the following is true in the case of the Access RDBMS?
    a. It is based on the client-server model.
    b. It is based on the direct file access model.
    c. It can act as a client to many client-server databases.
    d. It supports only a single-user environment.

2. Which of the following are important performance factors in a file-based RDBMS running in a multiuser environment?
    a. The processing speed and the cache size of the client machine
    b. The speed of the network
    c. The speed of the server
    d. All of the above

3. What components of Access actually manipulate a database file?
    a. The user interface
    b. The Access macros
    c. The Access programs
    d. The JET database engine

4. What does an Access database (`.MDB`) file hold?
    a. All the objects created for that database
    b. The user name and password information
    c. The data contained in the local tables
    d. All of the above

5. How do you find the names of the queries stored in an Access database file?
   a. By opening that file in a text editor and looking through the queries section
   b. By opening the database file in Access and typing **Show Queries** in the database container
   c. By opening the database file in Access and looking on the Queries tab of the database container
   d. All of the above

Complexity: Easy
   1. Read the topic "Introduction to Microsoft Access 97" in the online help for Access and describe how this section defines a database.

Complexity: Easy
   2. List the name of the queries contained in the **ORDERS.MDB** sample database provided with Access.

DATA TYPES AND FIELD PROPERTIES IN MICROSOFT ACCESS

In Chapter 3, you created a conceptual design of a calendar database to use for the Web calendar application. You will now convert this conceptual model into an Access database (which you will name **CALENDAR.MDB**) by following these main steps:

1. Create a new CALENDAR.MDB database file.

2. Create all the database tables and set the field properties.

3. Establish relationships and referential integrity between related tables.

This lesson covers the first step and lays out the premises for the next step (covered in the next lesson) by describing the data types and the field properties supported by Access and how they map to the generic data types you studied in Chapter 3 (refer to Table 3-1).

Creating the Calendar Database in Access

Follow the steps given below to create a blank `CALENDAR.MDB` database file:

1. Start Microsoft Access.

   Access displays the opening dialog box, as shown in Figure 4-5.

2. Select the Blank Database option.

   Access displays the File New Database dialog box.

3. In the Save In box of this dialog box, locate the `C:\WEBSITE\HTDOCS\WDBIC\ CHAP04\LESSON2\` directory and type `CALENDAR.MDB` in the file name text box, as shown in Figure 4-7.

4. Press the Create button.

   Access creates the `CALENDAR.MDB` database file and displays its empty container, as shown in Figure 4-8.

Data Types Supported by Access

Access supports a comprehensive set of data types that you can use to represent almost any type of data value. Here, we list these data types and provide a brief description of the kind of data they can represent.

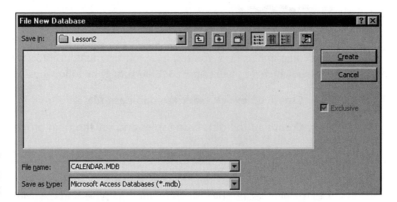

Figure 4-7
The Save In dialog box

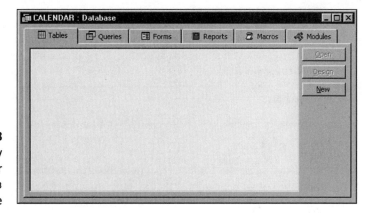

Figure 4-8
The empty
database container
of the CALENDAR.MDB
database

Text

This data type can hold alphanumeric characters and is useful for storing names, addresses, phone numbers, postal codes, and other nondescriptive text attributes. This is one of the most versatile and commonly used data types, with one limitation—you can store only up to 255 characters in a **Text** field.

Memo

This data type eliminates the 255-character limit of the **Text** data type by allowing you to store up to 64,000 characters, but you cannot sort or index a **Memo** field. You use this data type for notes, remarks, explanations, and other descriptive fields.

Number

This is a generic data type used to store numeric values with a field size of **Byte**, **Integer**, **Long Integer**, **Single**, or **Double**. You can use the fields of this data type in mathematical calculations.

Currency

This data type is used for storing numbers involving money. It represents a scaled integer that can handle large monetary values with great precision. Accuracy is maintained up to four decimal places.

Date/Time

This data type allows you to represent fields that signify a date and time value. Sorting on this type of field produces a chronological order of the records. Access also provides several built-in functions that can be applied to **Date/Time** field values, many of which are described in Chapter 5, "Sorting and Searching: Simple Select Queries."

AutoNumber

This data type is equivalent to a long integer, except Access automatically provides unique numbers (usually in a numeric sequence) for each record. You cannot edit a value in the `AutoNumber` field.

Yes/No

This data type is used for fields that hold logical values such as yes/no and true/false.

OLE Object

This data type is used for fields that hold pictures, graphs, sound, video, or other program objects, which can be linked or embedded in Access.

Hyperlink

This data type is used to store text or combinations of text and numbers that symbolize a hyperlink address. This address can point to a local document or an information resource on the Web. Lesson 5 covers the characteristics of this data type in more detail.

Field Properties

In addition to specifying the data type, you can also characterize the nature and appearance of the field data through the field properties, which are described below.

Field Size

For `Number` and `Text` fields, the `Field Size` property describes the maximum range (for numeric) or the maximum length (for text) of data values.

Format

This property specifies how Access should display the field data through its user interface. For example, a `MediumDate` format on a date value of 7/1/96 will force Access to show the date as `1-Jul-96`.

Decimal Places

This property applies only to `Number` and `Currency` fields and specifies the number of digits Access should display after the decimal separator.

Input Mask

This property helps you specify a pattern for all the data to be entered in a field. Access then flags an error any time the data does not match that pattern. Just like the `Format` and `Decimal Places` properties, this property is put in effect when you enter data through its user interface. If you import data or add data programmatically (as in the case of data entered using Visual Basic), then Access ignores this property.

Caption

This property specifies how Access displays the field heading when you view the table records. If you do not specify a value for the field's `Caption` property, Access uses the field name as the default caption for that field.

Default Value

This property holds the value (or an expression) that you want Access to fill in automatically for that field when a new record is entered. For example, if you want USA to be default country if no country is specified for an event location, then you can list `1` as the default value for the `CountryID` field of the `tblLocations` table (assuming ID `1` is assigned to USA in the `tblLocationsCountries_Lkp` table).

Validation Rule

The `Validation Rule` property allows you to add constraints on the field data values by requiring the data to follow specific rules. You can test for individual values, data ranges, and even multiple conditions on that field.

For example, if you want to ensure that the date entered in the `EventDate` field of the `tblEventsLocations` table (refer to Table 3-11) is always greater than the current date, you can enter `>=Date()` in the `Validation Rule` property of this field, as explained in Lesson 3. The `Date()` function is just one of the many built-in functions of Access that you can use to create a validation rule. These built-in functions are explained further in Chapter 5, "Sorting and Searching: Simple Select Queries."

Validation Text

The `Validation Text` property holds the message that you want Access to display if the user entered data does not meet the validation rule. For instance, you can specify the validation text for the `EventDate` field as `The start date of your event must be later than today's date`. Then anytime you try to enter an event date prior to the current date, Access will flag an error containing this validation text.

Required

This property tells Access to ensure that a data value is always specified for that field before it stores the record in the table.

Allow Zero Length

This property, which applies only to `Text`, `Memo`, and `Hyperlink` fields, is used to specify if Access will allow a zero-length string (`""`) as a valid entry for a field. Normally, this property should be set to `No`, in which case Access automatically puts a `Null` value if you do not specify any data for that field.

Indexed

The **Indexed** property tells Access to index the field for faster data retrieval and searches based on that field. This property can accept three values:

● No

● Yes (Duplicates OK)

● Yes (No Duplicates)

For example, the Web calendar application allows users to search events by their date. To make the search process efficient, you can set the **Indexed** property of the **StartDate** field of the **tblEventsLocations** table to **Yes (Duplicates OK)** (because the **EventDate** field can have duplicate values in the **tblEventsLocations** table).

The Scope of the Field Properties

Although these properties give you a lot of field customization options, it is important to recognize where exactly Access applies these properties. Some properties such as **Format**, **Decimal Places**, **Input Mask**, and **Caption** are effective only at the user interface level of Access, whereas the **Validation Rule** and other properties are enforced by the JET engine itself. For example, if you display a **Single** field formatted as **Currency** through the user interface, all values in that field will show up with a **$** prefix. However, if you access that field's data programmatically, Access will return the dollar values as raw numbers.

Because most of this book is based on working with Access databases using Visual Basic programs, don't worry about the user interface level properties and concentrate on those properties that are applicable even at the JET engine level.

Mapping Access Data Types to Generic Data Types

As you can see, Access supports all the common data types mentioned in Table 3-1, although it uses different names and in some cases a different way of specifying them. For example, the **SMALLINT**, **LONGINT**, **FLOAT**, and **REAL** data types are all specified as **Number** data with the **Field Size** property set differently. Table 4-1 shows how you can map the Access data types to the generic data types of Table 3-1.

Table 4-1 Data types in Access

Data Type	Field Size Property	Generic Data Type
Text	1-255	VARCHAR
Memo	Not Applicable	LONGVARCHAR
Number	Byte	BYTE
Number	Integer	SMALLINT

Data Type	Field Size Property	Generic Data Type
Number	Long Integer	LONGINT
Number	Single	REAL
Number	Double	FLOAT
Currency	Not Applicable	CURRENCY
Date/Time	Not Applicable	TIMESTAMP
Yes/No	Not Applicable	BOOLEAN
OLE Object	Not Applicable	LONGBINARY
AutoNumber	Long Integer	A LONGINT autoincrementing field
Hyperlink	Not Applicable	A special case of VARCHAR

Table 4-2 shows the Access-compatible version of the sponsor table given in Table 3-15. Note that because the **SponsorID** is a primary key (of the **LONGINT** type), you can use the **AUTONUMBER** data type of Access for this field.

Table 4-2 The Access-compatible version of the tblSponsors table

Field Name	Access Data Type	Field Size Property
SponsorID	AutoNumber	
SponsorName	Text	100
SponsorTypeID	Number	Byte
WebAddress	Hyperlink	
UserName	Text	20
Password	Text	20

Lesson Summary

In this lesson you learned how to construct a blank database file, how to give it a name, and how to save it in a directory. A good understanding of the data types supported by Access is essential for creating relevant tables in the database. This lesson describes all the data types used by Access to represent almost any type of data value and shows how you can map them with the generic data types of a RDBMS discussed in Chapter 3.

Each data type is further complemented by a set of field properties that help characterize the nature and appearance of the field data. This lesson explains the role of these field properties and at what level they are enforced. You set these properties when you create a table in Access, as described in the next lesson.

For your reference, a blank `CALENDAR.MDB` database file is provided in the `C:\`
`WEBSITE\HTDOCS\WDBIC\CHAP04\LESSON2\RESULTS` directory.

1. When you create a new database in Access, what visible objects does it contain
   by default?
   a. No objects
   b. A sample table object
   c. A help object
   d. An AutoExec macro object

2. List the data types (in the same order) that would be appropriate for the `Name`,
   `AuthorID`, and `Bibliography` fields of an author table.
   a. `Text, Number, Memo`
   b. `Text, AutoNumber, Memo`
   c. `Text, Text, Text`
   d. `Memo, Number, Text`

3. Which data types can you use for linking charts in Access Power Point to your
   database table?
   a. `Hyperlink`
   b. `Number`
   c. `OLE Object`
   d. `Text`

4. What field size would you specify for an event date in your event calendar?
   a. `Byte`
   b. `Long Integer`
   c. `Double`
   d. `Not applicable`

5. Which field property would be most appropriate to ensure that the data entered
   follows a consistent style?
   a. `Input mask`
   b. `Default Value`
   c. `Validation Rule`
   d. `Validation Text`

Complexity: Easy
1. Create a new database named **BOOKS.MDB** in the
C:\WEBSITE\HTDOCS\WDBIC\CHAP04\LESSON2 directory.

Complexity: Moderate
2. Map the data types for the following tables of the book database.

Table 4-A tblPublishers

Field Name	Data Type
PublisherID	LONGINT (Primary Key)
PublisherName	VARCHAR(255)
PublisherEmail	VARCHAR(255)
PublisherURL	VARCHAR(255)

Table 4-B tblBooks

Field Name	Data Type
ISBN	VARCHAR(13) (Primary Key)
Title	VARCHAR(100)
PublisherID	LONGINT (Foreign Key)
Editorial	LONGVARCHAR
Pages	SMALLINT
Price	CURRENCY
SubjectID	BYTE

Table 4-C tblAuthors

Field Name	Data Type
AuthorID	LONGINT (Primary Key)
FirstName	VARCHAR(50)
LastName	VARCHAR(50)
Biblio	LONGVARCHAR

Table 4-D `tblSubjects_lkp`

Field Name	Data Type
ID	BYTE (Primary Key)
Description	VARCHAR(50)

Table 4-E `tblBooksAuthors`

Field Name	Data Type
ISBN	VARCHAR(13) (First Primary Key Field)
AuthorID	LONGINT (Second Primary Key Field)

CREATING TABLES IN ACCESS

As shown in Chapter 3, the normalized calendar database organizes data through several tables containing fields associated with generic data types. The previous lesson explained how you can map the generic data types with the data types of Access and described the various field properties supported by Access. In this lesson, we show how you can use the Access data types and set appropriate field properties to reproduce the structure of all the conceptual tables defined for the calendar database.

Let's begin by creating the **tblsponsor** table based on the table structure defined in Table 3-15.

1. Copy the CALENDAR.MDB database file residing in the
   C:\WEBSITE\HTDOCS\WDBIC\CHAP04\LESSON2\RESULTS directory to the
   C:\WEBSITE\HTDOCS\WDBIC\CHAP04\LESSON3 directory.

2. Open the C:\WEBSITE\HTDOCS\WDBIC\CHAP04\LESSON3\CALENDAR.MDB database file
   in Access.

3. Click the Tables tab of the empty database container, and then press the
   New button.

   Access displays a list of table creation options, as shown in Figure 4-9.

4. Double-click on the Design View option.

   Access displays a new table named Table1 in its design view, as shown in
   Figure 4-10.

Figure 4-9
Table creation
options

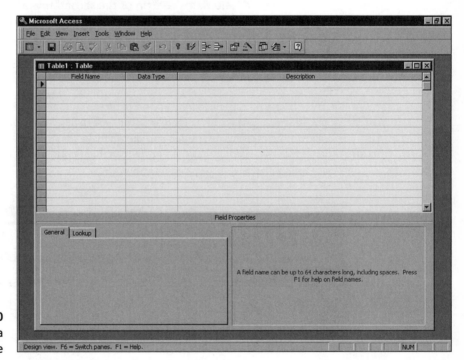

Figure 4-10
Design view of a
new table

5. Type SponsorID in the Field Name column of the first row and then press
   TAB.

   Access moves the cursor to the Data Type column and fills it with a default
   Text data type.

6. Click the arrow next to the Data Type column.

   Access displays a list of supported data types.

7. Set it to Access's AutoNumber data type and then press TAB.

The cursor moves to the Description column, where you can describe the purpose of your fields in more detail.

8. Type Unique ID for each sponsor in this column.

Now observe that at the lower portion of this table design window, Access displays a list of properties that you can customize for the SponsorID field. It even puts reasonable default values, which in the case of the SponsorID field are appropriate at this point and do not need to be changed. So let's move on to define the other fields of this table.

9. Click on the Field Name column of the second row and follow the previous steps to define the SponsorName field and set its properties as shown in Figure 4-11.

10. Similarly, define the rest of the fields and set their properties as shown in Figure 4-12.

There is no value specified for some properties of certain fields in Figure 4-12 (for example, the **Caption** property of the **SponsorTypeID** field or the **Default Value** property of all the fields). This means that you should make that property blank (erase any default value) for that field. Other field properties that are not listed in this figure should be left untouched (keep their default values).

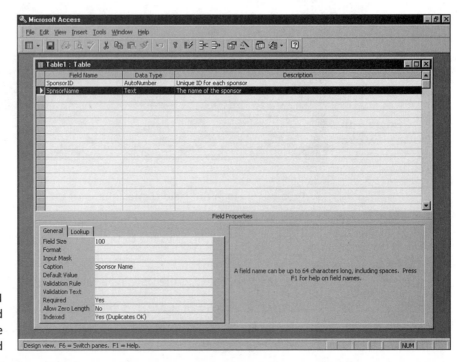

Figure 4-11
The data type and properties of the SponsorName field

Figure 4-12
Data types and
properties of the
other fields of the
sponsor table

Field Name	Data Type	Description	Field Size	Caption	Default Value	Required
SponsorTypeID	Number	Foreign key to tblSponsorsTypes_lkp	Byte			Yes
WebAddress	Hyperlink	URL for that sponsor		Web URL		No
UserName	Text	For authentication purpose	20	User Name		Yes
Password	Text	For authentication purpose (can be null)	20			No

11. Now you need to tell Access that the SponsorID field is also the primary key of this table. (Setting it to AutoNumber data type does not automatically make it the primary key.) Place the cursor on the SponsorID row and select the Primary Key option from the Edit menu.

Access shows a key symbol beside the SponsorID field and automatically sets the Index property to Yes (No Duplicates), as shown in Figure 4-13.

12. Finally, select the Save option from the File menu and save the table as tblSponsors. Then close the table by selecting the Close option from the File menu.

Access now displays the name of this table in the database container.

You can also use the button toolbars instead of selecting the menu options for many table design operations. Move your cursor to each button of the toolbar to highlight its function.

The remainder of this lesson gives the structure and field properties of the rest of the calendar database tables. Use this information to create these tables in the **CALENDAR.MDB** file based on the table creation procedure described previously.

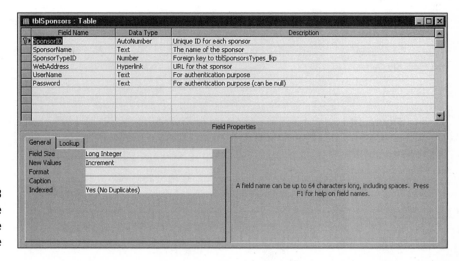

Figure 4-13
Establishing the
primary key in the
sponsor table

The `tblSponsorsContacts` **Table**

The basic structure of the `tblSponsorsContacts` table is given in Figure 4-14.

Figure 4-15 lists the relevant field properties of this table. Observe that the data type of the `SponsorID` foreign key field is set to `Long Integer`-sized `Number` instead of `AutoNumber` even though the `SponsorID` (the primary key) is set to `AutoNumber` in the `tblSponsors` table. You should never set a foreign key to `AutoNumber` data type because Access automatically generates unique values for `AutoNumber` fields and you cannot edit those values. (Lesson 5 provides further details on the characteristics of an `AutoNumber` field.)

You can only have one `AutoNumber` field per table.

Specifying Field-Level and Record-Level Validation Rules

In addition to these properties, you can also check whether the data entered for the `Email` field conforms to the standard Internet email address format by specifying the following validation rule and validation text properties for the `Email` field:

```
Validation Rule: InStr([Email],"@")>0 Or Is Null
Validation Text: The specified email address does not match the standard Internet⇐
email address format.
```

The first condition of the validation rule, (`InStr([Email],"@")>0`) uses the `InStr` function (described in Chapter 5, "Sorting and Searching: Simple Select Queries") to test for the existance of the `@` character in the `Email` field. The second condition (`Is Null`) allows for `Null` values in the `Email` field because this is not a required field.

Figure 4-14
Basic structure of the `tblSponsorsContacts` table

Field Name	Data Type	Description
SponsorContactID	AutoNumber	Unique ID for each contact
SponsorID	Number	Which sponsor this contact belongs to? (Foreign key to tblSponsors)
ContactName	Text	Full Name of the contact
Phone	Text	Phone number
Email	Text	Internet Email Address

Figure 4-15
Relevant field properties of the `tblSponsorsContacts` table

Field Name	DataType	Field Size	Caption	Default Value	Required	Indexed
SponsorContactID	AutoNumber	N/A		N/A	N/A	Yes (No Duplicates)
SponsorID	Number	Long Integer			Yes	Yes (Duplicates OK)
ContactName	Text	50	Contact Name		Yes	No
Phone	Text	50			No	No
Email	Text	255			No	No

As part of the record-level validation, though, you want to ensure that either the phone number or the email address for each contact is present. Specify this record-level condition through the table properties, as explained below:

1. While the `tblSponsorsContacts` is open in design view, select Properties from the View menu.

   Access pops up another window listing the table properties.

2. Specify the `Validation Rule` and `Validation Text` properties, as shown in Figure 4-16.

Note that if you want to refer to a field in your validation rule, then the name of that field must be enclosed within square brackets (`[]`).

Constraints on Defining Validation Rules in Access

Although Access gives you the ability to define field-level as well as the record-level validation rules, Access limits you to one expression up to 2,048 characters that can include only built-in functions for setting the `Validation Rule` property. For example, the current validation rule for the email address would consider an email address such as `abc@@@`

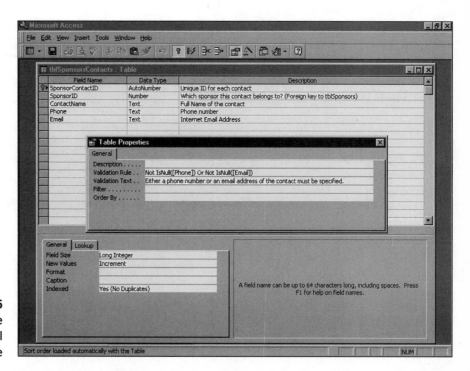

Figure 4-16
Specifying the
record-level
validation rule

a valid address. If you want to enforce a stricter rule, where an email address must conform to **xxx@aaa.bbb.ccc.ddd**-type pattern, it is very difficult to come up with an appropriate validation rule. In such cases, your best option is to validate data within your application before it reaches Access.

When setting the **Validation Rule** property of a field, you cannot refer to any other field.

Search for the keyword **ValidationRule** from the online help of Access for more information on this topic.

The **tblEvents** Table

The basic structure of the **tblEvents** table is shown in Figure 4-17.

Figure 4-18 lists the relevant field properties of this table.

Note that the **Required** property of the mandatory fields is set to **Yes**. The **Indexed** property of the **EventName** field is set to **Yes (Duplicates OK)** to search for events by their name efficiently. The **Indexed** property of all the foreign keys is also set to **Yes (Duplicates OK)** because Access uses these indexes to join related tables quickly. The joining of tables is explained in Chapter 5.

Figure 4-17
Basic structure of the tblEvents table

Field Name	Data Type	Description
EventID	AutoNumber	Unique ID for each event
EventName	Text	Name of the event
SponsorContactID	Number	Who is the contact person for this event? (Foreign key to tblSponsorsContacts)
EventTypeID	Number	The type of event (Foreign key to tblEventsTypes_lkp)
EventDescription	Memo	Details about this event

Figure 4-18
Relevant field properties of the tblEvents table

Field Name	DataType	Field Size	Caption	Default Value	Required	Indexed
EventID	AutoNumber	N/A		N/A	N/A	Yes (No Duplicates)
EventName	Text	100	Event Name		Yes	Yes (Duplicates OK)
SponsorContactID	Number	Long Integer			Yes	Yes (Duplicates OK)
EventTypeID	Number	Byte			Yes	Yes (Duplicates OK)
EventDescription	Memo	N/A	Event Description		No	N/A

The `tblLocations` Table

The basic structure of the `tblLocations` table is given in Figure 4-19.

Figure 4-20 lists the relevant field properties of this table. Note that the default value for the `CountryID` field is set to `1`, which will represent USA when you populate the `tblLocationsCountries` table in Lesson 6.

The `tblEventsLocations` Table

The basic structure of the `tblEventsLocations` table is give in Figure 4-21.

Figure 4-22 lists the relevant field properties of this table.

You can also specify the "Event date greater than current date" rule for the `EventDate` field as follows:

```
Validation Rule: >=Date()
Validation Text: The event date should be later than today's date.
```

Figure 4-19
Basic structure of the `tblLocations` table

Field Name	Data Type	Description
LocationID	AutoNumber	Unique ID for each location
LocationName	Text	Name of the location
Street	Text	First line of address
CityID	Number	City (Foreign key to tblLocationsCities_lkp)
StateID	Number	State (Foreign key to tblLocationsStates_lkp)
CountryID	Number	Country (Foreign key to tblLocationsCountries_lkp)
PostalCode	Text	Zip code

Figure 4-20
Relevant field properties of the `tblLocations` table

Field Name	DataType	Field Size	Caption	Default Value	Required	Indexed
LocationID	AutoNumber	N/A		N/A	N/A	Yes (No Duplicates)
LocationName	Text	100	Location Name		Yes	No
Street	Text	50			No	No
CityID	Number	Integer			No	Yes (Duplicates OK)
StateID	Number	Integer			No	Yes (Duplicates OK)
CountryID	Number	Byte		1	Yes	Yes (Duplicates OK)
PostalCode	Text	50	Postal Code		No	No

Figure 4-21
Basic structure of the `tblEventsLocations` table

Field Name	Data Type	Description
EventLocationID	AutoNumber	Unique ID for each record
EventID	Number	Which event this record belongs to? (Foreign key to tblEvents)
LocationID	Number	The location of this event (Foreign key to tblLocations)
EventDate	Date/Time	Date this event will occur
StartTime	Date/Time	Time when this event starts
EndTime	Date/Time	Time when this event ends

Figure 4-22
Relevant field properties of the `tblEventsLocations` table

Field Name	DataType	Field Size	Caption	Default Value	Required	Indexed
EventLocationID	AutoNumber	N/A		N/A	N/A	Yes (No Duplicates)
EventID	Number	Long Integer			Yes	Yes (Duplicates OK)
LocationID	Number	Long Integer			Yes	Yes (Duplicates OK)
EventDate	Date/Time	N/A	Event Date		Yes	Yes (Duplicates OK)
StartTime	Date/Time		Start Time		Yes	No
EndTime	Date/Time		End Time		No	No

Finally, you can specify the "Start time greater than end time" record-level validation rule through the following table properties:

```
Validation Rule: IIf(IsNull([EndTime]),True,[EndTime]>[StartTime])
Validation Text: The end time of an event must be greater than its start time.
```

Do not panic if this validation rule appears complicated. All it says is that if the EndTime field is not Null then ensure that EndTime is greater than StartTime. You will study the role of the Iif and IsNull built-in functions used in this rule in Chapter 5, "Sorting and Searching: Simple Select Queries."

The Lookup Tables

The basic structure of the tblSponsorTypes_lkp table is given in Figure 4-23.

Figure 4-24 lists the relevant field properties of this table. Note that the ID field (the primary key) is just a BYTE-sized Number field instead of the AutoIncrement type. This is because the AutoIncrement data type stores numbers as 32 bits, which is too large in this case. The Caption property of the Description field is set to Sponsor Type for further clarification and the Index property is set to Yes(No Duplicates) because it is a lookup table and should hold only one record per sponsor type.

Because all the lookup tables of the calendar database portray a common structure (except for the size of the ID field), they can be designed similar to the tblSponsorTypes_lkp table.

Tip Search the online help for creating new tables by copying the table structure of an existing table.

Lesson Summary

This lesson presented the step-by-step procedure for creating, naming, and saving a new table in a database. You open a new table in design view, enter all the field names, select appropriate data types for these fields, enter their brief descriptions, set the appropriate field properties, and specify the primary key. This lesson also explained through

Figure 4-23
Basic structure of the tblSponsorTypes_lkp table

Field Name	Data Type	Description
ID	Number	Unique ID of the lookup value
Description	Text	Description of the lookup value

Figure 4-24
Relevant field properties of the tblSponsorTypes_lkp table

Field Name	DataType	Field Size	Caption	Default Value	Required	Indexed
ID	Number	Byte			Yes	Yes (No Duplicates)
Description	Text	50	Sponsor Type		Yes	Yes (No Duplicates)

examples how to add constraints to certain field data values by setting the `Validation Rule` and `Validation Text` field and table properties.

Now that you have constructed all the tables of the calendar database defined in Chapter 3 in Access, all that remains is to identify and define table-level and database-level validations, which we will cover in the next lesson.

QUIZ 3

1. Why is the `Index` property set to `Yes(No Duplicates)` for the `SponsorID` field in the `tblsponsors` table?
   a. It helps in a quicker search of events by sponsor name.
   b. `SponsorID` is the `Primary Key` field.
   c. This is the default setting.
   d. All of the above.

2. What is the default data type in Access whenever you enter a field name?
   a. `Text`
   b. `Number`
   c. `Memo`
   d. `AutoNumber`

3. How can you tell Access that a table field must have a value in every record?
   a. Set the `Required` property of that field to `Yes`.
   b. Specify a non-`Null` value in the `Default` property of that field.
   c. Set the `Validation Rule` property of that field to `Is Not Null`.
   d. All of the above.

4. For an online ordering system, how would you make the `DeliveryDate` field greater than the `OrderingDate` field in the `tblOrders` table?
   a. By entering `>[DeliveryDate]` in the `Validation Rule` property of the `OrderingDate` field
   b. By entering `>[DeliveryDate]` in the `Validation Rule` property of the `OrderingDate` field and `<[OrderingDate]` in the `Validation Rule` property of the `DeliveryDate` field
   c. By entering `[DeliveryDate]>[OrderingDate]` in the `Validation Rule` property of the `tblOrders` table
   d. By entering `[OrderingDate]<[DeliveryDate]` in the `Validation Rule` property of the `tblOrders` table

5. Why is the primary key of the `tblSponsorTypes_lkp` table `BYTE` size?
   a. All primary keys are `BYTE` size.
   b. It is the most appropriate size for any primary key.
   c. `AutoIncrement` data type is too large in this case.
   d. Subject name in the `Description` field explains it.

Complexity: Moderate

1. How would you define the following validation rules in Access for the book database tables?

   1. The `Price` field must be a positive value.

   2. The `ISBN` field must hold data values that are 13 characters long. (Hint: Search for help on the `Len` function.)

   3. The `Price` field must be greater than $30.00 if the number of pages is more than 500.

Complexity: Advanced

2. Create all the tables of the book database based on the results of the second exercise of Lesson 2. Add the validation rules listed in the previous exercise.

DEFINING INDEXES, RELATIONSHIPS, AND REFERENTIAL INTEGRITY IN ACCESS

So far, you have created the necessary Access tables for building the calendar database and defined the field and record-level validation rules through the appropriate field and table properties. Furthermore, by establishing the primary key field in each table, you inadvertently defined a table-level validation rule of keeping the primary key field unique. Access does not provide any explicit properties to specify table-level validation rules. You can have Access perform the most common table validation rule of preventing duplicate values in a field (or in a set of fields), however, by defining a unique index on that field (or on that set).

Although defining a unique index on one field is a simple matter of setting that field's **Indexed** property to **Yes (No Duplicates)**, creating a composite index of multiple fields requires a different approach, which is explained in this lesson. This lesson also describes how to create table relationships and specify standard database-level validation (referential integrity) rules in Access.

Defining a Composite Index

A composite index is an index that involves more than one field. You define a composite index when you need to search or sort on multiple fields in a particular order. For example, say you have a customer table where the customer name is split into two fields, **LastName** and **FirstName**, and you want records in that table to be sorted first by last name and then by first name. In that case, a composite index consisting of the **LastName** and **FirstName** fields (in that particular order) would speed up the sorting process.

Not only does Access allow you establish one or more composite indexes on a table, but you can specify if each of those indexes allows **Null** values in the participating fields or only unique values in the combination of those fields. By setting the uniqueness constraint on a composite index, you can make Access flag an error anytime this constraint is violated. A good example of this is the **tblEventsLocations** table in the calendar database, where you would like to ensure that there is only one record for an event occurring on a particular date at a specific location. Essentially, you want the combination of the **EventID**, **StartDate**, and **LocationID** to stay unique. So you need to create a composite index of these fields. The following steps show how to carry out this task:

1. Copy the CALENDAR.MDB database file residing in the
   C:\WEBSITE\HTDOCS\WDBIC\CHAP04\LESSON3\RESULTS directory to the
   C:\WEBSITE\HTDOCS\WDBIC\CHAP04\LESSON4 directory.

2. Open the C:\WEBSITE\HTDOCS\WDBIC\CHAP04\LESSON4\CALENDAR.MDB database file in Access.

3. Click on the tblEventsLocations table listed in the database container to highlight it and then click on the Design button.

   Access opens this table in design view.

4. Select the Indexes option from the View menu.

   Access pops up another window displaying the current indexes set for this table, as shown in Figure 4-25. Note that all these indexes are one-field indexes created through the Index property of those fields and they all have a name. The EventLocationID has a special index name called the Primary Key.

5. To set the composite index consisting of the EventID, EventDate, and the EventDate fields, click on the Index Name column of the blank row and type EventDateLocation as the name of this index.

6. Press ENTER to move the cursor to the Field Name column of that row and type EventID in that column.

7. Type EventDate and LocationID in the Field Name column of the next two blank rows, as shown in Figure 4-26.

8. Move your cursor back to the EventDateLocation column to display the Index properties and set them as shown in Figure 4-26.

9. Because EventID is the first field in this composite index, the original single-field index set for this field becomes redundant and you can delete that index. To do that, click on the gray selector box next to the Index Name column that says EventID.

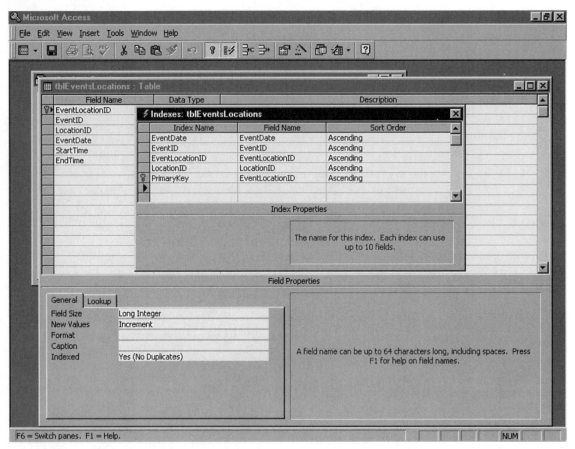

Figure 4-25
Current indexes in the `tblEventsLocations` table

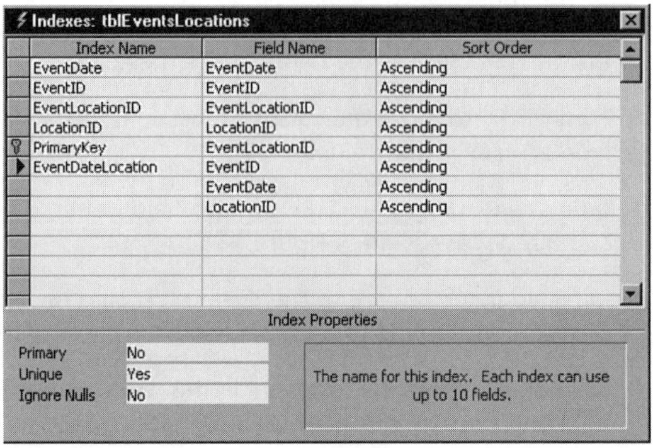

Figure 4-26
Specifying the
`EventDateLocation`
composite index

Access highlights that row.

10. Press (DELETE) to delete that index.

11. Finally, close this pop-up Index window, save the modified table design, and close this table design window.

You cannot delete the individual indexes for the `EventDate` and `LocationID` fields because they are the secondary fields of the composite index.

Creating Relationships and Defining Referential Integrity Among Tables

In Access, you can specify the exact relationships that exist among database tables. Explicitly defining these relationships not only documents your database but also helps Access conduct faster data searches. You define a relationship by adding the tables you want to relate to the Relationship window and then dragging the key field from one table and dropping it on the key field in the other table. As an illustration, the following steps show how you can create a one-to-many relationship between the `tblSponsors` table and the `tblSponsorsContacts` table.

1. Open the `c:\WEBSITE\HTDOCS\WDBIC\CHAP04\LESSON4\CALENDAR.MDB` database in Access if it is not already open.

2. Select the Relationships... option from the Tools menu.

   Access opens up a blank Relationship window.

3. Select the Show Table... option from the Relationships menu.

   Access pops up the Show Table dialog box listing the names of all the tables in the database, as shown in Figure 4-27.

4. Double-click on `tblSponsors` and `tblSponsorsContacts` from this dialog box and then press the Close button to remove this box.

   Access displays two list boxes in the Relationship window depicting the fields of these two tables. The primary key of each table is in bold.

5. Click on the `SponsorID` field of the `tblSponsors` table and drag it over to the `SponsorID` field of the `tblSponsorsContacts` table, as shown in Figure 4-28.

   Access pops up the Relationships dialog box listing further options, as shown in Figure 4-29. One of those options is a checkbox that asks if you want to establish any referential integrity between these tables.

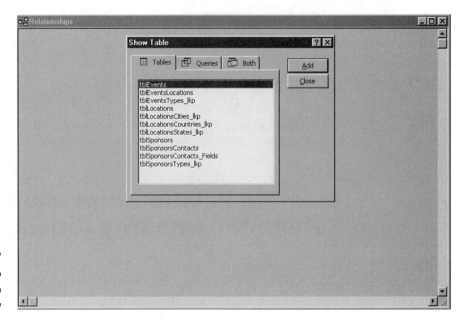

Figure 4-27
Adding tables to the Relationship window

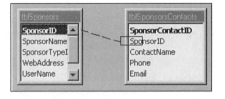

Figure 4-28
Linking the primary key to the foreign key

6. As a recommended practice, you should always establish referential integrity among your related tables. (See Chapter 3, Lesson 5, for a discussion of referential integrity.) Click on the referential integrity checkbox to indicate to Access that it must maintain referential integrity between the records of the tblSponsors and tblSponsorsContacts tables.

   Access enables the two referential integrity choices that allow you to specify what action it should take when someone tries to break the integrity.

7. In this case, select both Cascade Update and Cascade Delete.

   This means that if the SponsorID of a sponsor is changed in the tblSponsors table for any reason, then Access should automatically change the SponsorID field of all the related contact records. Furthermore, if a sponsor record is deleted, then Access should automatically delete all related contact records.

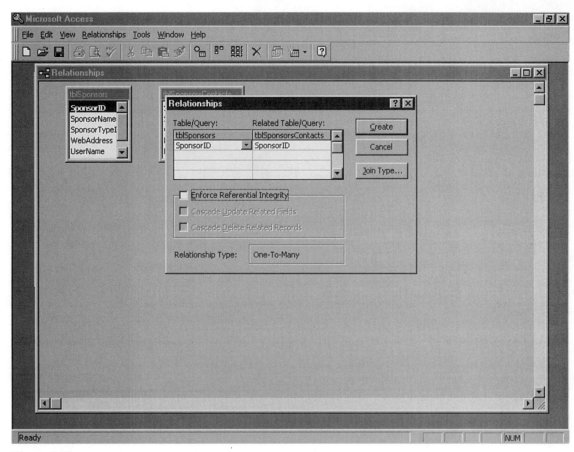

Figure 4-29
The Relationships dialog box

8. Finally, click on the OK button to accept these options and close the Relationships dialog box.

   Access displays the one-to-many relationship between the two tables in the Relationship window, as shown in Figure 4-30.

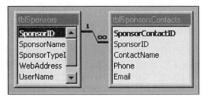

Figure 4-30
The Relationships
dialog box

Similarly, you can follow the above steps to create the rest of the relationships of the calendar database, as given in Table 4-3.

Table 4-3 Relationships for the `CALENDAR.MDB` database

Primary Table	Related Table	Primary Key	Foreign Key	Ref. Integrity
tblSponsorsContacts	tblEvents	SponsorContactID	SponsorContactID	Cascade Update & Delete
tblEvents	tblEventsLocations	EventID	EventID	Cascade Update & Delete
tblLocations	tblEventsLocations	LocationID	LocationID	Cascade Update
tblSponsorsTypes_lkp	tblSponsors	ID	SponsorTypeID	Cascade Update
tblEventsTypes_lkp	tblEvents	ID	EventTypeID	Cascade Update
tblLocationsCities_lkp	tblLocations	ID	CityID	Cascade Update
tblLocationsStates_lkp	tblLocations	ID	StateID	Cascade Update
tblLocationsCountries_lkp	tblLocations	ID	CountryID	Cascade Update

Note that according to these relationships, if you delete a sponsor from the `tblSponsors` table, then Access will automatically delete all the related records from `tblSponsorsContacts`, `tblEvents`, and `tblEventsLocations` records.

Establishing Business Rules

Besides referential integrity, Access does not provide any native mechanism for enforcing other database-specific integrity rules (also called *business rules*) discussed in Chapter 3, Lesson 5. The best option for handling those business rules is to list them clearly on a sheet of paper and then enforce them through the front end (the user interface you build for data entry) of your database application.

For the Web calendar database, let's go with the following two business rules:

● Each sponsor record in the `tblSponsors` table must have at least one related sponsor contact record in the `tblSponsorsContacts` table.

● Each event record in the `tblEvents` table must have at least one related record in the `tblEventsLocations` table (otherwise, you will end up having an event with no location and date information).

In Chapter 11, "Populating Tables: Web-Based Data Entry," we discuss how to enforce these rules when designing the data entry interface of the Web-based event calendar application.

The referential integrity feature allows you to ensure that there are no orphan records (child records without any parent record) in a table. The above two business rules help ensure the reverse—that there are no childless records in **tblSponsor** and **tblEvents**. Note that we do permit storing a sponsor and contact record without any associated event records.

Lesson Summary

In this lesson, you learned how to define a composite index in order to carry out search or sort on multiple fields in a particular order. A composite index can be made to accept duplicate field values, as in the case of multiple customers with the same name in a customer table, or set to accept only unique values in the combination of these fields. This uniqueness constraint was demonstrated in this lesson through a step-by-step procedure for enforcing a unique combination of **EventID**, **StartDate**, and **LocationID** fields in **tblEventsLocations** to ensure that there is only one record for an event occurring on a particular date at a particular location.

This lesson further showed how to specify relationships among database tables and define referential integrity. This helps Access conduct faster data searches and cascade related field updates or deletions. Finally, this lesson listed two database-level business rules that we would like to enforce in the Web calendar database. Unfortunately, Access does not provide any native support for defining these rules as part of the database design and so they must be enforced through the data entry interface that we will create (in Chapters 11, "Populating Tables: Web-Based Data Entry," and 12, "Creating a Data-Entry Wizard: Advanced Data Entry and Maintenance") for this calendar database.

For your reference, the resulting **CALENDAR.MDB** database file is provided in the **C:\ WEBSITE\HTDOCS\WDBIC\CHAP04\LESSON4\RESULTS** directory.

1. Under what circumstances do you need a composite index in Access?
   a. When you want to ensure that each field has a unique index property
   b. When you want to ensure that each field has a **Null** value
   c. When you want to ensure that each field has a unique value
   d. When you want to ensure that the combination of those fields has a unique value

2. Which of the following is true when you set a composite index?
   a. You have to retain the original index of the first field.
   b. You can delete the individual indexes of the secondary fields.
   c. Individual indexes of the secondary fields have to be retained.
   d. Index of the first field is redundant.

3. Which of the following features of Access helps in conducting faster data searches?
   a. Composite indexes
   b. Table relationships
   c. Referential integrity
   d. All of the above

4. Which of the following steps helps you in defining relationships between tables of a database?
   a. Selecting the relationships option from the View menu
   b. Adding the tables to be related to the Relationship window
   c. Dragging the key field of one table and dropping it on the key field of the other related table
   d. Dragging the key field of one table and dropping it on any key of the other related table

5. A change in the `SponsorsContactID` in the `tblSponsorsContacts` table would be reflected in which other table in the calendar database?
   a. `tblSponsors`
   b. `tblEvents`
   c. `tblEventsLocations`
   d. `tblLocations`

EXERCISE **4**

Complexity: Moderate

1. Create the composite (nonunique) index on the `LastName` and the `FirstName` fields of the `tblAuthors` table of the `BOOKS.MDB` database you created in the second exercise of Lesson 3.

Complexity: Advanced

2. Create all the relationships and set the appropriate referential integrity options between the tables of the `BOOKS.MDB` database.

LESSON **5**

ADDING, EDITING, AND DELETING RECORDS THROUGH ACCESS

Besides helping you create the structure of a relational database (as described in the previous lessons), Access also allows you to populate it with data through its graphical user interface. You can use this feature of Access to test the design of your database before linking it with your Web application. In addition, you can populate the lookup tables that you don't want users to change (such as tblCountries_Lkp) with predefined values directly from Access.

Access provides two main options for creating, displaying, and editing records—opening the table in datasheet view or creating a custom form. The table datasheet view presents the records and fields of a table as rows and columns, just like a spreadsheet. Through a custom form, you can display and work with table data according to your own layout and subject the data to advanced validation that otherwise is not feasible through the Validation Rule table and field properties. The coverage of Access forms is beyond the scope of this book because for most Web applications, you use HTML-based data entry forms described in Chapter 1. In this lesson, we show how you can use the table datasheet interface of Access to add, manipulate, and view data in any table. We will also look at how Access handles the AutoNumber field and what it expects in the Hyperlink fields.

Adding Records in the
tblSponsorsTypes_Lkp **Table**

To populate the tables of a database with new records, you must start with the table that does not have a parent table. This way, when you add a record in that table, you do not break any referential integrity. The tblSponsorTypes_Lkp table is a good example. Follow the steps given below to add a few sponsor types in this table:

1. Copy the CALENDAR.MDB database file residing in the
   C:\WEBSITE\HTDOCS\WDBIC\CHAP04\LESSON4\RESULTS directory to the
   C:\WEBSITE\HTDOCS\WDBIC\CHAP04\LESSON5 directory.

2. Open the C:\WEBSITE\HTDOCS\WDBIC\CHAP04\LESSON5\CALENDAR.MDB database file in Access.

3. Click on the tblSponsorsTypes_Lkp table listed in the database container to highlight it and then click on the Open button.

   Access opens this table in datasheet view, displaying a blank record as shown in Figure 4-31. Note that the second column is titled Sponsor Type, which is the text specified in the Caption property of the Description field.

4. Place your cursor in the ID column, type 1, and then press ENTER.

   Access moves the cursor to the Sponsor Type column. Note that the record selector shows a pencil sign indicating that the record is *dirty* (not saved yet).

5. Type Arts in the description column and press ENTER.

   Access saves this record and moves the cursor to the next blank record.

6. Repeat the above steps to enter the sponsor types given in Table 4-4 and then close this table.

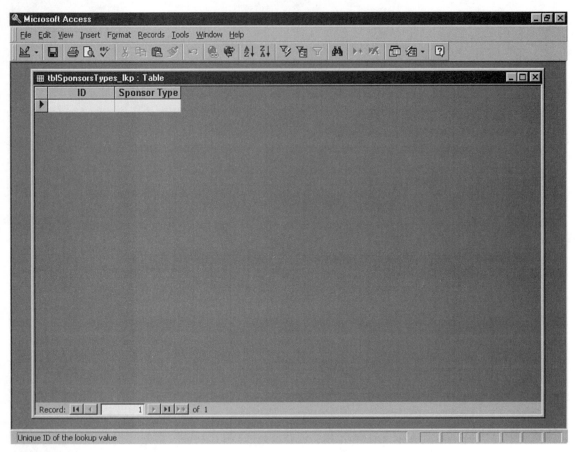

Figure 4-31
The blank `tblSponsorTypes_lkp` table in datasheet view

Table 4-4 List of sponsor types

ID	Sponsor Type
2	Business
3	Information technology
4	Cultural
5	Education
6	Foundation/trust
7	Professional
8	Social
9	Scientific

ID	Sponsor Type
10	Sports
11	Public interest groups
12	Energy
13	Other

Adding Records in the `tblSponsors` Table

Now that you have a predefined list of sponsor types, you can populate the **tblSponsors** table as follows:

1. Open the `tblSponsors` table in datasheet view.

   Access displays just one blank record, as shown in Figure 4-32.

2. Note that the text (AutoNumber) appears under the SponsorID column. This is how Access indicates that you cannot enter any data in this AutoNumber field. Place your cursor in the Sponsor Name field, type Amateur Athletics Association, and then press ENTER.

   Access moves the cursor to the SponsorTypeID field. Note that it also automatically adds the number 1 in the SponsorID field.

3. Type 10 in this field and then press ENTER again.

   Access moves the cursor to the Web URL field.

4. Type www.amaa.org in this field and press ENTER.

   Note that Access automatically underlines this address, indicating that it is a hyperlink.

5. Type John and amaa123 in the User Name and Password fields respectively and then press ENTER to save this record.

6. Now let's see how Access reacts when you add a record without giving any value to the required User Name field. Type the following information in the next blank record and then press SHIFT-ENTER to force Access to save the record:

   ```
   Sponsor Name: Royal Art Gallery
     SponsorID: 1
     Web URL: royalgallery.com
   ```

   Access generates an error message indicating that it cannot allow a Null value in the User Name field, as shown in Figure 4-33.

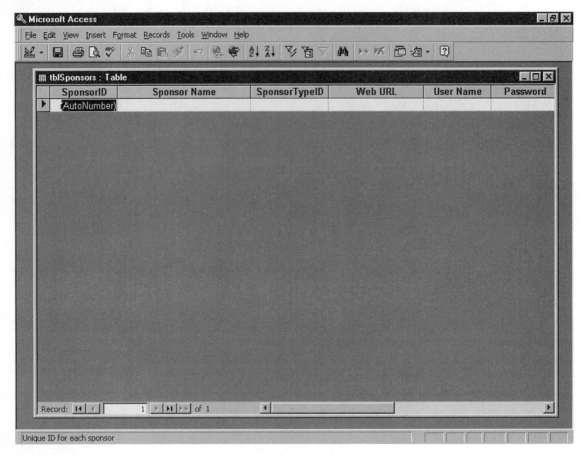

Figure 4-32
The blank `tblSponsors` table in datasheet view

7. Press the OK button to remove the error message box.

   Access still displays the current record as dirty, indicating that it has not been saved.

8. Place the cursor in the User Name field of this record and type royal. Then press ⎡SHIFT⎤-⎡ENTER⎤ again.

   This time Access does not complain and saves the record with a Null value in the Password field (whose Required property is set to No).

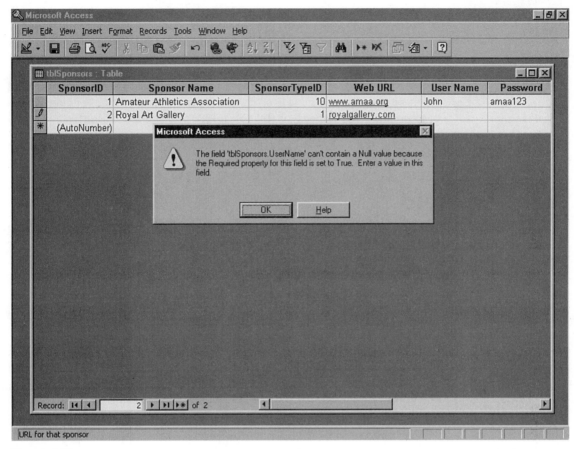

Figure 4-33
Error message indicating that no value has been provided in a required field

How Access Handles the `AutoNumber` Field

As you have seen, Access does not allow you to enter any data in the `AutoNumber` field, and automatically fills it with the next unique number in sequence the moment you try to add data to the blank record. Once a number is assigned to a saved record, Access does not allow you to change it. Now, you may wonder what will happen if you delete a record and add a new record. Will Access assign the number of the deleted record to that new record? The answer is no. Access keeps going with its original numeric sequence and does not try to fill the gap. Because `AutoNumber` is a 32-bit field, you will have to insert more than 4 billion records before Access will cycle back to find the first gap (and yes, it does cycle back!).

In a relational database, the possibility of a gap in the primary key sequence should not matter. As long as the required and unique properties of a primary key are met and the primary key value does not change once it is assigned to a record, your data meets all the requirements of a relational model.

If you want to ensure a regular numeric sequence for your key field, then an `AutoNumber` data type is not a good choice. Instead, you can define your key field as an appropriate-size `Number` type and design your own autonumbering method to add values to that field.

How Access Handles the `Hyperlink` Field

Although you just typed the URL address of the sponsors' Web sites in the Web address `Hyperlink` field of the `tblSponsors` table, the address can have up to three parts separated by the pound sign (`#`):

`displaytext#address#subaddress`

where `displaytext` is the text you want to appear in a field, `address` is the path to a file (UNC path) or a Web page (URL), and `subaddress` is the location within the file or page.

Access does not display all three parts of a `Hyperlink` field. Furthermore, if you click in that field using your mouse, Access tries to bring up the document indicated by that link. If you want to see the whole hyperlink address, put the cursor to an adjacent non-`Hyperlink` field and then use TAB to place the insertion bar in the `Hyperlink` field (so you don't follow the link) and then press F2. Access follows the following rule sequence on how it displays the data in the `Hyperlink` field:

1. If you enter display text, Microsoft Access does not show any of the rest of the address following the display text.

2. If you don't enter display text, Microsoft Access displays just the address.

3. It displays the subaddress only if there is no display text or address and if the subaddress points to an object in a Microsoft Access database and the object is in the current database.

Finally, if the text you enter in a `Hyperlink` field does not include a pound sign (`#`), a protocol (such as `http:`), or a reference to an object in the current database, Microsoft Access assumes the text entered is display text and appends the same text to `http://` for the address. For example, when you type `www.amma.com` for the Web URL of the first sponsor in the `tblSponsors` table, Access translates the address as `www.amma.com#http://www.amma.com#`.

Search for the phrase **Hyperlink addresses** from the online help for Access for more information on this data type.

Adding Records in the
tblSponsorsContacts **Table**

Now that you know how to populate a table, add two contacts for the Amateur Athletic Association and one contact for the Royal Art Gallery to the **tblSponsorsContacts** table, as shown in Figure 4-34.

Let's see how Access responds if you try to add a contact record for a sponsor that does not exist in the **tblSponsors** table. Try to insert the following record in the **tblSponsorsContacts** table:

```
SponsorID: 3
ContactName: Joe Smith
Phone: 123-123-1234
Email: smith@aol.com
```

Access will generate a referential integrity error, as shown in Figure 4-35.

Press OK to close this error message box and then press ESC twice to cancel the record insertion operation.

Editing a Record

The process of changing a field value of an existing record of a table is similar to that of adding a new record. The following steps show how you can modify the password of the Amateur Athletic Association from **aama123** to **marathon**:

1. Open the **tblSponsors** table in datasheet view.

2. Place the cursor in the **Password** field of the first record.

3. Press F2 to highlight the current password value.

4. Type the new password. Access overwrites the previous password.

5. Press SHIFT-ENTER to save the modified record.

Figure 4-34
Adding contacts into the **tblSponsors Contacts** table

▦ tblSponsorsContacts : Table				
SponsorContactID	**SponsorID**	**Contact Name**	**Phone**	**Email**
1	1	John Baker	(415)-210-1212	jb@amaa.org
2	1	Jeff Thomas	(415)-210-1214	jt@amaa.org
3	2	Manager		manager@royalgallery.com
(AutoNumber)				

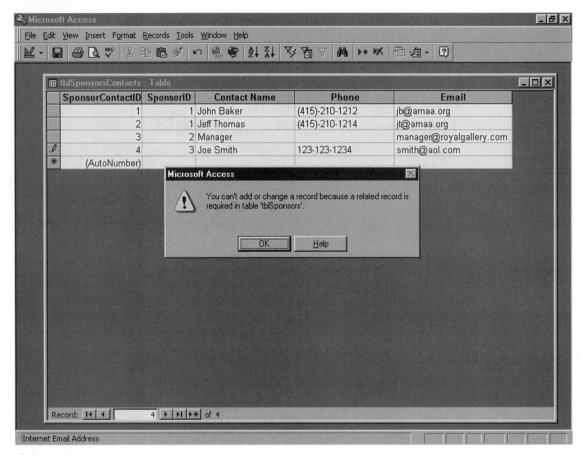

Figure 4-35
Access showing a referential integrity error

Deleting a Record

Deleting a record is also a simple process. Let's say the Royal Art Gallery is no longer your patron and you want to delete its record from the **tblSponsors** table. The following steps show how you can accomplish this task:

1. Open the **tblSponsors** table if it is not already open.

2. Select the record by clicking on the Record Selector button.

   Access highlights this record.

3. Press DEL.

   Access asks for your confirmation before deleting the record.

Note When you delete this record from the `tblSponsors` table, Access automatically deletes the associated contact record from the `tblSponsorsContacts` table due to the Cascade Delete option set between these two tables (see Lesson 4). You can open the `tblSponsorsContacts` table for verification.

Things to Consider During Data Editing

Here are some additional tips that you may find useful when editing data through Microsoft Access tables:

- Access supports a Multiple Document Interface, allowing you to open and edit multiple tables at a time.

- You can copy the data from one field and paste it into another field. To make a duplicate of an existing record, select a record and then choose the Copy command from the Edit menu. Then go to a new record, choose the Paste command from the Edit menu, and save the pasted record.

- If you make a mistake while editing and have not saved the record yet, press ⒺⓈⒸ once to undo the changes made in the current field. Pressing ⒺⓈⒸ twice will undo all the changes made to the current record. If you have already saved the record, select the Undo Saved Record command from the Edit menu to undo any changes.

- You can press ⓈⒽⒾⒻⓉ-Ⓕ⒉ to view or edit the data of a field in a zoom window.

- Two users on different machines can open the same database file and edit the records of the same table concurrently, provided neither user opens the database in the *exclusive* mode. Refer to the online help for Access for more information on multiuser data editing.

Lesson Summary

This lesson showed how you can open any Access table in datasheet view to add, edit, or delete records. When adding a record to a table containing an `AutoNumber` field, Access automatically supplies a unique value that you cannot change for that field. The special `Hyperlink` field allows you to specify three types of hyperlink-related information: display text, address, and subaddress—although none of these portions is mandatory. If you try to save a record that contains invalid data or that may breach referential integrity, Access generates an appropriate error message and does not save the record. To get out of this situation, you can either fix the problem or undo all your changes.

Although Access certainly makes it easy to enter data manually, this is not the only option for populating your tables. You can also use the import and linking facilities of Access to get data from an external data source, as explained in the next lesson.

1. Which tables should be populated before data can be added to the `tblEvents` table?
   a. `tblEventsTypes_lkp`
   b. `tblLocations`
   c. `tblCountries`
   d. `tblSponsorsContacts`

2. When does Access save a new or an edited record?
   a. When you add data in the last field
   b. When you move to another record
   c. When you press SHIFT-ENTER
   d. When you close the table

3. Which of the following holds true for an `AutoNumber` type field?
   a. You cannot enter any data in this field.
   b. It ensures a regular numeric sequence.
   c. It ensures uniqueness and is generally used as a primary key.
   d. It can be linked to a `Number` type foreign key of any size when creating a relationship.

4. What does Access store when you type `www.waite.com/waite` in a `Hyperlink` type field?
   a. `http://www.waite.com/waite`
   b. `www.waite.com#www.waite.com/waite#`
   c. `www.waite.com/waite#www.waite.com/waite#`
   d. `www.waite.com/waite#http://www.waite.com/waite#`

5. What happens when you try to save a record which has invalid data in one of its fields?
   a. Access warns about the invalid data and then saves that record with that data.
   b. Access warns about the invalid data and then saves that record with a Null value in that field.
   c. Access tries to correct the invalid data before saving the record.
   d. Access warns about the invalid data and does not save the record.

EXERCISE 5

Complexity: Easy

1. Populate the `CALENDAR.MDB` database with the following event:

```
Sponsor: Amateur Athletics Association
Contact: Jeff Thomas
```

```
Event Name: 9th Amateur Olympiad
Event Type: Sports Competetion
Location: Houston Olympic Stadium, 3130 N. Olympic Village, Houston,⇐
Texas - 12345, USA
Event Dates: 12/1/97 to 12/3/97 from 9:00 AM to 6:00 PM
Event Description: AMAO is organizing its ninth amateur olympiad.⇐
Interested participants
 may register with the listed contact before November 1st, 1997.
```

Complexity: Moderate

2. Test the various validation rules that have been set in the **CALENDAR.MDB** database by trying to add invalid data.

IMPORTING AND ATTACHING DATA

No database management system would be considered feature-rich if it did not provide good data import and export facilities. Access is no exception. It not only handles this aspect with elegance, but also supports a powerful table-linking capability by which you can directly work with data from other Microsoft Access databases (versions 1.x, 2.0, 7.0/95, and 8.0/97), as well as data from other programs and file formats, such as Microsoft Excel, dBASE, Microsoft FoxPro, and Paradox. You can also import or link (read-only) HTML tables and lists, which can reside on your local computer, a network server, or an Internet server. This lesson explains the difference between importing and linking and shows how these features work in Access. Although this does not happen too frequently, an Access database file can be corrupted or attain a size that is not proportional to the number of records in database. To help in such cases, Access provides database repair and compacting facilities, which are also covered in this lesson.

Import or Link?

When you import data from another source, Access creates a copy of that information in a new table of the currently opened database. The source table or file is not altered in this process. Linking data enables you to read and in most cases update data in the external data source without importing. The external data source's format is not altered, so you can continue to use the file with the program that originally created it but you can add, delete, or edit its data using Microsoft Access.

Importing Data from a Text File

Access allows you to import data from two types of text files—fixed width and character delimited. A fixed width text file contains fields whose data is organized in fixed width columns. A character delimited text file contains fields whose data is separated using a specified delimiter character. In addition, a text file can also include the field names as long as they are in the first row and follow the same format as the rest of the data.

As an example, let's say you have the list of sponsor types shown in Table 4-4 as a comma-delimited text file. Instead of manually typing that information, you could import data directly from that text file into the `tblSponsorTypes_lkp` table. To illustrate this procedure, we have provided that comma-delimited text file in the `C:\WEBSITE\HTDOCS\WDBIC\CHAP04\LESSON6` directory; it is named `SPTYPES.TXT`. The contents of this file are given in Listing 4-1.

Listing 4-1 Contents of the `SPTYPE.TXT` file

```
1,"Arts"
2,"Business"
3,"Information Technology"
4,"Cultural"
5,"Education"
6,"Foundation/Trust"
7,"Professional"
8,"Social"
9,"Scientific"
10,"Sports"
11,"Public Interest Groups"
12,"Energy"
13,"Other"
```

The following steps show how you could populate the `tblSponsorTypes_lkp` table from the data in this text file:

1. Copy the `CALENDAR.MDB` database file residing in the `C:\WEBSITE\HTDOCS\WDBIC\CHAP04\LESSON4\RESULTS` directory (the nonpopulated version) to the `C:\WEBSITE\HTDOCS\WDBIC\CHAP04\LESSON6` directory.

2. Open the `C:\WEBSITE\HTDOCS\WDBIC\CHAP04\LESSON6\CALENDAR.MDB` database file in Access.

3. Verify that the `tblSponsorTypes_lkp` table is empty.

4. Select the Get External Data option from the File menu.

    Access presents two options: Import... and Link Tables... in a submenu.

5. Select the Import... option.

    Action displays the Import window, which asks you to specify the path, name, and type of the data file you want to import.

6. Locate the `C:\WEBSITE\HTDOCS\WDBIC\CHAP04\LESSON6` directory in the Look In box.

7. Select the Text Files (*.txt,*.csc,*.tab,*.asc) option in the box labeled Files of type, type SPTYPES.TXT in the File Name box as shown in Figure 4-36, and then press the Import button.

Access displays the contents of that text file as shown in Figure 4-37.

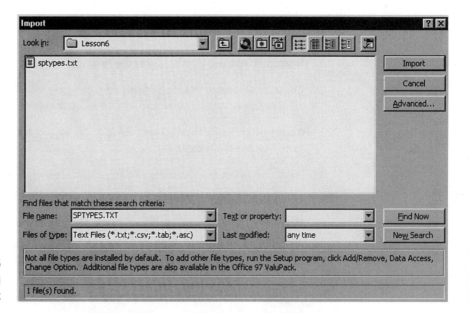

Figure 4-36
The Import dialog
box

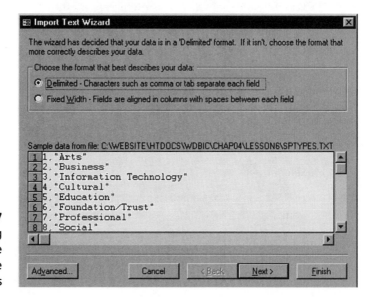

Figure 4-37
Access displaying
the contents of the
text file during the
import process

8. Because it appears to be the correct data file and the Delimited option is selected by default, press the Next button.

   Now Access shows another screen (see Figure 4-38) asking you for the appropriate import parameters.

9. In this case, the default parameter settings are correct. Press the Next button.

   Access now asks its final question: whether you want to import the data from this text file into a new table or append it to an existing table.

10. Choose the existing table option, select the tblSponsorTypes_lkp table in its adjacent text box, as shown in Figure 4-39, and then press the Next button.

    Access prompts its final screen, asking you to reconfirm tblSponsorTypes_lkp as the destination table.

11. Press the Finish button to reconfirm and start the import process.

    Access takes a few moments to import the data and then displays a message box indicating that the import is successful.

12. Press the OK button to close the message box and open the tblSponsorTypes_lkp table to verify that the data was imported correctly.

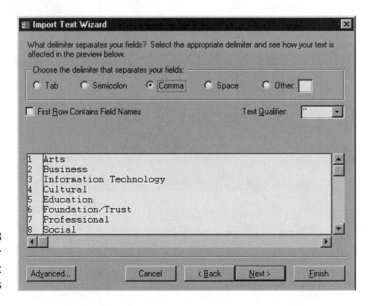

Figure 4-38
Access asking for the import parameters

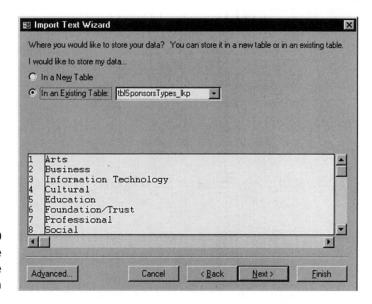

Figure 4-39
Specifying the destination of the imported data

The process of importing data from the fixed-width text file is similar to the procedure described. Just start the import wizard and follow its screens while specifying the appropriate options.

Linking to Tables from Another Access Database

When you import data from another source, Access creates a copy of that information in a new table of the currently opened database. The source table or file is not altered in this process. Linking data, however, enables you to read and, in most cases, update data in the external data source without importing. The external data source's format is not altered, so you can continue to use the file with the program that originally created it, but you can add, delete, or edit its data using Microsoft Access.

The biggest advantage of linking versus importing is that you can use Access as a homogeneous and dynamic front end in a heterogeneous database environment, where different portions of data are available in different formats. For example, let's say you have been assigned to design a Web-based ordering system for a company that stores the information about its products and their current prices in an Excel spreadsheet. That company needs all online orders to be made available to its order processing application that is written in FoxPro.

A good option would be to create an Access database that contains direct links to the Excel spreadsheet and the relevant FoxPro tables and then have your online ordering system dynamically access and manipulate those tables through the Access database engine. Chapter 13, "Using Client-Side Scripting Languages: JavaScript and VBScript," shows how to use this approach when making a data entry wizard for the Web calendar application. For now, let's look at a small example where you link an Excel file containing a detailed explanation of each sponsor type (`C:\WEBSITE\HTDOCS\WDBIC\CHAP04\LESSON6\SPTYPES_LIST.XLS`) into the `CALENDAR.MDB` database and show how to edit that file directly through Access. We are assuming that Excel 97 is installed on your computer. Follow these steps:

1. Open the `C:\WEBSITE\HTDOCS\WDBIC\CHAP04\LESSON6\SPTYPES_LIST.XLS` spreadsheet in Excel 97.

   Excel displays the list of sponsor types and their explanations, as shown in Figure 4-40.

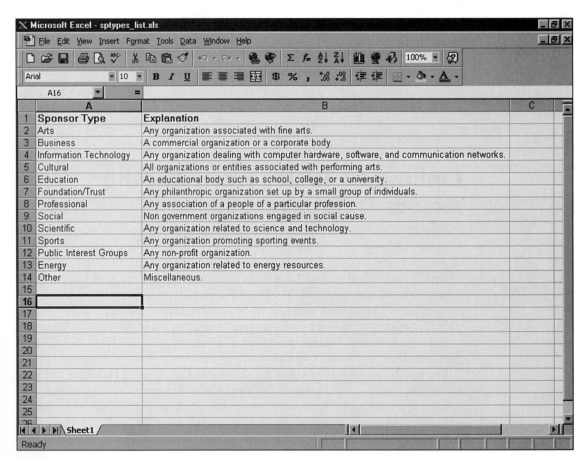

Figure 4-40
An Excel spreadsheet containing sponsor types and their explanations

2. Close this spreadsheet and open the `C:\WEBSITE\HTDOCS\WDBIC\CHAP04\LESSON6\CALENDAR.MDB` database file in Access (if it is not already open).

3. Select the Get External Data option from the File menu.

   Access presents two options—Import... and Link Tables...—in a submenu.

4. Select the Link Tables... option to start the Access table linking wizard.

   The wizard displays the Link window, which asks you to specify the path, name, and type of the data file you want to import. (Note that this window looks very similar to the Import window shown in Figure 4-36.)

5. Locate the `C:\WEBSITE\HTDOCS\WDBIC\CHAP04\LESSON6` directory in the Look In box.

6. Select the Microsoft Excel (*.xls) option in the box labeled Files of type, type `SPTYPES_LIST.XLS` in the File Name box, and then press the Link button.

   The link wizard displays the next screen, as shown in Figure 4-41.

7. Select the checkbox labeled First Row Contains Column Headings and then press the Next button.

   You are taken to the final screen, which asks for the name of the table that will represent this link, as shown in Figure 4-42.

8. Type `tblSponsorTypes_Explanations` in the Linked Table Name text box and then press the Finish button.

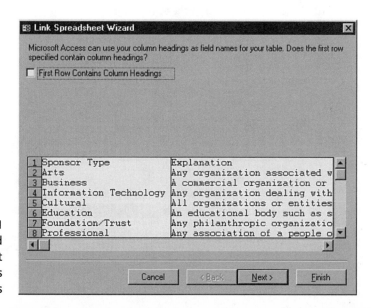

Figure 4-41
The link wizard asking if the first row contains column headings

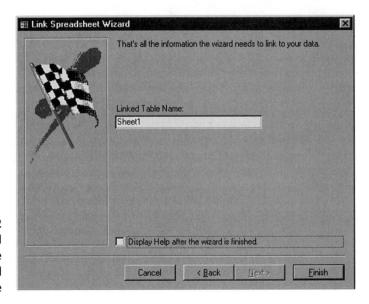

Figure 4-42
The link wizard
asking for the
name of the linked
table

The link wizard pops up a message box stating that the linking process is successful.

9. Press the OK button to close that message box.

   Access displays the linked table in the database container, as shown in Figure 4-43.

10. Click on the linked table to highlight it and then press the Open button.

    Access opens it just like a regular table, as shown in Figure 4-44.

11. As a test, change the explanation for the sponsor type Other to say `Any other organization` instead of `Miscellaneous` and save the record.

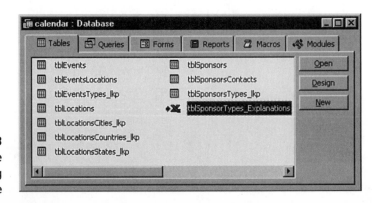

Figure 4-43
The database
container showing
the linked table

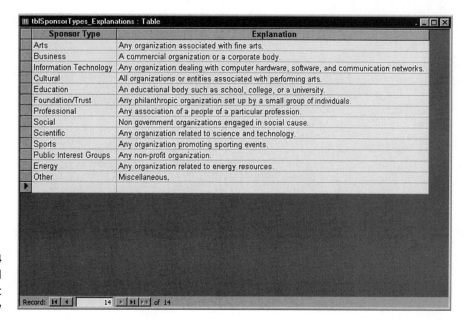

Figure 4-44
Opening a linked table in datasheet view

12. Close the `tblSponsorTypes_Explanations` table.

13. Now open the `c:\WEBSITE\HTDOCS\WDBIC\CHAP04\LESSON6\SPTYPES_LIST.XLS` spreadsheet in Excel 97.

    The modified explanation appears in the spreadsheet, as shown in Figure 4-45.

Things to Consider When Importing or Linking Data

When importing data or creating linked tables, you should remember the following points:

- When you import data from another Access, FoxPro, or any other supported database format, Access always creates a new table. You can import data into an existing table only using text files, spreadsheets, or HTML tables.

- To link to an HTML file residing on a Web server, start the link wizard, select HTML Documents (*.html, *.htm) in the box labeled Files of type:, specify the complete URL (`http://servername/path/filename`) in the File Name box, and then press the Link button. Note that your machine must be connected to the Web at that time.

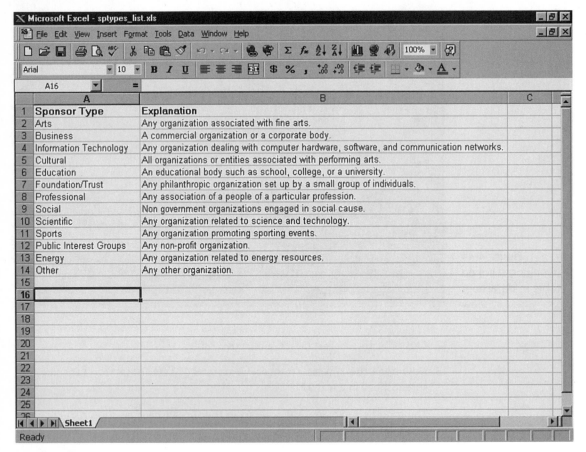

Figure 4-45
The linked spreadsheet displaying the modified explanation

- When you link to a local file, Access stores the absolute path of that file as the link information. You can open the linked table in design view and view the table properties to examine the stored path.

- You cannot establish referential integrity between regular tables and linked tables.

- You cannot manipulate data in a linked table that is based on a text or HTML file.

- Access also allows you to attach or import tables from a client-server database such as Microsoft SQL Server by specifying the relevant ODBC (Open Database Connectivity) information. Refer to the online help for Access for the exact instructions.

Compacting an Access Database

When you delete records from an Access database, the file size of that database does not decrease. With time, the file size can grow quite big. To recover the space taken by deleted records, Access provides a Compact feature that you use as follows:

1. Open the database in Access.

2. From the Tools menu, point to Database Utilities and then select the Compact Database option. (In a production environment, you should perform this step on a regularly scheduled basis after hours.)

Repairing an Access Database

Although it does not happen too frequently, an Access database can be corrupted due to unforeseeable reasons. In most cases, Microsoft Access will detect that a database is damaged when you try to open it, and it will allow you to repair the database at that time. In some situations, Access may not detect that a database is damaged. If a database behaves unpredictably, you can manually perform repairs using the following procedure:

1. Launch Access but do not open any database.

2. From the Tools menu, point to Database Utilities and then select the Repair Database option.

3. Specify the name and location of the database you want to repair and then press the Repair button. You will get a message box when the repair is done.

Lesson Summary

This lesson showed how to use the import and link wizards of Microsoft Access to import data and create table attachments from external data sources. The linking feature of Access comes in handy when you have to work in a heterogeneous database environment or when you want to use Access as a client to a database server. If you ever encounter a corrupt Access database file or a file that appears too large in size compared to the number of records it holds, you should try the repair and compact database features of Access, as explained in this lesson.

1. What is the format of a character-delimited text file?
    a. The data of each field must be of a fixed width.
    b. The data of each field must be separated by a consistent delimiter character.
    c. The data itself cannot contain the delimiter character, and if it does, it must be enclosed within a pair of double quotes or any other qualifier character.
    d. The first character of the first row specifies the delimiter character.

2. What information needs to be specified before the Access import wizard can start importing data?
    a. Path, name, and type of file to be imported
    b. Destination table
    c. Maintain referential integrity
    d. All of the above

3. What does Access do when you link to an external data source?
    a. It creates a copy of that information in a new table of the currently opened database.
    b. It allows you to read and update data in the external data source without changing its format.
    c. It allows you to change the table structure of the external data source.
    d. It stores the absolute path (or the ODBC information) of the external source as part of the linked table definition.

4. How can you link to an HTML file in Access?
    a. By specifying the local path of that file to the link wizard
    b. By specifying the Web path of that file
    c. By specifying the FTP path of that file
    d. All of the above

5. When do you need to compact an Access database?
    a. When the database contains too many records
    b. When some of the records get corrupted
    c. When the database starts behaving unpredictably
    d. When there are too many voids in the database because of deleted records but the file continues to hold the space of these records

Complexity: Moderate
1. The `C:\WEBSITE\HTDOCS\WDBIC\CHAP04\LESSON6\` directory contains the sponsor data in Excel 7 format (`SPONSORS.XLS`) and contact data in HTML format (`SPCONTACTS.HTM`). As you know, the sponsor types are in a text file named

SPTYPES.TXT. Copy the nonpopulated version of the **CALENDAR.MDB** database file from the **C:\WEBSITE\HTDOCS\WDBIC\CHAP04\LESSON4\RESULTS** directory into the **C:\WEBSITE\HTDOCS\WDBIC\CHAP04\LESSON6\EXERCISE1** directory. Then import the sponsor-related data from these files into this database file. Remember that the order in which you import the tables is very important.

Complexity: Easy

2. The **C:\WEBSITE\HTDOCS\WDBIC\CHAP04\LESSON6\EXERCISE2** directory contains an HTML-formatted table in a file named **SPTYPES.HTML**. Create a linked table named **tblSponsorTypes_html** that points to this file in the **CALENDER.MDB** database file of the previous exercise.

CHAPTER SUMMARY

This chapter highlighted the capabilities and modular architecture of Microsoft Access and showed how you can use its intuitive interface to construct the database for the Web calendar application from the conceptual design described in Chapter 3. The process is simple.

1. Start by creating a blank Access database.

2. Define each table by listing the names, data types, and relevant properties of all the fields.

3. Specify appropriate data validation criteria through the Validation Rule property of each field or the table itself.

4. Set the primary key.

5. Create the necessary composite indexes.

6. Establish relationships and referential integrity options among tables.

7. Finally, test the database design by populating it with sample data.

You can populate data manually through table datasheet view or import it from another source using the import wizard of Access. In addition, Access supports the capability of attaching to other data sources directly, which allows you to use the familiar and powerful interface of Access to work with different data formats. Using ODBC, you can also use Access as a front end to a database server, although this topic is beyond the scope of this book.

Here is a recap of the salient points covered in this chapter:

● To create a relational database, you normally use a relational database management system.

● Most relational database management systems can be classified as client-server or file based, depending on whether the database operations occur on a server or at each client's machine.

● Access is a powerful, multiuser, file-based RDBMS that can also act as a client to a server database due to its table-linking capability.

● An Access database file generally has an .MDB file extension and can store table, query, form, report, macro, and module objects as well as the data in all the nonlinked tables.

● Access uses the JET engine to manipulate the .MDB database files.

● Access not only supports all the generic data types but also provides special data types such as AutoNumber and Hyperlink.

● The AutoNumber data type, which is used mainly for the primary key field, is compatible to a Long Integer-sized Number field.

● You can specify that a data in a field is mandatory through the Required field property.

● Use the Validation Rule and Validation Text properties to list simple data validation rules.

● To prevent duplicate value in a combination of two or more fields, set a composite index of those fields with the Unique property set to Yes.

● You can establish relationships between tables in Access through the Relationship window.

● You can specify Cascade Update, Cascade Delete, neither, or both as the referential integrity options.

● You can add, edit, or delete data in an Access table by opening that table in datasheet view.

● You can import or link data from many popular data sources using the import and link wizards.

● In case your Access database file gets damaged or grows too big in size, try the repair and compact database utilities.

Now that you have created the **CALENDAR.MDB** database for the Web calendar application, we will look at how you can search, sort, and filter data from this database using Access queries, which is the topic of the next chapter.

CHAPTER 5

SORTING AND SEARCHING: SIMPLE SELECT QUERIES

This chapter explains how Microsoft Access's powerful query design interface can be used to construct queries and filters for sorting and searching data and for creating calculated fields. Concepts are illustrated using numerous examples. A full lesson is devoted to parameterized queries, which prove extremely useful in Web database application development. In particular, you will learn about

- How to specify the fields you want to display in the query result

- How to run and save a query

- The importance of the asterisk (*) field

- How to construct a calculated field

- How to sort table data on one or more fields

- The arithmetic and string operators

- The Between...And, IN, and Like criteria expressions

197

- How to detect records with a Null value in a field

- How to create queries with multiple criteria

- How to specify parameters in a query

WHAT IS AN ACCESS QUERY?

So far, you have seen how constructing a relational calendar database helps you organize and store event-related information in a meaningful and space-efficient manner. But all this is just one side of the information equation. On the other side, you want to use this information to generate desired results quickly. These results could be as simple as a list of events occurring within a certain date range or as complex as an event summary grouped by category, location, sponsor type, and year.

One possible way to get the results is to compute them manually or programmatically by browsing through the records of the appropriate database tables. For example, if you want to see which sponsors deal in the area of education, you can first look at the `tblSponsorsTypes_lkp` table to identify the `SponsorTypeID` value for the Education category and then navigate through the sponsor table to locate all the sponsor records with that `SponsorTypeID` value. As you can see, this is neither an easy nor an efficient way to extract specific information from the database, especially if that database is populated with thousands of records. Fortunately, most relational database management systems (RDBMSs) allow you to search, sort, and analyze information by specifying queries. Access, in particular, provides an extremely intuitive design interface that allows you to define your queries visually. This lesson introduces you to this powerful interface and shows how to use this interface to design and run a simple query quickly.

The Sample CALENDAR.MDB Database

For illustrating the query concepts discussed in this chapter, we have populated the **CALENDAR.MDB** database with 37 events taken from the Internet to act as our sample data. This data has been modified and is being used purely for the purpose of illustration. This prepopulated version of the **CALENDAR.MDB** file resides in the **C:\WEBSITE\HTDOCS\WDBIC\CHAP05\LESSON1\SAMPLES** directory. We recommend that you browse through the tables of this database to gain some familiarity with the sample data before you proceed to the next section.

Creating a Query in Access

To define a query in Access, you generally have to perform the following tasks:

1. Open the query design window.

2. Select the tables from which you want to query.

3. Specify what fields you want to display in your result.

4. Specify your search criteria and how you want to sort your query result.

To illustrate this procedure, let's create a query to list all the sponsors from the `CALENDAR.MDB` database that belong to the Education category. Follow the steps given below:

1. Copy the `CALENDAR.MDB` file residing in the `C:\WEBSITE\HTDOCS\WDBIC\CHAP05\SAMPLES` directory to the `C:\WEBSITE\HTDOCS\WDBIC\CHAP05\LESSON1` directory.

2. Open the `C:\WEBSITE\HTDOCS\WDBIC\CHAP05\LESSON1\CALENDAR.MDB` database file in Access.

3. Open the `tblSponsorTypes_lkp` table in datasheet view to determine the ID assigned to the Education category.

   As shown in Figure 5-1, the `Education` sponsor type has an `ID` of 5. So you need to list all the sponsor records from the `tblSponsors` table that have a `SponsorID` of 5.

4. Click on the Queries tab of the database container and then click on the New button.

   Access gives you the option of using either the four available query wizards or going directly into query design view, as shown in Figure 5-2.

5. Select the Design View option and then press the OK button.

   Access brings up the query design window and displays a list of tables in the calendar database, as shown in Figure 5-3.

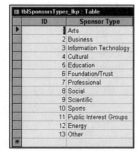

Figure 5-1
List of sponsor
types in the sample
CALENDAR.MDB
database

Figure 5-2
Options for
creating a new
query

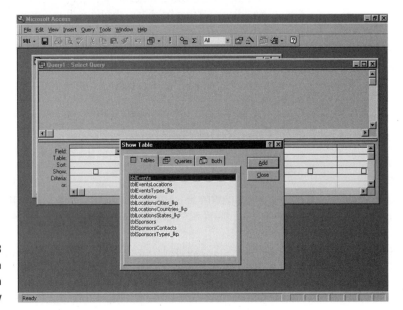

Figure 5-3
Adding a table in a
query design
window

Note

For most types of queries, the query wizards can give you a good head start. Eventually, each wizard takes you to the query design window, with major portions of the query predesigned based on the choices you made while using the wizard. However, it is ultimately through the query design window that you are able to exploit the tremendous power of Access.

6. Select the `tblSponsors` table from the displayed list and click on the Add button. Click on the Close button to hide the table list.

Access adds the `tblSponsors` table to the query design window, as shown in Figure 5-4.

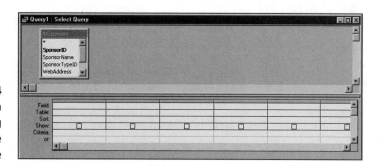

Figure 5-4
Query design
window displaying
the fields of the
selected table

7. Double-click on the asterisk (*) symbol in the tblSponsors table.

   Access adds that asterisk symbol in the first cell of the Field row, as shown in Figure 5-5. It also lists the table name in the first cell of the Table row and automatically selects the first Show checkbox.

8. Now double-click on the SponsorTypeID field displayed in the tblSponsors table.

   Access adds the SponsorTypeID to the second cell of the Field row and selects its Show checkbox by default, as shown in Figure 5-6.

9. Deselect the Show checkbox associated with the SponsorTypeID field and then type =5 in its Criteria cell, as shown in Figure 5-7.

Figure 5-5
Adding the asterisk
symbol to the field
row

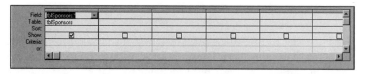

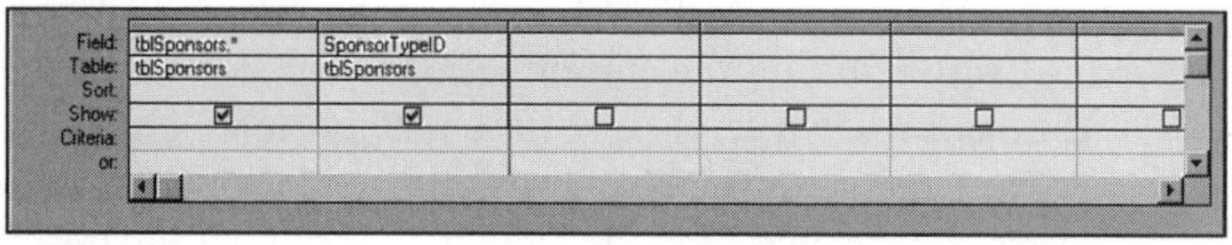

Figure 5-6
Adding the
SponsorTypeID field
to the Field row

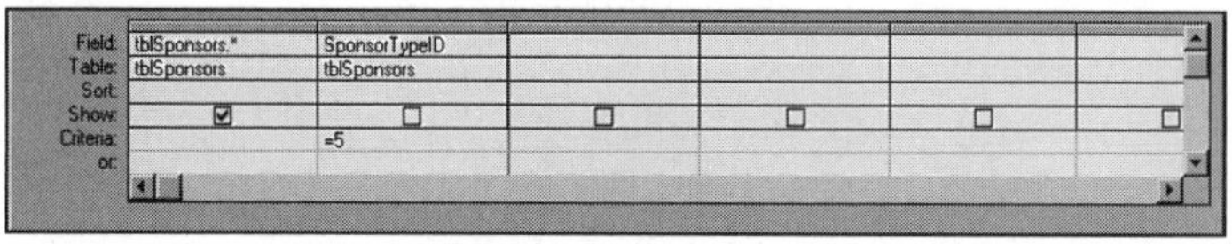

Figure 5-7
Specifying a
criterion for the
SponsorTypeID field

Query1 : Select Query

SponsorID	Sponsor Name	SponsorTypeID	Web URL	User Name	Password
12	International Sociological Associ	5	http://www.arch.vt.edu/ca	urban	housing
21	University of Michigan, Ann Arbo	5	http://www.dla.utexas.edu	tintin	comic
22	The Department of Mathematics,	5	http://icg.fas.harvard.edu/	teachers	teach
23	Miami-Dade Community College	5	http://www.mdcc.edu/boo	dades	books
30	Iowa State University	5	http://www.public.iastate.	students	teachers
(AutoNumber)					

Figure 5-8 Sponsors dealing with education

10. Finally, select the Run option from the Query menu.

    Access executes your query and returns a list of five sponsors affiliated with the area of education, as shown in Figure 5-8.

Note that Access presents the query result in a form similar to the datasheet view of a table. We will explain the reason behind this similarity later in this lesson. Let's first examine how this query is designed.

Examining the Query Design

As you can see from Figure 5-7, the query design window contains two main sections. The top section holds a rectangular box, representing your selected table, that acts as a data source of your query. The asterisk (*) symbol in the rectangular list box acts as a special field that stands for "all table fields." Use this special field whenever you want the query to display the data from all the table fields in its result.

The bottom section of the query design appears as a grid of rows and columns. Use this grid to specify the goal of your query. List the table fields you want to work with in the Field row. The Table row indicates which table each field listed in the Field row belongs to and is particularly helpful when you include multiple tables in your query, as you will see in Chapter 6, "Combining Tables and Grouping Data: Joins and Total Queries."

The Sort row (described further in the next lesson) is provided to generate the query result in either ascending or descending order by specifying one of these two Sort options available against one or more fields listed in the Sort row. Note that you cannot specify a Sort option for the asterisk field.

The checkboxes in the Show row let you select which fields you want to include in the query result. In the current example, we deselected the Show checkbox for the `tblSponsorsID` field because it was already represented by the asterisk field.

The Criteria row of the query design grid allows you to define the limiting criteria against any field listed in the Field row. Access applies the criteria to filter the records from the source table. The subsequent Or rows act as extensions of the Criteria row and are used to combine multiple criteria through the logical `OR` operator, as explained in Lesson 5.

Saving the Query Design

You can store your query design as a database object. This way you can run the query anytime in the future without having to redesign it. The result of the query is always based on the current data. To save your current query as **qrySponsors_EducationType**:

1. Select the Save option from the File menu.

   Access prompts you for a query name and displays Query1 as the default name.

2. Type qrySponsors_EducationType for the query name, and press the OK button.

   Access saves the query design as a query object named qrySponsors_EducationType.

Always use a consistent naming scheme for your query names. Because Access requires that a query name be different from a table name, we recommend that you add appropriate prefixes (**tbl** for a table and **qry** for a query) to your table and query names.

3. Select the Close option from the File menu.

   Access closes the Query Result window and displays the stored query object in the database container, as shown in Figure 5-9.

4. Click on the Open button in the database container.

   Access redisplays the filtered sponsor records.

When you save a query, Access stores only the query design, not the result of the query.

Figure 5-9
The database container displaying saved queries

Examining the Query Result

Refer to the query result shown in Figure 5-8. As you can see, this result contains the subset of sponsor records that meets the specified sponsor type criteria. By presenting this result in the form of a table datasheet, Access provides a familiar interface for browsing through filtered information. Furthermore, you can edit the data listed in this query result just like you can edit data in a table. Any changes made to this query result are reflected in the `tblSponsors` table itself, as demonstrated by the following:

1. Open the `qrySponsors_EducationType` query (if it is not already open) to display the query result shown in Figure 5-8.

2. Click in the Password field of the sponsor record with `SponsorID` 30, and change the data from `teachers` to `professors` in that field.

3. Press `SHIFT`-`ENTER` to save the record.

4. Close the Query Result window.

5. Select the Tables tab of the database container, and open the `tblSponsors` table in datasheet view.

6. Using the vertical scroll bar, locate the sponsor with `SponsorID` 30.

   The `Password` field of this sponsor record now contains the value `professors`, as shown in Figure 5-10.

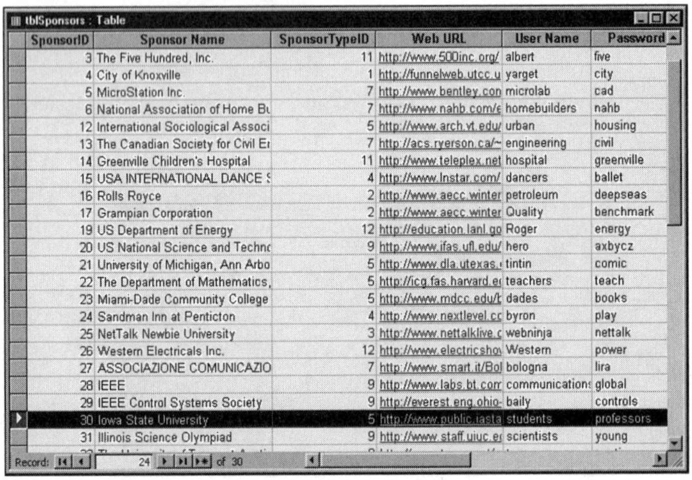

Figure 5-10
Editing table data
from the query
result

SponsorID	Sponsor Name	SponsorTypeID	Web URL	User Name	Password
3	The Five Hundred, Inc.	11	http://www.500inc.org/	albert	five
4	City of Knoxville	1	http://funnelweb.utcc.u	yarget	city
5	MicroStation Inc	7	http://www.bentley.con	microlab	cad
6	National Association of Home Bu	7	http://www.nahb.com/s	homebuilders	nahb
12	International Sociological Associ	5	http://www.arch.vt.edu/	urban	housing
13	The Canadian Society for Civil Er	7	http://acs.ryerson.ca/~	engineering	civil
14	Greenville Children's Hospital	11	http://www.teleplex.net	hospital	greenville
15	USA INTERNATIONAL DANCE S	4	http://www.lnstar.com/	dancers	ballet
16	Rolls Royce	2	http://www.aecc.winter	petroleum	deepseas
17	Grampian Corporation	2	http://www.aecc.winter	Quality	benchmark
19	US Department of Energy	12	http://education.lanl.go	energy	energy
20	US National Science and Techno	9	http://www.ifas.ufl.edu/	hero	axbycz
21	University of Michigan, Ann Arbo	5	http://www.dla.utexas.ı	tintin	comic
22	The Department of Mathematics,	5	http://icg.fas.harvard.er	teachers	teach
23	Miami-Dade Community College	5	http://www.mdcc.edu/t	dades	books
24	Sandman Inn at Penticton	4	http://www.nextlevel.cc	byron	play
25	NetTalk Newbie University	3	http://www.nettalklive.c	webninja	nettalk
26	Western Electricals Inc.	12	http://www.electricsho	Western	power
27	ASSOCIAZIONE COMUNICAZIO	7	http://www.smart.it/Bol	bologna	lira
28	IEEE	9	http://www.labs.bt.com	communications	global
29	IEEE Control Systems Society	9	http://everest.eng.ohio-	baily	controls
30	Iowa State University	5	http://www.public.iasta	students	professors
31	Illinois Science Olympiad	9	http://www.staff.uiuc.er	scientists	young

Record: 24 of 30

The preceding steps also illustrate how you can use this powerful feature of Access queries for *selective editing*, where you first filter your records of interest and then make changes to them. You can even add new sponsors. Access enforces all the field properties such as default values and validation rules defined in the table design during this data editing process.

An Experiment to Determine How the Query Result Is Affected When the Underlying Data Changes

Run the `qrySponsors_EducationType` query and change the `SponsorTypeID` of any sponsor in that result to **4** and save the record. What do you notice? Access does not automatically remove that sponsor from the query result, even though it does not meet the `SponsorTypeID=5` criterion anymore. Now close the Query Result window and reopen the query. This time, that sponsor is not included in the result. From this experiment, it is easy to conclude that Access does not automatically rerun a query if there is a change in the underlying data.

Viewing the SQL Statement Behind Your Query

Although Access allows you to define your query visually, it runs that query by passing the equivalent SQL statement to its JET engine. SQL stands for Structured Query Language and is a query-defining standard supported by most RDBMSs. SQL statements closely resemble English sentences. Although Access does not require you to know this language, it helps to have some understanding of SQL syntax when designing advanced queries (such as Union queries and subqueries, discussed in Chapter 6, "Combining Tables and Grouping Data: Joins and Total Queries"). Fortunately, the query design interface of Access can be a powerful teaching aid to gain this understanding because you can display the SQL statement this interface creates when you run your query. The following steps show how you can display the SQL statement behind the `qrySponsors_EducationType` query:

1. Highlight the `qrySponsors_EducationType` query in the database container.

2. Press the Design button to open this query in query design view.

3. Select the SQL View option from the View menu.

   Access lists the SQL statement corresponding to this query, as shown in Figure 5-11. Note how closely it resembles an English-like sentence. Because this SQL statement starts with the SELECT command, the `qrySponsors_EducationType` query is also classified as a Select query.

Figure 5-11
Displaying the SQL
statement behind a
query

qrySponsors_EducationType : Select Query

```
SELECT tblSponsors.*
FROM tblSponsors
WHERE (((tblSponsors.SponsorTypeID)=5));
```

Lesson Summary

This lesson introduced you to the query design interface of Access that makes the process of creating database queries quick and painless. Through this visual interface, you select the table you want to query, specify the output fields and your sorting and searching criteria, and then run the query. Behind the scenes, Access automatically creates the SQL statement, which the JET engine processes to produce the desired result.

If you want to display all the table fields in your query result, you can use the special asterisk (*) field. This way, if you store the query and later on change the design of the source table by adding or removing fields, the query result will automatically reflect the change. On the other hand, if you have an application program that processes five fields from Table X and you change Table X to include six fields, you must also remember to change your application program to process the sixth field.

In addition to displaying the data from the existing fields, you can also create new fields using a query. We will explore this capability of Access queries in the next lesson. For your reference, the **CALENDAR.MDB** database file resulting from this lesson is provided in the **C:\WEBSITE\HTDOCS\WDBIC\CHAP05\LESSON1\RESULTS** directory.

1. What is a query?
   a. It is a method by which you specify table relationships.
   b. It is a subset of data records.
   c. It is a wizard for finding data.
   d. It is a feature of most database management systems with which you can search, sort, and analyze data stored in the database.

2. What is the significance of the asterisk (*) symbol in Access query design?
   a. It is always displayed separately in the first cell of the Field row.
   b. It stands for "all tables."
   c. You use it whenever you want the query to display the data from all the table fields in its result.
   d. It automatically selects the Show checkbox.

3. Why do you need to deselect the Show checkbox associated with the **SponsorTypeID** field in the **qrySponsors_EducationType** defined in this lesson?
   a. You do not want the field name to be displayed in your query result.
   b. You want to enter a criterion in the Criteria cell of this field.
   c. You want to filter records.
   d. The asterisk field already represents this field.

4. What happens when you save a query in Access?
   a. Access saves the query design.
   b. Access saves the current result of the query.
   c. Access regenerates the result dynamically whenever you run the saved query.
   d. Access shows the SQL when you open the saved query.

5. How is an Access query executed?
   a. The visually designed Access query is first converted into an SQL statement.
   b. The Access JET engine generates SQL statements.
   c. The Access JET engine executes SQL statements passed to it.
   d. Access generates SQL statements.

Complexity: Easy
1. Design a query named `qryEvents_Musical` that lists all the musical-type events.

Complexity: Easy
2. Create a query named `qryContacts_NAHB` that lists only the names and email addresses of the contacts belonging to National Association of Home Builders (NAHB).

CREATING CALCULATED FIELDS

Often, there are times when you want information that has to be computed from original data. For example, if you want to list the event duration along with the start time and the end time of each record of the `tblEvents_Locations` table, then this duration information has to be derived from the `StartTime` and the `EndTime` fields. The way to handle this is by defining a calculated field in a query. This lesson explains how calculated fields are created and describes some of the frequently used built-in functions of Access that you can use in this process.

What Is a Calculated Field?

A *calculated field* is a query field created using the following syntax:

```
FieldName: FieldExpression
```

where `FieldName` is the name you want to assign to that calculated field and `FieldExpression` is a combination of operators, constants, functions, and existing table fields that evaluates to a single value. Each table field listed in the field expression must be enclosed within square brackets. Some examples of calculated fields are given below:

```
Tax: [Price]*[TaxRate]
TotalInvoiceAmount: [SalesAmount]+[TaxAmount]
FullName: [FirstName] & " " & [LastName]
EventYear: Year([EventDate])
EventDuration: DateDiff("h",[StartTime],[EndTime])
WebURL: HyperlinkPart([WebAddress],2)
```

Using Operators

Table 5-1 presents a list of operators that you can use to create calculated field expressions.

Table 5-1 Arithmetic and string operators

Operator	Purpose	Examples
+	Add or concatenate	2+2=4; "2"+"2"="22"; "2"+Null=Null
&	String concatenate	"2"&"2"="22"; "2" & Null= "2"
–	Subtract	3–2=1; 3–Null=Null
*	Multiply	3*5=15; 3*Null=Null
/	Divide	10/4=2.5; 10/Null=Null
\	Integer Divide	10\4=2; Null\10=Null
^	Exponent	2^3=8; 2^Null=Null; Null^3=Null
MOD	Remainder	10 MOD 4 = 2; 10 MOD Null = Null

Note that the main difference between the + and & operators is how they act when they encounter a `Null` value. If `A` is any string expression, then `A + Null` returns `Null`, whereas `A & Null` returns `A`.

If an expression involves multiple operators, then Access uses precedence rules to determine which portion of the expression is evaluated first. You can override the default precedence by enclosing the expression you want evaluated first in parentheses. For example, 2+3*4 would return 14, whereas (2+3)*4 would return 20.

Using Built-In Functions

Access supports numerous built-in functions to help you create the necessary field expressions for your calculated fields. The commonly used functions are listed below. You can seek online help on any function for its exact syntax, parameters, and purpose.

● `Abs`: This function returns the absolute value of a number. For example, `Abs(-4)` returns 4.

● `Date`: This function returns the current system date.

● `DateAdd`: This function adds a time interval (positive or negative) to a given date and returns the resulting date. For example, `DateAdd("d",2,#12/30/97#)` returns 1/1/98 (date that falls two days after 12/30/97). Note that a date literal must be enclosed between the pound (#) characters.

● `DateDiff`: This function returns the number of time intervals between two specified dates. For example, `DateDiff("h",#10:00AM#,#1:00PM#)` returns 3 (the number of hours between 1:00 PM and 10:00 AM).

● `DatePart`: This function returns a specified part of a given date. For example, `DatePart("yyyy",12/1/05)` returns 2005 (the year of this date). Note that you can also use the `Year` function for the same purpose.

● `DateSerial`: This function returns a date in Access's native date format (a double-sized number) for a specified year, month, and day. For example, `DateSerial(97,11,20)` returns 35754.

● `Format`: This function formats an expression according to instructions contained in a format expression. It is an extremely powerful function that helps you display your data in various ways. Some examples of this function follow:

```
Format(#1/1/98#,"m") returns "1"
Format(#1/1/98#,"mm") returns "01"
Format(#1/1/98#,"mmm") returns "Jan"
Format(#1/1/98#,"mmmm") returns "January"
Format (20.276,"Currency") returns $20.28.
Format (0.85,"Percent") returns 85%.
```

See Ms-Access Help on Format for all the available formatting options.

● `HyperlinkPart`: This function returns information about data stored as a `Hyperlink` data type. For example, if a `Hyperlink` field A contains the data `Waite Group Press#http://www.waite.com#`, then `HyperlinkPart([A],1)` returns `"Waite Group Press"` (the display text), whereas `HyperlinkPart([A],2)` returns `"http://www.waite.com"` (the hyperlink address).

● `Iif`: This function returns one of two parts based on the given expression. For example, `Iif([A]>[B],[A],[B])` returns the value of field [A] if it is greater than the value of field [B]; otherwise, it returns the value of field [B].

● `Instr`: This function returns the position of the first occurrence of one string within another. For example, `Instr("john@aol.com","@")` returns 5, whereas `Instr("abcde","@")` returns 0.

- IsNull: This function determines if an expression results in a Null value. For example, IsNull([EndTime]) returns -1 (True) if no value has been specified for the EndTime field; otherwise, it returns 0 (False).

- Mid: This function returns a specified number of characters from a string. For example, Mid("abcde",3,2) returns "cd" (two characters starting from the third character).

- Now: This function returns the current date and time according to the setting of your computer's system date and time.

    Note that the Date function returns only the current date (with time always set to 00:00 or 12:00 AM).

- Val: This function returns the numbers contained in a string. For example, Val("123a") returns 123.

Most of these functions that accept one or more parameters on encountering a Null value because their parameter will either return an error or a Null value.

An Example of Creating a Calculated Field

Now that you have gained some familiarity with the structure of a calculated field and the role of important built-in functions, let's see how you can design a query that lists the event duration along with all the fields of the tblEventsLocations table of the sample CALENDAR.MDB database. Follow the steps given below:

1. Copy the CALENDAR.MDB file residing in the
   C:\WEBSITE\HTDOCS\WDBIC\CHAP05\SAMPLES directory to the
   C:\WEBSITE\HTDOCS\WDBIC\CHAP05\LESSON2 directory.

2. Open the C:\WEBSITE\HTDOCS\WDBIC\CHAP05\LESSON2\CALENDAR.MDB database file in Access.

3. Open a new query in design view and list tblEventsLocations as the source table.

4. Add the asterisk field to the first cell of the Field row.

5. Place the cursor in the second cell of the Field row and type the following (You may press SHIFT-F2 to display that cell through a zoom window.):

   ```
   Duration: DateDiff("h",[StartTime],[EndTime])
   ```

6. Press ENTER after typing the above text.

   Access automatically selects the Show checkbox under this second cell, as shown in Figure 5-12.

7. Save this query as `qryEventsLocations_withDuration`.

8. Run this query.

   Access displays the event duration in hours in the query result, as shown in Figure 5-13.

Although Access ran this query successfully, there are two anomalies in this query result. First, the **Duration** field of many records does not contain any value (see the records with **EventLocationID** of **1**, **8**, and **9**). This anomaly is easy to explain because the **EndTime** field of these records is **Null** and the **DateDiff** function used to create the **Duration** field on getting the **Null** value from this field returns a **Null** value.

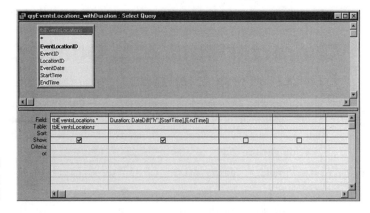

Figure 5-12 Creating a calculated field

qryEventsLocations_withDuration : Select Query

EventLocationID	EventID	LocationID	Event Date	Start Time	End Time	Duration
1	1	1	9/20/97	8:00:00 PM		
2	2	2	9/21/97	10:00:00 AM	5:00:00 PM	7
3	2	2	9/22/97	10:00:00 AM	5:00:00 PM	7
4	3	1	9/21/97	10:00:00 AM	12:00:00 PM	2
5	5	1	9/26/97	12:00:00 PM	1:30:00 PM	1
6	6	4	4/26/97	10:00:00 AM	8:00:00 PM	10
7	6	4	4/27/97	12:00:00 PM	6:00:00 PM	6
8	7	5	5/23/97	9:00:00 AM		
9	7	5	5/24/97	9:00:00 AM		
10	8	5	7/23/97	9:00:00 AM	7:00:00 PM	10
11	8	5	7/24/97	9:00:00 AM	7:00:00 PM	10
12	9	6	1/20/97	8:00:00 AM	6:00:00 PM	10
13	9	6	1/21/97	8:00:00 AM	6:00:00 PM	10
14	9	6	1/22/97	8:00:00 AM	3:00:00 PM	7
15	10	8	1/24/97	1:00:00 PM	4:00:00 PM	3
16	10	8	1/25/97	11:00:00 AM	1:00:00 PM	2
17	12	8	1/22/97	12:00:00 PM	3:00:00 PM	3
18	13	8	1/24/97	9:00:00 AM	12:00:00 PM	3

Record: 1 of 59

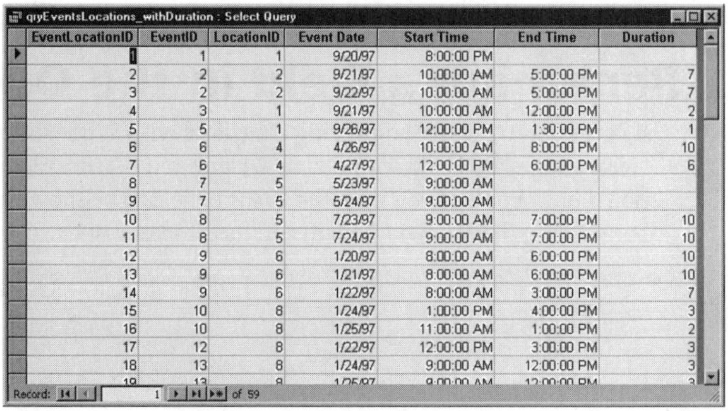

Figure 5-13 Query result showing information generated using a calculated field

The second anomaly shows up when the difference between the StartTime and the EndTime fields involves a fraction of an hour. The record with EventLocationID of 5 in Figure 5-13 serves as a good example. Note that although the start time is listed as 12:00 PM and the end time is listed as 1:30 PM, the Duration field displays 1 hour. This is because the DateDiff function always returns integral values of the time interval you ask. You have two options to resolve this anomaly:

● Create the Duration field by getting the time difference from the DateDiff function in minutes and then dividing that value by 60, as shown below:

```
Duration: DateDiff("n",[StartTime],[EndTime])/60
```

Using this method, the record with EventLocationID of 5 will display 1.5 for the Duration field.

● Create two calculated fields, DurationHours and DurationMinutes, that indicate the duration in hours and minutes. So for the sample record, the DurationHours field will be 1 and the DurationMinutes field will be 30. The expressions needed to create these fields are left as an exercise.

Characteristics of a Query Containing Calculated Fields

The query with calculated fields follows most of the attributes of a regular query. The SELECT SQL statement is modified to include the name and definition of the calculated field. For example, the Access-generated SQL statement for the qryEventsLocations _withDuration query of Figure 5-12 is as follows:

```
SELECT tblEventsLocations.*, DateDiff("n",[StartTime],[EndTime])/60 AS Duration
FROM tblEventsLocations;
```

You cannot edit the value of the calculated field in the query result. You can change the data of the source fields (such as StartTime or EndTime), in which case Access immediately recomputes the value of the corresponding calculated field.

Renaming a Field in the Query Result

If you want to display an existing table field with a different name in the query result, create a calculated field with that new name and list the original field as its field expression. For example, if you want the EventID field to be shown as Event ID in your query output, add the following calculated field to your query:

```
Event ID: [EventID]
```

For fields that have their `Caption` property set in their table design (for example, the `EventDate` field), Access always shows the caption for the field name in the query result even if you try to rename it using this calculated field method. However, this feature (or bug?) is limited to the scope of the Access user interface. The actual query result returned by the JET engine contains the calculated field name instead of the `Caption` property, as you will see in Chapter 9, "Accessing Database Records From Visual Basic: Data-Access Objects."

Lesson Summary

This lesson explained the importance of calculated fields. They go hand in hand with the third rule of normalization (see Chapter 3, "Organizing Data: Tables and Relationships"), which advocates that a table need not contain any field that is completely dependent on the other fields of that table. Instead, that field should be dynamically generated through a query, as shown in this lesson.

A calculated field has two components: a field name and a field expression separated by a colon. The field expression defines the formula consisting of existing table fields, operators, constants, and built-in functions, many of which were described in this lesson. Just remember that when you create a field expression, you need to make sure that it produces the expected result in all possible cases.

As mentioned in Lesson 1, one of the many options of Access queries is to specify the sort order in which you want the query result to be generated. We focus on this option in the next lesson. For your reference, the `CALENDAR.MDB` database file containing the `qryEventsLocations_withDuration` query created in this lesson is provided in the `C:\WEBSITE\HTDOCS\WDBIC\CHAP05\LESSON2\RESULTS` directory.

1. Which of the following holds true for a calculated field?
   a. It computes information from the original data.
   b. It has to be assigned a field name.
   c. The resulting information generated by the calculated field must have a single value.
   d. The field expression precedes the field name in a calculated field.

2. What value is returned by the following `DateAdd` expression?

   ```
   DateAdd("m",1,#31-Jan-96#)
   ```

   a. `31-Feb-96`
   b. `28-Feb-96`
   c. `29-Feb-96`
   d. `30-Feb-96`

3. How would you create a calculated field named `EmailAvailable` that returns
   -1 if a sponsor contact has an email address listed and 0 if not?
   a. `EmailAvailable: IIF([Email] = Null,0,-1)`
   b. `EmailAvailable: IsNull([Email])`
   c. `EmailAvailable: IsNull(Email)`
   d. `EmailAvailable: IIF(IsNull([Email]),0,-1)`

4. What does the following calculated field return if the `[Rate]` field contains a
   value `20.034`?

   `FormattedRate:Format([Rate],"Currency")`

   a. `20.034`
   b. `$20.034`
   c. `20.03`
   d. `$20.03`

5. What will the following calculated field return?

   `Test:("A"+Null) & "B"`

   a. `A`
   b. `B`
   c. `AB`
   d. `Null`

EXERCISE 2

Complexity: Easy

1. Design a query named `qryEventsLocations_YearMonth` that lists two fields
   named `EventMonth` and `EventYear` in addition to all the fields of the
   `tblEventLocations` table. The `EventMonth` field should display the full name
   of the month and the `EventYear` field should display the four-digit year corresponding to the `EventDate` field of each record.

Complexity: Moderate

2. Create a query named `qryEventsLocations_DurationHourMinutes` that lists
   the duration of each event in hours and minutes using two fields named
   `DurationHours` and `DurationMinutes`. Hint: For the `DurationMinutes` field,
   seek online help on the `MOD` operator.

SORTING DATA

Normally, Access shows the table records in the primary key order, whether you are viewing them from the table datasheet or as part of a query result. Often, though, there is a need to view the records in a different sort order. It helps in grouping similar information together. For example, when displaying the list of events, you may want to sort them by EventTypeID so that similar events appear together. In another instance, you may want to display the events chronologically, in which case you will have to sort them by the event date. And if you want to take this chronological order to its limits, for each date you can further sort the event records by their start time.

This lesson looks into some examples of how to specify the sort criteria in an Access query and then describes constraints and performance factors that you should be aware of when sorting your records.

Sorting on a Single Field

In this first sorting example, we show how you can list all the events in the sample CALENDAR.MDB database sorted by their event types:

1. Copy the CALENDAR.MDB file residing in the
   C:\WEBSITE\HTDOCS\WDBIC\CHAP05\SAMPLES directory to the
   C:\WEBSITE\HTDOCS\WDBIC\CHAP05\LESSON3 directory.

2. Open the C:\WEBSITE\HTDOCS\WDBIC\CHAP05\LESSON3\CALENDAR.MDB database file in Access.

3. Open a new query in design view and list tblEvents as the source table.

4. Add the asterisk field to the first cell of the Field row.

5. Add the EventTypeID field in the second cell of the Field row.

6. Specify Ascending in the Sort cell of the EventTypeID field and deselect its Show checkbox, as shown in Figure 5-14.

7. Save the query as qryEvents_SortedByEventType.

8. Run the query.

   Access lists the events sorted by the data in the EventTypeID field, as shown in Figure 5-15.

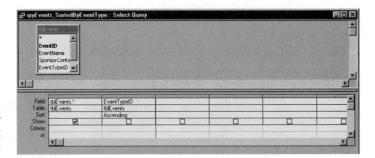

Figure 5-14 Specifying a sort field

EventID	Event Name	SponsorContactID	EventTypeID	Event Description
18	Memorial Day Weekend E	15	1	Make Plans now to attend Freedom Weekend Alot
1	Music Night	1	2	The Symphony Winds comprised of nine "Wind" p
5	Organ Recitals	1	2	
8	International Jubilee	4	2	Join the fun as the Sixth Annual International Jubil
2	Art Exhibition	1	3	Uxbridge Secondary School Auditorium will be trar
7	ARTFEST	3	3	ARTFEST is a Memorial Day weekend tradition wh
9	MicroStation FORUM & E	5	3	The World's Largest Educational Conference and E
3	Film Day	1	4	Film buffs will be interested in the program featurin
4	Troll Stories	8	4	This is an original play, written by Colleen Baskin.
27	1997 Okanagan Zone Dra	26	4	Hello! Penticton's Progress Theatre Company Soc
6	The 1997 Main Street Fes	2	5	The Fourteenth Annual Main Street Festival feature
19	USA International Ballet C	17	5	One of the world's most prestigious dance events,
10	Review of Existing Plans	6	6	Go beyond the seminars to hands-on education th
12	The Construction Industry	8	6	This three hour course helps participants understa
20	10th Annual Offshore Drill	18	6	The latest challenges in well technology as E&P e
29	Electric West-98	28	6	Don't miss out on your best opportunity of the yeai
30	Exhibition of Public Comn	29	6	Citizen information activities - Audiovisual equipme
33	The Iowa State Science a	32	6	The Iowa State Science and Technology Fair will b
38	Middle Tennessee Scienc	37	6	The Middle Tennessee Science and Engineering F
13	AIA Plan Review Worksho	9	7	In this workshop, architects and interior merchandi
15	Brick Sculpture - New Us	11	7	Brick sculpture has been used effectively to enhan
16	Housing in the 21st Centu	12	7	Confrence Agenda:The Future of Government and I
17	Durability of Buildings	14	7	Government and industry fund numerous surveys,
21	Seminar - Improving Oil ar	19	7	Industry experts from Gensym and Gensym Soluti
22	Space-Age Technologies	20	7	Includes presentations on the European Space Ag
23	HYDROGEN AND THE M	21	7	UPDATE 97 (NEW) will be the 11th annual worksh
24	National Science and Tec	22	7	A National Science and Technology Symposium is
25	SALSA V	23	7	Established four years ago, the Symposium About
26	International Conference c	24	7	The main objective of this International Conference

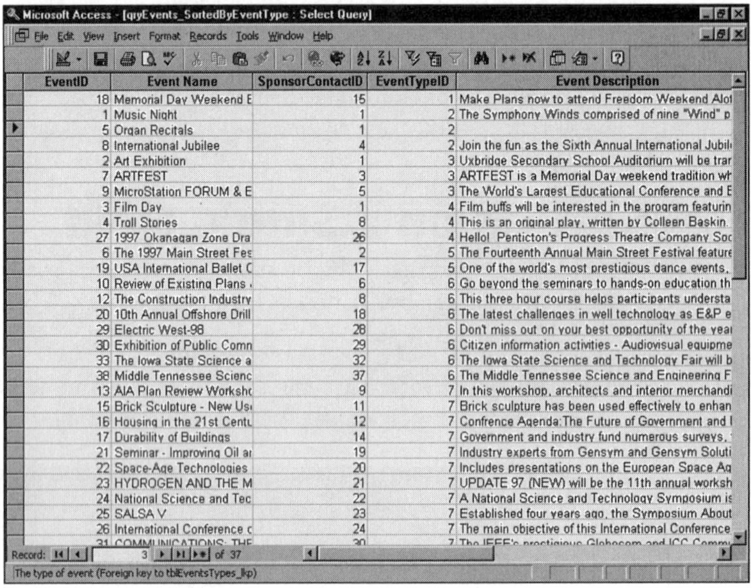

Figure 5-15 Query result of sorting events by `EventTypeID`

Sorting on Multiple Fields

In this example, we show how you can list all the records of the **`tblEventsLocations`** first sorted by the event date and then sorted by the start time:

1. Close the query created in the previous example.
2. Open a new query in design view and list `tblEventsLocations` as the source table.
3. Add the asterisk field to the first cell of the Field row.

4. Add the `EventDate` field in the second cell of the Field row, specify Ascending in its Sort cell, and deselect its Show checkbox.

5. Specify `StartTime` in the third cell of the Field row, specify `Ascending` in its Sort cell, and deselect its Show checkbox, as shown in Figure 5-16.

6. Save the query as `qryEvents_SortedByEventDateTime`.

7. Run the query.

   The query result shows the event location records sorted by date and time, as shown in Figure 5-17. (Note that the figure shows the middle portion of the query result, not the beginning.)

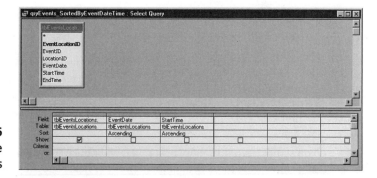

Figure 5-16 Specifying multiple sort fields

qryEvents_SortedByEventDateTime : Select Query

EventLocation	EventID	LocationID	Event Date	Start Time	End Time
28	18	16	5/24/97	1:00:00 PM	6:00:00 PM
29	18	16	5/25/97	10:00:00 AM	6:00:00 PM
22	16	14	6/11/97	9:00:00 AM	5:00:00 PM
23	16	14	6/12/97	9:00:00 AM	5:00:00 PM
24	16	14	6/13/97	9:00:00 AM	5:00:00 PM
25	16	14	6/14/97	9:00:00 AM	5:00:00 PM
10	8	5	7/23/97	9:00:00 AM	7:00:00 PM
11	8	5	7/24/97	9:00:00 AM	7:00:00 PM
58	4	2	9/1/97	10:00:00 AM	
52	36	35	9/6/97	4:00:00 PM	6:00:00 PM
41	28	27	9/10/97	9:00:00 PM	11:00:00 PM
46	32	31	9/15/97	10:00:00 AM	6:00:00 PM
47	32	31	9/16/97	10:00:00 AM	6:00:00 PM
43	30	29	9/17/97	9:00:00 AM	8:00:00 PM
1	1	1	9/20/97	8:00:00 PM	
4	3	1	9/21/97	10:00:00 AM	12:00:00 PM
2	2	2	9/21/97	10:00:00 AM	5:00:00 PM
3	2	2	9/22/97	10:00:00 AM	5:00:00 PM
5	5	1	9/26/97	12:00:00 PM	1:30:00 PM
44	31	30	10/16/97	8:00:00 AM	5:00:00 PM
45	31	30	10/17/97	8:00:00 AM	5:00:00 PM
35	23	21	10/27/97	9:30:00 AM	4:30:00 PM

Record: 1 of 59

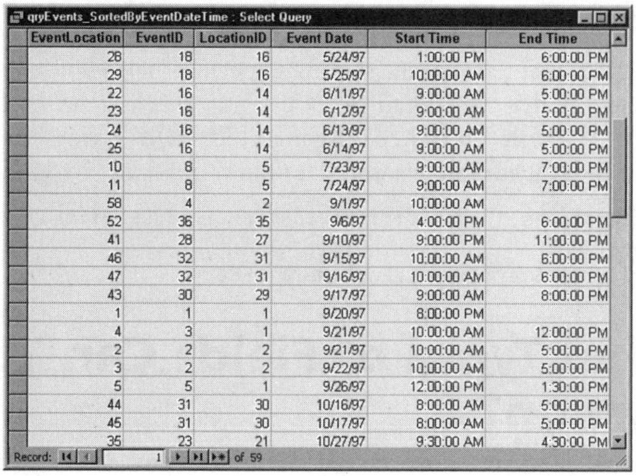

Figure 5-17 Query result of sorting on multiple fields

Sorting on a Calculated Field

In this example, we show how you can list all the records of the `tblEventsLocations` first sorted by the event duration, where the longer events are listed first:

1. Close the query created in the previous example.

2. Open a new query in the design view and list `tblEventsLocations` as the source table.

3. Add the asterisk field to the first cell of the Field row.

4. Add the following calculated field in the second cell of the Field row:

   ```
   Duration: DateDiff("n",[StartTime],[EndTime])
   ```

5. Specify Descending in the Sort cell of this calculated field, as shown in Figure 5-18. Leave the Show checkbox selected.

6. Save the query as `qryEvents_SortedByDuration_LongerFirst`.

7. Run the query.

   Figure 5-19 shows the query result returned by Access.

 Note
If you scroll down this query result, you will notice that the records whose `Duration` field is `Null` (due to no data in their `EndTime` field) show up in the end.

SQL Statement for a Sort Query

A query that returns data sorted by specified fields is also based on the `SELECT` SQL statement that contains an `ORDER BY` clause that lists the sort fields and their sort order. For example, the Access-generated SQL statement for the `qryEvents_SortedByDuration_LongerFirst` query of Figure 5-18 is as follows:

```
SELECT tblEventsLocations.*, DateDiff("n",[StartTime],[EndTime]) AS Duration
FROM tblEventsLocations
ORDER BY DateDiff("n",[StartTime],[EndTime]) DESC;
```

What Types of Fields Can You Sort on?

Access allows you to sort on one or more fields provided they are defined as `Text`, `Number`, `AutoNumber`, `Currency`, `Date/Time`, or `Yes/No` data type. You cannot sort on `Memo`, `Hyperlink`, or `OLE object` fields. You can also sort on calculated fields (as you saw in the last example above) as long as the fields fall between the parameters of the data types on which sorting is permitted.

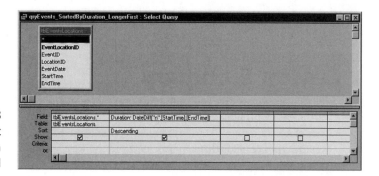

Figure 5-18 Specifying a sort order on a calculated field

qryEvents_SortedByDuration_LongerFirst : Select Query

EventLocation	EventID	LocationI	Event Date	Start Time	End Time	Duration
43	30	29	9/17/97	9:00:00 AM	8:00:00 PM	660
42	29	28	2/4/98	8:30:00 AM	7:00:00 PM	630
6	6	4	4/26/97	10:00:00 AM	8:00:00 PM	600
10	8	5	7/23/97	9:00:00 AM	7:00:00 PM	600
11	8	5	7/24/97	9:00:00 AM	7:00:00 PM	600
12	9	6	1/20/97	8:00:00 AM	6:00:00 PM	600
13	9	6	1/21/97	8:00:00 AM	6:00:00 PM	600
54	38	37	4/13/98	8:00:00 AM	6:00:00 PM	600
32	20	18	11/19/97	9:00:00 AM	6:00:00 PM	540
31	20	18	11/18/97	9:00:00 AM	6:00:00 PM	540
44	31	30	10/16/97	8:00:00 AM	5:00:00 PM	540
45	31	30	10/17/97	8:00:00 AM	5:00:00 PM	540
56	39	38	12/13/97	8:00:00 AM	5:00:00 PM	540
55	39	38	12/12/97	8:00:00 AM	5:00:00 PM	540
25	16	14	6/14/97	9:00:00 AM	5:00:00 PM	480
59	15	13	11/15/97	9:00:00 AM	5:00:00 PM	480
22	16	14	6/11/97	9:00:00 AM	5:00:00 PM	480
23	16	14	6/12/97	9:00:00 AM	5:00:00 PM	480
24	16	14	6/13/97	9:00:00 AM	5:00:00 PM	480
48	33	32	3/21/98	10:00:00 AM	6:00:00 PM	480

Record: 1 of 59

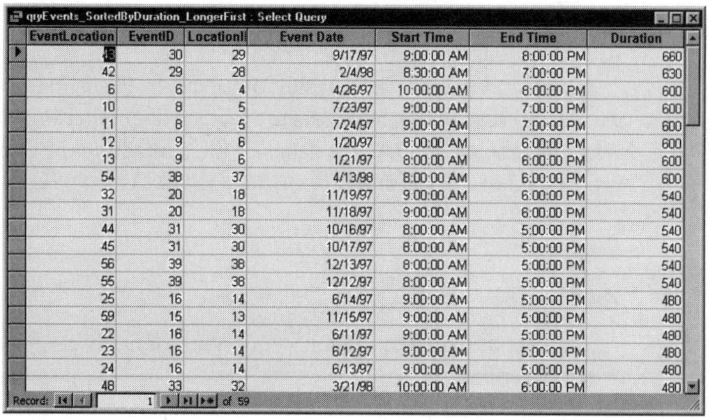

Figure 5-19 Query result of sorting on a calculated field

How Data Is Sorted

The way Access sorts data depends on the data type of the sort field. `Text` fields are sorted in alphabetical order, `Number` and `Currency` fields in numeric order, and `Date` fields in chronological order. So if you sort on a `Text` type field such as `Apartment#` that contains numeric values, then `1` will be followed by `10` and not `2`. When you sort a field in ascending order, any records in which that field is blank (contains a `Null` value) are listed first.

When sorting on multiple fields, the order in which you place these fields on the Field row decides which field is sorted on first. The leftmost sort field becomes the primary sort field, and so on.

Improving Sort Performance

When sorting on a field, you should index that field. If you are sorting on multiple fields, then establish a composite index on those fields, as explained in Chapter 4, "Constructing a Relational Database: The Microsoft Access Way," Lesson 4. It is difficult to improve performance when sorting on a calculated field because calculated fields cannot be indexed.

One option is to store the data of a calculated field in a regular table field and then index that field, although this goes against the third rule of normalization. (Under such circumstances, breaking the rule is justifiable!)

Lesson Summary

No matter what order you want to display your data in, one thing that stays consistent is the ease with which you can specify the sort order through the query design interface of Access, as proved by the examples in this lesson. However, there are certain restrictions on the types of fields that can be sorted and the way Access sorts them, especially when you are sorting on a text field that contains numeric data.

To improve sorting performance, you should index the sort fields. Where sorting is to be carried out on multiple fields, establish a composite index. This lesson showed how to sort on calculated fields. However, because calculated fields cannot be indexed, you may incur decreased query performance.

In the next lesson, we shall shift our focus from sorting to filtering data from a table; we will discuss the different ways to specify a filter criterion in an Access query. For your reference, the `CALENDAR.MDB` database file containing the queries created in this lesson is provided in the `C:\WEBSITE\HTDOCS\WDBIC\CHAP05\LESSON3\RESULTS` directory.

1. In Access, which of the following types of fields can you not sort on?
   a. `Text` fields
   b. `Memo` fields
   c. `Hyperlink` fields
   d. `Currency` fields

2. What construct of SQL is used for specifying the sort order?
   a. `GROUP BY`
   b. `SORT BY`
   c. `ORDER BY`
   d. `ASCENDING BY`

3. How will the following three records appear when you specify the Descending sort option on the `JoiningDate` text field?

```
ID    Joining Date
A     1/4/97
B     01/05/97
C     1/6/1997
```

   a. A first, B second, C third
   b. C first, B second, A third
   c. C first, A second, B third
   d. A first, C second, B third

4. When sorting in ascending order, where is a record with a `Null` value in the sort field listed?
   a. Not listed
   b. At the beginning
   c. In the end
   d. Randomly placed

5. Which of the following statements are true?
   a. Calculated fields cannot be sorted.
   b. Calculated fields cannot be indexed.
   c. When sorting on multiple fields, it helps if each sort field is individually indexed.
   d. When sorting on multiple fields, it helps if a composite index is established for these fields.

Complexity: Easy

1. Design a query named `qryLocations_ByCountryStateCityAndName` that lists all the location records grouped by country, state, city, and location name.

Complexity: Moderate

2. Create a query named `qrySponsors_SortedByWebAddress` that lists the sponsors sorted by their Web address. Remember that Access does not allow you to sort on a `HyperLink`-type field directly. Hint: Use the `HyperLinkPart` function to extract the address portion of the `WebAddress` field!

FILTERING DATA

Lesson 1 showed how you can quickly design a query in Access that lists sponsor records belonging to the Education category. That was just one small example of using an Access query to generate a subset of table records by matching a field against a particular value. There are many other ways to specify a criterion for filtering records. This lesson illustrates these techniques using relevant examples.

Using Comparison Operators

You use a comparison operator when you want to filter records by comparing the data of a field against a specific value. Records where the comparison evaluates to True are selected. The list of comparison operators supported by Access is given below:

- = (equal to)

- < (less than)

- <= (less than or equal to)

- > (greater than)

- >= (greater than or equal to)

- <> (not equal to)

The following example shows how you can use the >= operator to list the events occurring on or after November 11, 1997:

1. Copy the CALENDAR.MDB file residing in the
   C:\WEBSITE\HTDOCS\WDBIC\CHAP05\SAMPLES directory to the
   C:\WEBSITE\HTDOCS\WDBIC\CHAP05\LESSON4 directory.

2. Open the C:\WEBSITE\HTDOCS\WDBIC\CHAP05\LESSON4\CALENDAR.MDB database file in Access.

3. Open a new query in design view and list tblEventsLocations as the source table.

4. Add the asterisk field to the first cell of the Field row.

5. Add the EventDate field in the second cell of the Field row.

6. Type >=11/1/97 in the Criteria cell of the EventDate field and deselect its Show checkbox.

   You will notice that Access automatically puts # characters around the date value, as shown in Figure 5-20.

7. Save the query as qryEvents_OnOrAfter_Nov_1_1997.

8. Run the query.

   Access lists only those records that have an event date greater than or equal to November 1, 1997 in the query result.

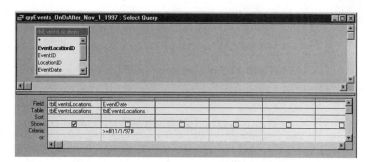

Figure 5-20
Specifying criteria
using a comparison
operator

The SQL Statement for a Filter Query

A query that returns filtered data is based on the **SELECT** SQL statement that contains a **WHERE** clause listing the filter criteria. For example, the Access-generated **SELECT** SQL statement for the query created in the previous example is as follows:

```
SELECT tblEventsLocations.*
FROM tblEventsLocations
WHERE (((tblEventsLocations.EventDate)>=#11/1/97#));
```

Using the Between...And Operator

Whenever you need to select records falling between (or outside) a specified range of values, you use the **Between...And** operator for your criterion using the following syntax:

```
[NOT] Between Value1 And Value2
```

where **Value1** and **Value2** define the end points of the criteria range. The end points **Value1** and **Value2** are also included as part of the criteria range. The **NOT** keyword is optional; if it is present, all records falling outside the specified limit will be selected.

The following example shows how you use this operator to list events occurring during the month of November 1997:

1. Close the query created in the previous example.

2. Open a new query in design view and list tblEventsLocations as the source table.

3. Add the asterisk field to the first cell of the Field row.

4. Add the EventDate field in the second cell of the Field row.

5. Type Between 11/1/97 And 11/30/97 in the Criteria cell of the EventDate field and deselect its Show checkbox.

6. Save the query as qryEvents_Nov_1997.

7. Run the query.

   Access lists all the November 1997 event records in the query result.

8. Select the SQL View option from the View menu.

   Access displays the following SQL statement corresponding to this query:

   ```
   SELECT tblEventsLocations.*
   FROM tblEventsLocations
   WHERE (((tblEventsLocations.EventDate) Between #11/1/97# And ⇐
   #11/30/97#));
   ```

It does not matter which of the two end values you list first in the **Between...And** operator. For example, the criterion **Between 11/30/97 And 11/1/97** would have produced the same result.

Using the IN *Operator*

The **IN** operator allows you to filter records against a list of discrete values. You use this operator when these discrete values cannot be defined as a range through the **Between...And** operator. The syntax of this operator is as follows:

```
[NOT] IN (Value1,Value2,...)
```

The optional **NOT** is used when you want to select records that do not contain any of the values specified in the **IN** expression.

As an example, if you want to list all the event locations in the states of Texas (**StateID=3**), Florida (**StateID=8**), and California (**StateID=11**), you can design a query using the **IN** operator as follows:

1. Close the query created in the previous example.

2. Open a new query in design view and list tblLocations as the source table.

3. Add the asterisk field to the first cell of the Field row.

4. Add the stateID field in the second cell of the Field row.

5. Type IN(3,8,11) in the Criteria cell of the stateID field and deselect its Show checkbox.

6. Save the query as qryLocations_TX_FL_CA.

7. Run the query.

   Access lists all the matching location records in the query result, as shown in Figure 5-21.

LocationID	Location Name	Street	CityID	StateID	CountryID
5	Fair Park		3	3	1
8	Astrodome USA	Outside Main En	6	3	1
13	Astrohall		6	3	1
22	Omni Rosen Hotel	9840 Internationa	13	8	1
23	Department of Linguis		5	3	1
25	Gray Exhibition Cent	300 N.E. 2nd Ave	15	8	1
27	Ft. Worth		17	8	1
28	Anaheim Convention		18	11	1
36	Jet Propulsion Labors	4800 Oak Grove	25	11	1
(AutoNumber)					

8. Select the SQL View option from the View menu.

Access displays the following SQL statement corresponding to this query:

```
SELECT tblLocations.*
FROM tblLocations
WHERE (((tblLocations.StateID) In (3,8,11)));
```

The order in which you list the values with the `IN` operator does not matter.

Finding Records Containing `Null` Values in a Field

All the previous filtering methods do not include records with a `Null` value in the criteria field. If you want to find which records contain a `Null` value for a particular field, you must use the `Is Null` criteria expression against that field. To do the reverse, use the `Is Not Null` expression.

The following example shows how you can list all the sponsor records that do not have any password:

1. Close the query created in the previous example.

2. Open a new query in design view and list `tblSponsors` as the source table.

3. Add the asterisk field to the first cell of the Field row.

4. Add the `Password` field in the second cell of the Field row.

5. Type `Is Null` in the Criteria cell of the `Password` field and deselect its Show checkbox, as shown in Figure 5-22.

6. Save the query as `qrySponsors_NoPassword`.

7. Run the query.

Access lists all the sponsor records without any password in the query result.

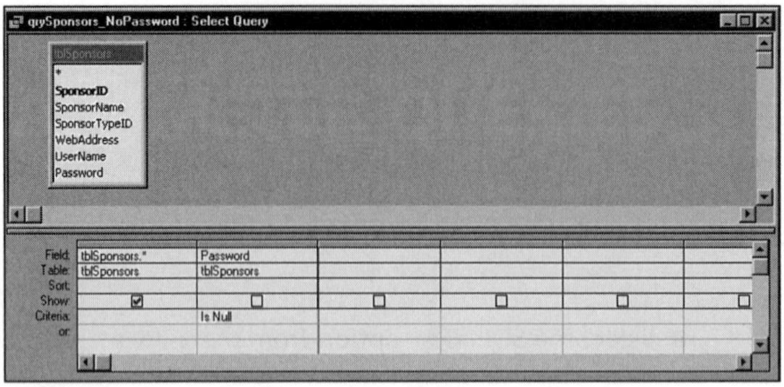

Figure 5-22

Using the Is Null criteria expression in a query

8. Select the SQL View option from the View menu.

Access displays the following SQL statement corresponding to this query:

```
SELECT tblSponsors.*
FROM tblSponsors
WHERE (((tblSponsors.Password) Is Null));
```

You cannot search for **Null** values using the **=Null** or **=""** criteria expressions.

Using Functions in a Criteria Expression

You can use any built-in function when specifying a criteria expression. Lesson 2 described some of those functions in detail. As an example, the following steps show how you can use the **Date()** function to list all the events occurring on or after the current date:

1. Close the query created in the previous example.

2. Open a new query in design view and list tblEventsLocations as the source table.

3. Add the asterisk field to the first cell of the Field row.

4. Add the EventDate field in the second cell of the Field row.

5. Type >=Date() in the Criteria cell of the EventDate field and deselect its Show checkbox.

6. Save the query as qryEventsLocations_CurrentEvents.

7. Run the query to list the current events.

8. Select the SQL View option from the View menu.

Access displays the following SQL statement corresponding to this query:

```
SELECT tblEventsLocations.*
FROM tblEventsLocations
WHERE (((tblEventsLocations.EventDate)>=Date()));
```

Lesson Summary

This lesson presented four important ways of specifying a criterion for filtering data using the Select query. The corresponding SQL statements of these queries contain a **WHERE** clause listing the filter criteria.

A comparison operator is used where you want to filter records by comparing the data of a field against a specific value and only those records where the comparison evaluates to **True** are returned. Whenever you want to filter records falling between (or outside) a specified range, you use the **Between...And** operator. Where you cannot define discrete values for your filter criterion using the **Between...And** operator, the **IN** operator is used. Use of **NOT** before the filter expression reverses the filter criterion. For filtering records having (or not having) a **Null** value in their criteria field, the **Is Null** (or **Is Not Null**) criteria expression is used. You can also use any of the built-in functions to create a criteria expression, as shown in this lesson.

So far, we have applied various criteria against a single field. In the next lesson, we shall move on to multiple field criteria and how to filter records that match a specified pattern. For your reference, the **CALENDAR.MDB** database file containing the queries created in this lesson is provided in the **C:\WEBSITE\HTDOCS\WDBIC\CHAP05\LESSON4\RESULTS** directory.

1. Which operators can you use when you want to filter records that match a particular value?
   a. **IN**
   b. **Between...And**
   c. **<>**
   d. **=**

2. Which of the following is the most appropriate operator for identifying all events occurring outside Canada and the USA?
   a. **Between...And**
   b. **Not In**
   c. **Is Not Null**
   d. **>=** operator

3. What criteria expressions can you use to filter records that have some data in a particular field?

   a. `<> Null` against that field
   b. `Is Not Null` against that field
   c. `<> ""` against that field
   d. `Not Is Null`

4. Which of the following are incorrect statements?

   a. The `WHERE` clause lists the filter criteria in a Select query.
   b. Records with `Null` value in the criteria field are not selected when the criteria expression involves any of the comparison operators.
   c. Interchanging the end values in the `Between'And` operator reverses the list of the filtered data.
   d. You can use only one built-in function to specify a filter criterion.

5. Which of the following are valid filter expressions?

   a. `=> "test"`
   b. `NOT BETWEEN 1 AND "2"`
   c. `IN(#12/1/97#,Date())`
   d. None of the above

EXERCISE 4

Complexity: Easy

1. Design a query named `qrySponsors_Art_and_Culture` that lists all sponsors belonging to either the Art or the Culture category.

Complexity: Moderate

2. Design a query named `qrySponsors_A_to_D` that lists all the sponsors whose names begin with the letter *A*, *B*, *C*, or *D*. Hint: Use the `Between...And` operator.

LESSON 5

PATTERN MATCHING AND MULTIFIELD CRITERIA

When you compare a field against a value using the equal to (=) comparison operator, Access performs an exact match. For example, if you list events containing the word `"Exhibition"` in their name, specifying the criterion `="Exhibition"` against the `EventName` field of the `tblEvents` table will not produce the desired result. Instead you need to use a criterion that tells Access to match the word **"exhibition"** with any part of the `EventName` field for each record and list all those records where this match succeeds. Such pattern-matching criteria are specified using the `Like` operator. In this lesson, we describe the syntax of this `Like` operator and then present some examples illustrating its use. Later, we show how to specify more than one criterion for a field and then extend that concept to multiple fields.

The `Like` **Operator**

A criteria expression involving the `Like` operator is specified as follows:

`Like "searchstring"`

The `searchstring` can be a regular text value or a text pattern created using the following wildcard characters:

- `*` stands for any number of alphanumeric characters.

- `?` represents any single character.

- `#` represents any single digit.

- `[charlist]` stands for any single character in `charlist`.

- `[!charlist]` stands for any character not in `charlist`.

You can use the `Like` operator to find values in a field that match the pattern you specify. Table 5-2 shows what type of patterns you can create.

Table 5-2 Examples of matches that can be performed with the `Like` operator

Kind of Match	Pattern	Matches	Does Not Match
Multiple characters	a*a	aa, aBa, aBBBa	aBC
	ab	abc, AABB, Xab	aZb, bac
Special character	a[*]a	a*a	aaa
Multiple characters	ab*	abcdefg, abc	cab, aab
Single character	a?a	aaa, a3a, aBa	aBBBa
Single digit	a#a	a0a, a1a, a2a	aaa, a10a
Range of characters	[a-z]	f, p, j	2, &
Outside a range	[!a-z]	9, &, %	b, a
Not a digit	[!0-9]	A, a, &, ~	0, 1, 9
Combined	a[!b-m]#	An9, az0, a99	abc, aj0

Searching for a Particular Word in Any Part of a Field

The following steps show how you can design a query that lists the events containing the word *Exhibition* anywhere in their event name:

1. Copy the CALENDAR.MDB file residing in the
   C:\WEBSITE\HTDOCS\WDBIC\CHAP05\SAMPLES directory to the
   C:\WEBSITE\HTDOCS\WDBIC\CHAP05\LESSON5 directory.

2. Open the C:\WEBSITE\HTDOCS\WDBIC\CHAP05\LESSON5\CALENDAR.MDB database file
   in Access.

3. Open a new query in design view and list tblEvents as the source table.

4. Add the asterisk field to the first cell of the Field row.

5. Add the EventName field in the second cell of the Field row.

6. Type Like "*Exhibition*" in the Criteria cell of the EventName field and deselect its Show checkbox, as shown in Figure 5-23.

7. Save the query as qryEvents_Exhibitions.

8. Run the query.

   Access displays the query result as shown in Figure 5-24.

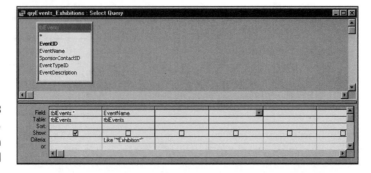

Figure 5-23
Using the Like operator to search any part of a field

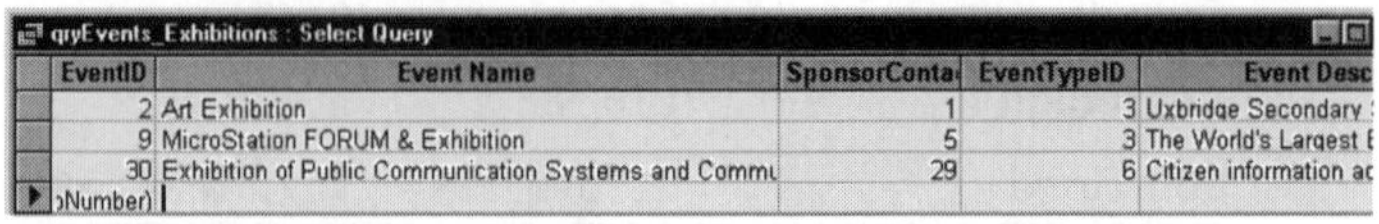

Figure 5-24
Result of the qryEvents_ Exhibitions query

9. Select the SQL View option from the View menu.

Access displays the following SQL statement corresponding to this query:

```
SELECT tblEvents.*
FROM tblEvents
WHERE (((tblEvents.EventName) Like "*Exhibition*"));
```

Searching for Text Beginning with a Specified Set of Characters

This example shows how you can list all the sponsors whose name begins with the letter *A*, *B*, *C*, or *D*.

1. Close the query created in the previous example.

2. Open a new query in design view and list `tblSponsors` as the source table.

3. Add the asterisk field to the first cell of the Field row.

4. Add the `SponsorName` field in the second cell of the Field row.

5. Type `Like "[A-D]*"` in the Criteria cell of the `SponsorName` field and deselect its Show checkbox.

6. Save the query as `qrySponsors_A_to_D`.

7. Run the query.

Access returns the query result as shown in Figure 5-25.

8. Select the SQL View option from the View menu.

Access displays the following SQL statement corresponding to this query:

```
SELECT tblSponsors.*
FROM tblSponsors
WHERE (((tblSponsors.SponsorName) Like "[A-D]*"));
```

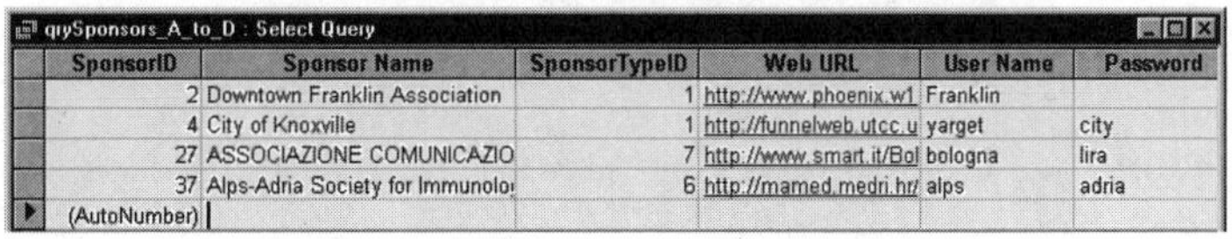

Figure 5-25
Result of the
qrySponsors_A_to_D
query

SponsorID	Sponsor Name	SponsorTypeID	Web URL	User Name	Password
2	Downtown Franklin Association	1	http://www.phoenix.w1	Franklin	
4	City of Knoxville	1	http://funnelweb.utcc.u	yarget	city
27	ASSOCIAZIONE COMUNICAZIO	7	http://www.smart.it/Bol	bologna	lira
37	Alps-Adria Society for Immunolo	6	http://mamed.medri.hr/	alps	adria
(AutoNumber)					

The AND and OR Logical Operators

You can design queries that contain multiple criteria expressions specified against one or more fields. The only additional thing you need to do is join these expressions using the AND or OR logical operators. Use the AND operator between criteria expressions when you want Access to filter records that meet all those criteria. Use the OR operator when you want Access to filter records that meet any of those criteria.

One Field with Two Criteria Expressions Combined Using the OR Operator

The following example shows how you can list the events that end at or before 5 PM or whose end time is not specified:

1. Close the query created in the previous example.

2. Open a new query in design view and list tblEventsLocations as the source table.

3. Add the asterisk field to the first cell of the Field row.

4. Add the EndTime field in the second cell of the Field row.

5. Type <= 5 PM in the Criteria cell of the EventTypeID field and deselect its Show checkbox.

   Access automatically changes this criteria to <= #5:00:00 PM#.

6. Type Is Null in the Or cell of the EndTime field, as shown in Figure 5-26.

6. Save the query as qryEvents_Before5PM_Or_Unknown.

7. Run the query.

   Access returns the query result that lists all events that end at or before 5 PM or whose end time is not available.

Figure 5-26
Creating a query with two criteria on a single field combined using the OR operator

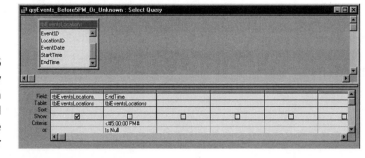

8. Select the SQL View option from the View menu.

Access displays the following SQL statement corresponding to this query:

```
SELECT tblEventsLocations.*
FROM tblEventsLocations
WHERE (((tblEventsLocations.EndTime)<#5:00:00 PM#)) OR ⇐
(((tblEventsLocations.EndTime) Is Null));
```

One Field with Two Criteria Expressions Combined Using the AND Operator

The following example shows how you can list all the events containing both the words *Annual* and *Conference* in their description:

1. Close the query created in the previous example.

2. Open a new query in design view and list tblEvents as the source table.

3. Add the asterisk field to the first cell of the Field row.

4. Add the EventDescription field in the second cell of the Field row.

5. Type Like "*Annual*" in the Criteria cell of this field and deselect its Show checkbox.

6. Add another copy of the EventDescription field in the third cell of the Field row by double-clicking on it in the Field List window.

7. Type Like "*Conference*" in the Criteria cell of this field and deselect its Show checkbox, as shown in Figure 5-27.

8. Save the query as qryEvents_AnnualConferences.

9. Run the query.

Access returns all the event records that have the words *Annual* and *Conference* in their EventDescription field.

Figure 5-27
Creating a query with two criteria on a single field combined using the AND operator

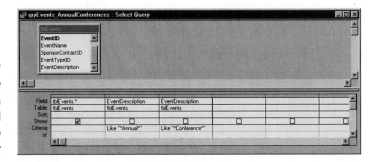

10. Select the SQL View option from the View menu.

Access displays the following SQL statement corresponding to this query:

```
SELECT tblEvents.*
FROM tblEvents
WHERE (((tblEvents.EventDescription) Like "*Annual*") AND ⇐
((tblEvents.EventDescription) Like "*Conference*"));
```

Using AND *and* OR *Operators with Criteria on Multiple Fields*

The following example shows how you can list events occurring in the months of November and December of 1997 that start after 8 AM but either end by 5 PM or do not have a specified end time:

1. Close the query created in the previous example.

2. Open a new query in design view and list tblEventsLocations as the source table.

3. Add the asterisk field to the first cell of the Field row.

4. Add the EventDate field in the second cell of the Field row.

5. Type Between 11/1/97 And 12/31/97 in the Criteria cell of this field and deselect its Show checkbox.

6. Add the StartTime field in the third cell of the Field row and deselect its Show checkbox.

7. Type >=8 AM in the criteria cell of this field.

8. Add the EndTime field in the fourth cell of the Field row and deselect its Show checkbox.

9. Type <=5 PM OR Is Null in the criteria row of this field, as shown in Figure 5-28.

10. Save the query as qryEvents_Nov_Dec_5to8.

11. Run the query.

Access returns the records that meet the all the above criteria in the query result, as shown in Figure 5-29.

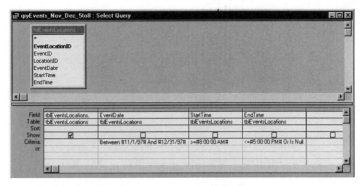

Figure 5-28
Creating a query
with criteria on
multiple fields
combined using the
AND and OR
operators

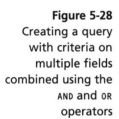

Figure 5-29
Result of the
qryEvents_Nov_Dec_
5to8 query

12. Select the SQL View option from the View menu.

Access displays the following SQL statement corresponding to this query:

```
SELECT tblEventsLocations.*
FROM tblEventsLocations
WHERE (((tblEventsLocations.EventDate) Between #11/1/97# And
#12/31/97#) AND ((tblEventsLocations.StartTime)>=#8:00:00 AM#) AND ⇐
((tblEventsLocations.EndTime)<=#5:00:00 PM# Or
(tblEventsLocations.EndTime) Is Null));
```

Criteria and Field Data Types

As you noticed in the previous example, Access automatically inserts the # characters when you specify the date or time value in your criterion. This is because it is important that the data value you list in your criteria match the data type of the field. Although Access tries to guess the appropriate syntax for the data value based on the type of the field it is being compared against, that guess can sometimes be incorrect. We recommend that you ensure proper syntax to guarantee the accuracy of your query, as described below:

● For a Date field, your date value must be surrounded by a pair of pound (#) characters.

● For a Text field, your text values must be bracketed by either a pair of single quotes (for example, 'Nebraska'), or a pair of double quotes (for example, "Nebraska").

Note that if you have a quote as part of your text data value, then you should replace that quote with two quotes (for example, "5"" Long") before specifying that data value in your criterion. Another way of getting around this situation is to use the other quote character around the data value (for example, '5" Long').

● For a Yes/No field, your criterion value must result in a True (-1) or a False (0) value.

● Numeric values (for example, 11) for a Number, Currency, or AutoNumber field do not need any special surrounding characters.

● You can also specify a criterion against a calculated field. In this case, though, you should try to evaluate the data type of the final field expression and then apply the appropriate syntax for your criterion.

For example, Month([EventDate]) must be set against a numeric criterion, whereas DateAdd("d",1,[EventDate]), which adds one day to each event's EventDate field, must be set against a date criterion.

● Although you cannot sort Memo or Hyperlink fields, Access allows you to specify filter criteria against them.

Lesson Summary

This lesson explained different ways of pattern matching in Access using criteria involving the Like operator. The search string can be a regular text value or a text pattern created using a wildcard character. Two examples illustrating the use of the Like operator to match any part of a field or matching the first character of a field with any specified character were presented.

Queries can also be designed using multiple criteria expressions specified against one or more fields. This lesson explains how to create such queries by joining the expressions using AND or OR (or both) logical operators. The AND operator is used when you want Access to filter records that meet all the criteria, whereas the OR operator filters records that meet any of those criteria. Examples of multiple field criteria using the logical operators for single as well as multiple fields were presented.

Although Access tries to guess the type of the data value that you list in your criteria based on the query field, we recommend that you ensure the proper syntax to guarantee the accuracy of your query, as explained in this lesson. In the next lesson, we shall show another area where determining the data type of the criteria plays a significant role when we discuss Parameter queries, which allow you to add parameters (variables) in their criteria. For your reference, the CALENDAR.MDB database file containing the queries created in this lesson is provided in the C:\WEBSITE\HTDOCS\WDBIC\CHAP05\LESSON5\RESULTS directory.

1. Which of the character strings matches the pattern of the following expression?

   `RA#S`

   a. `RA2S`
   b. `RA-S`
   c. `RA,S`
   d. `RA#S`

2. Which events would be returned if the following criteria is applied against the `EventName` field of the `tblEvents` table?

   `Like "Festival*"`

   a. All events with names ending with the word *Festival*
   b. All events having the word *Festival* listed anywhere in their name
   c. All events with names beginning with the word *Festival*
   d. All of the above

3. What result would be produced if you apply the criteria `Like "[!A-D]*"` to the `SponsorName` field of the `tblSponsors` table?
   a. List of all sponsors
   b. List of all sponsors whose name begins with an exclamation (!) character and is followed by the letter *A*, *B*, *C*, or *D*
   c. List of all sponsors whose name contains only alphanumeric characters
   d. List of all sponsors whose name does not begin with the letter *A*, *B*, *C*, or *D*

4. You wish to filter all event locations that do not have a `Null` value in their `Street` field and whose postal code begins with the letter *L* or the number 2. Which of the following statements are true in this case?
   a. This query applies multiple criteria on one field.
   b. This query requires the use of the `AND` operator.
   c. This query requires the use of the `OR` operator.
   d. This is an example of applying criteria to multiple fields using the logical operators.

5. Which of the following criteria expressions are valid?
   a. `>="$20"` against a `Currency`-type field
   b. `< 216.72` against a long integer sized `number` field
   c. `Year([EventDate])` set against a `Date/Time`-type field
   d. `Like '*"'` set against a `Memo` field

EXERCISE 5

Complexity: Moderate

1. Design a query named **qryEventsLocations_Upto2Hours** that lists all the events that either do not last more than two hours or where the duration information is not available.

Complexity: Moderate

2. Design a query named **qryEvents_MusicOrDance** that lists all the events that either belong to the Music or Dance category or have the words *Music* or *Dance* in either the **EventName** or **EventDescription** field.

LESSON 6

PARAMETER QUERIES

Until now, all the queries we have constructed have been static in nature. Their filtering criteria do not change and the only way to specify different criteria is by either creating a new query or changing the design of an existing query. If you find yourself repeatedly using the same query but with different values in your criteria, you can save time by creating a Parameter query. As the name implies, a *Parameter query* is one where you add parameters (or variables) to your query. By supplying different values to the parameters at the time of executing the query, you can dynamically change the target of the query. Let's create a Parameter query that allows you to filter events based on the event type that you specify at the time you run the query.

Step 1: Create a Regular Criteria Query

First, create an ordinary query containing the company and job tables and add a specific criterion against the company name, as described below:

1. Copy the **CALENDAR.MDB** file residing in the **C:\WEBSITE\HTDOCS\WDBIC\CHAP05\SAMPLES** directory to the **C:\WEBSITE\HTDOCS\WDBIC\CHAP05\LESSON6** directory.

2. Open the **C:\WEBSITE\HTDOCS\WDBIC\CHAP05\LESSON6\CALENDAR.MDB** database file in Access.

3. Open a new query in design view and list **tblEvents** as the source table.

4. Add the asterisk field to the first cell of the Field row.

5. Add the `EventTypeID` field in the second cell of the Field row.

6. Type 3 in the Criteria cell of the `EventTypeID` field and deselect its Show checkbox.

7. Run the query.

   The query returns all the events associated with `EventTypeID` 3.

Step 2: Replace the Criterion Value with a Parameter

1. Return to the query design window by selecting Design View from the View menu.

2. Change the criteria value 3 by substituting the following parameter, as shown in Figure 5-30:

   `[Enter Event Type ID]`

3. Save the query as `qryEvents_SelectedEventTypeID`.

4. Run the query again.

5. Access now prompts you to specify an `EventTypeID`.

6. Enter 3 in the input text box as shown in Figure 5-31 and click on the OK button.

   Access again displays the events of `EventTypeID` 3.

7. Now close the query result window.

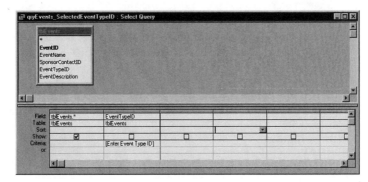

Figure 5-30
Designing a
Parameter query

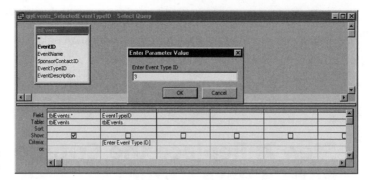

Figure 5-31
Running a
Parameter query

8. Run the `qryEvents_SelectedEventTypeID` query directly from the database container.

   Access again prompts you for the `EventTypeID`.

   This time, specify 5 in the input text box and click on the OK button.

   Access returns the event records for that event type. Dynamic, isn't it?

Syntax of Query Parameters

You place a parameter in a query by enclosing an alphanumeric prompt within square brackets (`[ ]`). The prompt can include spaces, and it becomes the name of the parameter. The parameter name must not match any field name of the underlying tables (that confuses Access!).

Specifying Multiple Parameters

You can add more than one parameter to the same query by specifying different parameter names at different places in the query. When you run the query with multiple parameters, Access prompts for the value of the first parameter by showing its name in the input box, then the second parameter, and so on. After substituting the values for each parameter, Access runs the query. The following example demonstrates a query that uses two parameters to display the events occurring within a specified date range:

1. Close the query opened in the previous example.

2. Open a new query in design view and list `tblEventsLocations` as the source table.

3. Add the asterisk field to the first cell of the Field row.

4. Add the `EventDate` field in the second cell of the Field row and deselect its Show checkbox.

5. Type `Between [Enter Starting Date] And [Enter Ending Date]` in the Criteria cell of this field.

6. Save the query as `qryEvents_Selected_DateRange`.

7. Run the query.

   Access prompts you for the starting date.

8. Enter 11/1/97 and click on the OK button. (Do not put any surrounding # characters.)

   Access now prompts you for the ending date.

9. Enter 11/30/97 and click on the OK button.

   Access displays all the events listed in November '97.

Specifying Multiple Occurrences of the Same Parameter

You can also repeat the same parameter name at different places in a query. When you run the query, Access recognizes that there are multiple occurrences of the same parameter and prompts for its value only once. It then faithfully substitutes that value wherever that parameter name appears in the query.

For example, say you want to design a Parameter query that prompts for a search keyword and finds all events that have that search keyword in either the `EventName` field or the `EventDescription` field. You can use two occurrences of the search parameter in this query as follows:

1. Close the query opened in the previous example.

2. Open a new query in design view and list `tblEvents` as the source table.

3. Add the asterisk field, `EventName` field, and `EventDescription` field to the first, second, and third column of the Field row, respectively.

4. Deselect the Show checkboxes of the `EventName` and the `EventDescription` fields.

5. Type the following criterion in the Criteria cell of the `EventName` field and the Or cell of the `EventDescription` field, as shown in Figure 5-32:

   `Like "*" & [Search For] & "*"`

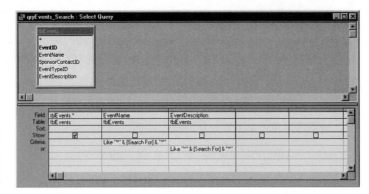

Figure 5-32
Query with two
occurrences of the
same parameter

6. Save the query as qryEvents_Search.

   Run the query.

7. Access prompts for the search word.

8. Enter National and click on the OK button.

   Access returns all the event records with the text string "National" occurring in either the EventName or the EventDescription field. Note that Access asked for the search parameter only once.

Specifying the Data Type of a Query Parameter

As you noticed in the examples, you do not need to add quotes around text value parameters or pound (#) signs around date value parameters. Access tries to guess the data type of a parameter value by its context. However, this guess can go wrong (especially when you apply a "parameterized" criterion against a calculated field) and you can end up with incorrect results or even an error message when running your query. To ensure correct results, you can inform access about the exact data type of each parameter, as explained in the following example:

1. Display the qryEvents_Search in design view.

2. Select Parameters... from the Query menu.

   Access displays the Query Parameters dialog box.

3. Type the exact parameter name [Search For] with its Text data type, as shown in Figure 5-33.

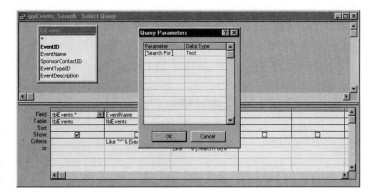

Figure 5-33
Specifying the data
type of a query
parameter

4. Click on the OK button to hide the Query Parameter window.

Select Save As/Export from the File menu and save the query as
`qrySearch_Events_Text`.

5. Run the query and enter 97 for the Search For prompt. Press OK.

Access returns the event records containing the string 97 in either the
`EventName` or the `EventDescription` field.

 Once you specify the parameters in the Query Parameters dialog box, Access always
prompts for a value of those parameters when you run that query, even though you may
eliminate some of the parameters in your query design.

Other Considerations About Parameters

Parameters cannot be used as a substitute for functions or any query options. For example, you cannot specify a parameter for a sort order. You can certainly specify a parameter to act as an argument of a function. You can use the following parameterized criteria against the `EventDate` field of the `tblEventsLocations` table to return all the events occurring within a specified number of days from the current date:

```
>=DateAdd("d",[Number of Days],Date())
```

Once you specify a parameter in the query design, Access always considers that parameter. For example, you cannot make Access ignore the parameter in a parameter-based criterion. If you do not specify a value for a parameter at the query execution time, Access assigns a `Null` value to that parameter and handles the query accordingly. So, if you do not enter any value for the `[Enter Event Type ID]` parameter for the `qryEvents_SelectedEventTypeID` query designed earlier in this lesson (see Figure 5-30), Access returns an empty query result.

If you want a `Null` parameter to mean all records, you can change the criterion for the `EventTypeID` field to

`=[Enter Event Type ID] OR [Enter Event Type ID] Is Null`

Lesson Summary

Parameter queries are the closest you can come to creating general-purpose queries in Access. They prove extremely useful for Web-based database searches and data publishing, as you will see in later chapters of this book. This lesson showed how you can construct a Parameter query by first creating and testing a regular query and then substituting the constant values in its criteria expression with a parameter name. All query parameters must be enclosed within square brackets (`[]`) and you should always list their data types through the Parameter window of that query. If you do not specify any value for a prompted parameter, Access automatically assigns a `Null` value to that parameter. You can use multiple parameters or multiple instances of the same parameter (or both) in your query.

Parameters cannot be used for specifying sort criteria or any other query properties, but they can be listed as function arguments. You can also add parameters when creating calculated fields, although this feature has not been covered in this lesson. You can refer to the online help for more information on this feature.

1. How does a Parameter query allow you to change filter criteria?
   a. By allowing you to assign one or more parameters in your criteria expression
   b. By allowing you to specify the filter criteria before execution
   c. By allowing you to specify the source table when you run the query
   d. All of the above

2. Which of the following are examples of correct parameter prompts assuming the source table has a field named `StateID`?
   a. `([StateID])`
   b. `[(StateID)]`
   c. `[enter StateID]`
   d. `[Enter State ID]`

3. What should be the data type of the parameters in the following criteria expression?

   `>(DateDiff([p1],[p2],Date()))`

    a. **p1** and **p2** should be of **Date/Time** type.

    b. **p1** should be **Text**, and **p2** should be **Date/Time** type.

    c. **p1** should be **Date/Time**, and **p2** should be **Text** type.

    d. **p1** and **p2** should be of **Text** type.

4. Identify the incorrect statements from the following.

    a. You can define a parameter to sort events by the event type ID in the **tblEvents** table of the, calendar database.

    b. Parameters once assigned cannot be changed.

    c. Parameters with **Null** values cannot be handled by Access.

    d. Parameters can be used as function arguments.

5. What is the response of running an Access query where the same parameter is applied to the criterion cell of two fields?

    a. Access displays an error message.

    b. Access displays a null result.

    c. Access asks for the value of the parameter only once and uses that value for the criterion of both fields.

    d. Access asks for the value of the parameter twice and uses the first value for the criterion of the first field and the second value for the criterion of the second field.

Complexity: Easy

1. Design a query named **qrySponsors_Selected** that lists all the sponsors whose name begins with the letter specified when you run the query.

Complexity: Moderate

2. Design a query named **qryEventsLocations_SelectedDuration** that lists all events less than or equal to a specified duration (in minutes).

CHAPTER SUMMARY

This chapter described how to design simple queries in Access using its user-friendly and visual query design interface. Each query has an SQL statement associated with it that is automatically constructed by Access from the visual query definition. The JET engine uses this SQL statement to process a query. A query used to filter data involves three main components:

● The data source

● The fields to display

● The sort and search criteria

Although most of these components must be specified when you design the query, you have some flexibility in changing the scope of the criteria through Parameter queries. Here is a recap of the salient points covered in this chapter:

- You can design a Select query to search, sort, group, or analyze data.

- The asterisk field is a special query field that stands for "all fields of a table."

- You specify which field to display by listing that field in the Field row of the query design interface and selecting its Show checkbox.

- You can specify the Ascending or Descending sort option on any field that is not a Memo, Hyperlink, or OLE type.

- When you save a query, Access saves only the query design, not the query result.

- You define a query criteria through the Criteria and Or rows of the query design interface.

- You can create calculated fields through a query using the syntax
  FieldName: FieldExpression.

- The main difference between the + and the & operators is how they act when they encounter a Null value as an operand. The + operator returns Null, whereas the & operator returns the other operand.

- You can use any built-in function in creating a calculated field or a criteria expression.

- You can specify a sort order on one or more fields. When sorting on multiple fields, the leftmost sort field in the field row becomes the primary sort field.

- To increase sort or search performance, index the field(s) that you sort or search on. You cannot index a calculated field.

- If you create an ascending sort on a field containing Null values, the records with Null values appear first.

- Use comparison operators when you want to filter records by comparing a field data against a particular value.

- Use the Between...And operator when you want to list records by comparing a field against a range of two values.

- Use the IN operator when you want to list records by comparing a field against a set of discrete values.

- Use the Is Null criteria expression to search for records that do not contain any data in a particular field.

- Use the Like operator when you want to query records by comparing a field against a pattern.

- You can specify multiple criteria on multiple fields by combining each criterion with the AND and OR logical operators.

- When specifying a value in a criteria expression, ensure that text values are surrounded by either single or double quotes and date values are surrounded by pound (#) characters.

- Create a Parameter query when you have to use different values in the query criteria.

- The parameter name must be enclosed within square brackets and cannot be same as the name of an existing table field.

- It is good to specify the data type of each parameter explicitly.

CHAPTER 6

COMBINING TABLES AND GROUPING DATA: JOINS AND TOTAL QUERIES

This chapter talks about multiple-table queries, table joins, and the use of aggregate functions to group data and calculate counts and totals. It also covers query performance issues and some advanced data analysis techniques that use Union queries, Nested queries, and subqueries. In particular, you will learn about the following:

- The difference between inner and outer table joins
- How to create multitable queries using inner and outer joins
- The application of sort and filter criteria in multitable queries
- How to create Subtract queries
- Grouping and aggregating data using Total queries.
- How to apply criteria in Total queries

● How to create Crosstab queries

● The functionality of subqueries and Union queries

● Tips for optimizing query performance

LESSON 1

INNER AND OUTER JOINS

The normalization technique that you applied to the calendar database in Chapter 4, "Constructing a Relational Database: The Microsoft Access Way," disintegrated large tables into several small and related tables to achieve the optimum database structure for modeling the real-world scenario. However, this normalization approach proves advantageous only if you have a way of combining the related tables and seeing all the information together. Fortunately, most relational database management systems (RDBMSs) do provide a way through a query technique known as *table joins*. This lesson explains this concept and describes how to construct joins using Access.

What Is a Table Join?

A table join is a link between a field in one table and a field of the same data type in another table, telling how data is related. Access supports two types of table joins:

● Inner join

● Outer join

In an *inner join*, the records from two tables are combined and added to the output only if a record in the first table matches a record in the second table. In an *outer join*, which must be directed from one table (source) to the other (destination), all records from the source are included in the output even if some of the records do not match the records of the destination table. Furthermore, records from the destination table are combined with the source table only when there are matching values in the joined fields.

To combine records from two or more tables in Access using either inner or outer joins, create a query with those tables defined as its record source. The rest of this lesson provides examples demonstrating the steps involved in creating these multitable queries.

Creating an Inner Join Between Two Tables in Access

The following example shows how you can list the sponsors and their sponsor types by creating an inner join between the `tblSponsors` and `tblSponsors_Types_lkp` tables:

1. Copy the `CALENDAR.MDB` file residing in the
   `C:\WEBSITE\HTDOCS\WDBIC\CHAP05\SAMPLES` directory to the
   `C:\WEBSITE\HTDOCS\WDBIC\CHAP06\LESSON1` directory.

2. Open the `C:\WEBSITE\HTDOCS\WDBIC\CHAP06\LESSON1\CALENDAR.MDB` database file in Access.

3. Select the Queries tab of the database container and press the New button to create a new query.

4. Select the Design View option.

   Access displays the query design interface and presents you with the table list to select the data source for the query.

5. Highlight `tblSponsors` from this list and then click on the Add button.

   Access places the `tblSponsors` table in the query design window.

6. Now highlight `tblSponsorsTypes_lkp` from this list and press the Add button again. Then click on the Close button to hide the table list.

   Access places the `tblSponsorsTypes_lkp` table next to the `tblSponsors` table in the query design window and displays a line connecting these two tables, as shown in Figure 6-1. This line, which Access automatically adds due to the one-to-many relationship defined between these two tables in Chapter 4 reflects the inner join between the tables.

7. Double-click on the asterisk field of the `tblSponsors` table.

   Access adds the asterisk field to the first cell of the Field row and lists `tblSponsors` in the first cell of the Table row.

8. Now double-click on the `Description` field of the `tblSponsorsTypes_lkp` table.

   Access adds the `Description` field to second cell of the Field row and lists `tblSponsorsTypes_lkp` in the second cell of the Table row, as shown in Figure 6-2.

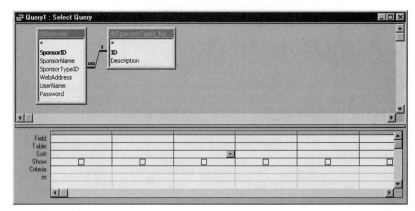

Figure 6-1
Adding two tables
to a query

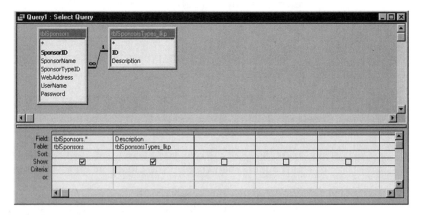

Figure 6-2
Adding fields from
the two tables

9. Save the query as `qrySponsors_withSponsorTypeDescription`.

10. Run the query.

11. Access displays the list of sponsors along with their description in the query result, as shown in Figure 6-3.

12. Select the SQL View option from the Query menu.

Access displays the following SELECT SQL statement it constructed for this query:

```
SELECT tblSponsors.*, tblSponsorsTypes_lkp.Description
FROM tblSponsorsTypes_lkp INNER JOIN tblSponsors ON
tblSponsorsTypes_lkp.ID = tblSponsors.SponsorTypeID;
```

As you can see, the SQL statement for a two-table inner join query includes additional keywords (**INNER JOIN** and **ON**) and the syntax is more complex than a single-table

SponsorID	Sponsor Name	SponsorTypeID	Web URL	User Name	Password	Sponsor Type
1	The Corporation of the T	1	http://www.uxbridge.	uxbridge	fsdgg	Arts
2	Downtown Franklin Asso	1	http://www.phoenix.w	Franklin		Arts
4	City of Knoxville	1	http://funnelweb.utcc	yarget	city	Arts
16	Rolls Royce	2	http://www.aecc.wint	petroleum	deepseas	Business
17	Grampian Corporation	2	http://www.aecc.wint	Quality	benchmark	Business
25	NetTalk Newbie Universi	3	http://www.nettalklive	webninja	nettalk	Information Technology
15	USA INTERNATIONAL D	4	http://www.Instar.cor	dancers	ballet	Cultural
24	Sandman Inn at Penticto	4	http://www.nextlevel.	byron	play	Cultural
12	International Sociologica	5	http://www.arch.vt.ed	urban	housing	Education
21	University of Michigan, A	5	http://www.dla.utexa:	tintin	comic	Education
22	The Department of Math	5	http://icg.fas.harvard	teachers	teach	Education
23	Miami-Dade Community	5	http://www.mdcc.edu	dades	books	Education
30	Iowa State University	5	http://www.public.ias	students	professors	Education
37	Alps-Adria Society for In	6	http://mamed.medri.l	alps	adria	Foundation/Trust
5	MicroStation Inc.	7	http://www.bentley.c	microlab	cad	Professional
6	National Association of I	7	http://www.nahb.corr	homebuilde	nahb	Professional

Record: 12 of 30

Figure 6-3
Result of the
qrySponsors_with
SponsorType
Description query

Select query. Fortunately, Access hides all this complexity from you through its powerful and intuitive query design interface.

Creating a Multitable Query Using Inner Joins

The previous example showed how to create a query that joins two tables. You can easily extend this concept to join multiple tables. The following example shows how you can link tblLocations, tblLocationsCities, tblLocationsStates_lkp, and tblLocationsCountries_lkp to display all the location records with their associated city, state, and country information:

1. Close the query created in the previous example.

2. Open a new query in design view and list tblLocations, tblLocationsCities_lkp, tblLocationsStates_lkp, and tblLocationsCountries_lkp as the source tables in the query design window.

   Access automatically creates an inner join between tblLocations and the three lookup tables based on the predefined relationships.

3. Expand the query design window and elongate the tblLocations table to display all the link fields of this table, as shown in Figure 6-4.

   Notice from this figure that Access has also created a join between the tblLocationsCities_lkp and the tblLocationsStates_lkp tables on their ID fields. This is because Access automatically tries to guess how different tables may be related. In this case, however, the join between the city and the state lookup tables is erroneous because these tables are not related. So this join has to be removed, which can be done by selecting the line representing this join with your mouse and then pressing DEL. But because this line is too close to the other join line, you may not be able to select your

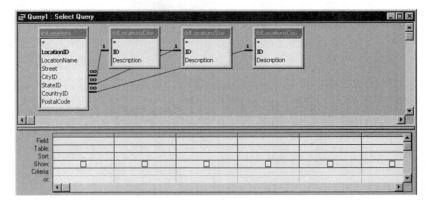

Figure 6-4
Access guessing a
table join not
based on a
predefined
relationship

target. To make the selection process easier, you can first separate these two lines by moving one of the two lookup tables, as described next.

4. Move the `tblLocationsStates_Lkp` table downward by dragging it with your mouse.

   Access automatically moves the associated join lines, as shown in Figure 6-5.

5. Click anywhere on the join line linking the `tblLocationsCities_Lkp` and the `tblLocationsStates_Lkp` tables.

   Access highlights that join line by making it thicker.

6. Press ⌁DEL⌁.

   Access removes that join line.

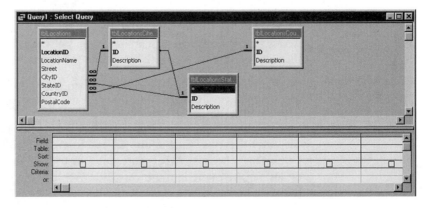

Figure 6-5
Moving a table and
its associated join
lines

As an alternative to removing undesirable join lines, you can tell Access not to guess and create automatic table joins that are not based on predefined relationships. Select Options from the Tools menu, click on the Tables/Queries tab, and uncheck the Enable AutoJoin checkbox.

7. Now that the proper joins are in place, add the asterisk field from the tblLocations table and the Description fields from the three lookup tables in the Field row, as shown in Figure 6-6.

8. Save the query as qryLocations_Cities_States_Countries.

9. Run the query.

Access displays the location records with their respective cities, states, and countries, as shown in Figure 6-7.

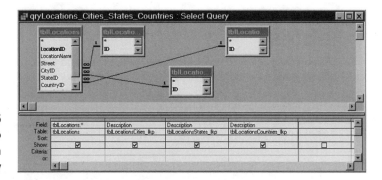

Figure 6-6
Adding fields to display in a multitable query

Figure 6-7
Result of the qryLocations_Cities _States_Countries query

10. Look at the record count shown in the navigation bar of this query result.

    It indicates that the query result contains only 30 records.

11. Now close this query and open the tblLocations table in datasheet view.

    Access displays a record count of 32 in this table's navigation bar, as shown in Figure 6-8.

So why did the query return 30 records instead of 32? The answer to this discrepancy originates from the fact that two location records (one with **LocationID 30** is visible in Figure 6-8) contain a **Null** value in the **StateID** field. Because this field is linked to the **tblLocationsStates_lkp** table with an inner join, these two records are not included in the result. Remember that the inner join produces only records where the linking fields match in *both* the tables. If you want to include these two records in your query result, you need to link the **tblLocations** and **tblLocationStates_lkp** tables with an outer join, as explained next.

Creating an Outer Join Between Two Tables

To create an outer join between **tblLocations** and **tblLocationsStates_lkp**, you need to modify the previous query as follows:

1. Close the tblLocations table.

2. Open the qryLocations_Cities_States_Countries query in design view.

	LocationID	Location Name	Street	CityID	StateID	CountryID	PostalCode
▶	1	Uxbridge Music Hall	16 Main Stre	1	1	2	L9P 1T1
	2	Uxbridge Secondary :	Third Avenue	1	1	2	
	3	Trinity United Church		1	1	2	
	4	Historic Franklin		2	2	1	
	5	Fair Park		3	3	1	
	6	Renaissance Austin H		4	2	1	
	8	Astrodome USA	Outside Mai	6	3	1	
	13	Astrohall		6	3	1	
	14	Radisson Hotell		7	4	1	24061-0205
	15	Toronto Airport Hilton	Airport Road	8	1	2	L4V 1N1
	16	Donaldson Industrial ,		9	5	1	
	17	Royal Ballet Centre		10	6	1	
	18	Aberdeen Exhibition {	Bridge of Dc	11	7	3	AB23 8BL
	21	SCHOOL OF TECHN		12	4	1	23504
	22	Omni Rosen Hotel	9840 Interna	13	8	1	
	23	Department of Linguis		5	3	1	
	24	Department of Mather		14	9	4	
	25	Gray Exhibition Centr	300 N.E. 2n	15	8	1	
	26	Cleland Theatre	Community	16	10	1	
	27	Ft. Worth		17	8	1	
	28	Anaheim Convention		18	11	1	
	29	Srl Via Tagliapietre	8/B - 40123	19	12	5	
	30	Queen Elizabeth II Cc	Westminste	20		3	
	31	Ritz-Carlton Dearborn		21	13	1	

Record: ◄ ◄   1 ► ►I ►* of 32

Figure 6-8

The tblLocations table in datasheet view

3. Double-click on the line representing the inner join between `tblLocations` and `tblLocationsStates_lkp`.

   Access displays the Join Properties dialog box, as shown in Figure 6-9.

4. Select the option (number 3) that says, `Include ALL records from 'tblLocations' and only those records from 'tblLocationsStates_lkp' where the joined fields are equal`, and then click on the OK button.

   Access now displays the link as a directed line pointing from the `tblLocations` table to the `tblLocationsStates_lkp` table, as shown in Figure 6-10.

The first option in the join properties recreates the inner join, whereas the second option creates an outer join in the other direction.

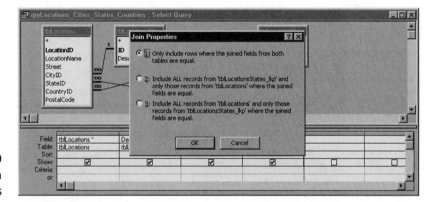

Figure 6-9
Displaying the join properties

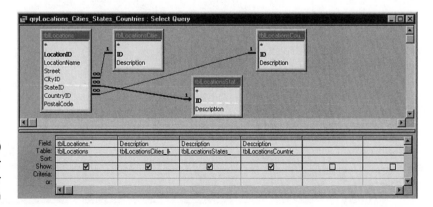

Figure 6-10
Changing an inner join to an outer join

5. Save the query as qryLocations_Cities_States_Countries_2.

6. Run the query.

Access displays all 32 records in the query result, as shown in Figure 6-11. Note that the State field of the record with LocationID 30 appears as Null.

7. Select the SQL View from the Query menu.

Access displays the following SQL statement corresponding to this query:

```
SELECT tblLocations.*, tblLocationsCities_lkp.Description,⇐
tblLocationsStates_lkp.Description,⇐
tblLocationsCountries_lkp.Description
FROM tblLocationsStates_lkp RIGHT JOIN (tblLocationsCountries_lkp⇐
INNER JOIN (tblLocationsCities_lkp INNER JOIN tblLocations ON⇐
tblLocationsCities_lkp.ID = tblLocations.CityID) ON⇐
tblLocationsCountries_lkp.ID = tblLocations.CountryID) ON⇐
tblLocationsStates_lkp.ID = tblLocations.StateID;
```

Because CityID is not a required field (just like the StateID field), it is a good idea to link the tblLocations and the tblLocationsCities_lkp tables with an outer join.

Multitable Editing

As with the single-table queries, Access allows you to edit the query result of a multi-table query. Changes are updated directly to the underlying tables. Try modifying the

Figure 6-11
Result of the
qryLocations_Cities
_States_Countries_2
query

LocationID	Location Name	Street	CityID	StateID	CountryID	Postal	City	State	Country
1	Uxbridge Music H:	16 Main S	1	1	2	L9P 1T	Uxbridge	Ontario	Canada
2	Uxbridge Seconda	Third Aver	1	1	2		Uxbridge	Ontario	Canada
3	Trinity United Chur		1	1	2		Uxbridge	Ontario	Canada
4	Historic Franklin		2	2	1		Franklin	Tennesse	USA
5	Fair Park		3	3	1		Dallas	Texas	USA
6	Renaissance Aust		4	2	1		Knoxville	Tennesse	USA
8	Astrodome USA	Outside N	6	3	1		Houston	Texas	USA
13	Astrohall		6	3	1		Houston	Texas	USA
14	Radisson Hotell		7	4	1	24061-l	Alexandria	Virginia	USA
15	Toronto Airport Hilt	Airport Ro	8	1	2	L4V 1N	Mississauga	Ontario	Canada
16	Donaldson Industri		9	5	1		Greenville	South Car	USA
17	Royal Ballet Centr		10	6	1		Jackson	Mississipp	USA
18	Aberdeen Exhibitic	Bridge of [	11	7	3	AB23 8	Aberdeen	Scotland	UK
21	SCHOOL OF TEC		12	4	1	23504	Norfolk	Virginia	USA
22	Omni Rosen Hotel	9840 Inter	13	8	1		Orlando	Florida	USA
23	Department of Ling		5	3	1		Austin	Texas	USA
24	Department of Mat		14	9	4		Samos	Samos	Greece
25	Gray Exhibition Ce	300 N.E. 2	15	8	1		Miami	Florida	USA
26	Cleland Theatre	Communit	16	10	1		Penticton	Missouri	USA
27	Ft. Worth		17	8	1		Ft. Worth	Florida	USA
28	Anaheim Conventic		18	11	1		Anaheim	California	USA
29	Srl Via Tagliapietre	8/B - 4012	19	12	5		Bologna	Bologna	Italy
30	Queen Elizabeth II	Westmins	20		3		London		UK
31	Ritz-Carlton Dearb		21	13	1		Dearborn	Michigan	USA

Record: 1 of 32

city of one of the location records in the result of your query and saving that record. You will see that this change is immediately reflected in the `City` field of all other locations in this city. If you open the `tblLocationsCities_lkp` table, you will see the changed city name.

Things to Consider When Creating Joins

When adding multiple tables to a query, consider the following:

- If you delete a join line by accident or want to link two tables on fields that are different from the ones specified in the predefined relationship, you can explicitly create a join by dragging the field from the first table to the linking field of the second table. Just make sure that the joined fields have compatible data types (for example, `Number` type is compatible with `Currency` type but not with `Text` type). Lesson 5 shows an example of manually creating a join.

- You can also create multiple-field joins (two or more fields of one table linked to the same number and type of fields of the second table). Just drag each linking field of the first table onto the associated field of the second table.

- If a query contains two tables with no join lines, then the result will be a *Cartesian product* of the two tables—every record of the first table will be linked with all records of the second table.

Lesson Summary

This lesson explained how information from various related tables can be viewed together using table joins, which are links between fields of one table and fields of another table. These joins indicate how data is related. You also learned in this lesson that Access supports two types of joins, inner joins and outer joins.

Two tables connected by an inner join combine and add to the output any record from the first table, which matches a record in the second table. On the other hand, in an outer join, which must be directed from one table (source) to the other (destination), all records from the source table are included in the output even if some of these records do not match records of the destination table. However, only those records from the source table, which have matching values in the joined fields, are combined with records from the destination table.

In Access, you create these joins by adding the related tables to the query design window and ensuring that appropriate join lines exist between these tables. Normally, Access automatically adds a join line based on the predefined relationship. Sometimes, it also adds extra join lines that may be undesirable and you must delete them before running the query. Otherwise, you may get incorrect results.

Like single-table queries, you can also add sort and filter criteria in multiple-table queries using fields from any of the source tables. The next lesson gives several examples explaining how this is done.

For your reference, the **CALENDAR.MDB** database file resulting from this lesson is provided in the **C:\WEBSITE\HTDOCS\WDBIC\CHAP06\LESSON1\RESULTS** directory.

1. What is a join?
    a. It is a link between two tables.
    b. It is a link between fields of one table and compatible fields of another table.
    c. It is a link between fields of multiple tables.
    d. All of the above.

2. What type of join can you create between the **tblEvents** and **tblEventsTypes_lkp** tables to list all the event records along with their type descriptions?
    a. Inner join between the **EventTypeID** field of **tblEvents** and the **ID** field of **tblEventsTypes_lkp**
    b. Outer join directed from the **EventTypeID** field of **tblEvents** to the **ID** field of **tblEventsTypes_lkp**
    c. Outer join directed from the **ID** field of **tblEventsTypes_lkp** to the **EventTypeID** of **tblEvents**
    d. Any of the above

3. What happens when two or more tables from a database are placed in the query design window?
    a. Access joins these tables based on their predefined relationships.
    b. Access joins these tables after guessing the relationships between them (unless this feature is disabled).
    c. Access does not automatically connect the tables.
    d. Access connects all the tables containing a field named **ID**.

4. If **tblLocations** has 20 records and **tblEventsLocations** has 30 records and you link them using an inner join in a query and display fields from both tables, how many records will that query produce?
    a. 20
    b. 30
    c. 50
    d. 600

5. What happens when you try to edit the result of a multiple-table query?
    a. Access does not permit editing of the query result.
    b. Changes in the query result are not reflected elsewhere.

c. These changes are lost when you save the query.

d. Changes in the query result are directly updated in the underlying query tables.

Complexity: Easy

1. Design a query named `qryEvents_withEventTypeDescription` that lists all the events with their event types.

Complexity: Moderate

2. Create a query named `qryLocations_Cities_States_Countries_3` that connects the city, state, and country tables with the location table using outer joins and displays the location ID, location name, street, city, state, country, and postal code of all the records.

SORTING AND FILTERING IN MULTIPLE TABLE QUERIES

The process of specifying sort and filter criteria in multiple-table queries is similar to the way you specify these criteria in single-table queries. The only extra advantage is that you can apply these criteria on fields from any of the source tables and limit records of one table based on the related data in the other tables. Because we covered the role of query criteria in detail in Chapter 4, here we will present several examples highlighting the sorting filtering process in multiple-table queries.

Sorting Events by Their Event Type Description

The following steps show how you can list events, their descriptions, and the names of their contacts and sponsors, sorted by the event type:

1. Copy the `CALENDAR.MDB` file residing in the `C:\WEBSITE\HTDOCS\WDBIC\CHAP05\SAMPLES` directory to the `C:\WEBSITE\HTDOCS\WDBIC\CHAP06\LESSON2` directory.

2. Open the `C:\WEBSITE\HTDOCS\WDBIC\CHAP06\LESSON2\CALENDAR.MDB` database file in Access.

3. Create a new query and select `tblSponsors`, `tblSponsorsContacts`, `tblEvents`, and `tblEventsTypes_Lkp` as the data sources.

   Access automatically creates inner joins between these tables based on their predefined relationships.

4. Add the following fields to the Field row:

   ```
   SponsorName from tblSponsors
   ContactName from tblSponsorsContacts
   EventName from tblEvents
   EventDescription from tblEvents
   Description from tblEventsTypes_Lkp
   ```

5. Select Ascending in the Sort cell of the `Description` field, as shown in Figure 6-12.

6. Save the query as `qryEvents_SortedByEventTypesDescriptions`.

7. Run the query.

   Figure 6-13 shows the query result.

8. Select the SQL View from the View menu.

   Access displays the following SQL statement corresponding to this query:

   ```
   SELECT tblSponsors.SponsorName, tblSponsorsContacts.ContactName,⇐
   tblEvents.EventName, tblEvents.EventDescription,⇐
   tblEventsTypes_Lkp.Description
   FROM tblEventsTypes_Lkp INNER JOIN ((tblSponsors INNER JOIN⇐
   tblSponsorsContacts ON tblSponsors.SponsorID =⇐
   tblSponsorsContacts.SponsorID) INNER JOIN tblEvents ON⇐
   tblSponsorsContacts.SponsorContactID = tblEvents.SponsorContactID) ON⇐
   tblEventsTypes_Lkp.ID = tblEvents.EventTypeID
   ORDER BY tblEventsTypes_Lkp.Description;
   ```

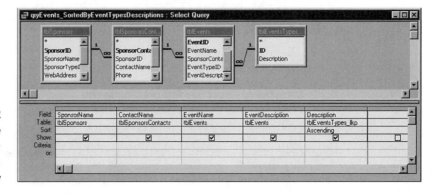

Figure 6-12
Design of the
`qryEvents_SortedBy`
`EventTypes`
`Descriptions` query

Sponsor Name	Contact Name	Event Name	Event Description	Event Type
The Corporation of the Tc	Administrative Officer	Art Exhibition	Uxbridge Secondary School A	Art Exhibition
The Five Hundred, Inc.	Albert Pinto	ARTFEST	ARTFEST is a Memorial Day v	Art Exhibition
MicroStation Inc.	James Moore	MicroStation FORUM & E	The World's Largest Education	Art Exhibition
The University of Texas a	Jesus T. Garcia	Texas Science Olympiad	The Science Olympiad was cr	Competetion
Illinois Science Olympiac	Brian Niece	Illinois Science Olympiad	The Illinois Science Olympiad	Competetion
NASA	JPL Space Exploration Pc	The Jet Propulsion Labora	This annual contest is about tc	Competetion
Downtown Franklin Assc	Festivals Office	The 1997 Main Street Fes	The Fourteenth Annual Main S	Dance
USA INTERNATIONAL C	Mary Joe	USA International Ballet C	One of the world's most presti	Dance
Vanderbilt University	Professor Ron Robertson	Middle Tennessee Scienc	The Middle Tennessee Scienc	Forum and exhibition
National Association of H	Convention Division Staff	Review of Existing Plans	Go beyond the seminars to ha	Forum and exhibition
National Association of H	Betty Norman	The Construction Industry	This three hour course helps p	Forum and exhibition
Rolls Royce	Peter Smith	10th Annual Offshore Drill	The latest challenges in well tc	Forum and exhibition
Western Electricals Inc.	Director	Electric West-98	Don't miss out on your best op	Forum and exhibition
ASSOCIAZIONE COMUI	Confrence Secretary	Exhibition of Public Comn	Citizen information activities -	Forum and exhibition
Iowa State University	Sean C. Murphy	The Iowa State Science a	The Iowa State Science and T	Forum and exhibition
The Corporation of the Tc	Administrative Officer	Music Night	The Symphony Winds compris	Musical
The Corporation of the Tc	Administrative Officer	Organ Recitals		Musical
City of Knoxville	Major	International Jubilee	Join the fun as the Sixth Annu	Musical
Greenville Children's Hos	Aloft Staff	Memorial Day Weekend E	Make Plans now to attend Fre	Sports
NetTalk Newbie Universit	Cool James	Net Talk Class - The Inter	You may now register "Online"	Talk Show
Sandman Inn at Penticto	Shirley Campbell	1997 Okanagan Zone Dra	Hello! Penticton's Progress Th	Theatre
The Corporation of the Tc	Administrative Officer	Film Day	Film buffs will be interested in	Theatre
National Association of H	Betty Norman	Troll Stories	This is an original play, written	Theatre
Alps-Adria Society for Im	Daniel Rukavina	4th International Meeting		Workshops, Conferen
National Institute of Envir	Claudia Thompson	A Decade of Improving He	Environmental exposures to ha	Workshops, Conferen
National Association of H	Donald Woodhead	AIA Plan Review Workshc	In this workshop, architects ar	Workshops, Conferen

Record: 18 of 37

Details about this event

Figure 6-13
Result of the `qryEvents_SortedByEventTypesDescriptions` query

Listing Information About Events of a Particular Type

The following steps show how you can list the location names and dates of all the musical events:

1. Close the query constructed in the previous example.

2. Create a new query and select `tblEventsTypes_lkp`, `tblEvents`, `tblEventsLocations`, and `tblLocations` as the data sources.

   Access automatically creates inner joins between these tables based on their predefined relationships.

3. Add the following fields to the Field row:

```
Description from tblEventsTypes_lkp
EventName from tblEvents
EventDescription from tblEvents
EventDate from tblEventsLocations
StartTime from tblEventsLocations
EndTime from tblEventsLocations
LocationName from tblLocations
```

4. Type ="Musical" in the Criteria cell of the Description field (of the tblEventsTypes_lkp table) as shown in Figure 6-14. (Note that Access automatically hides the = sign.)

5. Save the query as qryEvents_Info_Musical.

6. Run the query.

Figure 6-15 shows the query result.

7. Select the SQL View option from the View menu.

Access displays the following SQL statement corresponding to this query:

```
SELECT tblEventsTypes_lkp.Description, tblEvents.EventName,
tblEvents.EventDescription, tblEventsLocations.EventDate,
tblEventsLocations.StartTime, tblEventsLocations.EndTime,
tblLocations.LocationName
FROM tblLocations INNER JOIN ((tblEventsTypes_lkp INNER JOIN
tblEvents ON tblEventsTypes_lkp.ID = tblEvents.EventTypeID) INNER
JOIN tblEventsLocations ON tblEvents.EventID =
tblEventsLocations.EventID) ON tblLocations.LocationID =
tblEventsLocations.LocationID
WHERE (((tblEventsTypes_lkp.Description)="Musical"));
```

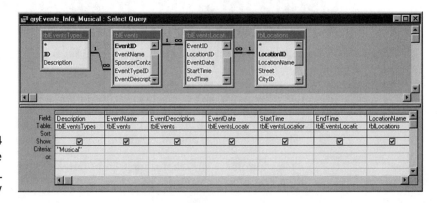

Figure 6-14
Design of the
qryEvents_Info_
Musical query

Figure 6-15
Result of the
`qryEvents_Info_`
`Musical` query

Event Type	Event Name	Event Description	Event Date	Start Time	End Time	Location Name
Musical	Music Night	The Symphony Winds com	9/20/97	8:00:00 PM		Uxbridge Music Hall
Musical	Organ Recitals		9/26/97	12:00:00 PM	1:30:00 PM	Uxbridge Music Hall
Musical	International Jubilee	Join the fun as the Sixth A	7/23/97	9:00:00 AM	7:00:00 PM	Fair Park
Musical	International Jubilee	Join the fun as the Sixth A	7/24/97	9:00:00 AM	7:00:00 PM	Fair Park

qryEvents_Info_Musical : Select Query

Listing Information About Events Matching a Specified Pattern Occurring Within a Specified Date Range

The following steps show how you can convert the query of the previous example to a multitable `Parameter` query that lists all the events falling within a given date range and whose names, descriptions, or types match a specified pattern:

1. Display the `qryEvents_Info_Musical` query in design view.

2. List the `Like "*" & [Find?] & "*"` criteria expression against the `Description`, `EventName`, and `EventDescription` fields and the `Between [StartDate?] And [EndDate?]` criteria expression against the `EventDate` field, as shown in Figure 6-16.

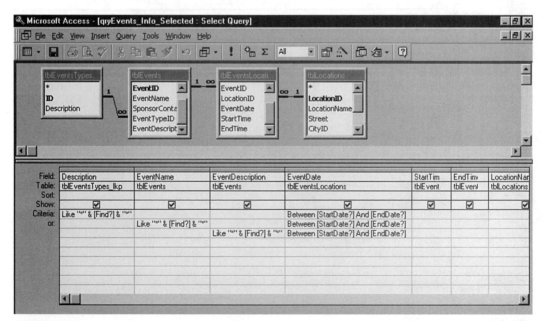

Figure 6-16
Design of the `qryEvents_Info_Selected` query

To understand how this query criteria works, think of it as follows:

```
(Event type containing the specified text AND EventDate Between⇐
specified date range) OR
(Event name containing the specified text AND EventDate Between⇐
specified date range) OR
(Event description containing the specified text AND EventDate⇐
Between specified date range)
```

3. Select Parameters... from the Query menu and specify the data types of the three parameters, as shown in Figure 6-17.

4. Save the query as qryEvents_Info_Selected.

5. Run the query.

   Access asks for the value of the [Find?] parameter.

6. Type Art and press the OK button.

   Access asks for the value of the [StartDate?] parameter.

7. Type Jan 1, 1997 and press the OK button.

   Access asks for the value of the [EndDate?] parameter.

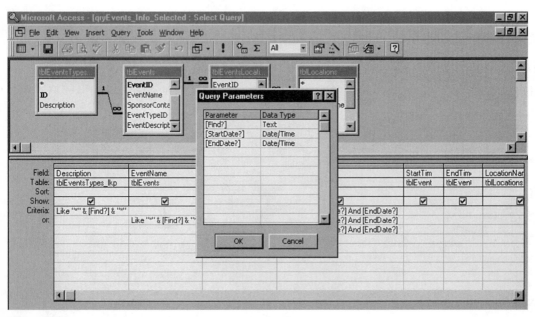

Figure 6-17
Specifying the data types of the query parameters

8. Type `Dec 31, 1997` and press the OK button.

   Access returns all the art-related events occurring in 1997 in the query result, as shown in Figure 6-18.

9. Select the SQL View option from the View menu.

   Access displays the following SQL statement corresponding to this query:

```
PARAMETERS [Find?] Text, [StartDate?] DateTime, [EndDate?] DateTime;
SELECT tblEventsTypes_lkp.Description, tblEvents.EventName,⇐
tblEvents.EventDescription, tblEventsLocations.EventDate,⇐
tblEventsLocations.StartTime, tblEventsLocations.EndTime,⇐
tblLocations.LocationName
FROM tblLocations INNER JOIN (tblEventsTypes_lkp INNER JOIN⇐
(tblEvents INNER JOIN tblEventsLocations ON tblEvents.EventID =⇐
tblEventsLocations.EventID) ON tblEventsTypes_lkp.ID =⇐
tblEvents.EventTypeID) ON tblLocations.LocationID =⇐
tblEventsLocations.LocationID
WHERE (((tblEventsTypes_lkp.Description) Like "*" & [Find?] & "*")⇐
AND ((tblEventsLocations.EventDate) Between [StartDate?] And
[EndDate?])) OR (((tblEvents.EventName) Like "*" & [Find?] & "*")⇐
AND ((tblEventsLocations.EventDate) Between [StartDate?] And⇐
[EndDate?])) OR (((tblEvents.EventDescription) Like "*" & [Find?] &⇐
"*") AND ((tblEventsLocations.EventDate) Between [StartDate?] And⇐
[EndDate?]));
```

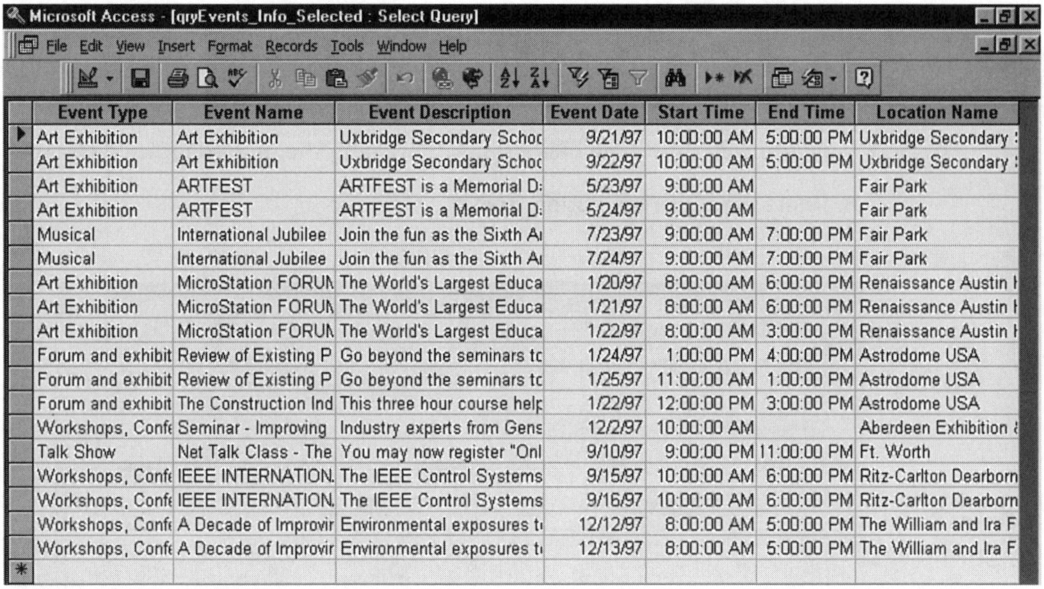

Event Type	Event Name	Event Description	Event Date	Start Time	End Time	Location Name
Art Exhibition	Art Exhibition	Uxbridge Secondary Schoc	9/21/97	10:00:00 AM	5:00:00 PM	Uxbridge Secondary :
Art Exhibition	Art Exhibition	Uxbridge Secondary Schoc	9/22/97	10:00:00 AM	5:00:00 PM	Uxbridge Secondary :
Art Exhibition	ARTFEST	ARTFEST is a Memorial D:	5/23/97	9:00:00 AM		Fair Park
Art Exhibition	ARTFEST	ARTFEST is a Memorial D:	5/24/97	9:00:00 AM		Fair Park
Musical	International Jubilee	Join the fun as the Sixth A	7/23/97	9:00:00 AM	7:00:00 PM	Fair Park
Musical	International Jubilee	Join the fun as the Sixth A	7/24/97	9:00:00 AM	7:00:00 PM	Fair Park
Art Exhibition	MicroStation FORUI	The World's Largest Educa	1/20/97	8:00:00 AM	6:00:00 PM	Renaissance Austin I
Art Exhibition	MicroStation FORUI	The World's Largest Educa	1/21/97	8:00:00 AM	6:00:00 PM	Renaissance Austin I
Art Exhibition	MicroStation FORUI	The World's Largest Educa	1/22/97	8:00:00 AM	3:00:00 PM	Renaissance Austin I
Forum and exhibit	Review of Existing P	Go beyond the seminars tc	1/24/97	1:00:00 PM	4:00:00 PM	Astrodome USA
Forum and exhibit	Review of Existing P	Go beyond the seminars tc	1/25/97	11:00:00 AM	1:00:00 PM	Astrodome USA
Forum and exhibit	The Construction Ind	This three hour course help	1/22/97	12:00:00 PM	3:00:00 PM	Astrodome USA
Workshops, Confe	Seminar - Improving	Industry experts from Gens	12/2/97	10:00:00 AM		Aberdeen Exhibition
Talk Show	Net Talk Class - The	You may now register "Onl	9/10/97	9:00:00 PM	11:00:00 PM	Ft. Worth
Workshops, Confe	IEEE INTERNATION	The IEEE Control Systems	9/15/97	10:00:00 AM	6:00:00 PM	Ritz-Carlton Dearborn
Workshops, Confe	IEEE INTERNATION	The IEEE Control Systems	9/16/97	10:00:00 AM	6:00:00 PM	Ritz-Carlton Dearborn
Workshops, Confe	A Decade of Improvir	Environmental exposures t	12/12/97	8:00:00 AM	5:00:00 PM	The William and Ira F
Workshops, Confe	A Decade of Improvir	Environmental exposures t	12/13/97	8:00:00 AM	5:00:00 PM	The William and Ira F
*						

Figure 6-18
Result of the `qryEvents_Info_Selected` query

Creating a Subtract Query

A *Subtract query* of two tables returns all records from one table that do not have any related records in the other table. This query comes in handy if you are looking for child-less records in the parent table. To construct a Subtract query, link the parent table with the child table using an outer join and then filter out all the parent records where the linking field of the child table is `Null`.

As an illustration, the `tblLocations` table of the sample calendar database contains location records not used by any record of the `tblEventsLocations` table. The following steps show how you can create a Subtract query to list those location records:

1. Close the query constructed in the previous example.

2. Create a new query and select `tblLocations` and `tblEventsLocations` as the data sources.

   Access automatically creates an inner join between the `LocationID` fields of these tables.

3. Change the inner join to an outer join directed from `tblLocations` to `tblEventsLocations`.

4. Add the asterisk field from `tblLocations` to the first cell of the Field row.

5. Add the `LocationID` field from `tblEventsLocations` to the second cell of the Field row and type `Is Null` in its Criteria cell, as shown in Figure 6-19.

6. Save the query as `qryLocations_NotUsed`.

7. Run the query.

   Figure 6-20 shows the query result containing the unused location records.

8. Select the SQL View option from the View menu.

Figure 6-19
Design of the
`qryLocations_Not`
`Used` query

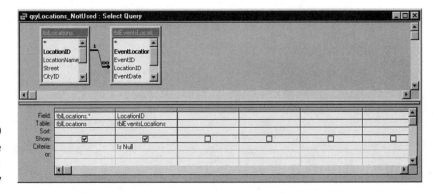

Figure 6-20
Result of the
qryLocations_Not
Used query

tblLocations.LocationID	Location Name	Street	CityID	State	Count	Posta	tblEventsLocations.LocationID
3	Trinity United Church		1	1	2		
25	Gray Exhibition Cent	300 N.E. 2n	15	8	1		
(AutoNumber)							

qryLocations_NotUsed : Select Query

Access displays the following SQL statement corresponding to this query:

```
SELECT tblLocations.*, tblEventsLocations.LocationID
FROM tblLocations LEFT JOIN tblEventsLocations ON
tblLocations.LocationID = tblEventsLocations.LocationID
WHERE (((tblEventsLocations.LocationID) Is Null));
```

Lesson Summary

This lesson showed how Access makes multiple-table queries a logical extension of single-table queries when it comes to specifying the sorting and filtering criteria and presented the following examples based on the calendar database:

● Use of sort criteria to generate a list of events with other pertinent information, sorted by the event type.

● Use of filtering criteria to generate information about a particular type of event.

● Use of a multitable Parameter query to list all events falling within a specified date range and whose names, descriptions, or type fields match a specified pattern.

● Use of a Subtract query on two tables to return all records from one table that do not have any related records in the second table.

In the next lesson, we shall talk about data analysis, where you design queries that group and aggregate data from various related fields.

For your reference, the **CALENDAR.MDB** database file resulting from this lesson is provided in the **C:\WEBSITE\HTDOCS\WDBIC\CHAP06\LESSON2\RESULTS** directory.

1. What would happen if you tried to sort by the **SponsorName** field of the **tblSponsors** table and the **Description** field of the **tblEventTypes_Lkp** table in the first example of this lesson?
   a. Access would display an error message.
   b. Access would sort based on both the fields.

    c. Access would sort only by the `SponsorName` field.

    d. Access would sort only by the `Description` field.

2. What criteria would you enter in the `Description` field of the second example of this lesson to list all musical- and dance-type events?

    a. `In (2,5)`

    b. `"Musical, Dance"`

    c. `In ("Musical","Dance")`

    d. `"Musical", "Dance"`

3. Suppose applying criteria A on Table A (containing 30 records) results in 10 records and applying criteria B on Table B (containing 40 records) results in 15 records. Further assume Table A and Table B form a one-to-many relationship. If you link these two tables with an inner join and apply criteria A and criteria B against each table in a query, how many records will this query produce?

    a. 10

    b. 15

    c. 10 or fewer

    d. 15 or fewer

4. What is the purpose of a Subtract query?

    a. It returns all records from one table that do not have any related records in the second table.

    b. It can be used to locate childless records in a parent table.

    c. It is used to carry out the mathematical subtract function on a query.

    d. None of the above.

5. How is a Subtract query performed?

    a. The parent table is linked to the child table by an inner join.

    b. The parent table is linked to the child table by an outer join.

    c. All parent records whose child record is `Null` are filtered out.

    d. All parent records whose child record is not `Null` are filtered out.

EXERCISE 2

Complexity: Moderate

1. Design a query named `qrySponsors_Events` that lists the names and descriptions of all the events sorted by the names of their sponsors.

Complexity: Advanced

2. Extend the `qryEvents_Info_Selected` query created in this lesson so that it includes a fourth parameter named `[Country?]` that allows you to filter events by a specified country. Additionally, if no value is entered for the `[Country?]` parameter, then this query should interpret it as `All Countries`. Name this modified query `qryEvents_Info_Selected_2`.

GROUPING AND AGGREGATING DATA

So far we have been looking at the calendar database from the narrow perspective of viewing part of the data through a table datasheet or selectively finding information through single-table or multiple-table queries. But this does not give us the big picture. The real power of an RDBMS lies in being able to analyze information from various standpoints to get a holistic view of the database. This lesson deals with this macroscopic view of information and explains how you can design queries in Access that help you group and aggregate data in a database.

Creating a Total Query

As the first step in the data analysis of the calendar database, let's find out how many events each sponsor is hosting. To generate this information, you will design a *Total query* in Access. Total queries allow you to calculate a sum, average, count, or total of a set of records.

1. Copy the CALENDAR.MDB file residing in the
   C:\WEBSITE\HTDOCS\WDBIC\CHAP05\SAMPLES directory to the
   C:\WEBSITE\HTDOCS\WDBIC\CHAP06\LESSON3 directory.

2. Open the C:\WEBSITE\HTDOCS\WDBIC\CHAP06\LESSON3\CALENDAR.MDB database file
   in Access.

3. Create a new query and select tblSponsors, tblSponsorsContacts, and
   tblEvents as the data sources.

   Access automatically creates inner joins between these tables based on
   their predefined relationships.

4. Add the SponsorName field from the tblSponsors table and the EventID field
   from the tblEvents table to the field row.

5. Select the Totals option from the View menu.

   Access adds a new row labeled Total: to the query design grid, as shown in
   Figure 6-21.

   This Total row shows the Group By function by default under the two selected fields.

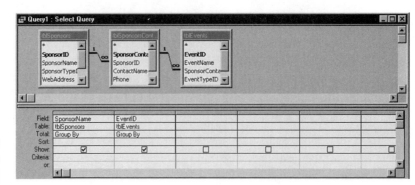

Figure 6-21
Adding the Total
row to the query
design grid

6. Change the Group By function to the Count function for the EventID field, as shown in Figure 6-22.

7. Save this query as qrySponsors_EventCount.

8. Run the query.

   The query result consists of two fields, as shown in Figure 6-23.

   The SponsorName field shows the name of each event sponsor, and the CountOfEventID field shows a count of all the events associated with each sponsor. In plain text, the query we just constructed can be described as: group all the events by their sponsor name and return a count of EventIDs for each group.

   Also notice that the records are shown in alphabetical order by sponsor name.

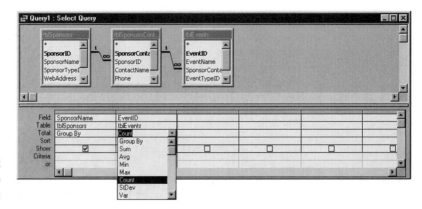

Figure 6-22
Specifying the
Count function

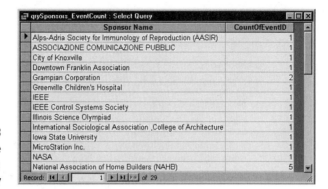

Figure 6-23
Result of the
qrySponsors_Event
Count query

9. Now select the Query Design option from the View menu to return to the query design window.

10. Specify a Descending sort option for the EventID field.

11. Select the Save As option from the File menu and save the modified query as qrySponsors_EventCount_Sorted.

12. Run the query again.

How did the result change? The sponsor with the highest event count is now listed first, as shown in Figure 6-24. There you have it! An easy way of not only producing the event count by each sponsor but also finding out which sponsor has listed the most events in the database.

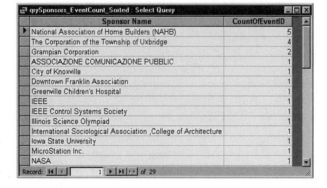

Figure 6-24
Result of the
qrySponsors_Event
Count_Sorted query

13. Select the SQL View option from the View menu.

Access displays the following SQL statement:

```
SELECT tblSponsors.SponsorName, tblSponsorsContacts.ContactName,⇐
Count(tblEvents.EventID) AS CountOfEventID
FROM tblSponsors INNER JOIN (tblSponsorsContacts INNER JOIN⇐
tblEvents ON tblSponsorsContacts.SponsorContactID =⇐
tblEvents.SponsorContactID) ON tblSponsors.SponsorID =⇐
tblSponsorsContacts.SponsorID
GROUP BY tblSponsors.SponsorName, tblSponsorsContacts.ContactName
ORDER BY Count(tblEvents.EventID) DESC;
```

Although a Total query shows its result in a datasheet view similar to other select queries, you cannot edit the data in that result.

The Group By **Function**

As you can see from the design of the `qrySponsors_EventCount_Sorted` query, the `Group By` function indicates the field you want to group in when performing calculations such as count, sum, and average. You can also group in multiple fields by specifying the `Group By` function for all those fields. In that case, the leftmost field becomes the primary grouping field. Say you want to rerun the previous example, but this time split the event count by each contact of the sponsor. All you need to do is group by the `SponsorName` and `ContactName` fields in the previous query, as explained below:

1. Return to the query design window from the Query Design option.

2. Highlight ContactName in the tblSponsorsContacts table, drag it, and drop it on to the second field cell.

    Notice that the EventID field moves over to the third field cell.

3. The Totals row of this field shows the Group By function by default.

4. Save this query as qrySponsors_Contacts_EventCount_Sorted.

5. Run the query.

    Access creates a subgroup of contact names associated with each sponsor name and lists their sorted event count, as shown in Figure 6-25.

A Total query with just one field in the Field row having a `Group By` function under its Total cell returns all the unique values of that field.

qrySponsors_Contacts_EventCount_Sorted : Select Query

Sponsor Name	Contact Name	CountOfEventID
The Corporation of the Township of Ux	Administrative Officer	4
National Association of Home Builder:	Betty Norman	2
NASA	JPL Space Exploration I	1
MicroStation Inc.	James Moore	1
Iowa State University	Sean C. Murphy	1
International Sociological Association	Dr. Patricia K. Edwards	1
Illinois Science Olympiad	Brian Niece	1
Alps-Adria Society for Immunology of	Daniel Rukavina	1
IEEE	Peter Harris	1
National Association of Home Builder:	Kelly A	1
Greenville Children's Hospital	Aloft Staff	1
Grampian Corporation	Sue Hay	1
Grampian Corporation	Claire Fitzpatrick	1
Downtown Franklin Association	Festivals Office	1

Record: 1 of 33

Figure 6-25 Result of the `qrySponsors_Contacts_EventCount_Sorted` query

Aggregate Functions

The kind of analysis carried out by a Total query depends on the aggregate functions specified in its Total row. These functions aggregate data within the grouping specified by the `Group By` function. In the query shown in Figure 6-23, the `Count` function counts the number of event IDs for each `SponsorName` group.

If you remove the `SponsorName` field from the Field row, then the query result returns a total count of the events listed by all sponsors. Would this query return the same result if you were to apply the `Count` function to any other field of the `tblEvents` table instead of the `EventID` field? Not necessarily, as shown in Figure 6-26, where the count for the sponsor in the first record decreases by 1 when we set the `Count` function on the `EventDescription` field.

Why did the count decrease? Because one event belonging to this sponsor did not have any data in the `EventDescription` field. The `Count` and other aggregate functions consider only records where the aggregated field is not `Null`. If you want to consider all your records for counting purposes, it is important to choose a field that is not `Null` in any record. The `EventID` field as the primary field is the ideal choice.

qrySponsors_Contacts_EventCount_Sorted_2 : Select Query

Sponsor Name	Contact Name	CountOfEventDescription
The Corporation of the Township of Uxbridge	Administrative Officer	3
National Association of Home Builders (NAH	Betty Norman	2
NASA	JPL Space Exploratior	1
MicroStation Inc.	James Moore	1
Iowa State University	Sean C. Murphy	1
International Sociological Association ,Colle	Dr. Patricia K. Edward	1
Illinois Science Olympiad	Brian Niece	1
Alps-Adria Society for Immunology of Repro	Daniel Rukavina	1
IEEE	Peter Harris	1
National Association of Home Builders (NAH	Kelly A	1
Greenville Children's Hospital	Aloft Staff	1
Grampian Corporation	Sue Hay	1
Grampian Corporation	Claire Fitzpatrick	1
Downtown Franklin Association	Festivals Office	1

Record: 1 of 33

Figure 6-26 Result of setting the `Count` function on the `EventDescription` field

Table 6-1 lists all the aggregate functions available for the Total row.

Table 6-1 Aggregate functions for a Total query

Function	Purpose	Applicable Data Types
Sum	Total of values in a row	Number, Date/Time, Currency, AutoNumber
Avg	Average of the values in a field	Number, Date/Time, Currency, AutoNumber
Min	Lowest value in a field	Text, Number, Date/Time, Currency, AutoNumber
Max	Highest value in a field	Text, Number, Date/Time, Currency, AutoNumber
Count	Number of non-Null values	All data types
StDev	Standard deviation	Number, Date/Time, Currency, AutoNumber
Var	Variance of the values in a field	Number, Date/Time, Currency, AutoNumber
First	Value of the first record in the group	All data types
Last	Value of the last record in the group	All data types

Lesson Summary

This lesson explained how you create Total queries in Access to perform various kinds of data analysis on your database and look at the database from a wider perspective. Total queries contain a row labeled **Total** in the query design window. In this row, you can specify the **Group By**, **Count**, **Sum**, and other aggregating options. The example of grouping events by the sponsor name and presenting a count of events for each group was used in this lesson to explain the application of this query. This lesson also illustrated how you can group on multiple fields.

The analysis carried out by a Total query depends on the aggregate function specified in the Total row. The role of each aggregate function was described in this lesson. It is important to remember that these functions ignore records that contain a **Null** value in the field being aggregated. If you want to include all records for aggregation, ensure that the field being aggregated has data in all records. For the **Count** function, the primary key field is always a good choice.

The next lesson shows what happens when you list multiple aggregate functions and filter criteria in a Total query and then describes how you can summarize the result of a Total query by creating a Crosstab query.

For your reference, the **CALENDAR.MDB** database file resulting from this lesson is provided in the **C:\WEBSITE\HTDOCS\WDBIC\CHAP06\LESSON3\RESULTS** directory.

1. What does the result of a Total query contain?
   a. Records of the source tables.
   b. Summary data based on the records of the source tables.
   c. Records of the source tables plus records containing their summary information.
   d. Records of the source tables matching the specified summary criteria.

2. Which of the following statements are true for aggregate functions?
   a. They are specified in the Total row of a Total query.
   b. They aggregate data within the grouping specified by the **Group By** function.
   c. **Sum** and **Sub** are two aggregate functions supported by Access.
   d. **Avg** and **Count** are two aggregate functions supported by Access.

3. Which of the following functions of a Total query ignore records with a **Null** value in the field on which they are applied?
   a. **Group By**
   b. **Count**
   c. **Sum**
   d. All of the above

4. What happens when you apply the **Sum** function to a **Text** field?
   a. Access concatenates this field's data from all the records.
   b. Access returns a count of all the records that have some data in this field.
   c. Access returns an error message.
   d. Access returns a **Null** value.

5. In a Total query that has multiple fields grouped together, how does Access determine the primary grouping field?
   a. The leftmost field containing the **Group By** function.
   b. The first field in the Field row.
   c. The rightmost field containing the **Group By** function.
   d. It picks one at random.

Complexity: Easy
1. Design a query named **qrySponsors_withPassword_Count** that returns the number of sponsors that have a specified (non-**Null**) password.

Complexity: Moderate

2. Design a query named `qryLocations_EventCount` that lists the number of occurrences of each event by location name and event name.

ADVANCED DATA ANALYSIS

In many cases, you can apply several aggregate functions at a time in a single Total query to get many answers in one go. Furthermore, you can limit the scope of your data being analyzed by specifying one or more criteria expressions. However, in a Total query, you have to be careful about whether the criteria gets applied before or after aggregating data, as you will see in this lesson. Access supports a special type of query known as the Crosstab query that helps you summarize the data in a compact form and make it more readable. This lesson demonstrates the difference between the results of a Total query and the results of a Crosstab query and shows an example of how you can convert a Total query into a Crosstab query.

Using Multiple Aggregate Functions in a Total Query

Let's say you want to examine the events in the calendar database and identify the total number of occurrences of each unique event, for example, how many of those occurrences are within the United States and their first and last occurrences. The following steps illustrate how you can design one Total query with multiple aggregate functions to get all the answers.

Step 1: Deciding on the Grouping Field(s)

The current data analysis task can be broken into four questions:

⚫ How many times is each event occurring?

⚫ How many times is each event occurring within the United States?

⚫ For each event, what is the date of the first occurrence?

⚫ For each event, what is the date of the last occurrence?

Observe the universal element among these questions. It is possible to respond to all these questions with just one query because they are all asking for information for each event. But what is an event? Is it an individual record of the `tblEvents` table or do all records having the same value for the `EventName` field constitute an event? For instance, say a sponsor holds an art exhibition every year and has two records in the `tblEvents` table with the event name listed as "Art Show." Would you consider each record a separate event or as belonging to the same event? In this case, it's all a matter of preference. For our example, we will treat each record of the `tblEvents` table as a separate event, use the `EventID` field (the primary key of `tblEvents`) as the primary grouping field, and design our query as follows:

1. Copy the `CALENDAR.MDB` file residing in the `C:\WEBSITE\HTDOCS\WDBIC\CHAP05\SAMPLES` directory to the `C:\WEBSITE\HTDOCS\WDBIC\CHAP06\LESSON4` directory.

2. Open the `C:\WEBSITE\HTDOCS\WDBIC\CHAP06\LESSON4\CALENDAR.MDB` database file in Access.

3. Open a new query in the query design window.

4. Add `tblEvents`, `tblEventsLocations`, and `tblLocations` to the query.

5. Select the Total option from the View menu.

6. Add the `EventID` and `EventName` fields from the `tblEvents` table to the first and second cell of the Field row, respectively.

   Access automatically sets the `Group By` function for these fields and selects their Show checkbox.

Step 2: Counting the Occurrences of Each Event

Now we can specify the `Count` function under the `EventLocationID` field to count the number of times each event occurs:

1. Add the `EventLocationID` field from the `tblEventsLocations` table to the Field row.

2. Set the `Count` function for this field in the Total row.

Step 3: Counting Occurrences in the United States of Each Event

How will you calculate how many occurrences of each event are within the United States? You cannot use the `Count` function on the `CountryID` field in the `tblLocations` table because it will return the same result as the total number of occurrences. Remember, the `Count` function simply counts the number of records with a non-`Null` value in the specified field; it does not distinguish between values. The way to handle this question is to employ the `Sum` function, as shown next:

1. Create a calculated field in the query's Field row (4th column) as follows:

   USCount: IIf([CountryID]=1,1,0)

   This calculated field returns a 1 if CountryID is 1 (the ID for the United States); otherwise it returns 0.

2. Set the Total row for this calculated field to the Sum function, as shown in Figure 6-27.

   The Sum function will add all the 1s and return an accurate reflection of the total U.S. occurrences of each event.

Step 4: Finding the Date of the First and Last Occurrences of Each Event

To find the dates of the first and last occurrences of each event:

1. Double-click on the EventDate field of the tblEventsLocations table.

   Access adds it to the Field row.

2. Set the total for this field to Min.

3. Double-click on the EventDate field of the tblEventsLocations table.

   Access adds another copy of this field to the Field row.

4. Set the Total cell of this copy to Max, as shown in Figure 6-28.

5. Save the query as qryEvents_Analysis.

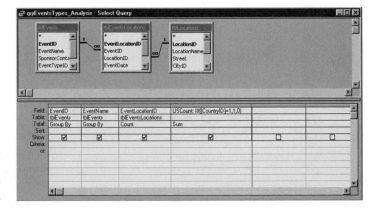

Figure 6-27
Calculating occurrences of each event within the United States

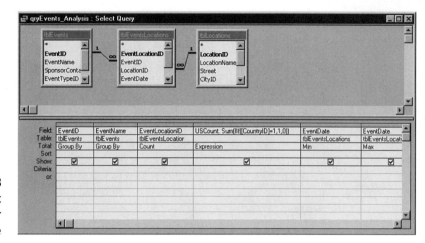

Figure 6-28
Calculating the first
and last dates for
each event type

Notice from Figure 6-28 that Access has automatically replaced the word `Sum` (that you entered for the `USCount` calculated field in the previous section) with the word `Expression`. This automatic conversion is a normal behavior of Access when you apply an aggregate function to a calculated field.

Step 5: Testing Your Query

Although it can be time consuming to test the exact numbers generated by this query, you should be able to verify its result at an intuitive level. Figure 6-29 shows the output of this query.

Figure 6-29
Result of the
`qryEvents_Analysis`
query

The query result lists the records sorted by the `EventID` field because no particular sort order was forced in the query design. The `CountOfEventLocationID` field shows the number of occurrences of each event type. Notice that this number is in some cases greater than the corresponding `USCount` value, which makes sense, because some events have their locations outside the United States. Also observe that for events occurring only once, the `MinOfEventDate` and `MaxOfEventDate` fields have the same date value.

How did the U.S. count field get the name `USCount`? Look at Figure 6-27 again and notice the expression `USCount:IIf([CountryID]=1,1,0)` used to construct this field. The label before the colon becomes the name of the resulting field. Similarly, if you do not like the name `CountOfEventID` and want to change it to `TotalEventCount`, just add the label `TotalEventCount:` before the `EventLocationID` field in the query design.

As a final step, select the SQL View option from the View menu. Access displays the following SQL statement it constructed for this query (whew!):

```
SELECT tblEvents.EventID, tblEvents.EventName,⇐
Count(tblEventsLocations.EventLocationID) AS CountOfEventLocationID,⇐
Sum(IIf([CountryID]=1,1,0)) AS USCount, Min(tblEventsLocations.EventDate) AS⇐
MinOfEventDate, Max(tblEventsLocations.EventDate) AS MaxOfEventDate
FROM tblLocations INNER JOIN (tblEvents INNER JOIN tblEventsLocations ON⇐
tblEvents.EventID = tblEventsLocations.EventID) ON tblLocations.LocationID =⇐
tblEventsLocations.LocationID
GROUP BY tblEvents.EventID, tblEvents.EventName;
```

You could have also used the `First` or `Last` function instead of the `Group By` function under the `EventName` field of this query without affecting its result.

Applying Criteria in Total Queries

In Total queries, you can specify two kinds of criteria: those that are applied before the records are aggregated (*precriteria*) and those that are applied after the records are aggregated (*postcriteria*). Which type of criteria you use depends on the objective of your query. Consider the following three data analysis tasks:

● Show all events that occur only once.

● Show the number of times an event occurs in the year 1997.

● Show all events that occur only once in 1997.

Specifying Postcriteria in a Total Query

To accomplish the first task, design a query that asks for all events that occur only once, as follows:

1. Construct a new Total query and select `tblEvents` and `tblEventsLocations` as the data sources.

2. Add `EventName` from the `tblEvents` table and `EventLocationID` from the `tblEventsLocations` table to the Field row and set the Total row of the `EventLocationID` field to `Count`.

3. Add `criteria =1` in the criteria cell of the `EventLocationID` field, as shown in Figure 6-30.

4. Save the query as `qryEvents_OneTimeOnly`.

5. Run the query.

Access first counts the number of events for each location and then applies =1 criteria to the resulting `EventLocationID` count, thereby returning all events that occur only once in the database, as indicated by the 19 records listed in the result of this query, shown in Figure 6-31.

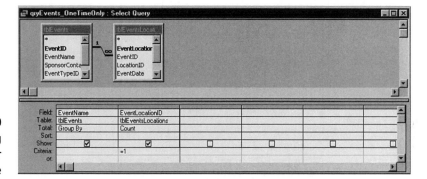

Figure 6-30
Query for listing events that occur only once

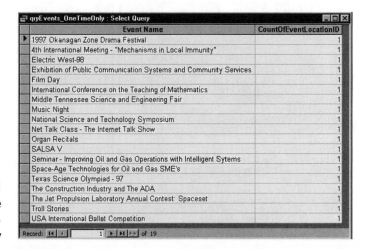

Figure 6-31
Result of the `qryEvents_OneTime Only` query

To handle the second task, make an event count query that considers only events happening in 1997. In other words, you have to list those events that occur between 1/1/97 and 12/31/97.

1. Construct a new query that lists events and their occurrences as explained in the first two steps of the previous example.

2. Add the `EventDate` field of the `tblEventsLocations` table to the Field row.

3. Select the `Where` option for the Total cell of this field.

   The `Where` option indicates to Access that it should apply the criteria before it starts counting the events.

4. Specify the `Between...And` date range criterion to its Criteria cell, as shown in Figure 6-32.

5. Save the query as `qryEvents_1997_Occurences`.

6. Run the query.

   Access displays the event names and the number of times they occur in 1997, as shown in Figure 6-33.

The names of the events that do not occur once in the year 1997 are not part of the query result.

The third task is a combination of the first two tasks. You can design its query by specifying both types of criteria in the basic event count query, as shown by the design of `qryEvents_OneTimeOnly_in_1997` in Figure 6-34.

Figure 6-35 shows the result of the above query.

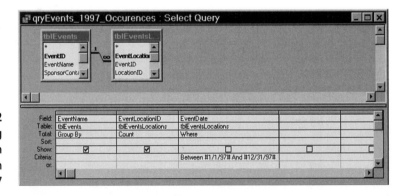

Figure 6-32
Query for listing number of times an event occurs in 1997

qryEvents_1997_Occurences : Select Query

Event Name	CountOfEventLocationID
10th Annual Offshore Drilling Technology Forum.	2
A Decade of Improving Health Through Multi-Disciplinary Research.	2
AIA Plan Review Workshop I	3
Art Exhibition	2
ARTFEST	2
Brick Sculpture - New Uses of Time Honored Materials Create Beauty and Sales	2
COMMUNICATIONS: THE KEY TO GLOBAL PROSPERITY	2
Durability of Buildings	2
Exhibition of Public Communication Systems and Community Services	1
Film Day	1
Housing in the 21st Century: Looking Forward.	4
HYDROGEN AND THE MATERIALS OF A SUSTAINABLE ENERGY FUTURE	2
IEEE INTERNATIONAL CONFERENCE ON CONTROL APPLICATIONS	2
International Jubilee	2
Memorial Day Weekend Balloning Festival	2
MicroStation FORUM & Exhibition	3
Music Night	1
Net Talk Class - The Internet Talk Show	1
Organ Recitals	1
Review of Existing Plans & Costs/Cost Saving Construction Techniques	2
Seminar - Improving Oil and Gas Operations with Intelligent Sytems	1
Space-Age Technologies for Oil and Gas SME's	1

Record: 1 of 27

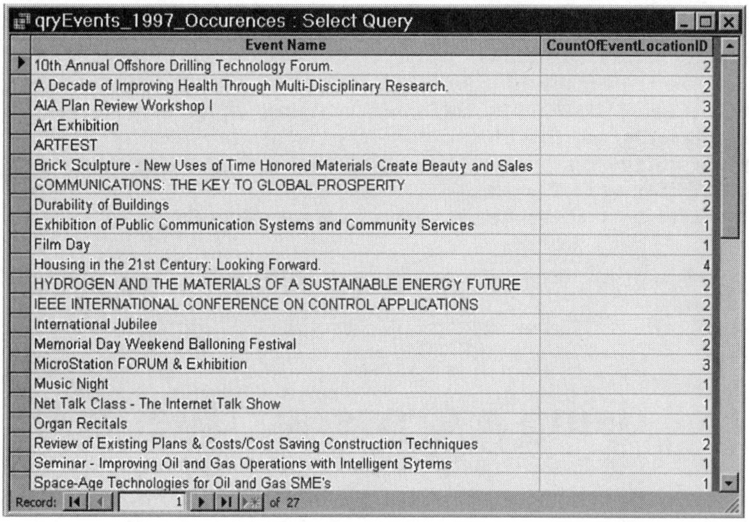

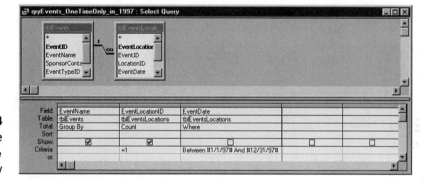

Figure 6-33 Event names and their occurrences in 1997

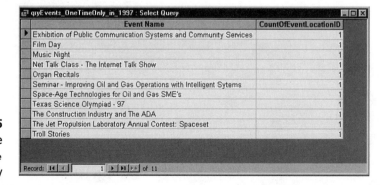

Figure 6-34 Design of the `qryEvents_OneTimeOnly_in_1997` query

qryEvents_OneTimeOnly_in_1997 : Select Query

Event Name	CountOfEventLocationID
Exhibition of Public Communication Systems and Community Services	1
Film Day	1
Music Night	1
Net Talk Class - The Internet Talk Show	1
Organ Recitals	1
Seminar - Improving Oil and Gas Operations with Intelligent Sytems	1
Space-Age Technologies for Oil and Gas SME's	1
Texas Science Olympiad - 97	1
The Construction Industry and The ADA	1
The Jet Propulsion Laboratory Annual Contest: Spaceset	1
Troll Stories	1

Record: 1 of 11

Figure 6-35 Result of the `qryEvents_OneTimeOnly_in_1997` query

The SQL statement constructed by Access for this query is given below:

```
SELECT tblEvents.EventName, Count(tblEventsLocations.EventLocationID) AS⇐
CountOfEventLocationID
FROM tblEvents INNER JOIN tblEventsLocations ON tblEvents.EventID =⇐
tblEventsLocations.EventID
WHERE (((tblEventsLocations.EventDate) Between #1/1/97# And #12/31/97#))
GROUP BY tblEvents.EventName
HAVING (((Count(tblEventsLocations.EventLocationID))=1));
```

 Tip In a Total query, any criteria listed against a field that does not have the word **Where** under its Total cell is treated as postcriteria.

Using a Crosstab Query

A Crosstab query is a specialized type of a Total query through which you aggregate data that is grouped by two types of information: one down the left side of the datasheet and another across the top. Figure 6-36 shows you results of the following

File Edit View Insert Format Records Tools Window Help

qryEvents_CountByTypeAndYear : Select Query

Event Type	Year	CountOfEventLocationID
Art Exhibition	1997	7
Competetion	1997	2
Competetion	1998	2
Dance	1997	2
Dance	1998	1
Forum and exhibition	1997	6
Forum and exhibition	1998	4
Musical	1997	4
Sports	1997	2
Talk Show	1997	1
Theatre	1997	2
Theatre	1998	1
Workshops, Conferences, and Seminars	1997	21
Workshops, Conferences, and Seminars	1998	4

Record: ⏮ ◀ 13 ▶ ▶▌ ▶* of 14

qryEvents_CountByTypeAndYear_Crosstab : C...

Event Type	1997	1998
Art Exhibition	7	
Competetion	2	2
Dance	2	1
Forum and exhibition	6	4
Musical	4	
Sports	2	
Talk Show	1	
Theatre	2	1
Workshops, Conferences, and Seminars	21	4

Record: ⏮ ◀ 1 ▶ ▶▌ ▶* of 9

Description of the lookup value

Figure 6-36
Result of a Total query and its equivalent Crosstab query

two queries that both show a count of event occurrences grouped by event type description and the year of their occurrence:

● A Total query named `qryEvents_CountByTypeAndYear`

● A Crosstab query named `qryEvents_CountByTypeAndYear_Crosstab`

As you can see, the Crosstab query compacts the result and makes it more readable. Figure 6-37 shows these two queries in their design view.

The design of the **qryEvents_CountByTypeAndYear** query shows a grouping on the **Description** field and the calculated field labeled **Year**, and a **Count** function applied to the **EventLocationID** field. The **Year** field is a calculated field that extracts the year from the **EventDate** field using the following expression:

```
Year: Year([EventDate])
```

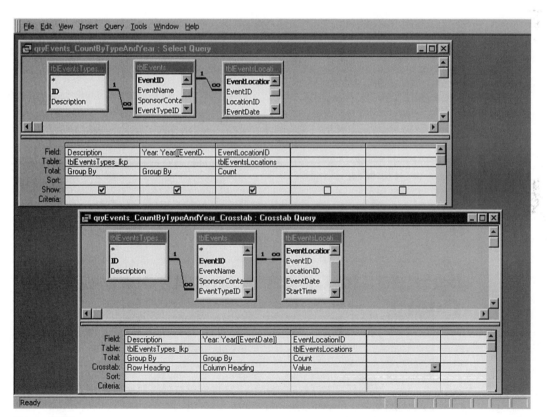

Figure 6-37
Design view of a Total query and its equivalent Crosstab query

The Crosstab query is essentially a derivative of the Total query with an extra Crosstab row in its design grid. You design this Crosstab query as follows:

1. Design a Total query similar to `qryEvents_CountByTypeAndYear`.

2. Display the Crosstab row on the query design grid by selecting the Crosstab option from the Query menu.

3. Select the Row Heading option for the Crosstab cell under the `Description` field.

4. Select the Column Heading option for the Crosstab cell under the `Year` field.

5. Select the Value option for the Crosstab cell under the `EventLocationID` field.

6. Save the query as `qryEvents_CountByTypeAndYear_Crosstab`.

7. Run the query to verify the results.

The Crosstab query defines which field becomes the row heading, which field's values act as the column heading, and which field's values to aggregate. You can specify a group of multiple fields for your row heading, but you can specify only one field as your column heading and one field for your Value option.

The SQL statement for the Crosstab query shown in Figure 6-37 is given below:

```
TRANSFORM Count(tblEventsLocations.EventLocationID) AS CountOfEventLocationID
SELECT tblEventsTypes_lkp.Description
FROM (tblEventsTypes_lkp INNER JOIN tblEvents ON tblEventsTypes_lkp.ID =⇐
tblEvents.EventTypeID) INNER JOIN tblEventsLocations ON tblEvents.EventID =⇐
tblEventsLocations.EventID
GROUP BY tblEventsTypes_lkp.Description
PIVOT Year([EventDate]);
```

Specifying Criteria in a Crosstab Query

You can add criteria to your Crosstab query just like you add criteria to a Total query, except that you cannot specify precriteria or postcriteria directly against the value field (Access does not allow it). There is, however, another way for specifying precriteria on the value field, as described below:

1. Add another copy of the value field to the Field row.

2. Select the `Where` function for its Total cell, and keep its Crosstab cell empty.

3. Set your criteria against this copy.

This criteria will be applied before totals are computed.

The easiest way to define a Crosstab query is to use the Crosstab Wizard option provided by Access when you start the design of a new query. For complete details on creating and using Crosstab queries, search **Crosstab** from the online help provided by Access.

Lesson Summary

This lesson dealt with those aspects of Total queries that not only make your data analysis more in depth and focused by limiting the scope of data being analyzed, but also provide answers to many questions about this data using just one query. The key lies in being able to break the data analysis task into smaller tasks and to identify the universal element among them. Having done that, you design queries for each of these smaller tasks and put them all together. The steps involved in creating such a Total query, which uses multiple aggregate functions, were explained in this lesson.

You can specify criteria in a Total query, which is applied either before (precriteria) or after (postcriteria) the records are aggregated. A criterion listed against a field that has the word **Where** under its Total cell is treated as precriteria; the absence of **Where** in the Total cell means postcriteria. You can apply both these criteria together in a Total query, as shown in this lesson.

This lesson also illustrated the use of a special type of Total query called the Crosstab query, which summarizes data by grouping one type of information down the left side of the datasheet (column) and another across the top (row). You have the flexibility to decide which field becomes the row heading, which field's value becomes the column heading, and which field's value to aggregate. Criteria specification in Crosstab queries is similar to that in Total queries, with the exception that you cannot list postcriteria on the value field.

If you look back at the design of the queries that have been created until now, you will see that several of these queries have many things in common, such as the tables as their data sources, output fields, and, in some cases, similar filter criteria. This phenomenon, where you end up repeating most of the query design when creating a new query, is not uncommon. To eliminate this design repetition task, Access supports a concept known as *query nesting*, by which you can create queries based on existing queries. We will explore this concept and show how it helps simplify the query design process in the next lesson.

For your reference, the **CALENDAR.MDB** database file resulting from this lesson is provided in the **C:\WEBSITE\HTDOCS\WDBIC\CHAP06\LESSON4\RESULTS** directory.

QUIZ 4

1. How do you decide the grouping field(s) while designing a Total query using multiple aggregate functions?
   a. By breaking the data analysis task into simpler tasks
   b. By selecting one or more fields from the source tables
   c. By looking for the common elements among the data analysis tasks
   d. All of the above

2. In the first example of this lesson, how would you get the count of events occurring in Canada under the field name `CountOfEventsInCanada`?
   a. Use the `Count` function under the `CountryID` value of the `tblLocationsCountries_Lkp` table.
   b. Use the `Sum` function under the calculated field expression `IIf([CountryID]=2,1,0)`.
   c. Use the `Count` function under the calculated field `CanadaCount: IIf([CountryID]=2,1,0)`.
   d. Use the `Sum` function under the calculated field `CountOfEventsInCanada:IIf([CountryID]=2,1,0)`.

3. How would you count the number of musical events (`EventTypeID = 2`) in a Total query containing `tblEvents` as a data source?
   a. List the `EventTypeID` field in the Field row, apply the `Count` function in its Total cell, and specify `=2` in its Criteria cell.
   b. List the `EventID` and `EventTypeID` fields in the Field row. Specify `Count` under the `EventID` field's Total cell and `Where` under the `EventTypeID` field's Total cell. Enter `=2` under the Criteria cell of the `EventTypeID` field.
   c. List the `EventID` and `EventTypeID` fields in the Field row. Specify `Count` under the `EventID` field's Total cell and `GroupBy` under the `EventTypeID` field's Total cell. Enter `=2` under the Criteria cell of the `EventTypeID` field.
   d. All of the above.

4. What happens if you specify the criteria expression `=1997` in the criteria cell of the `Year` field in the `qryEvents_CountByTypeAndYear_Crosstab` query created in this lesson?
   a. Access shows `Null` values in the 1998 column of the query result.
   b. Access does not list the 1998 column in the query result.
   c. Access produces an error message when you run the query.
   d. None of the above.

5. Which of the following statements holds true for Crosstab queries?
   a. You can specify more than one field to act as row headings.
   b. You can specify more than one field to act as column headings.
   c. You can specify the Value option for only one field.
   d. You cannot specify precriteria against a value field in a Crosstab query.

EXERCISE 4

Complexity: Moderate
1. Design a query named `qryMusicAndDanceEventCount_ByUSCities` that returns the number of occurrences of all the music and dance events in each city of the United States listed in the calendar database.

Complexity: Moderate
2. Design a Crosstab query named `qryEventCount_BySponsorAndEventTypes` that lists the event count (not the occurrence count) by sponsor type (row) and event type (column).

LESSON 5

NESTED QUERIES

Just when you may be thinking that we have covered some major query concepts, here is another power punch from Access: Nested queries. *Nested queries* are queries based on other queries (or a combination of queries and tables). This lesson explains how Nested queries are constructed and gives examples showing their usefulness in the following situations:

● Simplifying the query design through query reuse

● Easily propagating changes

● Performing advanced data analysis

Simplify Query Design Through Query Reuse

If you find yourself designing different queries that have a lot in common, you can first design a query that computes the common part, and then base other queries on that query. Once the common query is working correctly, you can concentrate on the extra requirements of the final query.

Many examples in the previous lessons used queries involving the **tblLocations** table. Whenever we needed to get the city, state, and country name information in those queries, we had to link the **tblLocations** table with the city, state, and country lookup tables. Wouldn't it be nice if you could link the **tblLocations** table with these lookup tables just once and then use that combination as the data source of your other queries? Nested queries help you do exactly that:

1. Copy the `CALENDAR.MDB` file residing in the `C:\WEBSITE\HTDOCS\WDBIC\CHAP05\SAMPLES` directory to the `C:\WEBSITE\HTDOCS\WDBIC\CHAP06\LESSON5` directory.
2. Open the `C:\WEBSITE\HTDOCS\WDBIC\CHAP06\LESSON5\CALENDAR.MDB` database file in Access.
3. Create a common query whose only purpose is to display all the fields from the `tblLocations` table and the `Description` fields from the city, state, and country lookup tables, as shown in Figure 6-38.
4. Save this query as `qryLocations`.
5. Run the query.

   Figure 6-39 shows the query result.

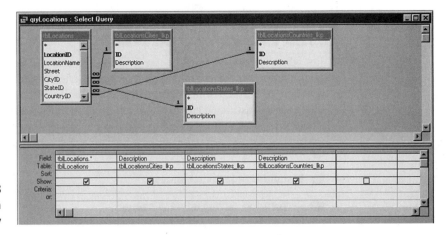

Figure 6-38 Creating a common query

LocationID	Location Name	Street	CityID	StateID	CountryID	PostalCode	City	State	Country
1	Uxbridge Music Ha	16 Main Stre	1	1	2	L9P 1T1	Uxbridge	Ontario	Canada
2	Uxbridge Seconda	Third Avenu	1	1	2		Uxbridge	Ontario	Canada
3	Trinity United Chur		1	1	2		Uxbridge	Ontario	Canada
4	Historic Franklin		2	2	1		Franklin	Tennessee	USA
5	Fair Park		3	3	1		Dallas	Texas	USA
6	Renaissance Aust		4	2	1		Knoxville	Tennessee	USA
8	Astrodome USA	Outside Mai	6	3	1		Houston	Texas	USA
13	Astrohall		6	3	1		Houston	Texas	USA
14	Radisson Hotell		7	4	1	24061-0205	Alexandri	Virginia	USA
15	Toronto Airport Hil	Airport Roac	8	1	2	L4V 1N1	Mississai	Ontario	Canada
16	Donaldson Industri		9	5	1		Greenville	South Caroli	USA
17	Royal Ballet Centr		10	6	1		Jackson	Mississippi	USA
18	Aberdeen Exhibitic	Bridge of Dc	11	7	3	AB23 8BL	Aberdeen	Scotland	UK
21	SCHOOL OF TEC		12	4	1	23504	Norfolk	Virginia	USA
22	Omni Rosen Hotel	9840 Interna	13	8	1		Orlando	Florida	USA
23	Department of Linç		5	3	1		Austin	Texas	USA
24	Department of Mat		14	9	4		Samos	Samos	Greece
25	Gray Exhibition Ce	300 N.E. 2n	15	8	1		Miami	Florida	USA

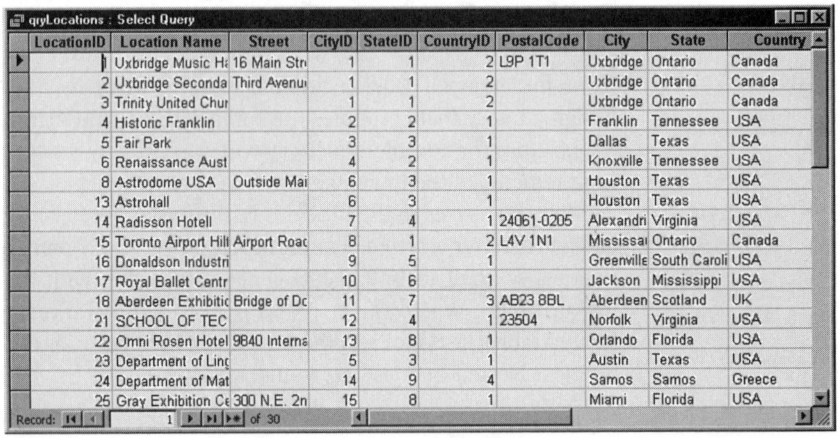

Figure 6-39 Result of `qryLocations`

6. Close the query result window.

Now say you want to design a Total query that lists the event occurrence count by country. You can reuse the `qryLocations` query as follows:

1. Open a new query in the query design window.

   Access displays the Show Table dialog box, prompting you to add tables for the query data source.

2. Add `tblEventsLocations` as one of the data sources of this query.

3. Now click on the Queries tab of this dialog box.

   Access shows the stored `qryLocations` query, as shown in Figure 6-40.

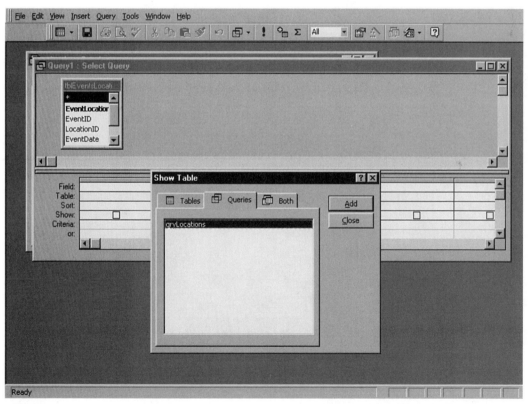

Figure 6-40
Adding a query as a data source

4. Click on the Add button.

   Access shows the field list box of this query next to the field list box of the tblEventsLocations table in the query design window. However, it does not automatically create a link between the LocationID fields of these two list boxes.

5. Click on the Close button to close the Show Table dialog box.

6. Expand the query design window and the two field list boxes and then drag the LocationID field from tblEventsLocations list box to the qryLocations list box.

7. Access creates an inner join between tblEventsLocations and qryLocations, as shown in Figure 6-41.

8. Select the Totals option from the View menu.

9. Add the field named tblEventsLocations_Countries_lkp.Description from the field list of qryLocations to the first cell of the Field row.

Even though Access displayed this field using the caption Country in the result of the qryLocations query shown in Figure 6-39, it does not show that caption in the field list. Instead it refers to this field by its full name (tblEventsLocations_Countries_lkp.Description) to distinguish it from the Description fields of the other two lookup tables.

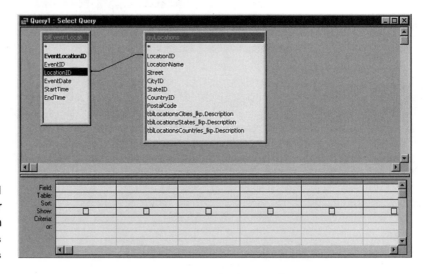

Figure 6-41
Creating an inner join between tblEventsLocations and qryLocations

10. Add the `EventLocationID` field from `tblEventsLocations` to the second cell of the Field row and select the `Count` function for its Total cell, as shown in Figure 6-42.

11. Save the query as `qryEventOccurrenceCount_ByCountry`.

12. Run the query.

    Access displays the event occurrence count by country, as shown in Figure 6-43.

13. Select the SQL View option from the View menu.

    Access displays the following SQL statement:

    ```
    SELECT qryLocations.tblLocationsCountries_lkp.Description,⇐
    Count(tblEventsLocations.EventLocationID) AS CountOfEventLocationID
    FROM tblEventsLocations INNER JOIN qryLocations ON⇐
    tblEventsLocations.LocationID = qryLocations.LocationID
    GROUP BY qryLocations.tblLocationsCountries_lkp.Description;
    ```

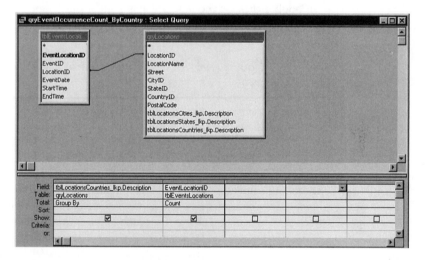

Figure 6-42
Design of
`qryEventOccurrence`
`Count_ByCountry`

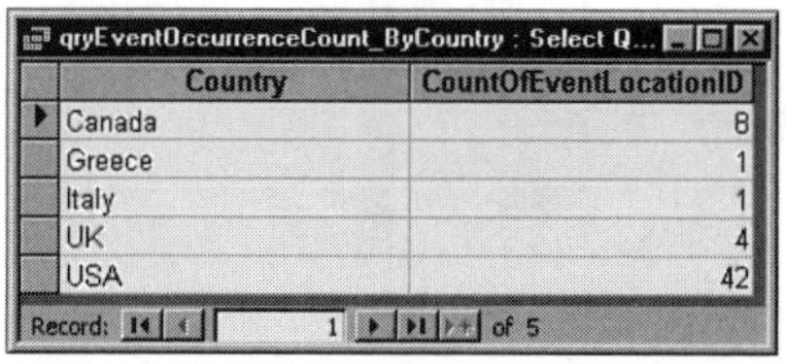

Figure 6-43
Result of
`qryEventOccurrence`
`Count_ByCountry`

Propagate Changes

Nested queries also help in propagating changes common among different queries. If many queries are based on one common query, any change you make to the common query is automatically reflected in all those dependent queries. How does this help?

Look at Figure 6-43. The numbers in the CountOfEventLocationID column, when added together, result in a total of 56 occurrences. If you open the **tblEventsLocations** table, it displays 59 records. Clearly, three records are not being counted. As explained in Lesson 1, this problem can be traced back to the inner join between **tblLocations** and **tblLocationsStates_lkp** that we used for the **qryLocations** query. If you look at the navigation bar of Figure 6-39, the **qryLocations** query produces 30 records, although there are 32 locations in the database; these 30 records link with 56 records of the **tblEventsLocations** table, as evident from Figure 6-43. To get the correct count from the **qryEventOccurrenceCount_ByCountry** query, you need to change the inner join between the location and state tables in **qryLocations** to an outer join:

1. Open the **qryLocations** query in the query design window.

2. Double-click on the link between **tblLocations** and **tblLocationsStates_lkp** and change that link to an outer join directed from **tblLocations** to **tblLocationsStates_lkp**.

3. Save the query (without changing its name) and close its query design window.

4. Run the **qryEventOccurrenceCount_ByCountry** query.

   Access now shows an event occurrence count that adds up to 59, as shown in Figure 6-44.

There is one limitation to the change propagation procedure. You cannot change the name of the common query and expect it to be propagated among dependent queries. In our example, if you change the name of the common query from **qryLocations** to qryLocations_New and try to run the dependent **qryEventOccurrenceCount_ByCountry** query, you will get an error.

Figure 6-44
New result of
qryEventOccurrence
Count_ByCountry

Country	CountOfEventLocationID
Canada	8
Croatia	1
Greece	1
Italy	1
UK	6
USA	42

Record: 1 of 6

If the common query contains parameters, then they automatically become the parameters of dependent queries.

Perform Advance Data Analysis

Certain types of data analysis questions cannot be answered with just one query. You have to use Nested queries in those cases. Consider the `qryEvents_Analysis` query constructed in Lesson 4 (see Figures 6-28 and 6-29). It lists the first and the last occurrence dates of each event. Say you want to include the start times of these two occurrences along with their dates. Instinctively, it appears that a simple modification of the query should do the trick. Just apply the `Min` and `Max` aggregate functions to two copies of the `StartTime` field. But that would return the earliest and the latest start times among all the occurrences of an event, not the start time of the first and last occurrence of an event. How can you modify the Total query? The answer is, you can't. This example is sufficient to make you realize that Total queries tend to lose the details when they produce their results.

To handle this apparently simple situation, you need to use Nested queries:

1. Close any query that you may have currently open.

2. Create the `qryEvents_Analysis` query, as shown in Figure 6-28 (or you can use the `GetExternalData` option from the File menu to import it from the `CALENDAR.MDB` file residing in the `C:\WEBSITE\HTDOCS\WDBIC\CHAP06\LESSON4\RESULTS` directory).

3. Open a new query in the query design window.

   Access displays the Show Table dialog box.

4. Highlight `tblEventsLocations` and press the Add button twice.

   Access puts two copies of the `tblEventsLocations` table on the query design window. (It automatically labels the second copy `tblEventsLocations_1`.)

5. Select the Queries tab and add `qryEvents_Analysis` to the query design window.

6. Click on the Close button to close the Show Table dialog box.

7. Enlarge the windows of the three data sources so that all their fields are visible.

8. Move `tblEventsLocations_1` to the right of `qryEvents_Analysis`, as shown in Figure 6-45.

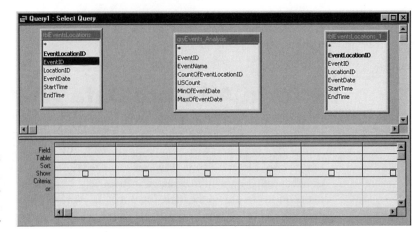

Figure 6-45
Laying out the data
sources in the
query design
window

9. Drag the EventID field from tblEventsLocations onto the EventID field of qryEvents_Analysis.

10. Drag the EventDate field from tblEventsLocations onto the MinOfEventDate field of qryEvents_Analysis.

11. Drag the EventID field from tblEventsLocations_1 onto the EventID field of qryEvents_Analysis.

12. Drag the EventDate field from tblEventsLocations_1 onto the MaxOfEventDate field of qryEvents_Analysis.

Access links the three data sources with inner joins, as shown in Figure 6-46.

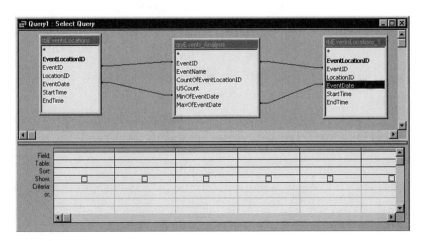

Figure 6-46
Linking the data
sources

13. Add the asterisk field of `qryEvents_Analysis`, the `StartTime` field of `tblEventsLocations`, and the `StartTime` field of `tblEventsLocations_1` to the Field row, as shown in Figure 6-47.

14. Save the query as `qryEvents_Analysis_withStartTimes`.

15. Run the query.

    Access displays the start times of the first and last occurrences of each event, along with the rest of the summary, as shown in Figure 6-48. (Observe the difference in the `StartTime` fields of the event with `EventID 10`.)

16. Select the SQL View option from the View menu.

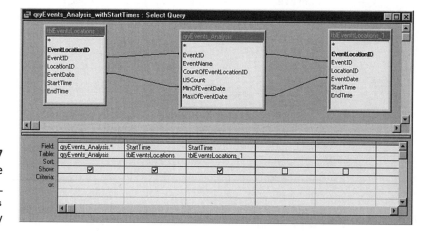

Figure 6-47
Design of the
`qryEvents_Analysis_`
`withStartTimes`
query

Figure 6-48
Result of the
`qryEvents_Analysis_`
`withStartTimes`
query

EventID	Event Name	Count	USCount	MinOfEventDate	MaxOfEventDate	Start Time	Start Time
1	Music Night	1	0	9/20/97	9/20/97	8:00:00 PM	8:00:00 PM
2	Art Exhibition	2	0	9/21/97	9/22/97	10:00:00 AM	10:00:00 AM
3	Film Day	1	0	9/21/97	9/21/97	10:00:00 AM	10:00:00 AM
5	Organ Recitals	1	0	9/26/97	9/26/97	12:00:00 PM	12:00:00 PM
6	The 1997 Main Street F	2	2	4/26/97	4/27/97	10:00:00 AM	12:00:00 PM
7	ARTFEST	2	2	5/23/97	5/24/97	9:00:00 AM	9:00:00 AM
8	International Jubilee	2	2	7/23/97	7/24/97	9:00:00 AM	9:00:00 AM
9	MicroStation FORUM &	3	3	1/20/97	1/22/97	8:00:00 AM	8:00:00 AM
10	Review of Existing Plan	2	2	1/24/97	1/25/97	1:00:00 PM	11:00:00 AM
12	The Construction Indust	1	1	1/22/97	1/22/97	12:00:00 PM	12:00:00 PM
13	AIA Plan Review Works	3	3	1/24/97	1/26/97	9:00:00 AM	9:00:00 AM
16	Housing in the 21st Cer	4	4	6/11/97	6/14/97	9:00:00 AM	9:00:00 AM
17	Durability of Buildings	2	0	3/20/97	3/21/97	10:00:00 AM	10:00:00 AM
18	Memorial Day Weekenc	2	2	5/24/97	5/25/97	1:00:00 PM	10:00:00 AM
19	USA International Balle	1	1	6/13/98	6/13/98	9:00:00 AM	9:00:00 AM
20	10th Annual Offshore D	2	0	11/18/97	11/19/97	9:00:00 AM	9:00:00 AM
21	Seminar - Improving Oil	1	0	12/2/97	12/2/97	10:00:00 AM	10:00:00 AM
22	Space-Age Technologie	1	0	12/22/97	12/22/97	10:00:00 AM	10:00:00 AM

Record: 1 of 37

Access displays the following SQL statement:

```
SELECT qryEvents_Analysis.*, tblEventsLocations.StartTime,⇐
tblEventsLocations_1.StartTime
FROM tblEventsLocations AS tblEventsLocations_1 INNER JOIN⇐
(tblEventsLocations INNER JOIN qryEvents_Analysis ON⇐
(tblEventsLocations.EventDate = qryEvents_Analysis.MinOfEventDate)⇐
AND (tblEventsLocations.EventID = qryEvents_Analysis.EventID)) ON⇐
(tblEventsLocations_1.EventDate = qryEvents_Analysis.MaxOfEventDate)⇐
AND (tblEventsLocations_1.EventID = qryEvents_Analysis.EventID);
```

The basic idea behind the design of this query is that there can be only one occurrence of an event on any particular date. So, when you join **tblEventsLocations** with **qryEvents_Analysis** on the **EventID** and **EventDate** (mapped to **MinOfEventDate** of **qryEvents_Analysis**) fields, Access pulls up the record belonging to the first occurrence of each event from **tblEventsLocations**. The logic behind the join of **tblEventsLocations_1** and **qryEvents_Analysis** is similar except that Access is pulling the last occurrence of each event in this case.

Lesson Summary

This lesson explained how query design can be simplified through a one-time activity of designing wide-ranging general-purpose queries and subsequently using them as a data source for other queries called Nested queries.

This concept of Nested query design was illustrated by first designing a query that links the **tblLocations** table with the city, state, and country lookup tables as the general-purpose query. Subsequently its field list box is added to the query design window of a new Total query and its relationship is established with a data table in the query design window.

Using examples based on the calendar database, this lesson also explained how Nested queries can help in propagating changes common among dependent queries by making changes in the general-purpose query. You cannot, however, make changes in the name of the general-purpose query, which destroys the link between the dependent query and the common query.

Quite often you will find that the data analysis that you want to carry out cannot be performed by a single query. This lesson showed how to perform advanced analysis using Nested queries. In the next lesson, we shall discuss some more types of Select queries that help in further expanding the scope of data analysis tasks.

For your reference, the **CALENDAR.MDB** database file resulting from this lesson is provided in the **C:\WEBSITE\HTDOCS\WDBIC\CHAP06\LESSON5\RESULTS** directory.

1. How does Access display the fields of a common query when it is used as a source of another query?
   a. It uses the syntax `TableName:FieldName` for each field.
   b. It uses the syntax `FieldName` for each unique field and the syntax `TableName:FieldName` for fields that share the same name.
   c. It uses the field caption for each field.
   d. It uses the syntax `FieldName` for each unique field and the syntax `TableName:Caption` for fields that share the same name.

2. What happens when you try to change the name of a query that is used as a data source of another query?
   a. Access does not allow you to make that change.
   b. Access automatically propagates that change.
   c. Access allows you to change the name but does not propagate that change into the dependent query.
   d. Access removes this Nested query from the dependent query.

3. Suppose Query A is nested in Query B and later on you add a new field to the result of Query A. Which of the following statements is true?
   a. The new field will automatically be displayed in the result of Query B.
   b. The new field will not be displayed in the result of Query B.
   c. The new field will automatically appear in the result of Query B only if the asterisk field of Query A is displayed in Query B.
   d. None of the above.

4. What happens when you try to add two copies of the same table to the query design window?
   a. Access generates an error message.
   b. Access displays both copies with the same table name.
   c. Access uses the name of the table as the name of the first copy.
   d. Access names the second copy by appending `1` to the table name.

5. Which of the following statements holds true in the case of Nested queries?
   a. The dependent query inherits the parameters of the source query.
   b. You can use a dependent query as a source of another query.
   c. You can easily generate the result produced by any Nested query using an equivalent query that is not nested.
   d. You can never edit data directly from the result of a dependent query.

Complexity: Easy

1. Design a Nested query named **qryEventsLocations** that is based on **qryLocations** and returns all the records from **tblEventsLocations**, along with the location name, street, city, state, country, and postal code.

Complexity: Advanced

2. Design a query named **qryEventsAnalysis_Cities** that lists the sponsor name, the event name, and the city of the first and last occurrences of each event. (Hint: Reuse two copies of the **qryEventsLocations** query created in the previous exercise.)

SUBQUERIES, UNION QUERIES, AND QUERY PERFORMANCE ISSUES

If you review the SQL statements of the queries we have constructed so far, you will notice they all fall under the category of Select queries. There are two more variations of Select queries: subqueries and Union queries. Because these two types of queries are not frequently used, this lesson introduces them by presenting an example of each and then concludes the discussion of Select queries by listing useful pointers for optimizing their performance.

What Is a Subquery?

A subquery is a **SELECT** statement nested inside another Select query. It works differently from a Nested query because you use it for specifying a filter criterion or a calculated field instead of a data source. The following example will help clarify this functionality.

Say you want to list the name and type of all the sponsors who are organizing music- and dance-type events. You can design a subquery to produce such a list, as shown below:

1. Copy the CALENDAR.MDB file residing in the
   C:\WEBSITE\HTDOCS\WDBIC\CHAP05\SAMPLES directory to the
   C:\WEBSITE\HTDOCS\WDBIC\CHAP06\LESSON6 directory.

2. Open the C:\WEBSITE\HTDOCS\WDBIC\CHAP06\LESSON6\CALENDAR.MDB database file in Access.

3. Create a new query and list `tblSponsorsTypes_Lkp`, `tblSponsors`, and `tblSponsorsContacts` as its data sources.

   Access automatically joins these tables based on the predefined relationships.

4. List the `Description` field from `tblSponsorsTypes_Lkp`, the `SponsorName` field from `tblSponsors`, and the `SponsorContactID` field from `tblSponsorsContacts` in the Field row.

5. Deselect the Show checkbox for the `SponsorContactID` field and place the cursor in its Criteria cell.

6. Press `SHIFT`-`F2`.

   Access displays a zoom window.

7. Type the criteria involving the Select subquery as shown in Figure 6-49.

8. Save the query as `qrySponsors_MusicAndDance`.

9. Run the query.

   Figure 6-50 shows the query result.

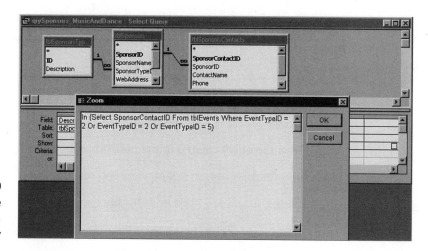

Figure 6-49
Design of the
`qrySponsors_Music`
`AndDance` query

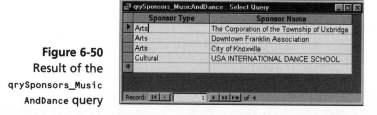

Figure 6-50
Result of the
`qrySponsors_Music`
`AndDance` query

10. Select the SQL View option from the View menu.

Access displays the following SQL statement:

```
SELECT tblSponsorsTypes_lkp.Description, tblSponsors.SponsorName
FROM tblSponsorsTypes_lkp INNER JOIN (tblSponsors INNER JOIN
tblSponsorsContacts ON tblSponsors.SponsorID =
tblSponsorsContacts.SponsorID) ON tblSponsorsTypes_lkp.ID =
tblSponsors.SponsorTypeID
WHERE (((tblSponsorsContacts.SponsorContactID) In (Select
SponsorContactID From tblEvents Where EventTypeID = 2 Or EventTypeID
= 2 Or EventTypeID = 5)));
```

In this example, the Select subquery populates the `IN` criteria (applied against the `SponsorContactID` field) with the `SponsorContactID`s of all the musical or dance events, causing Access to filter out sponsors that have at least one contact who listed these type of events.

Refer to the online documentation for more information on subqueries.

What Is a Union Query?

Union queries are used when you want to append the records from one data source to the records of another data source in your query result. The two data sources can be distantly related or completely nonrelated tables or queries. The only constraint is that for each field in the first data source, there must be a corresponding field (of a compatible data type) in the second data source.

As an example, say you want to create one list that includes the names of the sponsors belonging to the Arts or Cultural category and the names of the events that are marked as musical or dance. The following steps show how you can design a Union query to produce such a list:

1. Close the query created in the previous example.

2. Open a new query in design view and select `tblSponsors` as the data source.

3. List the `SponsorName` field and the `SponsorTypeID` field in the Field row.

4. Deselect the Show checkbox of the `SponsorTypeID` field and type `IN (1,4)` in its Criteria cell.

5. Add the following calculated field in the third cell of the Field row:

   `RecordType: "Sponsor"`

6. Select the SQL View option from the View menu.

Access displays the following SQL statement:

```
SELECT tblSponsors.SponsorName, "Sponsor" AS RecordType
FROM tblSponsors
WHERE (((tblSponsors.SponsorTypeID) In (1,4)));
```

7. Insert the cursor before the ending ; character and extend the above SQL statement as shown below:

```
SELECT tblSponsors.SponsorName, "Sponsor" AS RecordType
FROM tblSponsors
WHERE (((tblSponsors.SponsorTypeID) In (1,4))) UNION SELECT⇐
tblEvents.EventName, "Event" AS RecordType
FROM tblEvents
WHERE (((tblEvents.EventTypeID) In (2,5)));
```

8. Save this query as qrySponsorsAndEvents_Art_Related.

9. Select Run from the Query menu.

Access runs this Union query and returns the desired list, as shown in Figure 6-51.

The **RecordType** calculated field was added to help identify the data source of each record. Another thing to remember is that you cannot design a Union query in query design view. You have to enter the exact SQL in the query's SQL view. For more examples of Union queries, refer to the online documentation of Access.

Optimizing the Performance of Queries

Although Access is capable of employing state-of-the-art techniques for optimizing queries, a lot rests on your shoulders to help it exploit these techniques. Here is a list of pointers to make your queries execute faster:

⬤ Choose the smallest data type appropriate for a field during table design. If you are not particular about the precision of a numeric field, set the size of that field to Single instead of Double.

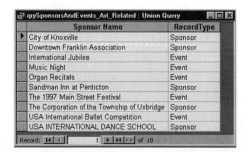

Figure 6-51
Result of the
qrySponsorsAnd
Events_Art_Related
query

● Index fields on both sides of a join, or better still, ensure that a relationship exists between the fields being linked. Access then automatically indexes them. Try to use joins between fields that have the same data type and size.

● When creating a query, add only the fields you need. Clear the Show checkbox of fields you used only to set criteria.

● Avoid restrictive query criteria on calculated and nonindexed columns whenever possible. The Rushmore technology that Access uses for fast index-based searches cannot work on such types of criteria.

For more information on Rushmore technology and when it can be applied, search for the keyword `Rushmore` from the online documentation for Access.

As an example, if you want to select events listed in the year 1997, use the `Between #1/1/97# And #12/31/97#` criterion directly on the `EventDate` field instead of first computing the year from the `EventDate` field using the `Year` function and then setting the criterion `=1997` on that calculated field.

● When creating Nested queries, do not put the calculated fields as part of your common query. Put them in your main queries.

● Index the fields that you use for sorting.

● Use the Performance Analyzer tool to have Access analyze your queries for potential improvements. It is available under the Tools, Analyze Performance menu option.

Lesson Summary

This lesson presented two more types of Select queries, subqueries and Union queries, and explained their application using examples based on the calendar database.

A subquery nests a **SELECT** statement inside another Select query and uses this **SELECT** statement for specifying the filter criteria. A Union query is used where you need to append records from one data source to records from another data source in your query result. However, you have to ensure that for every field in the first data source, there is a corresponding (compatible) field in the second data source.

This lesson concluded the discussion on Select queries by presenting some useful tips for optimizing query performance, which depends not only on your query design but also on the structure of your database.

For your reference, the **CALENDAR.MDB** database file resulting from this lesson is provided in the **C:\WEBSITE\HTDOCS\WDBIC\CHAP06\LESSON6\RESULTS** directory.

1. Where can you apply a subquery in a Select query?
   a. As a query data source
   b. As part of a filter criteria
   c. To create a calculated field as long as the subquery returns only one value
   d. In a sort cell as long as the subquery returns the words **Ascending** or **Descending** or a **Null** value

2. What are the names of the fields listed in the result of a Union query?
   a. Same as the name of the fields of the first data source.
   b. Same as the name of the fields of the last data source.
   c. Access assigns its own names, such as **Field1**, **Field2**, and so on.
   d. Access randomly picks up the field names from the data sources.

3. Which of the following statements holds true in the case of Union queries?
   a. You can unite only two data sources in one Union query.
   b. Each **SELECT** statement acting as the data source must end with a semicolon.
   c. In Access, you can develop a Union query only through the SQL view of its query design window.
   d. The corresponding fields of each data source must be of compatible types.

4. Suppose a query contains Table A and Table B as its data sources. Field 1 of Table A is linked with Field 2 of Table B with an outer join. Which of the following actions can help improve the performance of this query?
   a. Index Field 1.
   b. Index Field 2.
   c. Relate Table A and Table B using Field 1 and Field 2 as linking fields.
   d. All of the above.

5. A query contains the following calculated field:

```
DataPresent: IIF(IsNull([A]),False,True)
```

   The Show checkbox of this calculated field is turned off and the criterion **=True** is listed in its Criteria cell. What can you do to improve the performance of this query?
   a. Remove the **=True** criterion from this calculated field.
   b. Remove the calculated field.
   c. Specify the criterion **Is Not Null** against Field A.
   d. Index Field A.

Complexity: Easy

1. Design a subquery-based query named **qrySponsors_InfoExchange** that lists the names and types of all the sponsors who are organizing forums, exhibitions, workshops, conferences, and seminars.

Complexity: Advanced

2. Design a Union query named **qrySponsorsAndEvents_Professional** whose result includes the names of the sponsors belonging to the Professional category and the names of the events sponsored by each of those sponsors. The result should be formatted so that the event records follow the corresponding sponsor's record. (Hint: You can use an **ORDER BY** clause at the end of the last data source of a Union query to display the returned data in a specified order.)

CHAPTER SUMMARY

This chapter described how information from various tables of a database could be viewed together by linking them using table joins. This joining concept forms the basis of a wide variety of data analyses using various types of multiple-table Select queries such as Total queries, Crosstab queries, Nested queries, subqueries, and Union queries. Numerous examples based on the calendar database were presented to demonstrate the construction and application of each type of query. Here is a recap of the salient points covered in this chapter:

● A table join is a link between a field in one table and a field in another table.

● There are two types of table joins: inner joins and outer joins.

● Adding the related tables to the query design window creates these joins. Access automatically adds the join links based on predefined relationships.

● Sometimes Access tries to add extra join lines by trying to guess relationships between tables. Such lines may result in an error and should be deleted before you run the query.

● Sort and filter criteria can be applied to fields from any of the source tables. Filtering criteria helps generate information of a particular type.

● You can use the same criteria expression against multiple fields in a multi-table Parameter query.

● A Subtract query is used when you are looking for childless records in a parent table. This query returns all records from one table that do not have any related records in the second table.

● You can group and aggregate data using a Total query. A Total query allows you to calculate the sum, average, count, or total of a set of records.

● The Totals option is selected from the View menu of the query design window and adds a new row labeled Totals: to the query design grid and shows the Group By function by default under the selected fields.

● The analysis carried out by a Total query depends on the aggregate function specified in the Total row.

● You can get answers to many questions at once by applying several aggregate functions at a time in a single Total query.

● Criteria in a Total query can be specified either before (precriteria) or after (postcriteria) the records are aggregated, depending on the objective of your query.

● Crosstab queries help in summarizing data by grouping information in rows and columns and allowing you to specify the row heading, column heading, and value fields.

● The value field in a Crosstab query cannot have postcriteria.

● You can use a general-purpose query as a data source for another query— called a Nested query—and simplify its design.

● Any changes made in the query design are automatically propagated to the dependent queries.

● Nested queries can be used to perform advanced data analysis tasks that cannot be performed by a single query.

● A subquery is a SELECT statement nested inside another Select query.

● A Union query appends records from one data source to records from another data source in the query result. Records of these data sources should have the same data types.

● Query performance depends not only on the relational database management system that you use but also on your query design and database structure.

With this chapter, we conclude the discussion of Select queries. In the next chapter, we will look at the type of queries known as Action queries that allow you to perform bulk insertion, updates, and deletion of table records.

CHAPTER 7

DESIGNING QUERIES TO MAINTAIN DATA: ACTION QUERIES

There may be times when you have to make bulk changes in the tables of your database or move data among the tables. This can be performed through the user interface of Access or by moving through the records one row at a time and making the necessary changes. But when you think of a database containing thousands of records in which such changes need to be incorporated, this seems to be a formidable task. As usual, Access has an answer to this problem: It offers action queries, which are a simple, more efficient, and faster way of performing bulk updates to your records.

This chapter shows the use of action queries to update, append, and delete records from a database table and then presents some of their typical applications with relation to the calendar database. In particular, you will learn about:

311

● How to construct, save, and run an Update query

● How to use an expression to update a field

● How to use data from one table to update another

● How to specify criteria in an Update query

● How to construct a Delete query and preview its result

● Precautions to take when using Delete queries

● How to create tables using a Make-Table query

● How to populate tables using an Append query

● How to append records into tables with an `AutoNumber`-type field

● How to use a combination of action queries and temporary tables to perform a task

● How to use a subquery in an action query

● How to import data into multiple related tables

UPDATE QUERIES

Update queries are used to make bulk updates to the data in a table in an efficient manner. Update queries are exceptionally helpful in converting data imported from other sources into the format used by Access. Other useful applications of Update queries include making global changes, cascading changes from one table to another, and updating fields based on calculated values. This lesson lists the steps involved in constructing Update queries using examples illustrating their applications.

Constructing an Update Query

An Update query is constructed using the familiar query design interface. You specify the data source whose records you want to update, indicate to Access that you want to create an Update query, and then list the appropriate expressions for the fields you want updated. The following example will help illustrate this process.

Let's say you decide to add a field named `DateCreated` in the `tblEvents` table to keep track of when each event record was added to the calendar database. You modify the design of the `tblEvents` table as shown:

1. Copy the `CALENDAR.MDB` file residing in the `C:\WEBSITE\HTDOCS\WDBIC\CHAP05\SAMPLES` directory to the `C:\WEBSITE\HTDOCS\WDBIC\CHAP07\LESSON1` directory.

2. Open the `C:\WEBSITE\HTDOCS\WDBIC\CHAP07\LESSON1\CALENDAR.MDB` database file in Access.

3. Open the `tblEvents` table in design view.

4. Define a new `Date/Time` field named `DateCreated` after the `EventDescription` field and set its `DefaultValue` property to `=Date()`.

   The `DefaultValue` property ensures that anytime a record is added to the `tblEvents` table, the current date automatically is stored in this field.

5. Save the table design and open this table in datasheet view.

6. Access displays the `DateCreated` field as shown in Figure 7-1, but notice that it did not put any value in this field for the existing records. This is because Access applies the `DefaultValue` property only to new records.

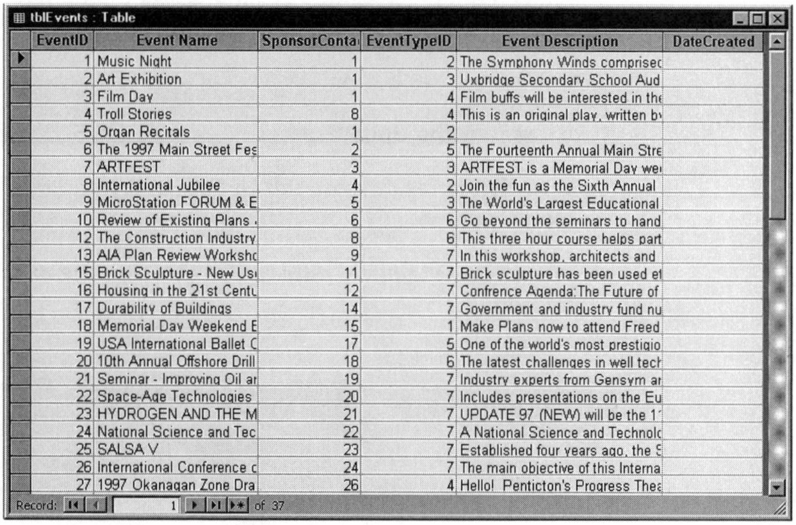

tblEvents : Table

EventID	Event Name	SponsorConta	EventTypeID	Event Description	DateCreated
1	Music Night	1	2	The Symphony Winds comprisec	
2	Art Exhibition	1	3	Uxbridge Secondary School Aud	
3	Film Day	1	4	Film buffs will be interested in the	
4	Troll Stories	8	4	This is an original play, written by	
5	Organ Recitals	1	2		
6	The 1997 Main Street Fes	2	5	The Fourteenth Annual Main Stre	
7	ARTFEST	3	3	ARTFEST is a Memorial Day we	
8	International Jubilee	4	2	Join the fun as the Sixth Annual	
9	MicroStation FORUM & E	5	3	The World's Largest Educational	
10	Review of Existing Plans .	6	6	Go beyond the seminars to hand	
12	The Construction Industry	8	6	This three hour course helps part	
13	AIA Plan Review Worksho	9	7	In this workshop, architects and	
15	Brick Sculpture - New Us	11	7	Brick sculpture has been used et	
16	Housing in the 21st Centu	12	7	Confrence Agenda:The Future of	
17	Durability of Buildings	14	7	Government and industry fund nu	
18	Memorial Day Weekend E	15	1	Make Plans now to attend Freed	
19	USA International Ballet C	17	5	One of the world's most prestigio	
20	10th Annual Offshore Drill	18	6	The latest challenges in well tech	
21	Seminar - Improving Oil ar	19	7	Industry experts from Gensym ar	
22	Space-Age Technologies	20	7	Includes presentations on the Eu	
23	HYDROGEN AND THE M	21	7	UPDATE 97 (NEW) will be the 1	
24	National Science and Tec	22	7	A National Science and Technolo	
25	SALSA V	23	7	Established four years ago, the S	
26	International Conference c	24	7	The main objective of this Interna	
27	1997 Okanagan Zone Dra	26	4	Hello! Penticton's Progress Thea	

Record: 1 of 37

Figure 7-1 Adding the `DateCreated` field to the `tblEvents` table

To populate the **DateCreated** field with some valid date value (say 1/1/97) for existing event records, you can create an Update query as follows:

1. Close the **tblEvents** table.

2. Open a new query in the query design window and add **tblEvents** as the data source.

3. Select the Update Query option from the Query menu.

   Access hides the Sort and Show rows and displays a new Update row in the bottom portion of the query design window.

4. Add the **DateCreated** field from **tblEvents** to the first cell of the Field row.

5. Enter **#1/1/97#** in the Update cell of this field, as shown in Figure 7-2.

6. Select Save from the File menu and save the query as **qryEvents_Update_DateCreated**.

7. Select Run from the Query menu.

   Access displays a message box indicating the number of records that will be updated and asking for a confirmation to proceed with the update.

8. Click on the Yes button.

   Access runs the Update query.

9. To verify the result, close this Update query and open **tblEvents** in datasheet view.

   The **DateCreated** field displays 1/1/97 in all the existing records, as shown in Figure 7-3.

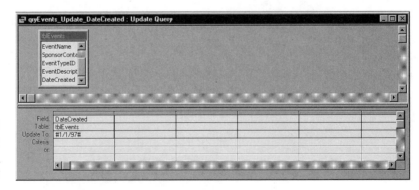

Figure 7-2
Creating the
qryEvents_Update_
DateCreated query

tblEvents : Table

EventID	Event Name	SponsorConta	EventTypeID	Event Description	DateCreated
1	Music Night	1	2	The Symphony Winds comprisec	1/1/97
2	Art Exhibition	1	3	Uxbridge Secondary School Aud	1/1/97
3	Film Day	1	4	Film buffs will be interested in the	1/1/97
4	Troll Stories	8	4	This is an original play, written b	1/1/97
5	Organ Recitals	1	2		1/1/97
6	The 1997 Main Street Fes	2	5	The Fourteenth Annual Main Stre	1/1/97
7	ARTFEST	3	3	ARTFEST is a Memorial Day we	1/1/97
8	International Jubilee	4	2	Join the fun as the Sixth Annual	1/1/97
9	MicroStation FORUM & E	5	3	The World's Largest Educational	1/1/97
10	Review of Existing Plans	6	6	Go beyond the seminars to hand	1/1/97
12	The Construction Industry	8	6	This three hour course helps part	1/1/97
13	AIA Plan Review Worksho	9	7	In this workshop, architects and	1/1/97
15	Brick Sculpture - New Us	11	7	Brick sculpture has been used e	1/1/97
16	Housing in the 21st Centu	12	7	Confrence Agenda:The Future of	1/1/97
17	Durability of Buildings	14	7	Government and industry fund nu	1/1/97
18	Memorial Day Weekend E	15	1	Make Plans now to attend Freed	1/1/97
19	USA International Ballet C	17	5	One of the world's most prestigio	1/1/97
20	10th Annual Offshore Drill	18	6	The latest challenges in well tech	1/1/97
21	Seminar - Improving Oil ar	19	7	Industry experts from Gensym ar	1/1/97
22	Space-Age Technologies	20	7	Includes presentations on the Eu	1/1/97
23	HYDROGEN AND THE M	21	7	UPDATE 97 (NEW) will be the 1	1/1/97
24	National Science and Tec	22	7	A National Science and Technolo	1/1/97
25	SALSA V	23	7	Established four years ago, the S	1/1/97
26	International Conference c	24	7	The main objective of this Interna	1/1/97
27	1997 Okanagan Zone Dra	26	4	Hello! Penticton's Progress Thea	1/1/97
28	Net Talk Class - The Inter	27	8	You may now register "Online" fc	1/1/97

Record: 1 of 37

Figure 7-3 Result of the `qryEvents_Update_DateCreated` query

As usual, Access creates an SQL statement from the specifications of the query design before running the query. However, this time the SQL statement begins with the keyword `UPDATE` instead of `SELECT`, which you can verify easily by displaying this SQL statement as follows:

1. **Close the `tblEvents` table.**
2. **Open the `qryEvents_Update_DateCreated` query in design view.**
3. **Select the SQL View option from the View menu.**

   Access displays the following SQL statement it constructed for this query:

   ```
   UPDATE tblEvents SET tblEvents.DateCreated = #1/1/97#;
   ```

Using an Expression to Update a Field

Any expression that can be used to create a calculated field can also be used to update an existing table field as long as the expression returns values that can be accepted by the data type of the field being updated. For example, say you want to set the `DateCreated` field of the existing records to one week before the current date. In that case, you can replace the `#1/1/97#` date value with the expression `DateAdd("ww", -1,Date())` in the `qryEvents_Update_DateCreated` query.

Using Data from One Table to Update Another

Access allows you to update multiple fields in a single Update query as long as they come from the same table. You can use the values in one table to update the values in another table, however. As an example, let's say you want to append a line indicating the sponsor's Web address at the end of the event description for each event. The following steps show how you can create a multiple table Update query to complete this task:

1. Close the query created in the previous example.

2. Open a new query in design view and list `tblSponsors`, `tblSponsorsContacts`, and `tblEvents` as the data sources.

   Access automatically links these tables with inner joins based on the predefined relationships.

3. Add the `EventDescription` field from `tblEvents` to the first cell of the Field row.

4. Add the following calculated field to the second cell of the Field row:
   `NewEventDescription: [EventDescription] & " Web Address: " & HyperlinkPart([WebAddress],2)`

   The expression in this calculated field uses the concatenation operator (&) to append the URL portion of the `WebAddress` hyperlink field to the original event description.

5. Select Run from the Query menu to run the query.

   Access displays two fields, `EventDescription` and `NewEventDescription`, in the query result.

6. Place the cursor in the `NewEventDescription` field of the first record and press `SHIFT`-`F2`.

   Access displays the value of the `NewEventDescription` field in a zoom window, as shown in Figure 7-4.

7. Return to the query design window.

8. Select Update Query from the Query menu.

   Access displays the Update row.

9. Enter the following expression in the Update cell of the `EventDescription` field (see Figure 7-5).

   `[EventDescription] & " Web Address: " & HyperlinkPart([WebAddress],2)`

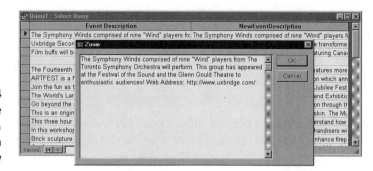

Figure 7-4
Displaying the
NewEventDescription
field in a zoom
window

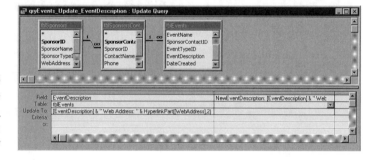

Figure 7-5
Design of the
qryEvents_Update_
EventDescription
query

You can also copy this expression from the **NewEventDescription** field and paste it to the Update cell.

10. Save this query as qryEvents_Update_EventDescription.

11. Select Run from the Query menu.

   Access displays a confirmation message box.

12. Select Yes.

   Access updates the EventDescription field of each event record. You can verify it by displaying its value from the datasheet view of the tblEvents table.

13. Select the SQL View option from the Query menu.

   Access displays the following SQL statement:

```
UPDATE (tblSponsors INNER JOIN tblSponsorsContacts ON⇐
tblSponsors.SponsorID = tblSponsorsContacts.SponsorID) INNER JOIN⇐
tblEvents ON tblSponsorsContacts.SponsorContactID =⇐
tblEvents.SponsorContactID SET tblEvents.EventDescription =⇐
```

```
[EventDescription] & " Web Address: " &⏎
HyperlinkPart([WebAddress],2);
```

This example also shows how you can first design a Select query to preview the change to the data you are about to make and then convert it to an Update query. Because the change made by an Update query (like all other action queries) is irreversible once you execute it, we recommend that you use this preview technique whenever in doubt.

Access ignores any field whose Update cell is empty and automatically removes it when you close the query. That is why we did not worry about the presence of the `NewEventDescription` field when we ran the Update query in this example.

Specifying Criteria in an Update Query

You can limit the records you want updated by specifying the appropriate criteria in the Criteria and Or rows of the query design window. Again, the approach is straight-forward:

1. First design a Select query containing the necessary filter criteria.

2. Verify that this Select query produces only records that you want to update.

3. Add the fields you want to update to the Field row.

4. Add their corresponding calculated fields that will return the new data.

5. Convert this Select query into an Update query.

6. List the field expression of each calculated field into the Update cell of its corresponding table field.

7. Leave the Update cells of all the other fields (that have a criteria expression or were used for preview) empty.

If two or more data sources in an Update query have fields with the same name and you want to use one of those fields in the Update cell, use the syntax `[TableName].[FieldName]` to represent that field uniquely. Note that the square brackets in this syntax are mandatory.

Lesson Summary

This lesson explained how bulk updates in data could be made in a simple and effi-cient manner using Update queries. To construct an Update query, you specify the data source whose records you want to update, select the Update query from the query menu bar, and build appropriate expressions for the fields to be updated. These steps were illustrated using a number of examples.

While building an Update query based on an expression, be careful that the value returned by this expression is acceptable by the data type of the field being updated. This lesson also showed how multiple fields from the same table could be updated using a single query. You can also limit the records you want to update by applying necessary criteria. Because the change made by an Update query is irreversible, this lesson explained how to preview this change before implementing it. Design a Select query containing calculated fields representing the changed data, verify the result of these calculated fields, and subsequently convert it into an Update query. In the next lesson, you will see how bulk deletes can be carried out in an efficient manner using the Delete query.

For your reference, the **CALENDAR.MDB** database file resulting from this lesson is provided in the **C:\WEBSITE\HTDOCS\WDBIC\CHAP07\LESSON1\RESULTS** directory.

1. An Update query would be useful in which of the following situations?
   a. When you need to add new records to a table
   b. When you need to add information to a particular field of one or more records of a table
   c. When you need to remove information from a particular field of one or more records of a table
   d. When you need to remove records from a particular table

2. Why does Access display a confirmation message box when you run an Update query?
   a. To indicate the number of records that will get updated
   b. It is a standard message generated for all types of queries
   c. To forewarn you that the changes made by an Update query are irreversible
   d. All of the above

3. Why is it advantageous to construct an Update query from a Select query?
   a. This is the only way to construct an Update query.
   b. Converting a Select query to an Update query is easy.
   c. You can preview the change to the data before running the Update query.
   d. All of the above.

4. Which of the following statements are true?
   a. You can update the **SponsorName**, **ContactName**, and **EventName** fields of the calendar database using a single Update query.
   b. You can list an expression containing the **SponsorName**, **ContactName**, and **EventName** fields of the calendar database in the Update cell of an Update query.

     c. When running an Update query, Access puts a `Null` value in any field listed in the Field row whose Update cell is empty.

     d. All of the above.

5. Which of the following expressions would you use to convert the data of a `Currency` field named `CostPrice` holding the amount in U.S. dollars to its equivalent Canadian dollars? (Assume $1 U.S. = $1.4 Canadian)

     a. `"* 1.4"`

     b. `"CostPrice" * 1.4`

     c. `[CostPrice] / 1.4`

     d. `[CostPrice] * 1.4`

Complexity: Easy

1. Design a query named `qrySponsors_UpdateUserName_ToUppercase` that changes the data in the `UserName` field of all the sponsor records to uppercase. (Hint: Use the `UCase` function.)

Complexity: Moderate

2. Create a query named `qryEvents_UpdateNullDescription` that adds the sponsor name, contact name, and Web address (in any appropriate format) to the `EventDescription` field wherever this field does not contain any data.

DELETE QUERIES

Whenever you need to delete batches of records from one or more tables, a Delete query is the way to go. As in the case of Update queries, a Delete query is usually more efficient than deleting records through the user interface. This lesson shows the steps involved in constructing Delete queries and then lists some important points that you should consider before running these types of queries.

Constructing a Delete Query

A Delete query allows you to delete selected records from any table. The process of constructing a Delete query is similar to that of constructing an Update query, as outlined in the following steps:

1. Create a Select query that generates all the records you want to delete.

2. Pick the Delete query option from the Query menu.

Access converts this query into a Delete query and displays a Delete row in the query design window.

3. Specify the asterisk (or any other) field of the source table in any cell of the Delete row.

Let's run through these steps using a simple example where we delete all the musical events from the sample calendar database.

1. Copy the CALENDAR.MDB file residing in the C:\WEBSITE\HTDOCS\WDBIC\CHAP05\SAMPLES directory to the C:\WEBSITE\HTDOCS\WDBIC\CHAP07\LESSON2 directory.

2. Open the C:\WEBSITE\HTDOCS\WDBIC\CHAP07\LESSON2\CALENDAR.MDB database file in Access.

3. Design a new query and list tblEvents and tblEventTypes_lkp as the data sources.

   Access automatically creates an inner join between these two tables based on the predefined relationship.

4. Add the asterisk field from tblEvents to the first cell of the Field row.

5. Add the Description field from tblEventsTypes_lkp to the second cell of the Field row.

6. Specify the criterion ="Musical" in the Criteria cell of the Description field.

7. Run the query.

   Access displays the list of all the musical events in the database.

8. Return to query design view and select the Delete Query option from the Query menu.

   Access hides the Sort and Show rows and displays a Delete row in the query design window. Furthermore, it automatically inserts the word From in the first cell and the word Where in the second cell of this row, as shown in Figure 7-6. This setup signifies the deletion of all records *from* tblEvents *where* the linked Description value is equal to Musical. This is exactly what we want from the Delete query.

9. Run the query by selecting Run from the Query menu.

   Access displays a message box asking you to confirm this deletion.

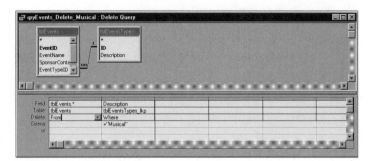

Figure 7-6
Design of the
qryEvents_Delete_
Musical query

10. Select Yes.

Access deletes all the musical event records from the tblEvents table.

11. Run the query again.

This time Access displays a message box indicating that no records will be deleted, which confirms that no musical event records are present in the database.

12. Save the query as qryEvents_Delete_Musical.

13. Select the SQL View option from the View menu.

Access shows the following SQL statement it constructed for this query. Note that it starts with the DELETE keyword.

```
DELETE tblEvents.*, tblEventsTypes_lkp.Description
FROM tblEventsTypes_lkp INNER JOIN tblEvents ON tblEventsTypes_lkp.ID
= tblEvents.EventTypeID
WHERE (((tblEventsTypes_lkp.Description)="Musical"));
```

Okay, so all the musical events have been deleted. But what about their related child records in tblEventsLocations table? As a matter of fact, Access deleted them, too, when you ran the previous query because you had set the Cascade Delete option at the time of establishing a relationship between these two tables. (See Chapter 5, Lesson 4.) Let's verify this claim:

1. Close the qryEvents_Delete_Musical query.

2. Create a new query and list tblEventsTypes_lkp, tblEvents, and tblEventsLocations as the data sources.

3. Add the asterisk (*) field from tblEventsLocations and the Description field from tblEventsTypes_lkp to the Field row.

4. Specify the criterion "=Musical" against the Description field.

5. Run the query.

No records are displayed in the query result.

This example illustrates that even though a Delete query allows you to specify only one data source as the target of deletion, you can in fact delete records from multiple tables using a single Delete query. What would happen if you tried to delete records from a parent table that has related records in the child table but the Cascade Delete option is not set between them? Access handles this case very sensibly, as illustrated by the following example:

1. Close the query of the previous example.

2. Create a new query and list tblEventsTypes_Lkp as the data source.

3. Add the asterisk field from tblEventsTypes_Lkp to the Field row.

4. Select the Delete Query option from the Query menu.

Access converts this Select query into a query that will delete all records from the tblEventsTypes_Lkp table, which has child records in the tblEvents table but does not have a cascade delete relationship with this table. Let's see how Access responds when you run this query.

5. Select Run from the Query menu.

Access displays a confirmation message indicating that nine records will be deleted.

6. Press Yes.

Instead of deleting the records, Access now produces a warning message indicating that it is unable to delete eight of those nine records due to key violations and asks if you still want to proceed with the deletion process (see Figure 7-7). The record that it is able to delete is the one whose Description is set to "Musical" because we deleted all the musical type events in the previous example.

Figure 7-7
Access giving a
warning message
when running a
Delete query

7. Press Yes again.

   Access completes the deletion process.

8. Save this query as qryEventTypes_DeleteUnused and close this query.

9. Open the tblEventsTypes_Lkp table in datasheet view.

   The eight event-type lookup values are intact and the record with the "Musical" value does not exist.

If you want to empty the tblEventsTypes_Lkp table completely, you will have to first delete all the records from tblEvents using another Delete query.

Important Considerations When Using a Delete Query

When creating and running a Delete query, keep the following points in mind:

- Once you delete records using a Delete query, you can't undo the operation. Therefore, you should preview the data the query selects for deletion before you run the query.

- You should maintain backup copies of your data at all times. If you delete the wrong records, you can retrieve them from your backup, as explained in the next lesson.

- As you have seen, running a Delete query might delete records in related tables, even if they're not included in the query. Be aware of the scope of your Delete query.

- You can delete records from any of the source tables in a Delete query as long as these tables form a one-to-one relationship.

- You can delete records only from the "many" table in a Delete query containing two tables forming a one-to-many relationship. You can, however, use the fields of the "one" table for specifying criteria. If you want to delete records from the "one" table using a criterion based on the fields of the "many" table, you have to use multiple queries, as explained in Lesson 5.

- You cannot execute a Delete query that is based on a nonupdateable data source such as a total query or a Crosstab query.

- If you start a Delete query on an attached Paradox, dBASE, or FoxPro table that's linked to your database, you can't cancel the query after you start running it.

Lesson Summary

In this lesson you learned a simple and efficient way to delete batches of records from one or more tables using the Delete query. You can construct a Delete query by first designing a Select query that generates all records that you want to delete and then converting it to a Delete query by selecting the Delete Query option from the Query menu. This process was explained using two examples.

Although you specify only one data source for deletion, the Delete query may delete records from multiple tables. This happens when you delete records from a parent table, which has related records in a child table, and the Cascade Delete Referential Integrity option is turned on. Access does not delete the records if the cascade delete is turned off.

Because of the irreversible consequences of executing a Delete query and its wider ramifications in a database having many related tables with cascade delete set on, this lesson concluded with some important points that you should bear in mind while executing a Delete query.

In the next lesson you will see how to create a new table using another type of action query known as the Make-Table query.

For your reference, the `CALENDAR.MDB` database file resulting from this lesson is provided in the `C:\WEBSITE\HTDOCS\WDBIC\CHAP07\LESSON2\RESULTS` directory.

1. What happens when a Select query is converted to a Delete query?
   a. A Delete row is added to the query grid.
   b. The Sort and Show rows are removed.
   c. Access automatically places `From` and `Where` keywords in the Delete row.
   d. Access pops up a warning message before converting the query into a Delete query.

2. When are records from multiple tables deleted when you run a Delete query?
   a. If a relationship exists between these tables
   b. If referential integrity has been established among these tables
   c. If the Cascade Delete option of the referential integrity is set
   d. All of the above

3. Suppose Table A has a one-to-many relationship with Table B, which has a one-to-many relationship with Table C. Further assume that the Cascade Delete option is turned on between Table A and Table B, but it is turned off between Table B and Table C. What happens when you execute a Delete query containing Table A as its data source?
   a. Access deletes all records from Table A, Table B, and Table C.
   b. Access deletes all records from Table A and Table B, but not from Table C.

c. Access does not delete any record from Table A, Table B, or Table C.

d. Access deletes only those records from Table A that either do not have a related record in Table B or have only related records in Table B that do not have any related record in Table C.

4. Which of the following statements are true for a Delete query?

a. Once you run the query, you cannot stop it.

b. Once the records are deleted, you cannot recover them.

c. Access does not allow you to delete records from the one table through a Delete query containing both the one table and the many table.

d. You can delete records from the multiple tables if you use a Delete query whose data source is another total query.

5. How will you delete data from specified fields?

a. Use a Delete query with a criterion.

b. Use an Update query.

c. Use a Select query.

d. None of the above.

EXERCISE 2

Complexity: Easy

1. Design a query named `qryLocations_Delete_Unused` that deletes all the location records that are not being used by any event in the calendar database.

Complexity: Easy

2. Create a Delete query named `qryEventsLocations_DeleteOld` that deletes all the event location records whose event dates are less than the current date.

LESSON 3

MAKE-TABLE QUERIES

Make-Table queries are used when you want to create tables from all or part of the data in one or more tables. These queries find their application in creating permanent, temporary, or archive tables. These queries are also very useful in converting imported data into a proper format. Fields in the new table can come from existing tables or queries or can be created using expressions. This lesson describes how to create a Make-Table query and then lists some of its applications.

Creating a Make-Table Query

The following steps outline the general procedure for constructing a Make-Table query:

1. Create a Select query that produces the data you want to put in the new table.

2. Convert it into a Make-Table query.

3. Specify the name of the new table and the name and path of the destination database.

Let's follow these steps to create a new table that copies all the events to a new table named **tblEvents_Backup**.

1. Copy the **CALENDAR.MDB** file residing in the **C:\WEBSITE\HTDOCS\WDBIC\CHAP05\SAMPLES** directory to the **C:\WEBSITE\HTDOCS\WDBIC\CHAP07\LESSON3** directory.

2. Open the **C:\WEBSITE\HTDOCS\WDBIC\CHAP07\LESSON3\CALENDAR.MDB** database file in Access.

3. Design a new query and list **tblEvents** as the data source.

4. Add the asterisk field to the Field row.

5. Select the Make-Table Query... option from the Query menu.

   Access displays a message box asking for the name of the new table and the location of the destination database. As you can see from Figure 7-8, the Current Database option is selected by default.

6. Enter **tblEvents_Backup** in the input box and then press the OK button.

   Access converts the Select query into a Make-Table query, as evident from the title of the query design window.

Figure 7-8
Access asking for the name of the new table in a Make-Table query

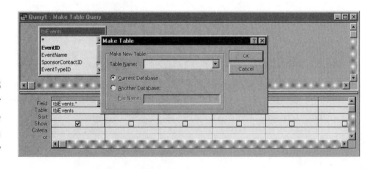

7. Save the query as qryEvents_MakeBackup.

8. Select Run from the Query menu to run the query.

   Access displays the number of records that will be added to the new table and asks for a confirmation to proceed.

9. Select Yes.

   Access executes the query.

Let's see if Access created a new table and how closely it resembles the original table in terms of data, field structure, and relationships.

1. Close the query design window.

2. Click on the Tables tab of the database container.

   The new table, tblEvents_Backup, is listed along with the other tables, as shown in Figure 7-9.

3. Open this table in datasheet view.

   The table contains an exact copy of all the event records.

4. Now select the Design View option from the View menu.

   Access displays the table structure as shown in Figure 7-10.

   Although the field structure of this table seems to be a duplicate of the original tblEvents table, the field properties are not. For example, the Required property of the EventName field in tblEvents is set to Yes, whereas in the new table, it is set to No. Also note that no primary key is defined for this table.

5. Close the Table Design window.

6. Select the Relationships... option from the Tools menu.

   Access opens up the Relationships window and displays all the relationships between existing tables as shown in Figure 7-11.

Figure 7-9
The database container displaying the new table created by the Make-Table query

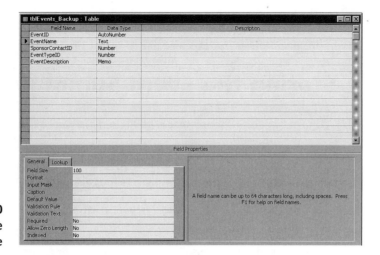

Figure 7-10
Structure of the
new table

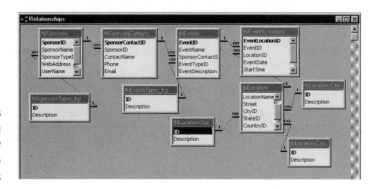

Figure 7-11
The Relationships
window displaying
the previously
saved layout of the
relationships

Notice that the new table is not displayed. This is because the Relationships window shows only the *previously saved layout* of the relationships. It does not automatically display all the tables or all the relationships in the database.

7. To display all the current relationships in the database, select the Show All option from the Relationships menu.

Nothing changes on the Relationships window, indicating that no relationships exist between the new table and the existing tables.

8. Close the Relationships window.

From this example, you can see that the table created by a Make-Table query mimics only the data and the data type of the fields of the original data source but not the field properties or the relationships. Next, we look at another example illustrating another common use of a Make-Table query.

When a Make-Table query creates a new table, it wipes out any existing table with the same name unless that existing table is participating in one or more relationships.

Storing the Event Summary

Let's say that, as part of the annual maintenance process, you want to purge all the events occurring in the previous year (say 1997) from the database. But before doing that, you want to store a summary of these events by event type. To do that, you create a Make-Table query as shown below:

1. Close the query created in the previous example if it is open.

2. Open a new query in design view and list `tblEventsLocations` as the data source.

3. Following the procedure explained in Chapter 6, Lesson 4, design a total query that lists the last occurrence date of all events by their event types, as shown in Figure 7-12.

4. Save the query as `qryEvents_LastOccurringDate`.

5. Open a new query in query design view and list `tblEventsTypes_Lkp`, `tblEvents`, and `qryEvents_LastOccurringDate` as the data sources.

   Access appropriately joins these data sources.

6. Add the `Description` field from `tblEventsTypes_Lkp`, the `EventID` field from `tblEvents`, and the `MaxOfEventDate` field from `qryEvents_LastOccurringDate` to the first three cells of the Field row respectively.

7. Convert this query into a Total query, as shown in Figure 7-13.

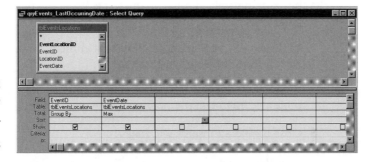

Figure 7-12
Design of the
`qryEvents_`
`LastOccurringDate`
query

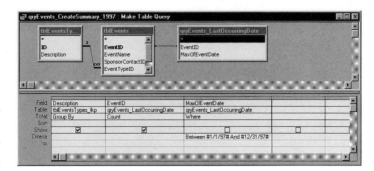

Figure 7-13
Total query
counting the 1997
events by their
event type

8. Run this query to verify the result and then switch back to Design mode.

9. Select the Make-Table Query... option from the Query menu.

   As before, Access displays a message box asking for the name of the new table and the location of the destination database.

10. Enter `tblEvents_Summary_1997` in the input box and then press the OK button.

    Access converts this total query into a Make-Table query.

11. Save the query as `qryEvents_CreateSummary_1997`.

12. Run the query.

    Access creates the `tblEvents_Summary_1997` table. Figure 7-14 displays this table in datasheet view.

Although you cannot edit the result of a total query, you can change the value of any field of the table created by the Make-Table query based on that total query.

Figure 7-14
The `tblEvents_Summary_1997` table in datasheet view

When Can You Use a Make-Table Query?

As you can see from the previous examples, a Make-Table query can be used to give persistence to the result of any Select query. This characteristic of a Make-Table query can be applied in a variety of applications, some of which are listed below:

- Making a backup copy of a table.

- Creating reports that display data from a specified point in time.

- Creating a table to export to other Microsoft Access databases. For example, you might want to create a table that contains fields from your sponsor and event tables, and then export that table to a database used by your invoicing department.

- Creating a history table that contains old records. For example, you could create a table that stores all your old events before deleting them from your current event table.

- Creating a temporary table to improve performance of tasks based on multiple table queries or SQL statements. For example, suppose you want to print multiple reports based on a five-table query that includes totals. You may be able to speed things up by first creating a Make-Table query that retrieves the records you need and stores them in one temporary table. Then you can base the reports on this table rather than rerunning the query for each report. However, the data in the table is frozen at the time you run the Make-Table query.

- Creating a temporary table to handle data manipulation tasks that cannot be easily accomplished by a single action query. Lesson 5 presents an example of this case.

Lesson Summary

A Make-Table query is used to create tables from existing data from one or more tables. It is constructed by first designing a Select query that produces the data you want in the new table and then converting it into a Make-Table query. The table is then saved after giving it a name and specifying the path and name of the database where it is to reside. These steps were illustrated in this lesson using examples based on the calendar database.

This lesson also demonstrated how a table created by the Make-Table query mimics only the data and data types of the fields of the original data source but not their properties or relationships. Some typical applications of Make-Table queries were also presented in this lesson.

If you want to append data to an existing table or a table created using a Make-Table query, you can do so using an Append query, whose construction and application are explained in the next lesson.

For your reference, the `CALENDAR.MDB` database file resulting from this lesson is provided in the `C:\WEBSITE\HTDOCS\WDBIC\CHAP07\LESSON3\RESULTS` directory.

1. You can use a Make-Table query for which of the following applications?
   a. When you want to import data from another database into an existing table of the current database
   b. When you want to export data to another database
   c. When you want to purge records from your database but want to maintain a backup summary of the records being purged
   d. All of the above

2. When does Access actually execute the Make-Table query?
   a. When you name your new table and specify its destination database
   b. When you select the Run command from the Query menu
   c. When you give your confirmation to proceed with creating the new table and add the identified records
   d. When you save the query

3. What type of queries can you use as the data source for a Make-Table query?
   a. Union query
   b. Total query
   c. Crosstab query
   d. Update query

4. Which of the following statements are true about the new table created by a Make-Table query?
   a. Its fields have the same names and data types as the fields in the result of the Select query on which this Make-Table query is based.
   b. Its fields have the same settings for their properties as the corresponding fields in the original tables.
   c. Relationships between the new table and the existing tables are automatically established.
   d. The new table does not have any primary key.

5. Under what circumstances would a Make-Table query not wipe out an existing table with the same name as the original table?
   a. When the existing table has data.
   b. When the existing table has a primary key.

c. When the existing table is participating in a relationship with other tables.

d. There are no such circumstances.

Complexity: Easy

1. Design a query named `qryLocations_BackupSponsors` that copies the data from the sponsor table to a new table named `tblSponsors_Backup`.

Complexity: Advanced

2. Create a query named `qryCreateSummaryByEventTypesAndYear` that creates a new table named `tblEventCountSummary_ByTypeandYear` listing the number of event occurrences by event type and year. The new table should have a field named `EventType` and a field for every relevant year (such as 1997, 1998, and so on). (Hint: Use a Crosstab query similar to the `qryEvents_CountByTypeAndYear_Crosstab` query created in Chapter 6, Lesson 4, as the data source of your Make-Table query.)

APPEND QUERIES

If you want to populate an existing table with data from one or multiple sources, use Append queries. You can also use an Append query to copy data to tables in other databases. Although Append queries are similar to Make-Table queries, what differentiates them is the fact that Append queries allow you to add records to an existing table, whereas Make-Table queries create a new table and, in the process, wipe out an existing table with the same name. Furthermore, an Append query would not know where to add the data if the target table did not exist. This lesson describes how to create an Append query and illustrates its applications with the help of examples. This lesson also presents some rules that should be followed when you want to append records with an `AutoNumber` field.

Creating an Append Query

The following steps outline the general procedure for constructing an Append query:

1. Create a Select query that produces the data you wish to append to an existing table.

2. Convert this query into an Append query.

3. Specify the name of the table and the name and path of the destination database.

4. Establish the correlation between the fields of the data source and the fields of the destination table.

Let's trace these steps through an example where we use an Append query to import some new sponsors into the `tblSponsors` table from a comma-delimited text file.

1. Copy the `CALENDAR.MDB` file residing in the `C:\WEBSITE\HTDOCS\WDBIC\CHAP05\SAMPLES` directory to the `C:\WEBSITE\HTDOCS\WDBIC\CHAP07\LESSON4` directory.

2. Open the `C:\WEBSITE\HTDOCS\WDBIC\CHAP07\LESSON4\CALENDAR.MDB` database file in Access.

3. Using the instructions given in Chapter 4, Lesson 6, import the comma-delimited text file named `SPONSORS.TXT` (residing in the `C:\WEBSITE\HTDOCS\WDBIC\CHAP07\LESSON4` directory) as a new table in the current database. Note that the first row of this text file contains the names of the fields and not the data.

   The import wizard should automatically name this table `SPONSORS`. Figure 7-15 shows the field names and the contents of this table.

4. Create a query and list the `SPONSORS` table as the data source.

5. Add the `SponsorName`, `SponsorTypeID`, and `WebAddress` fields to Field row.

6. Select the Append Query... option from the Query menu.

   Access asks for the name of the destination table.

7. In the Table Name box, enter `tblSponsors` and click OK.

   Access displays an Append To row in the query design grid and automatically fills it with names of the matching destination fields, as shown in Figure 7-16.

SPONSORS : Table

	ID	SponsorID	SponsorName	SponsorTypeI[	ContactName	Phone	Email	WebAddress
▶	1	1	Florence Histori	4	Mrs Florence	(402) 333-2322	florence@floren	http://www.florence.com/
	2	2	American Asso	7	Beck Marcia J	(607) 498- 5800	marcia@aao.co	http://www.aao.com
	3	3	Aero Internation	2	Steve Robinson		aero@aol.com	http://ail.aero.com
	4	4	L&M Motor Car	13	Jean P. Belman		Jean@lmm.com	http://lmm.lorenzo.com
	5	5	Smith Microsys	3	Clara Jhonson	117- 406-4423		
	6	6	Aero Manageme	2	A. B. Deol		abd@pmi.vsnl.n	
*	ıer)							

Figure 7-15
The `SPONSORS` table in datasheet view

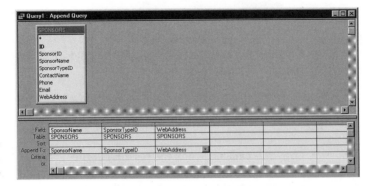

Figure 7-16
Designing an
Append query

What about the other fields such as `UserName` and `Password` that belong to the `tblSponsors` table but are not part of the imported table? If you do not list any corresponding field for these fields, Access will try to put in their default values (`Null`, in this case) in each inserted record. Let's see if that works.

1. Select Run from the Query menu.

   Access lists the number of records that will be appended once the query gets executed and asks for your confirmation.

2. Click Yes to confirm the execution of the query.

   Instead of running the query, Access displays an error message as shown in Figure 7-17. The message essentially says that none of the records can be appended due to the violation of a validation rule in one or more fields.

3. Select No to stop the execution of the query.

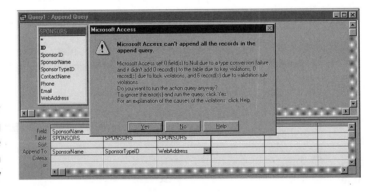

Figure 7-17
Access displaying
an error message
on running an
Append query

Although Access is not very specific about why the query fails to append the records, you can gain some insight once you review the properties of each field of the **tblSponsors** table. In this case, the error is caused due to the **Required** property being set for the **UserName** field. The Append query was trying to insert **Null** values in this field and that was not acceptable to the JET database engine. So now you have two choices. Either add a **UserName** field to the imported **SPONSORS** table with some valid data or supply some non-**Null** default value as a source for the **UserName** field of the **tblSponsors** table. Let's go with the second option for this example.

1. Add the following calculated field named **DefaultUserName** to the fourth cell of the Field row in the query design window.

   ```
   DefaultUserName: "None"
   ```

2. Select the UserName field in the Append To cell of this calculated field as shown in Figure 7-18.

3. Rerun the query.

   This time Access executes the query successfully.

4. Select the SQL View option from the View menu.

   Access displays the following SQL statement it constructed for this query:

   ```
   INSERT INTO tblSponsors ( SponsorName, SponsorTypeID, WebAddress,
   UserName )
   SELECT SPONSORS.SponsorName, SPONSORS.SponsorTypeID,
   SPONSORS.WebAddress, "None" AS DefaultUserName
   FROM SPONSORS;
   ```

5. Close this query after saving it as **qrySponsors_Import**.

Figure 7-18
Adding a default value for the **UserName** field

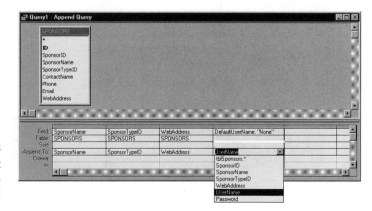

6. Open the `tblSponsors` table in datasheet view and scroll down to the end of the recordset.

Access lists the appended records as shown in Figure 7-19. Note how Access automatically supplies a unique value for the `SponsorID` field. Things would have been different if we had listed the `SponsorID` field from the `SPONSORS` table in the Field row of our Append query and correlated it with the `SponsorID` field of the `tblSponsors` table. The realization of this difference is important when you are appending records to a table whose primary key is an `AutoNumber` type field. We discuss this issue in more detail next.

Appending Records with an AutoNumber-Type Field

When you want to append records to a table with an **AutoNumber**-type field, it is advisable to keep the following in mind:

● If you don't include the `AutoNumber` field in your Append query, Access automatically assigns a `Counter` value for this field to each of the appended records.

● If you correlate a source field to the `AutoNumber` field in your Append query, Access accepts the source value as long as it does not match the value of any existing record. If the values do clash, Access will flag a key violations error.

Figure 7-19
Listing the appended records

You have already seen an example of how Access automatically assigns unique values in the **SponsorID** field of the **tblSponsors** table when you do not list this field in the Append To cell of an Append query. Let's take an example of the other case, where we force our own value for this field in an Append query (say the value **32**, which is not being used by any record, as you can see from Figure 7-19):

1. Close the **tblSponsors** table.

2. Open a new query in the query design window but do not select any data source.

3. Add the following calculated fields to the Field row:

```
SponsorID: 32
SponsorName: "Test Sponsor"
SponsorTypeID: 1
UserName: "Test"
```

4. Select the Append Query... option from the Query menu and enter **tblSponsors** as the destination table.

   Access automatically correlates these fields with the appropriate destination fields as shown in Figure 7-20.

5. Run the query.

   Access indicates that one record will be appended and asks for your confirmation.

6. Select Yes.

   Access successfully executes the query.

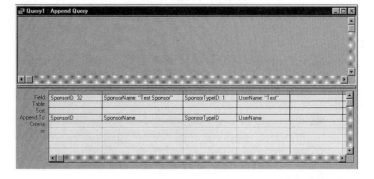

Figure 7-20
Supplying the
value for the
AutoNumber field in
an Append query

7. Select the SQL View option from the View menu.

Access displays the following SQL statement:

```
INSERT INTO tblSponsors ( SponsorID, SponsorName, SponsorTypeID,
UserName )
SELECT 32 AS SponsorID, "Test Sponsor" AS SponsorName, 1 AS
SponsorTypeID, "Test" AS UserName;
```

8. Close this query after saving it as qrySponsors_Import_Test.

9. Review the tblSponsors table in datasheet view.

You will see the test record included with the SponsorID value of 32.

The above example also illustrates how you can insert a new record into a table without supplying any existing data source. You can also use parameters instead of specific values to make it a general-purpose Append query.

Append Query Tips

When creating an Append query, consider the following points:

- If all the fields in both tables have the same names, you can just drag the asterisk (*) to the query design grid.

- If the fields you've selected have the same name in both tables, Microsoft Access automatically fills the matching name in the Append To row. If the fields in the two tables don't have the same name, enter the names of the fields in the table you're appending to in the Append To row.

- If fields of an Append query do not exactly match the fields in the target table, you can adjust the name of the target field in the Append To cell. You can also use a field to set criteria without sending its data to the target table by simply blanking out the field name in the Append To cell.

- To preview the records that the query will append, click View on the toolbar. To return to query design view, click View on the toolbar again. Make any changes you want in design view.

- If you try to append invalid data into a field, Access generates a warning message indicating that it will append the records but insert a Null value for that field.

- If you get a Key violation error message when running an Append query, chances are that either you are adding duplicate values into a field that must be unique or the records being appended are breaking the referential integrity constraints.

Lesson Summary

In this lesson you learned how to construct an Append query to append records to a table with data residing in a table in another database. The procedure was explained in a step-by-step manner with the help of examples. This lesson also demonstrated how Access automatically inserts the default value (or **Null** if none is specified) when you do not list all the destination fields in an Append query. In some cases this can cause Access to generate a violation of validation rule error if the unlisted field is a required field and its default value translates to **Null**.

This lesson also explained two possible scenarios of appending records into a table with an **AutoNumber** field. If you do not include the **AutoNumber** field in your Append query, Access takes care of it and automatically assigns a unique **Counter** value to this field to each record being appended. But if you correlate a source field with an **AutoNumber** field of the destination table, the source field values are accepted as long as they do not clash with any existing value. In the event of clash, Access flags a key violation error. Finally, this lesson presented some useful tips that you should consider while designing an Append query.

When dealing with real-world applications, you may find that a single action query may not suffice to produce the desired result. In the next lesson you will see two examples that require the services of multiple action queries used in a proper sequence.

For your reference, the **CALENDAR.MDB** database file resulting from this lesson is provided in the **C:\WEBSITE\HTDOCS\WDBIC\CHAP07\LESSON4\RESULTS** directory.

1. What does an Append query do?
   a. Populates a new table with data from the specified data source.
   b. Moves data from one table to another.
   c. Inserts data in an existing table without overwriting its existing data.
   d. Overwrites data already existing in a table before inserting the new data.

2. Under what circumstances does Access fail to append to records when you run an Append query?
   a. When the data types of the source fields and the corresponding destination fields are not compatible
   b. When the Append query tries to append records with primary key values that already exist
   c. When the Append query tries to violate the validation rules for a field or a record
   d. All of the above

3. How can you append records if the names of fields in the source table and destination table do match?
   a. Add an asterisk (*) in the first Field and Append To cells.
   b. Add an asterisk (*) in the Append To cell and add the field names of the source table in the Field cell.
   c. Add source fields in the Field cell and the name of the corresponding destination field in the Append To cell.
   d. All of the above.

4. What happens when you do not include an `AutoNumber` field in your `Append` query?
   a. Access tries to correlate the `AutoNumber` fields of the source table and the destination table.
   b. Access automatically assigns unique values for this field to the records being appended.
   c. The appended records appear at the end of the recordset.
   d. Access allocates missing values in the `AutoNumber` field and inserts the records in between the recordset.

5. Which of the following statements are true for Append queries?
   a. The destination table must be specified in an Append query.
   b. You can append records irrespective of the error messages flagged by Access.
   c. All the fields from the source table need not be listed in the Append query.
   d. Access automatically fills in the Append To cell if the field names of the source table and destination table match.

EXERCISE 4

Complexity: Moderate

1. Create a general purpose Append query named **qrySponsors_AddRecord** that allows you to insert any new record into the **tblSponsors** table. (Hint: Use parameters for the source fields.)

Complexity: Moderate

2. Design an Append query named **qrySponsorContacts_Import** that inserts the contact information of the first sponsor record of the imported **SPONSORS** table into the **tblSponsorsContacts** table. Ensure that the link between this contact record and its corresponding sponsor record in the **tblSponsors** table is maintained.

COMBINING ACTION QUERIES AND TEMPORARY TABLES TO PERFORM A TASK

Individually, each action query you have studied so far acts on only specified tables, although an Update or Delete query may have a cascading effect on other related tables. There are times, however, when the data manipulation task you want to perform cannot be easily accomplished by any single action query. It may be due to the narrow scope of the action query or just a limitation imposed by the JET engine. Either way, you have to use a sequence of two or more action queries to get the job done. This lesson presents two relevant examples from the calendar database where one action query does not easily work and you have to run multiple action queries as a group to accomplish the task. Finally, if you really are determined to explore a single query route for such cases, this lesson offers some insight on how you can go about it.

Marking Expired Events

Suppose you want to mark each event record in the **tblEvents** table as expired or not expired. An expired event is an event that has already occurred and does not have any future occurrences. To mark a record, you can add a **Yes/No**-type field named **Expired** in the **tblEvents** table. The question is how to set this field based on the data in the **tblEventsLocations** table. Let's first try the one action query approach and see what happens.

If you want to use one action query, it has to be an Update query. To create that Update query, first design a Select query that lists all the expired event records. To consider an event expired or not, you will need to identify the last occurrence date of each event and compare it with the current date. A total query such as **qryEvents_LastOccurringDate** that you designed in Lesson 3 (refer to Figure 7-12) can give you the last occurrence information. Let's see how we can use this query to create the Update query:

1. Copy the **CALENDAR.MDB** file residing in the
   C:\WEBSITE\HTDOCS\WDBIC\CHAP05\SAMPLES directory to the
   C:\WEBSITE\HTDOCS\WDBIC\CHAP07\LESSON5 directory.

2. Open the **C:\WEBSITE\HTDOCS\WDBIC\CHAP07\LESSON5\CALENDAR.MDB** database file in Access.

3. Add a **Yes/No**-type field named **Expired** to the **tblEvents** table.

4. Create the **qryEvents_LastOccurringDate** query as shown in Figure 7-12.

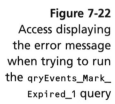
5. Create a new query listing tblEvents and qryEvents_LastOccurringDate as the data sources and containing the <Date() criterion against the MaxOfEventDate field, as shown in Figure 7-21.

6. Run the query.

   Access lists the expired event records.

7. Return to query design view and select the Update Query option from the Query menu.

8. Enter Yes in the Update cell of the Expired field.

9. Save the query as qryEvents_Mark_Expired_1.

10. Run the query.

    Instead of running the query, Access complains with an error message, as shown in Figure 7-22.

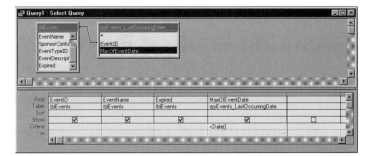

Figure 7-21
Designing a query
to list expired
event records

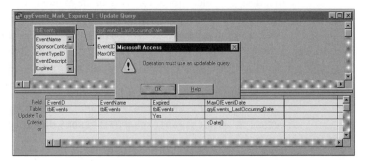

Figure 7-22
Access displaying
the error message
when trying to run
the qryEvents_Mark_
Expired_1 query

This error message says that Access cannot run an Update query that contains a nonup-dateable data source, which in this case happens to be the **qryEvents_LastOccurringDate** Total query. This is a serious limitation that Access imposes on the Update query. To work around this limitation, you can first use a Make-Table query to output the result of the **qryEvents_LastOccurringDate** query in a temporary table and then use an **Update** query that links this table with the **tblEvents** table, as described next:

1. Click OK to hide the error message and close the query.

2. Create a Make-Table query named qryEvents_Step01_StoreLastDates that outputs the result of the qryEvents_LastOccurringDate into a temporary table named tblTemp_Events_LastOccurringDate.

3. Run this Make-Table query.

   Access creates a new table named tblTemp_Events_LastOccurringDate that contains the last occurring date of each event.

4. Create a new Update query named qryEvents_Step02_UpdateExpired as shown in Figure 7-23.

5. Run this query.

6. This time Access successfully updates the Expired field of the selected records.

Notice how we have indicated a step number when labeling the above two action queries. This is because it is important that these queries be run in the proper order to generate the desired outcome.

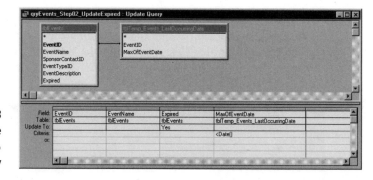

Figure 7-23
Design of the
qryEvents_Step02_Up
dateExpired query

Purging Expired Events

To prevent the `tblEvents` table from holding outdated data, it is a good idea to purge the expired event records as a regular maintenance task. Again, you can attempt to carry out this task with one action query, as follows:

1. Create a Delete query as shown in Figure 7-24 and save it as `qryEvents_DeleteExpired_1`.

2. Run this query.

   Access does not like this query design and displays the same `Operation must use an updateable query` error message, as in the case of the first Update query.

3. Close this query.

OK, so one query does not work (which you had probably guessed anyway!). Let's try to use the Make-Table approach like you did in the previous example. You already have the Make-Table query designed. You just need to design a Delete query that uses the temporary table created by this query instead of the total query.

1. Create a Delete query named `qryEvents_Step02_DeleteExpired` as shown in Figure 7-25.

2. Run this query.

   Access displays another error message that says `Couldn't delete from specified tables`.

3. Close this query.

Why did Access generate this error? Because it thinks that the `tblEvents` table and the `tblTemp_Events_LastOccurringDate` table are forming a one-to-many relationship and you are trying to delete records from the "one" table, which it does not permit. How does Access determine this relationship? Perhaps from the fact that these two tables

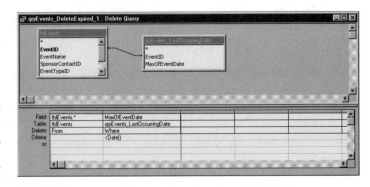

Figure 7-24
Design of the
`qryEvents_`
`DeleteExpired_1`
query

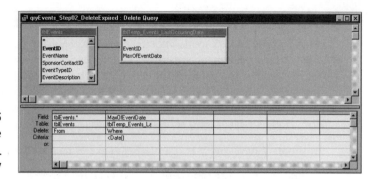

Figure 7-25
Design of the
qryEvents_Step02_
DeleteExpired query

are not linked in a one-to-one relationship because the **EventID** field of the **tblTemp_Events_LastOccurringDate** table is not set as the primary key. Recall from Lesson 3 that a Make-Table query does not set any primary key in the table it creates. What can be done?

One way is to set the **Expired** field of the event records that have expired using the two action queries designed in the previous example and then design a Delete query that deletes all these marked records, as shown in Figure 7-26.

There is also another approach you can consider:

1. Design a temporary table with two fields, **EventID** and **MaxOfEventDate**, and set the **EventID** field as its primary key.

2. Create an **Append** query to populate this table with the result of the **qryEvents_LastOccurringDate** query.

3. When you link this temporary table with the **tblEvents** table in your Delete query, Access will treat that link as a one-to-one relationship and permit the deletion of the records from the **tblEvents** table.

Note that because the Append query only appends data (without deleting the existing data), you need to ensure that the temporary table is empty before you run action queries. We leave the implementation of this approach as an exercise.

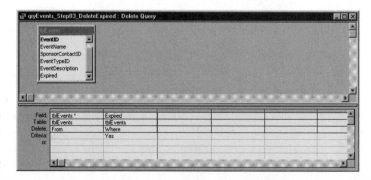

Figure 7-26
Design of the
qryEvents_Step03_De
leteExpired query

Using a Subquery in an Action Query

In Chapter 6, Lesson 6, we described the concept of a *subquery*, where you use the result of **SELECT** SQL statement as a criteria of another Select query. A subquery can also be used to specify a criteria in an action query, and it is this feature that you can use when trying to work around the above-mentioned constraints of action queries. As an illustration, the following steps show how you can update the **Expired** field with a single Update query containing a subquery.

1. Create a new query and add **tblEvents** as its data source.

2. Add the **EventID** field and the **Expired** field to the Field row.

3. Place your cursor in the Criteria cell of the **EventID** field and press SHIFT-F2.

   Access displays a zoomed text box.

4. Enter the following criteria expression in that text box:

   ```
   IN (Select EventID From qryEvents_LastOccurringDate Where
   MaxOfEventDate < Date())
   ```

5. Press OK to close the zoom window.

6. Select the Update Query... option from the Query menu.

7. Enter Yes in the Update cell of the **Expired** field.

8. Save the query as **qryEvents_MarkExpired_UsingSubquery**.

9. Run the query.

   Access does not generate any error message and indicates that zero rows will be updated.

Because all the expired records were deleted in the previous example, this makes sense. If you want to verify the effect of this query, execute it on another copy of the original calendar database after adding the **Expired** field to the **tblEvents** table and recreating the **qryEvents_LastOccurringDate** query.

The **CALENDAR.MDB** file residing in the **C:\WEBSITE\HTDOCS\WDBIC\CHAP07\ LESSON5\RESULTS** directory also has this query and the undeleted event data.

Lesson Summary

Quite often a single action query cannot accomplish the required data manipulation and you have to resort to a sequence of two or more action queries to carry out the task. This lesson used two examples from the calendar database to demonstrate this limitation of action queries and explained how to use multiple action queries.

In the first example, you marked all events whose last occurrence date was less than the current date as **Expired** in the **tblEvents** table. This was achieved by first creating a **Yes/No**-type field in the **tblEvents** table and then designing a Select query that listed all such events. The result of this query was stored in a temporary table using a Make-Table query; the **tblEvents** table was subsequently updated by linking the temporary table with it.

The second example carried the first example to its logical end by purging all the expired records. This example explained how even a combination of a Make-Table and a Delete query does not work in this case and demonstrated the need for yet another action query to carry out the task. You could use a Delete query on the **Expired** field set by the combination of the two action queries of the previous example. Alternatively, an Append query could be used to populate a temporary table with all the expired events, link it to the **tblEvents** table as a one-to-one relationship in a Delete query, and delete all the expired records. This lesson also explained how a subquery can be used to specify a criteria in an action query and to work around the constraints of action queries.

1. What type of action queries can you not run if you have a Total query as one of their data sources?
   a. Update query
   b. Delete query
   c. Make-Table query
   d. Append query

2. What would happen if you did not run the action queries of the examples presented in this lesson in the specified order?
   a. Access would not permit you to change the order.
   b. Access would generate an error message.
   c. You would not achieve the desired result.
   d. You would still get the same desired result.

3. If you get an **Operation must use an updateable query** error message when you run an Update query, what can you do to work around this problem?
   a. Replace all the nonupdateable data sources of this Update query with temporary tables containing the result of these data sources.
   b. Remove the nonupdateable data sources from this Update query and use subqueries based on these data sources in the query criteria.
   c. Convert the Update query into a Make-Table query.
   d. Convert the Update query into an Append query.

4. Assume that a Delete query has two tables, Table A and Table B, as its data sources. Furthermore, these two tables are joined on their primary keys, which are of the same data type. Which of the following statements are true, assuming that these two tables do not have any predefined relationship?

     a. Access will not allow you to delete records from either of these tables.
     b. Access will allow you to delete records from Table A but not from Table B.
     c. Access will allow you to delete records from Table B but not from Table A.
     d. Access will allow you to delete records from either of these two tables.

5. What should you normally ensure before you run an Append query to populate a temporary table that will be used by another Update query?
     a. The table should have a primary key.
     b. The table should have a predefined relationship with the tables that it will link to in the Update query.
     c. The table should be empty.
     d. All of the above.

Complexity: Moderate

1. Implement the Append query approach described in this lesson to delete the expired event records. Start the name of each action query with the prefix `qryDeleteEvents_Step_On`, w⁄.ere **n** represents the sequence number of that query. (Hint: Don't forget to create a Delete query that deletes all records from the temporary table first.)

Complexity: Moderate

2. Design a Delete query named `qryEvents_DeleteExpired_UsingSubquery` that employs a subquery to delete all the expired event records.

IMPORTING DATA INTO MULTIPLE RELATED TABLES

In Lesson 4, we demonstrated how an Append query could be used to import data from one table into another. By having an `AutoNumber`-type primary key field in the destination table, you don't have to worry about ensuring that the value in this key field stays unique for the inserted records. Access automatically takes care of it. The example in Lesson 4, where you appended the records from the `SPONSOR` table into the `tblSponsors` table, showed evidence of this autonumbering feature. For each of these inserted records, Access automatically assigned a new and unique value in its `SponsorID` field.

    Although autonumbering is a great feature when you are adding records to just one table, it can make things a little complicated if you have to fragment the source data and import these fragments into multiple related tables. For example, observe the fields and data of the **SPONSOR** table shown in Figure 7-15 (see Lesson 4). Besides the basic sponsor information, each record also contains the contact information.

Say you want to import this contact information into the `tblSponsorsContacts` table. What value will you assign to the linking `SponsorID` field of each added record? To keep the link intact with the data in the `tblSponsors` table, it has to be the value of the `SponsorID` field of the corresponding sponsor in the `tblSponsors` table. But how will you establish this match? As evident from Figure 7-19 (in Lesson 4), the `SponsorID` values of the imported sponsor records in the `tblSponsors` table have no correlation with the data in the `SponsorID` field of the **SPONSOR** table. So you cannot just copy the `SponsorID` field of the **SPONSOR** table into the `SponsorID` field of the `tblSponsorContacts` table. This lesson presents two techniques for determining the appropriate `SponsorID` value for each contact record and resolving this situation. Finally, it concludes with a brief discussion on importing data into tables that do not have a numeric ID field as a primary key. Lookup tables are a good example of such a case.

Method 1: Linking via Another Common Field

One way you can try to associate the Access-assigned `SponsorID` values with the contact records of the **SPONSOR** table is by linking the **SPONSOR** table and the `tblSponsors` table using another common field that stays unique. The `SponsorName` field would be a good candidate in this case. The following steps show how you can use this observation to import the contact information into the `tblSponsorsContacts` table:

1. Copy the `CALENDAR.MDB` file residing in the `C:\WEBSITE\HTDOCS\WDBIC\CHAP07\LESSON4\RESULTS` directory to the `C:\WEBSITE\HTDOCS\WDBIC\CHAP07\LESSON6` directory.

2. Open the `C:\WEBSITE\HTDOCS\WDBIC\CHAP07\LESSON6\CALENDAR.MDB` database file in Access.

   Notice that this database already contains the **SPONSOR** table. If you browse through the `tblSponsors` table, you will see that it holds the imported sponsor records as shown in Figure 7-19.

3. Create a new query and specify **SPONSORS** and `tblSponsors` as its data sources.

   Access automatically joins these tables on the `SponsorID` field.

4. Delete the line representing this join.

5. Add another join line that connects the `SponsorName` field of both the tables.

6. Add the `SponsorID` field from the `tblSponsors` table and the `ContactName`, `Phone`, and `Email` fields from the **SPONSORS** table to the Field row, as shown in Figure 7-27.

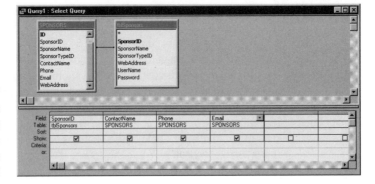

Figure 7-27
Joining the
tblSponsors table
and the SPONSORS
table on the
SponsorName field

7. Run the query.

   The correct SponsorID value appears with each contact record, as shown in Figure 7-28.

8. Select the Append Query... option from the Query menu and enter tblSponsorsContacts as the destination table.

   Access automatically fills in the destination fields corresponding to the source fields, as shown in Figure 7-29.

9. Save this query as qrySponsorsContacts_Import.

10. Run this query to completion.

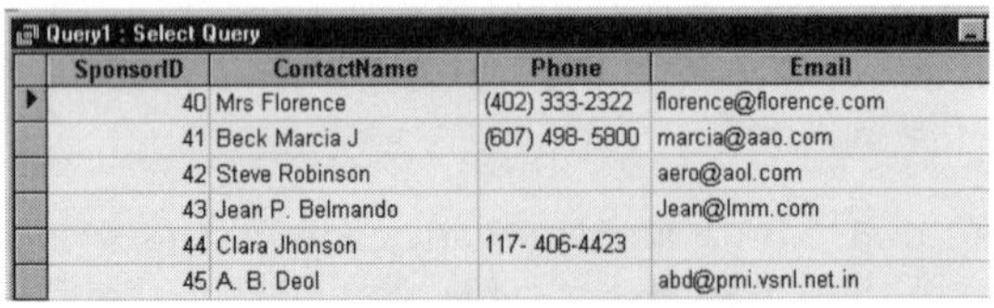

Figure 7-28
Query result
displaying the
correct SponsorID
value for each
contact record

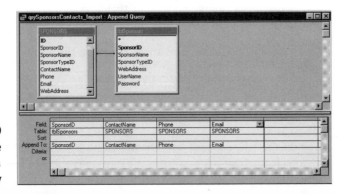

Figure 7-29
Design of the
qrySponsorsContacts
_Import query

Access appends the contact and the sponsor ID information to the `tblSponsorsContacts` table.

11. Close this query.

As you can see, this whole procedure is not hard to implement. The only caveat is that the common linking field is assumed to behave as a primary key. It must contain unique data for all records. Conversely, if two sponsor records happen to have the same sponsor name (the design of **tblSponsors** allows for it), there will be ambiguity and the procedure will fail. You can then try to use multiple common fields such as **SponsorName** and **UserName** to ensure uniqueness, but unfortunately, in this case the **UserName** information is not present in the **SPONSOR** table. The next method that we are going to describe gets around these limitations as long as the source table has a field that can act as a primary key, such as the **SponsorID** field of the **SPONSOR** table.

Method 2: Storing Old IDs Along with New IDs

In this method, you add another ID field in the destination table and then use this additional field to store the original ID of the source record being appended. This way, when Access assigns its own values to the main ID field (the primary key) during the append process, you can assign the original primary key value to this supplementary ID field. To illustrate how this method works, let's redo the sponsor and contact import process from the beginning:

1. Open the `tblSponsors` table in datasheet view and delete all the sponsor records imported from the `SPONSORS` table. The corresponding records in the `tblSponsorsContacts` table should automatically be deleted due to the `cascade delete` property set between these two tables.

2. Add a new `LongInteger`-sized `Number` field named `OldSponsorID` to the `tblSponsors` table.

3. Design an Append query named `qrySponsors_Import_withOldID` whose data source is the `SPONSORS` table and destination is the `tblSponsors` table.

4. Correlate the fields as shown in Figure 7-30. Note that the `SponsorID` source field of the `SPONSORS` table feeds the `OldSponsorID` field and not the `SponsorID` field of the destination table. The `SponsorID` destination field is not listed in this query at all.

5. Run this query to completion.

6. Close this query.

Open the `tblSponsors` table in datasheet view and scroll down to the last few records.

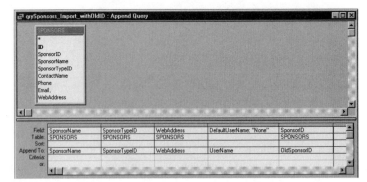

Figure 7-30
Design of the
qrySponsors_Import_
withOldID query

The imported records contain the original SponsorID values in the OldSponsorID field, as shown in Figure 7-31.

7. Now close this table and design a new Append query named qrySponsorsContacts_Import_withOldID, whose design is shown in Figure 7-32. This query is similar to the qrySponsorsContacts_Import query you made earlier except that the link is now between the SponsorID of the SPONSORS table and the OldSponsorID of the tblSponsors table.

8. Run the query to its completion.

Access appends all the contact records from the SPONSORS table into the tblSponsorsContacts table with the appropriate SponsorID field values.

9. Close this query and open the tblSponsorsContacts table in datasheet view to verify the result.

Although it is not obvious in this case, one more condition must be met before running this process, especially if you plan to import data repeatedly. The OldSponsorID field of the tblSponsors table must be Null for all the existing records before you append any new records. Again, the reason is simple. You do not want a situation where an existing record has the same OldSponsorID value as one of the newly inserted records. Luckily this can be easily accomplished by an Update query, shown in Figure 7-33, that you can run in the beginning of this process.

Importing Data into Tables That Do Not Have an AutoNumber-Type ID Field

How do you import data into tables that have a numeric ID field as their primary key but it is not an AutoNumber type? For example, let's say you have a list of some new cities that you want to import into the tblLocationsCities_lkp table, whose primary key (named ID) is an Integer-sized Number field. How do you assign new and unique

ID values without resorting to manual typing? Your first instinct may be, "Just design a query that lists an appropriate sequence number (created by a calculated field) along with each city name." Although this appears to be a simple task, you have just touched on one of the main limitations of SQL—dynamically assigning a sequence number to the records of a query result. The only reasonable way is to use looping techniques through a program designed in a language such as Visual Basic that can access table records one at a time. We will explain how this works in Chapter 9, "Accessing Database Records from Visual Basic: Data-Access Objects."

SponsorID	Sponsor Name	SponsorTypeID	Web URL	User Name	Password	OldSponsorID
22	The Department of Mathemati	5	http://icg.fas.ha	teachers	teach	
23	Miami-Dade Community Colle	5	http://www.mdc	dades	books	
24	Sandman Inn at Penticton	4	http://www.next	byron	play	
25	NetTalk Newbie University	3	http://www.nett	webninja	nettalk	
26	Western Electricals Inc.	12	http://www.elec	Western	power	
27	ASSOCIAZIONE COMUNICA	7	http://www.sma	bologna	lira	
28	IEEE	9	http://www.labs	communicat	global	
29	IEEE Control Systems Societ	9	http://everest.ei	baily	controls	
30	Iowa State University	5	http://www.publ	students	teachers	
31	Illinois Science Olympiad	9	http://www.staff	scientists	young	
32	Test Sponsor	1		Test		
33	The University of Texas at Au	9	http://www.texa	texas	austin	
34	NASA	9	http://www.nas.	explorers	stardust	
35	Vanderbilt University	9	http://cswww.vu	gloria	abcd	
36	National Institute of Environme	9	http://www.nieh	pascal	health	
37	Alps-Adria Society for Immuno	6	http://mamed.m	alps	adria	
47	Florence Historical Associatic	4	http://www.flore	None		1
48	American Association of Orth	7	http://www.aao.	None		2
49	Aero International Limited	2	http://ail.aero.c	None		3
50	L&M Motor Car Industries	13	http://lmm.lorer	None		4
51	Smith Microsystems Incorpor	3		None		5
52	Aero Management Institute	2		None		6
(AutoNumber)						0

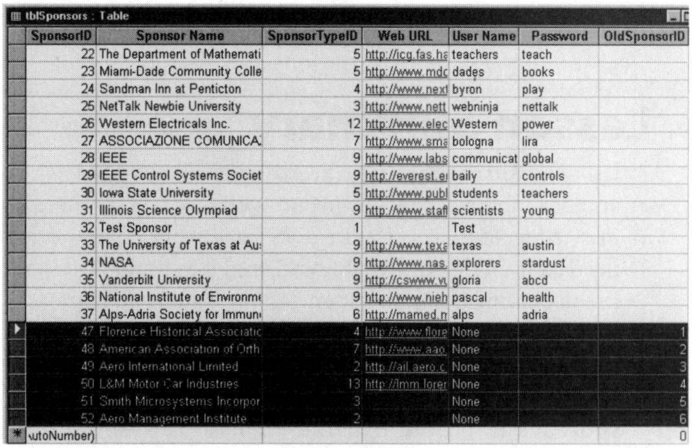

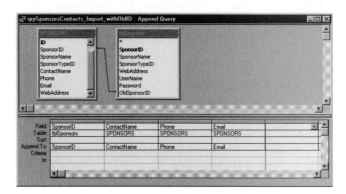

Figure 7-31 Displaying the imported sponsor records

Figure 7-32 Design of the `qrySponsorsContacts_Import_withOldID` query

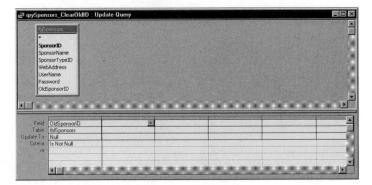

Figure 7-33
Design of the
`qrySponsors_`
`ClearOldID` query

Lesson Summary

Using an `AutoNumber`-type primary key allows you to import data from one table to another table without having to worry about the uniqueness of this field for the inserted records. This feature does cause some complexities when you try to fragment the data from the source table and send it to multiple destination tables, however. This lesson explained this limitation and presented two approaches to overcome it using the example of importing data from the **SPONSORS** table (which holds both the sponsor and contact information) to the **tblSponsors** table and the **tblSponsorsContacts** table, which are actually related in a one-to-many relationship. To maintain this relationship, you have to ensure that the **SponsorID** (the foreign key) of each record in **tblSponsorsContacts** (the many table) matches the **SponsorID** that Access assigns to the corresponding sponsor records in **tblSponsors** (the one table).

The first approach uses a common field other than the primary key field to link the source table (**SPONSORS**) and the one table (**tblSponsors**) get the correct value for this linking (**SponsorID**) field. The approach works well only if the common field behaves like a primary key in the one table. You can try to use multiple fields if one field does not meet this requirement.

The second approach is based on the assumption that the source table (**SPONSORS**) has a primary key (**ID**) field. You create an additional field in the one table (**tblSponsors**) and store the original ID of the source record being appended. Thus, although Access assigns its own values to the **ID** field of the destination table for the records being appended, the original **ID** value of the appended records remains intact in the new field. This field can then be used as the linking field between the source table and the one table.

For your reference, the **CALENDAR.MDB** database file resulting from this lesson is provided in the **C:\WEBSITE\HTDOCS\WDBIC\CHAP07\LESSON6\RESULTS** directory.

1. Let's say that **tblSponsors** already has a sponsor whose name is identical to the name of one of the sponsors in the **SPONSORS** table. What will happen if you apply the first import method?
   a. Access will generate an error when you run the Append query.
   b. Access will correctly append the contact records.
   c. Access will append one extra contact record.
   d. None of the above.

2. Suppose you have to import data to Tables A and B, related with a one-to-many relationship from a common source (say Table C) using the common field linking method. What should be the characteristics of the common field (say **F**)?
   a. **F** should be unique and non-**Null** in Table A.
   b. **F** should be unique and non-**Null** in Table B.
   c. **F** should be unique and non-**Null** in Table C.
   d. All of the above.

3. What is the alternative to the "common field" approach for importing data to multiple tables from one source table?
   a. Use a new field in the destination table.
   b. The **ID** field of the source table should feed the new field in the first destination table.
   c. The link between the **SourceID** field and the new field in the first destination table should be used to append records to the second destination table.
   d. Relate the source and destination tables with their primary keys.

4. What is the first step if you plan on repeatedly importing data into Tables A and B using the second import method described in this lesson? Assume Table A is the "one" table.
   a. Append the records into Table A.
   b. Append the records into Table B.
   c. Make the **OldID** field **Null** for all the records in Table A.
   d. None of the above.

5. Why is it difficult to import data into tables that have a **Number**-type **ID** field as their primary key?
   a. You have to supply valid values for this **ID** field.
   b. You cannot create a query that automatically generates a unique sequence number for each of the imported records.
   c. If you use Access to fill this **ID** field automatically for the imported records, there is no guarantee that these values will be unique.
   d. All of the above.

EXERCISE 6

Complexity: Advanced

1. The **C:\WEBSITE\HTDOCS\WDBIC\CHAP07\LAB6** directory has a text file named **EVENTS.TXT** that contains the basic information about the events offered by the sponsors in the **SPONSORS** table. For linking purposes, **EVENTS.TXT** file also contains two fields, **SponsorName** and **ContactName**, which hold the names of the sponsors and contacts of each event record. Import this text file into your **CALENDAR.MDB** database as a table named **EVENTS** and then copy the events from this table into the **tblEvents** table using the first method described in this lesson. For accurate results, use both the **SponsorName** and the **ContactName** fields as the common linking fields. Name all the queries you design for this exercise with the **qryEvents_Import_Method1_** prefix. (Hint: First create a Select query that produces **SponsorContactID**, **ContactName**, and **SponsorName** as its result and then link this query with the **EVENTS** table on the **ContactName** and **SponsorName** fields when designing the Append query.)

Complexity: Advanced

2. The **C:\WEBSITE\HTDOCS\WDBIC\CHAP07\LAB6** directory has another text file named **EVENTS2.TXT** that holds the same basic event information as the **EVENTS.TXT** file described in the previous exercise but contains the **SponsorID** field for linking back to the **SPONSORS** table. Import the events from this text file to the **tblEvents** table using the second method described in this lesson. Name all the queries you design for this exercise with the **qryEvents_Import_Method2_** prefix. (Hint: Add a field named **OldSponsorContactID** to the **tblSponsorsContacts** table; reimport the **SponsorContacts** records from the **SPONSORS** table into this table, putting **SponsorID** in this new field; and then link **OldSponsorContactID** with **SponsorID** of the **EVENTS2** table when designing your Append query.)

Note   You can either delete the imported records from your calendar database or you can make a copy of the **CALENDAR.MDB** file residing in the **C:\WEBSITE\HTDOCS\WDBIC\CHAP07\ LESSON6\RESULTS** directory and use it as a starting point for this exercise.

CHAPTER SUMMARY

This chapter presented a set of queries called action queries that allow you to carry out bulk changes to your tables or move data among them efficiently. A variety of examples were used to explain the construction and application of each type of action query. This chapter also demonstrated how a sequence of action queries and temporary tables could be used to perform data manipulation tasks that cannot be easily performed by a single action query. Techniques for importing data to multiple related tables were also detailed in this chapter. Specifically, the following points were covered:

⬤ Update queries are used to make bulk updates to data in a table and are constructed using the query design interface. Construction of Update queries was explained using a number of examples.

⬤ Update queries can be constructed that include expressions or criteria and update multiple fields of a table using a single query.

⬤ Delete queries offer a simple and efficient way to delete records from one or more tables. Their construction and application were explained using examples.

⬤ Although only one data source may be specified in the Delete query, data from multiple tables can be deleted due to the Cascade Delete Referential Integrity option being turned on.

⬤ Make-Table queries are used to create permanent, temporary, or archive tables from all or part of the data in one or more tables.

⬤ The table created by a Make-Table query is saved after you give it a name and specify the path and name of the database where it is to reside.

⬤ A Make-Table query mimics only the data and data type of the fields of the original data source and not its field properties or relationships.

⬤ A Make-Table query also can be used to create a time-specified snapshot summary report or improve performance of tasks based on multi-table queries.

⬤ Append queries populate existing tables with data from one or multiple tables.

⬤ Dragging the asterisk (*) to the query design grid automatically selects all the fields of the source and the destination table in an Append query.

⬤ The default values (or Null if none are specified) are automatically inserted by Access if all the destination fields are not specified in an Append query.

⬤ The problem of unmatched source and target fields in an Append query can be overcome by adjusting the name of the target fields in the Append To cell.

⬤ Key violation error messages are generated by Access when running an Append query if duplicate values are being added into a field that must be unique or the records being appended are breaking the referential integrity constraints.

⬤ When a single action query cannot easily accomplish the required data manipulation, resort to a sequence of two or more action queries to carry out the task.

- An Update query cannot be run on a nonupdateable data source. A temporary table created using a Make-Table query can be used in such a case.

- When using more than one action query to perform a task, you must use proper sequencing.

- Records from a "one" table cannot be deleted in a query based on multiple tables exhibiting one-to-many relationship.

- A subquery can be used to specify criteria in an action query to remove the constraints of action queries.

- Use of an AutoNumber-type primary key does not help when you try to fragment data from a source table and send it to multiple destination tables. You can apply the common field linking method or the original key duplication method to work around this problem.

With this chapter, we conclude our discussion about Access queries and Microsoft Access in general. We will revisit our calendar database in Chapter 9, "Accessing Database Records from Visual Basic: Data-Access Objects," when we describe how to run queries and access data through Visual Basic. In Chapter 8, "Creating Windows CGI Applications: The Visual Basic Framework," we switch our focus to the basic concepts of developing Windows CGI programs and describe how easy this process can be when you use the Visual Basic framework that comes with the WebSite server.

Fundamentals of Web-Database Application Development

PART III

CHAPTER 8

CREATING WINDOWS CGI APPLICATIONS: THE VISUAL BASIC FRAMEWORK

The chapter explains how to use the publicly available **CGI32.BAS** library module to create Windows CGI programs quickly in Visual Basic (VB). It gives step-by-step instructions for Visual Basic project setup, user data processing, CGI output generation, and program troubleshooting. In particular, you will learn about:

⬤ Basic operation of a typical Windows CGI program

⬤ How to choose a programming language for designing Windows CGI programs

⬤ The Visual Basic CGI framework

⬤ How to set up a Visual Basic project for constructing a Windows CGI program

⬤ Writing and compiling code and testing a Windows CGI program

⬤ How to access the CGI environment variables, Form fields, and other data present in the CGI profile (.INI) file from your Windows CGI program

361

WHAT IS A WINDOWS CGI PROGRAM?

In Chapter 2, Lesson 4, we explained how the WebSite server communicates with an external executable program using the Windows Common Gateway Interface (CGI) standard. This external program is called a Windows CGI program. In this lesson, you will learn how the WebSite server executes this program, what type of programming environment you should seek to develop such programs, and why Visual Basic is a good choice.

Basic Operation of a Typical Windows CGI Program

Although the phrase *Windows CGI program* may appear intimidating at the outset, the whole concept is actually not that complicated. A Windows CGI program is just a *noninteractive* executable program that essentially performs the following three tasks:

1. Reads data from the CGI content file and secondary input files.

2. Fulfills the CGI request based on the input data.

3. Generates CGI response in the designated output file and terminates.

The noninteractive attribute comes from the requirement that the program has to be designed so that the Web server can run it as a background process when it receives a request asking for the services of this program. Although we described the interaction process between the Web server and Windows CGI programs from the Web server's perspective in Chapter 2, "Handling User Requests: Static and Dynamic Response," let's now look at this process from the perspective of the Windows CGI program.

As you can see in Figure 8-1, a Windows CGI program expects the path and filename of the CGI profile file in its command-line argument. It assumes that the server has already created this file with the appropriate data formatted according to the Windows CGI standard and now its goal is to process that data and return its response to an output file, whose name and path are also listed in the CGI profile file. In the case of a **POST** request, a Windows CGI program may also have to read data from secondary input files such as the CGI content (**.INP**) file, as we will explain later in this chapter.

A Windows CGI program is not required to read all the data listed in the CGI content file unless the functionality of the CGI program depends on that data. At a minimum, the CGI program needs to get the path and filename of the CGI output file

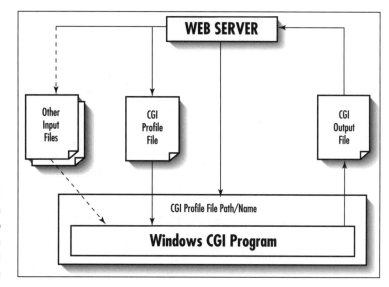

Figure 8-1
Interaction
between a Web
server and a
Windows CGI
program

from the CGI content file. The main objective of the Windows CGI program is to accomplish the desired task and produce a valid CGI response in the CGI output file in one of the output formats described in Chapter 2, Lesson 6.

How to Create a Windows CGI Program?

You can use any programming language to design a Windows CGI program as long as the development environment for that language allows the creation of a Windows executable (`.EXE`) file from the source code. The following questions serve as a good measure to determine which programming environment best suits your needs for developing a Windows CGI program:

- How easily can you pick up the language syntax?

- How user friendly is the development environment for that language?

- What debugging facilities are available through the development environment?

- Does the programming language provide support for accessing external databases?

- Are any libraries or tools available for the language environment to help in Windows CGI program development?

Why Visual Basic?

Visual Basic 5.0 (Professional Edition) earns high marks on all these factors. It is a popular language that has a simple syntax, comes with a powerful development environment with several user-friendly debugging facilities, and provides native support for accessing and manipulating Access databases. Besides, the WebSite server includes a Visual Basic CGI framework that simplifies and expedites the Windows CGI program development process. It is for these reasons that Visual Basic has been chosen as the development platform for the Windows CGI programs described in this book. This decision does not imply that other programming environments are any less suitable. They all have their strengths, and it may be possible to port the programming concepts discussed in this book to these environments.

What Is the Visual Basic CGI Framework?

The Visual Basic CGI framework that comes with the WebSite server is a VB library module named **CGI32.BAS** written by Robert Denny, the developer of the WebSite server. This module contains global declarations, functions, and procedures that come in handy when you develop a Windows CGI program. It takes care of handling common tasks such as opening input and output files, initializing variables and arrays based on the data from the CGI content file, and setting up a default error-handling mechanism. By using this module in your VB project, you can concentrate on the objective of your program instead of worry about the groundwork needed to handle the CGI communication details, as you will see in the next lesson.

The **CGI32.BAS** module helps you

● Declare and assign global VB variables representing the data listed in the CGI profile file.

● Open the CGI output file listed in the CGI profile file.

● Set up a default error handler for trapping the run-time errors.

● Provide utility procedures and functions related to CGI input and output operations.

Figure 8-2 shows the basic control structure you follow when you use this framework in your VB project.

The execution starts from the **Main** procedure, which resides in the **CGI32.BAS** module itself. The **Main** procedure takes care of the above-mentioned tasks and then passes control to the **CGI_Main** procedure, which becomes the starting point for your own code. Because **CGI32.BAS** can be shared by multiple CGI projects, it is best to include the **CGI_Main** and other subroutines specific to your project in a separate module, as

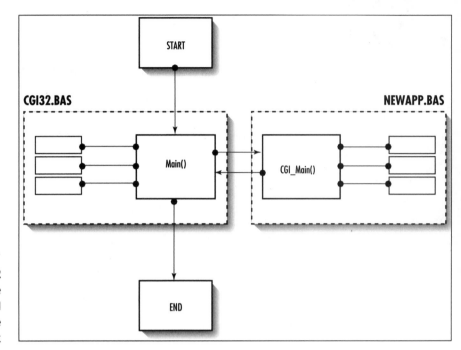

Figure 8-2
Control structure
of a Windows CGI
project using the
VB CGI framework

shown in Figure 8-2. When the `CGI_Main` procedure completes its objective, the control returns to the `Main` procedure, which then can perform the necessary cleanup operations. You will study the details of the `Main` and `CGI_Main` procedures later in this chapter.

Lesson Summary

This lesson explained the basic operation of a Windows CGI program and the tasks it performs while interacting with the Web server to fulfill a Web user's request. It receives the name and path of the CGI profile from the Web server as the only command-line argument, processes that data, and then submits its response in a valid output format to an output file whose name and path are listed in the profile file.

This lesson also presented several factors that you should consider when selecting a programming language for creating Windows CGI programs; it then identified Visual Basic 5.0 (Professional Edition) as a powerful development platform. The Visual Basic CGI framework included with the WebSite server in the form of a library module named `CGI32.BAS` relieves you of common CGI programming tasks such as handling CGI input/output, variable initialization, and error trapping. When you use this CGI framework, your program must follow a specific control structure, as outlined in this lesson.

In the next lesson you will explore this control structure in more detail when you construct your first Windows CGI application.

QUIZ 1

1. What are the general characteristics of a Windows CGI program?
   a. It should be an interactive program.
   b. It should be able to run noninteractively.
   c. It should be an executable file.
   d. It can be designed only using Visual Basic.

2. What does the Windows CGI program expect from the server when it is executed?
   a. Name and path of the CGI profile file
   b. Location of secondary input files
   c. Name and path of the output file
   d. All the data from the CGI profile file

3. What is the binding requirement on a programming language that you choose for designing Windows CGI programs?
   a. It should be easy to learn.
   b. It should be user friendly.
   c. It should allow the creation of Windows-executable (`.EXE`) files from the source code.
   d. It should offer support for accessing external databases.

4. What is the Visual Basic framework that is included with the WebSite server?
   a. It is an architecture that you can follow when designing multiple Windows CGI programs.
   b. It is a dynamic link library that you can use in your Windows CGI program.
   c. It is an error-handling mechanism.
   d. It is a VB library module named `CGI32.BAS` that you include in your Windows CGI projects.

5. What is the starting point of your program-specific code when you use the Visual Basic framework?
   a. The `Main` procedure
   b. The `CGI_Main` procedure
   c. The `Inter_Main` procedure
   d. None of the above

EXERCISE 1

Complexity: Easy
1. List all the steps involved in the communication process between a Web user and a Windows CGI program. Mention the protocol used, wherever appropriate.

Complexity: Moderate

2. Make a list of three other programming environments besides Visual Basic that can be used to create Windows CGI programs. Identify their strengths and weaknesses in terms of the programming factors listed in this lesson.

CREATING YOUR FIRST WINDOWS CGI PROGRAM

OK, enough talk! It's time to venture into the territory of Windows CGI programming and create your first Windows CGI program. What did you say? Is it going to be the traditional "Hello World" program? Kind of, except that you are going to greet the whole universe this time. After all, you should not exclude the possibility that the Web may one day extend its reach to other parts of the universe. In this lesson, you will learn how to set up the VB project for this program, what code to enter to make the program functional, and how to compile and test the program.

Setting Up a Visual Basic Project

In Visual Basic, you design a program by building a Visual Basic project. A *Visual Basic project* is a collection of files and configuration settings. The files represent the forms, custom controls, and library modules that you compile to create the executable program.

When you launch Visual Basic, you get several options (such as `Standard.EXE` and `ActiveX.Exe`) on the type of application you want to create. The `Standard.EXE` option is used to develop a regular executable program. When you select this option, VB's development environment automatically creates a new project containing a blank form and common custom controls, as shown in Figure 8-3. Visual Basic presets the environment options in this project with the assumption that you want to create a regular interactive application. However, these project settings do not work for a Windows CGI program, which is mainly a noninteractive application.

To create a project for the Windows CGI greeting program, you will use a template project file provided on the CD-ROM accompanying this book. This project file (`NEWAPP.VBP`) was copied to your local hard drive under the directory `C:\WEBSITE\CGI-WIN\WDBIC\NEWAPP\` during the Web server installation process.

The `NEWAPP.VBP` project file includes references to two module files: `CGI32.BAS` and `MYAPP.BAS`, both of which are also located in the same directory. As explained in the previous lesson, `CGI32.BAS` is a shareable library that contains the `Main()` procedure and the `MYAPP.BAS` is a template module in which you write code specific to your CGI program. To set up the project for the Greeting program from the `NEWAPP.VBP` project template, use the following steps:

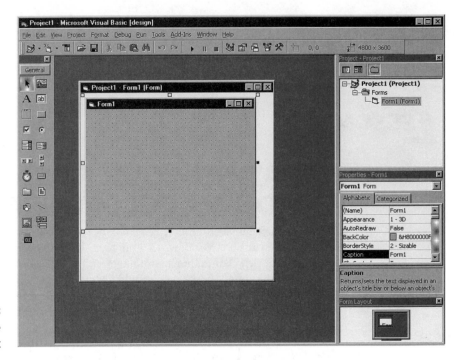

Figure 8-3
Layout of the
default VB project

1. Go to an MS-DOS prompt.

2. Create a new directory, `C:\WEBSITE\CGI-WIN\WDBIC\GREETING\`, by entering the following DOS commands:

   ```
   cd c:\website\cgi-win\wdbic [ENTER]
   md greeting [ENTER]
   ```

3. Copy the template project file to the GREETING directory as GREETING.VBP by entering the following command:

   ```
   copy newapp\newapp.vbp greeting\greeting.vbp [ENTER]
   ```

4. Copy `CGI32.BAS` and `MYAPP.BAS` module files to the GREETING directory by entering the following command:

   ```
   copy newapp\*.bas greeting [ENTER]
   ```

5. Verify that all the project-related files have been correctly copied by entering the following commands:

   ```
   cd greeting [ENTER]
   dir [ENTER]
   ```

The `Dir` command should list the following three files:

```
GREETING.VBP
CGI32.BAS
MYAPP.BAS
```

6. Close the MS-DOS window.

If everything appears to be in order, you can open the **GREETING.VBP** project in Visual Basic as follows:

1. Launch Visual Basic 5.0 (Professional Edition). VB asks if you want to open a new, existing, or recent project, as shown in Figure 8-4.

2. Click on the Existing tab. VB displays the standard file list dialog box listing the files and subdirectories under the VB directory.

3. Locate the `C:\WEBSITE\CGI-WIN\WDBIC\GREETING` directory from the Look In box. The file list box displays the `GREETING.VBP` project file as shown in Figure 8-5.

4. Double-click on the `GREETING.VBP` filename.

   VB loads this project file and displays the Project, Properties, and Form Layout windows. The Project window shows an entry labeled `Modules`, indicating that this project contains some modules.

5. Click on the + sign next to the Modules entry in the Project window.

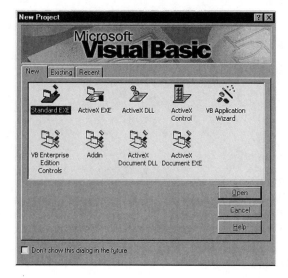

Figure 8-4
Selecting a new, existing, or recent VB project

VB displays the names of both the CGI32.BAS and MYAPP.BAS modules, as shown in Figure 8-6.

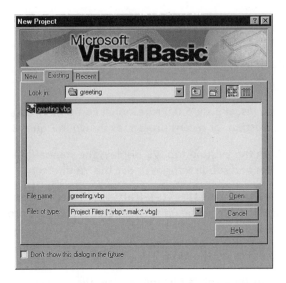

Figure 8-5
Opening the existing greeting project file

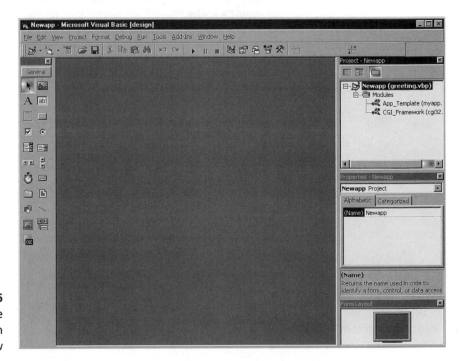

Figure 8-6
Displaying the module names in the Project window

Writing Code for Your CGI Program

The configuration options of this project are preset so that the **Main()** procedure acts as the designated starting point. You can verify this configuration setting by selecting the Newapp Properties... option from the Project menu. Visual Basic will display **Sub Main** as the Startup Object in the General section of the Project properties, as shown in Figure 8-7.

As mentioned in the previous lesson, the **CGI32.BAS** module comes with this **Main()** procedure, which, after performing the initialization tasks, calls the **CGI_Main()** procedure. The **CGI_Main()** procedure, which acts as the starting point for your code, is not part of the **CGI32.BAS** module, but a skeleton of it is included in the **MYAPP.BAS** module so you can directly start entering code, as explained below:

1. Press Cancel to hide the project properties.

2. Double-click on the name of the **MYAPP.BAS** module in the Project window.

   VB opens a Code window displaying the contents of this module.

3. Select the **CGI_Main** procedure from this window's procedure selection box as shown in Figure 8-8.

You can hide the toolbox (the leftmost window) to enlarge the size of the Code window.

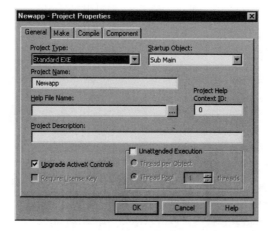

Figure 8-7
Displaying the
Project properties

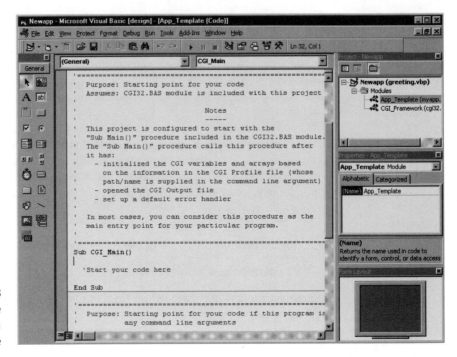

Figure 8-8
Displaying the
CGI_Main
procedure template

The `CGI_Main` procedure template has a Comment section and the following procedure definition:

```
Sub CGI_Main()

'Start your code here

End Sub
```

The Comment section lists the purpose, assumptions, and any notes related to the `CGI_Main` procedure. Although it is not required, it is good practice to keep the information in the Comment section up-to-date. In VB, all comments must start with an apostrophe symbol (`'`) or the `REM` instruction.

Now you can add the code to this `CGI_Main` procedure to generate the greeting message:

1. Type the following VB code below the comment line that says `Start your code here`:

```
Send "Content-type: text/html"
Send ""
Send "<HTML>"
Send "<HEAD>"
Send "<TITLE>Greetings</TITLE>"
```

```
Send "</HEAD>"
Send "<BODY>"
Send "<H1>Hello Universe!</H1>"
Send "</BODY>"
Send "</HTML>"
```

Figure 8-9 shows the CGI_Main procedure after you enter the preceding code. This code writes the HTML text for the greeting message to the CGI output file using the Send procedure provided in the CGI32.BAS module. The Send procedure is described further in Lesson 5.

2. Inspect your code again to ensure that there are no typing errors.

3. Save the MYAPP.BAS module by selecting the Save myapp.bas option from the File menu.

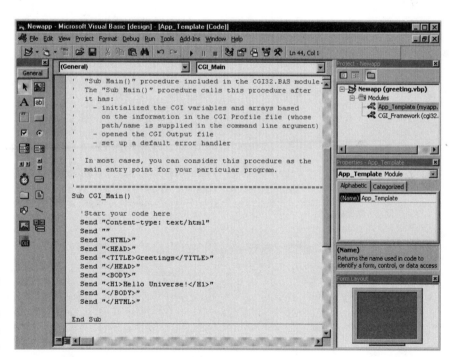

Figure 8-9
The CGI_Main procedure with the code for the greeting message

Compiling and Testing Your Program

A Windows CGI program has to be an executable (`.EXE`) file. You need to compile your Greeting project to create an executable file as follows:

1. Select the Make newapp.exe option from the File menu.

   VB prompts for the name of the executable file as shown in Figure 8-10. It lists NEWAPP.EXE under the C:\WEBSITE\CGI-WIN\WDBIC\GREETING directory as the default name.

2. Change NEWAPP.EXE to GREETING.EXE and click on the OK button.

   If your project is error free, then VB creates the GREETING.EXE executable file. If you encounter an error, then return to your code, correct the error, and recompile your project.

Once you have created the GREETING.EXE file, you can place a CGI request to test your Greeting program as follows:

1. Start your WebSite server if it is not already running.

2. Specify the following URL from your Web browser:

   `http://localhost/cgi-win/wdbic/greeting/greeting.exe`

   The browser should display the greeting message shown in Figure 8-11.

If your browser displays a `File Not Found` error message instead of the greeting message, then verify that you saved the Greeting program as GREETING.EXE in the C:\WEBSITE\CGI-WIN\WDBIC\GREETING directory and run this test again.

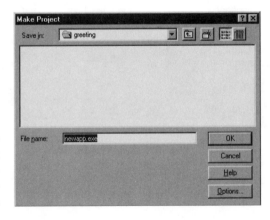

Figure 8-10
Dialog box prompting for the name of the executable file

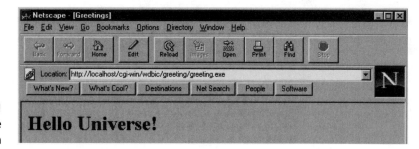

Figure 8-11
Response from the
Greeting program

In this example, we made a copy of the **CGI32.BAS** module in the **GREETING** directory even though we did not modify this module at all. Although **CGI32.BAS** is not a big file, copying the module was not necessary. It was done to simplify the steps involved in setting up the Windows CGI project. As an alternative, you can delete the **CGI32.BAS** file from the **GREETING** directory and just include the **CGI32.BAS** file residing in the **NEWAPP** directory or in the **C:\WEBSITE\CGI-SRC** directory (which is where the WebSite server puts its copy). Seek VB's online help on how to make this change.

Lesson Summary

This lesson explained how a Windows CGI program is created in Visual Basic using the **CGI32.BAS** library module. You set up a VB project, write the necessary code for the program, and compile the project to create an executable file.

Usually, when you start a new project in Visual Basic, it sets the default configuration of your project assuming that you want to create interactive applications. Because a Windows CGI program is noninteractive, this configuration does not work. You can either change the configuration parameters or base your project on a template project file (**NEWAPP.VBP**) containing the correct configuration settings, which is the approach we took in this lesson.

The **NEWAPP.VBP** project contains references to the **CGI32.BAS** and **MYAPP.BAS** modules and its configuration is preset to make the **Main** procedure the program's entry point. The **MYAPP.BAS** module contains a skeleton of the **CGI_Main** procedure, which is where you write code specific to your program. You do not change any part of the **CGI32.BAS** module. The complete process of developing a Windows CGI program using the above technique was demonstrated with the example of a Web-based Greeting program.

For reference, the results of this lesson are available in the **C:\WEBSITE\HTDOCS\ WDBIC\CHAP08\LESSON2\RESULTS** directory.

1. What is a Visual Basic project?
   a. It holds the configuration settings of your VB program.
   b. It is a collection of forms, custom controls, and library modules.
   c. It is a Visual Basic program.
   d. It is a collection of applications.

2. How did the **NEWAPP.VBP** project template help in creating the Greeting program?
   a. It contained the necessary configuration settings to create a noninteractive program.
   b. It included references to the **CGI32.BAS** and another template module.
   c. It contained the code to send the greeting response to the requesting Web user.
   d. All of the above.

3. What is the relationship between the **Main** and **CGI_Main** procedures?
   a. **CGI_Main** is called by the **Main** procedure.
   b. The **Main** procedure is called by the **CGI_Main** procedure.
   c. The **Main** procedure changes from one Windows CGI program to another.
   d. The **CGI_Main** procedure changes from one Windows CGI program to another.

4. What should you do when you have to modify the functionality of an existing Windows CGI program?
   a. Start a new Visual Basic project.
   b. Modify the source code of your Windows CGI program but do not recompile the project.
   c. Modify the source code of your Windows CGI program and recompile the project to recreate the executable file.
   d. Try to edit the existing executable file.

5. What would happen if you replaced the code in the **CGI_Main** procedure of the Greeting program with the following code and recompiled the project?

```
Send "Content-type: text/html"
Send ""
Send
"<HTML><HEAD><TITLE>Greetings</TITLE></HEAD><BODY><H1>Hello
Universe!</H1></BODY></HTML>"
```

   a. VB would generate a compilation error.
   b. The new **GREETING.EXE** program would generate a runtime error when it gets executed.
   c. The Web user would see a response that appears different from the response of the original **GREETING.EXE** program.
   d. Nothing would change from the Web user's perspective.

Complexity: Easy

1. Create a Windows CGI program named **MYNAME.EXE** in the **C:\WEBSITE\CGI-WIN\WDBIC\MYNAME** directory that displays your name.

Complexity: Moderate

2. Create a Windows CGI program named **DATE.EXE** in the **C:\WEBSITE\CGI-WIN\WDBIC\DATE** directory that displays the current date and time, the day of the week, and the name and path of the executable program. The current date and time should be displayed in the following format:

```
Wednesday, February 05, 1997 10:30 PM
```

(Hint: Use the **Now()** and **Format()** functions to format current date and time; use the **APP.ExeName** and **App.Path** properties to get the name and path of the executable file.)

LESSON 3

THE Main PROCEDURE

As indicated earlier, in a Windows CGI project, the entry point of a program is set to the **Main** procedure, which resides in the **CGI32.BAS** module and is responsible for performing common CGI-related tasks. In this lesson, we examine the construction of this **Main** procedure and then illustrate some of its main features through a demonstration.

How It Works

Listing 8-1 shows how the **Main** procedure is constructed.

Listing 8-1 The Main procedure

```
'---------------------------------------------------------------------
'
'    main() - CGI script back-end main procedure
'
' This is the main() for the VB back end. Note carefully how the error
' handling is set up, and how program cleanup is done. If no command
' line args are present, call Inter_Main() and exit.
'---------------------------------------------------------------------
Sub Main()
    On Error GoTo ErrorHandler

    If Trim$(Command$) = "" Then      ' Interactive start
```

continued on next page

continued from previous page

```
        Inter_Main              ' Call interactive main
        Exit Sub                ' Exit the program
    End If

    InitializeCGI        ' Create the CGI environment

    '===========
    CGI_Main             ' Execute the actual "script"
    '===========

Cleanup:
    Close #CGI_OutputFN
    Exit Sub                     ' End the program
'------------
ErrorHandler:
    Select Case Err              ' Decode our "user defined" errors
        Case ERR_NO_FIELD:
            ErrorString = "Unknown form field"
        Case Else:
            ErrorString = Error$    ' Must be VB error
    End Select

    ErrorString = ErrorString & " (error #" & Err & ")"
    On Error GoTo 0              ' Prevent recursion
    ErrorHandler (Err)          ' Generate HTTP error result
    Resume Cleanup
'------------
End Sub
```

The **Main** procedure works as follows:

1. Activate a default error handler.

2. Determine the program's run mode.

3. Initialize global variables and arrays.

4. Call the **CGI_Main** procedure and exit.

Now let's examine each step in more detail.

Step 1: Activate a Default Error Handler

The **On Error Goto ErrorHandler** line activates the error-handling routine to trap all run-time errors. If any error occurs during the execution of the program and no other error-handling routine is set to preempt the error, then the control goes to the line labeled **ErrorHandler** (listed toward the end of this procedure).

The error-handling code examines the value of the **Err** variable, an internal VB variable that holds the error number of the current error. Another string variable named **ErrorString** is set to the appropriate error message based on the value of this error number. Finally, a special procedure named **ErrorHandler** (included in the **CGI32.BAS** module) is called that overwrites the current contents of the CGI output file with the

HTML code listing the error message stored in the `ErrorString` variable. Listing 8-2 shows how the `ErrorHandler` procedure is constructed.

Listing 8-2 The `ErrorHandler` procedure

```vb
'------------------------------------------------------------------------
'
'     ErrorHandler() - Global error handler
'
' If a VB runtime error occurs dusing execution of the program, this
' procedure generates an HTTP/1.0 HTML-formatted error message into
' the output file, then exits the program.
'
' This should be armed immediately on entry to the program's main()
' procedure. Any errors that occur in the program are caught, and
' an HTTP/1.0 error messsage is generated into the output file. The
' presence of the HTTP/1.0 on the first line of the output file causes
' NCSA httpd for Windows to send the output file to the client with no
' interpretation or other header parsing.
'------------------------------------------------------------------------
Sub ErrorHandler(code As Integer)

    Seek #CGI_OutputFN, 1      ' Rewind output file just in case
    Send ("HTTP/1.0 500 Internal Error")
    Send ("Server: " + CGI_ServerSoftware)
    Send ("Date: " + WebDate(Now))
    Send ("Content-type: text/html")
    Send ("")
    Send ("<HTML><HEAD>")
    Send ("<TITLE>Error in " + CGI_ExecutablePath + "</TITLE>")
    Send ("</HEAD><BODY>")
    Send ("<H1>Error in " + CGI_ExecutablePath + "</H1>")
    Send ("An internal Visual Basic error has occurred⇐
in " + CGI_ExecutablePath + ".")
    Send ("<PRE>" + ErrorString + "</PRE>")
    Send ("<I>Please</I> note what you were doing when this problem occurred,")
    Send ("so we can identify and correct it. Write down the Web page you⇐
were using,")
    Send ("any data you may have entered into a form or search box, and")
    Send ("anything else that may help us duplicate the problem. Then contact the")
    Send ("administrator of this service: ")
    Send ("<A HREF=""mailto:" & CGI_ServerAdmin & """>")
    Send ("<ADDRESS>&lt;" + CGI_ServerAdmin + "&gt;</ADDRESS>")
    Send ("</A></BODY></HTML>")

    Close #CGI_OutputFN

    '======
    End                 ' Terminate the program
    '======
End Sub
```

Activating a default error handler ensures that your program always terminates properly. The subsequent example demonstrates how this feature works. Normally, you should provide your own error-trapping procedure to handle any runtime errors and use this default error handler as a last resort. This point is discussed further in Chapter 12, "Creating a Data Entry Wizard: Advanced Data Entry and Maintenance."

Step 2: Determine the Program's Run Mode

After setting the default error handler, the **Main** procedure examines the program's command line to determine the run mode of the program. This handles the possibility that someone may try to run that program directly, not knowing that it is a Windows CGI program designed to be run by a Web server as a background process. The method used to detect how this program has been executed is quite simple.

As explained in Lesson 1, when the Web server executes a Windows CGI program, it always passes the path and filename of the CGI content file as the command-line argument. If the command line is empty, this procedure assumes that the program has been launched in the interactive mode and passes control to the procedure named **Inter_Main**.

The **MYAPP.BAS** module that we provided with the sample Windows CGI project (**NEWAPP.VBP**) supplies a functional **Inter_Main** procedure as shown below:

```
Sub Inter_Main()

  MsgBox "This is a Windows CGI program."

End Sub
```

So if you run your **GREETING.EXE** program directly from Windows, you will get a message box as shown in Figure 8-12.

If other steps are required, you can easily modify this **Inter_Main** procedure to have your program perform other tasks in the interactive mode.

Step 3: Initialize Global Variables and Arrays

If the command line is not empty, the **Main** procedure assumes that the command-line argument contains a valid file path and filename of the CGI profile file. It then calls the **InitializeCGI** routine, which initializes the global variables and arrays based on the contents of the CGI profile file. The subsequent lessons describe these global VB variables and arrays. The **InitializeCGI** routine also opens the designated CGI output file.

Figure 8-12
Running the
Greeting program
directly from
Windows

Step 4: Call the `CGI_Main` *Procedure and Exit*

After successfully initializing the CGI environment, the `Main` procedure calls your `CGI_Main` procedure. All CGI global variables and arrays are directly accessible to the `CGI_Main` procedure. However, the variable assigned to the opened CGI output file (also called the *output file handle*) is not directly accessible and you need to use the `Send` procedure to write to this file, as demonstrated in the previous lesson.

Upon successful completion of the `CGI_Main` procedure (no errors), the `Main` procedure closes the CGI output file (as part of the cleanup operation) and exits, which also terminates the program.

A Demonstration of How the `Main` Procedure Functions

To demonstrate the functionality of the `Main` procedure, you will create a test program named `MAIN.EXE` that displays the values of some of the global variables this procedure initializes. Then you will modify the `MAIN.EXE` procedure so that a runtime error is generated after you display these global variables to see how the default error handling of the `Main` procedure works. Follow these steps:

1. Create a new project named `MAIN.VBP` in the `C:\WEBSITE\CGI-WIN\` `WDBIC\MAIN` directory from the `NEWAPP` project template as you did in the case of the Greeting project described in Lesson 2.

2. Open the `MAIN.VBP` project file in VB and modify the `CGI_Main` procedure of the `MYAPP.BAS` module as follows:

```
Sub CGI_Main()

    'Start your code here
    Send "Content-type: text/html"
    Send ""
    Send "<HTML>"
    Send "<HEAD>"
    Send "<TITLE>MAIN</TITLE>"
    Send "</HEAD>"
    Send "<BODY>"
    Send "<H2>Server Software: " & CGI_ServerSoftware
    Send "<BR>Remote Address: " & CGI_RemoteAddr & "</H2>"
    Send "</BODY>"
    Send "</HTML>"

End Sub
```

3. Compile this program to create an executable file named `MAIN.EXE` in the `MAIN` directory.

4. Start your Web server if it is not already running.

5. Enter the following URL in your Web browser:

```
http://localhost/cgi-win/wdbic/main/main.exe
```

The browser displays the values of two of the initialized CGI variables as shown in Figure 8-13. You will learn more about these CGI variables in the next lesson.

6. Now go back to your MAIN.VBP project and simulate a run-time error by using the Error command in the CGI_Main procedure as shown below:

```
Sub CGI_Main()

    'Start your code here
    Send "Content-type: text/html"
    Send ""
    Send "<HTML>"
    Send "<HEAD>"
    Send "<TITLE>MAIN</TITLE>"
    Send "</HEAD>"
    Send "<BODY>"
    Send "<H2>Server Software: " & CGI_ServerSoftware
    Send "<BR>Remote Address: " & CGI_RemoteAddr & "</H2>"
    Error ERR_NO_FIELD
    Send "</BODY>"
    Send "</HTML>"

End Sub
```

7. Recompile this program as MAIN1.EXE file residing in the MAIN directory.

8. Enter the following URL in your Web browser:

```
http://localhost/cgi-win/wdbic/main/main1.exe
```

This time, the browser displays the error message generated by the ErrorHandler procedure instead of the values of the two CGI variables, as shown in Figure 8-14.

Figure 8-13
Displaying the values of two CGI variables initialized by the Main procedure

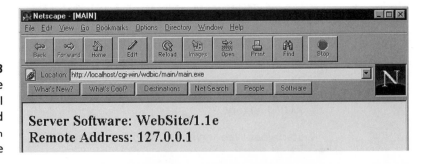

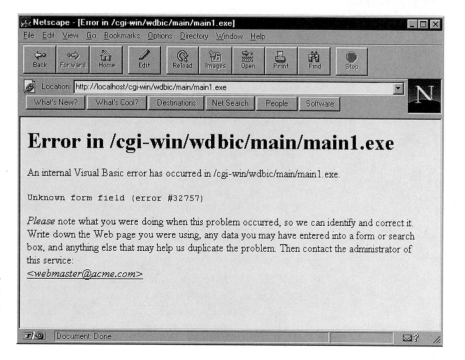

Netscape - [Error in /cgi-win/wdbic/main/main1.exe]

File Edit View Go Bookmarks Options Directory Window Help

Back Forward Home Edit Reload Images Open Print Find Stop

Location: http://localhost/cgi-win/wdbic/main/main1.exe

What's New? What's Cool? Destinations Net Search People Software

Error in /cgi-win/wdbic/main/main1.exe

An internal Visual Basic error has occurred in /cgi-win/wdbic/main/main1.exe.

```
Unknown form field (error #32757)
```

Please note what you were doing when this problem occurred, so we can identify and correct it. Write down the Web page you were using, any data you may have entered into a form or search box, and anything else that may help us duplicate the problem. Then contact the administrator of this service:
<u><webmaster@acme.com></u>

Document: Done

Figure 8-14
The error message
returned by the
ErrorHandler
procedure

Lesson Summary

This lesson provided insight into the construction and working of the **Main** procedure, which is the entry point of a Windows CGI project. From its code, we learned that it performed four important tasks.

The first task involves activating a default error handler to trap all run-time errors in case you do not set up your own error-handling mechanism. As its second task, the **Main** procedure determines the run mode of its program by inspecting the program's command line. If the command line is empty, the **Main** procedure assumes that the program is run interactively and passes control to the **Inter_Main** procedure.

However, if the command line is not empty, the **Main** procedure assumes that the first command-line argument contains a valid path and name of the CGI profile file and, as its third task, initializes the global variables and arrays based on the contents of that profile file.

Finally, the **Main** procedure calls the **CGI_Main** procedure, where you enter your code and write the response to the CGI output file using the **Send** procedure.

The lesson concluded with the construction of a small Windows CGI program demonstrating the functionality of the **Main** procedure and its error-trapping mechanism. For your reference, a copy of this program is available in the **C:\WEBSITE\HTDOCS\ WDBIC\CHAP08\LESSON3\RESULTS\MAIN** directory.

1. What is the advantage of setting up a default error handler?
   a. It prevents you from running the Windows CGI program in an interactive mode.
   b. It traps any unexpected run-time error generated by your program.
   c. It helps identify what run-time error (if any) was generated by a program.
   d. It ensures that a Windows CGI program always terminates properly.

2. What does the `ErrorHandler` procedure of the `CGI32.BAS` module do?
   a. It appends the HTML-coded error message to the CGI output file.
   b. It overwrites the current contents of the CGI output file with the HTML-coded error message.
   c. It displays the error message on the Web server machine.
   d. It terminates the program.

3. How does the `Main` procedure decide that a Windows CGI program has been started in an interactive mode?
   a. The command line contains an invalid path and filename.
   b. The command line is empty.
   c. The `Inter_Main` program determines it.
   d. The command line contains more than one argument.

4. Suppose the Web server gets a request for the `TEST.EXE` Windows CGI program and creates the following two input files to pass data to this program:

   ```
   C:\WEBSITE\CGI-TEMP\30WS.INI
   C:\WEBSITE\CGI-TEMP\30WS.INP
   ```

   What will the command line of the `TEST.EXE` program look like?
   a. `30WS.INI`
   b. `C:\WEBSITE\CGI-TEMP\30WS.INI`
   c. `C:\WEBSITE\CGI-TEMP\30WS.INP`
   d. `C:\WEBSITE\CGI-TEMP\30WS.INI 30WS.INP`

5. What does the `Main` procedure do as part of its cleanup operation?
   a. It initializes the global variables and arrays declared in the `CGI32.BAS` module.
   b. It appends the `"</BODY></HTML>"` string to the CGI output file.
   c. It closes the CGI output file.
   d. All of the above.

Complexity: Easy

1. Modify the **MAIN.EXE** program so that it also displays the values of the following CGI variables:

```
CGI_Version
CGI_RequestMethod
CGI_ExecutablePath
```

Complexity: Moderate

2. Modify the **MAIN.EXE** program containing the runtime error so that the error is listed after the values of the two CGI variables (appended to the current output). (Hint: Add your own error-handling mechanism within the **CGI_Main** procedure itself.)

ACCESSING THE CGI ENVIRONMENT VARIABLES

In Lesson 3, you saw that the **Main** procedure performs its CGI initialization process by calling the **InitializeCGI** procedure. The **InitializeCGI** procedure sets the values of the global variables and arrays declared in the Declarations section of the **CGI32.BAS** module based on the data in the specified CGI profile file. As explained in Chapter 2, Lesson 4, the CGI profile file is formatted as a Windows **.INI** file and can contain up to eight sections. In this lesson, we examine how the **InitializeCGI** procedure reads the contents of the first two sections of this CGI profile file (called the *CGI section* and the *System section*) and how you can use that data to perform some useful tasks.

Reading the CGI Section

The CGI section of the CGI profile file contains the names and values of all the CGI environment variables set by the Web server as follows:

```
[CGI]
Request Protocol=HTTP/1.0
Request Method=GET
Request Keep-Alive=No
Document Root=C:\WEBSITE\HTDOCS\
...
```

Refer to Chapter 2, Lesson 4, for a complete list of CGI variables listed in this section. For each of these CGI environment variables, the `CGI32.BAS` module declares a separate global variable in its Declarations section as follows:

```
Global CGI_ServerSoftware As String
Global CGI_ServerName As String
Global CGI_ServerPort As Integer
Global CGI_RequestProtocol As String
Global CGI_ServerAdmin As String
Global CGI_Version As String
Global CGI_RequestMethod As String
Global CGI_RequestKeepAlive As Integer
Global CGI_LogicalPath As String
Global CGI_PhysicalPath As String
Global CGI_ExecutablePath As String
Global CGI_QueryString As String
Global CGI_RequestRange As String
Global CGI_Referer As String
Global CGI_From As String
Global CGI_UserAgent As String
Global CGI_RemoteHost As String
Global CGI_RemoteAddr As String
Global CGI_AuthUser As String
Global CGI_AuthPass As String
Global CGI_AuthType As String
Global CGI_AuthRealm As String
Global CGI_ContentType As String
Global CGI_ContentLength As Long
```

Notice that the name of each of these variables begins with the `CGI_` prefix. This not only helps categorize these global variables but also decreases the possibility of name conflicts between these variables and your own variables that you may declare during the CGI program development process. Now let's look at how the `InitializeCGI` procedure reads the CGI section of the CGI profile file and sets these variables to their respective values.

Listing 8-3 shows the construction of the `InitializeCGI` procedure.

Listing 8-3 The `InitializeCGI` procedure

```
'---------------------------------------------------------------------------
'
'   InitializeCGI() - Fill in all of the CGI variables, etc.
'
' Read the profile filename from the command line, then fill in
' the CGI globals, the Accept type list and the Extra headers list.
' Then open the input and output files.
'
' Returns True if OK, False if some sort of error. See ReturnError()
' for info on how errors are handled.
'
' NOTE: Assumes that the CGI error handler has been armed with On Error
'---------------------------------------------------------------------------
Sub InitializeCGI()
```

```
Dim sect As String
Dim argc As Integer
Static argv(MAX_CMDARGS) As String
Dim buf As String

CGI_DebugMode = True      ' Initialization errors are very bad

'
' Parse the command line. We need the profile filename (duh!)
' and the output filename NOW, so we can return any errors we
' trap. The error handler writes to the output file.
'
argc = GetArgs(argv())
CGI_ProfileFile = argv(0)


sect = "CGI"
CGI_ServerSoftware = GetProfile(sect, "Server Software")
CGI_ServerName = GetProfile(sect, "Server Name")
CGI_RequestProtocol = GetProfile(sect, "Request Protocol")
CGI_ServerAdmin = GetProfile(sect, "Server Admin")
CGI_Version = GetProfile(sect, "CGI Version")
CGI_RequestMethod = GetProfile(sect, "Request Method")
buf = GetProfile(sect, "Request Keep-Alive")      ' Y or N
If (Left$(buf, 1) = "Y") Then                      ' Must start with Y
     CGI_RequestKeepAlive = True
Else
     CGI_RequestKeepAlive = False
End If
CGI_LogicalPath = GetProfile(sect, "Logical Path")
CGI_PhysicalPath = GetProfile(sect, "Physical Path")
CGI_ExecutablePath = GetProfile(sect, "Executable Path")
CGI_QueryString = GetProfile(sect, "Query String")
CGI_RemoteHost = GetProfile(sect, "Remote Host")
CGI_RemoteAddr = GetProfile(sect, "Remote Address")
CGI_RequestRange = GetProfile(sect, "Request Range")
CGI_Referer = GetProfile(sect, "Referer")
CGI_From = GetProfile(sect, "From")
CGI_UserAgent = GetProfile(sect, "User Agent")
CGI_AuthUser = GetProfile(sect, "Authenticated Username")
CGI_AuthPass = GetProfile(sect, "Authenticated Password")
CGI_AuthRealm = GetProfile(sect, "Authentication Realm")
CGI_AuthType = GetProfile(sect, "Authentication Method")
CGI_ContentType = GetProfile(sect, "Content Type")
buf = GetProfile(sect, "Content Length")
If buf = "" Then
     CGI_ContentLength = 0
Else
     CGI_ContentLength = CLng(buf)
End If
buf = GetProfile(sect, "Server Port")
If buf = "" Then
     CGI_ServerPort = -1
Else
```

continued on next page

continued from previous page

```
        CGI_ServerPort = CInt(buf)
    End If


    sect = "System"
    CGI_ContentFile = GetProfile(sect, "Content File")
    CGI_OutputFile = GetProfile(sect, "Output File")
    CGI_OutputFN = FreeFile
    Open CGI_OutputFile For Output Access Write As #CGI_OutputFN
    buf = GetProfile(sect, "GMT Offset")
    If buf <> "" Then                          ' Protect against errors
        CGI_GMTOffset = CVDate(Val(buf) / 86400#) ' Timeserial GMT offset
    Else
        CGI_GMTOffset = 0
    End If
    buf = GetProfile(sect, "Debug Mode")       ' Y or N
    If (Left$(buf, 1) = "Y") Then              ' Must start with Y
        CGI_DebugMode = True
    Else
        CGI_DebugMode = False
    End If


    GetAcceptTypes           ' Enumerate Accept: types into tuples
    GetExtraHeaders          ' Enumerate extra headers into tuples
    GetFormTuples            ' Decode any POST form input into tuples

End Sub
```

The following sections explain how this `InitializeCGI` procedure works.

Set the Debug Flag

After declaring some local variables, the first thing the `InitializeCGI` procedure does is set the value of the `CGI_DebugMode` variable to `True`. This variable is also called the *debug flag*. The idea is that if any error occurs during this initialization process and you want to add some extra code for debugging purposes, you can use this variable to make that code execute only when debugging is turned on, as follows:

```
'Debug code
If CGI_DebugMode Then
  'Add your debugging related code here
End If
```

Populate the argv *Array with the Command-Line Arguments*

After setting the `CGI_DebugMode` variable to `True`, the `InitializeCGI` procedure calls the `GetArgs` function to read the command-line arguments in the `argv` array and stores the argument count returned by the `GetArgs` function in the `argc` variable.

The `GetArgs` function essentially parses the command-line string (available in the `Command$` VB variable) and stores individual arguments into the elements of the specified array. Listing 8-4 presents the documented code of this function.

Listing 8-4 The GetArgs function

```
'-----------------------------------------------------------------------
'
'    GetArgs() - Parse the command line
'
' Chop up the command line, fill in the argument vector, return the
' argument count (similar to the Unix/C argc/argv handling)
'-----------------------------------------------------------------------
Private Function GetArgs(argv() As String) As Integer
    Dim buf As String
    Dim i As Integer, j As Integer, l As Integer, n As Integer

    buf = Trim$(Command$)                        ' Get command line

    l = Len(buf)                                 ' Length of command line
    If l = 0 Then                                ' If empty
        GetArgs = 0                              ' Return argc = 0
        Exit Function
    End If

    i = 1                                        ' Start at 1st character
    n = 0                                        ' Index in argvec
    Do While ((i < l) And (n < MAX_CMDARGS))     ' Safety stop here
        j = InStr(i, buf, " ")                   ' J -> next space
        If j = 0 Then Exit Do                    ' Exit loop on last arg
        argv(n) = Trim$(Mid$(buf, i, j - i))     ' Get this token, trim it
        i = j + 1                                ' Skip that blank
        Do While Mid$(buf, i, 1) = " "           ' Skip any additional whitespace
            i = i + 1
        Loop
        n = n + 1                                ' Bump array index
    Loop

    argv(n) = Trim$(Mid$(buf, i, (l - i + 1)))   ' Get last arg
    GetArgs = n + 1                              ' Return arg count

End Function
```

Identify the CGI Profile File

After the **GetArgs** function completes its job, the **InitializeCGI** variable sets the value of the first argument in the string variable named **CGI_ProfileFile**. This variable is not a global variable and is declared as a module-level variable within the Declarations section of the **CGI32.BAS** module as follows:

```
Dim CGI_ProfileFile As String          ' Profile file pathname
```

A *module level variable* is a variable that is considered global only within the scope of a module. It must be declared in the module's Declarations section and should not have the **Global** keyword in its dimension statement. As you can see, **CGI_OutputFN** and **ErrorString** are the only other module-level variables declared in the **CGI32.BAS** module.

Even though the **CGI32.BAS** module needs only one argument in the command line (the information about the CGI profile file), it does allow for the possibility of encountering multiple command-line arguments and handles them gracefully by selecting the first argument as the CGI profile file path name.

Setting the Global CGI Variables

After setting the path and name of the CGI profile file in the **CGI_ProfileFile** variable, the **InitializeCGI** procedure assigns the values of the CGI environment variables listed in that file's CGI section to their corresponding global variables using the **GetProfile** function, whose code is shown in Listing 8-5.

Listing 8-5 The GetProfile function

```
'-------------------------------------------------------------------------
'
'    GetProfile() - Get a value or enumerate keys in CGI_Profile file
'
' Get a value given the section and key, or enumerate keys given the
' section name and "" for the key. If enumerating, the list of keys for
' the given section is returned as a null-separated string, with a
' double null at the end.
'
' VB handles this with flair! I couldn't believe my eyes when I tried this.
'-------------------------------------------------------------------------
Private Function GetProfile(sSection As String, sKey As String) As String
    Dim retLen As Long
    Dim buf As String * ENUM_BUF_SIZE

    If sKey <> "" Then
        retLen = GetPrivateProfileString(sSection, sKey, "", buf, ENUM_BUF_SIZE,⇐
CGI_ProfileFile)
    Else
        retLen = GetPrivateProfileString(sSection, 0&, "", buf, ENUM_BUF_SIZE,⇐
CGI_ProfileFile)
    End If
    If retLen = 0 Then
        GetProfile = ""
    Else
        GetProfile = Left$(buf, retLen)
    End If

End Function
```

The **GetProfile** function takes two string parameters, **sSection** and **sKey**, that represent the names of the section and the key within that section. It then calls the **GetPrivateProfileString** Windows DLL function to extract the value of that key from the specified section of the CGI profile file. If the **sKey** parameter is an empty string, then the **GetProfile** function returns a list of keys within **sSection**, where each key is separated by a **Null** character (ASCII value 0).

The `GetPrivateProfileString` Windows DLL function is declared in the Declarations section of the `CGI32.BAS` module to handle both the 16-bit and 32-bit Windows environment as shown below (although the 16-bit programming environment is not recommended):

```
' ========================
' Windows API Declarations
' ========================
'
' NOTE: Declaration of GetPrivateProfileString is specially done to
' permit enumeration of keys by passing NULL key value. See GetProfile().
' Both the 16-bit and 32-bit flavors are given below. We DO NOT
' recommend using 16-bit VB4 with WebSite!
'
#If Win32 Then
Declare Function GetPrivateProfileString Lib "kernel32" _
    Alias "GetPrivateProfileStringA" _
   (ByVal lpApplicationName As String, _
    ByVal lpKeyName As Any, _
    ByVal lpDefault As String, _
    ByVal lpReturnedString As String, _
    ByVal nSize As Long, _
    ByVal lpFileName As String) As Long
#Else
Declare Function GetPrivateProfileString Lib "Kernel" _
   (ByVal lpSection As String, _
    ByVal lpKeyName As Any, _
    ByVal lpDefault As String, _
    ByVal lpReturnedString As String, _
    ByVal nSize As Integer, _
    ByVal lpFileName As String) As Integer
#End If
```

The `GetProfile` function always returns a string value, but some of the global CGI variables such as `CGI_RequestKeepAlive`, `CGI_ContentLength`, and `CGI_ServerPort` are declared as `Integer`. The `InitializeCGI` procedure automatically does the appropriate conversion before assigning values to such variables.

Reading the System Section

After setting all the global variables related to the CGI section of the CGI profile file, the `InitializeCGI` procedure extracts the names of the CGI content (`.INP`) file and the CGI output (`.OUT`) file from the System section. It then calls the `FreeFile` VB function for an available file handle number and sets it to the `CGI_OutputFN` variable, which it further uses to open the CGI output file. Note that `CGI_OutputFN` is a module-level variable, declared as follows:

```
Dim CGI_OutputFN As Integer              ' Output file number
```

This means that you cannot write to the CGI output file using `CGI_OutputFN` directly from your `CGI_Main` procedure. It is for this reason (and to make things simple) that the `CGI32.BAS` module provides the **Send** procedure, which is constructed as follows:

```
'--------------------------------------------------------------------
'
'   Send() - Shortcut for writing to output file
'
'--------------------------------------------------------------------
Sub Send(s As String)
    Print #CGI_OutputFN, s
End Sub
```

Overall, `InitializeCGI` sets the following system-related global variables based on their corresponding keys in the System section:

```
'  ------------------
'  System Variables
'  ------------------
'
Global CGI_GMTOffset As Variant      ' GMT offset (time serial)
Global CGI_ContentFile As String     ' Content/Input file pathname
Global CGI_OutputFile As String      ' Output file pathname
Global CGI_DebugMode As Integer      ' Script Tracing flag from server
```

Reading the Remaining Sections

After it is done reading the System section, the `InitializeCGI` procedure handles the remaining sections of the CGI profile file by calling three separate procedures, which we will examine in subsequent lessons. For now, let's see what interesting tasks you can accomplish based on the data provided by the server in the CGI and System section.

Listing Your Day of Birth

As your first example, you will create a Windows CGI program named `DAY.EXE` that returns the weekday (such as Monday or Tuesday) of any date listed in the query string portion of the requesting URL.

1. Create a new project named `DAY.VBP` in the `C:\WEBSITE\CGI-WIN\WDBIC\DAY` directory from the `NEWAPP` project template.

2. Open the `DAY.VBP` project file in VB and modify the `CGI_Main` procedure of the `MYAPP.BAS` module as follows:

```
Sub CGI_Main()

    Dim WeekDay As String
    Dim ReturnMessage As String

    If IsDate(CGI_QueryString) Then   'Check the validity of⇐
the input date
```

```
            'Get week day for the input date
            WeekDay = Format$(CGI_QueryString, "dddd")
            'Create message listing the corresponding weekday
            ReturnMessage = "The date " & CGI_QueryString & " falls on a "
    _
                & WeekDay & "."
        Else
            'Create an error message
            ReturnMessage = "Invalid Date: " & CGI_QueryString
        End If
        'Generate response
        Send "Content-type: text/html"
        Send ""
        Send "<HTML><HEAD><TITLE>"
        Send "DAY"
        Send "</TITLE></HEAD><BODY>"
        Send "<H2>" & ReturnMessage & "</H2>"   'Output return message
        Send "</BODY></HTML>"

    End Sub
```

3. Compile this program to create an executable file named DAY.EXE in the DAY directory.

4. Start your Web server if it is not already running.

5. Enter the following URL in your Web browser:

   `http://localhost/cgi-win/wdbic/day/day.exe?05/28/1956`

   The DAY.EXE program returns the corresponding day in its response as shown in Figure 8-15.

6. Save and close this VB project and try some other valid and invalid dates to test this DAY.EXE program.

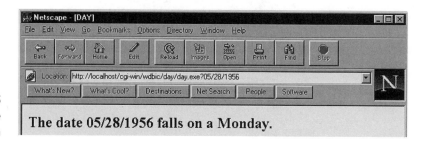

Figure 8-15
Response of the
DAY.EXE program

How the Day of Birth Program Works

The `CGI_Main` procedure of the `DAY.EXE` program first passes the user-specified date (available through the `CGI_QueryString` variable) to the `IsDate` function of VB to verify the date's validity. After ensuring that `CGI_QueryString` holds a valid date, this procedure uses the `Format$` function of VB to get the weekday corresponding to the input date. It then creates a message string containing that weekday and sends that string (after the `Content-type` and `HTML header` lines) to the CGI output file. In case of an invalid date, the `CGI_Main` procedure returns an appropriate error message.

Prompting for User Name and Password Information

In this example, you will create a Windows CGI program that authenticates the user through the browser's user name and password dialog box. The key here is to keep sending the status code `401` in the program's response until the program gets the correct combination. (Refer to Chapter 2, Lesson 6, for more information on the role of status code `401`.)

1. Create a new project named `PASS.VBP` in the `C:\WEBSITE\CGI-WIN\`
   `WDBIC\PASS` directory from the `NEWAPP` project template.

2. Open the `PASS.VBP` project file in VB and modify the `CGI_Main` procedure of the `MYAPP.BAS` module as follows:

```
Sub CGI_Main()

    'Check username and password combination
    If CGI_AuthUser = "Star" And CGI_AuthPass = "Ship" Then
        'Combination is valid, so send welcome message
        Send "Content-type: text/html"
        Send ""
        Send "<HTML><HEAD><TITLE>"
        Send "PASS"
        Send "</TITLE></HEAD><BODY>"
        Send "<H2>Welcome aboard!</H2>"   'Output success message
        Send "</BODY></HTML>"
    Else
        'Combination incorrect, so ask for authentication
        Send "HTTP/1.0 401 Unauthorized"
        Send "WWW-authenticate: basic realm = ""passtest"""
        Send ""
    End If

End Sub
```

3. Compile this program to create an executable file named `$PASS.EXE` in the `PASS` directory. Note that the `$` prefix is important here because otherwise the WebSite server would not supply the password information in the CGI profile file.

4. Start your Web server if it is not already running.

5. Enter the following URL in your Web browser:

   `http://localhost/cgi-win/wdbic/pass/$pass.exe`

   The browser displays the Username and Password dialog box as shown in Figure 8-16.

6. Press OK without entering any user name or password information.

   After a brief pause, the browser displays an `Authentication failed` message as shown in Figure 8-17 and asks if you want to try authenticating again.

7. Press OK to display the authentication dialog box and enter `Star` as the user name and `Ship` as the password. Note that the authentication check is case sensitive.

   This time the browser displays a success message as shown in Figure 8-18.

8. Save and close this VB project.

How does this authentication process work? When you first make the request for the `$PASS.EXE` program, the browser does not know that an authentication is needed; it simply passes the Windows CGI request to the Web server, which executes this program without passing any user name or password-related CGI variables in the `CGI_Profile` file. As a result, the `InitializeCGI` procedure of the program sets the `CGI_AuthUser` and `CGI_AuthPass` global variables to empty strings.

Figure 8-16
Browser displaying the Username and Password dialog box

Figure 8-17
Browser displaying the `Authentication failed` message

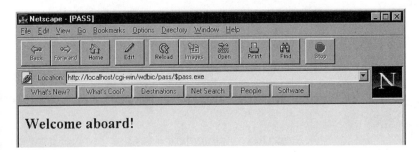

Figure 8-18
Browser displaying
the authentication
success message

When the `CGI_Main` procedure compares these two variables with the acceptable values, the test fails and it sends an HTTP response containing the status code **401**. The browser, on encountering that status code, displays the authentication dialog box. When you press the OK button, the browser again sends the original Windows CGI request but this time passes the user name and password information you supplied along with it. The program again validates that authentication information and, if the test fails, sends the **401** status-based response and the cycle continues until you either give up or enter the correct values.

Lesson Summary

This lesson reviewed the code of the `InitializeCGI` procedure, which the `Main` procedure calls to set the values of global variables and arrays (which all start with the `CGI_` prefix) based on the data supplied by the Web server in the CGI profile file.

The CGI profile file, which is formatted as a Windows `.INI` file, can contain up to eight sections. The first section of this file is named CGI and holds the names and values of the CGI environment variables. The `CGI32.BAS` module declares a separate global variable for each of these environment variables, which the `InitializeCGI` procedure appropriately assigns with the help of the `GetProfile` function, also included in the `CGI32.BAS` module.

After handling the CGI section, the `InitializeCGI` procedure reads the contents of the System section of the CGI profile file, which include the names of the CGI content file and the CGI output file from the System section. The procedure also opens the CGI output file in the write mode using a file handle (also called *file number*) variable named `CGI_OutputFN`. Because `CGI_OutputFN` is a module-level variable, you cannot use it to output data directly from your `CGI_Main` procedure (which resides in a different module). Instead, you call the `Send` procedure of the `CGI32.BAS` module, which then writes to the CGI output file through the `CGI_OutputFN` variable.

The `InitializeCGI` procedure deals with the remaining sections of the CGI profile file by calling additional procedures, which are discussed in subsequent lessons.

This lesson concluded by illustrating the use of some CGI-related global VB variables initialized by the `InitializeCGI` procedure. One such variable, named `CGI_QueryString`, is of particular importance because it contains the query string portion of the requesting URL that you use for passing parameters to your Windows CGI program.

For reference, the results of this lesson are available in the `C:\WEBSITE\HTDOCS\`
`WDBIC\CHAP08\LESSON4\RESULTS` directory.

1. Where does the `InitializeCGI` procedure store the value of the logical path
   CGI variable?
   a. In a local variable named `LogicalPath`
   b. In a module-level variable named `CGI_LogicalPath`
   c. In a global variable named `CGI_LogicalPath`
   d. As the first element of an array named `CGI_LogicalPath`

2. There are some CGI environment variables such as `Content Type` and `Content`
   `Length` that are sometimes absent from the CGI section of a CGI profile file (for
   example, if the request is a `GET` request). What does the `InitializeCGI` procedure do in such cases?
   a. It sets their corresponding VB variables to `Null` values.
   b. It sets their corresponding VB variables to an empty string.
   c. It sets their corresponding VB variables to `False`.
   d. None of the above.

3. Which of the following variables are declared as module level in the `CGI32.BAS`
   module?
   a. `CGI_ContentFile`
   b. `CGI_ProfileFile`
   c. `CGI_OutputFile`
   d. `CGI_OutputFN`

4. What will the `DAY.EXE` program do when you send the following Windows CGI
   request?

   `http://localhost/cgi-win/wdbic/day/day.exe?05 28 1956`

   a. It will return the corresponding day.
   b. It will return the invalid date message.
   c. It will return a runtime error message generated by the `ErrorHandler` proce-
      dure of its `CGI32.BAS` module.
   d. None of the above.

5. How many times may the `PASS.EXE` program have to run before you can get the
   `Welcome aboard!` message?
   a. 1
   b. 2
   c. 2 or more
   d. 3 or more

EXERCISE 4

Complexity: Easy

1. Modify the **DAY.EXE** program so that it displays the following message if no date is supplied in the query string portion of the requesting URL:

```
Usage: http://<Remote Address>/<URL_Path>?<Some Valid Date>
```

Note that the **Remote Address** and **URL Path** entries in the above message must be dynamically determined based on the values of their corresponding CGI variables.

Complexity: Moderate

2. Write a Windows CGI program named **REDIR.EXE** in the **C:\WEBSITE\CGI-WIN\WDBIC\REDIR** directory that takes a URL as its query string parameter and redirects the browser to that URL. For example, if you enter the following URL:

```
http://localhost/cgi-win/wdbic/redir/redir.exe?/wdbic/chap01/
lesson3/example1.htm
```

your browser should display the document corresponding to the following URL:

```
http://localhost/wdbic/chap01/lesson3/example1.htm
```

(Hint: Use the redirection-type HTTP response as explained in Chapter 2, Lesson 6.)

LESSON 5

ACCESSING ACCEPT TYPE AND EXTRA HEADER DATA

In Lesson 4, you saw how the **InitializeCGI** procedure assigns the values of the keys listed in the CGI and System section of the CGI profile file to their corresponding variables declared in the Declarations section of the **CGI32.BAS** module. Before terminating, this procedure also handles the other remaining sections of the CGI profile file by calling the following three procedures:

● **GetAcceptTypes**

● **GetExtraHeaders**

● **GetFormTuples**

As the names suggest, the `GetAcceptTypes` procedure deals with the Accept section, the `GetExtraHeaders` procedure deals with the Extra Headers section, and the `GetFormTuples` deals with all the form-related sections of the CGI profile file. In this lesson, we examine the construction of the `GetAcceptTypes` and `GetExtraHeaders` procedures and then describe the `CGI32.BAS` module's `FindExtraHeader` function that allows you to access the value of any extra header field. We will look at the `GetFormTuples` procedure in the next lesson.

The `GetAcceptTypes` Procedure

Listing 8-6 shows how the `GetAcceptTypes` procedure is constructed.

Listing 8-6 The `GetAcceptTypes` procedure

```
'-----------------------------------------------------------------------------
'
'    GetAcceptTypes() - Create the array of accept type structs
'
' Enumerate the keys in the [Accept] section of the profile file,
' then get the value for each of the keys.
'-----------------------------------------------------------------------------
Private Sub GetAcceptTypes()
    Dim sList As String
    Dim i As Integer, j As Integer, l As Integer, n As Integer

    sList = GetProfile("Accept", "") ' Get key list
    l = Len(sList)                            ' Length incl. trailing null
    i = 1                                     ' Start at 1st character
    n = 0                                     ' Index in array
    Do While ((i < l) And (n < MAX_ACCTYPE)) ' Safety stop here
        j = InStr(i, sList, Chr$(0))          ' J -> next null
        CGI_AcceptTypes(n).key = Mid$(sList, i, j - i) ' Get Key, then value
        CGI_AcceptTypes(n).value = GetProfile("Accept", CGI_AcceptTypes(n).key)
        i = j + 1                             ' Bump pointer
        n = n + 1                             ' Bump array index
    Loop
    CGI_NumAcceptTypes = n                    ' Fill in global count

End Sub
```

As explained in Chapter 2, Lesson 4, the Accept section lists the MIME types acceptable to the requesting browser in the following format:

```
[Accept]
*/*=Yes
text/html=Yes
text/plain=q=0.5
image/gif=Yes
```

The `GetAcceptType` procedure first calls the `GetProfile` function to get a list of keys present in the Accept section and stores that list in the `sList` variable. As mentioned in the previous lesson, these keys are separated by a `Null` character. Using this fact, the `GetAcceptType` procedure retrieves the name of each key from the `sList` variable and then again calls the `GetProfile` function to get their respective values. It stores the name and value of each key as elements of a global array named `CGI_AcceptTypes`, which is declared as follows:

```
Global CGI_AcceptTypes(MAX_ACCTYPE) As Tuple      ' Accept: types
```

The `MAX_ACCTYPE` is a constant, which is declared as follows:

```
Const MAX_ACCTYPE = 100      ' Max # of Accept: types in request
```

and `Tuple` is a special data type declared as follows:

```
Type Tuple                  ' Used for Accept: and "extra" headers
    key As String           ' and for holding POST form key=value pairs
    value As String
End Type
```

Essentially, `CGI_AcceptTypes` is a zero-based array of 101 elements (0–100) where each element has two parts, key and value, and the `GetAcceptType` procedure populates this array based on the information present in the Accept section of the CGI profile file. The `CGI_NumAcceptTypes` variable (initialized at the end of this procedure) is a global integer variable that indicates how many elements of the `CGI_AcceptTypes` array were filled.

The `GetExtraHeaders` **Procedure**

Listing 8-7 shows how the `GetExtraHeaders` procedure is constructed.

Listing 8-7 The `GetExtraHeaders` procedure

```
'----------------------------------------------------------------------
'
'    GetExtraHeaders() - Create the array of extra header structs
'
' Enumerate the keys in the [Extra Headers] section of the profile file,
' then get the value for each of the keys.
'----------------------------------------------------------------------
Private Sub GetExtraHeaders()
    Dim sList As String
    Dim i As Integer, j As Integer, l As Integer, n As Integer

    sList = GetProfile("Extra Headers", "") ' Get key list
    l = Len(sList)                           ' Length incl. trailing null
    i = 1                                    ' Start at 1st character
    n = 0                                    ' Index in array
    Do While ((i < l) And (n < MAX_XHDR))    ' Safety stop here
        j = InStr(i, sList, Chr$(0))         ' J -> next null
        CGI_ExtraHeaders(n).key = Mid$(sList, i, j - i) ' Get Key, then value
        CGI_ExtraHeaders(n).value = GetProfile("Extra Headers",
CGI_ExtraHeaders(n).key)
        i = j + 1                            ' Bump pointer
        n = n + 1                            ' Bump array index
    Loop
```

```
    CGI_NumExtraHeaders = n                    ' Fill in global count

End Sub
```

As you can see, the **GetExtraHeaders** procedure is constructed similar to the **GetAcceptTypes** procedure with only one difference: This procedure parses the Extra Headers section of the CGI profile file and stores the key and value pairs in an array named **CGI_ExtraHeaders**, which is declared as follows:

```
Const MAX_XHDR = 100           ' Max # of "extra" request headers
Global CGI_ExtraHeaders(MAX_XHDR) As Tuple       ' "Extra" headers
```

In this case, **CGI_NumExtraHeaders** is the global integer variable that holds a count of how many extra header key=value pairs were populated in the **CGI_ExtraHeaders** array.

The FindExtraHeader Function

The **CGI32.BAS** module includes a function named **FindExtraHeader** that you can use in your Windows CGI procedure to locate the value of any key present in the Extra Header section. Listing 8-8 shows how this function is constructed.

Listing 8-8 The FindExtraHeader function

```
'--------------------------------------------------------------------------
'
'    FindExtraHeader() - Get the text from an "extra" header
'
' Given the extra header's name, return the stuff after the ":"
' or an empty string if not there.
'--------------------------------------------------------------------------
Public Function FindExtraHeader(key As String) As String
    Dim i As Integer

    For i = 0 To (CGI_NumExtraHeaders - 1)
        If CGI_ExtraHeaders(i).key = key Then
            FindExtraHeader = Trim$(CGI_ExtraHeaders(i).value)
            Exit Function            ' ** DONE **
        End If
    Next i
    '
    ' Not present, return empty string
    '
    FindExtraHeader = ""
End Function
```

As you can see, this function accepts a string parameter named **key**, loops through all the populated elements of the **CGI_NumExtraHeaders** array (starting from element 0) to find one with the matching key, and then returns the value of that element. Note that the key-matching operation is case sensitive. Furthermore, this function trims all the leading and trailing spaces from the original value before returning it. In case no matching element is found, this function returns an empty string.

Now let's construct a small Windows CGI program to see how you can use this function to list the value of an extra header field specified in the query string portion of the requesting URL:

1. Create a new project named EXHDR.VBP in the C:\WEBSITE\CGI-WIN\ WDBIC\EXHDR directory from the NEWAPP project template.

2. Open the EXHDR.VBP project file in VB and modify the CGI_Main procedure of the MYAPP.BAS module as follows:

```
Sub CGI_Main()

    Dim KeyValue As String

    'Get value of the input extra header field
    KeyValue = FindExtraHeader(CGI_QueryString)
    Send "Content-type: text/html"
    Send ""
    Send "<HTML><HEAD><TITLE>"
    Send "EXHDR"
    Send "</TITLE></HEAD><BODY>"
    'Show the key value
    Send "<H3>" & CGI_QueryString & " = " & KeyValue & "</H3>"
    Send "</BODY></HTML>"

End Sub
```

3. Compile this program to create an executable file named EXHDR.EXE in the EXHDR directory.

4. Start your Web server if it is not already running.

5. Enter the following URL in your Web browser. Note that the H in the query string parameter is uppercase.

   `http://localhost/cgi-win/wdbic/exhdr/exhdr.exe?Host`

The browser displays the name and value of the Host extra header field as shown in Figure 8-19.

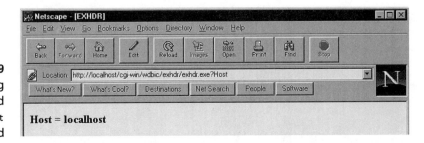

Figure 8-19
Browser displaying the name and value of the Host extra header field

6. Now enter the following URL in your Web browser. Note that the word host is lowercase.

```
http://localhost/cgi-win/wdbic/exhdr/exhdr.exe?host
```

This time the browser displays an empty string as the value of the host field, confirming that the case of extra header fields is important.

7. Save and close this project.

If you get a blank value in both cases, you are probably using a browser that does not send the host field to the Web server.

Lesson Summary

This lesson explained how the GetAcceptTypes and GetExtraHeaders procedures handle the Accept and Extra Headers sections of the CGI profile file respectively. The construction of both procedures is similar. Both store the key and value pairs listed under their respective sections into global arrays. In the case of GetAcceptTypes, the array is called CGI_AcceptTypes, whereas in the case of GetExtraHeaders, the array is called CGI_ExtraHeaders. Both arrays are declared to hold up to 101 elements (indexed as 0–100), and each element has two components, key and value. So, if you want to access the key name of the third entry under the Extra Headers section in your program, you can use the following syntax:

```
CGI_ExtraHeaders(3).Key
```

But what if the Extra Headers section contains only two entries? For that, you can first refer to the CGI_NumAcceptTypes and CGI_NumExtraHeaders global variables, which hold the count of entries in their respective sections.

To help you quickly locate the value of an extra header field, the CGI32.BAS module provides the FindExtraHeader function, whose usage was demonstrated in this lesson through a small Windows CGI program, a copy of which is available in the C:\ WEBSITE\HTDOCS\WDBIC\CHAP08\LESSON5\RESULTS directory for your reference.

In the next lesson we shall look into the GetFormTuples procedure, which is responsible for handling the form-related sections of the CGI profile file.

1. What is a Tuple, according to the CGI32.BAS module?
   a. It is a global variable.
   b. It is a two-dimensional global array.
   c. It is a user-defined data type composed of two string type elements.
   d. It is a global constant.

2. What will `CGI_AcceptTypes(2).Value` hold if the CGI profile file has the following entries in the Accept section and `GetAcceptTypes` procedure has completed its task?

```
[Accept]
*/*=Yes
text/html=Yes
text/plain=q=0.5
image/gif=Yes
```

   a. `*/*`
   b. `Yes`
   c. `-1`
   d. `g=0.5`

3. Referring to the example in the previous question, what will be the value of the `CGI_NumAcceptTypes` variable after the `GetAcceptTypes` procedure has completed its task?

   a. `0`
   b. `2`
   c. `4`
   d. `5`

4. Assume that the CGI profile file contains the following entries in its Extra Headers section:

```
[Extra Headers]
host=www.acme.com
pragma=no-cache
cookie=username=abc
```

   Which of the following expressions would return the string **"abc"** when it is evaluated?

   a. `FindExtraHeaders("username")`
   b. `CGI_ExtraHeaders(2).Value`
   c. `Mid$(FindExtraHeaders("cookie"),10)`
   d. `Mid$(CGI_ExtraHeaders(2).Value,10)`

5. Referring to the example in the previous question, which of the following expressions would evaluate to `True`?

   a. `CGI_NumExtraHeaders = 3`
   b. `FindExtraHeader("Pragma") = "no-cache"`
   c. `FindExtraHeader("HOST") = ""`
   d. `CGI_ExtraHeaders(0).value = "www.acme.com"`

EXERCISE 5

Complexity: Easy

1. Write a Windows CGI program named **EXHDR2.EXE** in the **C:\WEBSITE\CGI-WIN\WDBIC\EXHDR2** directory that functions similar to the original **EXHDR.EXE** program with the exception that the case of the specified header field is now irrelevant.

Complexity: Easy

2. Create a Windows CGI program named **LISTATEH.EXE** in the **C:\WEBSITE\CGI-WIN\WDBIC\LISTATEH** directory that lists the keys and values appearing in the Accept and Extra Headers section of its CGI profile file in a tabular form. Use HTML tables in the program's output.

LESSON 6

HANDLING FORM DATA

In the past two lessons, we have covered the functionality of the **InitializeCGI** procedure and explained how it sets the various global variables and arrays based on the data listed in the CGI profile file. The only step left unexplored is the call this procedure makes to the **GetFormTuples** procedure, which is responsible for handling the data in the form-related sections of the CGI profile file. In this lesson, we examine the construction of the **GetFormTuples** procedure and then demonstrate how you can access different portions of the form data sent in a Windows CGI request from your Windows CGI program.

Before you proceed with this lesson, we recommend that you review Chapter 2, Lesson 5, about the role and contents of the four form-related sections of the CGI profile file.

The GetFormTuples Procedure

Listing 8-9 shows how the **GetFormTuples** procedure is constructed.

Listing 8-9 The GetFormTuples procedure

```
'-----------------------------------------------------------------------
'
'   GetFormTuples() - Create the array of POST form input key=value pairs
'
'-----------------------------------------------------------------------
Private Sub GetFormTuples()
```

continued on next page

continued from previous page

```vb
Dim sList As String
Dim i As Integer, j As Integer, k As Integer
Dim l As Integer, m As Integer, n As Integer
Dim s As Long
Dim buf As String
Dim extName As String
Dim extFile As Integer
Dim extlen As Long

n = 0                                           ' Index in array


'
' Do the easy one first: [Form Literal]
'
sList = GetProfile("Form Literal", "")          ' Get key list
l = Len(sList)                                   ' Length incl. trailing null
i = 1                                            ' Start at 1st character
Do While ((i < l) And (n < MAX_FORM_TUPLES))    ' Safety stop here
    j = InStr(i, sList, Chr$(0))                 ' J -> next null
    CGI_FormTuples(n).key = Mid$(sList, i, j - i) ' Get Key, then value
    CGI_FormTuples(n).value = GetProfile("Form Literal", CGI_FormTuples(n).key)
    i = j + 1                                    ' Bump pointer
    n = n + 1                                    ' Bump array index
Loop
'
' Now do the external ones: [Form External]
'
sList = GetProfile("Form External", "")         ' Get key list
l = Len(sList)                                   ' Length incl. trailing null
i = 1                                            ' Start at 1st character
extFile = FreeFile
Do While ((i < l) And (n < MAX_FORM_TUPLES))    ' Safety stop here
    j = InStr(i, sList, Chr$(0))          ' J -> next null
    CGI_FormTuples(n).key = Mid$(sList, i, j - i) ' Get Key, then pathname
    buf = GetProfile("Form External", CGI_FormTuples(n).key)
    k = InStr(buf, " ")                          ' Split file & length
    extName = Mid$(buf, 1, k - 1)                ' Pathname
    k = k + 1
    extlen = CLng(Mid$(buf, k, Len(buf) - k + 1)) ' Length
    '
    ' Use feature of GET to read content in one call
    '
    Open extName For Binary Access Read As #extFile
    CGI_FormTuples(n).value = String$(extlen, " ")' Breathe in...
    Get #extFile, , CGI_FormTuples(n).value 'GULP!
    Close #extFile
    i = j + 1                                    ' Bump pointer
    n = n + 1                                    ' Bump array index
Loop

CGI_NumFormTuples = n                            ' Number of fields decoded
n = 0                                            ' Reset counter
'
```

```
' Next, the [Form Huge] section. Will this ever get executed?
'
sList = GetProfile("Form Huge", "")              ' Get key list
l = Len(sList)                                   ' Length incl. trailing null
i = 1                                            ' Start at 1st character
Do While ((i < l) And (n < MAX_FORM_TUPLES))     ' Safety stop here
    j = InStr(i, sList, Chr$(0))                 ' J -> next null
    CGI_HugeTuples(n).key = Mid$(sList, i, j - i) ' Get Key
    buf = GetProfile("Form Huge", CGI_HugeTuples(n).key) ' "offset length"
    k = InStr(buf, " ")                          ' Delimiter
    CGI_HugeTuples(n).offset = CLng(Mid$(buf, 1, (k - 1)))
    CGI_HugeTuples(n).length = CLng(Mid$(buf, k, (Len(buf) - k + 1)))
    i = j + 1                                    ' Bump pointer
    n = n + 1                                    ' Bump array index
Loop

CGI_NumHugeTuples = n                            ' Fill in global count

n = 0                                            ' Reset counter
'
' Finally, the [Form File] section.
'
sList = GetProfile("Form File", "")              ' Get key list
l = Len(sList)                                   ' Length incl. trailing null
i = 1                                            ' Start at 1st character
Do While ((i < l) And (n < MAX_FILE_TUPLES))     ' Safety stop here
    j = InStr(i, sList, Chr$(0))                 ' J -> next null
    CGI_FileTuples(n).key = Mid$(sList, i, j - i) ' Get Key
    buf = GetProfile("Form File", CGI_FileTuples(n).key)
    ParseFileValue buf, CGI_FileTuples(n)        ' Complicated, use Sub
    i = j + 1                                    ' Bump pointer
    n = n + 1                                    ' Bump array index
Loop

CGI_NumFileTuples = n                            ' Fill in global count

End Sub
```

The GetFormTuples procedure can be easily broken into four sections; for clarity, we have highlighted the comment at the beginning of each section. The first section contains code that looks similar to the code of the GetAcceptTypes and GetExtraHeaders procedures examined in the previous lesson. It essentially populates the CGI_FormTuples array with the key=value pairs found in the Form Literal section of the CGI profile file. The CGI_FormTuples array and its related constants and variables are declared as follows:

```
Const MAX_FORM_TUPLES = 100 ' Max # form key=value pairs
Global CGI_FormTuples(MAX_FORM_TUPLES) As Tuple  ' POST form key=value pairs
Global CGI_NumFormTuples As Integer              ' # of live entries in array
```

The next section, which deals with the Form External section, also appends entries into the CGI_FormTuples array, but works differently than the previous section. Remember (from Chapter 2, Lesson 5) that the value in each key=value pair listed under the Form External section does not hold the original field data but the path name and length of the secondary input file that contains that data. So in this section, the GetFormTuples procedure retrieves the key name first and then the path name and length of the specified input file; it then reads (gulps!) the actual data from that file into the value component of the current element of the CGI_FormTuples array.

The third section of the GetFormTuples procedure reads data from the Form Huge section of the CGI profile and populates the CGI_HugeTuples array. This array and all its related constants, data types, and variables are declared in the CGI32.BAS module as follows:

```
Const MAX_HUGE_TUPLES = 16   ' Max # "huge" form fields

Type HugeTuple              ' Used for "huge" form fields
    key As String           ' Keyword (decoded)
    offset As Long          ' Byte offset into Content File of value
    length As Long          ' Length of value, bytes
End Type

Global CGI_HugeTuples(MAX_HUGE_TUPLES) As HugeTuple ' Form "huge tuples
Global CGI_NumHugeTuples As Integer                 ' # of live entries in array
```

As you can see, each element of the CGI_HugeTuple array contains three components—*key*, *offset*, and *length*—that correspond to the data components that appear in each entry of the Form Huge section. Note that the actual data corresponding to the form fields listed in this section is not read here. That data resides in the CGI content (.INP) file; CGI32.BAS leaves it as your responsibility to retrieve its data as and when needed.

The last section of the GetFormTuples procedure populates the CGI_FileTuples array based on the entries listed in the Form File section of the CGI profile file. This array and all its related constants, data types, and variables are declared in the CGI32.BAS module as follows:

```
Const MAX_FILE_TUPLES = 16   ' Max # of uploaded file tuples

Type FileTuple              ' Used for form-based file uploads
    key As String           ' Form field name
    file As String          ' Local tempfile containing uploaded file
    length As Long          ' Length in bytes of uploaded file
    type As String          ' Content type of uploaded file
    encoding As String      ' Content-transfer encoding of uploaded file
    name As String          ' Original name of uploaded file
End Type

Global CGI_FileTuples(MAX_FILE_TUPLES) As FileTuple ' File upload tuples
Global CGI_NumFileTuples As Integer                 ' # of live entries in array
```

The GetFormTuples procedure calls another procedure named ParseFileValue (not described here) to separate the value of each key read from the CGI profile file into individual components of the current element of the CGI_FileTuples array. Once again, the actual contents of the specified file are not read by this procedure.

The `FieldPresent` and `GetSmallField` Functions

Similar to the `FindExtraHeader` function (described in the previous lesson), the `FieldPresent` and `GetSmallField` functions allow you to search and access form data held by the `CGI_FormTuples` array.

Listing 8-10 shows how the `FieldPresent` function is constructed.

Listing 8-10 The `FieldPresent` function

```
'--------------------------------------------------------------------
'
' Return True/False depending on whether a form field is present.
' Typically used to detect if a checkbox in a form is checked or
' not. Unchecked checkboxes are omitted from the form content.
'
'--------------------------------------------------------------------
Function FieldPresent(key As String) As Integer
    Dim i As Integer

    FieldPresent = False            ' Assume failure

    For i = 0 To (CGI_NumFormTuples - 1)
        If CGI_FormTuples(i).key = key Then
            FieldPresent = True     ' Found it
            Exit Function           ' ** DONE **
        End If
    Next i
                                    ' Exit with FieldPresent still False
End Function
```

The code of this function is easy to follow. This function takes a string parameter named **key** and returns a **True (-1)** or **False (0)** value depending on the presence or absence of an element with a matching key in the `CGI_FormTuples` array. As the introductory comments indicate, this function proves useful when you want to find out if a particular form field even came with the CGI request, which is important when you want to determine if a checkbox-type field was selected or not.

The `GetSmallField` function complements the `FieldPresent` function by returning the value associated with a specified key (after removing any leading or following white space characters from that value using the `Trim$` function). Listing 8-11 shows how this function is constructed.

Listing 8-11 The `GetSmallField` function

```
'--------------------------------------------------------------------
'
' Get the value of a "small" form field given the key
'
' Signals an error if field does not exist
'
```

continued on next page

continued from previous page

```
'-----------------------------------------------------------------
Function GetSmallField(key As String) As String
    Dim i As Integer

    For i = 0 To (CGI_NumFormTuples - 1)
        If CGI_FormTuples(i).key = key Then
            GetSmallField = Trim$(CGI_FormTuples(i).value)
            Exit Function              ' ** DONE **
        End If
    Next i
    '
    ' Field does not exist
    '
    Error ERR_NO_FIELD
End Function
```

As you can see from this code, the key-matching process is case sensitive and this function generates an error if no element matching the given key is found. In fact, by trapping this error, you can easily create an alternative version of the **FieldPresent** function from this function as follows:

```
Function FieldPresent2(key as String)
    Dim FieldValue As String

    On Error Resume Next
    FieldValue = GetSmallField(key)
    FieldPresent2 = (Err = 0)
End Function
```

To demonstrate the application of the **FieldPresent** and the **GetSmallField** functions, let's create a Windows CGI program named **FORM.EXE** that accepts data from the HTML form shown in Figure 8-20.

This form resides in the following URL:

```
http://localhost/wdbic/chap08/lesson6/example1.htm
```

and contains the following **<FORM>** tag options:

```
<FORM ACTION="/cgi-win/wdbic/form/form.exe" METHOD="POST">
```

The fields of this form are named as follows:

```
YourName (textbox)
Password (textbox)
Age (radio group)
C++ (check box)
VB (check box)
Pascal (check box)
Preferred Language (selection list)
Remarks (text area)
```

Follow these steps to construct the **FORM.EXE** program:

1. Create a new project named **FORM.VBP** in the `C:\WEBSITE\CGI-WIN\WDBIC\FORM` directory from the **NEWAPP** project template.

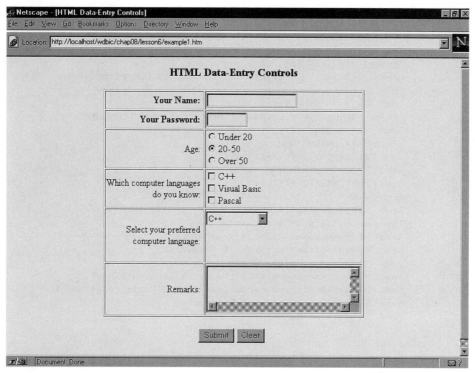

Figure 8-20
Form displaying various HTML data entry controls

2. Open the FORM.VBP project file in VB and modify the CGI_Main procedure of the MYAPP.BAS module as follows:

```
Sub CGI_Main()

    'Define variable for form fields
    Dim YourName As String
    Dim Password As String
    Dim Age As String
    Dim chkBox1 As Boolean, chkBox2 As Boolean, chkBox3 As Boolean
    Dim LanguagesKnown As String
    Dim PreferredLanguage As String
    Dim Remarks As String

    'Read field values into corresponding variables
    YourName = GetSmallField("YourName")
    Password = GetSmallField("Password")
    Age = GetSmallField("Age")
    'Check boxes can be handled by the FieldPresent function
    If FieldPresent("C++") Then LanguagesKnown = "C++, "
    If FieldPresent("VB") Then LanguagesKnown = LanguagesKnown + "VB,
```

```
                "
    If FieldPresent("Pascal") Then
       LanguagesKnown = LanguagesKnown & "Pascal, "
    End If
    'Remove the trailing comma and space
    LanguagesKnown = Left$(LanguagesKnown, Len(LanguagesKnown) - 2)

    'Get the remaining two fields
    PreferredLanguage = GetSmallField("Preferred Language")
    Remarks = GetSmallField("Remarks")
    'Output response
    Send "Content-type: text/html"
    Send ""
    Send "<HTML><HEAD><TITLE>"
    Send "FORM"
    Send "</TITLE></HEAD><BODY>"
    'Show each field on a separate line
    Send "<B>Your Name: </B>" & YourName
    Send "<BR><B>Password: </B>" & Password
    Send "<BR><B>Age: </B>" & Age
    Send "<BR><B>Languages Known: </B>" & LanguagesKnown
    Send "<BR><B>Preferred Language: </B>" & PreferredLanguage
    Send "<BR><B>Remarks: </B>" & Remarks
    Send "</BODY></HTML>"

End Sub
```

3. Compile this program to create an executable file named FORM.EXE in the FORM directory.

4. Start your Web server if it is not already running.

5. Enter the following URL in your Web browser to display the form shown in Figure 8-20.

   http://localhost/wdbic/chap08/lesson6/example1.htm

6. Fill out this form as follows:

```
             Your Name: John Smith
         Your Password: abc (although it will appear as a string
of asterisks)
                   Age: 20-50
       Known Languages: C++ and Visual Basic
    Preferred Language: Visual Basic
               Remarks: I prefer Visual Basic because
                        it is simple yet powerful.
```

7. Submit the form.

   Figure 8-21 shows the response of the FORM.EXE program.

8. Save and close your FORM.VBP project.

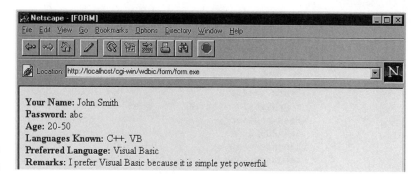

Figure 8-21
Response of the
FORM.EXE program

Lesson Summary

This lesson concluded the discussion on the **InitialzeCGI** procedure by explaining how it handles the form-related sections of the CGI profile file through the **GetFormTuples** procedure.

The **GetFormTuples** procedure performs four main tasks. As its first task, it populates the **CGI_FormTuples** array with key=value pairs found in the Form Literal section of the CGI profile file. As its second task, it retrieves data from the secondary input files corresponding to each key listed in the Form External section and populates additional elements of the **CGI_FormTuples** array. The **CGI_NumFormTuples** stores the final count.

After dealing with the Form Literal and Form External sections, the **GetFormTuples** procedure stores the entries listed in the Form Huge section into a global array named **CGI_HugeTuples**. Each element of this array has three components called key, offset, and length, where offset and length indicate the starting position and the size of the data in the CGI content (**.INP**) file that corresponds to the key portion of each element.

As its last step, the **GetFormTuples** procedure parses the entries of the Form File section and stores them in the **CGI_FileTuples** array, whose elements have keys and five (uploaded) file-related components, as described in this lesson.

This lesson also presented two other functions named **FieldPresent** and **GetSmallField**, which allow you to search and access data present in the **CGI_FormTuples** array. Their application was explained in this lesson with the help of a small Windows CGI program named **FORM.EXE**, a copy of which is available in the **C:\WEBSITE\HTDOCS\WDBIC\CHAP08\LESSON6\RESULTS\FORM** directory.

1. What sections of the CGI profile file are populated into the **CGI_FormTuples** array by the **GetFormTuples** procedure?
    a. Form Literal
    b. Form External

    c. Form Huge

    d. Form File

2. Assume that the CGI profile file has the following data in its form-related sections.

```
[Form Literal]
YourName=John Smith
Password=abc
Age=20-50
Language=on
Language_1=on
Preferred Language=Visual Basic
SUBMIT=Submit

[Form External]
Remarks=C:\WEBSITE\CGI-TEMP\9EWS.000 57
Address=C:\WEBSITE\CGI-TEMP\9EWS.001 25

[Form Huge]
Digital Signature=152 2048

[Form File]
picture=[C:\WEBSITE\CGI-TEMP\9EWS.002] 11387 text/html binary
[C:\Personal\pic.gif]
```

What will be the expression `CGI_FormTuples(7).Key` returns?

    a. Empty string

    b. `SUBMIT`

    c. Remarks

    d. Address

3. Referring to the example in the previous question, what will be the value of the following expression?

```
GetSmallField("Address")
```

    a. Empty string

    b. `C:\WEBSITE\CGI-TEMP\9EWS.001`

    c. `25`

    d. Contents of the file named `C:\WEBSITE\CGI-TEMP\9EWS.001`

4. Referring to the CGI profile file example of Question 2, which of the following statements are correct?

    a. `CGI_FormTuples(4).Value = "on"`

    b. `CGI_FormTuples(4).Value = -1`

    c. `CGI_HugeTuples(0).Offset = 152`

    d. `CGI_FileTuples(0).File =` Contents of the file named `C:\WEBSITE\CGI-TEMP\9EWS.002`

5. Referring to the CGI profile file example of Question 2, what will the following statement do?

```
Signature=GetSmallField("Digital Signature")
```

a. Store the string **"152"** in the **Signature** variable.
b. Store an empty string in the **Signature** variable.
c. Store 2048 bytes of the CGI content (**.INP**) file starting from the offset 152 in the **Signature** variable.
d. Generate an error.

EXERCISE 6

Complexity: Easy

1. Write a general purpose Windows CGI program named **FORMLIST.EXE** in the **C:\WEBSITE\CGI-WIN\WDBIC\FORMLIST** directory that lists the form data of any HTML form referring to this program. You may limit the output to just the Form Literal and Form External sections of its associated CGI profile file. Use tables to present the response and test your program with different HTML forms designed in Chapter 2, "Handling User Requests: Static and Dynamic Response."

Complexity: Moderate

2. Create a Windows CGI program named **CALC.EXE** in the **C:\WEBSITE\CGI-WIN\WDBIC\CALC** directory that takes three form fields named **Value1**, **Operator**, and **Value2** and calculates the result of **Value1** and **Value2** based on **Operator**. For example, if **Value1 = 10**, **Operator = "*"**, and **Value2 = 30**, then the program should return the value **300** as part of its response. Assume that the operator can be either **+**, **−**, *****, or **/** and that **Value1** and **Value2** hold numeric data. Also, design a corresponding HTML form to test your program.

CHAPTER SUMMARY

This chapter presented the basic operation of a Windows CGI program and showed how it is constructed using the Visual Basic framework. This framework, which essentially involves the use of a general purpose **CGI32.BAS** Visual Basic library module, was examined at length. A number of examples were used for better understanding of various features of this framework. The main points covered in this chapter are:

● A Windows CGI program is a noninteractive program that reads data from the CGI content file and secondary input files, fulfills the CGI request based on this input data, and generates CGI-formatted output in a designated output file and terminates.

● The Visual Basic CGI framework is a VB library module named **CGI32.BAS**, which contains global declarations, functions, and procedures that you can use while developing a Windows CGI program.

● A Visual Basic project is a collection of files and configuration settings.

● The `CGI32.BAS` module includes a `Main` procedure, which calls the `CGI_Main` procedure after performing the initialization tasks.

● You write your code in the `CGI_Main` procedure.

● The `Main` procedure activates a default error handler to trap run-time errors.

● A Windows CGI program's run mode can be determined from its command line. An empty command line indicates the program has been run in the interactive mode.

● The `Send` procedure of the `CGI32.BAS` module is used to write to the output file.

● The `CGI32.BAS` module declares global VB variables for all the environment variables that can be present in the CGI section of the CGI profile file. The `InitializeCGI` procedure initializes those variables.

● The `InitializeCGI` procedure stores the entries in the Accept and Extra Headers section in global arrays named `CGI_AcceptTypes` and `CGI_ExtraHeaders`, respectively.

● The entries in the Form Literal and Form External sections of the CGI profile file are stored in the global `CGI_FormTuples` array. In case of the Form External section, the contents of the specified files are read and stored in the value portion of the array element.

● The `CGI_AcceptTypes`, `CGI_ExtraHeaders`, and `CGI_FormTuples` are zero-based arrays whose elements have two components, key and value.

● The entries in the Form Huge section are stored in the `CGI_HugeTuples` array. The actual data from the CGI content file is not read.

● The entries in the Form File section are stored in the `CGI_FileTuples` array. Again, the actual contents of the listed files are not read.

● The `CGI32.BAS` module provides the `FindExtraHeader`, `FieldPresent`, and `GetSmallField` utility functions to search the `CGI_ExtraHeader` and `CGI_FormTuples` arrays quickly.

Until now, all the Windows CGI programs you have constructed simply demonstrated how to access the input data and how to send a response. In the next lesson, we will look at how to link an Access database with your Windows CGI program and process database-related requests.

ACCESSING DATABASE RECORDS FROM VISUAL BASIC: DATA-ACCESS OBJECTS

This chapter explains the recordset and other data access objects (DAOs) provided in Visual Basic (Professional and Enterprise editions) and shows how Windows CGI programs can use these objects to search and display records of one or more database tables. In particular, you will learn about:

- The Data Access Object (DAO) model; its hierarchy and important data access objects needed for accessing an Access database

- How to create a DAO

- The role of the `DBEngine`, `Workspace`, `Database`, `Recordset`, `QueryDef`, and `Field` objects

- The concept of a current record and listing it from a Windows CGI program

- Determining the field names and field count of a recordset

- Navigating through a recordset using the Move methods

- Displaying database records based on Select and Parameter queries

- How to trace and debug Windows CGI programs

THE DATA ACCESS OBJECT (DAO) MODEL

One major factor in the popularity of Visual Basic is its direct support for handling Access databases (and all other database formats that you can attach to within Access). This means that you can access and manipulate data of any supported external database right from your Visual Basic application and work with that data in any fashion you like. (You can even create new databases and tables from VB, but it's a lot easier with the user-friendly interface of Access.)

Visual Basic uses several programming objects (collectively called the *data access objects*, or DAOs) to provide hooks into an external database. These objects, which reflect the object-oriented programming methodology promoted by Visual Basic, give a natural outlook to how different database elements are related and what type of operations you can perform on them. In this lesson, we describe two main DAOs, DBEngine and Workspace, which are essential starting points to any database-related actions you want to perform. But first, let's review the basic concepts of object-oriented programming.

What Is an Object?

In the object-oriented programming (OOP) paradigm, an *object* is a programming entity that combines the data and the procedures that you can use to operate on that data. In many ways, a programming object functions similarly to a real-world object. Consider a car, for example (see Figure 9-1). It is a distinct object that has attributes such as color, make, model, (current) speed, and (current) direction.

If you have to create a car, each of these attributes will have to be given a value. Furthermore, for your car to behave like a car, you will have to provide it with the capabilities to start, move, and change directions, which could in turn affect the value of some of its attributes (such as speed and direction).

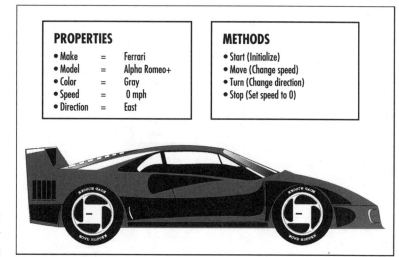

PROPERTIES
- Make = Ferrari
- Model = Alpha Romeo+
- Color = Gray
- Speed = 0 mph
- Direction = East

METHODS
- Start (Initialize)
- Move (Change speed)
- Turn (Change direction)
- Stop (Set speed to 0)

Figure 9-1
Properties and methods of a car object

Although we have listed only a few attributes and capabilities, a car is a complicated object that holds many other objects such as a steering wheel, an engine, and seats. These objects themselves have many characteristics and methods and are composed of additional smaller objects; you can keep going on until you reach the level of what you may call a *root object* (an atom, for example). The hierarchy in real-world objects, as you can see, is not easy to formulate.

Fortunately, programming objects are not that complex, although they can have hierarchical relationships with other objects. A good understanding of this hierarchy (also called an *object model*) is extremely important if you want to use these objects to their full potential. To review the data access objects of Visual Basic, we will not only examine the attributes (also called *properties*) and procedures (also called *methods*) of many of these objects, but we will also look at how they are related to each other.

The DBEngine **Object: The Starting Point of DAO**

In Visual Basic, data access objects follow a hierarchy that originates with a special object called the *DBEngine*. Figure 9-2 shows the beginning of this hierarchy.

The **DBEngine** object represents the Microsoft JET database engine, which is responsible for handling all the database management operations. As explained in Chapter 4, Lesson 1, Microsoft Access is also built on this JET engine.

The DAO Collections

From Figure 9-2, you can see that **DBEngine** holds two objects named **Workspaces** and **Errors**. These two objects are also referred to as *collection objects* because they

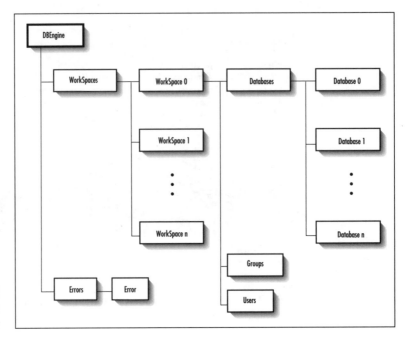

Figure 9-2
Beginning of the
DAO hierarchy

represent a collection of a particular type of objects (just like an array of elements, except each element is now an object). For instance, the `Workspaces` object is a collection of one or more `Workspace` objects.

Each collection object in DAO supports one property called `Count`, which indicates the number of elements that collection is currently holding. For example, the `Count` property of the `Workspaces` collection of the `DBEngine` object, accessed using the following expression, will return the number of `Workspace` objects currently in that collection:

```
DBEngine.Workspaces.Count
```

The syntax of this expression is quite simple. You start with the `DBEngine` object and use a dot (`.`) to go to the next level in the hierarchy, where you refer to the `Workspaces` collection object. Then you use the dot and the property name to refer to a particular property supported by that object.

Initial DAOs

Just because the objects shown in Figure 9-2 follow a hierarchy does not imply that these objects preexist in your application. This hierarchy simply indicates the order in which you can create these objects within your application. The only exception to this fact is the `DBEngine` object, which is created automatically the first time you refer to this object in your code.

Once the `DBEngine` object is created, it further creates the `Workspaces` and `Errors` collection, as well as a default `Workspace` object. The creation of any additional

`Workspace` objects or any child objects of the default workspace is the responsibility of your program. VB just gives you a jump start, as shown in Figure 9-3.

The `Workspace` Object

A `Workspace` object defines a named session for a user. It holds open databases and provides mechanisms for simultaneous transactions (explained further in Chapter 11, "Populating Tables: Web-Based Data Entry") and secure workgroup support. Right now, think of a workspace as a means of identifying yourself before you open any secured database.

The default `Workspace` object that `DBEngine` creates is an unsecure workspace, opened with the user name `Admin` and an empty (blank) password. You can use this default workspace to open any database (such as the sample `CALENDAR.MDB` database) that does not require authentication. However, if your application needs to work with a database that can only be opened with user name `John` and password `noble`, you must first create a secure `Workspace` object (as explained in the following section) and then use the `OpenDatabase` method of this `Workspace` object to open the secured database. The use of the `OpenDatabase` method is described later in this lesson.

Creating a New `Workspace` Object

To create a new `Workspace` object, you call the `CreateWorkspace` method of the `DBEngine` object using the following syntax:

```
Set workspace = DBEngine.CreateWorkspace(Name, UserName, Password, Type)
```

where *workspace* is an object variable that represents the workspace you want to create, *Name* is a string that uniquely names the new workspace object, *UserName* is a string that identifies the owner of the new workspace, *Password* is a string containing the password for the new workspace object, and *Type* is an optional attribute describing the type of workspace (JET or ODBC) you want to create. Because this book covers only JET-based DAOs, this parameter is not important in this context and can be omitted.

Figure 9-3
Initial DAOs created when you first refer to `DBEngine` in your code

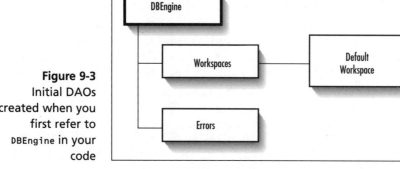

The following code shows how to use the above syntax to create a new workspace named **Protected** with **John** and **noble** as the user name and password, respectively:

```
Dim pws As Workspace      'Declare a workspace object variable named pws
Set pws = DBEngine.CreateWorkspace("Protected", "John", "noble")    'Create workspace
```

Note that the user name and password must be a valid combination, according to the information in the system database (**SYSTEM.MDA**). If this combination is incorrect, the above code will generate a run-time error.

To Set or Not to Set

In the previous code example, you declared the **pws Workspace** object variable, just like you would declare any other variable in Visual Basic:

```
Dim variablename As variabletype
```

However, observe that when you had to assign this variable, you had to use the **Set** keyword in the assignment statement. This is because VB requires you to specify the **Set** keyword anytime you want to associate an object variable with an object. VB signals a compilation error if you specify the object-assignment statement without the **Set** keyword, as shown below:

```
pws = DBEngine.CreateWorkspace("Protected", "John", "noble")    'Need the Set keyword
```

As a general rule, you do not need a **Set** keyword in your assignment statement if you are assigning a regular (nonobject) variable or if you are assigning an object variable to another object variable of the same object type. For example, the following code would not generate a compilation error:

```
Dim strName As String
Dim pws1 As Workspace
Dim pws2 As Workspace

strName = "Protected"    'Set not needed as strName is a string variable
Set pws1 = DBEngine.CreateWorkspace(strName, "John", "noble")    'Need the Set keyword
pws2 = pws1  'Set not needed as pws1 and pws2 are both object variables
```

Properties of a Workspace Object

A **Workspace** object is a nonpersistent object, which means you cannot save a workspace to disk. It contains properties such as **Name**, **UserName**, **Type**, and some others that are important only in the context of ODBC-type workspaces. Most of these properties get their initial values when you create the **Workspace** object. To access the value of any property of your **Workspace** object, use the following syntax:

```
workspace.PropertyName
```

where *workspace* is a workspace object variable pointing to your workspace and *PropertyName* is the name of the property you want to access. The following example shows how you can retrieve the values of the **Name** and **UserName** properties of your secure **Workspace** object and store them in the **strName** and **strUserName** string variables, respectively:

```
Dim strName As String, strUserName As String,
strName = pws.Name          'strName will get the value "Protected"
strUserName = pws.UserName  'strUserName will get the value "John"
```

The **Workspace** object does not support a **Password** property, which means you cannot retrieve the password used to create a **Workspace** object from that object.

Read-Only Properties

Although you can read the value of any predefined property of any existing **Workspace** object, you cannot change their values once the object has been created, with the **Name** property being the only exception. So if you want to change the name of your secure workspace from **Protected** to **Secure**, you can use the following statement:

```
pws.Name = "Secure"
```

On the other hand, if you try to change the **UserName** property, a run-time error will be generated.

As you will see in subsequent lessons, all DAOs support some properties that are read-only and some properties that can be changed after the objects have been created. In some cases, the value of a read-only property can change as a side effect of executing one or more methods of that object, as illustrated in the following section.

Appending a Workspace Object to the Workspaces Collection

When you create a new **Workspace** object, it does not automatically become a part of the **Workspaces** collection. This means that to refer to that object, you must have access to its object variable (**pws** in this case). In case you want to give your workspace global scope, you can either declare **pws** as a global variable

```
Global pws As Workspace
```

or add the **Workspace** object to the **Workspaces** collection using the collection's **Append** method, as shown below:

```
DBEngine.Workspaces.Append pws  'Append it after the default workspace
```

Append is a method supported by the **Workspaces** collection and its role is simply to add the specified object (pointed by its object variable) to the collection. As an indirect side effect, the value of the collection's **Count** property is incremented by 1.

Once your workspace becomes part of the **Workspaces** collection, you can refer to any of its properties (say the **UserName** property) in any of the following ways:

```
pws.UserName                              'Use the workspace variable
DBEngine.Workspaces(1).UserName           'Use the index in the workspaces collection
DBEngine.Workspaces("Protected").UserName 'Use the string expression representing the⇐
name
DBEngine!Workspaces!Protected.UserName    'Use the name directly with the ! operator
DBEngine(1).UserName                       'No need to specify the Workspaces keyword
DBEngine("Protected").UserName             'No need to specify the Workspaces keyword
```

Note that because your secure workspace is the second **Workspace** object (the default workspace is the first one), it holds the second position in the **Workspaces** collection and is thus accessed using the index value of 1. All DAO collections are like zero-based arrays with an additional feature that, instead of the index position, you can also refer to their held objects by object name. This is why **DBEngine. Workspaces ("Protected").UserName** is a valid syntax to access the **UserName** property of your secure workspace. As a final comment, VB allows you to skip the **Workspaces** keyword from your expression if you don't use the dot (**.**) after the **DBEngine** keyword. So **DBEngine(1)** and **DBEngine.Workspaces(1)** are synonymous expressions wherever you want to refer to the second workspace of the **Workspaces** collection.

Once you append a **Workspace** object to the **Workspaces** collection, you cannot change its **Name** property anymore.

Lesson Summary

This lesson introduced object-oriented programming (OOP) concepts and showed how Visual Basic follows these concepts to represent database-related entities through its data access objects.

In an OOP environment, an object is a programming element that combines both data and procedures operating on that data. The exposed portions of that data are called properties, whereas the exposed procedures (the ones you can use) are called methods. Like real-world objects, programming objects follow a hierarchical relationship, which generally starts with a root object.

In DAO, this root object is called **DBEngine**, which stands for the JET database engine. **DBEngine**, in addition to several predefined properties and methods, holds two types of collections, **Workspaces** and **Errors**, which are collections of **Workspace** and **Error** objects, respectively. A workspace represents a session that you plan to conduct with the external databases belonging to your workgroup (which is represented by the **SYSTEM.MDW** system database). An **Error** object simply represents any error that may occur during a DAO operation.

The **DBEngine** object is created automatically the first time your program refers to it during execution. The **DBEngine** further creates a default **Workspace** object, which essentially represents an unsecure user session. To create a new secure workspace, you use the **CreateWorkspace** method of **DBEngine** as described in this lesson. Furthermore, if you append that **Workspace** object to the **Workspaces** collection through the collection's **Append** method, you can refer to any property of that workspace using one of the many ways listed in this lesson.

In the next lesson, we will look at the general process of creating a DAO and show how it can be used to create a **Database** object representing the sample calendar database.

 **QUIZ 1**

1. What are the distinct elements of a programming object?
   a. Names
   b. Properties
   c. Methods
   d. All of the above

2. How can you refer to the **Version** property of the **DBEngine** object?
   a. `DBEngine.Property.Version`
   b. `Version`
   c. `DBEngine(0).Version`
   d. `DBEngine.Version`

3. What are the characteristics of the default **Workspace** object?
   a. It represents an unsecure session.
   b. VB provides a global **Workspace**-type object variable named **dws** to refer to this object.
   c. You can refer to this workspace as **DBEngine(0)**.
   d. It has the value **Admin** in its **Name** property.

4. Suppose your program contains the following lines of code:

   ```
   Dim ws As Workspace

   Set ws = DBEngine.CreateWorkspace("Owner","gupt")
   ```

   Which of the following statements would generate an error, assuming **strUserName** and **strPassword** are string variables?
   a. `strUserName = ws.UserName`
   b. `strPassword = ws.Password`
   c. `strUserName = ws.Name`
   d. `strUserName = DBEngine(1).UserName`

5. Referring to the example in the previous question, what will be the value of the **DBEngine.Workspaces.Count** expression once the code is executed?
   a. **0**
   b. **1**
   c. **2**
   d. The expression will generate an error.

EXERCISE 1

Complexity: Easy
   1. List all the methods and properties supported by the **DBEngine** object. (Hint: Read VB's online help on the **DBEngine** Object Summary.)

Complexity: Moderate
   2. Write a VB function named **WSLIST()** that returns a comma-delimited list of all the names of all the workspaces in the **Workspaces** collection.

LESSON 2

OPENING A DATABASE

In VB's DAO model, an external database is represented by the DAO's **Database** object, which, according to Figure 9-2, is a subordinate of the **Workspace** object. Therefore, to open an existing database in your VB program, you need to create a **Database** object that will represent it. The process is similar to how you created the new **Workspace** object in the previous lesson, except you need to consider some additional details. In fact, there are standard steps you can follow to create any DAO. In this lesson, we will outline those standard steps and then apply them to create a **Database** object that represents the sample calendar Access database.

Creating a DAO

The steps to create any DAO are as follows:

1. Declare a variable for your new object.

2. Determine the parent object of the object you want to create according to the DAO hierarchy.

3. Ensure that the parent object already exists.

4. Identify the appropriate child object's creation method from the parent object's list of supported methods and use that method to create the child object.

The Parent Object

The parent object of any DAO (say, Object A) is the first noncollection-type object you encounter if you traverse upward in the DAO hierarchy from Object A. So referring to Figure 9-2, the **DBEngine** is the parent object of a **Workspace** object. A **Workspace** object is the parent object of a **Database** object, which is the parent object of many other objects, as you will see later in this chapter. Note that collection-type objects such as **Workspaces** and **Databases** are not considered applicable parent objects. Also, it is fairly easy to distinguish a collection object from a regular object, thanks to DAO's consistent naming conventions. A collection object's name has an "s" on the end, such as **Workspaces**, **Databases**, and **Errors**.

Creating a Database Object

Now that you have a general outline of how to create any DAO, let's follow these steps to create a **Database** object that will represent the sample **CALENDAR.MDB** database residing in the **C:\WEBSITE\HTDOCS\WDBIC\CHAP05\SAMPLES** directory.

Step 1: Declare a Variable for Your New Object

Any time you create an object, it needs to be assigned to a variable declared to be of that object type. So before you create the **Database** object, you must declare a **Database** object variable as follows:

```
Dim db As Database
```

Step 2: Identify the Parent Object

According to the DAO model, the parent object of a **Database** object is a **Workspace** object. Because the calendar database that you want to open is not a secure database, you can use the default workspace as its parent object.

Step 3: Ensure that the Parent Object Exists

As mentioned in Lesson 1, the default workspace is automatically created by the **DBEngine** object and stored as the first element of the **Workspaces** collection. So the answer to the question "Does the default **Workspace** object exist?" is affirmative, and you can refer to this workspace as **DBEngine.Workspaces(0)**, or simply **DBEngine(0)**.

Step 4: Identify the Appropriate Object Creation Method from the Parent's List of Supported Methods

This is probably the most interesting step: finding out the exact name and syntax of the method you need to use to create your **Database** object. The best way is to search VB's online help on the methods supported by the parent object. In this case, search for **Workspace Object** from the Help index and then select the Workspace Object, Workspaces Collection Summary (DAO) help topic, as shown in Figure 9-4.

Figure 9-5 shows the online help page corresponding to the selected help topic.

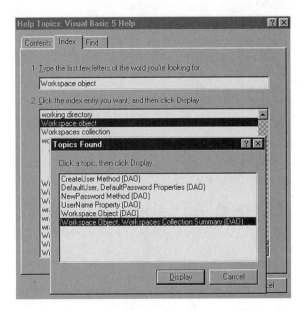

Figure 9-4
Seeking help on
the summary of a
Workspace object

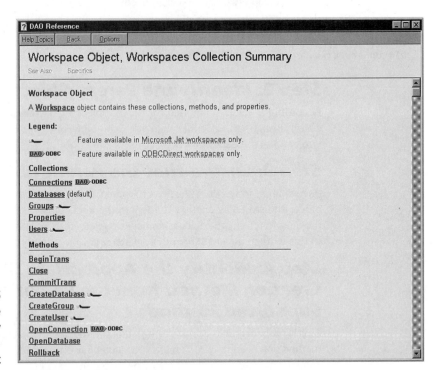

Figure 9-5
Online help page
listing the summary
of a Workspace
object

Notice in Figure 9-5 that the `Workspace` object supports the `CreateDatabase` and `OpenDatabase` methods. Both these methods create a `Database` object. The only difference is that the `CreateDatabase` method creates a new (blank) database, whereas the `OpenDatabase` method opens an existing database. Because in this case you want to open the existing calendar database, use the `OpenDatabase` method, which has the following syntax:

```
Set database = workspace.OpenDatabase (dbname, [options], [read-only], [connect])
```

where *database* is a database object variable, *workspace* is a *Workspace* object, *dbname* is the path and name of the existing database file, and *options*, *read-only*, and *connect* are optional parameters that you can use to classify how to open the database. If you omit these optional parameters, the database will be opened in a shared mode with full read/write privileges. For this example, we will use these default settings to create the `Database` object as follows:

```
Set db = DBEngine(0).OpenDatabase("C:\WEBSITE\HTDOCS\WDBIC\CHAP05\SAMPLES\⇐
CALENDAR.MDB")
```

Note that you could have also used the following lines of code to achieve the same result:

```
Dim ws As Workspace
Dim db As Database

Set ws = DBEngine(0)
Set db = ws.OpenDatabase("C:\WEBSITE\HTDOCS\WDBIC\CHAP05\SAMPLES\CALENDAR.MDB")
```

The database filename that you specify when you create this `Database` object becomes the value of its `Name` property.

In some cases, you can also create a new DAO using a method supported by either a peer object (for example, a `Recordset` object from a `QueryDef` object) or an ancestor object (for example, a `Database` object from the `DBEngine`). However, this is more an exception than a norm. There are also some objects (such as the `Field` object) that have multiple parent objects; in these cases, only one of those parent objects generally supports the object creation method.

Referring to a Database Object

Unlike a `Workspace` object, where you open an existing database through a `Database` object, the `Database` object automatically is appended to the `Databases` collection. This means that you can refer to your `Database` object in any of the following ways:

```
db                      'Using the database object variable
DBEngine.Workspaces(0).Databases(0)    'First database of the first workspace of⇐
DBEngine
DBEngine(0)(0)    'Workspaces and Databases keywords assumed by default
DBEngine(0)("C:\WEBSITE\HTDOCS\WDBIC\CHAP05\SAMPLES\CALENDAR.MDB")     'By Database⇐
Name
ws.Databases(0)  'In case you declared ws as the default workspace
ws(0)                'Databases keyword assumed by default
```

Opening the Calendar Database in Your Windows CGI Program

Now that you know how to create a **Database** object that opens the calendar database, let's create a simple Windows CGI program to list some of that object's properties.

1. Create a new project named DBTEST.VBP in the C:\WEBSITE\CGI-WIN\ WDBIC\DBTEST directory from the NEWAPP project template, as explained in Chapter 8, Lesson 2.

2. Open the DBTEST.VBP project file in VB.

3. Select References... from the Project menu.

   VB displays the available and selected object libraries for this project as shown in Figure 9-6.

   Note that the Microsoft DAO 3.5 Object Library is one of the selected options. Having this library selected is important if you are planning to work with DAOs within your VB application. Fortunately, the NEWAPP.VBP project template has this library preselected as part of its configuration, so you do not need to worry about it if you design your Windows CGI projects based on this template. Just be aware that this is a critical requirement in case you get a compilation error such as Object-type not defined when you declare a DAO variable in your program.

4. Modify the CGI_Main procedure of the MYAPP.BAS module, as shown in Listing 9-1.

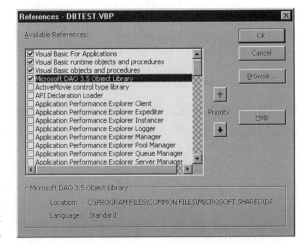

Figure 9-6
Selected and available object libraries

Listing 9-1 The `CGI_Main` procedure of the `DBTEST.EXE` program

```
Sub CGI_Main()

   Dim db As Database

   Set db =
DBEngine(0).OpenDatabase("C:\WEBSITE\HTDOCS\WDBIC\CHAP05\SAMPLES\CALENDAR.MDB")
   Send "Content-type: text/html"
   Send ""
   Send "<HTML>"
   Send "<HEAD><TITLE>DBOPEN</TITLE></HEAD><BODY>"
   Send "<B>Default workspace name: </B> " & DBEngine(0).name
   Send "<BR><B>Default workspace username: </B> " & DBEngine(0).UserName
   Send "<BR><B>Workspaces collection count: </B> " & DBEngine.Workspaces.Count
   Send "<BR><B>Database name: </B>" & db.name
   Send "<BR><B>Database collating order: </B>" & db.CollatingOrder
   Send "<BR><B>Database version: </B>" & db.Version
   Send "<BR><B>Database Updatable: </B>" & db.Updatable
   Send "<BR><B>Count of open databases in the default workspace: </B>"
   Send DBEngine(0).Databases.Count
   Send "<BR><B>DBEngine(0)(0).Name = </B>" & DBEngine(0)(0).name
   Send "</BODY></HTML>"

End Sub
```

5. Compile this program to create an executable file named DBTEST.EXE in the DBTEST directory.

6. Start your Web server if it is not already running.

7. Enter the following URL in your Web browser:

   `http://localhost/cgi-win/wdbic/dbtest/dbtest.exe`

   The program returns the values of some workspace- and database-related properties, as shown in Figure 9-7. Note that the default workspace has a name of #Default Workspace#.

Lesson Summary

This lesson described the steps for creating a data access object and how to follow those steps to create a **Database** object representing an existing database. The DAO creation process involves setting up a variable for that new object and using the DAO hierarchy to identify its parent object, which must already exist. The collection-type objects such as **Workspaces** and **Databases** are not applicable candidates for being a parent object.

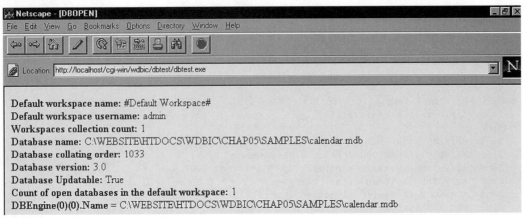

Figure 9-7
Response of the DBTEST.EXE program

Once you identify the parent object, you should inspect its list of supported methods to determine which methods produce a new child object. For example, in the case of a **Workspace** object, you could use either the **CreateDatabase** or **OpenDatabase** to create a new **Database** object. The former creates a new (blank) database, and the latter opens an existing database. This lesson showed how to apply the **OpenDatabase** method to create a **Database** object representing the sample calendar database and how to list some of its key properties through a Windows CGI program.

From Chapters 4, "Constructing a Relational Database: The Microsoft Access Way," and 5, "Sorting and Searching: Simple Select Queries," you already know that an Access database contains tables and **Select** queries, which appear quite similar when seen in their datasheet view. This is not just a coincidence but a reflection of the versatile capabilities of the DAO's **Recordset** object, which we will examine in the next lesson.

For your reference, a copy of the **DBTEST** program created in this lesson is available in the **C:\WEBSITE\HTDOCS\WDBIC\CHAP09\LESSON2\RESULTS** directory.

1. What are the applicable parent objects of a **Database** object?
   a. **DBEngine**
   b. The default workspace
   c. The **Workspaces** collection
   d. The **Error** object

2. Suppose your VB program contains the following lines of code:

```
Dim ws As Workspace
Dim pws As Workspace
Dim db As Database
Dim dbName As String
Dim DefaultDBName As String

dbName = "C:\WEBSITE\HTDOCS\WDBIC\CHAPO5\SAMPLES\CALENDAR.MDB"
Set ws = DBEngine.Workspaces(0)
```

Which of the following statements would generate an error if they were listed after the last line of the above code?

a. `Set db = ws.OpenDatabase(dbName)`

b. `Set db = DBEngine(0).OpenDatabase(dbName)`

c. `Set db = pws.OpenDatabase(dbName)`

d. `DefaultDBName = ws.Databases(0).Name`

3. Which of the following expressions will evaluate to `True` after the following code is executed?

```
Dim db1 As Database
Dim db2 As Database
Dim db3 As Database
Dim dbName

dbName = "C:\WEBSITE\HTDOCS\WDBIC\CHAPO5\SAMPLES\CALENDAR.MDB"
Set db1 = DBEngine(0).OpenDatabase(dbName)
Set db2 = DBEngine(0).CreateDatabase("C:\WEBSITE\HTDOCS\WDBIC\⇐
TEST.MDB", dbLangGeneral)
Set db3 = DBEngine(0).OpenDatabase(dbName)
```

a. `db2.Name = "C:\WEBSITE\HTDOCS\WDBIC\TEST.MDB"`

b. `db3.Name = db1.Name`

c. `db1.Updatable = False`

d. All of the above

4. Refer to the code example of the previous question. What will be the value of `DBEngine(0).Databases.Count` after the last line of that code is executed?

a. `0`

b. `1`

c. `2`

d. `3`

5. What should you do if you get an `Object-type not defined` or similar compilation error message on the following line of your code?

```
Dim db As Database
```

 a. Remove this line.
 b. Change `Database` to `Databases` in this line.
 c. Ensure that the DAO 3.5 Object Library has been selected as one of the references in your VB project.
 d. Switch to another programming language.

Complexity: Easy

 1. List all the methods and properties supported by the `Workspace` object. (Hint: Read VB's online help on the `Workspace` Object Summary.)

Complexity: Moderate

 2. The `Database` object contains a collection named `TableDefs`, which holds the definitions of all the tables stored in the database represented by that `Database` object. Write a Windows CGI program named `NUMTABLES.EXE` (in the `C:\WEBSITE\CGI-WIN\WDBIC\NUMTABLES` directory) that returns the number of tables in an Access database whose path and name are provided in the query string portion of the requesting URL. For example, the following URL should return the number of tables present in the `C:\WEBSITE\HTDOCS\WDBIC\CHAP05\SAMPLES\CALENDAR.MDB` database:

```
http://localhost/cgi-win/wdbic/numtables/numtables.exe?c:\website
\htdocs\wdbic\chap05\samples\calendar.mdb
```

LESSON 3

THE Recordset OBJECT

A `Recordset` object is the most widely used DAO component because it not only gives you access to virtually any data field but also lets you work with individual records of a table or a query result as if they were array elements. Through a `Recordset` object, you can add, update, and quickly find records with minimal programming effort. This lesson describes the different types of `Recordset` objects that VB supports, how to create a table-based `Recordset` object, and how to use that object to list the first record of the sponsor table of the sample calendar database through a Windows CGI program.

Types of Recordsets

A `Recordset` object represents a collection of records. It can be based on a table, a query, or an SQL statement that returns records. Depending on the nature of the record source and the sort of operations you want to perform, the **Recordset** object can be one of the following types (in the context of JET-based workspaces):

● *Table-type recordset*, where records are based on a single table. This is the most efficient way of accessing records.

● *Dynaset-type recordset*, where the record source is generally a query that returns updatable records. The query can be based on one or more tables.

● *Snapshot-type recordset*, which holds a static copy of the records. These records cannot be updated.

● *Forward-only-type recordset*, where you can move in only one (forward) direction when navigating through the records.

Why are there so many types of recordsets? Mainly to allow both flexibility and efficiency. For example, a table-type recordset takes minimum memory and can use user-specified indexes for quick searches. However, it lacks flexibility, because this recordset can be based only on a single database table. On the other hand, the dynaset-type recordset can originate from queries involving multiple tables but is not as efficient (relatively speaking) as the table-type recordset.

Creating a Recordset **Object**

Figure 9-8 shows where **Recordset** objects fit within the DAO model.

As you can see from Figure 9-8, a **Recordset** object is associatd with the **Recordsets** collection, which belongs to a **Database** object. This means that the **Database** object is the only parent object of a **Recordset** object (based on the definition of the parent object given in Lesson 2) and hence it must support a method to create a new **Recordset** object. If you examine the list of methods supported by a **Database** object from VB's online help, you will see that such a method does exist. It is the **OpenRecordset** method and has the following syntax:

```
Set recordset = database.OpenRecordset (source [,type] [,options] [,lockedits])
```

In this syntax, *recordset* stands for a **Recordset**–type object variable and *database* stands for a **Database**-type variable pointing to an existing **Database** object. The *source* argument is a string expression identifying the source of the data, which can be a table name, query name, or a valid **SELECT** SQL statement. The optional *type* argument indicates the type of recordset you want to create and can be set to any of the four constants listed in Table 9-1. Note that if you do not specify the **Type** parameter at all, a table-type recordset is returned if the **source** is the name of a table. If the **source** is a query name or an SQL string, the **OpenRecordset** method returns a dynaset-type **Recordset** object by default.

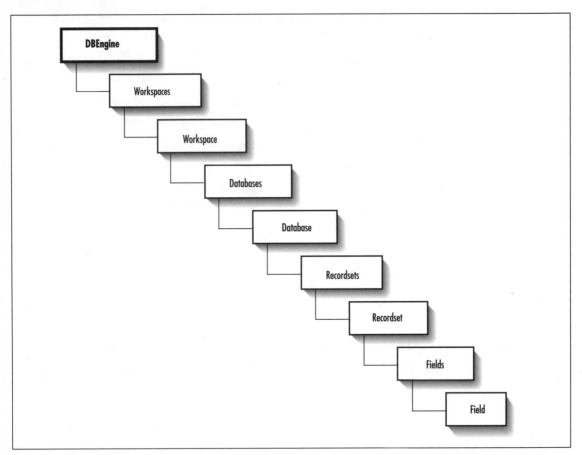

Figure 9-8
Position of `Recordset` objects within the DAO model

Table 9-1 Constants for defining a recordset type

Constant Name	Used to Open
dbOpenTable	Table-type recordset
dbOpenDynaset	Dynaset-type recordset
dbOpenSnapshot	Snapshot-type recordset
dbOpenForwardOnly	Forward-only-type recordset

The `Options` argument of the `OpenRecordset` method is a combination of constants that allows you to further characterize the `Recordset` object (such as restrictions on other users' ability to edit and view records while your recordset is active). Table 9-2 lists some important options that you may specify when creating a `Recordset` object.

If your recordset will support data editing capabilities, then the lockedits argument specifies the type of locking mechanism (dbPessimistic or dbOptimistic) that you want to use to handle multiuser editing conflicts. The difference between pessimistic and optimistic locking schemes is explained in Chapter 3, Lesson 6.

Table 9-2 Constants for defining a recordset option

Constant Name	Use
dbDenyWrite	To keep other users from modifying or adding records while the recordset is active
dbDenyRead	To keep other users from viewing records (table-type recordset only)
dbReadOnly	To allow you only to view records; other users can modify them
dbAppendOnly	To allow you only to append new records (dynaset-type recordset only)
dbSeeChanges	To generate a run-time error if the record you are editing through your recordset was recently modified by another user
dbInconsistent	To update records from all tables in a multiple table dynaset-type recordset
dbConsistent	To update records from only the many table in a multiple table dynaset-type recordset

The following code example shows how you can create a **Recordset** object representing the records of the **Sponsor** table of the sample calendar database.

```
Dim dbCalendar As Database  'Declare database variable
Dim rsSponsor As Recordset  'Delcare recordset variable
Dim dbName As String        'Path and name of the calendar database
Dim TableName As String     'Name of the table within the calendar database

DbName = "C:\WEBSITE\HTDOCS\WDBIC\CHAP05\SAMPLES\CALENDAR.MDB"
TableName = "tblSponsors"
Set dbCalendar = dbEngine(0).OpenDatabase(dbName)    'Open the database
Set rsSponsor = dbCalendar.OpenRecordset(TableName)  'Open a recordset from the table
```

The Concept of Current Record

A **Recordset** object can be perceived as a virtual table consisting of records and fields with the capability to access and manipulate data *one record at a time*. Think of it as a book, where you must go to a specific page before you can read the contents of that page. Figure 9-9 shows a visual representation of the **Recordset** object that you created based on the **Sponsor** table in the previous example.

SponsorID	Sponsor Name	SponsorTypeID	Web URL	User Name	Password
1	The Corporation of the Township	1	http://www.uxbridge.co	uxbridge	fsdgg
2	Downtown Franklin Association	1	http://www.phoenix.w1	Franklin	
3	The Five Hundred, Inc.	11	http://www.500inc.org/	albert	five
4	City of Knoxville	1	http://funnelweb.utcc.u	yarget	city
5	MicroStation Inc.	7	http://www.bentley.con	microlab	cad
6	National Association of Home Bu	7	http://www.nahb.com/e	homebuilders	nahb
12	International Sociological Associ	5	http://www.arch.vt.edu/	urban	housing
13	The Canadian Society for Civil Er	7	http://acs.ryerson.ca/~	engineering	civil
14	Greenville Children's Hospital	11	http://www.teleplex.net	hospital	greenville
15	USA INTERNATIONAL DANCE ⟨	4	http://www.Instar.com/	dancers	ballet
16	Rolls Royce	2	http://www.aecc.winter	petroleum	deepseas
17	Grampian Corporation	2	http://www.aecc.winter	Quality	benchmark
19	US Department of Energy	12	http://education.lanl.go	Roger	energy
20	US National Science and Techno	9	http://www.ifas.ufl.edu/	hero	axbycz
21	University of Michigan, Ann Arbo	5	http://www.dla.utexas.	tintin	comic
22	The Department of Mathematics,	5	http://icg.fas.harvard.e	teachers	teach
23	Miami-Dade Community College	5	http://www.mdcc.edu/t	dades	books

Figure 9-9
A visual representation of the recordset based on the Sponsor table

When you create a **Recordset** object, the first record of the underlying record source is automatically set as the current record of the recordset. You can then retrieve the data of any field of this current record by its field name or by its field position in the following ways:

● recordset!FieldName (or recordset![FieldName] if FieldName contains spaces or hyphens).

● recordset(FieldNameString), where FieldNameString is a string constant or a string variable that evaluates to the name of the field.

● recordset(FieldPostionNumber), where FieldPostionNumber identifies the numeric position of a field in the underlying source. The first field (left-most) is considered to have a FieldPositionNumber of 0.

Note that this nomenclature is a direct consequence of the fact that the fields of a **Recordset** object are automatically stored in its **Fields** collection, as shown in Figure 9-8. The following examples show how you can use the preceding methods to access the value of the **SponsorName** field of the current (first) record of the recordset shown in Figure 9-9.

```
rsSponsors!SponsorName        'Direct reference to the field name
rsSponsors![SponsorName]      'Also, if field name has spaces or hyphens
rs("SponsorName")            'Using a string constant
rs("Sponsor" + "Name")       'Using a string expression
rs(strFieldName)             'Where strFieldName = "SponsorName"
rs(1)                        'SponsorName is the second field
rs(intFieldPos)              'Where intFieldPos = 1
```

A Windows CGI Program that Lists the First Sponsor Record

Now that you know how to create a recordset based on the **tblSponsors** table and the various ways of accessing the fields of its first (current) record, let's design a Windows CGI program named **SPONSOR1.EXE** that will display this record as its response.

1. Create a new project named SPONSOR1.VBP in the C:\WEBSITE\CGI-WIN\ WDBIC\SPONSOR1 directory from the NEWAPP project template.

2. Open the SPONSOR1.VBP project file in VB.

3. Modify the CGI_Main procedure of the MYAPP.BAS module, as shown in Listing 9-2.

Listing 9-2 The CGI_Main procedure of the SPONSOR1.EXE program

```
Sub CGI_Main()

    Dim dbCalendar As Database    'Declare database variable
    Dim rsSponsor As Recordset    'Delcare recordset variable
    Dim dbName As String          'Path and name of the calendar database
    Dim TableName As String       'Name of the table within the calendar database
    Dim FieldCount As Integer     'Count of fields in the recordset

    dbName = "C:\WEBSITE\HTDOCS\WDBIC\CHAP05\SAMPLES\CALENDAR.MDB"
    TableName = "tblSponsors"
    Set dbCalendar = DBEngine(0).OpenDatabase(dbName)     'Open the database
    Set rsSponsor = dbCalendar.OpenRecordset(TableName)   'Open a recordset from the table
    'Generate response
    Send "Content-type: text/html"
    Send ""
    Send "<HTML><HEAD><TITLE>SPONSOR1</TITLE></HEAD><BODY>"
    Send "<TABLE BORDER=1 CELLSPACING=5 CELLPADDING=5>"
    Send "<CAPTION>First record of the sponsor table</CAPTION>"
    Send "<TR><TH>Field Name</TH><TH>Field Value</TH></TR>"
    Send "<TR><TD>Sponsor ID: </TD><TD>" & rsSponsor!SponsorID & "</TD></TR>"
    Send "<TR><TD>Sponsor Name: </TD><TD>" & rsSponsor![SponsorName] & "</TD></TR>"
    Send "<TR><TD>Sponsor TypeID: </TD><TD>" & rsSponsor(2) & "</TD></TR>"
    Send "<TR><TD>Web URL: </TD><TD>" & rsSponsor("WebAddress") & "</TD></TR>"
    Send "<TR><TD>Username: </TD><TD>" & rsSponsor("User" + "Name") & "</TD></TR>"
    FieldCount = 6    'Sponsor table contains 6 fields
    'Send last field
    Send "<TR><TD>Password: </TD><TD>" & rsSponsor(FieldCount - 1) & "</TD></TR>"
    Send "</TABLE>"
    Send "</BODY></HTML>"

End Sub
```

4. Compile this program to create an executable file named SPONSOR1.EXE in the SPONSOR1 directory.

5. Start your Web server if it is not already running.

6. Enter the following URL in your Web browser:

   http://localhost/cgi-win/wdbic/sponsor1/sponsor1.exe

   The response contains the data from the first sponsor record as shown in Figure 9-10.

If you get an error message saying Item not found in the collection instead of the first record as your response, chances are you mistyped one of the field names. Correct any field name typos in your code and then recompile and retest the program.

Determining the Field Names and the Field Count of a Recordset

For the CGI_Main procedure of the SPONSOR1.EXE program, you had to explicitly type the name of each field. In a recordset with few fields, this may not be a big concern.

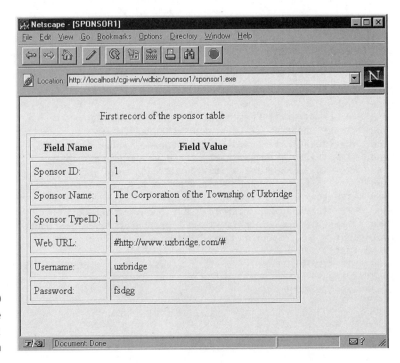

Figure 9-10
Response of the
SPONSOR1.EXE
program

However, if the underlying data source of your recordset has several fields, this process of listing field names can become cumbersome. Furthermore, if you want to write a general purpose procedure that lists the current record of any given recordset, how will you know the names of its fields in advance? Fortunately, the answer in both cases lies in the use of the **Fields** collection of that recordset.

As we briefly mentioned earlier, the **Fields** collection of a **Recordset** object contains **Field** objects representing the fields of the recordset's underlying data source. Like every other collection, the **Fields** collection contains a **Count** property that indicates the number of such objects currently held by the collection.

The **Field** object supports several properties, many of which are the same as the field properties that you set for an Access table (see Chapter 4, Lesson 2). One key property of the **Field** object is the **Name** property, which identifies the name of the field represented by that **Field** object. So if you know the field position, you can access the name of any field through this **Fields** collection as **recordset.Fields(FieldPosition).Name**, or simply **recordset(FieldPosition).Name** (because **Fields** is the default collection of a **Recordset** object).

As a demonstration of the above feature, create another Windows CGI project named **SPONSOR2.VBP** in the **C:\WEBSITE\CGI-WIN\WDBIC\SPONSOR2** directory and design its **CGI_Main** procedure as shown in Listing 9-3.

Listing 9-3 The **CGI_Main** procedure of the **SPONSOR2.EXE** program

```
Sub CGI_Main()

    Dim dbCalendar As Database    'Declare database variable
    Dim rsSponsor As Recordset    'Delcare recordset variable
    Dim dbName As String          'Path and name of the calendar database
    Dim TableName As String       'Name of the table within the calendar database
    Dim FieldCount As Integer     'Count of fields in the recordset
    Dim i As Integer,             'Index variable

    dbName = "C:\WEBSITE\HTDOCS\WDBIC\CHAP05\SAMPLES\CALENDAR.MDB"
    TableName = "tblSponsors"
    Set dbCalendar = DBEngine(0).OpenDatabase(dbName)    'Open the database
    Set rsSponsor = dbCalendar.OpenRecordset(TableName) 'Open a recordset from the table
    'Generate response
    Send "Content-type: text/html"
    Send ""
    Send "<HTML><HEAD><TITLE>SPONSOR2</TITLE></HEAD><BODY>"
    Send "<TABLE BORDER=1 CELLSPACING=5 CELLPADDING=5>"   'Begin table
    Send "<CAPTION>First record of the sponsor table</CAPTION>"
    Send "<TR><TH>Field Name</TH><TH>Field Value</TH></TR>"   'Table heading
    FieldCount = rsSponsor.Fields.Count          'Get Field count
    For i = 0 To FieldCount - 1                   'Remember collection is 0-based
      Send "<TR>"                                 'Start new table row
      Send "<TD>" & rsSponsor(i).name & "</TD>"  'Send field name
      Send "<TD>" & rsSponsor(i) & "</TD>"       'Send field value
```

continued on next page

continued from previous page

```
        Send  "</TR>"                          'End table row
    Next
    Send  "</TABLE>"                           'End table
    Send  "</BODY></HTML>"

End Sub
```

Compile this program as `SPONSOR2.EXE` and test it by entering the following URL:

`http://localhost/cgi-win/wdbic/sponsor2/sponsor2.exe`

Figure 9-11 shows the response of this program, which now contains the field names as specified in the sponsor table.

The `Name` property of a `Field` object is *not* related to the `Caption` property of an Access table field. In fact, the `Caption` property is an Access-only property and not part of the JET engine, which means it is not a predefined property of the `Field` object and cannot be accessed using the standard syntax. We will show how you to retrieve the value of the `Caption` property in the next lesson.

Lesson Summary

This lesson described the concept of a recordset, which can represent the records contained in a database table or returned by a query. In the realm of a JET workspace (the

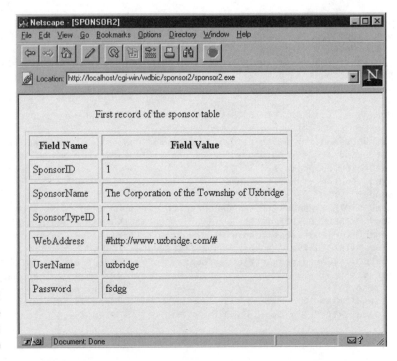

Figure 9-11
Response of the
`SPONSOR2.EXE`
program

other type of workspace supported by VB is the ODBC type, which is not covered in this book), you can create four types of recordsets based on whether performance or versatility is your main objective. The simplest and fastest recordset is a table-type record-set, but it must be based on a single table.

If you create a recordset from a query or an SQL string (as will be shown in the next lesson), then it must be either a dynaset-type, a snapshot-type, or a forward-only-type recordset. By default, the `OpenRecordset` method of the `Database` object, which you normally use to create a `Recordset` object, creates a dynaset-type recordset if the record-set source is not the name of a single table. Note that you can create a dynaset-type recordset to represent a single table, as you will see in the next lesson.

Once you create a `Recordset` object, the first record of the underlying source becomes its current record. The `Fields` collection of that recordset is populated with the `Field` objects representing the fields of that recordset. The `Count` property of that collection returns the total number of recordset fields. You can retrieve data from a recordset field using any of following ways:

```
recordset![FieldName]
recordset("FieldName")
recordset(FieldPosition)
```

Because a field is represented through a `Field` object, you can access many field-related properties by typing a dot (.) and the property name after any of the above expressions. For example, to retrieve the name of the third recordset field, you can use the following syntax:

```
recordset(3).Name
```

This lesson demonstrated two ways of creating a Windows CGI program that lists the first record of the sponsor table as its response. In the next lesson, we will show how you can navigate through a recordset to list all or selected records of a record source from a Windows CGI program.

The project for this exercise is stored in the `C:\WEBSITE\HTDOCS\WDBIC\CHAP09\` `LESSON3\` directory.

1. What type of recordset is created in the `SPONSOR1.EXE` program?
   a. Table-type
   b. Dynaset-type
   c. Snapshot-type
   d. Forward-only-type

2. When you create a new `Recordset` object, which record of underlying source becomes the current record of that recordset?
   a. None
   b. The first record
   c. Any record, chosen at random
   d. The last record

3. How do you create a dynaset-type recordset that only allows you to read records?
   a. Set the `type` argument of the `OpenRecordset` method to `dbDynasetType`.
   b. Set the `type` argument of the `OpenRecordset` method to `dbOpenDynaset`.
   c. Set the `options` argument of the `OpenRecordset` method to `dbDenyWrite`.
   d. Set the `options` argument of the `OpenRecordset` method to `dbReadOnly`.

4. Referring to the code of the `SPONSOR1.EXE` program, which of the following expressions will return the value of the `Required` property of the `SponsorName` field?
   a. `rsSponsors.SponsorName.Required`
   b. `rsSponsors!SponsorName.Required`
   c. `rsSponsors.SponsorName!Required`
   d. `rsSponsors("SponsorName").Required`

5. What does the following expression return, assuming `rs` is a `Recordset` object variable pointing to an open recordset?

   ```
   rs(rs.Fields.Count - 1).Name
   ```

   a. A run-time error
   b. The name of the second-last field of the recordset referred to by the `rs` variable.
   c. The name of the last field of the recordset referred to by the `rs` variable.
   d. The name of the last recordset in the `Databases` collection of the default workspace.

EXERCISE 3

Complexity: Easy
1. Create a Windows CGI program named `SPCONTACT.EXE` in the `C:\WEBSITE\CGI-WIN\WDBIC\SPCONTACT` directory that returns the first record of the `tblSponsorsContacts` table of the sample calendar database when called using the following URL:

   ```
   http://localhost/cgi-win/wdbic/spcontact/spcontact.exe
   ```

Complexity: Moderate
2. Create a Windows CGI program named `FIRSTREC.EXE` in the `C:\WEBSITE\CGI-WIN\WDBIC\FIRSTREC` directory that returns the first record of any table of the sample calendar database whose name is provided in the

query string portion of a URL. For example, the following CGI request should return the first record of the **tblEvents** table:

```
http://localhost/cgi-win/wdbic/firstrec/firstrec.exe?tblEvents
```

NAVIGATING THROUGH A RECORDSET

In Lesson 3, we discussed how a **Recordset** object can represent the records of any data source, whether that source is a database table or a query result based on multiple tables. You learned how to create a **Recordset** object based on a single database table.

We also mentioned that a recordset allows you to access one record at a time by supporting the concept of a current record. So if you want to list the information of the fifth record of your recordset, you must first make that fifth record the current record. To help you accomplish this and other recordset navigation tasks, the **Recordset** object supports several useful methods and properties, which we will discuss in this lesson. We will also show how to create **Recordset** objects that are based on stored (nonparameterized) queries. You will be able to display the records of any database table or **Select** query (except for a **Parameter** query) through a Windows CGI program after you are done with this lesson.

The Move **Methods**

The previous lesson demonstrated that when you create a new **Recordset** object, the first record of its underlying record source automatically becomes its current record. To set another record as the current record, you can use the following methods with your **Recordset** object:

```
recordset.MoveFirst     'Make the first record as the current record
recordset.MoveLast      'Make the last record as the current record
recordset.MoveNext      'Make the next record as the current record
recordset.MovePrevious  'Make the previous record as the current record
```

where *recordset* stands for a **Recordset** object variable. In addition, the **Recordset** object also supports the plain **Move** method, which allows you to move the current record a specific number of records up or down. The syntax of the **Move** method is as follows:

```
recordset.Move rows, [start]
```

where the **rows** parameter specifies the number of rows to move (positive value for down, negative value for up), and the optional **start** parameter indicates the record relative to which the move should occur. If you do not specify the **start** parameter, then the move is made relative to the current record.

Note that the **start** parameter is defined in terms of a *bookmark*, which is a unique string assigned by the JET engine to every record in the recordset. A bookmark, as the name suggests, is used as a placeholder whenever you need to work on some other records without losing track of your current position within the recordset. The detailed coverage of how the bookmark feature works is beyond the scope of this book. Refer to VB's online help for more information.

The BOF and EOF Properties

What happens if the recordset does not contain any records and you try to access a field, or if you execute the **MovePrevious** method from the first record of a nonempty recordset and then try to access a field value? In both cases, you will get a run-time error. To prevent you from getting into these situations, the **Recordset** object supports two properties, **BOF** and **EOF** ("beginning of file" and "end of file"), that help determine if the current record has moved beyond the limits of the recordset.

The **BOF** property is a Boolean (**True/False**-type) value that indicates if the current record position is before the first record. The **EOF** property indicates if the current record is after the last record. If the recordset contains no records, then both properties return as **True** values.

You can use these properties along with the **Move** methods to navigate through all the records of a nonempty recordset, as illustrated by the following code templates:

```
'Move from first to last
rs!MoveFirst
Do Until rs.EOF
    'Process the current record
    rs.MoveNext
Loop

'Move from last to first
rs!MoveLast
Do Until rs.BOF
    'Process the current record
    rs.MovePrevious
Loop
```

Listing All the Records of the Sponsor Table

The **SPONSOR2.EXE** program that you created in the previous lesson listed only the first record of the sponsor table of the sample calendar database. Using the first-to-last record-navigation code template presented here, let's create another version of this Windows CGI program, **SPONSOR3.EXE**, that lists all the records of the sponsor table as its response.

1. Create a new directory named SPONSOR3 under the c:\WEBSITE\CGI-WIN\WDBIC directory.

2. Copy the SPONSOR2.VBP project file and the CGI32.BAS and MYAPP.BAS module files from the C:\WEBSITE\HTDOCS\WDBIC\CHAP09\LESSON3\RESULTS\SPONSOR2 directory into this SPONSOR3 directory.

3. Rename the (copied) SPONSOR2.VBP project file in the SPONSOR3 directory SPONSOR3.VBP and open it in VB.

4. Modify the CGI_Main procedure of the MYAPP.BAS module as shown in Listing 9-4. The highlighted lines indicate that they have been either inserted or changed in this modified version; some lines have been indented for readability.

Listing 9-4 The CGI_Main procedure of the SPONSOR3.EXE program

```
Sub CGI_Main()

    Dim dbCalendar As Database    'Declare database variable
    Dim rsSponsor As Recordset    'Delcare recordset variable
    Dim dbName As String          'Path and name of the calendar database
    Dim TableName As String       'Name of the table within the calendar database
    Dim FieldCount As Integer     'Count of fields in the recordset
    Dim i As Integer              'Index variable

    dbName = "C:\WEBSITE\HTDOCS\WDBIC\CHAP05\SAMPLES\CALENDAR.MDB"
    TableName = "tblSponsors"
    Set dbCalendar = DBEngine(0).OpenDatabase(dbName)    'Open the database
    Set rsSponsor = dbCalendar.OpenRecordset(TableName) 'Open a recordset from the table
    'Generate response
    Send "Content-type: text/html"
    Send ""
    Send "<HTML><HEAD><TITLE>SPONSOR3</TITLE></HEAD><BODY>"
    Do Until rsSponsor.EOF 'Loop until current record goes beyond last record
        Send "<TABLE BORDER=1 CELLSPACING=5 CELLPADDING=5>"  'Begin table
        Send "<CAPTION>SponsorID " & rsSponsor!SponsorID & "</CAPTION>"
        Send "<TR><TH>Field Name</TH><TH>Field Value</TH></TR>"  'Table heading
        FieldCount = rsSponsor.Fields.Count          'Get Field count
        For i = 0 To FieldCount - 1                  'Remember collection is 0-based
            Send "<TR>"                              'Start new table row
            Send "<TD>" & rsSponsor(i).name & "</TD>" 'Send field name
            Send "<TD>" & rsSponsor(i) & "</TD>"     'Send field value
            Send "</TR>"                             'End table row
        Next
        Send "</TABLE>"                                          'End table
        Send "<HR>"                 'Record separator
        rsSponsor.MoveNext          'Move to next record
    Loop                            'End of the Do Until loop
    Send "</BODY></HTML>"


End Sub
```

5. Compile this program to create an executable file named SPONSOR3.EXE in the SPONSOR3 directory.

6. Start your Web server if it is not already running.

7. Enter the following URL in your Web browser:

   http://localhost/cgi-win/wdbic/sponsor3/sponsor3.exe

   The program lists all the sponsor records, as shown in Figure 9-12.

As you can see from Figure 9-12, **SPONSOR3.EXE** takes a lot of vertical space to display each record. A more reasonable presentation would be to display the fields of each record similar to the datasheet view of an Access table. That is just a matter of using the right HTML layout within your Windows CGI program. Not much is going to change in terms of the code associated with the database access. The next example not only demonstrates how to achieve this datasheet view presentation but also sorts the sponsor records by sponsor name field.

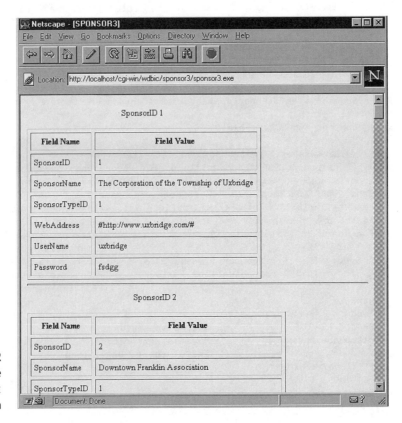

Figure 9-12
Response of the
SPONSOR3.EXE
program

Listing All the Sponsor Records Sorted by Their Sponsor Names

As explained in Chapter 5, Lesson 3, you can easily create a query in Access that generates the sponsor records sorted by the **SponsorName** field. For this example, we have provided a copy of the **CALENDAR.MDB** database file in the **C:\WEBSITE\HTDOCS\WDBIC\CHAP09\LESSON4** directory that contains such a query. This query is named **qrySponsors_SortedByName**, and its design is shown in Figure 9-13.

To create a Windows CGI program that displays the sponsor records in the order of their sponsor names, you just need to use a recordset based on the **qrySponsors_SortedByName** query. Let's make our task a bit more challenging. Let's make this program list the field captions instead of the field names as part of its response. In Lesson 3, we briefly mentioned that **Caption** is an Access-only **Field** property (not a standard JET property), so it cannot be accessed via the syntax you have been using until now.

The **Caption** and other Access-only properties of a field can be accessed through the **Properties** collection of its corresponding **Field** object as follows:

field`.Properties!`*AccessPropertyName*

where *field* represents a **Field** object or a variable pointing to a **Field** object. As an example, you would use the following syntax to access the caption of the **SponsorName** field in the **SPONSOR3.EXE** program:

`rsSponsors!SponsorName.Properties!Caption`

What happens if a field (such as **SponsorID**) does not have any value for the **Caption** property specified in the table design? If you try to access the **Caption** property of such fields using the above syntax, a run-time error occurs. Think of it this way: If nothing is specified in the **Caption** property of a field during table design, the property itself is not stored in the database, and when you try to access it, an error is signaled.

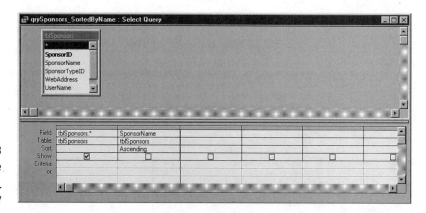

Figure 9-13
Design of the
qrySponsors_
SortedByName query

So, how do you get the captions for fields where the `Caption` property does exist without causing the program to crash? The answer lies in the proper use of the error-trapping features of VB as shown in the `GetCaption` function (see Listing 9-5), which takes a `Field` object variable as its argument and returns its caption if the caption exists; otherwise, it simply returns the name of the field.

Listing 9-5 The `GetCaption` function

```
Function GetCaption(F As Field)

  On Error Resume Next                  'Ignore all run-time errors
  GetCaption = F.Properties!Caption     'Try to retrieve the caption property
  If Err <> 0 Then GetCaption = F.Name  'If previous statement generated error,⇐
return field name

End Function
```

The `GetCaption` function works as follows. The `On Error Resume Next` line tells VB to ignore all run-time errors generated during the execution of this procedure. If an error does get generated, then VB simply stores the error number of the most recent error in the `Err` variable. In the next line, it tries to set the value of the `GetCaption` function to the `Caption` property of the given field object. If that property exists, then no error is generated, which it checks in the next line. If an error does occur (indicated by `Err` not being equal to `0`), then it simply returns the `Name` property (which always exists) of the given `Field` object.

Now let's use this function and the **qrySponsors_SortedByName** query to list the sponsor records in the desired layout and order through a Windows CGI program. Follow the steps given below:

1. Create a new project named SPONSOR4.VBP in the C:\WEBSITE\CGI-WIN\ WDBIC\SPONSOR4 directory from the NEWAPP project template.

2. Open the SPONSOR4.VBP project file in VB.

3. Display the Code window of the MYAPP.BAS module.

4. Select Add Procedure... from the Tools menu.

   VB pops up the Add Procedure dialog box, as shown in Figure 9-14.

Figure 9-14
The Add Procedure
dialog box

5. Enter GetCaption in the Name text box, select Function for the Type parameter, and then press the OK button.

   VB creates the template for the GetCaption function.

6. Enter F As Field as this function's argument declaration and then type its code as shown in Listing 9-5.

7. Insert another procedure named ShowRecordsAsDatasheet (and of the type Sub), as shown in Listing 9-6.

Listing 9-6 The ShowRecordsAsDatasheet procedure

```
Public Sub ShowRecordsAsDatasheet(rs As Recordset)
  'Displays the records of the given recordset in the datasheet format

  Dim i As Integer          'Index variable
  Dim F As Field            'Field object variable
  Dim FieldCount As Integer  'Number of fields in the recordset

  FieldCount = rs.Fields.Count
  'Begin table
  Send "<TABLE BORDER=1 CELLSPACING=5 CELLPADDING=5>"
  'Show Field captions
  Send "<TR>"   'Start first table row
  For i = 0 To FieldCount - 1
    Set F = rs(i)                              'Set F to the ith field object
    Send "<TH>" & GetCaption(F) & "</TH>"      'Send caption of that field
  Next
  Send "</TR>" 'End first table row
  'Now show one row for each record, starting from the current record
  Do Until rs.EOF
    Send "<TR>"   'Start row
    For i = 0 To FieldCount - 1
      Send "<TD>" & rs(i) & "</TD>"   'Send value of the ith field
    Next
    Send "</TR>" 'End row
    rs.MoveNext   'Goto next record
  Loop
  'End table
  Send "</TABLE>"

End Sub
```

The ShowRecordsAsDatasheet procedure is a general purpose procedure that generates the HTML code to display the records of any given recordset in a datasheet format. Note how it makes use of the GetCaption function.

8. Finally, enter the code for the CGI_Main procedure shown in Listing 9-7 and compile your program to create an executable file named SPONSOR4.EXE in the SPONSOR4 directory.

Listing 9-7 The `CGI_Main` procedure of the `SPONSOR4.EXE` program

```
Sub CGI_Main()

    Dim dbCalendar As Database    'Declare database variable
    Dim rsSponsor As Recordset    'Delcare recordset variable
    Dim dbName As String          'Path and name of the calendar database
    Dim RecordSource As String    'Source of the recordset

    dbName = "C:\WEBSITE\HTDOCS\WDBIC\CHAP09\LESSON4\CALENDAR.MDB"
    RecordSource = "qrySponsors_SortedByName"
    Set dbCalendar = DBEngine(0).OpenDatabase(dbName)        'Open the database
    Set rsSponsor = dbCalendar.OpenRecordset(RecordSource) 'Open a recordset from the⇐
table
    'Generate response
    Send "Content-type: text/html"
    Send ""
    Send "<HTML><HEAD><TITLE>SPONSOR4</TITLE></HEAD><BODY>"
    ShowRecordsAsDatasheet rsSponsor    'Call the general-purpose procedure
    Send "</BODY></HTML>"

End Sub
```

9. Start your Web server if it is not already running.

10. Enter the following URL in your Web browser:

    ```
    http://localhost/cgi-win/wdbic/sponsor4/sponsor4.exe
    ```

    The program lists all the sponsor records sorted by the sponsor name field, as shown in Figure 9-15. Notice that the field captions are displayed wherever available.

Lesson Summary

This lesson explained how a recordset could be created from a nonparameterized Select query and how to use its various **Move** methods to navigate through all its records.

The **Move** methods, namely **MoveFirst**, **MoveLast**, **MoveNext**, and **MovePrevious**, allow you to make the first, last, previous, or next record (with reference to the current record) of a recordset the current record. In addition, you can also use the **Move** methods to move the current record up or down by a specific number of records. To avoid run-time errors while trying to move beyond the limits of a recordset, use the **BOF** and **EOF** recordset properties. Using these properties as a termination condition of a **Do** loop, you can easily present all the records of your recordset through a Windows CGI program, as shown in this lesson. In the next lesson, we will describe how to create a recordset based on a Parameter query and how to display selected records of a database table.

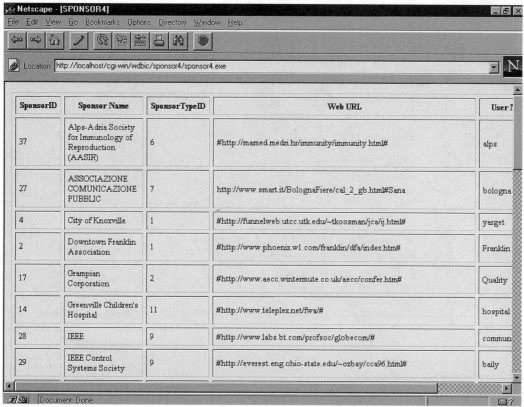

Figure 9-15
Response of the SPONSOR4.EXE program

The programs created in this lesson are stored in the **C:\WEBSITE\HTDOCS\WDBIC\ CHAP09\LESSON4\RESULTS** directory.

1. How would you go to the fifth record of a recordset pointed to by a **Recordset** object variable named **rs**? Assume that this recordset contains more than five records.
   a. **rs.MoveFirst 5**
   b. **rs.MoveNext 5**
   c. **rs.MoveFirst** and then list **rs.MoveNext** statement five times
   d. **rs.MoveFirst** and then **rs.Move 5**

2. Under what circumstances will the **BOF** property return a **True** value?
   a. When the **EOF** property is **False**
   b. When the first record is the current record
   c. When you try to move the current record before the first record
   d. When the recordset does not contain any records

3. What will the following function do, assuming **rs** is a **Recordset** object variable that points to an existing nonempty recordset?

```
Dim i As Integer

i = 0
rs.MoveFirst
Do Until rs.EOF
  i = i + 1
Loop
```

   a. Count the number of records in the recordset.
   b. Generate an overflow run-time error.
   c. Generate a compilation error.
   d. None of the above.

4. What does the **GetCaption** function return when it receives a **Field** object representing the **WebAddress** field of the **tblSponsors** table?
   a. **WebAddress**
   b. **Web Address**
   c. **Web URL**
   d. A run-time error

5. What will the **ShowRecordsAsDatasheet** procedure do if the recordset it receives as its parameter does not contain any records?
   a. Generate a run-time error.
   b. Not send anything to the CGI output file.
   c. Just send a table with one row listing the field captions (or field names as appropriate).
   d. Send a **No Records Found** message to the CGI output file.

EXERCISE 4

Complexity: Easy
   1. Modify the **SPONSOR4.EXE** program so that it returns all the sponsor records sorted by sponsor-type description. List this description along with the rest of the sponsor information.

Complexity: Advanced
   2. Create a Windows CGI program named **BROWSE.EXE** in the **C:\WEBSITE\CGI-WIN\WDBIC\BROWSE** directory that responds to the following URL template

```
http://localhost/cgi-win/wdbic/browse/browse.exe⇐
/LogicalDatabasePath?RecordSourceName
```

in the following manner:

1. The program interprets the extra path portion of this URL
   (`LogicalDatabasePath`) as the logical directory path to the CALENDAR.MDB
   database.

2. The program interprets the query string portion of the URL as the name
   of the table or query belonging to the CALENDAR.MDB database whose
   logical directory path was specified as described in step 1.

3. After determining the exact location of the CALENDAR.MDB file and the
   name of the record source, the program lists all the records of that
   record source as its response.

As an example, the following URL:

```
http://localhost/cgi-win/wdbic/browse/browse.exe/wdbic/chap09/lesson4?qrySponsors_⇐
SortedByName
```

should return the datasheet-formatted result of the **qrySponsors_SortedByName**
query belonging to the **CALENDAR.MDB** database residing in the
C:\WEBSITE\HTDOCS\WDBIC\CHAP09\LESSON4 directory. Also test your program with
the following URL:

```
http://localhost/cgi-win/wdbic/browse/browse.exe/wdbic/chap05/samples?tblSponsors
```

(Hint: To get the physical directory path of the specified **CALENDAR.MDB** database, use
the **CGI_PhysicalPath** variable within your program.)

CREATING RECORDSETS BASED ON A PARAMETER QUERY

The previous lesson showed how easily you can construct a recordset based on a database table or a non-Parameter query. You can also create a recordset from a Parameter
query, but the process is not as straightforward. In this case, you have to seek the help
of another DAO called the **QueryDef** object, as explained in the following section. This
lesson describes the role of the **QueryDef** object and then shows how it is used to create a Parameter-query–based **Recordset** object.

The `QueryDef` Object

A `QueryDef` object represents a stored database query; Figure 9-16 shows its position within the DAO model.

When you open a database (by creating a **Database** object), all the queries stored in that database become part of that **Database** object's **QueryDefs** collection. You can then refer to any stored query through the **QueryDefs** collections by any of the standard methods of referring to a collection item. For example, to refer to a stored query by its name, you can use either one of the following syntaxes:

```
db.QueryDefs!QueryName (or db.QueryDefs![QueryName] if QueryName contains spaces or⇐
hyphens)
db.QueryDefs("QueryName")
```

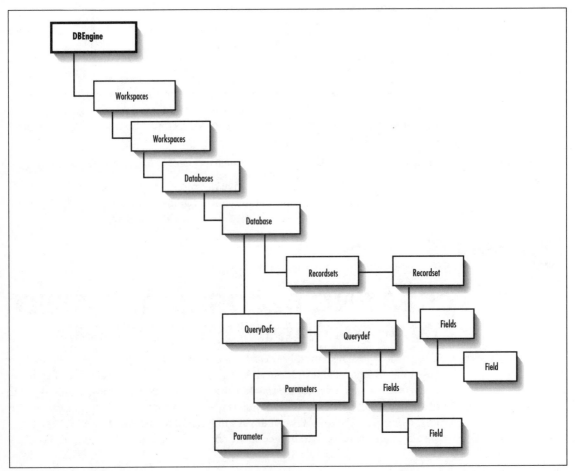

Figure 9-16

Position of the Querydefs collection and QueryDef object in the DAO model

where **db** points to the database holding the specified query. The `QueryDef` object contains a `Parameters` collection (the default collection), which holds all the parameters of a Parameter query. This collection is empty for a non-Parameter query.

Creating a Recordset Based on a Parameter Query

As you can see, the only difference between a Parameter query and a non-Parameter query is that a Parameter query contains parameters, which can be listed as part of its criteria or as calculated field expressions.

The `CALENDAR.MDB` file residing in the `C:\WEBSITE\HTDOCS\WDBIC\CHAP05\` `LESSON6\RESULTS` directory contains a Parameter query named `qryEvents_` `Selected_DateRange` with the following two parameters:

```
Enter Starting Date
Enter Ending Date
```

Figure 9-17 shows the design of this query.

To create a recordset based on this query, you will first need to supply a value for this parameter through a `QueryDef` object, as outlined below:

1. Declare a variable for a `QueryDef` object as follows:

   ```
   Dim qd As QueryDef
   ```

2. Set the `qd` variable to refer to the Parameter query in either of the following ways:

   ```
   Set qd = db.QueryDefs!qryEvents_Selected_DateRange
   Set qd = db.QueryDefs("qryEvents_Selected_DateRange")
   ```

3. Assign values to the query parameters:

   ```
   qd![Enter Starting Date] = #11/1/97#
   qd![Enter Ending Date] = #11/30/97#
   ```

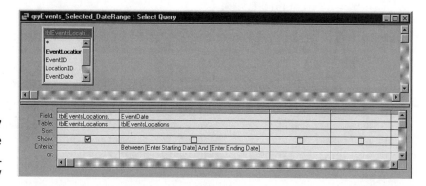

Figure 9-17
Design of the
`qryEvents_Selected_`
`DateRange` query

Note that if you use a date constant, it must be surrounded by the # characters.

4. Create the recordset based on the Parameter query by using the `OpenRecordset` method of the `QueryDef` object as follows:

```
Set rs = qd.OpenRecordset()
```

Now the recordset pointed to by the `rs` recordset variable will contain all the records returned by `qryEvents_Selected_DateRange` based on the specified date range.

Creating a Windows CGI Program that Uses a Parameter Query

The following example demonstrates how you can use the technique outlined above to create a Windows CGI program that lists the event occurrences within the specified date range. We will name this program `EVENT1.EXE` and will assume that the two dates are provided in the URL's query string portion, as shown below:

```
http://localhost/cgi-win/wdbic/event1/event1.exe?11/1/97+11/30/97
```

Follow these steps to design the `EVENT1.EXE` program:

1. Create a new directory named `EVENT1` under the `C:\WEBSITE\CGI-WIN\WDBIC` directory.

2. Copy the `SPONSOR4.VBP` project file and the `CGI32.BAS` and `MYAPP.BAS` module files from the `C:\WEBSITE\HTDOCS\WDBIC\CHAP09\LESSON4\RESULTS\SPONSOR4` directory into this `EVENT1` directory.

3. Rename the (copied) `SPONSOR4.VBP` project file in the `EVENT1` directory `EVENT1.VBP` and open it in VB.

4. Modify the `CGI_Main` procedure of the `MYAPP.BAS` module, as shown in Listing 9-8.

Listing 9-8 The `CGI_Main` procedure of the `EVENT1.EXE` program

```
Sub CGI_Main()

    Dim dbCalendar As Database    'Declare database variable
    Dim rs As Recordset           'Delcare recordset variable
    Dim qd As QueryDef            'Declare querydef variable
    Dim dbName As String          'Path and name of the calendar database
    Dim pQueryName As String      'Name of the parameter query
    Dim StartDate As String       'Start date parameter value
    Dim EndDate As String         'End date parameter value
```

```
Dim DelimiterPos As Integer 'Delimiter Position

'Get the position of the + delimiter within query string
DelimiterPos = InStr(CGI_QueryString, "+")
'Get start date and end date from query string
StartDate = Left$(CGI_QueryString, DelimiterPos - 1)
EndDate = Mid$(CGI_QueryString, DelimiterPos + 1)
'Open database and recordset
dbName = "C:\WEBSITE\HTDOCS\WDBIC\CHAP05\LESSON6\RESULTS\CALENDAR.MDB"
pQueryName = "qryEvents_Selected_DateRange"
Set dbCalendar = DBEngine(0).OpenDatabase(dbName)    'Open the database
Set qd = dbCalendar.QueryDefs(pQueryName)            'Create querydef object
'Set parameters
qd![Enter Starting Date] = CVDate(StartDate)         'CVDate converts string to date
qd![Enter Ending Date] = CVDate(EndDate)
Set rs = qd.OpenRecordset()                          'Open recordset from querydef
'Generate response
Send "Content-type: text/html"
Send ""
Send "<HTML><HEAD><TITLE>EVENT1</TITLE></HEAD><BODY>"
ShowRecordsAsDatasheet rs   'Call the general-purpose procedure
Send "</BODY></HTML>"

End Sub
```

5. Compile this program to create an executable file named EVENT1.EXE in the EVENT1 directory.

6. Start your Web server if it is not already running.

7. Enter the following URL in your Web browser:

   http://localhost/cgi-win/wdbic/event1/event1.exe?11/1/97+11/30/97

   The EVENT1.EXE program returns the appropriate records from the tblEventsLocations table, as shown in Figure 9-18.

Lesson Summary

This lesson described how to create a recordset from a Parameter query within a Windows CGI program. The process involves using a new DAO called **QueryDef**, which essentially represents a database query definition.

When you create a **Database** object to represent an existing database, all the database queries (actually the **QueryDef** objects representing those queries) become part of the **QueryDefs** collection of that **Database** object. You can then declare a **QueryDef** variable and point it to the **QueryDef** object representing your Parameter query by accessing the **QueyDefs** collection using the name of that Parameter query.

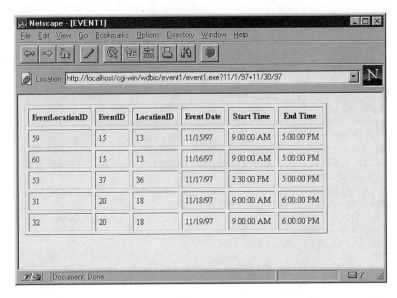

Figure 9-18
Response of the
EVENT1.EXE program

Once the **QueryDef** variable has been assigned to the appropriate Parameter query's **QueryDef** object, you can assign values to the parameters of that object, as shown in this lesson. Finally, you can create the desired recordset by using the **OpenRecordset** of that **QueryDef** object.

This whole process was illustrated in this lesson through a practical construction of a Windows CGI program that used a Parameter query for listing all the event occurrences within a user-specified date range. In the next lesson, you will see how to design a Windows CGI program that allows you to filter events not just by a date range but by any user-specified SQL criteria.

The programs created in this lesson are stored in the **C:\WEBSITE\HTDOCS\WDBIC\ CHAP09\LESSON4\RESULTS** directory.

1. Which of the following objects is the parent object of a **QueryDef** object?
   a. **QueryDef**s
   b. **Databases**
   c. **Database**
   d. **RecordSet**

2. How can you refer to the following Parameter query in your VB code?

`qryEvents-SelectedLocation`

  a. `db.QueryDefs!qryEvents-SelectedLocation`
  b. `db.QueryDefs("qryEvents-SelectedLocation")`
  c. `db.QueryDefs![qryEvents-SelectedLocation]`
  d. Any of the above

3. Which of the following DAOs support the `OpenRecordset` method?
  a. `Workspace`
  b. `Database`
  c. `QueryDef`
  d. All of the above

4. What would happen if you entered the following URL from your browser?

`http://localhost/cgi-win/wdbic/event1/event1.exe?11/1/97`

  a. The `EVENT1.EXE` program would return all the event occurrences, starting from 11/1/97.
  b. The `EVENT1.EXE` program would return all the event occurrences, up until 11/1/97.
  c. The `EVENT1.EXE` program would return a run-time error.
  d. None of the above.

5. What would happen if you entered the following URL from your browser?

`http://localhost/cgi-win/wdbic/event1/event1.exe?November-1,1997+⇐`
`November-30,1997`

  a. The browser would generate an error.
  b. The `EVENT1.EXE` program would return all the event occurrences between 11/1/97 and 11/30/97.
  c. The `EVENT1.EXE` program would return a run-time error.
  d. None of the above.

EXERCISE 5

Complexity: Easy
1. Create a Windows CGI program named `EVENT2.EXE` in the `C:\WEBSITE\CGI-WIN\WDBIC\EVENT2` directory that returns all the event records based on the `EventTypeID` entered in the query string portion of the URL. (Hint: Use the Parameter query `qryEvents_SelectedEventTypeID` from the `CALENDAR.MDB` file residing in the `C:\WEBSITE\HTDOCS\WDBIC\CHAP05\LESSON6\RESULTS` directory.)

Complexity: Moderate

2. Extend the **EVENT1.EXE** program so that it accepts a third parameter, representing the search pattern, in the URL's query string and responds by listing all the events and their occurrences that fall within the given date range and whose name, description, or type matches a specified pattern. Save the modified VB project as **EVENT3.VBP** in the **C:\WEBSITE\CGI-WIN\WDBIC\EVENT3** directory and name the executable file **EVENT3.EXE**. Test this program with the following URL:

```
http://localhost/cgi-win/wdbic/event3/event3.exe?1/1/97+12/31⇐
/97+music
```

(Hint: Use the **qryEvents_Info_Selected** Parameter query stored in the **C:\WEBSITE\HTDOCS\WDBIC\CHAP06\LESSON2\RESULTS\CALENDAR.MDB** database file.)

TROUBLESHOOTING WINDOWS CGI PROGRAMMING ERRORS

When creating a Windows CGI program (or any program), programmers may make programming errors. The error might originate from a simple typing mistake or a flaw in logic. Programming errors do and will occur. The key is to know how to identify these errors and how to fix them.

Programming errors can be categorized into three main categories, depending on when and how they occur:

- Compilation errors

- Run-time errors

- Logical errors

This lesson describes what types of errors fall in these categories and what techniques you can use to fix them.

Compilation Errors

A *compilation error* is generally due to the use of invalid programming syntax or by not meeting some other language or compiler's requirement. For example, the following **CGI_Main** procedure contains a compilation error in line 4 where the **Database** object variable is being assigned to a new **Database** object without using the **Set** keyword.

```
Sub CGI_Main()

   Dim db As Database                                                  'Line 1
   Dim dbName As String                                                'Line 2

   dbName = "C:\WEBSITE\HTDOCS\WDBIC\CHAP05\SAMPLE\CALENDAR.MDB"        'Line 3
   db = DBEngine(0).OpenDatabase(dbName)                               'Line 4

End Sub
```

Compilation errors are easy to locate because a compiler will catch them for you when you try to compile your program to create an executable file. For instance, if you try to compile a Windows CGI program containing the above `CGI_Main` procedure, the compiler will flag an error message on line 4 and will not create the executable file. You must correct the error before recompiling your program.

Run-Time Errors

Run-time errors cannot be trapped at compile time and occur when you run your program. For example, a Windows CGI program containing the following `CGI_Main` procedure will compile just fine but will generate an **invalid path** error when it is executed.

```
Sub CGI_Main()

   Dim db As Database                                                  'Line 1
   Dim dbName As String                                                'Line 2

   dbName = "C:\WEBSITE\HTDOCS\WDBIC\CHAP05\SAMPLE\CALENDAR.MDB"        'Line 3
   Set db = DBEngine(0).OpenDatabase(dbName)                           'Line 4

End Sub
```

Line 4 is where the run-time error occurs. This is because the database file path specified in line 3 refers to the **CALENDAR.MDB** file in the **SAMPLE** subdirectory, which does not exist. In fact, the **CALENDAR.MDB** database resides in the **SAMPLES** directory and the path listed in line 3 may be a typing oversight, but that is immaterial when this program is executing.

The problem with run-time errors is that they occur only after you run the Windows CGI program; unless you have added a proper error-handling mechanism within your program, these errors will cause your program either to terminate abruptly or to display the error message on the server machine. If the program is terminated abruptly without writing any response into the CGI output file, the Web server will simply pass on a **500 Server Error** message to the user.

However, if the run-time error causes the program to display an error message on the server's screen and to wait for someone to press the OK button, the Web server will think that the program is still executing. In other words, the Web user who made a request for this program will be left hanging without ever knowing if something went wrong with the program or if the program was just taking a long time to complete its task. Hence, it is imperative that you trap all the run-time errors that can possibly occur within your Windows CGI program and ensure that your program terminates under all such circumstances.

Fortunately, Windows CGI programs using the **CGI32.BAS** module are preequipped with a default error-handling mechanism that takes care of this problem, as explained in Chapter 8, Lesson 3. But the fact remains that run-time errors are not a good sign and all efforts should be made to prevent them from occurring in the first place. Most of the Windows CGI programs we have designed so far do not include much code for error anticipation or prevention because they were designed to illustrate programming concepts. When designing a professional-level Web application, you should always put as many checks and balances in your program as you can. We will cover this aspect in more detail in Chapter 10, "Presenting Information: Web Database Publishing."

Logical Errors

Logical errors cause a program to return incorrect results. The compiler cannot catch them, and they do not crash your program. They are an indication of any logical flaw in the program's design. Let's demonstrate the concept of a logical programming error through a practical example.

Say you want to design a Windows CGI program named **SPONSOR5.EXE** that first lists the record count and then the records of the **tblSponsors** table of the sample calendar database. Based on the concepts you have studied so far, you modify the **CGI_Main** procedure of the **SPONSOR4.EXE** program, as shown in Listing 9-9.

Listing 9-9 The **CGI_Main** procedure for the **SPONSOR5.EXE** program

```
Sub CGI_Main()

  Dim db As Database, rs As Recordset                               'Line 1
  Dim dbName As String, NumRecords As Long                          'Line 2

  dbName = "C:\WEBSITE\HTDOCS\WDBIC\CHAP05\SAMPLES\CALENDAR.MDB"     'Line 3
  Set db = DBEngine(0).OpenDatabase(dbName)                         'Line 4
  Set rs = db.OpenRecordset("tblEvents")
  NumRecords = 0                                                    'Line 5
  Do Until rs.EOF                                                   'Line 6
    NumRecords = NumRecords + 1                                     'Line 7
    rs.MoveNext                                                     'Line 8
  Loop                                                              'Line 9
  Send "Content-type: text/html"                                   'Line 10
  Send ""                                                           'Line 11
  Send "<HTML><HEAD><TITLE>EVENT3</TITLE></HEAD><BODY>"            'Line 12
  Send "The sponsor table contains " & NumRecords & " records."   'Line 13
  Send "<P>"                                                       'Line 14
  ShowRecordsAsDatasheet rs                                        'Line 15
  Send "</BODY></HTML>"                                            'Line 16

End Sub
```

At first glance, the program seems to have all the code necessary to generate the desired result. However, if you compile and test it, you may be surprised by what you get. Let's see what that surprise is.

For your convenience, we have provided the project for this program in the **C:\WEBSITE\HTDOCS\WDBIC\CHAP09\LESSON6\SPONSOR5** directory. Follow these steps to compile and test this program:

1. Create a new directory named SPONSOR5 under the C:\WEBSITE\CGI-WIN\WDBIC directory.

2. Copy the SPONSOR5.VBP project file and the CGI32.BAS and MYAPP.BAS module files from the C:\WEBSITE\HTDOCS\WDBIC\CHAP09\LESSON6\SPONSOR5 directory into this SPONSOR5 directory.

3. Open the copied SPONSOR5.VBP project file in VB.

4. Display the CGI_Main procedure of MYAPP.BAS and verify that its code is identical to Listing 9-3.

5. Compile this program to create an executable file named SPONSOR5.EXE in the project's directory.

6. Start your Web server if it is not already running.

7. Enter the following URL in your Web browser:

   `http://localhost/cgi-win/wdbic/sponsor5/sponsor5.exe`

   The SPONSOR5.EXE program returns its response, as shown in Figure 9-19.

Observe that, although the response has the correct record count, it does not contain any sponsor records. What happened? The program did run successfully. You just witnessed the evidence of a logical error in the **SPONSOR5.EXE** program. So how do you determine where the fault lies? It's time to put on your debugging hat!

Figure 9-19
Response of the
SPONSOR5.EXE
program

Tracing Through a Windows CGI Program

The `CGI_Main` procedure of the `SPONSOR5.EXE` program is not a big procedure. To identify the logical flaw in this program, you can manually inspect the procedure code line by line to see why things are not turning out as expected. In such small programs, this is not a bad way to start. On large-sized programs, however, this option can become time-consuming and stressful. There is another option, though, one that makes you glad that you picked the Windows CGI standard instead of the standard CGI for your Web applications. This option involves using the integrated debugging environment of VB to trace through the code and inspect the state of the program during the tracing process. This process requires that you simulate the environment created by the Web server when it launches the Windows CGI program. To enact this simulation:

1. Capture the CGI profile (.INI) file created by the Web server for the Windows CGI request that caused the program to produce the logical error.

2. Configure the environment options of your program's project to specify the path and filename of the T.INI file as the command-line argument.

3. Trace the Windows CGI program within the development environment while monitoring the control flow and the values of the declared variables.

Let's examine each step in more detail.

Capturing the CGI Profile File

You capture the CGI profile file by enabling the CGI tracing configuration of your WebSite server and resubmitting the CGI request that caused your program to return incorrect results. Once the CGI tracing option is enabled, the WebSite server does not automatically delete the temporary files it creates for communicating with the Windows CGI program. The complete procedure for enabling the CGI tracing option was explained in Chapter 6, Lesson 4. Go through that procedure if you have not already done so and ensure that this option is currently set. Then follow these steps to resubmit the CGI request and capture its associated CGI profile file:

1. Delete all the previous temporary files from the c:\WEBSITE\CGI-TEMP directory, using the following MS-DOS commands:

```
cd c:\website\cgi-temp
del *.*
```

2. Ensure that your WebSite server is running.

3. Resubmit the following URL from your Web browser:

```
http://localhost/cgi-win/wdbic/sponsor5/sponsor5.exe
```

4. Using the MS-DOS prompt, list the new temporary files created by the server, as shown in Figure 9-20.

Your temporary files may have different names.

5. Rename the temporary .INI file T.INI. You can also review the contents of this .INI file to ensure that the Web server is passing appropriate data based on the above request.

There is nothing special about the **T.INI** name. You can use any other name instead or directly refer to the name of the CGI profile file in the project's command-line argument option.

Configuring the Environment Options of Your VB Project

Next, you need to tell Visual Basic what command-line argument to supply when you trace your program within VB's development environment. To configure this option in the **SPONSOR5.VBP** project:

1. Load the **SPONSOR5.VBP** project file residing in the **C:\WEBSITE\CGI-WIN\WDBIC\SPONSOR5** directory in VB if it is not already loaded.

2. Select the **Make Sponsor5.exe...** option from VB's file menu.

   VB displays the Make Project dialog box, which contains an Options... button.

Figure 9-20
Temporary files created during the processing of the Windows CGI request

```
MS-DOS Prompt                                          _ □ ×

  8 x 12 ▼

Microsoft(R) Windows 95
   (C)Copyright Microsoft Corp 1981-1995.

C:\WIN95>cd c:\website\cgi-temp

C:\WebSite\cgi-temp>dir

 Volume in drive C is RESEARCH
 Volume Serial Number is 3065-18FC
 Directory of C:\WebSite\cgi-temp

.              <DIR>        12-11-96 12:00p .
..             <DIR>        12-11-96 12:00p ..
B2WS     INP          0     02-22-97  7:56p b2ws.inp
B2WS     INI        593     02-22-97  7:56p b2ws.ini
B2WS     OUT        321     02-22-97  7:56p b2ws.out
         3 file(s)             914 bytes
         2 dir(s)       35,487,744 bytes free

C:\WebSite\cgi-temp>
```

3. Press this Options... button to display the Project Properties... dialog box and enter c:\WEBSITE\CGI-TEMP\T.INI in the CommandLine Arguments text box, as shown in Figure 9-21.

4. Press OK to close this dialog box.

5. Press Cancel to close the Make project dialog box without recompiling the project.

Tracing the Windows CGI Program Execution

The Visual Basic development environment allows you to trace each step of your program's execution and monitor the values of the variables at each step. The following procedure describes how you can use these tracing features to debug the SPONSOR5.EXE program:

1. Go to the CGI_Main procedure of the NEWAPP.BAS module and place the cursor on line 1.

2. Press F9 to insert a break point on this line. (See Figure 9-22.)

3. Press F5 to start executing this program.

   VB starts with the Main procedure of the CGI32.BAS module and then stops at the break point inserted in the CGI_Main procedure.

   From here, you can single-step through the program using F8 or have the execution stop at another break point. Because you know that the record count is being calculated correctly, chances are that the Do loop is

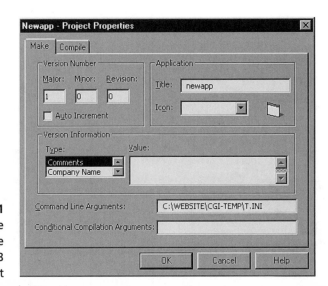

Figure 9-21
Specifying the command-line arguments of a VB project

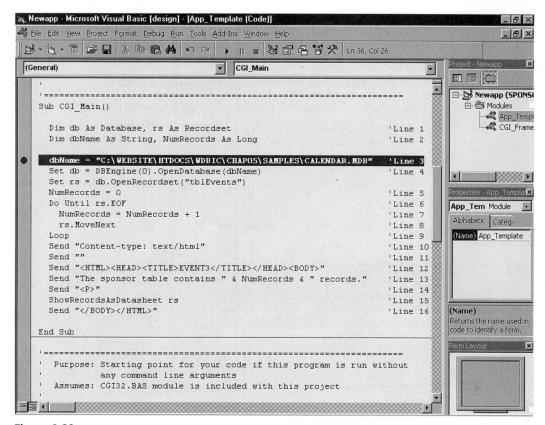

Figure 9-22
Inserting a break point in the `CGI_Main` procedure

functioning properly. So let's have the program execute until the end of this `Do` loop and see how things look after that.

4. Place the cursor on line 10 of the `CGI_Main` procedure and press F9 to add a break point on that line.

5. Press F5 to continue execution.

   The program now halts on line 10.

6. Move your mouse pointer on the `NumRecords` variable in line 7.

   VB flashes a text box showing the value of this `NumRecords` variable as 37.

7. Everything looks good so far. Press SHIFT-F8 to step over to the next line. Keep pressing SHIFT-F8 until you reach line 15.

Note   If you accidentally stepped over line 15, select End from the Run menu and start again from step 1.

8. Press F8 to enter into the ShowRecordsAsDatasheet procedure.

   Because you know that the field descriptions are being listed in the response, it is apparent that the For loop responsible for creating that portion of that response is functioning correctly. So let's quickly get this For loop executed.

9. Place a break point on the line right after the For loop, as shown in Figure 9-23.

10. Press F5 to stop at that break point.

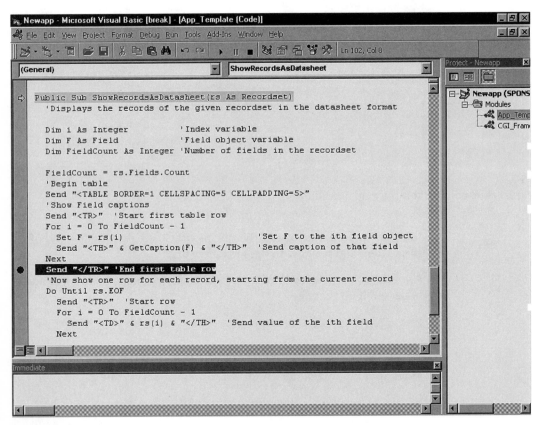

Figure 9-23
Inserting a break point in the ShowRecordsAsDatasheet procedure

11. Press SHIFT-F8 to step over to the beginning of the Do loop responsible for listing the sponsor records. Let's see why the records are not listed.

12. Press SHIFT-F8 to go to the next line.

The execution stops at the last line of this procedure, skipping the Do loop completely.

What does this imply? That the termination condition of the loop (the recordset's EOF property) was True to begin with. You can verify this by examining the value of this EOF property. Select End from the Run menu to halt this program.

How did this EOF property become True? If you look back at the CGI_Main procedure, you will see that the Do loop used for counting the records already made the EOF property of rs to True and there is no following instruction that sets the current record of rs back to the first record. This is exactly why the program is behaving erroneously. The fix for this problem is relatively simple and is left as an exercise.

Lesson Summary

This chapter explained the three different types of errors you can encounter while designing a Windows CGI program and how to troubleshoot them. The compilation error is the easiest one to fix because it is detected during the program compile time. Run-time errors occur after the program is executed. If you plan on designing professional-quality Windows CGI programs, you should take extra measures to anticipate and prevent the possibility of any run-time error, even though the CGI32.BAS module provides a default mechanism. Once you have eliminated compilation and run-time errors from a program, you must ensure that it does not have any logical flaw in it.

Although this lesson presented simple examples of run-time and logical errors, these errors can consume substantial amounts of programming time, especially when the program behaves erratically under certain input cases. Once you are able to locate such cases, however, you can easily trace through the program execution to get to the bottom of the problem, as described in this lesson.

1. Identify all the possible compilation errors in the following procedure.

```
Sub Test

    Dim ws As Variant          'Line 1
    Dim db As Database         'Line 2
    Dim wsName As String       'Line 3

    On Error Goto Err_Test     'Line 4
    Set ws = DBEngine(0)       'Line 5
    wsName = ws.Name           'Line 6

End Sub
```

   a. Line 1 has an error because **ws** cannot be declared as a variant.

   b. Line 4 has an error because no line labeled **Err_Test** is defined in this procedure.

   c. Line 5 has an error because **ws** was not declared as a **Workspace** variable.

   d. Line 6 has an error because it does not start with the **Set** keyword.

2. Identify all the possible run-time errors in the following procedure.

```
Sub CGI_Main

    Dim db As Database                                  'Line 1
    Dim LastwsName As String                            'Line 2
    Dim wsCount As Integer                              'Line 3

    wsCount = DBEngine.Workspaces.Count                 'Line 4
    LastwsName = DBEngine.Workspaces(wsCount).Name      'Line 5
    Set db = DBEngine(0).OpenDatabase(CGI_QueryString)  'Line 6

End Sub
```

   a. Line 4 will generate an error because there are no open workspaces.

   b. Line 5 will generate an error because the specified collection index will always be beyond limits.

   c. Line 6 can generate an error if the query string portion of the URL is empty or contains an invalid database file path name.

   d. All of the above.

3. What does the Web user see when the requested Windows CGI program generates a run-time error and waits for a response to terminate?

   a. A **500-Server** error message

   b. The run-time error sent by the Web server

   c. A browser error

   d. Indication from the browser that it is waiting for a reply

4. How do you capture a CGI profile file for debugging a Windows CGI program?

   a. Set the CGI tracing option in the Web server's configuration.

   b. Resubmit the CGI request that causes the program to fail while the Web server is running.

   c. Resubmit the CGI request that causes the program to fail while the Web server is not running.

   d. Use a screen-capturing program.

5. How do you prevent tracing through all the iterations of a loop while debugging a program?

   a. Use F8.

   b. Use SHIFT-F8.

   c. Set a break point on the line following the loop and then press F5.

   d. Place your mouse cursor on the line following the loop and press F5.

EXERCISE 6

Complexity: Easy

1. Fix the **SPONSOR5.EXE** program so that it responds as expected and does not cause any run-time errors if the sponsor table happens to be empty.

Complexity: Advanced

2. The **EVENT1.EXE** program that you created in Lesson 5 generates run-time errors if the start and end dates are not specified correctly in the requesting URL's query string. Modify this program so that it anticipates such possibilities and uses the current date whenever it cannot determine either the start date or the end date. Test this program with the following URLs:

```
http://localhost/cgi-win/wdbic/event1/event1.exe
http://localhost/cgi-win/wdbic/event1/event1.exe?1/1/97
http://localhost/cgi-win/wdbic/event1/event1.exe?+12/31/97
http://localhost/cgi-win/wdbic/event1/event1.exe?1/1+12/31
```

(Hint: Use an **On Error Resume Next** statement to ignore errors when processing the query string for start date and end date values. Then test the **Err** variable to see if any error was generated during the process and use the default current date as necessary.)

CHAPTER SUMMARY

This chapter described how you could access and manipulate data from an Access database using the data access objects provided in Visual Basic. Different record navigation techniques and procedures for displaying selected records from a database using regular queries, Parameter queries, and the steps for debugging a faulty Windows CGI program were presented. Following are the main points covered in this chapter:

● In the object-oriented programming paradigm, an object is a programming entity that combines data and procedures operating on that data.

● DAOs follow a hierarchy that originates from the DBEngine object, which represents the Microsoft JET database engine.

● All DAOs support a Name property.

● The DBEngine holds two collection objects called Workspaces and Errors.

● A collection object is like a zero-based array that can hold objects of the same type. You can refer to any object within a collection c using any of the following syntaxes:

```
c!ObjectName or c![ObjectName] if ObjectName has spaces or hyphens
c("ObjectName")
c(IndexPositionOfObject)
```

● The DBEngine on startup creates a default Workspace object, which automatically gets appended to the Workspaces collection. The default workspace is not a secure workspace.

● You can open an existing database in VB as follows:

```
Dim db As Database
Set db = DBEngine(0).OpenDatabase(DatabaseFilePathAndName)
```

● A Recordset object represents a collection of records that can be based on a table, query, or SQL statement. You can use the OpenRecordset method of the parent Database object to create a new recordset.

● There are four types of recordsets in the JET workspaces environment, among which the dynaset-type recordset is the most flexible.

● The first record of the underlying data source of a newly created recordset automatically becomes its current record.

● All fields of a recordset are stored as Field objects in the Fields collection of that recordset.

● The Move method is used to set any record of a recordset as its current record. BOF and EOF properties can help ensure that the current record does not move beyond the limits of the recordset.

● Using the MoveFirst and MoveNext methods and the EOF property as the termination condition of a Do loop, you can navigate through all the records of a recordset.

● You have to use the QueryDef object to create a recordset based on a Parameter query.

● QueryDefs is a collection of all QueryDef objects representing the stored queries of a database.

● Although the compile can help identify compilation errors, you generally need to trace through a Windows CGI program to locate the cause of run-time and logical errors.

This chapter covered the fundamentals of how to search and display database records through a Windows CGI program. Although these are the foundation for creating database-based Web applications, you still have to cover some distance before you can create applications that are practical as well as Web-friendly. The next chapter brings several factors to light that play a significant role in achieving this objective.

Fundamentals of Web-Database Publishing and Maintenance

CHAPTER 10

PRESENTING INFORMATION: WEB DATABASE PUBLISHING

This chapter discusses the different approaches you can consider when creating a Web publication from a database and presents techniques for implementing them. In particular, you will learn about:

- Differences between data browsing and data searching

- What pitfalls to avoid when publishing large databases

- How to use Access's Web publishing wizard

- How to present information as a series of linked pages

- How to implement the drill-down browsing technique

- How to group and format database information presented through a Web page

- How to program field-based search capability in a Web database application

WEB DATABASE PUBLISHING APPROACHES

In Chapter 9, "Accessing Database Records from Visual Basic: Data-Access Objects," you learned how to access and search your database through a Windows CGI program. Now it is time to consider extending the reach of this database to all corners of the globe by putting it on the Web. The power of Web database publishing lies in its capability to make this information available to any person having access to the Web, any time, anywhere in the world. The user can either browse through the entire database or search for specific information of interest, depending on how the database is published on the Web. This lesson presents an overview of various approaches that can be used for Web database publishing. The subsequent lessons will examine each approach in more detail.

Browsing Versus Searching

When designing a Web database application, you can have users browse through the available information, you can provide a way to search for the desired information, or you can do both.

The Browse Approach

Under the *browse approach*, you have two distinct options. You can either present data from individual tables of your application's database as separate HTML pages or you can combine information from related tables and then present that combined dataset on a single page. In a multiple table database (such as the calendar database), however, neither of these options works well by itself.

For example, if you show each table on a separate page, users will have a hard time linking the related information. On the other hand, if you provide every bit of information from all the tables in one page, you may put the user in a state of information overload.

One remedy to overcome these difficulties is to compromise. In other words, achieve a balance between these two approaches. For example, in the Web calendar application, you could go for the following breakdown of information:

● A sponsor list that includes the sponsor and sponsor-type information

● An event list that contains the event, sponsor name, event-type, and contact information

● An event calendar that contains the event name, date, and location information

Although this breakdown is a good starting point, it will start showing the signs of the above-mentioned data-browsing problems once your database is heavily populated. You can try to split each list further into smaller HTML pages so that the user gets only a portion of the list at a time, which at least economizes the bandwidth utilization. The other option is to use the *drill-down technique*, in which the user gets to see related pieces of information by following a series of hyperlinks.

The Drill-Down Technique

The drill-down technique is one of the widely used techniques of presenting information on the Web. Look at how most regular Web sites are designed. They start with a home page, which generally acts as the main menu supporting links to other pages. These pages may further contain links to pages that provide more detailed information on a particular topic. The drill-down technique is simply about organizing and presenting information in a hierarchical manner. In the Web setting, nothing prevents you from establishing cross-links between this hierarchy. After all, that is the definition of the Web, isn't it?

The drill-down technique, when applied in Web database applications, helps eliminate the information overload problem while keeping the related information connected. For example, in the Web calendar application, you could have users start with the list of sponsor types, with a hyperlink under each sponsor type leading to a list of appropriate sponsors and their contacts. Clicking on the name of any sponsor could then bring up all the associated events with the date and location information; if the desired information is not found, the user can easily use the Back button of the browser to follow a different path.

One obstacle in implementing the drill-down browsing technique in the Web database environment is the large number of individual data pages that needs to be generated, not to mention the proportionally large number of links required to connect these pages. From a Web user's perspective, the main drawback is that if the levels are either too deep or too broad, it may take several back and forth movements before the desired information is found. The answer to this problem lies in giving users the ability to get to the information directly using a search mechanism.

The Search Approach

In the *search approach*, a Web database application provides information that matches user-specified search criteria. The search can be a keyword-based search or a field-based search or a combination of both. A *keyword-based search* allows users to retrieve any portion of the database information that matches specified keywords. For example, a user can get a list of all the events that have anything to do with energy, irrespective of whether the word "energy" appears in the event name, event description, sponsor name, or location name.

The *field-based approach* lets users specify criteria against individual fields of one or more tables—similar to what you do when designing a query in Access. As mentioned earlier, you can merge the keyword and field-based search into one general purpose search to give users the ultimate flexibility. For example, getting a list of all energy-related events within a certain date range would be a good candidate for this general purpose search feature. However, such flexibility does incur a cost in terms of both a decrease in search performance and an increase in the implementation effort, as you will see later in this chapter.

What do you do if the user's search criterion is too broad and the search result holds too much information? In this case, you may have to apply the drill-down technique to the search result itself. You can even reverse this approach—give users an option to search within a drill-down path.

The Static Versus Dynamic Approach

You can also look at Web database publishing from another perspective: whether the data being published is generated statically or dynamically. The *static approach* involves creating and storing data pages beforehand as static files and letting the Web user serve those files per user request. There is no direct interaction between the user and the database.

The biggest benefit of the static approach is high performance. But this approach never guarantees that the user will get the latest information. However, you can apply one of the following two synchronization techniques to keep the information somewhat current:

- Time-bound synchronization

- Event-based synchronization

The *time-bound synchronization* technique involves re-creation of data pages from the database at regular time intervals. The *event-based synchronization* involves recreation of (appropriate) data pages whenever the database is updated. Needless to say, both these techniques require some kind of automation.

The alternative to the static approach is the *dynamic approach*, in which your application makes use of the back-end CGI programs to provide data pages that are generated on the fly based on the current database information. If you are considering using the drill-down technique and providing a search facility within your Web database application, then think dynamic. You do incur a performance penalty when running a CGI-dependent application, but what you gain in flexibility and timeliness generally makes up for it. Again, we recommend you consider ways and techniques that help you strike a reasonable balance between the static and dynamic approach when designing the front end of your Web application. We will shed some light on this aspect in Chapter 11, "Populating Tables: Web-Based Data Entry".

Lesson Summary

This lesson presented an overview of the different approaches to Web database publishing. Their suitability for the Web calendar application was determined and the relative strengths and weaknesses of each approach were analyzed.

From the angle of locating desired information, the choice lies between using the browse or the search approach. In a heavily populated multiple table database environment, the drill-down browsing technique with a suitable search mechanism can yield the best result in terms of application usability and bandwidth utilization.

The other perspective of Web database publishing is the method used for generating database information being published. Here you can use either the static or the dynamic approach. The static approach, which has the performance advantage, has to be further supplemented with either the time-bound or event-based synchronization procedure so that the information presented is reasonably up to date. The dynamic approach, which involves creating back-end CGI programs to generate the requested information on the fly, is best when implementing the drill-down and search features for your application. As a recommended practice, it is always beneficial to design a Web application that includes a mix of static and dynamic pages. In the next lesson, you will see how to create static HTML pages using the tools provided in Access.

1. What are the disadvantages of combining information from all tables of the calendar database into one static page for publishing on the Web?
   a. The network bandwidth requirements for each Web request would increase.
   b. Users would receive a lot more information than they are looking for.
   c. Information from various tables cannot be combined in one page.
   d. It is not an easy approach to implement.

2. How does the drill-down technique help prevent information overload to the user?
   a. It allows the user to follow a series of links to see pieces of related information.
   b. It organizes data in a hierarchical manner.
   c. It provides information using small data pages.
   d. It allows users to create their own links while navigating through individual pages.

3. Which would be the best approach to locate next month's events occurring in France?
   a. The keyword-based search
   b. The field-based search
   c. The event-based static approach
   d. None of the above

4. Under what circumstances may the search technique not prove very useful?
   a. When there is too little information in the database
   b. When there is too much information in the database
   c. When the scope of the data in the database is not known
   d. All of the above

5. What technique or approach would you consider for your Web calendar application offering search and drill-down facilities, where new upcoming events are added frequently and each month's events have to be listed separately?
   a. The time-bound synchronization technique
   b. The event-based synchronization technique
   c. The dynamic approach using a back-end CGI program
   d. A combination of static and dynamic approaches

Complexity: Easy
   1. For each of the following cases, list the name of a popular Web site that acts as a good example:
      a. Drill-down technique
      b. Keyword-based search
      c. Field-based search
      d. Combination of drill-down technique and keyword-based search

Complexity: Easy
   2. What approach (time-bound static, event-based static, or dynamic) would you use in the following cases:
      a. Main menu of the Web calendar application
      b. Previous year's event summary
      c. List of sponsor types
      d. Pages containing the list of sponsors belonging to each sponsor-type category
      e. Input form for keyword-based event search
      f. Criteria input form for field-based event search
      g. Event search result

STATIC PUBLISHING USING ACCESS

The previous lesson provided a conceptual background of different approaches for Web database publishing. This lesson takes you right to the scene of the action and shows you how to publish statically the calendar database using Access. You will learn how to create a Web page for each table or query of this database and how to tie them all together through a home page. You will also learn about the format of Access template files that you can create to customize the basic layout of your static pages.

Publishing All Database Tables

As ever, the genius of Access makes static publishing of any database seem like a piece of cake—all because of its built-in and intuitive publish to the Web wizard. This wizard enables you to create a Web publication from any set of database tables or queries as it walks you through the entire process. To give a quick demonstration, let's publish all the tables of the sample calendar database using this wizard:

1. Open the CALENDAR.MDB database residing in the
   C:\WEBSITE\HTDOCS\WDBIC\CHAP10\LESSON2 directory in Access.

2. Select the Save As HTML option from the File menu.

   Access brings up the Publish to the Web Wizard screen shown in Figure 10-1. This screen introduces the wizard and lists its main capabilities.

3. Press the Next button provided at the bottom of this screen.

   The wizard brings up the next screen, which indicates what it can do and asks what you want to publish, as shown in Figure 10-2.

4. Click on the Tables tab and then click on Select All to select all the tables of the database.

5. Press the Next button to move on to the third screen.

   This screen asks for a template for formatting your Web pages. Ignore this feature for the time being. The use of templates is described later in this lesson.

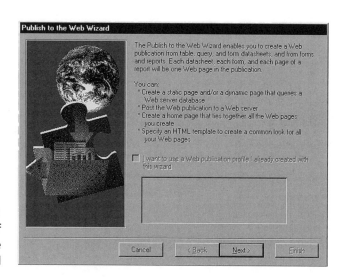

Figure 10-1
The first screen of the publish to the Web wizard

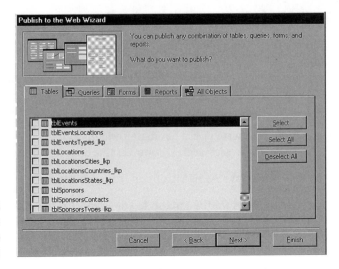

Figure 10-2
The second screen
of the publish to
the Web wizard

6. Press the Next button to move on to the fourth screen.

The wizard now asks what default format type you want to create and selects the Static HTML option by default, as shown in Figure 10-3.

The other two format options allow you to create dynamic Web pages but work only with a Microsoft Internet Information Server (IIS)-compatible Web server. The detailed explanation of these options is beyond the scope of this book.

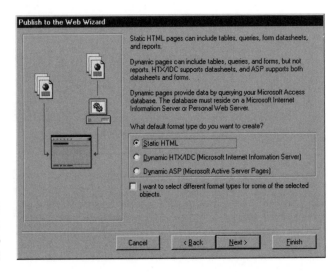

Figure 10-3
The fourth screen
of the publish to
the Web wizard

7. Because you are interested in creating static pages for this demonstration, retain the default option. Press the Next button to move to the next screen.

The wizard now wants to know the location of the directory where you want to publish your documents. Note that this directory must reside under the domain of the document root directory of the WebSite server; otherwise, you will have to create a document mapping as explained in Chapter 2, Lesson 2.

8. For this demonstration, use the STATIC1 directory already residing under the C:\WEBSITE\HTDOCS\WDBIC directory path. Enter C:\WEBSITE\HTDOCS\WDBIC\STATIC1 in the current screen and then press the Next button.

The wizard now gives you the option to create a home page for your publication. The home page will contain links to the HTML pages created by this wizard.

9. Select the Yes, I want to create a home page option and enter index as the filename of this home page as shown in Figure 10-4. Then press the Next button.

The wizard now gives you the option to save the information provided in the previous screens to a Web publication file, which you can use later to republish this set of objects quickly.

10. Because this is a one-time demonstration, you can skip this option for now and just press the Finish button.

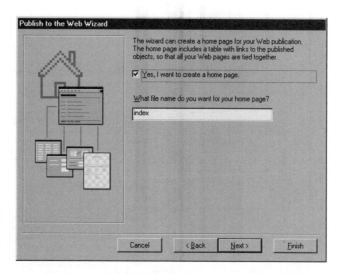

Figure 10-4
The sixth screen of the publish to the Web wizard

The wizard should be ready with your first Web publication within a few moments. To view this:

1. Start your WebSite server if it is not already started.

2. Enter the following URL from your Web browser:

   `http://localhost/wdbic/static1/index.html`

   The home page of your publication will appear on your browser as shown in Figure 10-5.

3. Click on the link associated with the tblEvents table.

   The browser displays the HTML-formatted records of this table as shown in Figure 10-6.

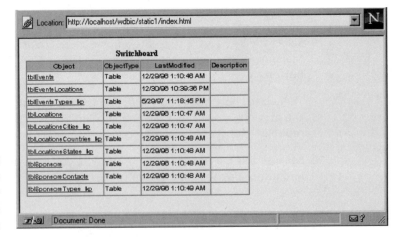

Figure 10-5
Home page of the Web calendar database publication

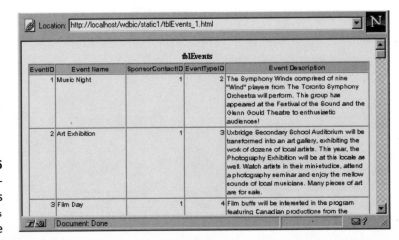

Figure 10-6
The HTML-formatted records of the tblEvents table

The Web publishing wizard creates one HTML page per selected data source under the specified publishing directory. The files corresponding to these HTML pages go by the following naming convention:

```
DataSourceName_1.html
```

where *DataSourceName* represents the name of the data source object (which can be either a table or query). So the HTML file for `tblEvents` would be named as follows:

```
tblEvents_1.html
```

Using a Predefined Template

The layout that the Web publishing wizard used for creating the data pages in the previous demonstration was plain and simple. You can customize these pages with a better background pattern, your own logo or company name as the header, and uniform navigation buttons as the footer of each page, and anything else you can think of to make these pages look more appealing and catchy. To perform this customization, you make use of the *format template file* feature of the Web publishing wizard.

A format template file is an HTML document that contains special tokens unique to Microsoft Access to indicate where to insert data. For example, the following two tokens are interpreted by the publishing wizard as placeholders for the name and content of the data object being published:

```
<!--AccessTemplate_Title-->
<!--AccessTemplate_Body-->
```

 All the other tokens supported by Access are relevant only when you are creating HTML pages from Access reports, which are not discussed in this book.

For your convenience, Access provides many predefined template files that you can choose from in the `C:\Program Files\Microsoft Office\Templates\Access` directory. For example, Figure 10-7 shows how the records of `tblEvents` would appear if you used the `stones.htm` template file provided by Access.

The contents of the `stones.htm` file are listed below:

```
<HTML>
<TITLE><!--ACCESSTEMPLATE_TITLE--></TITLE>
<BODY leftmargin = 110 background = stones.jpg>
<!--ACCESSTEMPLATE_BODY-->
</BODY>
<BR><BR>
<IMG SRC = "msaccess.jpg">
</HTML>
```

Note that the image files specified in this template have to be placed in the publication directory for the HTML page to work correctly.

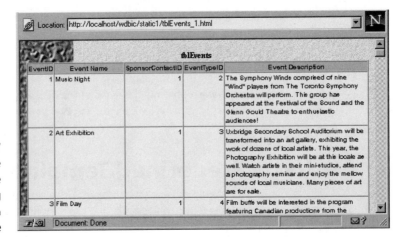

Figure 10-7
Records of the
`tblEvents` table
formatted using
the `stones.htm`
template file

How the Web Publishing Wizard Handles the Special Characters of HTML

The Web publishing wizard converts all the special characters of HTML to their equivalent markup codes when creating the data pages. A double-quote character in a data field is replaced by the `&quot;` HTML markup code, the `<` character is replaced by the `&lt;` markup code, and so on. The Web publishing wizard ensures that all these characters are correctly presented as part of the published data and not interpreted by the Web browser as part of HTML tags. Although this is a nice feature, it does prevent you from embedding HTML tags as part of your source data. In other words, if your data contains the following text:

`<B>Urgent</B>`

then this text will be converted as follows:

`&lt;B&gt;Urgent&lt;/B&gt;`

and it will appear as `<B>Urgent</B>` in your browser instead of the bold-faced word `Urgent`. It would be nice if the wizard gave an option that prevents it from this conversion in case you want to publish a database that contains HTML-aware data.

Note

The Web wizard does present the data stored in a `Hyperlink`-type field as an HTML hyperlink and not in its raw format.

Lesson Summary

This lesson explained how a static Web publication can be created from any set of tables or queries of an Access database using its built-in Web publishing wizard. The process was demonstrated by creating a Web publication using all the tables of the calendar database.

The visual appeal of HTML pages designed using this wizard can be further enhanced and customized using the format template feature of the Web publishing wizard. This is an HTML document that contains special tokens unique to Access that, for example, tell the wizard where exactly on the HTML page to place the name or content of the data object being published. Access provides many predefined template files that you can choose from for your Web publication.

Although the Web wizard creates appropriate HTML links for the data stored in the `Hyperlink`-type field, you cannot embed HTML tags in your data source because the wizard converts all the special characters of HTML as data using HTML markup codes.

Having covered static publishing procedures in this lesson, we will switch over to dynamic browsing techniques in the next lesson.

QUIZ 2

1. Which of the following jobs can the Web publishing wizard perform?
   a. Create static pages.
   b. Create a home page of the Web publication it is creating.
   c. Create HTML template files.
   d. All of the above.

2. What will be the name and path of the HTML file created by the Web publishing wizard for a query named `qryEvents`? Assume that the wizard has been given `c:\website\htdocs` and `stones.htm` as the values for the publication directory and the name of the template file, respectively.
   a. `c:\website\htdocs\stones.html`
   b. `c:\website\htdocs\stones_1.html`
   c. `c:\website\htdocs\qryEvents.html`
   d. `c:\website\htdocs\qryEvents_1.html`

3. Which of the following statements are true for the Web publishing wizard?
   a. It creates a separate HTML page for each selected data source.
   b. It allows the use of only one template file for all the selected data sources in one session.
   c. It presents the data of a `Hyperlink`-type field as an HTML hyperlink.
   d. All of the above.

4. What is a Format Template file?
   a. An image file
   b. An Access database file containing HTML tags
   c. A text file that includes HTML tags and other tokens unique to Access
   d. None of the above

5. How will the following HTML tag in the data source of your Web publication appear in your browser?

`<BR><BR>`

a. It will appear as a blank row.
b. It will appear as `&lt;BR&gt;&lt;BR&gt;`.
c. It will appear as `<BR><BR>`.
d. None of the above.

EXERCISE 2

Complexity: Easy
1. Republish all the tables of the calendar database in the `C:\WEBSITE\HTDOCS\WDBIC\STATIC1` directory using the `100.htm` template file.

Complexity: Moderate
2. Publish the calendar database using only three pages containing the following information:

● A sponsor list that includes the sponsor and sponsor-type information

● An event list that contains the event, sponsor name, event-type, and contact information

● An event calendar that contains the event name, date, and location information

LESSON 3

DYNAMIC BROWSING AND CREATING PAGE BREAKS

If users are presented with the static Web publication that you created in the previous lesson for the calendar database, they will be overwhelmed with a huge amount of information. Presenting information about all events, whether past, present, or future, in one page is not the right approach; you must break it up into smaller packets, pruning the irrelevant and dated information in the process.

If you want to continue with the static approach, the only way the Web publishing wizard allows you to publish a data source using multiple pages is through Access reports. Access reports allow you to group, sort, and format the records of any data source so that it looks good when printed on a hard copy. However, because a detailed discussion of the features and design procedures of these reports could require a series of chapters and because these reports help only with static publications, we do not cover them in this book.

On the other hand, the dynamic approach using Windows CGI gives you all the power and flexiblility you need, and you will find it more appealing once you get comfortable with it. A simple requirement, such as a current list of upcoming events, may take considerable management and automation effort with the static approach but can be accomplished easily through dynamic publishing. However, lengthy data pages, inclusion of undesired information, and other performance and bandwidth-related issues can become as much of a concern in the dynamic approach as they are in the static approach. As mentioned in Lesson 1, there are two standard techniques to optimize the amount of information being presented at any given time:

● List records from the same data source as a series of linked pages

● Use the drill-down technique

This lesson explains how you can implement the first technique when dynamically publishing the list of upcoming events. We shall focus on the implementation of the drill-down alternative in the next lesson.

Listing Upcoming Events as a Series of Linked Pages

Chapter 9, "Accessing Database Records from Visual Basic: Data-Access Objects," covered the basic programming concepts needed to publish all upcoming event records dymamically through a Windows CGI program. As a recap, the basic steps are outlined below:

1. Create a query that generates a list of events whose event date is later than the current date.

2. Create a recordset based on this query in the Windows CGI program.

3. Use the `MoveFirst` and `MoveNext` methods of that recordset to send the information of each record of that recordset in the program's response.

If you want Web users to receive the query result in small segments, you have to modify your program so that it lists only a subset of the result for any incoming request and provides links for fetching the next or previous subset. To accomplish this task, the program must require each request to send the necessary parameters that define which subset the Windows CGI program should send.

One approach to indicating the desired subset could be in terms of specifying short date ranges. For example, the first page could list the events occuring within three days of the current date, the second page could list the events of the subsequent three days, and so on. The only problem is that this approach does not guarantee uniformity in page size.

To get uniform-sized pages, you could limit the number of records passed in each request irrespective of how many days they represent. In this case, you would define the desired subset by passing the following two parameters with each Web request:

● The position of the record in the query result that defines the beginning of the subset, called the *starting record position*

● The number of records to fetch

You can eliminate the need for the second parameter if you decide that your subsets are going to always be of the same size—say 20 records (except for the last subset, whose size may be less). However, when using this approach, you need to ensure that the source query always returns the records in the same order. In our case, we could have the query sort the events by their event date and start time to meet this requirement.

Running the UPCOMING.EXE Program

Now that we have analyzed our options, let's look at a Windows CGI program named **UPCOMING.EXE** that lists upcoming events from the sample calendar database as a series of linked pages. This program resides in the **C:\WEBSITE\CGI-WIN\WDBIC\HTDOCS** directory:

1. Start your Web server if it is not already started.

2. Enter the following URL from your Web browser:

   `http://localhost/cgi-win/wdbic/upcoming/upcoming.exe`

   The UPCOMING.EXE program returns three upcoming events and provides a hyperlink labeled Next, as shown in Figure 10-8.

Event Name	Event Date	Start Time	End Time	Location Name	Sponsor Name	Contact Name	Event Type	Street	City	State	Countr
Durability of Buildings - Design, Maintenance, Codes, and Practices	3/20/97	10:00:00 AM	5:00:00 PM	Toronto Airport Hilton	The Canadian Society for Civil Engineering (CSCE)	Hitesh Doshi	Workshops, Conferences, and Seminars	Airport Road	Mississauga	Ontario	Canada
Durability of Buildings - Design, Maintenance, Codes, and Practices	3/21/97	10:00:00 AM	5:00:00 PM	Toronto Airport Hilton	The Canadian Society for Civil Engineering (CSCE)	Hitesh Doshi	Workshops, Conferences, and Seminars	Airport Road	Mississauga	Ontario	Canada
The 1997 Main Street Festival	4/26/97	10:00:00 AM	8:00:00 PM	Historic Franklin	Downtown Franklin Association	Festivals Office	Dance		Franklin	Tennessee	USA

Next

Figure 10-8
First response of the UPCOMING.EXE program

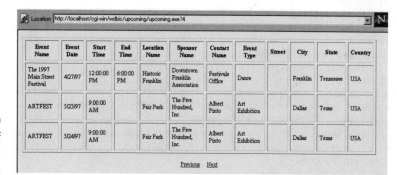

Figure 10-9
Second response of
the UPCOMING.EXE
program

Note that you may get a different set of records depending upon your current date. (If you do not get any records, you can temporarily change your computer's system date to 03/01/97 and rerun this experiment.)

3. Click on the Next hyperlink.

The response contains another three upcoming events with two hyperlinks labeled Previous and Next, respectively, as shown in Figure 10-9.

Observe that the URL listed in the Location window of the browser again points back to the **UPCOMING.EXE** program but now has the number 4 listed in its query string. Also note that the events are listed in chronological order.

If you keep following the **Next** link, you will be able to traverse through all the upcoming events currently listed in the database.

Examining the Design of the UPCOMING.EXE **Program**

The **UPCOMING.EXE** program contains the **CGI_Main** procedure shown in Listing 10-1.

Listing 10-1 The CGI_Main procedure of the UPCOMING.EXE program

```
Sub CGI_Main()

    Dim dbCalendar As Database      'Declare database variable
    Dim rs As Recordset             'Declare recordset variable
    Dim dbName As String            'Path and name of the calendar database
    Dim RecordSource As String      'Source of the recordset
    Dim StartRecordPos As Long      'Position of the first record to list
    Const NUMRECORDS = 3            'Number of records to list


    'Get starting record position from URL's query string
```

continued on next page

continued from previous page

```
If CGI_QueryString = "" Then      'If no starting position specified
   StartRecordPos = 1             'then start from the first record
Else                             'else get the starting position parameter
   StartRecordPos = CLng(CGI_QueryString)
   If StartRecordPos < 1 Then StartRecordPos = 1
End If
'Open database and recordset
dbName = "C:\WEBSITE\HTDOCS\WDBIC\CHAP10\LESSON3\CALENDAR.MDB"
RecordSource = "qryEvents_Upcoming"
Set dbCalendar = DBEngine(0).OpenDatabase(dbName)   'Open the database
Set rs = dbCalendar.OpenRecordset(RecordSource)     'Open a recordset from the table
'Generate response
Send "Content-type: text/html"
Send ""
Send "<HTML><HEAD><TITLE>UPCOMING</TITLE></HEAD><BODY>"
'Send the specified records
ShowRecordsSubset rs, StartRecordPos, NUMRECORDS
'Send the link for getting previous and next set of records
Send "<P><CENTER>"
ShowPreviousSubsetLink rs, StartRecordPos, NUMRECORDS
Send "   "  'Add three spaces between the two links
ShowNextSubsetLink rs, StartRecordPos, NUMRECORDS
Send "</CENTER>"
Send "</BODY></HTML>"

End Sub
```

The `CGI_Main` procedure starts by extracting the starting record position from the URL's query string. If no position is specified, then it assumes that you want to start from the first (most recent) upcoming event. The `NUMRECORDS` constant, which is set to **3**, indicates the number of records to list in the response.

Next, `CGI_Main` opens a recordset from the `qryEvents_Upcoming` query of the calendar database residing in the `C:\WEBSITE\HTDOCS\WDBIC\CHAP10\LESSON3` directory. The `qryEvents_Upcoming` query produces a list of all the chronologically sorted upcoming events. Its design is shown in Figure 10-10.

Note that the `qryEvents_Upcoming` query is based on the `tblEvents_Locations` table and two other queries named `qryEvents` and `qryLocations`. The `qryEvents` query generates a list of all event records from `tblEvents` along with pertinent information from related tables. The `qryLocations` query produces location records linked with the city, state, and country lookup tables. You can open these queries in Access to review their design.

After populating the recordset with the result of the `qryEvents_Upcoming query`, `CGI_Main` sends the usual HTML starting headers to the CGI output file and then calls the `ShowRecordsSubset` procedure (described next) to list the specified subset of records. After that it calls the `ShowPreviousSubsetLink` and `ShowNextSubsetLink` procedures to add the **Previous** and **Next** hyperlinks (as appropriate) to the response; it ends the response with the closing HTML tags.

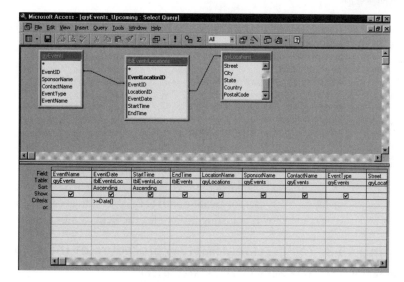

Figure 10-10
Design of the
qryEvents_Upcoming
query

The ShowRecordsSubset *Procedure*

The design of the **ShowRecordsSubset** procedure is shown in Listing 10-2. In many ways, the **ShowRecordsSubset** procedure is similar to the **ShowRecordsAsDatasheet** procedure discussed in Chapter 9.

Listing 10-2 The ShowRecordsSubset procedure of the UPCOMING.EXE program

```
Public Sub ShowRecordsSubset(rs As Recordset, StartPos As Long, NumRecords As Long)
    'Displays the specified number of records of the given recordset
    'in the datasheet format starting from the record located at the
    'StartPos position.

    Dim i As Integer        'Index variables

    'Begin table
    Send "<TABLE BORDER=1 CELLSPACING=5 CELLPADDING=5>"
    'Show Field captions
    ListFieldCaptions rs
    'Make the record at the StartPos position as the current record
    On Error Resume Next        'Ignore all errors generated by the following lines
    rs.MoveFirst                'Set first record as current record
    If StartPos > 1 Then
        rs.Move StartPos - 1    'Set record at StartPos as current record
    End If
    On Error GoTo 0             'Return to the default error handler
    'Now list NumRecords starting from the current record.
```

continued on next page

continued from previous page

```
For i = 1 To NumRecords
  'Do not continue with this loop if recordset has no records left
  If rs.EOF Then Exit For
  'Display current record
  ListCurrentRecord rs
  rs.MoveNext   'Goto next record
Next
'End table
Send "</TABLE>"

End Sub
```

The `ShowRecordsSubset` procedure, which accepts two additional parameters (`StartPos` and `NumRecords`) besides the `Recordset` object, starts by sending the appropriate tags for creating an HTML table. It then calls the `ListFieldCaptions` procedure shown in Listing 10-3 to list the field captions of the passed recordset.

Listing 10-3 The `ListFieldCaptions` procedure of the UPCOMING.EXE program

```
Public Sub ListFieldCaptions(rs As Recordset)
  'Lists the field captions of rs as a table row
  Dim i As Integer         'Index variable
  Dim F As Field           'Field object variable


  Send "<TR>"  'Start first table row
  For i = 0 To rs.Fields.Count - 1
    Set F = rs(i)                              'Set F to the ith field object
    Send "<TH>" & GetCaption(F) & "</TH>"      'Send caption of that field
  Next
  Send "</TR>" 'End first table row

End Sub
```

After listing the field captions, the `ShowRecordsSubset` procedure makes the record at the position indicated by the `StartPos` parameter the current record of the recordset. It does that by first setting the current record to the first record using the `MoveFirst` method and then skipping `StartPos -1` records using the `Move` method. After setting the current record, the remaining code uses a `For` loop to list only the number or records specified by the `NumRecords` parameter. The loop terminates if the recordset reaches its end prematurely.

Note that before setting the current record, the program executes the `On Error Resume Next` line to ignore any potential run-time errors in the subsequent statements. This is a neat technique that helps you handle the possibility of an empty recordset (in case there are no upcoming events) without requiring any additional code. For example, if the recordset is empty, then both the `rs.MoveFirst` and `rs.Move StartPos -1` statements will generate run-time errors. However, if you simply ignore these errors, the rest of the code will function as desired.

The `ShowRecordsSubset` procedure calls the `ListCurrentRecord` procedure to send the data of the current record to the CGI output file. The design of the `ListCurrentRecord` procedure is shown in Listing 10-4.

Listing 10-4 The `ListCurrentRecord` procedure of the UPCOMING.EXE program

```
Public Sub ListCurrentRecord(rs As Recordset)
  'Lists the current record of rs as a table row

  Dim i As Integer              'Index variable

  Send "<TR>"  'Start row
  For i = 0 To rs.Fields.Count - 1
    'Send value of the ith field, replacing it with   if Null
    Send "<TD>" & IIf(IsNull(rs(i)), " ", rs(i)) & "</TD>"
  Next
  Send "</TR>" 'End row

End Sub
```

One good thing about this procedure is that it sends the ` ` code (HTML command for a no-break space) every time it encounters a field with a `Null` value. This code tells the browser to display empty cells for `Null` field values (see Figure 10-9).

The ShowPreviousSubsetLink *and* ShowNextSubsetLink *Procedures*

The `ShowPreviousSubsetLink` and `ShowNextSubsetLink` procedures are small procedures that add a hyperlink to call the UPCOMING.EXE program with the starting record position of the previous and next subset, respectively. Listing 10-5 shows the design of these procedures.

Listing 10-5 The `ShowPreviousSubsetLink` and `ShowNextSubsetLink` procedures of the UPCOMING.EXE program

```
Public Sub ShowPreviousSubsetLink(rs As Recordset, StartPos As Long, NumRecords As Long)
  'Sends an HTML link for requesting the previous set of records
  Dim PreviousStartPos As Long

  If StartPos = 1 Then Exit Sub  'Already at the beginning, so no link required
  'Get starting position of the previous subset
```

continued on next page

continued from previous page

```
    PreviousStartPos = StartPos - NumRecords
    'Ensure that PreviousStartPos is positive
    If PreviousStartPos < 1 Then PreviousStartPos = 1
    'Send link
    Send "<A HREF=""" & CGI_ExecutablePath & "?" & PreviousStartPos & """>"
    'Send text associated with this link and close anchor tag
    Send "Previous</A>"

End Sub

Public Sub ShowNextSubsetLink(rs As Recordset, StartPos As Long, NumRecords As Long)
    'Sends an HTML link for requesting the next set of records
    Dim NextStartPos As Long

    If rs.EOF Then Exit Sub  'Already at the end, so no link required
    'Get starting position of the next subset
    NextStartPos = StartPos + NumRecords
    'Send link
    Send "<A HREF=""" & CGI_ExecutablePath & "?" & NextStartPos & """>"
    'Send text associated with this link and close anchor tag
    Send "Next</A>"

End Sub
```

Note that the procedures add the hyperlink only if needed. This is why Figure 10-8 does not contain the **Previous** link. Further note that both these procedures use the **CGI_ExecutablePath** variable to refer to the URL path of the **UPCOMING.EXE** program. This helps ensure that the **UPCOMING.EXE** program will function normally if you move it to a different directory.

Lesson Summary

This lesson showed how to present the records of any data source dynamically through a series of linked pages. The technique involves passing the record-range-related parameter records as part of the URL request to the Windows CGI program. These parameters can be related in terms of the data itself (for example, specifying the date range) or independent of the underlying data source. In the latter case, you generally specify the starting position of the first record and the number of records that you want listed from the data source.

The advantage of this approach is that you can easily produce (almost) uniform-sized data pages by fixing the number of records that are sent with any request. The disadvantage is that for every request, the program has to recreate the recordset containing all the records first and then select the specified range of records, as evident from the design of the **UPCOMING.EXE** program. The drill-down browsing approach helps overcome this disadvantage, as you will see in the next lesson.

Quiz 3

1. What happens when you request the **UPCOMING.EXE** program with the following URL, assuming that the sample calendar database contains a total of 50 event occurrences?

   `http://localhost/cgi-win/wdbic/upcoming/upcoming.exe?51`

   a. The **UPCOMING.EXE** program returns a run-time error.
   b. The **UPCOMING.EXE** program returns the last three upcoming events.
   c. The **UPCOMING.EXE** program returns only the field captions with the **Previous** link.
   d. The **UPCOMING.EXE** program returns only the field captions with both **Previous** and **Next** links.

2. How would you generate five upcoming events on each response of the **UPCOMING.EXE** program instead of the present three?
   a. Enter **5** as the second parameter of the URL's query string.
   b. Set the constant **NUMRECORDS** to **5** in **CGI_Main** and recompile the **UPCOMING.EXE** program.
   c. Set the constant **NUMRECORDS** to **5** in **CGI_Main** but do not recompile the **UPCOMING.EXE** program.
   d. None of the above.

3. How does the **UPCOMING.EXE** program list a field containing a **Null** value?
   a. The program generates a run-time error if it encounters a field containing a **Null** value.
   b. The program generates the text **"<Null>"** in place of the **Null** value.
   c. The program lists an empty string (**""**).
   d. The program generates the text **" "** in place of the **Null** value.

4. Which of the following URLs will list the three most recent upcoming events?
   a. `http://localhost/cgi-win/wdbic/upcoming/upcoming.exe`
   b. `http://localhost/cgi-win/wdbic/upcoming/upcoming.exe?1`
   c. `http://localhost/cgi-win/wdbic/upcoming/upcoming.exe?1+3`
   d. `http://localhost/cgi-win/wdbic/upcoming/upcoming.exe?3`

5. Which of the following statements are true?
   a. The **qryEvents_Upcoming** query returns up to three records based on the value of the **StartRecordPos** variable and **NUMRECORDS** constant.
   b. The **UPCOMING.EXE** program behaves normally even if there are no upcoming events in the calendar database.
   c. You can also create uniform-sized data pages if you use fixed-size date ranges for selecting the desired subset of records.
   d. When creating linked uniform-sized data pages, you must make sure that the record source used by the Windows CGI program always returns records in the same order.

EXERCISE 3

Complexity: Moderate

1. Create a Windows CGI program named `UPCOMING1.EXE` in the `C:\WEBSITE\CGI-WIN\WDBIC\UPCOMING1` directory that accepts two parameters in the requesting URL's query string in the following format:

```
http://localhost/cgi-win/wdbic/upcoming2
/upcoming2.exe?StartPos+NumRecords
```

The `StartPos` parameter indicates the position of the first record to be listed in the current response and the `NumRecords` parameter indicates the maximum number of records to be listed in this response and the subsequent responses generated by `Next` and `Previous` hyperlinks. Assume the default values of `1` and `5` for the `StartPos` and `NumRecords` respectively, if either of these parameters are absent from the requesting URL.

Complexity: Advanced

2. Create a Windows CGI program named `UPCOMING2.EXE` in the `C:\WEBSITE\CGI-WIN\WDBIC\UPCOMING2` directory so that it presents the upcoming events one month at a time. (Hint: Use the `qryEvents_SelectedDateRange` Parameter query provided in the `C:\WEBSITE\HTDOCS\WDBIC\CHAP10\LESSON3\CALENDAR.MDB` database file.)

LESSON 4

DRILL-DOWN BROWSING

The previous lesson showed how a Web user could be saved from information overload with the dynamic presentation of data through a series of linked pages. Although this is certainly better than presenting the entire information in one go as in static publishing, it could still test a user's patience; the user may have to browse through a large number of pages while looking for a specific piece of information. In such circumstances, the drill-down technique, which organizes data in a hierarchical manner and allows a user to narrow down the context of desired information quickly, is the right choice, as you will see in this lesson.

Developing the Drill-Down Hierarchy Scheme

The simplest way of developing the drill-down hierarchy for a database publication is to mimic the relationship that exists between the tables of that database. For instance, in the case of the calendar database, users could start from a page listing the **sponsor**-types stored in the `tblSponsorTypes_lkp` table. Each **sponsor**-type description would have a hyperlink that would take the user to a page listing the sponsors (from `tblSponsors`) belonging to that `sponsor`-type. Clicking on the name of any sponsor would take the user to a page listing all the associated sponsor contacts (from `tblSponsorsContacts`), and each contact would further generate a page of associated events. Finally, clicking on the name of any event would lead the user to a page providing the complete time and location details of that event.

Although the above scheme appears quite logical, it requires a user to traverse several intermediate levels before getting to the details of the desired events. This can become time consuming if the user is looking for more than one event and has to move back and forth several times. As a rule of thumb, the drill-down technique loses its effectiveness if the hierarchy scheme is either too deep or too broad. It is essential to strike a balance between the number of levels used and the information provided in each level. A good example of this balance can be achieved for the Web calendar, as shown in Figure 10-11.

Here we have combined `tblSponsorContacts` and `tblEvents` into one level (Level 3). Now the link under each sponsor (Level 2) presents all the events (and their sponsor contacts) belonging to that sponsor. For example, if a sponsor has two sponsor contacts and each contact lists three events, then Level 3 presents all six events.

Developing the Link Structure Format

Once you have finalized the number of levels for drill-down browsing, the next step is to create a format for the hyperlinks used to move from one level to another. You need to develop a consistent structure to address the following two link-related factors:

● The URL path for accessing each level

● The parameter(s) passed to each level

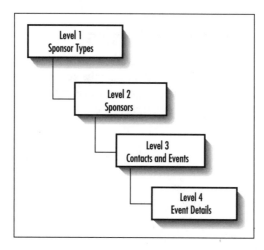

Figure 10-11
A balanced hierarchy for the calendar database

The URL path for accessing each level depends on whether you are planning to call a different Windows CGI program for each level or one Windows CGI program for all the levels. If you want to create a separate Windows CGI program for each level, then each program's URL path will be sufficient to indicate which level you are trying to access. If, however, you want to create only one program for all levels, then you need to pass the level identifier as a parameter to that program. A good way to pass this parameter is by attaching it to the tail of the program's URL path (as the extra parameter), as shown below:

```
ProgramURLPath/sptypes          'For level 1
ProgramURLPath/sponsors         'For level 2
ProgramURLPath/events           'For level 3
ProgramURLPath/eventdetails     'For level 4
```

After establishing the URL path to access each level, you then have to identify what additional parameters are required to retrieve the appropriate information from each level. For example, Level 1, which always presents a complete list of the available **sponsor**-types, does not need any parameters. However, Level 2, where we present sponsors belonging to a specified sponsor type, requires `SponsorTypeID` as an additional parameter. Similarly, Level 3 needs `SponsorID` and Level 4 needs `EventID` as parameters. It is not hard to see that these parameters are nothing but the linking fields used in the database to relate the tables.

As you have seen in previous chapters, the query string portion of a URL is well suited for passing additional parameters. For example, if you are using one Windows CGI program and the extra path to identify the level, then the exact format for the link to each level will be as follows:

```
ProgramURLPath/sptypes                'For level 1
ProgramURLPath/sponsors?sptypeid      'For level 2
ProgramURLPath/events?sponsorid       'For level 3
ProgramURLPath/eventdetails?eventid   'For level 4
```

Associating the Links

With the format of the link for each level established, you now have to determine how you want to display these links. Let's consider the **sponsor**-type (Level 1) page, for example. It lists all the **sponsor**-types currently in the calendar database, preferably in alphabetical order. For each **sponsor**-type, you have to provide the following hyperlink on that page:

```
ProgramURLPath/sponsors?sptypeid
```

where `sptypeid` is the ID of that **sponsor**-type. One good choice is to associate this link with the description of each **sponsor**-type so the appropriate link is triggered based on which **sponsor**-type the user clicks on. The other option is to place a small (but same) image depicting an icon of a link button next to each **sponsor**-type and add the appropriate link to each image. Whichever option you choose, you need to formulate the exact syntax for creating and associating the hyperlink. For example, if you want each sponsor type description to have a hyperlink, then the syntax of that hyperlink will be as follows:

```
<A HREF="ProgramURLPath/sponsors?sptypeid">SponsorTypeDescription</A>
```

Similarly, if you want to associate the hyperlinks with the sponsor name and event name in Level 2 and Level 3 pages, respectively, the syntax of their hyperlinks will be as follows:

```
<A HREF=" ProgramURLPath/events?sponsorid">SponsorName</A>
<A HREF=" ProgramURLPath/eventdetails?eventid">EventName</A>
```

Creating Source Queries

Because each drill-down level represents a different entity, it requires its own distinct record source. For maximum flexibility, you should design database queries to act as these record sources. For example, in case of the Level 1 record source, you may be tempted to use the `tblSponsorTypes_lkp` table directly. However, then you will not be able to present the **sponsor**-types in alphabetical order because the records of a table are, by default, ordered by their primary key (in this case, the ID of each sponsor type). On the other hand, a Select query based on the `tblSponsorsTypes_lkp` table will allow you to specify the desired sort order.

For Level 2 and above, you could have your source queries filter records based on the value of a specified linking field (passed as the query string parameter). A Parameter query approach is an ideal choice for creating such source queries. For example, the Parameter query shown in Figure 10-12 lists all the sponsor names belonging to the **sponsor**-type whose ID is specified through the `[pSponsorTypeID]` parameter and would work well as a data source for generating the Level 2 page.

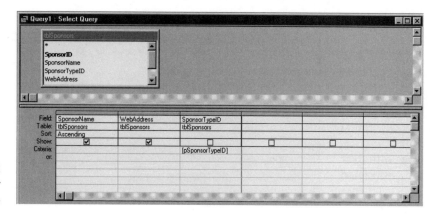

Figure 10-12
Source query for
the Level 2 page

Generating Hyperlinks Within Source Queries

As long as you are designing a query as the record source for each level, you could also have that query generate the complete hyperlink that needs to be attached to each record for moving to the next level. For example, the source query for the Level 1 page could generate the result shown in Figure 10-13. To create the Level 1 page, your Windows CGI program (**DRILL.EXE**, according to the figure) has to do nothing more than simply output the records of that query in its response.

One thing the Level 1 source query needs to produce in the hyperlinks is the URL path to access the Level 2 page. For example, the query result shown in Figure 10-13 contains the following URL path:

```
/cgi-win/wdbic/drill/drill.exe/sponsors
```

But this URL path is dependent on the name and location of your Windows CGI program. Does that mean that every time you change the name or location of this program you will also have to modify the query design to adapt to that change? Fortunately, the Parameter query approach provides a reasonable solution to this problem, too. Just use a query parameter for the URL path and have the Windows CGI program supply its correct value when the program runs this Parameter query.

Figure 10-14 shows how the Parameter query can be designed to produce the result shown in Figure 10-13:

The first column of this query creates a calculated field named **Sponsor Types** using the following expression:

```
"<A HREF=""" & [pSponsorLinkPath] & "?" & [ID] & """>" & [Description] & "</A>"
```

This expression, which generates the hyperlinks shown in Figure 10-12, is formed by concatenating the following string expressions:

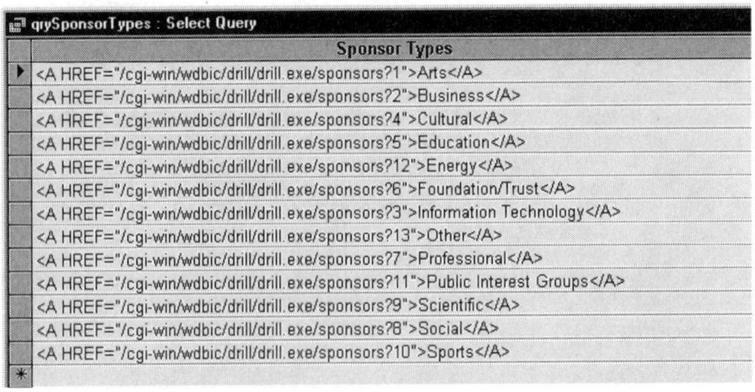

Figure 10-13
Query generating the list of sponsor-types with their associated hyperlinks

Sponsor Types
<A HREF="/cgi-win/wdbic/drill/drill.exe/sponsors?1">Arts</A>
<A HREF="/cgi-win/wdbic/drill/drill.exe/sponsors?2">Business</A>
<A HREF="/cgi-win/wdbic/drill/drill.exe/sponsors?4">Cultural</A>
<A HREF="/cgi-win/wdbic/drill/drill.exe/sponsors?5">Education</A>
<A HREF="/cgi-win/wdbic/drill/drill.exe/sponsors?12">Energy</A>
<A HREF="/cgi-win/wdbic/drill/drill.exe/sponsors?6">Foundation/Trust</A>
<A HREF="/cgi-win/wdbic/drill/drill.exe/sponsors?3">Information Technology</A>
<A HREF="/cgi-win/wdbic/drill/drill.exe/sponsors?13">Other</A>
<A HREF="/cgi-win/wdbic/drill/drill.exe/sponsors?7">Professional</A>
<A HREF="/cgi-win/wdbic/drill/drill.exe/sponsors?11">Public Interest Groups</A>
<A HREF="/cgi-win/wdbic/drill/drill.exe/sponsors?9">Scientific</A>
<A HREF="/cgi-win/wdbic/drill/drill.exe/sponsors?8">Social</A>
<A HREF="/cgi-win/wdbic/drill/drill.exe/sponsors?10">Sports</A>

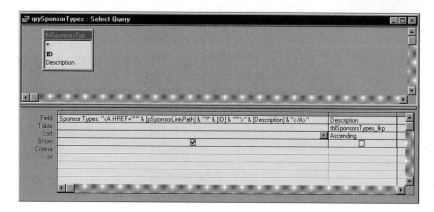

Figure 10-14
Design of the query
generating the list
of sponsor-types
with their
associated
hyperlinks

```
"<A HREF="""            which results in <A HREF="
[pSponsorLinkPath]      which represents the URL path of the Level 2 page
"?"                     which results in ?
[ID]                    the sponsor type ID of the current record
"""">"                  which results in ">
[Description]           the sponsor type description of the current record
"</A>"                  which results in </A>
```

The second column of this query specifies the Ascending sort order on the **Description** field. Note that the Show checkbox in this column is unchecked because the calculated field already contains the HTML text necessary to display the sponsor type description.

This same hyperlink-generation concept can be applied to the source queries of Level 2 and Level 3. The **CALENDAR.MDB** database residing in the **C:\WEBSITE\HTDOCS\WDBIC\CHAP10\LESSON4** directory contains the following four queries that follow the above concepts and can be used as the source queries for the four drill-down levels of the calendar database:

```
qrySponsorTypes                        (for Level 1)
qrySponsors_SelectedSponsorTypeID      (for Level 2)
qryEvents_SelectedSponsorID            (for Level 3)
qryEventDetails_SelectedEventID        (for Level 4)
```

At this point, we suggest that you go through the design of these queries before proceeding to the next section.

Running the DRILL.EXE Program

As a practical demonstration of the drill-down browsing technique, we have provided a Windows CGI program, **DRILL.EXE**, in the **C:\WEBSITE\CGI-WIN\WDBIC\DRILL** directory. This program uses most of the drill-down implementation concepts discussed so far. The following steps present a test run of this program:

1. Start your WebSite server if it is not already started and enter the following URL from your browser:

   `http://localhost/cgi-win/wdbic/drill/drill.exe/sptypes`

   The program returns a list of hyperlinked `sponsor-types` as shown in Figure 10-15.

2. Click on the Arts `sponsor-type`.

   The program returns all sponsors related to the Art category as shown in Figure 10-16. Notice that the URL in the Location window of the browser contains the text `sponsors` as the extra path and a `SponsorID` of 1 as its query string parameter.

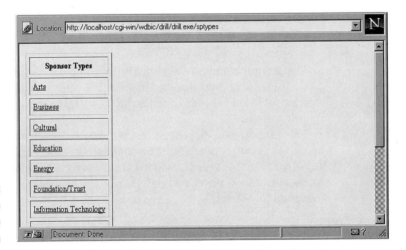

Figure 10-15
Level 1 page
returned by the
DRILL.EXE program

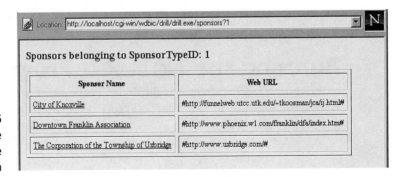

Figure 10-16
Level 2 page
returned by the
DRILL.EXE program

3. Click on the sponsor named The Corporation of the Township of Uxbridge.

   The program returns all the events hosted by this sponsor, as shown in Figure 10-17.

4. Click on the event named Arts Exhibition.

   The program returns all the occurrences of this event, as shown in Figure 10-18.

5. Using the Back button of your browser, trace through some other paths to get familiar with the functionality of this program.

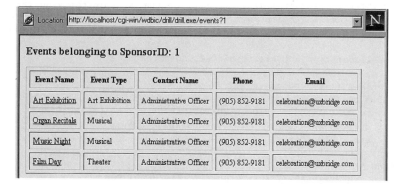

Figure 10-17
Level 3 page
returned by the
DRILL.EXE program

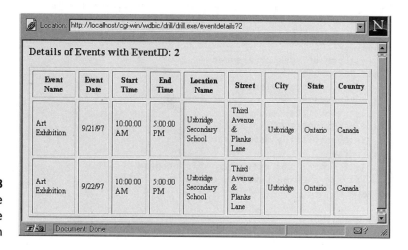

Figure 10-18
Level 4 page
returned by the
DRILL.EXE program

Examining the Design of the
DRILL.EXE **Program**

The DRILL.EXE program contains the CGI_Main procedure shown in Listing 10-6.

Listing 10-6 The CGI_Main procedure of the DRILL.EXE program

```
Sub CGI_Main()

    Dim dbCalendar As Database    'Declare database variable
    Dim dbName As String          'Path and name of the calendar database
    Dim LevelIdentifier As String 'The extra path parameter

    'Get level identifier from the URL's extra path by removing the leading
    'slash from CGI_LogicalPath. For example:
    'if CGI_LogicalPath = "/sptypes" then LevelIdentifier would become SPTYPES

    LevelIdentifier = UCase$(Mid$(CGI_LogicalPath, 2))

    'Perform tasks common to all levels
    'Open database
    dbName = "C:\WEBSITE\HTDOCS\WDBIC\CHAP10\LESSON4\CALENDAR.MDB"
    Set dbCalendar = DBEngine(0).OpenDatabase(dbName)      'Open the database
    'Generate HTML header
    Send "Content-type: text/html"
    Send ""
    Send "<HTML><HEAD><TITLE>DRILL</TITLE></HEAD><BODY>"

    'Call the appropriate procedure based on LevelIdentifier's value

    Select Case LevelIdentifier
      Case "SPTYPES"
        ListSponsorTypes dbCalendar
      Case "SPONSORS"
        ListSponsors dbCalendar
      Case "EVENTS"
        ListEvents dbCalendar
      Case "EVENTDETAILS"
        ListEventDetails dbCalendar
      Case Else
        'Tell how to correctly run this program
        ListProgramUsage LevelIdentifier
    End Select

    'Send HTML footer
    Send "</BODY></HTML>"

End Sub
```

The CGI_Main procedure first gets the identifier of the level being sought from the CGI_LogicalPath CGI variable (which always holds the extra path portion of the requesting URL). It then opens the calendar database containing the source queries and sends the HTML header common to all the levels. Based on the value of the level identifier, `CGI_Main` calls the appropriate procedure to generate the body of the response. After the called procedure does its job, the `CGI_Main` procedure appends the HTML footer to the CGI output file and terminates.

The ListSponsorType *Procedure*

The design of the `ListSponsorType` procedure is shown in Listing 10-7.

Listing 10-7 The `ListSponsorType` procedure of the `DRILL.EXE` program

```
Public Sub ListSponsorTypes(db As Database)

  Dim qd As QueryDef, rs As Recordset

  Set qd = db.QueryDefs!qrySponsorTypes              'Open source query
  qd!pSponsorLinkPath = CGI_ExecutablePath & "/sponsors"   'Path to Level 2
  Set rs = qd.OpenRecordset()                        'Get sponsor types
  'Send the result of this query
  ShowRecordsAsDatasheet rs

End Sub
```

The `ListSponsorType` procedure opens the `qrySponsorTypes` query and provides the URL path for accessing the Level 2 page to the query's `pSponsorLinkPath` parameter. It then creates a recordset based on the result of this query and calls the `ShowRecordsAsDatasheet` procedure (explained in Chapter 9, Lesson 4) to list the records of that recordset. This query result (which looks similar to Figure 10-13) is displayed by the browser as shown in Figure 10-15.

The ListSponsors, ListEvents, *and* ListEventDetails *Procedures*

The design of the `ListSponsors` procedure is shown in Listing 10-8.

Listing 10-8 The `ListSponsors` procedure of the `DRILL.EXE` program

```
Public Sub ListSponsors(db As Database)

  Dim qd As QueryDef, rs As Recordset

  Set qd = db.QueryDefs!qrySponsors_SelectedSponsorTypeID   'Open source query
  qd!pEventLinkPath = CGI_ExecutablePath & "/events"        'Path to Level 3
  qd!pSponsorTypeID = CByte(CGI_QueryString)                'Set SponsorTypeID criteria
  Set rs = qd.OpenRecordset()                               'Get applicable sponsors
  'Send the result of this query
  Send "<H2>Sponsors belonging to SponsorTypeID: " & CGI_QueryString & "</H2>"
  ShowRecordsAsDatasheet rs

End Sub
```

The ListSponsors procedure works similar to the ListSponsorTypes procedure, except that it provides the value of the SponsorTypeID present in the requesting URL's query string to the second parameter (pSponsorTypeID) of the source query. Again, the result of that query is directly fed back to the browser, which displays it as shown in Figure 10-16.

The ListEvents and ListEventsDetails procedures also follow similar logic to return the third- and fourth-level pages shown in Figures 10-17 and 10-18. You can view the design of these procedures by opening the DRILL.VBP project in VB.

The ListProgramUsage *Procedure*

The ListProgramUsage is called if the program receives an invalid or no value in the requesting URL's extra path portion. This procedure, whose design is shown in Listing 10-9, simply returns an error message and provides a link to get to the Level 1 page.

Listing 10-9 The ListProgramUsage procedure of the DRILL.EXE program

```
Public Sub ListProgramUsage(LevelIdentifier As String)

    Dim UsageLink As String   'Link to correctly start this program

    UsageLink = """" & CGI_ExecutablePath & "/sptypes"""
    Send "<H2>Unknown Level Identifier: '" & LevelIdentifier & "'<BR>"
    Send "<A HREF=" & UsageLink & ">"
    Send "Click here to start browsing."
    Send "</A>"
    Send "</H2>"

End Sub
```

Lesson Summary

This lesson showed how to implement the drill-down browsing technique by developing an appropriate hierarchical structure. The key lies in establishing a balance between the number of levels of this hierarchy and the information presented at each level. Further tasks for implementing this technique can be broken up into the following steps:

● Determine the URL path for accessing each level.

● If only one Windows CGI program is used for all levels, pass the level identifier as the URL's additional path.

● Identify additional parameters to retrieve appropriate information from each level and pass them as the query string of the program's URL.

● Determine how to display the links between various levels and formulate their syntax.

Each drill-down level represents a different entity and thus needs its own record source, which can be generated through database queries. These queries can also be used to generate the complete hyperlink needed for moving to the next level, in which case the Windows CGI program has to output the result of that query to generate the data pages. The design of the **DRILL.EXE** program described in this lesson demonstrated how these concepts can be implemented.

In the next lesson you will see how to improve the usability of the **DRILL.EXE** program by focusing on issues related to grouping and formatting of information.

1. What should be the guiding principle for developing the drill-down hierarchy scheme?
   a. Simply mimic the table relationships of the database.
   b. Keep the number of levels low and present as much information at each level as possible.
   c. Strike a balance between the number of levels and the amount of information at each level.
   d. None of the above.

2. What are the options available for formatting hyperlinks to navigate between various levels of the drill-down hierarchy?
   a. Use a different Windows CGI program for each level.
   b. Use one Windows CGI program for all levels and pass the level identifier parameter in the URL's query string.
   c. Use one Windows CGI program for all levels and pass the level identifier parameter in the URL's extra path.
   d. All of the above.

3. What would be the extra path and query string parameters of a URL that makes the **DRILL.EXE** program return a list of all business-type (**SponsorTypeID = 2**) sponsors?
   a. **sptypes+2**
   b. **sptypes?2**
   c. **sponsors+2**
   d. **sponsors?2**

4. What does the **DRILL.EXE** program return when you enter the following URL?

   `http://localhost/cgi-win/wdbic/drill/drill.exe?2`

   a. A run-time error message
   b. A message saying that an invalid extra path has been specified
   c. The correct URL path to request the Level 1 page
   d. The list of sponsor types (Level 1 page)

5. What are the parameters of the **qryEvents_SelectedSponsorID** query?
   a. **pSponsorTypeID**
   b. **pSponsorID**
   c. **pEventLinkPath**
   d. **pEventDetailsLinkPath**

EXERCISE 4

Complexity: Moderate

1. Create a Windows CGI program named **DRILL1.EXE** in the **C:\WEBSITE\ CGI-WIN\WDBIC\DRILL1** directory that enhances the **DRILL.EXE** program by incorporating the following two features:

   ● The program should return the Level 1 page if no extra path is attached to the requesting URL.

   ● The Level 1 page should list an additional field indicating the number of sponsors belonging to each sponsor type.

Complexity: Advanced

2. Create a Windows CGI program named **DRILL2.EXE** in the **C:\WEBSITE\ CGI-WIN\WDBIC\DRILL2** directory that will let you browse through the calendar database using the following hierarchy:

```
Level 1: Countries
Level 2: Cities
Level 3: EventDetails
Level 4: Event
```

Level 1 will contain the country list sorted alphabetically by country name. Level 2 will list the cities for the selected country. Level 3 will list all the event occurrences (date and location) in the selected city of the selected country. Level 4 will list the sponsor and other related information of the event selected in Level 3.

GROUPING AND FORMATTING DATA PAGES

The **DRILL.EXE** program we examined in Lesson 4 is a far cry from the professional-looking browsing interface that you would like to put on the Web. The tabular structure in which data is presented makes the Web pages generated by this program insipid. Furthermore, the program allows a user to follow only a set path while looking for information, offering little flexibility to move to other related information along the way. A number of possible enhancements come to mind that could improve the appeal of the program.

To start with, you could provide cross-links that help users quickly jump to other related pages without having to retrace the path to those pages. For example, you could list the sponsor type in the details of an event (Level 4); clicking on that name could take the user back to the list of all the sponsors belonging to that sponsor type. You could also provide a `Next` and `Previous` link in the event detail page that automatically takes the user to the details of the next or previous event listed in Level 3. These refinements are not difficult to incorporate by following the general concepts presented in Lessons 3 and 4.

The issue of record formatting and layout still needs to be addressed, however. Is table (datasheet) view the best way of presenting all types of database information? Should the data in each cell always be left-aligned? Does the browser determine the correct width of each table column? Although these questions are not very difficult to address, they do play a significant role in the kind of load balance you want to establish between the Windows CGI program and the source queries it employs. For example, in Lesson 4, the source queries were made to do all the hard work and the `DRILL.EXE` program simply returned the results of each query using the `ShowRecordsAsDataSheet` general purpose procedure.

Although this approach provides the flexibility to make changes to the program's output without having to recompile the program itself, it takes away the flexibility to generate custom layout for each page. This lesson shows how you can transfer some of the load from the source queries back to the Windows CGI program to achieve better control of the overall layout of the program's responses.

Adding Group Levels Within a Data Page

A closer examination of the `DRILL.EXE` program reveals that you perhaps do not need four levels of browsing for the Web calendar. Grouping certain information between levels would improve program usability.

For example, in the Level 4 page of the `DRILL.EXE` program (see Figure 10-18), the event name and the location are repeated on each row, thereby adding redundancy on that page. Furthermore, the Level 3 page (see Figure 10-17) contains only peripheral information about each event. If you group this peripheral information with the corresponding event details and then present each event in a concise manner, you can easily merge Level 3 and Level 4 pages into one level containing events and their location and timing details, as shown in Figure 10-19.

The key thing to note here is that each event record has a Header section and a Detail section. The Header section (up to the Web URL line) contains the event information common to all the occurrences of that event. The Detail section, indicated by the location and date columns, displays the information specific to each event occurrence. Although not evident from Figure 10-19, this Detail section is broken down into another header/detail level to group the event occurrences by location, as you will see later in this lesson.

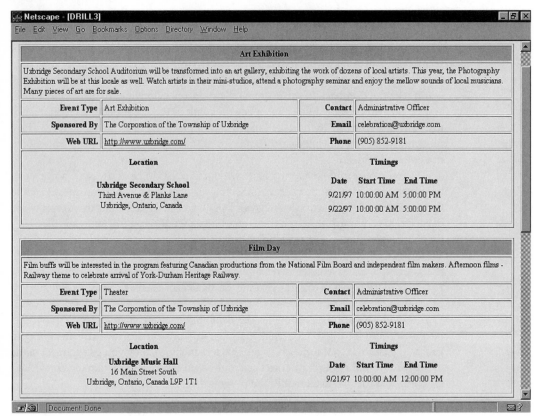

Figure 10-19
Third-level page returned by the DRILL.EXE program

Column Widths and Data Alignment

Figure 10-19 also shows how page readability improves if you assign appropriate widths to data fields. For example, the cells representing the EventName and EventDescription fields have been given the whole page width. Further note that these fields do not have a field caption. The placement and alignment of these fields hints about the kind of information they are presenting.

Coming up with an effective layout is not always easy and can take several iterations of moving and rearranging the fields. On top of that, you have to operate within the scope of HTML formatting capabilities. To make this experimentation process fast and painless, it works best if you use a good HTML editor to lay out some sample data and then methodologically replace that data with the actual field data in the Windows CGI program. You will see evidence of this process when we examine the modified DRILL.EXE program (DRILL3.EXE) in this lesson.

Handling Hyperlink-Type Fields

In Chapter 4, Lesson 5, we explained that Access supports a Hyperlink data type for hyperlink-related information. This is why it made sense to set the WebAddress field of the tblSponsors table to this data type. Moreover, Access treats the data of Hyperlink-type fields in a special way. For example, when you statically publish a table containing a Hyperlink-type field, Access automatically creates an HTML hyperlink for the data in that field (see Lesson 2).

When you access a Hyperlink-type field from a recordset created through Visual Basic, the picture becomes slightly different. The data you get is in its raw format—three parts separated by the pound signs, as shown below:

```
displaytext#address#subaddress
```

The role of each part was explained in Chapter 4, Lesson 5. To extract any individual part from this raw format, Access supports a special function named HyperlinkPart whose syntax was explained in Chapter 5, Lesson 2. Unfortunately, there is no equivalent function in Visual Basic. This also means that if you try to create a calculated field based on this function in an Access query and then try to create a recordset based on the query, you will get a run-time error. So you need to create your functions in VB to access and manipulate the different parts of the raw data returned by the Hyperlink field. A sample function to do this is shown later in this lesson.

 If you run a query using the Hyperlink function directly from Access, that query will run just fine. This is an important factor that you must consider when creating queries for your Windows CGI program. Not all queries that run perfectly in Access may run in VB, mainly because VB does not support all the functions available in Access.

Examining the DRILL3.EXE Program

To illustrate the concepts discussed above, we have provided a Windows CGI program named DRILL3.EXE in the C:\WEBSITE\CGI-WIN\DRILL3 directory. This program functions identically to the DRILL.EXE program you studied in the previous lesson for the first two drill-down levels. However, when you request the third drill-down level, the DRILL3.EXE program groups and formats the selected events and their occurrence details, as shown in Figure 10-19. At this point, we recommend that you run this program using the following URL to see how DRILL3.EXE differs from DRILL.EXE:

```
http://localhost/cgi-win/wdbic/drill3/drill3.exe/sptypes
```

Once you are comfortable with this program's functionality, open the DRILL3.VBP project in VB to examine its design. You will notice that its CGI_Main procedure has not changed much from the CGI_Main procedure of the DRILL.EXE program, except that the Case statement now handles three levels instead of four, as shown below:

```
Select Case LevelIdentifier
    Case "SPTYPES"
        ListSponsorTypes dbCalendar
```

continued on next page

continued from previous page

```
      Case "SPONSORS"
         ListSponsors dbCalendar
      Case "EVENTS"
         ListEvents dbCalendar
      Case Else
         'Tell how to correctly run this program
         ListProgramUsage LevelIdentifier
   End Select
```

The ListEvents *Procedure*

The ListEvents procedure of this program, shown in Listing 10-10, also differs from the ListEvents procedure of the DRILL.EXE program.

Listing 10-10 The ListEvents procedure of the DRILL3.EXE program

```
Public Sub ListEvents(db As Database)
   Dim qd As QueryDef, rs As Recordset

   Set qd = db.QueryDefs!qryEvents_SelectedSponsorID      'Open source query
   qd!pSponsorID = CLng(CGI_QueryString)                  'Set sponsorID criteria
   Set rs = qd.OpenRecordset()                            'Get applicable sponsors
   'Send the result of this query
   Send "<CENTER><H2>Sponsored Events</H2></CENTER>"
   'Now List each event and its location and timing details
   Do Until rs.EOF
      ShowEvent rs, rs![EventID]
      Send "<P>"
   Loop
End Sub
```

The qryEvents_SelectedSponsorID source query used by this procedure is in the CALENDAR.MDB file residing in the C:\WEBSITE\HTDOCS\WDBIC\CHAP10\LESSON5 directory. This query lists all the event occurrences and all the other related information for the events of the sponsor whose SponsorID is specified through the pSponsorID parameter. Its design is shown in Figure 10-20.

Note that the records are sorted in the following order:

```
EventName
EventID
LocationID
EventDate
StartTime
```

This ensures that all the event occurrence records belonging to the same event are adjacent to each other and, within those records, that all the records occurring at the same location are adjacent to each other. Maintaining this sort order is crucial to the proper functioning of the ListEvents procedure, which repeatedly calls the ShowEvent procedure to list each event in the format shown in Figure 10-19. Note that the Do loop used by the ListEvents procedure does not contain the rs.MoveNext statement even

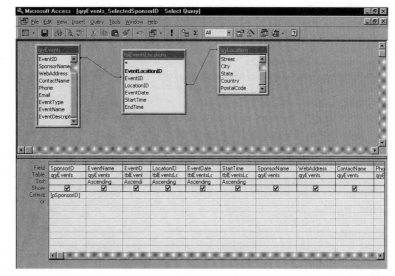

Figure 10-20
Design of the
qryEvents_SelectedS
ponsorID query
used by the
ListEvents
procedure of the
DRILL3.EXE program

though the terminating criteria of this loop depend on the assumption that the **rs** record-set will reach its end. This is not a problem because the current record of **rs** is moved forward during the execution of the **ShowEvent** procedure.

The ShowEvent *Procedure*

The **ShowEvent** procedure receives the **rs** recordset and the **EventID** of that record-set's current record as its parameters. The objective of this procedure is to go through the current record and all the subsequent records of **rs** having the same **EventID** value and generate the HTML code for presenting the event represented by that **EventID**. Listing 10-11 shows the design of the **ShowEvent** procedure.

Listing 10-11 The ShowEvent procedure of the DRILL3.EXE program

```
Public Sub ShowEvent(rs As Recordset, EventID As Long)
   Dim WebURL As String

   'Begin main table
   Send "<TABLE BORDER=1 CELLPADDING=3 WIDTH=100%>"
   'Display event header section from the current record
      'Event name
```

continued on next page

continued from previous page

```
    Send "<TR><TH ALIGN=CENTER COLSPAN=4 BGCOLOR=#COCOCO>"
    Send rs![EventName] & "</TH></TR>"
    'Event Description
    Send "<TR><TD COLSPAN=4>" & rs![EventDescription] & "</TD></TR>"
    'Event type and Contact Name
    Send "<TR><TH ALIGN=RIGHT>Event Type</TH><TD>" & rs![EventType] & "</TD>"
    Send "<TH ALIGN=RIGHT>Contact</TH><TD>" & rs![ContactName] & "</TD></TR>"
    'Sponsor name and Email; if Email is Null then send  
    Send "<TR><TH ALIGN=RIGHT>Sponsored By</TH><TD>" & rs![SponsorName] & "</TD>"
    Send "<TH ALIGN=RIGHT>Email</TH><TD>" & N2S(rs![Email]) & "</TD></TR>"
    'Display WebAddress field (with a hyperlink) and phone on the same row
    Send "<TR><TH ALIGN=RIGHT>Web URL</TH>"
    If Not IsNull(rs![WebAddress]) Then
       WebURL = HyperLinkPart(rs![WebAddress], 2)
       Send "<TD><A HREF=""" & WebURL & """>" & WebURL & "</A></TD>"
    Else
       Send "<TD> </TD>"
    End If
    Send "<TH ALIGN=RIGHT>Phone</TH><TD>" & N2S(rs![Phone]) & "</TD></TR>"
    'Now send event details from current and subsequent records having
    '  this EventID as one big cell of the next row
    Send "<TR><TD COLSPAN=4>"
    Do Until rs![EventID] <> EventID
       'Show event dates and times grouped by location for the current event
       ShowLocationAndDate rs, rs!EventID, rs!LocationID
       If rs.EOF Then Exit Do  'Exit if recordset has ended
    Loop
    Send "</TD><TR>"
    Send "</TABLE>"  'Close event table

End Sub
```

The majority of this procedure deals with sending the HTML instructions responsible for formatting the Event Header section and placing the data from the header fields at appropriate places. The **N2S** (**Null-to-Space**) function that this procedure applies to the **Email** and **Phone** fields handles the possibility of these fields having **Null** values by converting those **Null** values to the ** ** HTML code. Remember that the ** ** code helps in displaying an empty cell of a table in the same format as all the other table cells. The design of the **N2S** function is shown in Listing 10-12.

Listing 10-12 The N2S function of the DRILL3.EXE program

```
Public Function N2S(Value As Variant) As Variant
   'Return Value if it is not null; otherwise return the text " "
   If IsNull(Value) Then N2S = " " Else N2S = Value
End Function
```

The `ShowEvent` procedure also creates an HTML hyperlink for the `WebAddress` field of the sponsor of the current event. As mentioned earlier in the lesson, VB does not provide a built-in `HyperLinkPart` function as Access does, so we created an almost equivalent function to retrieve the address portion from the `WebAddress` field and used that address to generate the HTML hyperlink. The design of this new `HyperLinkPart` function is shown in Listing 10-13.

Listing 10-13 The `HyperLinkPart` function of the `DRILL3.EXE` program

```
Public Function HyperLinkPart(Value As Variant, PartNumber As Byte) As Variant
   Dim FirstPoundPos As Integer
   Dim SecondPoundPos As Integer

   If IsNull(Value) Then HyperLinkPart = Null
   FirstPoundPos = InStr(Value, "#")
   SecondPoundPos = InStr(FirstPoundPos + 1, Value, "#")
   If SecondPoundPos = 0 Then SecondPoundPos = Len(value) + 1
   Select Case PartNumber
    Case 1  'Return Display Text Portion
       HyperLinkPart = Left$(Value, FirstPoundPos - 1)
    Case 2  'Return Address Portion
      HyperLinkPart = Mid$(Value, FirstPoundPos + 1, SecondPoundPos - FirstPoundPos - 1)
     Case 3  'Return SubAddress Portion
       HyperLinkPart = Mid$(Value, SecondPoundPos + 1)
   End Select

End Function
```

Once the Header section for the current event is complete, the `ShowEvent` procedure repeatedly calls the `ShowLocationAndDate` procedure to generate the Detail section of this event. Note that again the `Do` loop used by the `ShowEvent` procedure does not contain an `rs.MoveNext` statement. You will see this statement being executed in the `ShowLocationAndDate` procedure.

The ShowLocationAndDate *Procedure*

The design of the `ShowLocationAndDate` procedure is shown in Listing 10-14.

Listing 10-14 The `ShowLocationAndDate` procedure of the `DRILL3.EXE` program

```
Public Sub ShowLocationAndDate(rs As Recordset, EventID As Long, LocationID As Long)
   'Begin event location and timing table
   Send "<TABLE CELLPADDING=2 WIDTH=100%>"
   'Send column titles
   Send "<TR>"
   Send "<TH ALIGN=CENTER WIDTH=50%>Location</TH>"
```

continued on next page

continued from previous page

```
Send "<TH ALIGN=CENTER>Timings</TH>"
Send "</TR>"
'Send location and timing data
Send "<TR>"
'Send location info as one cell with a subtable
Send "<TD ALIGN=CENTER>"
Send "<TABLE><TR><TD>"
Send "<B>" & rs![LocationName] & "</B><BR>"
If Not IsNull(rs![Street]) Then Send rs![Street] & "<BR>"
If Not IsNull(rs![City]) Then Send rs![City] & ","
If Not IsNull(rs![State]) Then Send rs![State] & ","
Send rs![Country]
Send "</TD></TR></TABLE>" 'Close location subtable
Send "</TD>"                'Close location data cell
'Send Timings as one cell with a subtable
Send "<TD ALIGN=CENTER>"
Send "<TABLE>"
'Show headings in the first row of this subtable
Send "<TR>"
Send "<TH ALIGN=CENTER>Date</TH>"
Send "<TH ALIGN=CENTER>Start Time</TH>"
Send "<TH ALIGN=CENTER>End Time</TH>"
Send "</TR>"
'Show dates and times for this location, one day per row
Do Until rs![EventID] <> EventID Or rs![LocationID] <> LocationID
  Send "<TR><TD ALIGN=CENTER>" & rs![EventDate] & "</TD>"
  Send "<TD ALIGN=CENTER>" & rs![StartTime] & "</TD>"
  Send "<TD ALIGN=CENTER>" & rs![EndTime] & "</TH></TR>"
  'Goto next date
  rs.MoveNext
  If rs.EOF Then Exit Do  'Exit if recordset has ended
Loop
Send "</TABLE>"  'Close timing subtable
Send "</TD>"       'Close timing data cell
Send "</TR></TABLE>" 'Close location and date table

End Sub
```

This **ShowLocationAndDate** procedure sends HTML instructions for displaying one table row for each unique location of the given event. The first cell of that table lists the location information and the second cell uses another subtable to list all the dates and times the event is occurring at that location. Notice that the current record of **rs** is moved to the next record after each detail line (the event date and time information) for the current location has been listed.

Lesson Summary

This lesson showed that proper load balance between the Windows CGI program and Access queries helps in better control of the overall layout of the program's responses. Using **DRILL.EXE** as the starting point, this lesson demonstrated how grouping information by merging certain levels of the drill-down hierarchy and appropriately formatting the program response prevents redundancy and improves readability. Coming up with a good layout requires patience, however; you must try out a number of prototype layouts, and a good HTML editor can prove to be an indispensable tool for this experimentation.

This lesson presented the design of the **DRILL3.EXE** program, which uses common grouping and formatting techniques to list events and their occurrence details on the same page. The key to accomplishing such grouping lies in using the correct sort order in the source query to ensure that records belonging to all occurrences of a particular event are contiguous. In addition, this lesson, using the example of the **HyperLinkPart** function, exposed the fact that not all functions provided in Access are supported by VB and you may have to build your own functions to perform the desired task.

In the next lesson, we will show how to implement the SQL search capability in the Web calendar application.

1. How can you avoid redundancy in the result of your Windows CGI program?
   a. By improving the formatting of the program result
   b. By increasing the number of hierarchies for drill-down browsing
   c. By grouping information together and merging certain levels of the drill-down hierarchy
   d. By avoiding peripheral information

2. What happens when you try to create a recordset in VB using an Access query that has a calculated field based on the **HyperLinkPart** function?
   a. VB automatically creates a hyperlink for the data in that field.
   b. The program generates a run-time error.
   c. VB returns the data in the raw format.
   d. None of the above.

3. Why is it important to sort the records of the **qryEvents_SelectedSponsorID** (source query for **DRILL3.EXE** program) in a certain specific order?
   a. To ensure that all event occurrence records belonging to a particular event are adjacent to each other
   b. To ensure proper functioning of the **ListEvents** procedure
   c. To ensure proper functioning of the **ShowEvent** procedure
   d. All of the above

4. What is the function of the **N2S** function in the **DRILL3.EXE** program?
   a. It is used to handle fields that may contain a **Null** value.
   b. It returns ** ** on receiving a **Null** value.
   c. It returns ** ** on receiving a **Null** value.
   d. All of the above.

5. How many times will an event be displayed by the **DRILL3.EXE** program in its Level 3 page if that event occurs at two different locations?
   a. The event will not be displayed at all.
   b. The event will be displayed only once, with both locations listed in its detail section.
   c. The event will be displayed twice, once for each location.
   d. The **DRILL.EXE** program will generate a run-time error.

EXERCISE 5

Complexity: Easy

1. Create a Windows CGI program named **DRILL4.EXE** in the **C:\WEBSITE\CGI-WIN\WDBIC\DRILL4** directory that enhances the **DRILL3.EXE** program by incorporating the following two features:

   ● The Level 1 page should list the sponsor-types in four columns.

   ● The Level 2 page should display the selected sponsor-type description (not the sponsor-type ID) as its first line and the Web address field should have an attached hyperlink.

Complexity: Advanced

2. Create a Windows CGI program named **DRILL5.EXE** in the **C:\WEBSITE\ CGI-WIN\WDBIC\DRILL5** directory that will let you browse through the calendar database using the following hierarchy:

   ```
   Level 1: Countries
   Level 2: Cities
   Level 3: Events
   ```

   Level 1 will contain the country list sorted alphabetically by country name. Level 2 will list the cities for the selected country. Level 3 will list all the current events and their occurrences in the selected city of the selected country in the format shown in Figure 10-19.

SQL-BASED SEARCHING

Any Web database application dealing with a potentially large database is expected to support a search feature to help the user quickly locate information of interest. As described in Lesson 1, this feature can be provided in two ways:

● Keyword-based text search of the complete database

● Field-based search of database tables

The keyword-based search of the complete database requires the creation of a word index based on the information in the database. As a simple example, if two events are named **Art Exhibition** and **Art Show**, respectively, then your word index will include the words **Art**, **Exhibition**, and **Show**. The database will also have to contain information that links the word **Art** to both these events and the words **Exhibition** and **Show** to their respective events.

This process of creating a word index and the corresponding link information can be static or dynamic. In either case, the implementation of this process and the associated keyword-search mechanism requires a good knowledge of text-retrieval techniques and algorithms, which is a complete subject by itself.

The field-based search feature allows users to specify criteria against specific database fields. Compared to the text-based search, this feature is relatively easy to implement for a database that supports SQL-based queries.

This lesson describes the features and design of the **SEARCH.EXE** Windows CGI program that acts as an example of how the field-based search can be implemented for the Web calendar application. This program also shows how you can incorporate a limited keyword-based text search capability as a special case of the field-based search, although doing this can lead to a drop in the overall search performance, as we will explain later in this lesson.

Running the SEARCH.EXE Program

Before we examine the design of the **SEARCH.EXE** program, let's subject it to a test run to see how it works:

1. Start your WebSite server if it is not already started and enter the following URL through your browser:

   ```
   http://localhost/wdbic/chap10/lesson6/search.htm
   ```

   The browser displays an event search form as shown in Figure 10-21. This search form acts as a front end to the SEARCH.EXE program.

2. Enter the following criteria in the event search form and press the Search button:

   ```
   Event type: Workshops, Conferences, and Seminars
   Event name or description contains text: home
   Start date: 1/25/97
   Cities: Houston, Knoxville
   ```

   The browser sends the form data to the SEARCH.EXE program, which responds as shown in Figure 10-22.

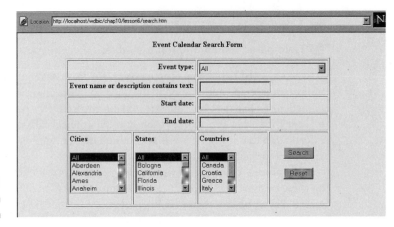

Figure 10-21
The event search
form

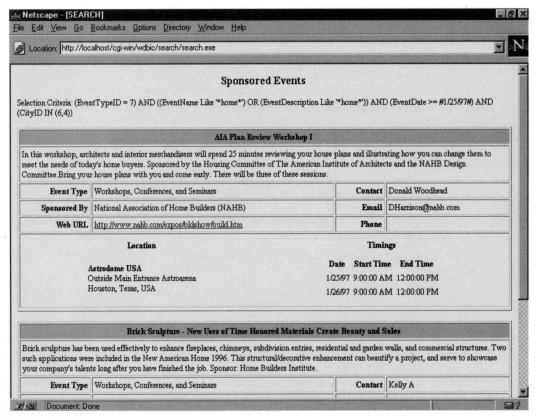

Figure 10-22
Response of the EVENT.EXE program

The response contains all the workshop-, conference-, and seminar-type events occurring on or after 1/25/97 in either Houston or Knoxville and having the word home in either their event name or event description. Note that the criteria used to search the events are also listed in the beginning of the response.

At this point, you can return to the event search form and test the program using various criteria.

The Event Search Form

The event search form is a static HTML form whose form tag is set as follows:

```
<form action="/cgi-win/wdbic/search/search.exe" method="POST">
```

In addition, this form contains the following input fields:

```
EventTypeID: Pop-down selection list
Keyword: Text
StartDate: Text
EndDate: Text
CityID: Multiple-selection list
StateID: Multiple-selection list
CountryID: Multiple-selection list
```

The option values for the four selection-list-type fields are populated from their associated lookup tables in the calendar database. For example, the CountryID field is designed as follows:

```
<td><strong>Countries</strong><p><select
name="CountryID" multiple size="5">
     <option selected value="-1">All</option>
     <option value="2">Canada</option>
     <option value="6">Croatia</option>
     <option value="4">Greece</option>
     <option value="5">Italy</option>
     <option value="3">UK</option>
     <option value="1">USA</option>
     </select></p>
</td>
```

Note that the All option (the default selection) returns the value of −1, whereas all other options, when selected, return the ID corresponding to the country name to the SEARCH.EXE program. The other three selection-list-type fields of this event search form are constructed using the same concept.

Examining the Design of the SEARCH.EXE Program

The SEARCH.EXE program is designed to search and show events that meet all the specified field criteria. In other words, individual criteria expressions are concatenated using the logical **AND** operator. Any text-type search field that is left blank (for example, the **EndDate** in the test run) or any selection-list-type field whose All option is selected is ignored when querying the database. This means that not just the criteria values but the fields themselves can change in the search criteria. Therefore, you cannot apply the Parameter query technique (used in the previous two lessons) to select the appropriate events.

The key to handling situations where the number of fields in the query criteria differ is to build the SQL string containing the desired criteria dynamically within your Windows CGI program. Then you can create a recordset based on that SQL string to filter out the appropriate records. The simplest way to generate the SQL string is using the following syntax:

```
SELECT RecordSourceName.* FROM RecordSourceName WHERE SQLCriteria;
```

In this syntax, **RecordSourceName** can be the name of any table or non-Parameter query of the database that outputs all the fields needed to list or search the information. **SQLCriteria** is any valid SQL criteria that can be applied to the specified record source. It is also referred to as the **WhereClause** of the SQL statement.

SEARCH.EXE essentially applies this SQL generation technique to conduct all the searches. Its **CGI_Main** program is coded as shown in Listing 10-15.

Listing 10-15 The CGI_Main procedure of the SEARCH.EXE program

```
Sub CGI_Main()

    Dim dbCalendar As Database      'Declare database variable
    Dim dbName As String            'Path and name of the calendar database
    Dim LevelIdentifier As String   'The extra path parameter

    'Get level identifier from the URL's extra path by removing the leading
    'slash from CGI_LogicalPath. For example:
    'if CGI_LogicalPath = "/sptypes" then LevelIdentifier would become SPTYPES

    LevelIdentifier = UCase$(Mid$(CGI_LogicalPath, 2))

    'Perform tasks common to all levels
    'Open database
    dbName = "C:\WEBSITE\HTDOCS\WDBIC\CHAP10\LESSON6\CALENDAR.MDB"
    Set dbCalendar = DBEngine(0).OpenDatabase(dbName)        'Open the database
    'Generate HTML header
    Send "Content-type: text/html"
    Send ""
    Send "<HTML><HEAD><TITLE>SEARCH</TITLE></HEAD><BODY>"
    ListEvents dbCalendar
    'Send HTML footer
    Send "</BODY></HTML>"

End Sub
```

As you can see, the `CGI_Main` procedure, after taking care of the preliminary initialization tasks, passes control to the `ListEvents` procedure to search the database and return the results.

The `ListEvents` *Procedure*

The design of the `ListEvents` procedure is shown in Listing 10-16.

Listing 10-16 The `ListEvents` procedure of the `SEARCH.EXE` program

```
Public Sub ListEvents(db As Database)
   Dim BaseSQL As String      ' Record source portion of SQL
   Dim WhereClause As String  ' Criteria portion of SQL
   Dim SQL As String          ' Complete SQL statement
   Dim rs As Recordset        ' Recordset based on the SQL statement


   BaseSQL = "SELECT qryEvents_Locations.* From qryEvents_Locations"
   WhereClause = GenerateSQLCriteria()
   If WhereClause <> "" Then
     SQL = BaseSQL & " WHERE " & WhereClause & ";"
   Else
     SQL = BaseSQL & ";"
   End If
   Set rs = db.OpenRecordset(SQL)
   'Send the result of this query
   Send "<CENTER><H2>Sponsored Events</H2></CENTER>"
   Send "Selection Criteria: " & WhereClause & "<P>"
   'Now List each event and its location and timing details
   Do Until rs.EOF
     ShowEvent rs, rs![EventID]
     Send "<P>"
   Loop
End Sub
```

The `ListEvents` procedure first creates the portion of the SQL statement that defines `qryEvents_Locations` as the record source to be used for the search. The `qryEvents_Locations` query simply generates one row for each event occurrence record (from `tblEvents_Locations`), along with all the related information from other database tables in the sort order needed to present the event header and the occurrence details as one unit. As such, the query itself does not contain any sort criteria.

After setting the base SQL, the `ListEvents` procedure calls the `GenerateSQLCriteria` function to return the SQL criteria based on the information entered on the event search form and then appends it to the base SQL to create a complete SQL statement. If a user does not specify any search criteria, the `GenerateSQLCriteria` function returns an empty string, in which case the `ListEvents` procedure makes the base SQL the final SQL statement (essentially returning all the events stored in the database).

Once the SQL statement has been formed, the `ListEvents` procedure creates a record-set from that SQL statement. Next, it outputs the selection criteria in the response and then repeatedly calls the `ShowEvent` procedure (described in Lesson 4) to list all the selected events and their details in the format shown in Figure 10-21.

The `GenerateSQLCriteria` *Function*

The `GenerateSQLCriteria` function interprets the information entered on the event search form and converts it to a valid SQL criteria expression. The design of this function is presented in Listing 10-17.

Listing 10-17 The `GenerateSQLCriteria` function of the `SEARCH.EXE` program

```
Public Function GenerateSQLCriteria() As String
  Dim C As String    'Criteria String
  Dim F As Variant   'A form field

  C = ""
  'Handle EventTypeID form field
  F = GetSmallField("EventTypeID")
  If F <> "-1" Then C = C & "(EventTypeID = " & F & ")"
  'Handle Keyword form field
  F = GetSmallField("Keyword")
  If F <> "" Then
    'Replace each quote in data with two double quotes
    F = ReplaceString(F, "'", "''")
    C = C & " AND ((EventName Like '*" & F & "*') OR (EventDescription⇐
Like '*" & F & "*'))"
  End If
  'Handle StartDate form field
  F = GetSmallField("StartDate")
  If F <> "" Then
    F = CVDate(F)
    C = C & " AND (EventDate >= #" & F & "#)"
  End If
  'Handle EndDate form field
  F = GetSmallField("EndDate")
  If F <> "" Then
    F = CVDate(F)
    C = C & " AND (EventDate <= #" & F & "#)"
  End If
  MakeMultiListCriteria C, "CityID"
  MakeMultiListCriteria C, "StateID"
  MakeMultiListCriteria C, "CountryID"
  'Remove the leading AND (if any) from the criteria
  If Left$(C, 5) = " AND " Then
    C = Mid$(C, 6)
  End If
  GenerateSQLCriteria = C

End Function
```

Because the request generated through the event search form comes via the **POST** method, the **GenerateSQLCriteria** function calls on the **GetSmallField** function of the **CGI32.BAS** module to retrieve the value of each form field. The construction of the **GetSmallField** function was explained in Chapter 8, Lesson 6.

The **GenerateSQLCriteria** function starts with an empty criteria string (represented by the variable **C**). Then it incrementally concatenates the individual field criteria expressions to this string using the **AND** logical operator for all fields that have a criteria value other than **ALL (-1)** or an empty string. The criteria generation procedure for the **Keyword** input field needs some further explanation.

When the **GenerateSQLCriteria** function retrieves the value of the **Keyword** input field in the variable **F** and finds it to be a nonempty string, it calls the **ReplaceString** function to replace all the single quotes in that value with two single quotes. This is an important requirement because the SQL criteria expressions involving the **EventName** and **EventDescription** fields have this value listed within a pair of single quotes, as shown below:

```
EventName Like '*KeywordValue*'
EventDescription Like '*KeywordValue*'
```

If the **KeywordValue** itself contains a single quote (say **"Mozart's symphony"**) and you place that value directly into the expressions as follows:

```
EventName Like '*Mozart's symphony*'
EventDescription Like '* Mozart's symphony*'
```

then the expressions will become syntactically incorrect. The correct way of representing a single quote within a text value is by embedding two single quotes in its place. Note that if you use a pair of double quotes to enclose a text value in a criteria expression, then you will have to ensure that each double-quote character within that value is replaced by two double-quote characters.

For **CityID**, **StateID**, and **CountryID** input fields that can take multiple values, the **GenerateSQLCriteria** function calls the **MakeMultiListCriteria** procedure to append the appropriate criteria expression to the current criteria string. The **MakeMultiListCriteria** procedure (described in the next section) uses the **IN** operator to create the criteria expression. For example, when you selected Houston (**CityID = 6**) and Knoxville (**CityID = 4**) as the desired cities in the test run of the **SEARCH.EXE** program, the **MakeMultiListCriteria** created the following expression for the **CityID** field:

```
CityID IN (6,4)
```

The design of the **MakeMultiListCriteria** is presented in Listing 10-18.

Listing 10-18 The `MakeMultiListCriteria` procedure of the `SEARCH.EXE` program

```
Public Sub MakeMultiListCriteria(C As String, FieldName As String)

    Dim IDList As String    'The arguments of the IN operator
    Dim i As Integer        'Index variable
    Dim F As String         'Field value

    'Remember that the multiple values are stored in form-fields
    ' in the format: FieldName, FieldName_1, FieldName_2, and so on

    'Get the first value of the multi-select field
    F = GetSmallField(FieldName)
    If F <> "-1" Then    'If the All option is not selected
        IDList = F          'then add the first value to IDList
        i = 1               'Index for the second value of the current field
        On Error Resume Next   'Ignore error for the following code
        Do Until False      'Continue looping
            'Get the field value number i+1
            F = GetSmallField(FieldName & "_" & i)
            'If that field value doesn't exist, then terminate loop
            If Err <> 0 Then Exit Do
            'Otherwise add that value to IDList
            IDList = IDList & "," & F
            'Increment index
            i = i + 1
        Loop
        'Append this field's criteria expression to the current criteria string
        C = C & " AND (" & FieldName & " IN (" & IDList & "))"
    End If

End Sub
```

The `MakeMultiListCriteria` procedure, which has the current value of the criteria string and the name of the multiselect input field as its parameters, modifies the criteria string only if the first value of the specified field is not **-1**. Remember that **-1** means **All** in our front end. If the first value is other than **-1**, then the `MakeMultiListCriteria` procedure gathers all the values of that field that were passed on with the form request into a comma-delimited list held by the `IDList` variable. It then creates a criteria expression by passing the `IDList` through the **IN** operator and appends that expression to the criteria string.

Finally, when the criteria string is fully formed, the `GenerateSQLCriteria` function makes a final check to see if that string begins with the **AND** operator. This case will occur whenever the user selects the All option for the **Event**-type input field. If the criteria string does begin with the **AND** operator, the `GenerateSQLCriteria` function simply removes it and returns the remaining string back to the calling (`ListEvents`) procedure.

Performance Issues

As you can see, the SQL statement used by the `SEARCH.EXE` program applies criteria to the `qryEvents_Locations` query, which produces a big virtual table of all the event occurrence records and their related fields from other tables. You may think that this will slow down the performance because the JET engine will have to create that virtual table first and then filter records based on the specified criteria for every request. Fortunately, the JET engine is smart enough not to do that. As long as you are applying criteria directly to table fields and not to any calculated field, the JET engine is generally able to apply the filter criteria before it combines information from multiple tables, thereby making the search process quite efficient.

The only performance bottleneck that you may incur would be due to the use of the `Like` operator for searching events containing the specified keyword value. This is because the JET engine has to go through a pattern-matching process for the names and descriptions of all the events; setting an index on the `EventName` field does not help. (The `EventDescription` field, being a `Memo` data type, cannot be indexed.) This is where word-indexing and text-retrieval concepts come in handy, but they require a lot more programming effort. The book *Web Database Construction Kit*, published by Waite Group Press, presents a step-by-step process for incorporating the word-indexing technique for performing efficient keyword-based searches of Access databases.

Lesson Summary

Any Web application dealing with a large database should support a search feature to locate desired information quickly. This search feature can be provided in the form of keyword-based text search of the complete database or a field-based search of the data tables or a combination of both. Although the former requires complex text-retrieval mechanisms and algorithms beyond the scope of this book, the latter was demonstrated in this lesson through the `SEARCH.EXE` program, based on the calendar database. This program does offer limited keyword-based text search, however, though at the expense of overall search performance.

The search application uses an HTML form containing the search fields as the front end of the `SEARCH.EXE` program. The user is not required to supply a criteria value for each field, however. Only the fields where the criteria value is given are made part of the search criteria. This feature, where the number of search fields can easily vary, cannot be implemented using the Parameter query technique and requires that an SQL string containing the appropriate criteria is generated dynamically by the Windows CGI program. Once that is done, then the program can use the standard recordset-based techniques to retrieve the matching records from the database and present them to the requesting user.

1. Why is it not possible to use a Parameter query for the **SEARCH.EXE** program described in this lesson?
   a. You cannot use a Parameter query for dynamically generating the search criteria.
   b. You cannot use a Parameter query to carry out both field-based and text-based searches.
   c. You cannot use a Parameter query where the criteria fields can change.
   d. You cannot use a Parameter query when the SQL string for the query criteria is to be built dynamically through the Windows CGI program.

2. What happens if you submit the event search form without specifying any criteria?
   a. The program does not list any events.
   b. The program lists all the events.
   c. The program displays a message asking for at least one valid search criteria.
   d. The program returns a run-time error.

3. What search criteria string will the **SEARCH.EXE** program use if you ask for all the events occurring between 1/1/98 and 1/31/98 in the USA (**CountryID = 1**) through the event search form?
   a. `(EventDate Between #1/1/98# And #1/31/98#) AND (CountryID = 1)`
   b. `(EventDate Between #1/1/98# And #1/31/98#) AND (CountryID IN (1))`
   c. `(EventDate >= #1/1/98# OR EventDate <= #1/31/98#) AND (CountryID = 1)`
   d. `(EventDate >= #1/1/98#) AND (EventDate <= #1/31/98#) AND (CountryID IN (1))`

4. What will the **SEARCH.EXE** program return if you select the All option and the Houston option from the cities selection list and submit the event search form?
   a. All events sorted by the their event name
   b. Events occurring in Houston
   c. All events occurring in Houston followed by the rest of the events
   d. No events

5. Which of the following search criteria strings can be used to search the events containing the text **"Dancin' in the Street"** in the event description? (Note that the double quotes are included in the text.)
   a. `EventDescription Like "*Dancin' in the Street*"`
   b. `EventDescription Like '*"Dancin'' in the Street"*'`
   c. `EventDescription Like "*"Dancin'' in the Street"*"`
   d. `EventDescription Like "*""Dancin' in the Street""*"`

EXERCISE 6

Complexity: Easy

1. The **SEARCH.EXE** program returns a run-time error if it receives an invalid date in the **Start date** or **End date** input fields. Modify this program so that it returns an appropriate message when this condition happens.

Complexity: Moderate

2. Create a Windows CGI program named **SEARCH1.EXE** (in the **C:\WEBSITE\ CGI-WIN\WDBIC\SEARCH1** directory) and its corresponding search form named **SEARCH1.HTM** (in the **C:\WEBSITE\HTDOCS\WDBIC\CHAP10\LAB6** directory) that adds the following two features to the original **SEARCH.EXE** program discussed in this lesson:

● The user should be able to select more than one event type in the event search form.

● The search keyword should also apply to the sponsor name of an event.

CHAPTER SUMMARY

This lesson presented various approaches and techniques that can be used to put a database on the Web as either a static or a dynamic publication. It further showed how you can design your Web publication so that it offers the ability to browse through the database or use search techniques to get to the information of interest directly. Each technique was discussed in detail and strategies to improve the presentation of the pages returned by such a publication were described. Here is a recap of the salient points covered in this chapter:

● When designing a Web database application, you can have users browse through the available information or search for the desired information or both.

● Using the browse approach, you can present data from your application's database as separate HTML pages or combine information from related tables and then present the combined dataset on a single page. A good choice is to achieve a balance between the two to avoid information overload.

● The drill-down technique helps avoid information overload while keeping the related information connected. It requires a large number of individual data pages to be generated along with their links, however.

- A Web database application offering the search approach allows a user to specify a keyword-based or field-based search or a combination of both.

- Web database publishing can be carried out statically or dynamically. Static publishing involves creating and storing data pages beforehand as static files, serving them per user request.

- You can apply time-bound or event-based synchronization techniques to keep the statically generated information up to date within some level.

- The dynamic approach uses back-end CGI programs to provide data pages that are generated on the fly based on current database information.

- Static publishing in Access is easy to carry out because of the built-in and intuitive publish to the Web wizard.

- The Web publishing wizard creates one HTML page per selected data source under the specified publishing directory. You can also use the format template file feature of this wizard to customize your Web pages.

- While using the dynamic approach, you can make your Windows CGI program list only a subset of any incoming request and provide links for fetching next and previous subsets.

- Whenever using the drill-down technique, you must strike a balance between the number of levels and the information provided in each level.

- The URL path for accessing each level of the drill-down hierarchy depends on whether a different Windows CGI program is called for each level or the same program is used for all levels.

- When using a single program, you can pass the level identifier as a parameter attached to the tail end of the program's URL path.

- Each drill-down level represents a separate identity requiring its own record source, which may be a database query.

- These database queries can also be used to generate the hyperlinks attached to each record for moving to the next level.

- A good load balance between source queries and the Windows CGI program allows better control of the overall layout of the program's response.

- Creating an effective layout is not always easy and can take several iterations. A good HTML editor can help make this job easier.

● All functions supported by Access are not supported by VB.

● Parameter queries cannot be used where fields change in the search criteria.

Besides publishing database information, most Web applications also have to provide an interface to add new information to that database. Unfortunately, the stateless nature of the Web does not make this an easy task. The next chapter explains why this is difficult and what techniques you can apply to overcome this difficulty.

CHAPTER 11

POPULATING TABLES: WEB-BASED DATA ENTRY

Most Web database applications require that the database be kept up to date in order to be useful. The widespread availability of Web browsers and the data input support of HTML make the Web a perfect medium for accepting new information to be stored in a database. However, the stateless nature of the Web poses some difficulties when the database is made up of many related tables. This chapter looks at these difficulties and presents commonly used techniques for overcoming them. In particular, you will learn about:

● Adding a record to a single database table

● Desirable characteristics of a data entry form and the back-end Windows CGI program for adding new records

● How to create front-end HTML forms and understand the design of Windows CGI programs for single and multitable data entry

- How to design front ends and back ends involving static and dynamic lookup tables

- Constraints and advantages of using one form for multiple table data entry

- Processing multiple table data entry requests submitted through a single input form

- Implementing transaction processing

SINGLE TABLE DATA ENTRY

The simplest form of Web-based data entry involves adding a new record to a single table. You create an HTML form containing input controls representing the table fields and feed that form to a CGI program, which then appends the user-entered data to the appropriate table. This lesson explains this process by showing how you can add a new sponsor record to the **tblSponsors** table of the calendar database through the Web interface.

Desirable Characteristics of a Data Entry Form

The first step in implementing the Web-based data entry process is to create a proper user interface for accepting the field values of the new record. The user interface, which is normally an HTML form, should have the following attributes:

- Provide an appropriate input control for each table field that a user can fill in.

- Label each input control to explain its purpose and the type of data values it expects.

- Supply default values wherever possible.

- Provide a clear distinction between required and optional fields.

Note that the database table being populated may contain additional fields that are system maintained. A good example of a system-maintained field is the **AutoNumber**-type **ID** field or a field that holds the creation date of a new record. These system-maintained fields generally should not be part of the user interface; if they are, then the user should not be able to edit them.

Overall, the layout of the user interface should be intuitive so that it helps project the field characteristics and any dependency relationship that may exist within the fields. For example, you may have a case where a value in Field B is expected only if Field A is given a specific value. In such a case, Field B is dependent on Field A and the data entry form should be laid out to reflect this dependency clearly. For example, you could display the input control for Field B under Field A with some indentation or add a border enclosing both the fields.

Characteristics of the Program Responsible for Adding a New Record

The back-end program, which will be receiving the data from the data entry user interface, needs to perform the following three tasks:

- Validate the input data.

- Generate the values for the system-maintained fields, wherever required.

- Open the database and add the new record to the destination table in a multiuser environment setting.

Validating Input Data

The data validation task has to do with ensuring that valid data has been received through the data entry form. This generally involves making the following checks:

- The data type of the incoming values should match the data type of their corresponding fields.

- The incoming values should meet all the validation rules specified for their corresponding fields.

- A nonempty value should be received for each required field that does not have a default value defined for it.

- Record-level validation rules (if any) should be met.

- Table-level validation rules (if any) should be met.

- Referential integrity and other database-level validation rules should be met.

Note that most of these validation rules and data integrity checks may already be part of the database design and enforced by the database engine itself. However, for faster processing, it is a good idea to have the back-end program perform as many checks as possible before even opening the database. Besides, this *precheck* gives your program more control on how to proceed if invalid data is received and detected before passing it on to the database engine.

The details of validation rules from field level up to database level are covered in Chapter 4, "Constructing a Relational Database: The Microsoft Access Way."

Handling System-Maintained Fields

The only system-maintained table fields that a Windows CGI program has to handle are the ones not automatically maintained by the database engine itself. For example, if the ID field of the destination table is an AutoNumber-type field, then the program need not worry about it. However, if the ID field is a Number field (for example, in case of the lookup tables), then the program has to generate a unique value for that field before it adds the new record.

Similarly, if there is a system-maintained field for the record creation date and its default value has been set to the Date() function as part of the table design, then it does not need any extra attention. However, if no default value has been preset, then the Windows CGI program has to determine the current date for this field.

Adding a New Record in a Multiuser Environment Setting

Once valid data for the user-maintained fields and the appropriate process for the system-maintained fields have been established, you can add the new record using the following steps:

1. Create a recordset representing the destination table with the optimistic-locking option enabled. (See Chapter 3, Lesson 6, for more information on optimistic locking schemes.)

2. Execute the AddNew method of that recordset.

3. Assign each user-maintained table field (referred through the recordset) to its corresponding value.

4. Assign each system-maintained table field whose value has to be determined by the program to its corresponding value.

5. Execute the Update method of the recordset.

6. If a primary key duplication error is generated, then recalculate the new primary key value based on the current information stored in the database and repeat step 5 for up to a specified number of times.

7. If the primary key duplication error cannot be resolved in the specified number of times or if another error is generated, then return an appropriate error message to the user.

8. If the Update method did not generate any error, then return a Success message to the user.

Note that the primary key duplication error will never occur if the table has an **AutoNumber**-type primary key field. However, if the primary key is a numeric **ID** field (as in the case of the lookup tables of the calendar database) and the program is designed to select the next available value for the **ID** field, then the possibility of generating an ID duplication error exists.

For example, if two copies of this program are executed simultaneously, then each copy will identify the same next available value. When saving the record with that next available value, the first copy will succeed but the second copy will fail. In that case, the second copy will have to recalculate the next available value and succeed the second time it tries to save the record.

Following the above user interface and CGI programming considerations, let's implement the Web-based data entry process for the **tblSponsors** table of the calendar database.

Creating the Sponsor Entry Form

The **tblSponsors** table contains the following fields:

```
SponsorID        (AutoNumber)
SponsorName      (100 char Text and required)
SponsorTypeID    (Byte-sized Number, required, and related to tblSponsorTypes_lkp)
WebAddress       (Hyperlink and optional)
UserName         (20 char Text and required)
Password         (20 char Text and optional)
```

The **SponsorID** field is a system-maintained field that is assigned at the time the new record is inserted in the sponsor table. Therefore we will not show this field on the data entry form. The rest of the fields are best represented using the following HTML input controls:

```
SponsorName      (Text box of size 50 and MaxLength 100)
SponsorTypeID    (Drop-down Selection List with options from tblSponsorTypes_lkp)
WebAddress       (Text box of size 50 and MaxLength 100)
UserName         (Text box of size 20 and MaxLength 20)
Password         (Password box of size 20 and MaxLength 20)
VerifyPassword   (Password box of size 20 and MaxLength 20)
```

Note that we have assigned two input controls named **Password** and **VerifyPassword** to handle the **Password** field. This will help catch any typing error that a user may make while supplying the value for the **Password** field.

To differentiate between the required and optional fields, we can boldface the labels for the required fields and give a suitable message indicating this distinction in the beginning of the form.

The option values of the **SponsorTypeID** selection list can be specified using the following format:

```
<option value="SponsorTypeID">SponsorTypeDescription/option>
```

This way, the destination Windows CGI program (**SPENTRY.EXE**) will receive the ID of the selected sponsor type while the browser displays the sponsor type descriptions in the selection list.

Building on this framework, you can use an HTML editor to design the new sponsor entry form as shown in Figure 11-1.

For this example, we will submit this form to the **SPENTRY.EXE** Windows CGI program residing in the **C:\WEBSITE\CGI-WIN\WDBIC\SPENTRY** directory by starting this form with the following **<FORM>** tag:

```
<form action="/cgi-win/wdbic/spentry/spentry.exe" method="POST">
```

A copy of this form is provided in the file named **SPENTRY.HTM** residing in the **C:\WEBSITE\HTDOCS\WDBIC\CHAP11\LESSON1** directory. At this point, we recommend that you review the contents of this file to fully understand the design of this form.

Running the SPENTRY.EXE Program

As mentioned, the **SPENTRY.EXE** program is the back-end program for handling the Web requests send through the sponsor entry form. This program resides in the **C:\WEBSITE\CGI-WIN\WDBIC\SPENTRY** directory; before we examine its construction, let's see how it works:

1. Start your Web server if it is not already running and enter the following URL in your Web browser:

   ```
   http://localhost/wdbic/chap11/lesson1/spentry.htm
   ```

   The browser displays the new sponsor entry form as shown in Figure 11-1.

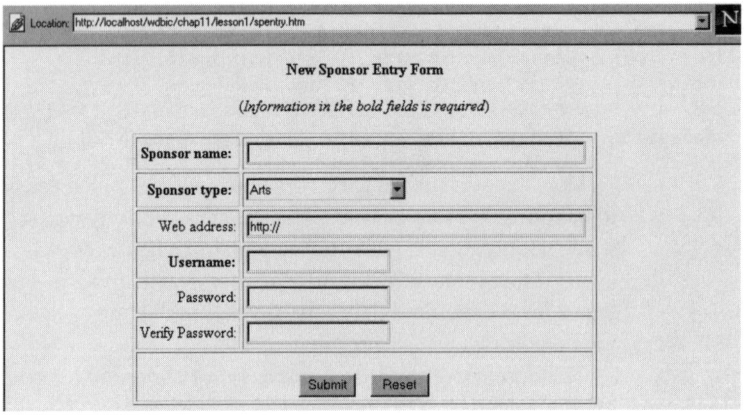

Figure 11-1
The new sponsor
entry form

2. Fill out this form as follows and then press the Submit button:

```
    Sponsor name: XYZ Corporation
    Sponsor type: Business
     Web address: http://www.xyzcorp.com
        Username: webmaster
        Password: zyx
 Verify Password: zyx
```

The SPENTRY.EXE program adds a new sponsor record with this data in the tblSponsors table of the CALENDAR.MDB database file residing in the C:\ WEBSITE\HTDOCS\WDBIC\CHAP11 directory and responds by returning the SponsorID assigned to this record, as shown in Figure 11-2.

3. Now open the tblSponsors table of the CALENDAR.MDB database file in Access.

You will see that it contains the record you just added.

At this point, you can perform some more test runs by submitting different entries through the sponsor entry form. Also see what happens if you submit the form without entering any value for one or more required fields.

Examining the Design of the
SPENTRY.EXE **Program**

The **SPENTRY.EXE** program follows the standard Windows CGI program format that you have been using so far. However, instead of declaring the variables within each procedure, the program is declaring most of the variables used in this program in the Declarations section of its **MYAPP.BAS** module, as shown in Listing 11-1.

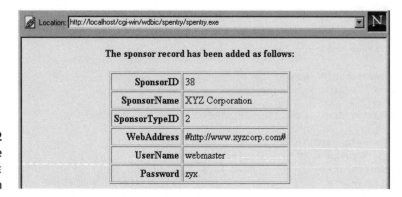

Figure 11-2
Response of the
SPENTRY.EXE
program

Listing 11-1 The Declarations section of the MYAPP.BAS module of the SPENTRY.EXE program

```
Option Explicit        'Force explicit declaration of all variables
'String Variable for each input control of the sponsor entry form
Dim SponsorName As String
Dim SponsorTypeID As String
Dim WebAddress As String
Dim UserName As String
Dim Password As String
Dim VerifyPassword As String

'Database related variables
Dim dbCalendar As Database    'Declare database variable
Dim rsSponsor As Recordset    'Delcare recordset variable
Dim dbName As String          'Path and name of the calendar database
Dim TableName As String       'Name of the table within the calendar database

'Error Handling variables
Dim ErrorMessage As String    'Error message to be returned
```

By declaring them in the Declarations section, the program gives these variables a module-level scope so they can be accessed by any procedure listed within the MYAPP.BAS module.

The CGI_Main *Procedure of the* SPENTRY.EXE *Program*

The CGI_Main procedure, which highlights the main steps of the SPENTRY.EXE program, is shown in Listing 11-2.

Listing 11-2 The CGI_Main procedure of the SPENTRY.EXE program

```
Sub CGI_Main()

  'Add Error Handler
  On Error GoTo Err_CGI_Main

  'Generate HTML header
  Send "Content-type: text/html"
  Send ""
  Send "<HTML><HEAD><TITLE>SPENTRY</TITLE></HEAD><BODY>"

  'The main steps
  ErrorMessage = ""      'Initially no error
  ReadFormData           'Read form data in the declared variables
  ValidateData           'Check for required fields and enforce validation rules
  ProcessData            'Perform any required data processing before saving data
  AddDataToDatabase      'Store data into the database
  GenerateResponse       'Send appropriate response

Exit_CGI_Main:
```

```
    'Send HTML footer and exit
    Send "</BODY></HTML>"
    Exit Sub

'Error Handling Section
Err_CGI_Main:
    HandleError              'Handle error gracefully
    Resume Exit_CGI_Main     'Return to the Exit_CGI_Main section

End Sub
```

As you can see, the `CGI_Main` procedure uses its own error-handling scheme by identifying the location of the error-handling section as its first step. Next, it outputs the HTML header string and initializes the `ErrorMessage` variable to an empty string. We will explain the role of this variable later in this lesson.

Next, the `CGI_Main` procedure calls the `ReadFormData` and other procedures to process the form request. If everything goes smoothly, the `CGI_Main` procedure outputs the HTML footer string and terminates. But if any of the procedure called by `CGI_Main` signals an error, the control passes to the `CGI_Main` procedure's error-handling section (labeled `Err_CGI_Main`), which calls the `HandleError` procedure (shown in Listing 11-3) to return the appropriate error message. The control is then returned to the Exit section to send the HTML footer string and terminate the procedure.

Listing 11-3 The `HandleError` procedure of the SPENTRY.EXE program

```
Public Sub HandleError()

    If ErrorMessage = "" Then
        Send Error$          'Send VB's error message
    Else
        Send ErrorMessage    'Send custom error message
    End If

End Sub
```

The `ReadFormData` *Procedure of the* SPENTRY.EXE *Program*

The `ReadFormData` procedure simply assigns each input field value received with the Web request to its corresponding VB variable as shown in Listing 11-4. This way, the other procedures can directly use these variables to access or manipulate these field values.

Listing 11-4 The `ReadFormData` procedure of the SPENTRY.EXE program

```
Public Sub ReadFormData()

    SponsorName = GetSmallField("SponsorName")
    SponsorTypeID = GetSmallField("SponsorTypeID")
```

continued on next page

continued from previous page

```
WebAddress = GetSmallField("WebAddress")
UserName = GetSmallField("UserName")
Password = GetSmallField("Password")
VerifyPassword = GetSmallField("VerifyPassword")

End Sub
```

The ValidateData *Procedure of the* SPENTRY.EXE *Program*

The design of the ValidateData procedure is shown in Listing 11-5.

Listing 11-5 The ValidateData procedure of the SPENTRY.EXE program

```
Public Sub ValidateData()
   'Handle Required Fields
   CheckRequiredField SponsorName, "sponsor name"
   CheckRequiredField SponsorTypeID, "sponsor type"
   CheckRequiredField UserName, "username"

  'Handle any other data validations
   If Password <> VerifyPassword Then
      ErrorMessage = "The password could not be verified."
      Error ERR_BAD_REQUEST
   End If

End Sub
```

The ValidateData procedure performs the required-field test by repeatedly calling the CheckRequiredField procedure (shown in Listing 11-6) for each required field, ensures that the incoming SponsorTypeID field is a byte value, and then verifies the password value.

Listing 11-6 The CheckRequiredField procedure of the SPENTRY.EXE program

```
Public Sub CheckRequiredField (FieldValue As String, FieldCaption As String)

   If FieldValue = "" Then   'Empty field
      ErrorMessage = "A value for the <B>" & FieldCaption & "</B> field must be speci-
fied."
      Error ERR_BAD_REQUEST
   End If

End Sub
```

Note that during the execution of the ValidateData procedure, an ERR_BAD_REQUEST error is generated anytime something wrong with the input data. The reason is listed in the ErrorMessage VB variable. The ERR_BAD_REQUEST is a global constant defined in the CGI32.BAS module.

The signaling of the error causes the flow control to go to the error-handling section of the CGI_Main procedure immediately, where the HandleError procedure (described later) takes over. Observe that when such a situation occurs, the `ProcessData` and remaining procedures are automatically bypassed and the program terminates without opening the calendar database.

The `ProcessData` *Procedure of the* `SPENTRY.EXE` *Program*

The `ProcessData` procedure takes care of any data preprocessing tasks that need to be performed before saving the new record. In general, this is where you look after the system-maintained fields. However, in this example, the `SponsorID` field is the only system-maintained field and, being an `AutoNumber` field, it does not need special attention. On the other hand, the `WebAddress` input field does require some manipulation.

First, note that the sponsor entry form supplies the string `"http://"` as the default value for this field. This helps ensure that the user does not miss the `http://` prefix when entering the URL for the Web address. But if the sponsor does not have any Web address then it is possible that this `http://` prefix may be the only value that is sent to the program (in case the user does not erase the default value). Second, the `WebAddress` field is defined as a `Hyperlink`-type field in the calendar database. This means that the address URL must be enclosed within two pound (#) signs (see Figure 11-2). All this is handled by the `ProcessData` procedure, whose design is given in Listing 11-7.

Listing 11-7 The `ProcessData` procedure of the `SPENTRY.EXE` program

```
Public Sub ProcessData()
   'Process the Web address field
   If WebAddress = "http://" Then
     'No web address specified
     WebAddress = ""
   Else
     'Insert the address portion within the pound (#)signs
     'as required by a Hyperlink-type field
     WebAddress = "#" & WebAddress & "#"
   End If
End Sub
```

The `AddDataToDatabase` *and* `GenerateResponse` *Procedures of the* `SPENTRY.EXE` *Program*

The `AddDataToDatabase` procedure, shown in Listing 11-8, follows the record insertion steps described earlier in this lesson.

Listing 11-8 The `AddDataToDatabase` procedure of the `SPENTRY.EXE` program

```
Public Sub AddDataToDatabase()

   dbName = "C:\WEBSITE\HTDOCS\WDBIC\CHAP11\CALENDAR.MDB"
   TableName = "tblSponsors"
```

continued on next page

continued from previous page

```
'Open the database
Set dbCalendar = DBEngine(0).OpenDatabase(dbName)
'Open a recordset from the table
'using the (default) optimistic locking scheme
Set rsSponsor = dbCalendar.OpenRecordset(TableName)
With rsSponsor
   'Start a new record
   .AddNew
   'Assign values to the fields of the new record
   !SponsorName = SponsorName
   !SponsorTypeID = CByte(SponsorTypeID)
   !WebAddress = EmptyToNull(WebAddress)
   !UserName = UserName
   !Password = EmptyToNull(Password)
   'Save the new record
   .Update
   'Make the new record as the current record
   .Bookmark = .LastModified
End With

End Sub
```

The **AddDataToDatabase** procedure first creates the **rsSponsor** recordset based on the **tblSponsors** table. The optimistic locking scheme is used by default for this recordset, so no extra options need to be listed when you are opening this recordset. Next, this procedure applies the **With** operator to the **rsSponsor Recordset** object. This operator allows you to execute a series of statements for this object without requalifying the name of the object with each statement. For example, the **.AddNew** statement within the **With** block is equivalent to the **rsSponsor.AddNew** statement.

The **AddNew** method reserves temporary space for adding a new record. Because the optimistic locking scheme is being used, this method will not fail even if other records are being added to the sponsor table simultaneously. After executing the **AddNew** method, the **AddDataToDatabase** procedure sets the recordset fields to their appropriate values.

One thing to remember is that even though the **WebAddress** and **Password** fields of the sponsor table are not set as required fields, they cannot accept an empty string. This is because we set their **Allow Zero Length String** property to **No** when defining these fields in Chapter 4, Lesson 3. So before assigning any values to these fields, **AddDataToDatabase** ensures that an empty string is converted to a **Null** value through the help of the **EmptyToNull** function shown in Listing 11-9.

Listing 11-9 The EmptyToNull function of the SPENTRY.EXE program

```
Public Function EmptyToNull(Value As String)
   'Returns Null if input argument is an empty string
   EmptyToNull = IIf(Value = "", Null, Value)

End Function
```

Once all the fields of the new sponsor record have been assigned, the `AddDataToDatabase` procedure executes the recordset's `Update` method to save the record. This is when a lock is placed on the `tblSponsors` table for a very brief moment and the possibility of encountering a locking conflict becomes extremely remote, which is why we do not need to put extra code for handling lock conflicts in the program.

The successful completion of the `Update` method is an indication that the new record has been saved in the underlying sponsor table with the automatically assigned `SponsorID` value. However, this new record does not automatically become the current record of the `rsSponsor` recordset. If you want to determine the `SponsorID` value that was assigned to this new record, you must first make this record the current record. This can be done by setting the recordset's `Bookmark` property to the bookmark of the last modified record, which can be retrieved through the `LastModified` property of that recordset.

Once the new record is made the current record, the `GenerateResponse` procedure outputs the field names and field values of that record, as shown in Listing 11-10.

Listing 11-10 The `GenerateResponse` function of the `SPENTRY.EXE` program

```
Public Sub GenerateResponse()
  Dim i As Long   'Index Variable

  Send "<CENTER>"
  Send "<B>The sponsor record has been added as follows:</B><P>"
  Send "<TABLE BORDER=1 CELLPADDING=3>"
  'List fields and their values for the added record
  For i = 0 To rsSponsor.Fields.Count - 1
    Send "<TR>"
    Send "<TH ALIGN=RIGHT>" & rsSponsor(i).name & "</TH>"
    Send "<TD>" & IIf(IsNull(rsSponsor(i)), "Null", rsSponsor(i)) & "</TD>"
    Send "</TR>"
  Next
  Send "</TABLE>"
  Send "</CENTER>"

End Sub
```

Lesson Summary

This lesson explained Web-based data entry in its simplest form by showing how to add a new record to a single database table. The process involves designing a user interface (an HTML form) for accepting the field values of the new record and creating a back-end Windows CGI program that validates the input data and then adds this record to the destination table assuming a multiuser environment setting. The desirable characteristics of the user interface and the back-end program were explained in detail. The whole process was demonstrated by describing the design of a new sponsor entry form and its corresponding back-end Windows CGI program called `SPENTRY.EXE` that either adds a new sponsor record to the `tblSponsors` table or returns an appropriate error message.

All the variables of the **SPENTRY.EXE** program were given module-level scope by declaring them in the Declarations section of the **MYAPP.BAS** module. The **CGI_Main** procedure uses its own error-handling mechanism and calls the **ReadFormData** and other procedures to process the form request. All the procedures used by this program were explained and their listings were provided in this lesson. The optimistic locking option used for adding the new record ensures that the record insertion process does not fail even if other records are being added to the sponsor table simultaneously.

In the next lesson, we will address some more locking and multiuser issues when we focus on lookup tables and the role these tables play in the development of a Web database application.

QUIZ 1

1. What are the features of a good HTML form for Web-based data entry?
   a. Labeled input controls for each table field to be filled in by the user
   b. Allowing users to edit system-maintained fields
   c. Providing default values wherever possible
   d. Economizing the use of page space

2. How does the **SPENTRY.EXE** program respond if you submit the sponsor entry form in its default state?
   a. It appends an empty record to the sponsor table.
   b. The program returns a message stating that a value for the sponsor name field must be specified.
   c. The program returns a message stating that a value for all required fields must be specified.
   d. None of the above.

3. How does the **SPENTRY.EXE** program respond if you submit a completed sponsor entry form twice without modifications?
   a. The program appends the same record twice to the **tblSponsors** table.
   b. The program appends the entered record the first time and ignores the second submission.
   c. The program appends the entered record the first time and generates a run-time error the second time.
   d. The program does not append any record and generates a run-time error each time.

4. Assuming that **Password** is a required field, how would you incorporate this change?
   a. Make the **Password** field boldfaced in the new sponsor entry form.
   b. Introduce **Password** as a **Checkrequired** field in the **ValidateData** procedure of the **SPONSOR.EXE** program.

    c. Remove the `VerifyPassword` label and input box from the new sponsor entry form.

    d. All of the above.

5. Why does the `SPENTRY.EXE` program pass the `WebAddress` and `Password` fields through the `EmptyToNull` function before assigning it to the appropriate table fields?

    a. `WebAddress` and `Password` are required fields.

    b. `WebAddress` and `Password` are not required fields.

    c. The `Allow Zero Length` property of these fields is set to `Yes`.

    d. The `Allow Zero Length` property of these fields is set to `No`.

Complexity: Easy

1. Design an HTML form named `CONTACTENTRY.HTM` that contains input controls representing the fields of the `tblSponsorsContacts` table. The form should submit its data to the `CONTACTENTRY.EXE` program residing in the `C:\WEBSITE\CGI-WIN\WDBIC\CONTACTENTRY` directory. Save this form in the `C:\WEBSITE\HTDOCS\WDBIC\CHAP11\LESSON1` directory. For this exercise, assume that the user will enter the `SponsorID` value of the related sponsor in a text control.

Complexity: Moderate

2. Design a Windows CGI program named `CONTACTENTRY.EXE` in the `C:\WEBSITE\CGI-WIN\WDBIC\CONTACTENTRY` directory. This program will accept valid sponsor contact information submitted through the `CONTACTENTRY.HTM` form (designed in exercise 1) and save that information in the `tblSponsorsContacts` table of the `CALENDAR.MDB` database residing in the `C:\WEBSITE\HTDOCS\WDBIC\CHAP11` directory.

DEVELOPING FRONT ENDS INVOLVING LOOKUP VALUES

As you have seen so far, the sole purpose of a lookup table in a database is to help control the data values that are stored in a particular field of another database table. For example, the `tblSponsorTypes_lkp` table is a lookup table that limits what is added to the **SponsorTypeID** field of the **tblSponsors** table. Depending on how a lookup table is maintained, most lookup tables can be classified under one of the following two categories:

● Static lookup tables

● Dynamic lookup tables

A *static lookup table* is a lookup table that contains a predefined list of lookup values. Web users are not supposed to update or populate this table. Only database administrators can change its contents. A *dynamic lookup table,* on the other hand, is a lookup table that can accept new (but unique) lookup values directly from Web users as part of the Web-based data entry process. In some cases, users might be permitted to edit or delete the existing values in dynamic lookup tables.

Classifying a lookup table as static or dynamic can have a considerable effect on the complexity and performance of your Web application. This lesson explains the nature of this effect when you are developing the front end of a Web application. In the next lesson, we will look into how the lookup table classification affects the back-end development and what extra steps your CGI program needs to take to support dynamic lookup tables.

Static Lookup Tables

Static lookup tables present two big advantages when developing a Web database application:

● They promote the use of HTML forms that can be generated statically.

● They are extremely easy to incorporate within a Web application.

The sponsor data entry process described in Lesson 1 illustrates the above advantages if we classify the **tblSponsorTypes_lkp** table as a static lookup table. First, the sponsor entry form that we used as the front end for this process needs to be generated only once and can be stored as a static HTML file. Second, the **SPENTRY.EXE** program does not have to worry about handling new sponsor types, which, as you will see in Lesson 3, can require a lot of coding effort.

Although static lookup tables make implementation simple, they do so with a compromise in flexibility. What if none of the choices defined in a static lookup table matches exactly what a user is looking for? In that case, the only option a user has is to settle for the closest choice, which may cause ambiguity or even change the whole meaning of what the user wants to say. One thing you can do to avoid this problem is to include Other or None as a last choice in your lookup tables. This gives users who are not comfortable using any of your predefined choices an alternative option.

Dynamic Lookup Tables

There are times when it is hard to generate the values of a lookup table beforehand. It may not be possible to determine a comprehensive set of predefined values or the set of values the lookup table can take may be too large. The city lookup table (`tblLocationsCities_Lkp`) of the calendar database is a good example of this case. You can initially populate this table with a select group of cities, but you will have to give users the ability to add new cities as the need arises. The concept of selecting the closest city or the "other" city (that is generally applied when using static lookup tables) would not work well in this case.

Handling a dynamic lookup table in a Web application requires two things:

● That any HTML form containing the lookup values from this table be generated on the fly and provide an option for adding a new value

● That the back-end CGI program receiving data from that form be able to detect and add new lookup values to this table before adding any other related records using that new value

These requirements can best be demonstrated using the example of the `LOCATIONENTRY.EXE` Windows CGI program, which allows users to add a new location record in the `tblLocations` table of the calendar database. In addition, it lets users enter a new city name if the new location does not fall in any of the existing cities.

Running the `LOCATIONENTRY.EXE` Program

The `LOCATIONENTRY.EXE` Windows CGI program (residing in the `C:\WEBSITE\CGI-WIN\WDBIC\LOCATIONENTRY` directory) performs two tasks, depending on the method used to request this program:

● It returns a (dynamically generated) location entry form on receiving a GET request. This form contains the most current list of existing cities and provides the user with an option to specify a new city.

● It validates and adds the new location record on receiving a POST request. If a new city is specified in that location, then the program also inserts that city name into the city lookup table.

Let's go through a test run of this program:

1. Start the Web server if it is not already running.

2. Enter the following URL from the Web browser:

   `http://localhost/cgi-win/wdbic/locationentry/locationentry.exe`

   The `LOCATIONENTRY.EXE` program returns the location entry form as shown in Figure 11-3. If you open the selection lists, you will see that they are populated with the currently available lookup values for the CityID, StateID, and CountryID fields of the location table. You will also notice that the last value of the city selection list is listed as (New City).

3. For this test run, fill out this form as follows and then press the Submit button.

```
Location name: Towerbridge Center
Street: 123 XYZ Street
City: (New City)
New City Name: Towerbridge
State: Iowa
Country: USA
Postal Code: 12345-7891
```

The LOCATIONENTRY.EXE program adds the new city name to the tblLocationCities_Lkp table, then adds this new location record to the tblLocations table, and finally returns the complete information of the added location record, as shown in Figure 11-4.

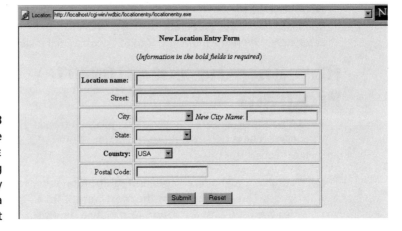

Figure 11-3
The
LOCATIONENTRY.EXE
program returning
the location entry
form on receiving a
GET request

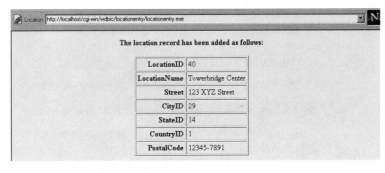

Figure 11-4
Response of the
LOCATIONENTRY.EXE
program on
receiving a POST
request

4. Open the `tblLocationsCities_Lkp` table and the `tblLocations` table of the `CALENDAR.MDB` file residing in the `c:\WEBSITE\HTDOCS\WDBIC\CHAP11` directory to verify the presence of the new city record and the new location record.

5. Resubmit the GET request (step 2) to the `LOCATIONENTRY.EXE` program and examine the values of the city selection list in the location entry form returned by the program.

   You will notice that the new city appears as one of the values of this selection list.

At this point, we suggest that you perform some more test runs of this program.

Examining How the `LOCATIONENTRY.EXE` Program Generates the Location Entry Form

The location entry form that the `LOCATIONENTRY.EXE` program generates is a regular HTML-based form except that the city values in its city selection list can change dynamically. In other words, the HTML text that comes before the first city option and the HTML text that comes after the last city option always stay the same. We made use of this fact when constructing the `LOCATIONENTRY.EXE` program.

First, we used an HTML editor to create an HTML file named `LOCATIONENTRY.HTM`, which, when displayed in the browser, produced the data entry form that looks similar to the one shown in Figure 11-3. The table row containing the city selection list control of this form was created as follows:

```
<td align="right">City:</td>
<td valign="top"><select name="CityID" size="1">
    <option value=""></option>
    <option value="CityID_1">CityName_1</option>
    <option value="CityID_2">CityName_2</option>
            ...
    <option value="CityID_n">CityName_n</option>
    <option value="New">(New City)</option>
</select>
```

Notice that the first city option is an empty string and the last city option allows users to indicate that they are supplying a new city name. The empty string option is needed because `CityID` is not a required field in the location table of the calendar database.

After creating this static entry form, we separated its HTML file into three separate files:

● `LOCATIONENTRY_1.HTM`, which contains all the HTML text up to the first (blank) option.

● `LOCATIONENTRY_2.HTM`, which contains all the option values representing `City_1` through `City_n`. Note that this file represents the dynamic section of the location entry form.

● LOCATIONENTRY_3.HTM, which starts from the last city option and holds the rest of the HTML text.

Now the LOCATIONENTRY.EXE program can send the location entry form by carrying out the following step sequence:

1. Send the contents of the LOCATIONENTRY_1.HTM file without modifications.

2. Dynamically generate and send the city option values based on the city lookup table of the calendar database in a format similar to the format of the LOCATIONENTRY_2.HTM file.

3. Send the contents of the LOCATIONENTRY_3.HTM file without modifications.

Using this file-based approach to generate an HTML form dynamically helps in two ways. First, you do not need to hard-code the HTML text that never changes. Second, you have a lot of flexibility to modify the layout of the form without having to modify the program. To see how we have implemented this approach in the LOCATIONENTRY.EXE program, let's start by looking at this program's CGI_Main procedure, which is shown in Listing 11-1.

Listing 11-11 The CGI_Main procedure of the LOCATIONENTRY.EXE program

```
Sub CGI_Main()

   'Add Error Handler
   On Error GoTo Err_CGI_Main

   If UCase$(CGI_RequestMethod) = "GET" Then
      SendLocationEntryForm
      Exit Sub
   End If

   'Generate HTML header
   Send "Content-type: text/html"
   Send ""
   Send "<HTML><HEAD><TITLE>Location Entry</TITLE></HEAD><BODY>"

   'The main steps
   ErrorMessage = ""        'Initially no error
   ReadFormData             'Read form data in the declared variables
   ValidateData             'Check for required fields and enforce validation rules
   ProcessData              'Perform any required data processing before saving data
   AddDataToDatabase        'Store data into the database
   GenerateResponse         'Send appropriate response

Exit_CGI_Main:
   'Send HTML footer and exit
```

```
Send "</BODY></HTML>"
Exit Sub

'Error Handling Section
Err_CGI_Main:
   HandleError            'Handle error gracefully
   Resume Exit_CGI_Main   'Return to the Exit_CGI_Main section

End Sub
```

Structurally, this procedure is designed similar to the `CGI_Main` procedure of the **SPENTRY.EXE** program discussed in Lesson 1. The only extra code that was added is in the beginning, where this procedure checks to see if the incoming request was made using the `GET` method. If that check holds true, then the procedure calls the `SendLocationEntryForm` procedure and terminates.

The `SendLocationEntryForm` procedure, which closely follows the steps outlined above, is shown in Listing 11-12.

Listing 11-12 The `SendLocationEntryForm` procedure of the `LOCATIONENTRY.EXE` program

```
Public Sub SendLocationEntryForm()

   'Begin response indicating that an html document is being returned
   Send "Content-type: text/html"
   Send ""
   'Send the HTML text that comes before the first city option
   SendFile "\WEBSITE\HTDOCS\WDBIC\CHAP11\LESSON2\LOCATIONENTRY_1.HTM"
   'Send the list of cities as HTML option tags
   OpenCalendarDatabase
   Set rsCity = dbCalendar.OpenRecordset("qryLocationsCites_lkp")
   Do Until rsCity.EOF
      Send "<option value=""" & rsCity!ID & """>" & rsCity![Description] & "</option>"
      rsCity.MoveNext
   Loop
   'Send the HTML text that comes after the last city option
   SendFile "\WEBSITE\HTDOCS\WDBIC\CHAP11\LESSON2\LOCATIONENTRY_3.HTM"

End Sub
```

The **qryLocationsCites_lkp** query used by this procedure returns city records sorted alphabetically by city name. The **OpenCalendarDatabase** procedure opens the calendar database if it is not already open. This "not already open" check is important when multiple procedures of the program may need to open the same database and you want them to share the same database object. You will see an evidence of this in the next lesson.

The **SendFile** procedure simply appends the contents of a specified file to the program's response. The design of the **OpenCalendarDatabase** procedure and the **SendFile** procedure is shown in Listing 11-13.

Listing 11-13 The `OpenCalendarDatabase` and `SendFile` procedures of the `LOCATIONENTRY.EXE` program

```
Public Sub OpenCalendarDatabase()

   Dim TempName As String     'Temporary variable

   dbName = "C:\WEBSITE\HTDOCS\WDBIC\CHAP11\CALENDAR.MDB"
   On Error Resume Next
   'See if database is open by accessing its name property
   TempName = dbCalendar.name
   If Err <> 0 Then   'Database is not open
      'So open it
      Set dbCalendar = DBEngine(0).OpenDatabase(dbName)
   End If

End Sub

Public Sub SendFile(FilePathAndName)
   Dim FN As Integer          'File handle
   Dim FileContent As String  'File contents

   'Open file
   FN = FreeFile
   Open FilePathAndName For Binary Access Read As #FN
   FileContent = String$(LOF(FN), " ")  'Allocate storage
   Get #FN, , FileContent               'Read file contents
   Close #FN                            'Close File Handle
   Send FileContent

End Sub
```

At this point, we recommend that you go through the contents of the `LOCATIONENTRY_1.HTM` and `LOCATIONENTRY_3.HTM` files and verify that everything ties together.

Lesson Summary

This lesson explained how the choice of a static or dynamic lookup table affects the design of a Web database application. Static lookup tables can be handled through statically generated front-end HTML forms and are easy to incorporate within the Web application. However, certain situations warrant that a lookup table be maintained dynamically. This affects the Web application's performance and design complexity, because every HTML form displaying the values of that dynamic lookup table must be generated on the fly. Besides, the back-end Windows CGI program must provide complete support for adding new lookup values to this table as needed.

This lesson demonstrated the functionality of the `LOCATIONENTRY.EXE` program, which allows users to select an existing city or add a new city while adding a new location to the `tblLocations` table of the calendar database. The `LOCATIONENTRY.EXE` program examines the method of the Web request to determine whether a user wants a new location entry form or is submitting one. The approach this program uses to generate the location entry form depends on separating the static and dynamic portions of the HTML text and was explained in detail. In the next lesson, we will examine the other procedures of this program to see how it handles new city values that a user may supply with the new location information.

QUIZ 2

1. What are the advantages of using static lookup tables within a Web application?
   a. They provide maximum flexibility.
   b. The back-end CGI programs generally do not require extra coding effort to handle these lookup tables.
   c. They allow Web users to add new but unique lookup values.
   d. The front-end HTML forms supporting these lookup tables do not need to be generated on the fly.

2. When should you use a dynamic lookup table?
   a. When you cannot determine beforehand all the lookup values that may be needed.
   b. When you want to improve your Web application's performance.
   c. When the lookup table represents discrete entities and it is not possible to generalize these entities using a small subset of values.
   d. It does not really matter whether you use static or dynamic lookup tables.

3. What happens if you request the location entry form from the `LOCATIONENTRY.EXE` program, specify a new location record with a new city name and submit this form, and then use the Back button of your browser?
   a. The browser displays the empty location entry form with the original city selection list.
   b. The browser displays the filled-out location entry form with the original city selection list.
   c. The browser displays the empty location entry form with the new city added to the city selection list.
   d. The browser displays the filled-out location entry form with the new city added to the city selection list.

4. Which files would you modify to change the layout of the location entry form returned by the `LOCATIONENTRY.EXE` program?
   a. `LOCATIONENTRY.HTM`
   b. `LOCATIONENTRY_1.HTM`
   c. `LOCATIONENTRY_2.HTM`
   d. `LOCATIONENTRY_3.HTM`

5. Why does the `CityID` selection list have a blank option?
   a. The `CityID` is a required field in the city lookup table of the calendar database.
   b. The `CityID` is not a required field in the location table of the calendar database.
   c. All selection lists are required to have a blank option.
   d. None of the above.

EXERCISE 2

Complexity: Easy

1. List the modifications that you would make to the location data entry process to incorporate the following features:

   a. **All users to select** `Other` **as a choice for the state and country selection list**

   b. **Force users to select an existing city or specify a new city**

   (Hint: You can incorporate these features without changing the `LOCATIONENTRY.EXE` program.)

Complexity: Moderate

2. Create a Windows CGI program named `LOCATIONENTRY1.EXE` in the `C:\WEBSITE\CGI-WIN\WDBIC\LOCATIONENTRY1` directory that generates the location entry form assuming that both city and state lookup tables are to be dynamically maintained.

LESSON 3

MAINTAINING DYNAMIC LOOKUP TABLES

The previous lesson showed how the front end is affected if you incorporate dynamic lookup tables in your Web application. The HTML form displaying the values from a dynamic lookup table has to be generated dynamically so that the list of these values stays current. Furthermore, if the form is used for data entry, then it must provide an option for specifying a new lookup value. These requirements were explained through the example of the location entry form; we described the approach taken by the `LOCATIONENTRY.EXE` program to create this form.

Besides acting as a form generator, the `LOCATIONENTRY.EXE` program also plays the role of the form recepient. It determines which role to play for its current request by inspecting the method used to send that request. The `GET` method causes it to send the location entry form, whereas the POST method puts it into the form-processing mode, in which it not only handles the new location data but also maintains the city lookup table. In this lesson, we shall examine what issues this program has to address to make all this work and then examine its design to see how it deals with those issues.

Issues Involved with Handling and Maintaining Dynamic Lookup Tables

If you review the CGI_Main procedure of the LOCATIONENTRY.EXE program presented in Listing 11-1, you can see that this program follows the standard data input and data validation issues (discussed in Lesson 1) by calling the ReadFormData and ValidateData procedures, which are shown in Listing 11-14.

Listing 11-14 The ReadFormData and ValidateData procedures of the LOCATIONENTRY.EXE program

```
Public Sub ReadFormData()

  LocationName = GetSmallField("LocationName")
  Street = GetSmallField("Street")
  CityID = GetSmallField("CityID")
  NewCityName = GetSmallField("NewCityName")
  StateID = GetSmallField("StateID")
  CountryID = GetSmallField("CountryID")
  PostalCode = GetSmallField("PostalCode")

End Sub

Public Sub ValidateData()
  'Handle Required Fields
  CheckRequiredField LocationName, "location name"
  If CityID = "New" Then
    CheckRequiredField NewCityName, "new city name"
  End If
  CheckRequiredField CountryID, "country"

End Sub
```

However, due to the possibility of a user supplying a new city value instead of selecting an existing one from the city selection list, the LOCATIONENTRY.EXE program now has to deal with the following additional issues:

● The new city value has to be added to the city lookup table before adding the new location record to the location table to stay within the referential integrity constraint that exists between the two tables.

● The ID field (primary key) of the city lookup table is not an AutoNumber-type field and the program has to determine a new and unique value for it for every new city it adds to the city lookup table.

● The user can specify a new city value that may already exist in the city selection list.

● Multiple users may concurrently send new city values and some of those values may be the same.

On receiving a new city value in the incoming POST request, LOCATIONENTRY.EXE uses the following approach to handle the above issues:

1. Check if the new city value already exists in the city lookup table. If it does, then determine the ID already assigned to this city and set the cityID of the new location record to that ID. Then go directly to step 6.

2. If the new city does not exist in the city lookup table, then determine the maximum value of the cityID field in that table.

3. Set the ID of the new city to one more than that maximum value and try to add the new city record in the city lookup table.

4. If an error occurs while adding the record, then some other new city (supplied by a concurrent user) must have just received this ID. In that case, wait a random amount of time and start over from step 1. Repeat this error detection and retry process up to a set number of times, and if you don't have success, then return an error message to the user and have the user try again some other time.

5. If no error occurs in step 3, then set the cityID of the location record to this new ID value.

6. Save the new location record with the cityID of the new city determined from the previous steps.

Let us now examine how the LOCATIONENTRY.EXE program implements these steps.

Examining the Section of the LOCATIONENTRY.EXE Program Responsible for Handling the POST Request

Refer to the CGI_Main procedure shown in Listing 11-1. Once the LOCATIONENTRY.EXE program reads the data that came with the incoming POSTrequest (the ReadFormData procedure) and ensures that all the required values are present (the ValidateData procedure), it calls the ProcessData procedure. The objective of the ProcessData procedure is to determine the correct value to be used for the

CityID field (of the location record) depending on whether the requesting user select-ed an existing city or specified a new one. To achieve this objective, the ProcessData procedure calls another procedure named ProcessLookupValue with the appropriate arguments, as shown in Listing 11-15.

Listing 11-15 The ProcessData procedure of the LOCATIONENTRY.EXE program

```
Public Sub ProcessData()

  'Determine the CityID associated with the city selected or specifies by the user
  ProcessLookupValue CityID, "tblLocationsCities_lkp", NewCityName

End Sub
```

The first argument passed to ProcessLookupValue is the CityID variable, which currently contains the value selected in the city selection list of the location entry form (thanks to the ReadFormData procedure). If the user selects the (first) blank option, then the value of the CityID variable will be an empty string. If the user selects the (New City) option, then this variable will have the value New; in every other case, this vari-able will hold the ID of the selected city.

The second argument passed to the ProcessLookupValue is the name of the city lookup table itself; the third argument is the name of the new city specified by the request-ing user (an empty string if none is specified).

The ProcessLookupValue *Procedure and the* GetID *Function of the* LOCATIONENTRY.EXE *Program*

The ProcessLookupValue procedure is a general purpose procedure designed to handle and maintain dynamic lookup tables. The design of this procedure is shown in Listing 11-16.

Listing 11-16 The ProcessLookupValue procedure of the LOCATIONENTRY.EXE program

```
Public Sub ProcessLookupValue(IDVariable As String, LookupTable As String, NewValue As
String)

'This procedure handles and maintains the specified lookup table.
'It accepts a variable named IDVariable and gets into action only
'if a value of "New" was passed to this procedure through this
'variable. The "New" value of IDVariable indicates that the value
'stored in the NewValue (third) argument has to be added to the
'lookup table. For that, it repeatedly calls the services of GetID
'function until either the record with the new value gets saved
'successfully or max-try limit (indicated by MAXTRIES constant) is
'reached.
```

continued on next page

continued from previous page

```
Dim i As Long
Dim ReturnError As Integer
Dim ReturnErrorMsg As String

Const MAXTRIES = 5
Const MAXLOOPCOUNT = 50

If IDVariable = "New" Then
  On Error Resume Next
  'Get ID for the new value
  For i = 1 To MAXTRIES
    Err = 0
    IDVariable = GetID(LookupTable, NewValue)
    If Err = 0 Then Exit For
    'Wait a random amount of time (max of 50 loop iterations)
    WaitRandom MAXLOOPCOUNT
    'Now, try getting the ID again (up to 5 times max)
  Next
  'Check if the ID determination process was successful by
  'testing if loop was terminated prematurely
  If i <= MAXTRIES Then Exit Sub  'If successful, then exit

  'Otherwise;
  'Get the error information that existed at loop termination
  ReturnError = Err
  ReturnErrorMsg = Error$
  'Set the current error handler to the calling procedure's error handler
  On Error GoTo 0
  'Return the error message
  ErrorMessage = "Unable to add the new city into the city table. " &
ReturnErrorMsg
  Error ReturnError
End If

End Sub
```

As you can see, this procedure does not do anything if it receives any value other than New in the CityID variable (passed as the IDVariable argument). In other words, the ProcessLookupValue procedure assumes that the CityID variable already contains the correct ID and leaves it alone. On the other hand, if the CityID variable is set to New, then this procedure overwrites that value with the ID that it assigns to the new city by calling the GetID function.

The design of the GetID function is shown in Listing 11-17.

Listing 11-17 The GetID function of the LOCATIONENTRY.EXE program

```
Public Function GetID(TableName As String, NewValue As String) As String

  Dim rs As Recordset      'Recordset based on the specified lookup table
  Dim NextID As Variant    'Next available ID

  OpenCalendarDatabase     'Open database if not already open
```

```
'Open the dynaset-type recordset representing the lookup table
Set rs = dbCalendar.OpenRecordset(TableName, dbOpenDynaset)
If Not rs.EOF Then        'If the lookup table already has some records
   'then check if the new value already exists
   rs.FindFirst "Description = '" & ReplaceString(NewValue, "'", "''") & "'"
   If Not rs.NoMatch Then        'If matching record found
      GetID = CStr(rs![ID])      'then return ID of that record
      Exit Function              'and exit immediately
   End If
   rs.MoveLast                   'Otherwise goto the last record
   NextID = rs![ID] + 1          'and add 1 to its ID to get next ID
Else
   'Lookup table does not have any records so start with 1
   NextID = 1
End If
'Now add the new record and return the new ID
rs.AddNew
rs!ID = NextID
rs!Description = NewValue
rs.Update
GetID = CStr(NextID)

End Function
```

The **GetID** function creates a dynaset-type recordset representing the city lookup table. If the recordset is not empty, then the function uses the **FindFirst** method of that recordset to search for an existing city record with the same city name.

The **FindFirst** method, which is available only for **dynaset**-type and **snapshot**-type recordsets, accepts any valid SQL criteria string as its argument and sets the current record pointer position to the first record that meets the specified criteria. In this case, the criteria expression involves searching the **NewValue** in the **Description** field of the recordset. The **NewValue** is passed through the **ReplaceString** function to handle the possibility of any single quotes in that **NewValue** itself. (See Chapter 10, Lesson 6, for more information about handling single quotes in a criteria value.)

The success or failure of the **FindFirst** method is indicated by the recordset's **NoMatch** property. This is why the **GetID** function checks to see if this property is returning a **False** value, in which case the function simply returns the ID of the found city record (after converting it to a string value) and terminates.

If the **FindFirst** method does not find any existing record, then the **GetID** function gets the ID value of the last city record, which also represents the highest number used by the ID field in the city lookup table. It then adds 1 to this maximum value to establish the ID of the new city value.

If the recordset was empty to start with, then the **GetID** function sets the ID of the new city to 1.

Once the ID of the new city has been established, the **GetID** function proceeds to add the record with this ID and the new city value into the city lookup table. This is where the possibility of a primary key can occur if another new city record with the same ID value was added to the city lookup table *after* the **GetID** function created the city recordset.

Note that the new record does not automatically become a part of this recordset. To include that record in this recordset, you would have to execute the recordset's **Requery** method or recreate the recordset. We took the latter approach and simply returned the error to the calling **ProcessLookupValue** procedure, which, on detecting the error, called the **GetID** function hoping that this time the function would succeed.

The **ProcessLookupValue** procedure waits a random length of time after each try by calling the **WaitRandom** procedure (shown in Listing 11-18) and eventually gives up after consistently receiving error signals from the **GetID** function. This ensures that the user always gets some response (even if it is an error message) within a reasonable length of time.

Listing 11-18 The WaitRandom procedure of the LOCATIONENTRY.EXE program

```
Public Sub WaitRandom(MaxIterations As Integer)

  Dim i As Integer

  Randomize    'Initialize the seed for random number generation
  For i = 0 To MaxIterations * Rnd    'Loop random number of times
    DoEvents 'Yield control to the operating system
  Next

End Sub
```

The random wait helps avoid the possibility of deadlock that might occur due to multiple concurrent updates.

Finally, once the **ProcessData** procedure is over and the correct **CityID** value has been determined, the **CGI_Main** procedure calls the **AddDataToDatabase** procedure to add the new location record to the location table and then returns complete information on how the record was added by calling the **GenerateResponse** procedure. These procedures are designed similar to the **AddDataToDatabase** and **GenerateResponse** procedures of the **SPENTRY.EXE** program discussed in Lesson 1.

Lesson Summary

This lesson continued the examination of the **LOCATIONENTRY.EXE** program (introduced in the previous lesson) and presented how it handled the data entry process involving the dynamic city lookup table.

Upon receiving the new city value in the incoming **POST** request, the **LOCATIONENTRY.EXE** program, using the **ProcessData** and **ProcessLookupValue** procedures, first confirms that the value received does not already exist in the city lookup table. If it does, the ID of the matching city is set as the incoming **CityID** field. If the new city does not match any of the existing lookup values, it is added to the city lookup table after assigning it the next available ID.

In a multiuser environment, the possibility of two or more new cities being added at the same time using the same value for the next available ID can easily occur. This would cause a primary key duplication error in some of those programs. The **LOCATIONENTRY.EXE** program handles such errors by waiting a random amount of time and then recalculating the next available ID for the new city it is trying to add. This retry process is carried out a fixed number of times and if the error still is not resolved, the program returns an error message to the user.

The simultaneous data entry in a dynamic lookup table and another related table is just one example of how you can use one form to accept information stored in multiple tables. In the next lesson we shall examine some more issues involved with multiple table data entry using one form.

1. What critical issues, apart from data input and data validation, does the
   LOCATIONENTRY.EXE program have to address for successfully processing the
   form data?
   a. The program has to ensure that the referential integrity constraints between
      the city lookup table and the location table are not violated.
   b. The program has to ensure that users always select an existing city.
   c. The program has to generate a unique ID number for each new city entered.
   d. The program has to resolve locking errors that may occur in a multiuser envi-
      ronment.

2. What happens if a user enters a city that is already listed in the city lookup table
   as a new city?
   a. The city is assigned a new city ID.
   b. The city entered is assigned the ID value of the matching city from the city
      lookup table.
   c. The program generates an error message asking the user to select the appro-
      priate city from existing lookup values.
   d. The program assigns a **Null** value to the **CityID** field of the location record
      being saved.

3. Which city will the **LCOATIONENTRY.EXE** program use when saving the location
   record if you select an existing city from the city selection list and specify a new
   city in the New City Name text box?
   a. The city selected from the selection list.
   b. The new city specified in the New City Name text box.
   c. The program will return an error indicating that there is ambiguity in the
      input data.
   d. The program will randomly select among the two.

4. What happens when the **GetID** function applies the **FindFirst** method on the
   city recordset, assuming the new city already exists in the city lookup table?
   a. The **NoMatch** property is set to **True**.
   b. The **NoMatch** property is set to **False**.
   c. The current record position of the city recordset is set to the matching city
      record.
   d. The current record position of the city recordset does not change.

5. Assume that two users concurrently submit the location entry form and specify the same new city for the location information. What response will each user get?

   a. The first user will get a response containing the information about the saved location record, whereas the other will get an error message.

   b. Both users will get a response containing the information about their saved location record, and the value of the `CityID` field in both cases will be the same.

   c. Both users will get a response containing the information about their saved location record and the value of `CityID` field will be different.

   d. Both users will get an error message.

EXERCISE 3

Complexity: Easy

1. One way to simulate the primary key duplication error generally caused due to the multiuser environment setting is as follows:

   1. Replace the `NextID = rs![ID] + 1` line in the `GetID` function of the `LOCATIONENTRY.EXE` program with the following line:

      ```
      NextID = rs![ID]
      ```

   2. Recompile the `LOCATIONENTRY.EXE` program.

   3. Get the location entry form from this program, fill out a new location and a new city value, and then submit this form.

   Implement these steps and list the response returned by this program. (Note: Don't forget to return the program to its original code after you are done with this exercise.)

Complexity: Moderate

2. Create a Windows CGI program named `LOCATIONENTRY2.EXE` in the `C:\WEBSITE\CGI-WIN\WDBIC\LOCATIONENTRY2` directory that performs the following two tasks:

   ● Generates the location entry form assuming both city and state lookup tables are to be dynamically maintained.

   ● Appropriately handles the new city and state values a user may specify when entering the new location.

MULTIPLE TABLE DATA ENTRY USING ONE FORM

The division of information into multiple related tables is a practice that is highly recommended when designing a database because it promotes higher storage efficiency by preventing data redundancy. However, there is a negative side to this table division scheme. Populating the database can become an elaborate task. Not only do you have to feed the appropriate portions of information to the right tables but you also have to ensure that proper links are maintained between these portions. Let's look at the calendar database for an example.

To Web users who want to enter information about their events into this calendar database, the event is the main entity. The name of the event, its location, and the date and time are generally considered the basic requirements when presenting that event to other interested users. Everything else, such as the sponsor's name, the Web address, and the contact information, is additional information that plays a supporting role in describing the event. However, from the perspective of a database, this support information must be specified (and stored) in the appropriate tables before entering the basic information.

This duality in perspective causes a dilemma when determining how to design an intuitive user interface for accepting information that must be ultimately stored in multiple database tables. Furthermore, using HTML-based forms for rendering such an interface adds another level of complexity due to their passive nature. Once an HTML form is loaded in the browser, all it does is accept information in a sequential manner. The number and attributes of the input controls cannot be changed and there is no "intelligence" or active adaptability that you can depict through that form.

This last statement is not exactly true, because you can use JavaScript or VBScript to add some life to an HTML form, as explained in Chapter 13, "Using Client-Side Scripting Languages: JavaScript and VBScript." But not all browsers provide built-in support for a scripting language, and often you are restricted to sticking with the lowest common denominator supported by most Web browsers. The basic HTML forms described in Chapter 1, "Gathering User-Data: Forms and Queries," generally prove to be a safe bet.

You can explore two avenues when constructing HTML form-based user interface for accepting multiple table information as one transaction:

- Using one long HTML form that contains input controls representing the fields of all the tables so that all the information is sent as one big request

- Using a series of linked HTML forms (such as a data entry wizard) that accept information in stages and pass it to the Web application's back end through multiple requests

The first avenue is relatively easy to design and implement but imposes a lot of constraints on the data entry process. The second avenue offers far more flexibility but requires considerable implementation effort. In this lesson, we explore the first avenue, describing the type of constraints it presents and what approaches you can opt for when implementing the user interface following this path. We shall explore the second avenue in Chapter 12, "Creating a Data Entry Wizard: Advanced Data Entry and Maintenance."

Constraints of Using One Form for Multiple Table Data Entry

The biggest constraint of using one HTML form for multiple table data entry is when these tables hold a one-to-many or a many-to-many relationship. This is a common occurrence in the case of the calendar database. One sponsor (in `tblSponsors`) can have many sponsor contacts (in `tblSponsorsContacts`), each contact can enter many events (in `tblEvents`), and each event can occur on multiple dates at multiple locations (as specified in `tblEventsLocations`). As you can see, the one-to-many link is several levels deep in the calendar database; as such, the database design does not impose any restrictions on how many child records you can enter for each parent record.

However, this "unlimited child records" feature cannot be supported when you are using only one HTML form simply because the number of input controls you can put on an HTML form must be determined at design time, which limits the amount of data a user can input through that form. Let's take a simple example from the `tblSponsors` and `tblSponsorContacts` tables. According to the calendar database, one sponsor can have any number of contacts. But if you try to create one form to allow the data entry of these two tables, you will have to draw a maximum limit on the number of contacts a user can enter on that form. Figure 11-5 shows an example of such a form, where this maximum limit is set to two contacts.

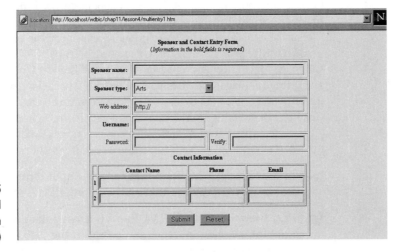

Figure 11-5
Sponsor and contact entry form
(`MULTIENTRY1.HTM`)

You can display this form in your browser using the following URL:

`http://localhost/wdbic/chap11/lesson4/multientry1.htm`

The HTML code used to construct this form is shown in Listing 11-19.

Listing 11-19 Design of the sponsor and contact entry form

```html
<form action="/cgi-win/wdbic/multientry1/multientry1.exe" method="POST">
    <div align="center"><center><table border="1" cellpadding="3"
    cellspacing="3">
        <tr>
            <th align="right" nowrap>Sponsor name: </th>
            <td colspan="3"><input type="text" size="50"
            maxlength="100" name="SponsorName"> </td>
        </tr>
        <tr>
            <th align="right">Sponsor type: </th>
            <td colspan="3"><select name="SponsorTypeID" size="1">
                <option value="1">Arts</option>
                <option value="2">Business</option>
                <option value="4">Cultural</option>
                <option value="5">Education</option>
                <option value="12">Energy</option>
                <option value="6">Foundation/Trust</option>
                <option value="3">Information Technology</option>
                <option value="7">Professional</option>
                <option value="11">Public Interest Groups</option>
                <option value="9">Scientific</option>
                <option value="8">Social</option>
                <option value="10">Sports</option>
                <option value="13">Other</option>
            </select></td>
        </tr>
        <tr>
            <td align="right">Web address:</td>
            <td colspan="3"><input type="text" size="50"
            maxlength="100" name="WebAddress" value="http://"></td>
        </tr>
        <tr>
            <th align="right">Username:</th>
            <td colspan="3"><input type="text" size="20"
            maxlength="20" name="UserName"></td>
        </tr>
        <tr>
            <td align="right">Password:</td>
            <td><input type="password" size="20" maxlength="20"
            name="Password"></td>
            <td align="right">Verify:</td>
            <td><input type="password" size="20" maxlength="20"
            name="VerifyPassword"></td>
        </tr>
```

continued on next page

continued from previous page

```
<tr>
    <td align="center" colspan="4"><table border="1"
    width="100%">
        <caption align="top"><strong>Contact Information</strong></caption>
        <tr>
            <th> </th>
            <th>Contact Name</th>
            <th>Phone</th>
            <th>Email</th>
        </tr>
        <tr>
            <th><strong>1</strong></th>
            <td align="center"><input type="text"
            size="25" maxlength="50" name="ContactName_1"></td>
            <td align="center"><input type="text"
            size="15" maxlength="50" name="Phone_1"></td>
            <td align="center"><input type="text"
            size="15" maxlength="255" name="Email_1"></td>
        </tr>
        <tr>
            <th><strong>2</strong></th>
            <td align="center"><input type="text"
            size="25" maxlength="50" name="ContactName_2"></td>
            <td align="center"><input type="text"
            size="15" maxlength="50" name="Phone_2"></td>
            <td align="center"><input type="text"
            size="15" maxlength="255" name="Email_2"></td>
        </tr>
    </table>
    <p><input type="submit" name="Submit" value="Submit">
       <input type="reset" name="Reset"
    value=" Reset "></p>
    </td>
</tr>
</table>
```

As you can see, the name of each contact-related input control ends with a numeric value to help identify which contact record that control belongs to. For example, the two input controls for the `ContactName` field are named `ContactName_1` and `ContactName_2`.

Let's say you want to go one level deeper and allow the entry of the event header information for each sponsor contact. This time you will have to not only limit the number of event records (let's say, 3) per contact but also provide six copies of each event field on the form, as shown in Figure 11-6. (We have omitted the `EventDescription` field for clarity.)

You can display this form in your browser using the following URL:

`http://localhost/wdbic/chap11/lesson4/multientry2.htm`

In Figure 11-6, you can clearly see that as you add more one-to-many levels to the same form, you increase the complexity and readability of that form. Furthermore, if

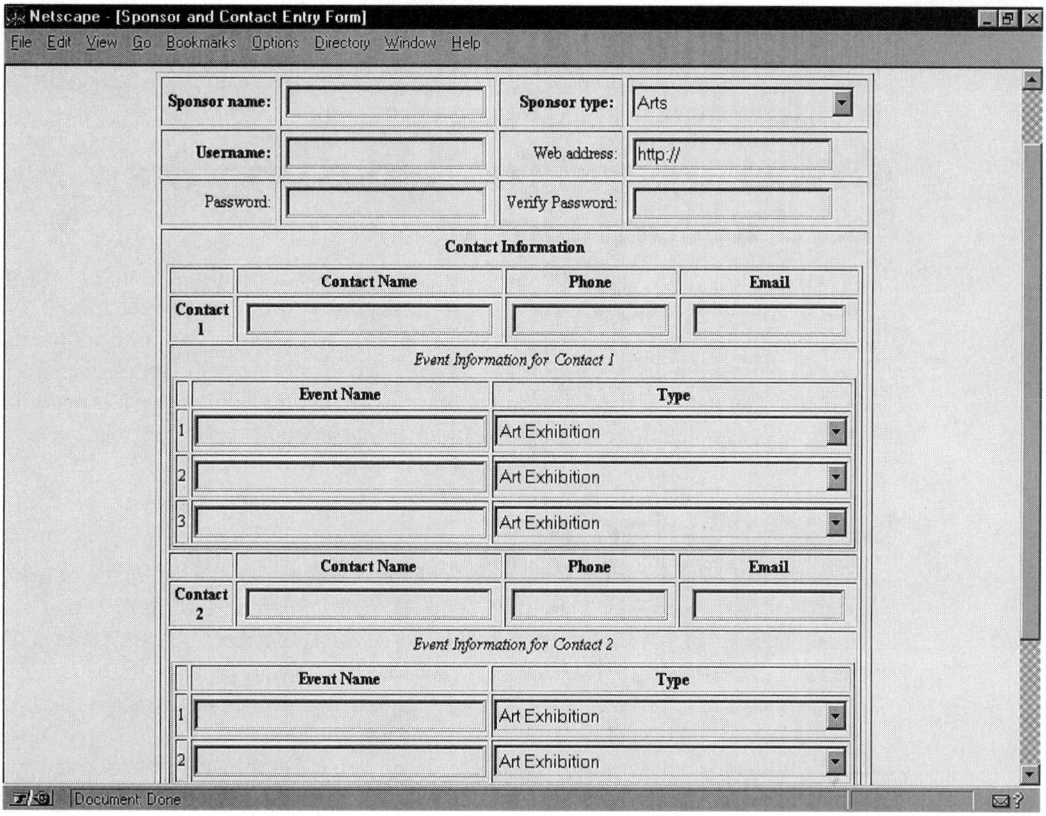

Figure 11-6
Sponsor, contact, and event entry form (MULTIENTRY2.HTM)

one of the sublevels contains a selection-list–type control (for example, the Event-type control in this case), then you have to supply the same option values for each copy of that control, thereby not only increasing the size of the HTML document but also introducing data repetition.

Advantages of Using One Form for Multiple Table Data Entry

In spite of all the constraints and complexities that you have to deal with when using one form as a data entry interface for multiple tables, one big advantage makes all this effort and compromise worth the hassle. This advantage has to do with the back-end CGI program receiving all the user-entered information (belonging to related tables) as one packet. Then the program simply has to disseminate this information and store the relevant portions in the appropriate tables to complete the data entry transaction.

The dissemination process is fairly easy to implement because each input control on the input form can be given a distinct name, which can then help determine exactly what data was supplied and how it is related. We will discuss the implementation details of this dissemination process in the next lesson.

A Workaround for Bypassing the Fixed-Record Limit

Although the form capabilities of HTML do not directly support the concept of accepting an undefined number of records through one form, you can get around this fixed-record constraint by using a multiple line text box control. Each line of this text box can represent a discrete record, and a comma or any other delimiter character can delimit individual field data. The only problem with this approach is that it is not intuitive and it is a lot more error-prone than using separate input controls for each record field.

Lesson Summary

Although splitting information into several related tables is the hallmark of good database design, populating multiple tables of such a database presents several challenges. These challenges are further compounded when the user interface for data entry has to be created using HTML forms, which do not allow any change in the number or type of input controls once they are loaded into the browser. To meet these challenges, you can either solicit data for all the tables using just one form or design a series of linked forms simulating a data entry wizard. This lesson looked at the pros and cons of using the first approach by presenting the design of two multiple table data entry forms for populating the calendar database. The issues involved with processing these types of forms through the back-end Windows CGI programs are examined in the next lesson.

1. Why are HTML forms generally termed "passive" user interfaces?
   a. Because once these forms are designed, the attributes of the input control cannot be changed
   b. Because these forms are difficult to design
   c. Because the process of sending data through an HTML form is considerably slower than sending data through the query string portion of a hyperlink
   d. Because the input controls cannot be made to react differently based on user input

2. What are the different options available for designing an HTML-based user interface for data entry to a multiple-table relational database?
   a. Use one form having a limited number of controls representing important fields of different tables of the database.
   b. Use one long form having input controls to enter a fixed amount of records into all the tables of the database.
   c. Use an independent form for each table of the database.
   d. Use a series of linked forms.

3. Why is it not possible to support the entry of unlimited records through an HTML form?
   a. This is an inherent constraint imposed by a Web browser.
   b. The size of the form becomes unmanageable.
   c. The database design does not support such a feature.
   d. The number of input controls to be put on the form has to be fixed at the form design stage.

4. One-to-many relationships between various tables of a database pose what constraints to an HTML-based user interface?
   a. The form design becomes too complex.
   b. The options for the selection lists used by the many side have to be repeated.
   c. The implementation of the back-end Windows CGI program becomes extremely difficult.
   d. All of the above.

5. What are the advantages of using one HTML form for multiple table data entry?
   a. The back-end program receives the entire information in one go.
   b. The back-end program receives the related information as multiple requests.
   c. It is easy to establish how the input data is related.
   d. It is easy to list the input controls for all the database tables on one form.

EXERCISE 4

Complexity: Easy
1. Modify the sponsor and contact entry form (shown in Figure 11-5) so that it allows a maximum of five contacts per sponsor.

Complexity: Moderate
2. Modify the sponsor, contact, and event entry form (shown in Figure 11-6) so that it includes the `Event Description` field and allows a maximum of four events per sponsor contact.

PROCESSING SINGLE-FORM–BASED MULTIPLE TABLE DATA ENTRY REQUESTS

In the previous lesson, we indicated that using a single form for handling the simultaneous data entry of multiple table requests has one main advantage—all the related data is sent to the receiving CGI program at the same time as one bundle. Why is this an advantage? This will become clear in this lesson when you see how easy the job of that CGI program becomes knowing the fact that the user has provided *all* the information to populate the database tables.

Running the `MULTIENTRY1.EXE` Program

The sponsor and contact entry form shown in Figure 11-5 and listed in Listing 11-19 is a simple example of simultaneously accepting user data for two tables (`tblSponsors` and `tblSponsorsContacts`) related through a one-to-many relationship. The requests submitted through this form are directed to the `MULTIENTRY1.EXE` program residing in the `C:\WEBSITE\CGI-WIN\WDBIC\MULTIENTRY1` directory. Let's go through a sample run of how this program processes these requests:

1. Load the sponsor and contact entry form in your browser using the following URL:

   `http://localhost/wdbic/chap11/lesson4/multientry1.htm`

2. Fill this form as follows and then press the Submit button.

   ```
   Sponsor name: XYZ Corporation
      Sponsor type: Business
        Web address: http://www.xyzcorp.com
            Username: webmaster
            Password: zyx
   Verify Password: zyx
      ContactName_1: Robert Smith
             Phone_1: 808-555-1234
             Email_1: bob@xyzcorp.com
      ContactName_2: Verla Roelle
             Phone_2: 808-555-1256
             Email_2: verla@xyzcorp.com
   ```

   The `MULTIENTRY1.EXE` program adds the sponsor record to the `tblSponsors` table and the two contact records to the `tblSponsorsContacts` table and then returns the exact details of these saved records in its response, as shown in Figure 11-7. You can open these two tables of the CALENDAR.MDB file located in the C:\WEBSITE\HTDOCS\WDBIC\CHAP11\LESSON5 directory to verify that the records were actually saved as this program indicates.

At this point, we suggest that you test run this two-table data entry process with some more sample data.

Examining the Design of the
MULTIENTRY1.EXE **Program**

On receiving the form-data, the **MULTIENTRY1.EXE** program first examines the sponsor-related fields to ensure that the sponsor information is valid. Next, it must validate the information provided for each contact record. According to the entry form, a user can list up to two sponsors. But how should the program determine exactly how many contacts have been listed for that sponsor? Remember that the browser will always send the same number of name=value pairs to the **MULTIENTRY1.EXE** program even though the user may not enter anything for the second contact record.

The **MULTIENTRY1.EXE** program resolves this issue by following a simple rule. If the **ContactName** input field of a contact row is blank, then the whole row will be ignored. This means that if a user lists a phone number but not the contact name in the second contact row, then the program will assume that no second contact has been specified. What if the user specifies the contact name in the second row but not in the first row? In this case, the **MULTIENTRY1.EXE** program assumes that only one contact has been specified and adds a contact record to the database based on the information given in the second row.

Finally, the user may not enter any contact information at all and fill in only the sponsor fields. Should the **MULTIENTRY1.EXE** program accept such a case? The answer depends on whether there is another way a user can add the contact information for an existing sponsor. If this is the only form available to add new sponsors and their contacts to the calendar database (which is what we assume in this particular case), then the **MULTIENTRY1.EXE** program must ensure that at least one contact has been specified for

Figure 11-7
Response of the
MULTIENTRY1.EXE
program

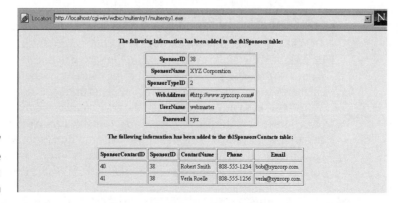

Location: http://localhost/cgi-win/wdbic/multientry1/multientry1.exe

The following information has been added to the tblSponsors table:

SponsorID	38
SponsorName	XYZ Corporation
SponsorTypeID	2
WebAddress	#http://www.xyzcorp.com#
UserName	webmaster
Password	zyx

The following information has been added to the tblSponsorsContacts table:

SponsorContactID	SponsorID	ContactName	Phone	Email
40	38	Robert Smith	808-555-1234	bob@xyzcorp.com
41	38	Verla Roelle	808-555-1256	verla@xyzcorp.com

that sponsor. This is necessary because the calendar database links an event to a sponsor through the sponsor contact; in the absence of the sponsor contact link, the whole purpose of adding the sponsor information is defeated.

Keeping these issues in perspective, the implementation of the `MULTIENTRY1.EXE` program is not hard to understand. Let's start by looking at the Declarations section of its `MYAPP.BAS` module, shown in Listing 11-20.

Listing 11-20 The Declarations section of the `MYAPP.BAS` module of the `MULTIENTRY1.EXE` program

```
Option Explicit        'Force explicit declaration of all variables
'String variable for each input control of the sponsor and contact entry form
Dim SponsorName As String, SponsorTypeID As String
Dim WebAddress As String, UserName As String
Dim Password As String, VerifyPassword As String
Const MAX_CONTACTS_PER_SPONSOR = 2
Dim ContactName(MAX_CONTACTS_PER_SPONSOR) As String
Dim Phone(MAX_CONTACTS_PER_SPONSOR) As String
Dim Email(MAX_CONTACTS_PER_SPONSOR) As String
Dim ContactCount As Long      'Number of contacts that came with the request
Dim SponsorContactID(MAX_CONTACTS_PER_SPONSOR) As Long 'ID of added contacts

'Database related variables
Dim dbCalendar As Database   'Declare database variable
Dim rsSponsor As Recordset   'Declare recordset variables
Dim rsSpContact As Recordset
Dim dbName As String          'Path and name of the calendar database

'Other variables
Dim ErrorMessage As String   'Error message to be returned
Dim i As Long                 'Index variable
```

The key thing to note here is that `ContactName`, `Phone`, and `Email` are declared as arrays whose size is defined by the maximum number of contact records that may accompany the incoming request.

The `CGI_Main` *and the* `ReadFormData` *Procedures of the* `MULTIENTRY1.EXE` *Program*

The `CGI_Main` procedure of the `MULTIENTRY.EXE` program is identical to the `CGI_Main` procedure of the `SPENTRY.EXE` program presented in Listing 11-2 (see Lesson 1). This is because the basic steps for processing the data entry submissions for populating one table or multiple tables are the same as long as all the data is received through one request.

The `CGI_Main` procedure first sets the error handler and then calls the `ReadFormData` procedure to read the data from the input form fields into the appropriate VB variables and arrays. The design of the `ReadFormData` procedure is shown in Listing 11-21. Note how it takes advantage of the consistent and array-like naming scheme used for the contact-related input controls of the sponsor and contact entry form.

Listing 11-21 The `ReadFormData` procedure of the `MULTIENTRY1.EXE` program

```
Public Sub ReadFormData()

   Dim i As Long

   'Get fields for the sponsor record
   SponsorName = GetSmallField("SponsorName")
   SponsorTypeID = GetSmallField("SponsorTypeID")
   WebAddress = GetSmallField("WebAddress")
   UserName = GetSmallField("UserName")
   Password = GetSmallField("Password")
   VerifyPassword = GetSmallField("VerifyPassword")
   'Get fields for the contact record
   For i = 1 To MAX_CONTACTS_PER_SPONSOR
      ContactName(i) = GetSmallField("ContactName_" & i)
      Phone(i) = GetSmallField("Phone_" & i)
      Email(i) = GetSmallField("Email_" & i)
   Next

End Sub
```

The `ValidateData` *and the* `ProcessData` *Procedures of the* `MULTIENTRY1.EXE` *Program*

After reading the form data, the `CGI_Main` procedure passes control to the `ValidateData` procedure, which is shown in Listing 11-22.

Listing 11-22 The `ValidateData` procedure of the `MULTIENTRY1.EXE` program

```
Public Sub ValidateData()
   'Validate sponsor data
   CheckRequiredField SponsorName, "sponsor name"
   CheckRequiredField SponsorTypeID, "sponsor type"
   CheckRequiredField UserName, "username"
   If Password <> VerifyPassword Then
      ErrorMessage = "The password could not be verified."
      Error ERR_BAD_REQUEST
   End If
   'Validate contact data -- at least one contact must be specified
   ContactCount = 0    'Initialize
   For i = 1 To MAX_CONTACTS_PER_SPONSOR
      If ContactName(i) <> "" Then
         'Ensure that either email or phone is specified
         If Phone(i) = "" And Email(i) = "" Then
            CheckRequiredField Phone(i), "phone or email for contact " & i
         End If
         'Check if email-address is valid
         If Email(i) <> "" Then
            If InStr(Email(i), "@") = 0 Then
```

continued on next page

continued from previous page

```
            ErrorMessage = "Please specify a valid internet email address for contact
" & i & "."
            Error ERR_BAD_REQUEST
          End If
        End If
        'Everything Ok so increment contact count
        ContactCount = ContactCount + 1
      End If
    Next
    'Return error if no contact information listed
    If ContactCount = 0 Then
      ErrorMessage = "At least one contact name must be specified for this sponsor."
      Error ERR_BAD_REQUEST
    End If

End Sub
```

The `ValidateData` procedure first ensures that valid and required sponsor information has been provided. After the sponsor information passes all the necessary tests, the procedure then validates each contact record whose `ContactName` field is not empty. While validating, it also keeps a contact count, which it inspects in the end to ensure that the user has entered at least one valid contact. Following the principles discussed in Lesson 1, this `ValidateData` procedure is also designed to signal an error (with an appropriate error message) the moment any validation check fails.

The `ProcessData` procedure, which `CGI_Main` calls after the `ValidateData` procedure has terminated normally, handles the necessary postprocessing of the `WebAddress` field of the sponsor record. The design of this procedure is identical to the `ProcessData` procedure of the `SPENTRY.EXE` program listed in Listing 11-7 (see Lesson 1).

The `AddDataToDatabase`*,* `AddSponsor`*, and Other Related Procedures of the* `MULTIENTRY1.EXE` *Program*

Once the data has been validated and processed for storage, the `CGI_Main` procedure passes control to the `AddDataToDatabase` procedure to open the calendar database and store the data in appropriate tables. The design of the `AddDataToDatabase` procedure is presented in Listing 11-23.

Listing 11-23 The `AddDataToDatabase` procedure of the `MULTIENTRY1.EXE` program

```
Public Sub AddDataToDatabase()

  OpenCalendarDatabase
  AddSponsor
  AddSponsorContacts

End Sub
```

The `AddDataToDatabase` procedure performs its job by calling three other procedures. The `OpenCalendarDatabase` procedure (discussed in Lesson 3) opens the calendar database (in this case, the **CALENDAR.MDB** file residing in the **C:\WEBSITE\HTDOCS\WDBIC\CHAP11\LESSON5** directory). The `AddSponsor` procedure creates a new sponsor record in the **tblSponsors** table and sets that new record as the current record of the **rsSponsor** recordset. The `AddSponsorContacts` procedure then uses the value of the **SponsorID** field of that new (current) record to create the related contact records in the **tblSponsorsContacts** table. The design of these two procedures is shown in Listing 11-24.

Listing 11-24 The `AddSponsor` and `AddSponsorContacts` procedures of the MULTIENTRY1.EXE program

```
Public Sub AddSponsor()

  Set rsSponsor = dbCalendar.OpenRecordset("tblSponsors")
  With rsSponsor
    'Start a new record
    .AddNew
    'Assign values to the fields of the new record
    !SponsorName = SponsorName
    !SponsorTypeID = CByte(SponsorTypeID)
    !WebAddress = EmptyToNull(WebAddress)
    !UserName = UserName
    !Password = EmptyToNull(Password)
    'Save the new record
    .Update
    'Make the new record as the current record
    .Bookmark = .LastModified
  End With

End Sub


Public Sub AddSponsorContacts()

  'The following recordset is opened as a dynaset because
  'the GenerateResponse uses its findfirst method
  Set rsSpContact = dbCalendar.OpenRecordset("tblSponsorsContacts", dbOpenDynaset)
  'Now add the contact records to the contact table through this recordset
  For i = 1 To MAX_CONTACTS_PER_SPONSOR
    If ContactName(i) <> "" Then
      With rsSpContact
        'Start a new record
        .AddNew
        'Assign values to the fields of the new record
        !SponsorID = rsSponsor!SponsorID
        !ContactName = ContactName(i)
        !Phone = EmptyToNull(Phone(i))
        !Email = EmptyToNull(Email(i))
```

continued on next page

continued from previous page

```
                'Save the new record
                .Update
                'Make the new record as the current record
                .Bookmark = .LastModified
                'Store the SponsorContactID assigned to this record
                SponsorContactID(i) = rsSpContact!SponsorContactID
            End With
        End If
    Next

End Sub
```

Note how the **AddSponsorContacts** procedure creates the contact records only in cases where the contact information contains a nonempty contact name and stores their **SponsorContactIDs** in the **SponsorContactID** array. This array is used by the **GenerateResponse** procedure shown in Listing 11-25 to search and present the stored contact information back to the user, as shown in Figure 11-7.

Listing 11-25 The GenerateResponse procedures of the MULTIENTRY1.EXE program

```
Public Sub GenerateResponse()
    Dim Criteria As String
    Dim FieldValue As Variant
    Dim j As Long

    Send "<CENTER>"
    Send "<B>The following information has been added to the tblSponsors table:</B><P>"
    Send "<TABLE BORDER=1 CELLPADDING=3>"
    'List fields and their values for the added sponsor record
    For i = 0 To rsSponsor.Fields.Count - 1
        Send "<TR>"
        Send "<TH ALIGN=RIGHT>" & rsSponsor(i).name & "</TH>"
        Send "<TD>" & IIf(IsNull(rsSponsor(i)), "Null", rsSponsor(i)) & "</TD>"
        Send "</TR>"
    Next
    Send "</TABLE>"
    Send "<BR>"
    Send "<B>The following information has been added to the tblSponsorsContacts
table:</B><P>"
    'List fields and their values for the added contact records
    Send "<TABLE BORDER=1 CELLPADDING=3>"
    'List field names of tblSponsorsContacts
    Send "<TR>"
    For i = 0 To rsSpContact.Fields.Count - 1
        Send "<TH>" & rsSpContact(i).name & "</TH>"
    Next
    Send "</TR>"
    'Send contact records
    For j = 1 To MAX_CONTACTS_PER_SPONSOR
        If ContactName(j) <> "" Then
            'Set the criteria for finding the related contact records
```

```
        Criteria = "SponsorContactID = " & SponsorContactID(j)
        rsSpContact.FindFirst Criteria    'Find the first contact
        If Not rsSpContact.NoMatch Then 'List current contact
          Send "<TR>"
          For i = 0 To rsSpContact.Fields.Count - 1
            FieldValue = rsSpContact(i)
            Send "<TD>" & IIf(IsNull(FieldValue), "Null", FieldValue) & "</TD>"
          Next
          Send "</TR>"
        End If
      End If
    Next
    Send "</TABLE>"
    Send "</CENTER>"

  End Sub
```

Lesson Summary

Continuing with the example of the sponsor and contact entry form developed in the previous lesson as a front end to simultaneously accepting user data for the **tblSponsors** and **tblSponsorsContacts** tables, this lesson explained the design and functioning of the associated back-end Windows CGI program called **MULTIENTRY1.EXE**. The program first validates the furnished sponsor and contact information and ensures that a minimum of one valid contact record is specified in the incoming request. A contact record is not even considered for validation if the user leaves its contact name field blank.

Because the entire information is being received as one request, the basic steps involved for processing it are similar to handling a one-table data entry request except that each step now has to be extended individually to recognize the multitable situation.

One issue that the **MULTIENTRY1.EXE** program does not address is the possibility of a run-time error that may cause only a portion of the incoming information to be saved. Because the addition of the sponsor record and the contact records requires two discrete steps (highlighted by the **AddSponsor** procedure and the **AddSponsorContacts** procedure), it is possible that the second step may fail due to a locking or some other unexpected error. But the first step has already saved the sponsor information, which puts the database in an inconsistent state. The next lesson examines this situation further and shows how to apply the transaction processing concepts to prevent this problem.

 **QUIZ 5**

1. Why is it important to specify at least one contact name and its associated information along with the new sponsor record?
   a. Because **ContactName**, **Phone**, and **Email** are required fields.
   b. Because the event and sponsor records can be linked only through the contact information.

c. Because `ContactName`, `Phone`, and `Email` are declared as arrays whose size is determined by the number of contact records that accompany the incoming request.

d. All of the above.

2. How does the `MULTIENTRY1.EXE` program respond if it receives only the phone and email information along with valid sponsor information?

a. The sponsor information is added to the sponsor table and the phone and email information is added to the contact table.

b. The program ignores the incoming request and returns a blank form.

c. The program generates an error, asking for at least one contact name for the specified sponsor.

d. The program adds only the validated sponsor information but ignores the contact information.

3. How does the `MULTIENTRY1.EXE` program determine the number of contacts specified in the incoming user request?

a. By declaring `ContactName`, `Phone`, and `Email` as variables in the Declarations section of the `MYAPP.BAS` module.

b. By specifying a constant for a maximum number of contact records.

c. By declaring `ContactName`, `Phone`, and `Email` as arrays.

d. By counting the number of contact name input fields with a nonempty string value.

4. Which of the following statements are true?

a. The basic steps involved in processing a Web request containing data for populating a single table or multiple tables are the same.

b. The `MULTIENTRY1.EXE` program requires that two contacts must be specified for each new sponsor.

c. Submitting a sponsor and contact entry form with contact information only in the second contact row will result in a run-time error.

d. The `SponsorContactID` array holds the `SponsorContactID` of each added contact.

5. What tasks are carried out by the `ValidateData` procedure of the `MULTIENTRY1.EXE` program?

a. It validates sponsor information.

b. It validates information specified in each contact row irrespective of the contact name being specified or not.

c. It validates a contact row only if the `ContactName` field is not empty.

d. It keeps a count of valid and invalid contact records and uses that count to ensure that no invalid contact record came with the incoming request.

Complexity: Easy

1. The sponsor and contact entry form represented by the **MULTIENTRY1.HTM** file residing in the **C:\WEBSITE\HTDOCS\WDBIC\CHAP11\LAB5** directory allows the data entry of a new sponsor and a maximum of five contacts. Modify the **MULTIENTRY1.EXE** program so that it can correctly process the requests sent through this form.

Complexity: Advanced

2. Design a Windows CGI program named **MULTIENTRY2.EXE** in the **C:\ WEBSITE\CGI-WIN\WDBIC\MULTIENTRY2** directory to handle the data entry requests sent through the sponsor, contact, and event entry form (**MULTIENTRY2.HTM**) presented in Lesson 4. Use the following rules when designing this program.

- An event record should be ignored if it has an empty value in its event name input field.

- A sponsor contact record should be ignored only if it has an empty value in its contact name input field and no events are listed for it.

- The case where a contact is specified but no associated events are listed should be treated as an acceptable case.

TRANSACTION PROCESSING

Whenever you are dealing with a situation that involves a sequence of updating multiple tables, you must ask yourself, "Would the failure of any of these update steps cause the database to get into an inconsistent state?" An inconsistent state implies that the information in that database could cause a potential violation of one or more database-level business rules.

For example, when designing the calendar database in Chapter 4, Lesson 6, we established a business rule that each event must be linked to its sponsor record through the sponsor contact table. In other words, there must be at least one contact record present for each sponsor record stored in the calander database before you store any events in that database. If you add a new sponsor record into that database without adding any associated contact records, the database will get into an inconsistent state. Similarly, having an event in the **tblEvents** table without any information about its timings and locations listed in the **tblEventsLocations** table is in violation of the business rule that we established for the calendar database in Chapter 4, Lesson 6.

Note that having a database in an inconsistent state is not always perceived as a bad thing. It just presents the *possibility* of a business rule violation. For example, you may decide to collect the contact information when the user lists an event. In that case, you are able to ensure that the business rule of requiring a sponsor-event link is satisfied. But as a rule of thumb, you should try to avoid this possibility wherever possible.

Let's analyze the simultaneous multiple table update scenario from the perspective of the user initiating that update. How will it affect that user if all the updates are not carried through successfully? For instance, say a user enters information about a new sponsor and its two contacts through the sponsor and contact entry form. The receiving CGI program (**MULTIENTRY1.EXE**) adds the sponsor record to the **tblSponsors** table, then adds the first contact record to the **tblSponsorsContact** table, but is unable to add the second contact record due to locking conflict or some other unexpected error. The program informs the user that something went wrong while saving the information.

How will a typical user react on receiving this error message? Most probably, the user will try to resubmit the original data hoping that this time the information will be saved successfully. But that will cause partial duplication of information in the database, which is undesirable. How do you handle this situation? You could try informing the user exactly how much data was saved while processing the first request and then have that user submit only the remaining data in the next request. However, this approach requires considerable error trapping and implementation. The easier and better approach to such a situation is the concept of transaction processing.

Through transaction processing, you can make the database engine treat multiple database update operations as one transaction. If any of these operations fail, you can then force the whole transaction to roll back as if none of these operations had occurred. Using this technique, you can make sure that in any request that comes from the sponsor and contact entry form, either all the information is saved or nothing is saved if an error occurs. This way, when the user receives an error message and resubmits the original data, the data duplication scenario will not occur.

Implementing Transaction Processing

To group multiple database update operations within a transaction, use the **BeginTrans**, **CommitTrans**, and **Rollback** methods of a **Workspace** object. The following code template shows how these methods are typically applied together:

```
DBEngine(0).BeginTrans        'Begin the transaction using the default workspace
On Error Resume Next          'Trap all run-time errors
'-----------------------------------------------------------------
'Now, perform all database operations that are grouped as one transaction
'-----------------------------------------------------------------
'Check to see if any operation generated an error
If Err = 0 Then               'All operations were successful
   DBEngine(0).CommitTranas   'So commit the transaction
Else                          'otherwise
   DBEngine(0).Rollback       'Undo the effect of these operations
End IF
```

Indicate the start of a transaction using the `BeginTrans` method. Next, conduct all the database operations that you want considered part of this transaction. On successful completion of these operations, you can execute the workspace's `CommitTrans` method to make the effect of these operations permanent. However, if you detect an error, the `Rollback` method allows you to undo the changes made by these operations.

Things to Consider When Implementing Transaction Processing

The `BeginTrans`, `CommitTrans`, and `Rollback` methods make the process of implementing transaction processing appear simple—as long as you remember some key facts:

Transaction Processing Is a Workspace Feature

All three transaction-processing methods are associated with a `Workspace` object, not a `Database` object. This means that you can group update operations on different databases as one transaction.

Nothing Is Committed Until Specifically Said So

The changes made by all the database operations within the transaction are a reflection of how you plan to update the database. You will not see the effect of these changes until the `CommitTrans` method is executed.

All Validation and Referential Integrity Rules Are Enforced During a Transaction

Each database operation conducted within a transaction goes through the same validation and referential integrity checks as a normal database operation does. However, the effect of all the database operations that have previously occurred within that transaction is considered when performing those checks. For example, if you add a new sponsor record within a transaction and use its `SponsorID` to add the related contact records within the same transaction, you will not get a referential integrity failure error because of using a `SponsorID` that does not permanently exist in the database.

Changes Occurring Within One Transaction Are Not Visible to Other Concurrent Transactions

Another program (or another copy of the same program) cannot sense any change you make within a transaction until that transaction is committed. This means if the first program adds a new sponsor record within a transaction and another program tries to add the related contact records before the first program commits its transaction, the second program will get a referential integrity error from the database engine.

Transaction Processing Causes Table and Record Locking

Adding a new record to a database table within a transaction prevents other concurrent transactions from adding records to the same table until the first transaction is committed. For example, if one transaction (say Transaction A) adds a sponsor record and then another concurrent transaction (say Transaction B) tries to add another record in the **tblSponsors** table while Transaction A is still in process, Transaction B will receive a locking error. Specifically, it will receive error number **3260**, which goes as follows:

```
Couldn't update; currently locked by user "user name" on machine "machine name"
```

Note that if both transactions were using an optimistic locking scheme for data insertion, then Transaction B would get an error when it executed the recordset's **Update** method, not the **AddNew** method.

As you can see, this is a big constraint when implementing transaction processing in a multiuser environment. This is why we recommend that transactions should be kept as small as possible. Another solution to work around this constraint is to trap error **3260** and keep retrying a few times, similar to the approach followed for handling dynamic lookup tables in Lesson 3.

Examining the Design of the MULTIENTRY3.EXE **Program**

The **MULTIENTRY3.EXE** program (provided in the **C:\WEBSITE\CGI-WIN\WDBIC\ MULTIENTRY3** directory) replicates the functionality of the **MULTIENTRY1.EXE** program except that it uses transaction processing to add the sponsor and associated contact records. You can test run this new version using the sponsor and contact entry form accessed through the following URL:

```
http://localhost/wdbic/chap11/lesson6/multientry3.htm
```

The **MULTIENTRY3.EXE** program implements the transaction processing by modifying the **AddDataToDatabase** procedure of the **MULTIENTRY1.EXE** program, as shown in Listing 11-26.

Listing 11-26 The AddDataToDatabase procedure of the MULTIENTRY3.EXE program

```
Public Sub AddDataToDatabase()

    OpenCalendarDatabase
    'Begin transaction
    DBEngine(0).BeginTrans
    AddSponsor
    AddSponsorContacts
    'Commit the transaction
    DBEngine(0).CommitTrans

End Sub
```

Notice that the transaction is started before adding the sponsor record and ended after adding all the contact records. However, no `Rollback` method is used in this procedure to roll back the transaction in case of an error. This is because the `Rollback` method is executed by the general purpose `HandleError` procedure, shown in Listing 11-27.

Listing 11-27 The `HandleError` procedure of the `MULTIENTRY3.EXE` program

```
Public Sub HandleError()

  If ErrorMessage = "" Then
    Send Error$          'Send VB's error message
  Else
    Send ErrorMessage    'Send custom error message
  End If
  'Roll back any transaction in process when this error occurred
  On Error Resume Next
  DBEngine(0).Rollback

End Sub
```

The `On Error Resume Next` line is listed to ignore the error generated by the `Rollback` method in case the `HandleError` procedure is called before the transaction is started (by the failure of the `ValidateData` procedure, for example).

The `MULTIENTRY3.EXE` program also addresses the possibility of locking conflict that can occur if two copies of this program are executed concurrently and the users try to add a new record to the database table while neither user has closed his or her transactions. Clearly, the copy that tries first will get a lock on the table while the other one will get an error (**3260**). The `MULTIENTRY3.EXE` program is designed so that this second copy senses this error, waits a short time, and then tries again hoping that the first copy has completed its transaction by that time. To see how this scheme is implemented, let's look at the `AddSponsor` procedure of this program, presented in Listing 11-28.

Listing 11-28 The `AddSponsor` procedure of the `MULTIENTRY3.EXE` program

```
Public Sub AddSponsor()
  Dim i As Long

  Set rsSponsor = dbCalendar.OpenRecordset("tblSponsors")
  With rsSponsor
    'Start a new record
    .AddNew
    'Assign values to the fields of the new record
    !SponsorName = SponsorName
    !SponsorTypeID = CByte(SponsorTypeID)
    !WebAddress = EmptyToNull(WebAddress)
    !UserName = UserName
    !Password = EmptyToNull(Password)
    'Save the new record
    UpdateRecord rsSponsor
    'Make the new record as the current record
```

continued on next page

continued from previous page

```
      .Bookmark = .LastModified
   End With

End Sub
```

This **AddSponsor** procedure differs from the **AddSponsor** procedure of the
MULTIENTRY1.EXE program in just one statement, where it updates the **rsSponsor** recordset by calling the **UpdateRecord** procedure instead of directly executing the recordset's
Update method. Similarly, the **AddSponsorContacts** procedure (not shown) also
calls the **UpdateRecord** procedure to execute the **Update** operation of the **rsSpContact**
recordset.

The design of the **UpdateRecord** procedure is shown in Listing 11-29.

Listing 11-29 The **UpdateRecord** procedure of the **MULTIENTRY3.EXE** program

```
Public Sub UpdateRecord(rs As Recordset)

   Dim i As Long              'Index variable
   Dim ErrNo As Integer       'Error number returned by the Update operation
   Const MAX_TRIES = 5        'Maximum number of Update retries

   On Error Resume Next
   For i = 1 To MAX_TRIES
      rs.Update                        'Execute the Update operation
      ErrNo = Err                      'Get the error returned by this operation
      If ErrNo = 0 Then Exit Sub       'If no error then success, so quit
      If ErrNo <> 3260 Then            'If not locking error then
         On Error GoTo 0               'signal error to the calling procedure
         Error ErrNo
      End If
      WaitRandom 50                    'otherwise, wait a random amount of time
      ' Call the Idle method to release unneeded locks, force
      ' pending writes, and refresh the memory with the current
      ' data in the .mdb file.
      DBEngine.Idle dbRefreshCache
   Next                                'and try again
   On Error GoTo 0                     'All tries failed, so return error
   Error ErrNo

End Sub
```

The **UpdateRecord** repeatedly executes the **Update** method of the passed recordset until either the update succeeds, an error other than **3260** occurs, or the number
of iterations exceeds the retry limit. The procedure notifies the update failure by signaling the error back to the calling procedure; that error finally is handled by the **HandleError**
procedure, which sends the error message to the user and also rolls back the transaction.

Lesson Summary

This lesson presented some possible multiple table data entry scenarios that could bring the database to an inconsistent state. Having a database in this state can not only cause a potential database business rule violation but also make the user entering the data take actions that might lead to the duplication of information.

Transaction processing, in which you treat multiple database update operations as a single transaction, helps avoid the above situations by either saving the entire information coming with the update request or, in case of an error, aborting and leaving no trace of the update operations.

The multiple database update operations are grouped within a transaction using the **BeginTrans**, **CommitTrans**, and **Rollback** methods of a **Workspace** object. Before you apply these methods, you must be aware of several key issues related to transaction processing presented in this lesson. Transactions should be kept as small as possible and no changes made during the transaction should be visible to other users until that transaction is committed.

This lesson discussed a standard way of implementing transaction processing in a multiuser environment setting by describing the design of the **MULTIENTRY3.EXE** program, which replicates the functionality of the **MULTIENTRY1.EXE** program discussed in the previous lesson and performs all the record insertion operations within a transaction. The transaction is started with the **BeginTrans** method and is committed using the **CommitTrans** method. The **Rollback** method is used in the error-handling procedure to roll back any partial update if an error occurring before the transaction is committed. The program also uses the standard retry after random wait technique to resolve locking conflicts in a reasonable amount of time. Most procedures of **MULTIENTRY3.EXE** that used these transaction processing methods and techniques were listed and explained in this lesson.

1. Which of the following situations would benefit from transaction processing?
   a. Adding a new database record to only one table
   b. Simultaneously updating two fields of the same record
   c. Updating the same field of two records of the same table
   d. Adding a record to one table and deleting a record in another table

2. What happens if a program terminates in the middle of a transaction processing session without executing the **Rollback** method?
   a. The database gets corrupted.
   b. The database is automatically rolled back.
   c. The changes that have already been made in that transaction are saved.
   d. None of the above.

3. Which of the following statements are true in the case of transaction processing?
   a. Update operations on different databases can be grouped as one transaction.
   b. Database operations conducted within a transaction are not constrained by validation and referential integrity checks until the transaction is committed.
   c. The changes are made to a database only when the transaction is committed.
   d. Transactions should generally be as long as possible.

4. What will happen if the **GenerateResponse** procedure of the **MULTIENTRY3.EXE** program generates a run-time error?
   a. The sponsor and contact information will be saved in the database.
   b. The sponsor and contact information will not be saved in the database.
   c. The amount of information saved will depend on where the error occurred in the **GenerateResponse** procedure.
   d. None of the above.

5. When does the **UpdateRecord** procedure notify an error to its calling procedure in the **MULTIENTRY3.EXE** program?
   a. When error **3260** occurs
   b. When any error other than **3260** occurs
   c. When the number of iterations exceeds the retry limit
   d. All of the above

Complexity: Easy
1. Open two instances of your browser and display the sponsor and contact entry form (**MULTIENTRY3.HTM** file residing in the **C:\WEBSITE\HTDOCS\WDBIC\CHAP11\LESSON6** directory) in each instance. Fill out each entry form with some valid sample data and then submit both forms in quick succession. What response do you receive for each submission and why?

Complexity: Easy
2. Modify the **AddDataToDatabase** procedure of the **MULTIENTRY3.EXE** program to simulate the occurrence of an error between the **AddSponsor** and **AddSponsorContacts** procedure as follows and then recompile the program:

```
Public Sub AddDataToDatabase()

    OpenCalendarDatabase
    'Begin transaction
    DBEngine(0).BeginTrans
    AddSponsor
    ErrorMessage = "Error after adding sponsor but before adding the
contact records."
    Error ERR_BAD_REQUEST
```

```
AddSponsorContacts
'Commit the transaction
DBEngine(0).CommitTrans
```

End Sub

Now submit the sponsor and contact entry form (`MULTIENTRY3.HTM` file) after filling it with some sample sponsor and contact data. What response do you get? How is the calendar database (`CALENDAR.MDB` file residing in the `C:\WEBSITE\HTDOCS\WDBIC\CHAP11\LESSON5` directory) affected by the processing of this form request?

CHAPTER SUMMARY

This chapter presented some techniques for populating one or more tables of a database using Web-based data entry mechanisms. The process involves designing front-end HTML-based data entry forms, which can be generated statically or dynamically, and the corresponding back-end Windows CGI programs for processing the update requests. The main points covered in this chapter are listed below:

- The simplest form of Web-based data entry is to add a new record to a single table.

- The first step in implementing the Web-based data entry process is to create a proper user interface, which is normally an HTML-based form for accepting the field values of the record to be entered.

- The layout of the user interface should be intuitive so that it helps project the field characteristics and any dependency relationship that may exist within the fields.

- The back-end Windows CGI program validates the input data, generates values for system-maintained fields, opens the database, and adds the new record to the destination table in a multiuser environment.

- Prechecking validation and integrity rules by the back-end program provides more control over how to proceed if invalid data is received and detected before passing it on to the database engine.

- The only system-maintained table fields that a Windows CGI program has to handle are the ones not automatically maintained by the database engine itself.

- A primary key duplication error will occur only if it is a numeric ID field (as in the case of the lookup tables of the calendar database) and the program is designed to select the next available value for the ID field.

- The variables used by various procedures of the back-end Windows CGI program are given module-level scope by declaring them in the Declarations section of the MYAPP.BAS module.

- A static lookup table is a lookup table that contains a predefined list of lookup values; only database administrators can change the contents of such a table.

- A dynamic lookup table can accept new (but unique) lookup values directly from Web users as part of the Web-based data entry process.

- Classifying a lookup table as static or dynamic has a considerable effect on the complexity and performance of a Web application.

- Static lookup tables allow the use of HTML forms that are generated statically and are easy to incorporate within a Web application. However, they compromise flexibility.

- Dynamic lookup tables require HTML forms that are generated on the fly that provide the option for adding a new value to the form. Similarly, the back-end program should be able to detect and add new lookup values to this table before adding any other related records using that new value.

- Using a file-based approach, the static and dynamic portions of the HTML text of the front-end form can be separated to achieve greater flexibility and avoid the need to hard-code the HTML text that never changes.

- The GET method of the incoming request causes the Windows CGI program to send the front-end form, whereas the POST method puts it into the form-processing mode.

- In a multiuser environment setting, the possibility of two or more new fields being added at the same time and using the same value for the next available ID can occur and cause a primary key violation.

- The program handles the problem of primary key violation by waiting a random amount of time and then recalculating the next available ID of the field being added.

- Populating multiple related tables of a database is an elaborate task because appropriate portions of the information have to be fed to the correct tables and proper links have to be maintained.

- Once loaded in the browser, an HTML form accepts information in a sequential manner and generally does not possess any "intelligence" or active adaptability that you can depict through that form.

- You can either use one long form for all tables of the database or design a series of linked forms simulating a data entry wizard.

- One-to-one or one-to-many relationships between tables of a database are a big constraint when you are using one HTML form for data entry.

- Unlimited child records cannot be supported when you are using only one HTML form because the number of input controls to be presented on the form have to be determined at the design stage.

- A single HTML form has the advantage of passing the entire information to the back-end program as one package.

- The basic steps for processing the data entry submissions for populating one table or multiple tables are the same as long as all the data is received through one request, except that each step has to be extended individually to recognize the multitable situation.

- Violation of one or more database-level business rules can cause the database to be in an inconsistent state.

- Transaction processing makes the database engine treat multiple database update operations as one transaction. Thus, either all the information being passed in a transaction gets saved or nothing gets saved.

- The `BeginTrans`, `CommitTrans`, and `Rollback` methods of a `Workspace` object are used to group multiple database update operations within one transaction.

- The transaction is completed only when the `CommitTrans` method commits it.

- Transaction processing causes table and record locking. Hence, transactions should be kept as small as possible.

This chapter concluded with a discussion of transaction processing, which is an important concept that is generally applied when a multiple database operation needs to be performed to complete a task. In the next chapter we shall look at some advanced Web-based data entry techniques such as implementing a data entry wizard and handling data security issues.

CREATING A DATA ENTRY WIZARD: ADVANCED DATA ENTRY AND MAINTENANCE

This chapter shows how you can use and implement the concept of a data entry wizard to create an interface for populating and maintaining multiple database tables. It also describes standard session-building techniques using hidden fields and persistent cookies, which play an important role in the wizard implemention. In particular, you will learn about

- Objectives and design features of the event entry wizard

- The template design approach for generating dynamic input forms

- Self-contained application design

- Adding user security and maintaining state using hidden fields

- Implementing security using the browser's Username and Password dialog box

- Linking forms through hidden fields

- Persistent cookies—what they are and how they are set

- Differences between cookies and the browser's authentication mechanism

- Using cookies in a data entry wizard

- Editing and deleting existing data over the Web

DESIGNING A DATA ENTRY WIZARD

In Chapter 11, "Populating Tables: Web-Based Data Entry," Lesson 4, we described the two approaches available for accepting Web-based user input that is stored in multiple tables of a relational database. The first approach uses a single Web form for accepting all pieces of the input at the same time; the pieces are then sent to the back-end program via a single request. Getting all pieces of input together helps simplify the process of enforcing business database rules involving multiple tables and allows transaction processing. However, this simplification comes at the cost of flexibility. You always have to set a maximum limit of how many records a user can enter through one form.

This maximum-limit constraint can be overcome by following the second approach, in which you accept user input in stages using a series of linked input forms. Each form is dynamically generated based on the information provided in the previous form and may carry some of that information to maintain continuity. Furthermore, some of these forms may be used repeatedly (in a loop) to gather multiple records of the same type of input.

The data import wizard (described in Chapter 4, "Constructing a Relational Database: The Microsoft Access Way," Lesson 6) and the Web publishing Wizard (described in Chapter 10, "Presenting Information: Web Database Publishing," Lesson 2) of Microsoft Access essentially follow this second approach to acquiring information from the user. However, implementing this second approach is generally more difficult than implementing the single-form approach due to the following reasons:

- Most forms need to be generated dynamically.

- The stateless nature of the Web, where all Web transactions are conducted independent of each other, does not lend itself as an ideal medium for maintaining continuity between linked forms.

- A mechanism may be required for temporarily storing the partial information received for individual forms while the wizard is in progress.

● The issue of multiple users using the data entry wizard has to be addressed.

● The possibility of a user leaving the wizard in the middle of a session and then starting all over again has to be addressed.

The implementation hurdles created by each of the aforementioned reasons vary from application to application. We will show what effect they have on the Web calendar application when we try to build an event entry wizard for populating the sponsor and event information in the calendar database. This lesson describes the main objectives of this wizard and then goes over the functionality and layout of the input forms it needs to meet those objectives.

The Objectives of the Event Entry Wizard

The main objective of the event entry wizard is to allow users to enter new sponsor and event information easily without imposing any artificial constraints. In addition, the wizard should incorporate the following features:

● Allow existing sponsors to add new contacts and upcoming events after authenticating the users providing this information.

● Optimize the number of input forms used by this wizard without losing the *unlimited records* flexibility. This means the user should not get the feeling of being unnecessarily burdened by the wizard.

● Economize on the size of each input form to stay bandwidth-friendly. This means that the number of selection list controls and the number of options within a selection list control should be kept within a reasonable limit.

● Promote the use of the Back button of the browser to enter multiple events or multiple occurrences of an event. This way, a user will not have to request a new form from the back-end CGI program every time he or she wants to add a new child record linked to the same parent record.

These objectives will become clearer once we discuss the layout of the event entry wizard in the next section.

Laying Out the Event Entry Wizard

A good way to start the design process of a data entry wizard is by applying the modular approach. In this approach, you first identify the main input tasks performed by that wizard and where they fit in the overall input flow model, and then you figure out the input forms necessary for implementing these tasks. For example, the event entry wizard can be attributed with the following two main tasks, performed in the manner shown in Figure 12-1:

1. **Get the sponsor and contact information.**

2. **Get the events for the selected sponsor contact.**

Note that getting the sponsor and contact information does not just mean asking the user for a new sponsor and its new contact. It also includes allowing a user to specify a new contact for an existing sponsor or to select an existing contact. The ultimate goal of the first task is to produce a valid **SponsorContactID** that can then be used to link all the new events entered for that contact.

One question you may ask is why did we use the sponsor contact as the point of separation for establishing the two main tasks of the event entry wizard? This decision was made based on two reasons. First, we are subdividing the event entry wizard into its *main* input tasks only. Second, this separation point was chosen after determining when it would be appropriate to store the provided information in the calendar database permanently without disturbing any database business rules.

For example, say a user enters a new sponsor and a new contact through this first task. If we let the wizard permanently store that sponsor and contact information in the calendar database and determine the **SponsorContactID** of that new contact, it can then keep track of that contact using this ID for conducting the second task. Having the sponsor and contact information in the database without any associated events is an acceptable scenario as long as the user can easily select that contact at another point of time to enter new related events.

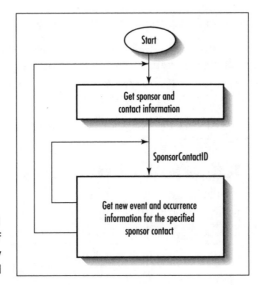

Figure 12-1
The main tasks of the event entry wizard

Establishing the Sponsor Contact for the New Events

The event entry wizard should give a user three options to establish the sponsor contact that can then be associated with all the new events subsequently added through that wizard:

1. Select an existing contact for an existing sponsor.

2. Add a new contact for an existing sponsor.

3. Add a new contact for a new sponsor.

The first two options require the user to select a sponsor that already exists in the calendar database. This is where we need to consider two other requirements of the event entry wizard: security and bandwidth friendliness.

As part of the security requirement, the event entry wizard must ensure that the user enters the correct user name and password combination for the selected sponsor before adding any new information. The bandwidth-friendliness requirement forces us to think twice if we are considering having the user choose an existing sponsor by listing the names (and **SponsorIDs**) of all the existing sponsors in a selection list control. Imagine what will happen when the calendar database grows big and contains thousands of sponsor records. A lot of data will then have to be sent to each requesting user, consuming both time and bandwidth.

To work around this problem, you can make the task of sponsor selection a two-step process. First, have a user enter the first few characters of the sponsor name through a static input form. Then generate a form containing the sponsor selection list that is populated with only sponsors whose names begin with the specified characters. This list should be a lot smaller than the total sponsor count. Also note that because the sponsor name field is indexed in the calendar database, searching the matching sponsor names and sending the ones that match over the Net is a lot quicker than sending the complete sponsor list. We will look further into this aspect in Lesson 2.

Now that you have established a process for selecting an existing sponsor, you can merge this process with the option of adding a new sponsor to conduct the first main task of the event entry wizard, as follows:

1. Start the user with a static input form that prompts for the first few characters of the sponsor name, irrespective of whether that user wants to select an existing sponsor or add a new one.

2. Send the user a dynamically generated input form displaying a selection list of matching sponsors and providing input fields for adding a new sponsor and up to three associated contacts.

3. If the user selects a sponsor from the selection list, go to step 4. If the user adds a new sponsor, go to step 5.

4. Ask for the user name and password set for that sponsor. Go to step 5 for getting the correct combination; otherwise, repeat this step.

5. Verify that at least one valid contact has been specified for that new sponsor and then add the sponsor and contact information to the calendar database.

6. If only one new contact was added with this sponsor, then make that contact the selected contact and go to step 9; otherwise, make this newly added sponsor the selected sponsor and go to step 7.

7. Send the user a dynamically generated form displaying a selection list of all the sponsor contacts associated with the selected sponsor, and provide input fields to add a new sponsor contact.

8. If the user enters a new sponsor contact, then add it to the database and make it the selected sponsor contact.

9. Pass the `SponsorContactID` of the selected sponsor contact to the first form of the second main task of the event entry wizard.

Figure 12-2 outlines the logical flow of the above steps, which potentially update only two tables of the calendar database, `tblSponsors` and `tblSponsorsContacts`. Note that there is no input form for user authentication. This is because we will request the `username` and `password` values using the authentication dialog box of the browser, as demonstrated in the next lesson.

Adding New Events for the Specified Sponsor Contact

The second main task of the event entry wizard deals with accepting information about new events for the sponsor contact established through the first main task. Designing an input flow model for this second task requires more elaborate analysis than the first one because now you are dealing with the simultaneous data entry of more than two tables. For each new event, you have to ensure that the user provides the following information:

● The header information, which is stored in the `tblEvents` table.

● The name and address of each new location where this event is occurring. These new locations, which should not already exist in the `tblLocations` table, are then added to the `tblLocations` table and assigned a unique `LocationID` value.

● The event occurrence information in the form of one or more records of the `LocationID`, `date`, and `time` values that are eventually stored in the `tblEventsLocations` table.

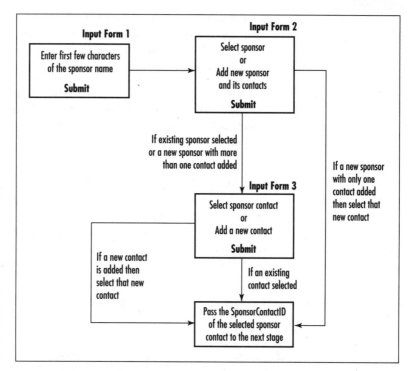

Figure 12-2
Conducting the first main task of the event entry wizard

In addition to the preceding input requirements, you need to ensure that the header information of the new event is not permanently saved in the **tblEvents** table until at least one associated occurrence record is saved in the **tblEventsLocation** table simultaneously.

Based on this requirement analysis and considering the standard objectives of the event entry wizard, you can conduct the second main task using the following plan:

1. Send the user an input form for accepting only the event header information.

2. Temporarily store this header information.

3. Send the user an input form prompting for the city in which the event will be occurring. Also have the form ask for the number of times the event will be occurring in that city.

4. Send the user an input form displaying a selection list containing the names of all the known locations in that city, the appropriate input controls to accept information of a new location, and an array of input controls to accept multiple date and time values. The size of this array should depend on the number of occasions specified in the previous form.

5. Once the user submits one instance of the location and timing information, permanently store the event header and this instance in the calendar database. For each additional instance, use the `EventID` assigned to this event to store that instance permanently.

6. Inform the user to use the Back button to return to any of the previous screens to add more information. For example, the user can return to the form presented in step 4 to add a new location in the same city as the previous location.

Figure 12-3 outlines the logical flow of the above steps.

Note that the information requested in step 3 is mainly used to customize the input form sent in step 4. This neat technique, in which a form is used to generate another form dynamically, is the closest you can come to reaping the benefits of having all the input controls on one single form without constraining the number of records a user can enter through that form. We will examine the implementation of this technique and other concepts needed to execute the above plan properly in Lesson 4.

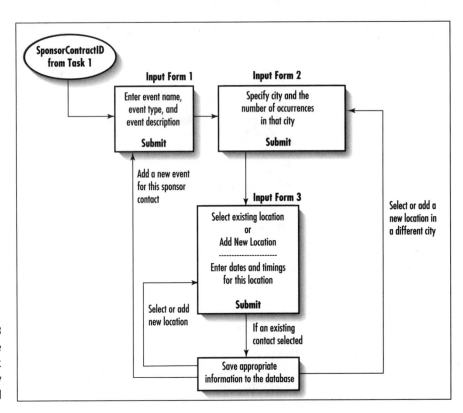

Figure 12-3
Conducting the second main task of the event entry wizard

Lesson Summary

This lesson described the overall objectives of a Web-based event entry wizard that allows users to enter sponsor and event information through a series of linked forms. Many of these forms are dynamically generated based on the information received from the previous form, thereby removing the constraints posed by the single-form-based data entry approach discussed in Chapter 11, "Populating Tables: Web-Based Data Entry."

The whole process of executing the event entry wizard was divided into two main tasks. The first task deals with getting the sponsor and contact information; the second task gets the event information for the specified sponsor contact. The exact sequence of events for both tasks was explained in detail. In the next lesson you will see a practical demonstration of the first main task of the event entry wizard and we will discuss its implementation.

 **QUIZ 1**

1. What makes the implementation of the Web-based event entry wizard a difficult task?
    a. The unlimited records flexibility requires a large number of forms to be generated dynamically.
    b. The stateless nature of the Web makes it difficult to maintain continuity between the linked forms.
    c. Each input form used by the wizard becomes quite lengthy.
    d. All of the above.

2. Why is the sponsor contact chosen as the point of separation for establishing the two main tasks of the event entry wizard?
    a. The contact information and the event information are independent of each other.
    b. The contact information links sponsor information with event information.
    c. Having the sponsor and contact information in the database without the associated event information does not disturb the database business rules.
    d. All of the above.

3. How is the issue of bandwidth friendliness resolved for selecting an existing sponsor in the event entry wizard?
    a. By listing only the names of the existing sponsors in the sponsor selection list
    b. By making the user enter the first few characters of the sponsor name and then listing only those sponsors whose names start with those characters
    c. By making the user enter the full sponsor name and then matching it with an existing sponsor name
    d. None of the above

4 . How will the event entry wizard respond if a user adds a new sponsor?
   a. It will temporarily store the sponsor information without verifying the contact details.
   b. It will add the sponsor information to the database.
   c. It will verify at least one valid contact information for that sponsor before adding it to the calendar database.
   d. It will send the user a list of all existing sponsor contacts.

5. When does the event entry wizard permanently store the event header information?
   a. As soon as the user submits the header data
   b. After the user specifies the city of the event location
   c. After the user submits one instance of the event location and timing information
   d. After the user submits all instances of the event location and timing information

Complexity: Moderate
1. Design the static version of the three HTML forms needed to conduct the first main task of the event entry wizard. Name these forms `evententry_1.htm`, `evententry_2.htm`, and `evententry_3.htm`.

Complexity: Moderate
2. Design the static version of the three HTML forms needed to conduct the second main task of the event entry wizard. Name these forms `evententry_4.htm`, `evententry_5.htm`, and `evententry_6.htm`.

GENERATING DYNAMIC INPUT FORMS

As discussed in Lesson 1, the design of the event entry wizard can be thought of as a two-phase process. The first phase establishes the sponsor and contact of the new event, and the second phase deals with obtaining the event header, location, and occurrence information. Figures 12-2 and 12-3 depict how each phase can be conducted using a series of linked forms where each form is dynamically generated based on the information provided in the previous form.

A dynamically generated form (or a *dynamic form*) can be thought of as an HTML document comprising a sequence of static and dynamic sections. An easy way to create a dynamic form is to use the *break-and-combine approach*, in which you store the static sections in separate external files and then programmatically combine the contents of these files with the dynamic portions. You saw an implementation of this approach in the example of the location entry form presented in Chapter 11, Lesson 2.

The main advantage of this approach is that you have the flexibility to change the layout of the resulting form by modifying the external files without having to touch the CGI program. However, this approach also has a couple of drawbacks that come about as a result of segregating one HTML document into multiple files. The first drawback is that the creation of a dynamic form with many noncontiguous dynamic sections requires several external files. Furthermore, if you plan on using many dynamic forms in your Web application, you might end up with a lot of small external files, which can become hard to manage.

The second drawback of this approach is that editing these individual external files in an HTML editor to make several form layout changes is not easy. On the other hand, if you edit the original (and complete) HTML document representing that form, you will have to recreate the external files once again, which could be a tedious process.

In this lesson, we shall show you an easier approach for creating dynamic forms. This approach, called the *template file approach*, follows the template file scheme that Access uses in its Web publishing wizard. (See Chapter 10, Lesson 2, for details on the Web publishing wizard.)

The Template File Approach

The idea behind the template file approach is simple. You create the static version (a text file) of the HTML document that you want to publish dynamically. Then you embed special markup codes (sometimes also called *tokens*) in this text file as place holders for the dynamic sections. Finally, you make your CGI program read this text file and replace each special markup code with the appropriate dynamic content. The main advantage of this approach is that you can edit the template text file with the embedded markup codes directly through your HTML editor. We will discuss the implementation of this approach later in this lesson when we examine the design of the $EVENTENTRY.EXE Windows CGI program that represents the event entry wizard.

Self-Contained Application Design

If a Web application is based mostly on generating dynamic responses (such as the event entry wizard), then you should also consider making this application self-contained and adaptive to its environment. A *self-contained and adaptive application* keeps all the external files used by its back-end programs along with the programs themselves. Only the static documents used for the application's front end are placed under the Web server's document root directory hierarchy. In addition, absolute paths that refer to any external file are never hard-coded within the back-end program. Either the paths are determined automatically (as you will see later in this lesson) or they are read from an external file whose file path can be determined automatically.

The principle of path independence is applicable not only to the back end but also to the front end of the Web application. For example, if the back-end program sends a dynamic form that should submit the request back to that same program, then the form's destination URL path should be set based on the current location of that program.

The biggest advantage of self-contained and adaptive applications is that you can create and run multiple versions of that application at the same time by putting each version in a different directory. Furthermore, each version can be independently customized without affecting the other versions.

The example Web applications that we have discussed in past chapters are not good examples of self-contained or adaptive applications. All external files used by these applications were placed under the hierarchy of the WebSite server's document root directory (**C:\WEBSITE\HTDOCS**), even though some of these files (the **CALENDAR.MDB** file, for example) were used only by their back-end Windows CGI programs. Furthermore, the paths to the **CALENDAR.MDB** file and all other external files were hard-coded within their Windows CGI programs. This means that if you move the database or any other external file into a different directory or if your Web server is installed on a drive other than the C drive, most of these applications will not work unless you modify the paths and recompile the Windows CGI programs.

The reason we took this hard-coded path approach for these earlier applications was to keep things simple and consistent so that you could focus on the individual Web database concepts rather than worrying about how each application was laid out. The **$EVENTENTRY.EXE** program that we will examine next is based on the principles of a self-contained and adaptive Web application and uses the template file approach to create the dynamic forms. Before we get into the implementation details, let's take a quick peek at how this program conducts the first phase of the event entry wizard. We will go over its second phase in Lesson 4.

Note The idea of designing true self-contained applications contradicts the idea of striking a balance between static and dynamic publishing discussed in Chapter 10.

Demonstrating the First Phase of the Event Entry Wizard

The **$EVENTENTRY.EXE** Windows CGI program resides in the **C:\WEBSITE\CGI-WIN\WDBIC\EVENTENTRY** directory and performs all the tasks of the event entry wizard. Follow the steps below to run the first phase of this wizard:

1. Start your WebSite server if it is not already running and request the following URL from your Web browser:

   ```
   http://localhost/cgi-win/wdbic/evententry/$evententry.exe
   ```

   The program responds by returning the first input form of the event entry wizard, as shown in Figure 12-4. As you can see, this form contains a text box asking for the first few characters of the name of the sponsor holding the new event.

2. Enter Gr in the text box and then press the Next button.

The program now returns the second input form, as shown in Figure 12-5.

This form contains a selection list displaying the known sponsor names beginning with the characters Gr and an option to select a new sponsor. If you select the new sponsor option, then the form instructs you to enter information about the new sponsor and at least one associated contact, as shown in Figure 12-6.

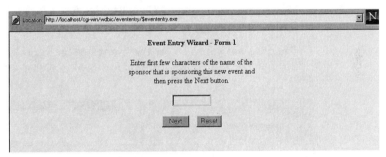

Figure 12-4
The first input form of the event entry wizard

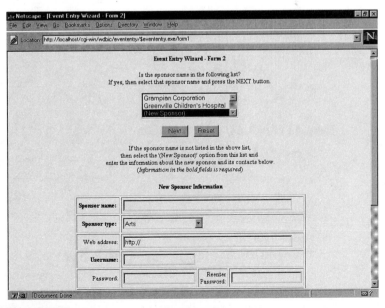

Figure 12-5
The second input form of the event entry wizard

3. For this demonstration, select Grampian Corporation from the sponsor selection list and then press the Next button.

   The browser prompts for the user name and password combination for this sponsor, as shown in Figure 12-7.

4. Enter Quality for the user name and benchmark for the password and then press the OK button.

   The $EVENTENTRY.EXE program now returns the third input form, listing the known contacts and an option to add a new contact for the selected sponsor, as shown in Figure 12-8.

5. Select the second contact (Sue Hay) from this list and press the Next button.

   The program now asks for the event header information of the new event through the fourth input form, as shown in Figure 12-9.

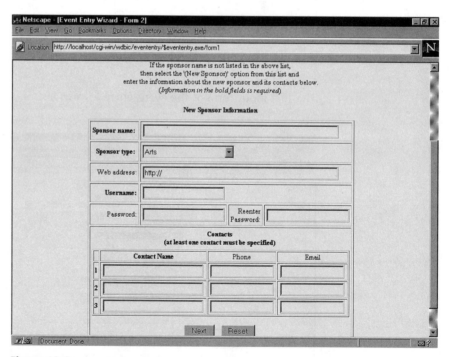

Figure 12-6
The new sponsor and contact entry section of the second input form of the event entry wizard

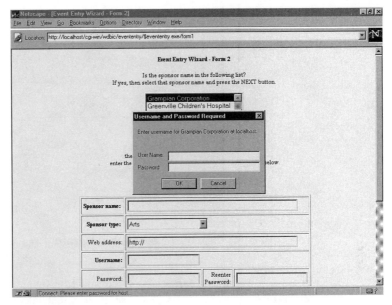

Figure 12-7
The browser prompting for the user name and password
combination for the selected sponsor

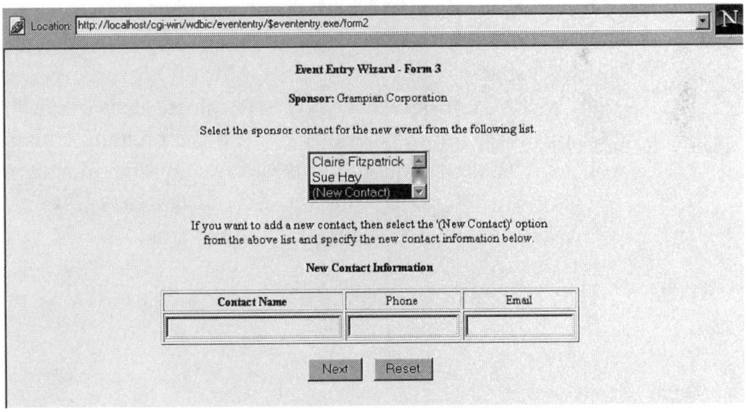

Figure 12-8
The third input form of the event entry wizard

This fourth form marks the beginning of the second main task of the event entry wizard, so we will stop here. We will explore the subsequent input forms of this wizard in the next lesson. At this point, we recommend that you go to the first form and try some other input combinations. Add some new sponsors (through input form 2)

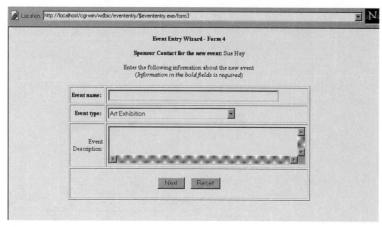

Figure 12-9
The fourth input form of the event entry wizard

and some new contacts of the existing sponsors (through input form 3). Examine the contents of the sponsor and contact tables of the **CALENDAR.MDB** file residing in the **C:\ WEBSITE\CGI-WIN\WDBIC\EVENTENTRY** directory after each form submission.

Implementation of the First Phase of the Event Entry Wizard

The **$EVENTENTRY.EXE** program is designed so that the complete response is stored in a string variable, and then the final value of this variable is sent to the CGI output file right before the program is ready to terminate. This use of an intermediate string variable provides a lot of flexibility for how the program constructs its response because you can change the value of this variable anytime during processing to modify your response. The **CGI_Main** procedure of the **$EVENTENTRY.EXE** program, presented in Listing 12-1, shows how this technique is implemented.

Listing 12-1 The **CGI_Main** procedure of the **$EVENTENTRY.EXE** program

```
Sub CGI_Main()

  'Add Error Handler
  On Error GoTo Err_CGI_Main

  'Get form identifier from the URL's extra path by removing the leading
  'slash from CGI_LogicalPath.
  TaskIdentifier = UCase$(Mid$(CGI_LogicalPath, 2))

  'Call the appropriate procedure based on TaskIdentifier's value
  Select Case TaskIdentifier
    Case "FORM1"
      HandleForm1
```

```
        Case "FORM2"
            HandleForm2
        Case "FORM3"
            HandleForm3
        Case "FORM4"
            HandleForm4
        Case "FORM5"
            HandleForm5
        Case "FORM6"
            HandleForm6
        Case Else
            SendForm1
    End Select

Exit_CGI_Main:
    Send Result
    Exit Sub

'Error Handling Section
Err_CGI_Main:
    HandleError              'Handle error gracefully
    Resume Exit_CGI_Main 'Return to the Exit_CGI_Mainsection

End Sub
```

The **CGI_Main** procedure uses the extra path portion of the requesting URL to determine which step of the event entry wizard the user is on. If the extra path portion is empty, the procedure starts the user with the first input form of the wizard by calling the **SendForm1** procedure. In other cases, **CGI_Main** passes control to the appropriate procedures, which not only process the incoming request but also store the response in the **Result** string variable. The **CGI_Main** procedure (before it exits) sends the value of this **Result** variable as its last statement before terminating.

The **Result** variable, like most other variables used in this program, was declared in the Declarations section of the **MYAPP.BAS** module to give it module-level scope.

What happens if a procedure called by the **CGI_Main** procedure signals back a run-time error? As you can see from Listing 12-1, control is passed to the **HandleError** procedure, shown in Listing 12-2.

Listing 12-2 The HandleError procedure of the $EVENTENTRY.EXE program

```
Public Sub HandleError()

Dim NL As String

    If Err = ERR_FAILED_SECURITY Then Exit Sub  'Result already generated

    NL = Chr(13) & Chr(10)          'Newline characters
    Result = HTMLContentType()      'Initialize result with the content-type lines
    Result = Result & "<HTML><HEAD><TITLE>Event Entry Wizard</TITLE></HEAD>"
    If ErrorMessage = "" Then
        Result = Result & NL & Error$         'Send VB's error message
```

continued on next page

continued from previous page

```
Else
  Result = Result & NL & ErrorMessage     'Send custom error message
End If
Result = Result & NL & "</BODY></HTML>"
'Rollback the current transaction (if any)
On Error Resume Next
DBEngine(0).Rollback

End Sub
```

Unless a security failure error has been signaled (the details of which we shall discuss in the next lesson), the `HandleError` procedure simply overwrites the current value of the `Result` variable with its own CGI response containing the error message. This way, no matter where and how the run-time error occurs, the user will always get a properly formed error message. The `HTMLContentType` function used by the `HandleError` procedure and shown in Listing 12-3 returns a string containing the Content-type header lines needed to start an HTML-formatted CGI response.

Listing 12-3 The `HTMLContentType` function of the `$EVENTENTRY.EXE` program

```
Public Function HTMLContentType()

  'Start the CGI output for an HTML-based response
  HTMLContentType = "Content-type: text/html" & Chr(13) & Chr(10) & Chr(13) & Chr(10)

End Function
```

The `SendForm1` *Procedure of the* `$EVENTENTRY.EXE` *Program*

The `CGI_Main` procedure calls the `SendForm1` procedure to send the first input form of the event entry wizard. The `SendForm1` procedure, presented in Listing 12-4, handles this job by using the `EVENTENTRY_1.HTM` text file as a template.

Listing 12-4 The `SendForm1` procedure of the `$EVENTENTRY.EXE` program

```
Public Sub SendForm1()

  'Creates the first input form of the event entry wizard
  Result = HTMLContentType()    'Start with the content type line
  Result = Result & ReadFile(App.Path & "\Responses\evententry_1.htm")
  Result = ReplaceString(Result, "**CGI_ExecutablePath**", CGI_ExecutablePath)

End Sub
```

The `EVENTENTRY_1.HTM` file (and every other template file used by this program) is stored in a subdirectory (named `Responses`) of the directory that holds this program. Any VB program can refer to its directory path through the `Path` property of the `App` object; the `SendForm1` procedure utilizes this `App.Path` information to determine the location of the `EVENTENTRY_1.HTM` file automatically. The `ReadFile` function, which simply returns the contents of the specified file as a string value to the calling procedure, is designed similar to the `SendFile` procedure shown in Listing 11-13 (see Chapter 11, Lesson 2).

The first input form of the event entry wizard is essentially a static form except that it must submit its request back to the `$EVENTENTRY.EXE` program. This means that the destination URL path of this input form should be based on the program's current location. To achieve this functionality, a special markup code, `**CGI_ExecutablePath**`, is placed in the `<FORM>` tag of the `EVENTENTRY_1.HTM` file:

```
<form action="**CGI_ExecutablePath**/form1" method="POST" name="Event Entry Form 1">
```

The `SendForm1` procedure then replaces this markup code with the program's current URL path (available through the `CGI_ExecutablePath` VB variable) by calling the `ReplaceString` function.

The `ReplaceString` function tries to substitute every occurrence of the search string (its second argument) in the source string (its first argument) with the replacement string (its third argument). So it is important to ensure that the markup code the program uses as place holders for dynamic substitutions is distinct from the regular HTML text stored in your template file.

The `HandleForm1` *Procedure of the* `$EVENTENTRY.EXE` *Program*

When the user enters the first few characters of the sponsor name in the `SponsorName` input field of the first input form, the request is submitted back to the `$EVENTENTRY.EXE` program with the requesting URL's extra path portion set to `/Form1`. The `CGI_Main` procedure, on receiving this extra path value, calls the `HandleForm1` procedure presented in Listing 12-5.

Listing 12-5 The `HandleForm1` procedure of the `$EVENTENTRY.EXE` program

```
Public Sub HandleForm1()

  'Create a recordset of matching sponsor names
  OpenCalendarDatabase     'Open the calendar database residing in the program direc⟸
tory
  Set qd = dbCalendar.QueryDefs("qrySponsors_Matching")
  qd!pSponsorName = GetSmallField("SponsorName")
  Set rs = qd.OpenRecordset()
  'Make an HTML option list of matching sponsor names
  MatchingSponsors = ""
  Do Until rs.EOF
    MatchingSponsors = MatchingSponsors & "<option value=""" & rs!SponsorID & """>"
    MatchingSponsors = MatchingSponsors & rs!SponsorName & "</option>" & Chr$(13) &⟸
Chr$(10)
```

continued on next page

continued from previous page

```
        rs.MoveNext
    Loop
    'Send the second input form
    SendForm2

End Sub
```

The `HandleForm1` procedure first opens the calendar database residing in the program directory by calling the `OpenCalendarDatabase` procedure. It then uses the Parameter query named `qrySponsors_Matching` (stored in that database) to generate a recordset containing a list of sponsors beginning with characters specified in the `SponsorName` input field of the first input form. The recordset is then used to create an HTML option list of matching sponsors. This list is stored in the `MatchingSponsors` string variable and is used by the `SendForm2` procedure to create the second input form based on the `EVENTENTRY_2.HTM` template file.

The `SendForm2` *Procedure of the* $EVENTENTRY.EXE *Program*

The design of the `SendForm2` procedure is shown in Listing 12-6.

Listing 12-6 The `SendForm2` procedure of the $EVENTENTRY.EXE program

```
Public Sub SendForm2()

    'Creates the second input form of the event entry wizard
    Result = HTMLContentType()     'Start with the content type line
    Result = Result & ReadFile(App.Path & "\Responses\evententry_2.htm")
    Result = ReplaceString(Result, "**CGI_ExecutablePath**", CGI_ExecutablePath)
    Result = ReplaceString(Result, "<option>**MatchingSponsors**</option>",⇐
MatchingSponsors)

End Sub
```

Note that the markup code used for representing the matching sponsor option list in the second input form is the string `<option>**MatchingSponsor**</option>` and not just `**MatchingSponsors**`. This is because if you display the contents of the `EVENT ENTRY_2.HTM` file, you will see that it creates the sponsor name selection list as follows:

```
<select name="SponsorID" size="3">
        <option>**MatchingSponsors**</option>
        <option selected value="New">(New Sponsor)</option>
</select>
```

Creating markup codes with embedded HTML tags helps keep the integrity of the HTML document when you display the template file directly through a browser or an HTML editor. For example, Figure 12-10 shows how the FrontPage HTML editor treats our markup code as just another valid option of the sponsor name list.

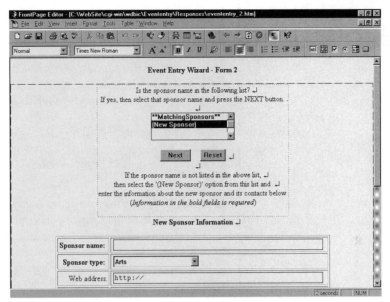

Figure 12-10
The EVENTENTRY_2.HTM file opened in FrontPage

Lesson Summary

This lesson discussed some of the disadvantages of the make-and-combine approach for generating dynamic HTML forms and presented the template file approach, which overcomes these disadvantages and is relatively easy to implement. In this approach, special markup codes are embedded as place markers for the dynamic sections of the form in the static version of the HTML document, called the template file. The CGI program reads this template file and replaces each markup code with the appropriate dynamic content.

The $EVENTENTRY.EXE program presented in this lesson shows a practical implementation of this approach. The program also demonstrates the principles of self-contained and adaptive Web applications by logically placing the external files and avoiding the use of hard-coded paths. This lesson limited its discussion to how the $EVENTENTRY.EXE program conducts the first phase of the event entry wizard, in which the sponsor and contact information of a new event is established. In the next lesson, we shall look at how this program deals with user security issues and how it passes information from one input form to the next in the first phase.

QUIZ 2

1. What are the disadvantages of dynamically generated HTML forms using the break-and-combine approach?
   a. The CGI program has to be modified every time the external files are modified.
   b. Each form may require several external files.
   c. Every time the HTML document representing a dynamically generated form is edited, the external files have to be recreated.
   d. All of the above.

2. What are the requirements for the markup codes used by the **$EVENTENTRY.EXE** program in its implementation of the template file approach?
   a. Each markup code must be placed within an HTML comment.
   b. Each markup code must start and end with two asterisk (*****) characters.
   c. Each markup code must be distinct from the regular HTML text.
   d. All of the above.

3. What are the characteristics of self-contained and adaptive Web applications?
   a. They keep all external files used by the back-end program with the back-end program so that multiple versions of the application can be developed easily and independently.
   b. The front-end forms of these applications are static in nature and kept under the document root directory hierarchy so that they can be directly accessed by the user without having to request the back-end programs.
   c. They offer path independence by avoiding the use of hard-coded absolute paths in their back-end programs.
   d. All of the above.

4. What will happen if **$EVENTENTRY.EXE** tries to replace a markup code that appears at two different places in the template file?
   a. A run-time error will be generated.
   b. Only the first occurrence of the markup code will be replaced.
   c. Only the second occurrence of the markup code will be replaced.
   d. Both occurrences of the markup code will be replaced.

5. What happens when you submit the first form of the event entry wizard without entering any character in the sponsor name input box?
   a. The wizard returns an error message specifying that at least one character must be specified in the sponsor name input box.
   b. The wizard shows only the (New Sponsor) option in the sponsor selection list of the second input form.
   c. The wizard returns the second input form with its sponsor selection list displaying the names of all the known sponsors.
   d. The wizard asks for the user name and password information.

Complexity: Easy

1. Modify the **$EVENTENTRY.EXE** program so that it displays the (New Sponsor) option as the first option in the sponsor selection list of the second input form.

Complexity: Moderate

2. Create a new version of the event entry wizard (**$EVENTENTRY2.EXE** in the **C:\WEB-SITE\CGI-WIN\WDBIC\EVENTENTRY2** directory with its own calendar database) that uses an external template file named **ERROR.HTM** to format its error messages. Design a sample **ERROR.HTM** file to test this version.

ADDING USER SECURITY AND MAINTAINING STATE USING HIDDEN FIELDS

Security should be an important consideration when you are designing Web applications that allow online data entry in a multiuser environment. Essentially, you want to protect one user's data from being tampered with by another user. As explained in Chapter 3, "Organizing Data: Tables and Relationships," Lesson 5, you can take different approaches to handling data security. One common approach is to link each dataset with a user name and password combination and allow only users who provide the right combination the appropriate control to that dataset.

Having **Username** and **Password** fields in the database is not the only step. Where you place these fields is also important. For example, in our calendar database, we added the **Username** and **Password** fields to the sponsor table. This permits any contact of that sponsor to add events associated with any other contact. If we wanted to limit contacts to their own events, the **Username** and **Password** fields would then have to be placed with the sponsor contact table.

Once the appropriate security model has been incorporated into the database structure, the data entry process should be designed so that it enforces security at appropriate check points. Note that if you conduct the data entry process through a series of linked input forms (like in a wizard), you may need to do a security check after each form submission or whenever you want to ensure that the requests are coming from the same user.

The requirement of placing multiple security check points during the same data entry session originates mainly because the Web follows a sessionless model. Each request sent to the Web server is independent of all other requests, and you have no way of knowing if the same user is sending all the requests during a particular data entry session unless you verify the user with each request. Does that mean that the user should be asked for authentication information (the user name and password combination) with each input form? That would certainly annoy most users.

The proper approach is to require authentication information only once (the first time) and have this information silently (and automatically) relayed back with each subsequent request. In other words, have your Web application maintain a link between user requests and implement virtual user sessions over the sessionless Web model. This lesson describes two approaches to maintaining this link and shows how they are implemented in the event entry wizard. The first approach uses the browser's Username and Password dialog box, whereas the second approach uses hidden fields to pass information between subsequent requests.

Implementing Security Using the Browser's Username and Password Dialog Box

As you saw in Lesson 2, the event entry wizard (implemented through the $EVENTENTRY.EXE program) has a security check point located between the second and third input form, when the user selects an existing sponsor from the sponsor selection list. As you will see in the next lesson, the wizard also has another security check point before it tries to save the new event information.

The wizard gathers the user authentication information for these security checks using the browser's built-in Username and Password dialog box. The main advantage of using the browser's dialog box (instead of adding the `Username` and `Password` input fields to the input forms) is that the browser automatically supplies the user name and password combination with every subsequent request a user makes during that session. To see how this browser-based security is implemented within the event entry wizard, let's continue with our examination of the $EVENTENTRY.EXE program (from the previous lesson) and see how it handles the request submitted through the second input form.

Examining the `HandleForm2` Procedure of the $EVENTENTRY.EXE Program

The second input form of the event entry wizard (see Figure 12-5 in Lesson 2) is designed to send its data back to the $MULTIENTRY.EXE program with the extra path portion of the requesting URL set to `Form2`. The `CGI_Main` procedure of the $EVENTENTRY.EXE program (see Listing 12-1), on detecting this extra path value, passes control to the `HandleForm2` procedure, which is presented in Listing 12-7.

Listing 12-7 The `HandleForm2` procedure of the $EVENTENTRY.EXE program

```
Public Sub HandleForm2()

    'Get the option selected in the sponsor selection list
    SponsorID = GetSmallField("SponsorID")
    If SponsorID = "New" Then   'If new sponsor option is selected
```

```
      AddNewSponsor                'then add the new sponsor and its contacts to database
      If ContactCount = 1 Then 'If only one contact was specified for this new sponsor
         SendForm4                 'then proceed directly to input form 4
         Exit Sub                  'and exit
      End If
   Else
      'An existing sponsor was selected so ask for and verify
      'username and password information by calling the following procedure
      AuthenticateUser             'Signals error if unable to authenticate user
   End If
   'If here, then the user has passed authentication
   'so, make an HTML option list of matching contacts and
   'send the third input form
   OpenCalendarDatabase
   Set qd = dbCalendar.QueryDefs("qrySponsorsContacts_SelectedSponsorID")
   qd!pSponsorID = rsSponsor!SponsorID
   Set rs = qd.OpenRecordset()
   MatchingContacts = ""
   Do Until rs.EOF
      MatchingContacts = MatchingContacts & "<option value=""" & rs!SponsorContactID &⇐
""">"
      MatchingContacts = MatchingContacts & rs!ContactName & "</option>" & Chr$(13) &⇐
Chr$(10)
      rs.MoveNext
   Loop
   SendForm3

End Sub
```

The **HandleForm2** procedure first checks to see if the user selected the (New Sponsor) option from the sponsor selection list, in which case it calls the **AddNewSponsor** procedure to validate the new sponsor and contact information and add it to the database. The **AddNewSponsor** procedure (not shown here) essentially follows the logic of the **MULTIENTRY3.EXE** program discussed in Chapter 11, Lesson 6, except that it does not create any response and signals an error on encountering invalid data or if it fails for any other reason.

After calling the **AddNewSponsor** procedure, the **HandleForm2** procedure inspects the **ContactCount** variable (whose value is set by the **AddNewSponsor** procedure) to determine the number of contacts entered for the new sponsor. If only one contact was entered, then the **HandleForm2** procedure calls the **SendForm4** procedure to send the fourth input form (one that asks about event header information). We will cover the design of the **SendForm4** procedure later in this lesson.

If the user selects an existing sponsor from the sponsor selection list, then the **HandleForm2** procedure calls the **AuthenticateUser** procedure to determine if the user has the access to perform data entry for the selected sponsor. If the **AuthenticateUser** procedure does not generate any error, then the **HandleForm2** procedure creates an HTML-formatted option list of the matching contacts and calls the **SendForm3** procedure, which uses this list to create the third input form. The **SendForm3** procedure is examined later in this lesson. Let's now look at how the **AuthenticateUser** procedure works.

Examining the AuthenticateUser *Procedure of the* $EVENTENTRY.EXE *Program*

The design of the AuthenticateUser procedure is shown in Listing 12-8.

Listing 12-8 The AuthenticateUser procedure of the $EVENTENTRY.EXE program

```
Public Sub AuthenticateUser()

  'Retrieve the username and password of the selected sponsor from the database
  OpenCalendarDatabase
  Set rsSponsor = dbCalendar.OpenRecordset("tblSponsors", dbOpenDynaset)
  rsSponsor.FindFirst "SponsorID = " & SponsorID
  UserName = rsSponsor!UserName
  Password = NullToEmpty(rsSponsor!Password)
  'Match the stored username and password combination with the
  'combination that came with the incoming request
  If CGI_AuthUser <> UserName Or CGI_AuthPass <> Password Then
     'Combination incorrect, so create a response asking for authentication
     Result = ReadFile(App.Path & "\Responses\authenticate.txt")
     Result = ReplaceString(Result, "**SponsorName**", rsSponsor!SponsorName)
     Error ERR_FAILED_SECURITY
  End If

End Sub
```

The AuthenticateUser procedure first opens a dynaset-type recordset based on the sponsor table and applies the FindFirst method to locate the record of the selected sponsor. It then compares the values of the Username and Password fields stored in that record (after converting a Null password value to an empty string) with the user name and password combination (CGI_AuthUser and CGI_AuthPass) that came with the request. If the security check fails, then this procedure first creates a response that makes the browser display its Username and Password dialog box (using the authenticate.txt template file listed in Listing 12-9) and then signals the ERR_FAILED_SECURITY error to the calling procedure.

Listing 12-9 Contents of the authenticate.txt file

```
HTTP/1.0 401 Unauthorized
WWW-authenticate: basic realm="**SponsorName**"

<HTML>
<HEAD><TITLE>User Authentication Failed</TITLE></HEAD>
<BODY>
You must specify the correct username and password combination
in order to enter new events for this sponsor.
</BODY>
</HTML>
```

The HandleError procedure that eventually processes all the run-time errors is designed so that it does nothing on receiving the ERR_FAILED_SECURITY error signal. (See Listing

12-2 in Lesson 2 for the code of the **HandleError** procedure.) As a result, the **CGI_Main** procedure (see Listing 12-1) ends up sending the response created by the **AuthenticateUser** procedure back to the user.

The details of how this browser-based authentication process works were explained in Chapter 8, Lesson 4. Essentially, when the user first submits the second input form, no user name and password information is available to the browser and it sends the form data without any authentication information. As a result, the **CGI_AuthUser** and **CGI_AuthPass** CGI variables are blank ("") the first time the **AuthenticateUser** procedure is called.

Because every sponsor in the database has a nonempty user name (the **Username** field of the sponsor table is a required field), the security check in the **AuthenticateUser** procedure fails, causing it to send the HTTP response with the authentication required status code. The browser, on receiving this response, prompts the user for the user name and password information. After receiving that information, it then automatically resubmits the original form request with this authentication information. The request again goes through the **AuthenticateUser** procedure of another instance of the **$EVENTENTRY.EXE** program (because the first instance already terminated); if the authentication information is correct, the **AuthenticateUser** procedure simply terminates, allowing the calling procedure to proceed normally.

The browser keeps sending the current authentication information with each subsequent request until either the user terminates the browser program or the browser receives another **Authentication required** message from the Web server.

Linking Forms Through Hidden Fields

As mentioned earlier in this lesson, the **HandleForm2** procedure either adds a new sponsor and the associated contacts to the database or verifies if the user has the right user name and password combination if that user selected an existing contact from the sponsor selection list. The outcome in either case is that the **SponsorID** VB variable is set to the **SponsorID** of the specified sponsor as reflected in the calendar database. After the **HandleForm2** procedure is done handling the sponsor, it prepares an HTML-formatted option list of the associated contacts and then calls the **SendForm3** procedure to generate the third input form. Before we examine the design of the **SendForm3** procedure, let's revisit the functionality of the third input form.

As you can see from Figure 12-8 in Lesson 2, the third input form allows a user either to pick an existing contact for the specified sponsor or to add a new contact for that sponsor through the provided input fields. If the user selects an existing contact from the contact selection list and submits this form, the receiving program gets the **SponsorContactID** of the selected contact in the form request, which is all the program needs to determine everything about the contact and its sponsor. However, if the user specifies a new contact through this form, then to add that contact to the database, the receiving program needs to know the **SponsorID** of the sponsor selected in the second input form. But how does the program know about this **SponsorID**?

One way may be to use the user name and password combination the browser sends with the form request. Search the sponsor table for the sponsor having that combination and use the **SponsorID** of that sponsor. There are two obvious problems with this approach. First, the browser will not send any authentication information if the user enters a new sponsor in the second input form instead of selecting an existing sponsor. Notice in Figure 12-7 that for the new sponsor, the user name and password information is accepted through two form input fields and not through the browser's authentication dialog box. The second problem arises if there is another sponsor with the same user name and password combination as the selected sponsor. Remember that there is no uniqueness requirement on the **Username** and **Password** fields in the calendar database.

A more suitable way to propagate information from one form to the next is through hidden fields. As explained in Chapter 1, Lesson 4, hidden fields are special text fields not visible on the HTML form but sent along with the rest of the form fields when the user submits the form. The event entry wizard applies this hidden field approach to pass on the **SponsorID** value from the second input form to the third input form. This will become clear once we look at the **SendForm3** procedure, which is shown in Listing 12-10.

Listing 12-10 The `SendForm3` procedure of the `$EVENTENTRY.EXE` program

```
Public Sub SendForm3()

    Result = HTMLContentType()   'Start with the content type line
    Result = Result & ReadFile(App.Path & "\Responses\evententry_3.htm")
    'Set the form's destination path
    Result = ReplaceString(Result, "**CGI_ExecutablePath**", CGI_ExecutablePath)
    'Set the value of the SponsorContactID hidden field
    Result = ReplaceString(Result, "**SponsorID**", SponsorID)
    'Set the name of the selected contact
    Result = ReplaceString(Result, "**SponsorName**", rsSponsor!SponsorName)
    'Add the list of knows contacts to the contact selection list of the input form
    Result = ReplaceString(Result, "<option>**MatchingContacts**</option>",
MatchingContacts)

End Sub
```

As you can see in Listing 12-10, **SendForm3** creates the third input form based on the **EVENTENTRY_3.HTM** template file. This template file contains a **SponsorID** hidden field, which is constructed as follows:

```
<input type="hidden" name="SponsorID" value="**SponsorID**">
```

SendForm3 substitutes the ****SponsorID**** special markup code in the above line with the value of the **SponsorID** variable determined by **HandleForm2** procedure. This way, when the third input form is sent back to the user, it contains the appropriate value in its **SponsorID** hidden field. This same hidden field concept is used to propagate the **SponsorContactID** value selected through the third input form to the fourth input form.

The HandleForm3 and SendForm4 procedures, which implement this step and are designed similar to the HandleForm2 and SendForm3 procedures, are shown in Listing 12-11.

Listing 12-11 The HandleForm3 and SendForm4 procedures of the $EVENTENTRY.EXE program

```
Public Sub HandleForm3()

  'Handle request sent from the third input form
  SpContactID = GetSmallField("SponsorContactID")
  If SpContactID = "New" Then
    AddNewSponsorContact
  Else
    SelectSponsorContact
  End If
  SendForm4

End Sub

Public Sub SendForm4()

  Result = HTMLContentType()    'Start with the content type line
  Result = Result & ReadFile(App.Path & "\Responses\evententry_4.htm")
  'Set the form's destination path
  Result = ReplaceString(Result, "**CGI_ExecutablePath**", CGI_ExecutablePath)
  'Set the value of the SponsorContactID hidden field
  Result = ReplaceString(Result, "**SponsorContactID**", rsSpContact!SponsorContactID)
  'Set the name of the selected contact
  Result = ReplaceString(Result, "**ContactName**", rsSpContact!ContactName)

End Sub
```

Lesson Summary

This lesson discussed the importance of building appropriate security controls within Web applications that allow online data entry in a multiuser environment. Two approaches that help maintain a link between user requests and implement virtual user sessions over the otherwise sessionless Web model were introduced and their implementation within the $EVENTENTRY.EXE program was explained.

The first approach uses the browser's Username and Password dialog box, which the wizard uses to gather user authentication information. The browser automatically passes the user name and password combination with every subsequent request a user makes during that session. To link the sponsor information submitted through the second input form with the new contact information supplied through the third input form, the $EVENTENTRY.EXE program uses the hidden field approach, in which the SponsorID value is passed from the second form to the third as a hidden field. In the next lesson, we will look at the concept of persistent cookies, yet another (and perhaps the most versatile) technique for maintaining state in the Web environment.

1. Why is it important to have multiple security check points during the same data entry session?
   a. Because of the sessionless model of the Web
   b. To ensure that the requests are coming from the same user
   c. Because the requests are linked with each other
   d. Because the requests are dependent on each other

2. What is the advantage of using the browser's dialog box for user authentication?
   a. It eliminates the need to add the `username` and `password` input fields to the input forms.
   b. The browser automatically supplies the user name and password combination with every subsequent request.
   c. It helps reduce the number of requests that have to be made to the back-end CGI program.
   d. All of the above.

3. In which of the following cases will the browser display its authentication dialog box?
   a. When you select an existing sponsor from the sponsor selection list
   b. When you select the (New Sponsor) option from the sponsor selection list and enter the new sponsor and contact information (including user name and password data) through the fields provided on the second input form
   c. When you select the (New Sponsor) option from the sponsor selection list and enter the new sponsor and contact information except for the user name and password
   d. All of the above.

4. What hidden information is passed through the third input form of the event entry wizard?
   a. `SponsorID`
   b. `SponsorContactID`
   c. `Username`
   d. `Password`

5. What hidden information is passed through the fourth input form of the event entry wizard?
   a. `SponsorID`
   b. `SponsorContactID`
   c. `EventID`
   d. All of the above

Complexity: Easy

1. If you press the Cancel button when the browser displays its Username and Password dialog box, the browser automatically displays the following message:

```
You must specify the correct username and password combination
in order to enter new events for this sponsor.
```

Modify the **$EVENTENTRY.EXE** program so that it causes the browser to display the name of the selected sponsor in the above message.

Complexity: Moderate

2. Modify the **$EVENTENTRY.EXE** program so that it passes the user name and password values of the new sponsor entered in the second input form to the fourth input form through hidden fields.

PERSISTENT COOKIES

The hidden field approach described in the previous lesson is best suited for passing information between form requests when the flow of information occurs in only one direction: forward. This is because the hidden field is the attribute of the input form, and if the user goes back to an intermediate form containing a hidden field (using the browser's Back button) and then resubmits that form, the same original value of that hidden field is transmitted. In most cases, this is not a problem. However, there are times when you may not want this to happen, especially if the information being re-sent conflicts with the information expected by the back end.

This lesson presents an example of one such case that occurs in the second phase of the event entry wizard, where the hidden field approach does not work well. It then describes the concept of persistent cookies, which can be used to address some of the limitations of the hidden field approach. In the next lesson, you will see how the **$EVENTENTRY.EXE** program uses this concept for conducting the second phase of the event entry wizard.

Exploring the Second Phase of the Event Entry Wizard

Lesson 2 presented a demonstration of how the **$EVENTENTRY.EXE** program conducts the first phase of the event entry wizard. We will continue this demonstration to explore the second phase of the wizard. Follow the steps given below:

1. Start the event entry wizard by entering the following URL from your Web browser:

   ```
   http://localhost/cgi-win/wdbic/evententry/$evententry.exe
   ```

2. Enter Gr in the first input form and press the Next button.

3. Select Grampian Corporation from the sponsor selection list of the second input form and press the Next button.

4. Specify Quality and benchmark for the Username and Password fields of the browser's authentication dialog box.

5. Select Sue Hay from the sponsor contact list of the third input form and press the Next button.

6. Enter the following information in the fourth input form and press the Next button:

   ```
          Event Name: The Internet Update
          Event Type: Workshops, Conferences, and Seminars
   Event Description: An annual workshop on the current state of
                      Internet and related technologies. Last
                      date of registration: 6/15/98. First 100
                      registrants receive 10% discount on their
                      registration fee.
   ```

   The wizard displays the fifth input form, asking for the name of the city where this event occurs and the number of times it occurs in that city (see Figure 12-11).

7. Enter Houston for the city name and 2 for the number of occurrences.

   The wizard now displays the sixth input form, as shown in Figure 12-12.

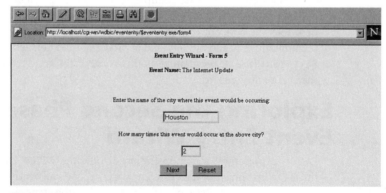

Figure 12-11
The fifth input form of the event entry wizard

The sixth (and final) input form contains a location selection list displaying a list of known locations in Houston and provides input controls for specifying a new location. If you scroll down this form, you will see that it provides input controls for specifying up to two records of date and time information (see Figure 12-13).

8. Select the second location (AstroHall – Texas) from the location selection list.

9. Enter the following information in the date and time rows and then press the Next button.

```
Row 1
Event Date: 11/1/98
Start Time: 9:00 AM
  End Time: 5:00 PM


Row 2
Event Date: 11/2/98
Start Time: 9:00 AM
  End Time: 5:00 PM
```

The wizard responds with a page displaying the complete information entered so far about the new event, as shown in Figure 12-14.

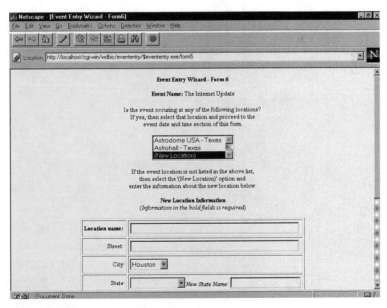

Figure 12-12
The top portion of the sixth input form of the event entry wizard

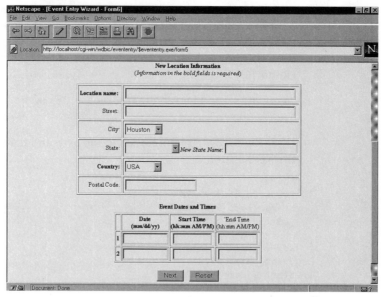

Figure 12-13
The bottom portion of the sixth input form of the event entry wizard

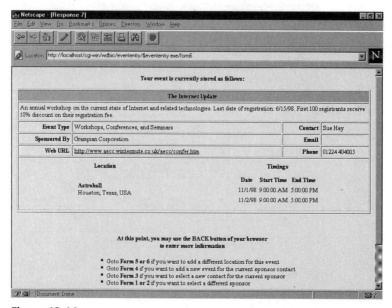

Figure 12-14
The wizard displaying the complete information about the new event

Note that the response also contains instructions on how the user can return to any of the previous input forms, using the browser's Back button, to add more information about this current event or add a new event for the currently selected contact or sponsor. Let's specify a new location for the event you just entered.

10. Use your browser's Back button to go to the fifth input form and press the Reset button.

11. Specify Dallas for the city name and enter 3 for the number of occurrences.

    This time the wizard displays its sixth input form showing the known locations in Dallas and provides three rows for specifying the date and time information.

12. Select Fair Park, Texas, for the location and enter the following information date and time information:

    ```
    Row 1
    Event Date: 12/1/98
    Start Time: 9:00 AM
      End Time: 5:00 PM

    Row 2
    Event Date: 12/2/98
    Start Time: 9:00 AM
      End Time: 5:00 PM

    Row 3
    Event Date: 12/3/98
    Start Time: 9:00 AM
      End Time: 5:00 PM
    ```

    This wizard attaches this information to the current event as indicated by its response, shown in Figure 12-15.

At this point, we recommend that you add some more events through this wizard to familiarize yourself with its complete functionality.

How Information Passing Occurs in the Second Phase of the Event Entry Wizard

As described in Lesson 2, the event entry wizard cannot store the event header information in the calendar database unless it has at least some occurrence information to go along with it. This means that when the user submits the event header information through the fourth input form, the $EVENTENTRY.EXE program must somehow retain

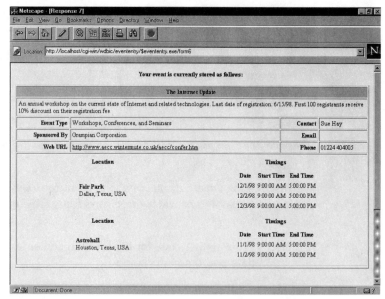

Figure 12-15
The wizard displaying the currently stored information about the event being added

that information in a temporary place until the user supplies the location and timing information through the sixth input form.

One way is to propagate this information to the sixth input form through hidden fields; when the user submits the sixth input form, the program has all the information it needs to store it in the calendar database. But then what will happen when the user submits the sixth input form the second time with another set of location and timing information by using the Back button method demonstrated earlier? The program will again receive the complete event header information through the hidden fields because the user is using the same sequence of forms. How will the program know that this is the second location of the event submitted earlier and not another new event?

As you can see, this is the kind of situation where the hidden field approach does not work very well. The way to handle this situation is to use the *persistent cookie* feature of the Web browser. The rest of this lesson explains the concept of persistent cookies; in the next lesson, we will describe how the **$EVENTENTRY.EXE** program uses this concept to conduct the second phase of the event entry wizard.

What Are Persistent Cookies?

Technically, persistent cookies (short for persistent client-state HTTP cookies) are a general mechanism that server-side connections (such as CGI programs) can use to both store and retrieve information on the client side of the connection. In layperson terms, a cookie is a piece of information (a name=value pair) that the CGI program can have the browser supply with each request that meets certain characteristics.

Difference Between Cookies and Browser's Authentication Mechanism

Functionally, the idea of cookies is similar to the idea of the browser's authentication mechanism presented in the previous lesson. In both cases, the browser automatically supplies some information with each request. However, the big difference between these two ideas is who provides that information. A cookie is set by the CGI program, whereas the authentication information is provided by the Web user. Furthermore, cookies provide more flexibility and can live longer than a user session.

How Are Cookies Set?

A CGI program, when returning an HTTP response to the browser, may also send a `Set-Cookie` header field formatted as follows:

```
Set-Cookie: Name=Value; expires=Date; path=URL_path; domain=Domain_Name; secure
```

The parameters in the above line have the following meanings:

Name=Value

This string is a sequence of characters excluding semicolons, commas, and white space. If there is a need to place such data in the name or value, some encoding method such as URL-style %XX encoding is recommended, though no encoding is defined or required. This is the only required attribute on the `Set-Cookie` header.

expires=Date

The `expires` attribute specifies a date string that defines the valid lifetime of that cookie. Once the expiration date has been reached, the cookie will no longer be stored or given out. The date string is formatted as

```
Weekday, DD-Mon-YYYY HH:MM:SS GMT
```

The `expires` attribute is optional. If this attribute is not specified, the cookie will expire when the user's session ends.

domain=Domain_Name

The `domain` attribute defines the Internet domain name of the host that must be specified while making the request in order to send the cookie. Note that you can set the domain attribute to `acme.com` if you want the cookie to be sent to hosts named `host1.acme.com` and `host1.division1.acme.com`.

Only hosts within the specified domain can set a cookie for a domain and domains must have at least two (2) or three (3) periods in them to prevent domains of the form `.com`, `.edu`, and `va.us`. Any domain that falls within one of the seven special top-level domains (`COM`, `EDU`, `NET`, `ORG`, `GOV`, `MIL`, and `INT`) requires two periods. Any other domain requires at least three.

The default value of domain is the host name of the server that generated the cookie response.

Path=*URL_Path*

The **Path** attribute is used to specify the subset of URLs in a domain for which the cookie is valid. If a cookie has already passed the domain criteria, then the path component of the URL is compared with the value of the **Path** attribute, and if there is a match, the cookie is considered valid and is sent along with the URL request. The path **/foo** matches **/foobar** and **/foo/bar.html**. The path **/** is the most general path.

If the path is not specified, it is assumed to be the same path as the document being described by the header that contains the cookie.

Secure

If a cookie is marked **Secure**, it will be transmitted only if the communications channel with the host is a secure one. If **Secure** is not specified, a cookie is considered safe to be sent over unsecured channels.

How Are Cookies Transmitted?

When requesting a URL from an HTTP server, the browser will match the URL against all cookies and if any of them match, a **Cookie** header field containing the name=value pairs of all matching cookies will be included in the HTTP request using the following format:

```
Cookie: Name1=Value1; Name2=Value2 ...
```

An Example of How Cookies Are Set and Transmitted

Let's say the browser sends a request to a Windows CGI program named **TEST.EXE** using the following URL:

```
http://localhost/cgi-win/test.exe/task1
```

and the Windows CGI program returns the following response:

```
Content-type: text/html
Set-Cookie: SessionID=xcv123

<HTML>
...Rest of HTML document
</HTML>
```

If you make the browser resend the above request, the browser will send the **Cookie** header field as follows:

```
Cookie: SessionID=xcv123
```

The Web server will make this header field available to the **TEST.EXE** program by adding the following line in the Extra Headers section of the CGI profile (**.INI**) file it creates for that request:

```
Cookie=SessionID=xcv123
```

Let's say this time the **TEST.EXE** sends two cookies using the following response:

```
Content-type: text/html
Set-Cookie: SessionID=
Set-Cookie: DateUpdated=12-23-1998; path=/cgi-win/test.exe

<HTML>
...Rest of HTML document
</HTML>
```

If you resend the same request to the program, it will receive the following line in the Extra Headers section of its CGI profile file:

```
Cookie=SessionID=; DateUpdated=12-23-1998
```

However, if you send the following request to the **TEST.EXE** program:

```
http://localhost/cgi-win/test.exe/task2
```

the program will receive the following cookie line:

```
Cookie=DateUpdated=12-23-1998
```

The browser will not send the **SessionID** cookie because the URL path listed for that cookie (**/cgi-win/test.exe/task1**) does not match the URL path of the above request.

The following points summarize the observations that can be made from this example:

● A CGI program can set multiple cookies in a single response by sending multiple Set-Cookie header lines.

● The value of an existing cookie is overwritten only if the CGI program sends another cookie with the same name and path attributes.

● When sending cookies to a server, the browser sends cookies with more specific path mapping before cookies with less specific path mapping.

Lesson Summary

This lesson explained why the hidden field approach is unsuitable for passing information from one input form to the other in the second phase of the event entry wizard. This is because once you return an input form containing a hidden field to the user, the back-end program cannot change that value. Every time the user uses that input form (using the Back button of the browser) to supply additional information, the program receives the same value of the hidden field and thus is not able to make a distinction between the first and second submission. The ability to make this distinction is essential for properly conducting the second phase of the event entry wizard.

A way to handle this situation is to use an approach based on persistent cookies, which are informational objects CGI programs can use to both store and retrieve information on the client side of the connection. Although functionally similar to the browser's authentication mechanism, a cookie is set from the server end (by the CGI program), whereas authentication information is provided by the Web user.

To set a cookie, the server must pass a **Set-Cookie** header field formatted as follows in its HTTP response:

```
Set-Cookie: Name=Value; expires=Date; path=URL_path; domain=Domain_Name; secure
```

This lesson explained the function of each parameter elaborated the process of how cookies are set and transmitted. In the next lesson we shall discuss how the **$EVENTENTRY.EXE** program uses persistent cookies to conduct the second phase of the event entry wizard.

1. How can a CGI program change the value of a hidden field in an input form?
   a. By sending a **Set-Hidden field** header field in its response
   b. The CGI program cannot change the value of a hidden field in the input form that has already been sent to the user
   c. By sending another copy of that input form
   d. All of the above

2. How do persistent cookies differ from the browser's authentication mechanism?
   a. The CGI program sets a cookie, whereas the Web user provides authentication information.
   b. The browser supplies authentication information only when the CGI program asks for it, but it sends cookie information with each request.
   c. Cookies provide more flexibility than the browser's authentication mechanism.
   d. The life of a cookie can be longer (or shorter) than a browser session, whereas authentication information lasts only until the end of the browser session.

3. What will the browser do when it gets the following **Set-Cookie** header lines with the HTML document sent by the Web server, assuming that this transaction occurs in 1998?

```
Set-Cookie: CartID=1.3; path=/cgi-win/shop.exe; expires=Friday, 04-Apr-1980 17:00:00
GMT
Set-Cookie: OrderID=2300; path=/cgi-win/shop.exe; domain=cookie.com
```

   a. It will immediately send the **OrderID=2300** cookie value back to all the Web servers serving under the **cookie.com** domain.
   b. It will generate a message box telling the user that two cookies were sent with the response.
   c. It will display the HTML document as if nothing special has occurred and wait for the next action from the Web user.
   d. None of the above.

4. Continuing with the example presented in Question 3, what cookie information will the browser send when the user makes the following request?

```
http://www.cookie.com/cgi-win/shop.exe/makepayment
```

   a. The browser does not send any cookies.
   b. `OrderID=2300`
   c. `CartID=1.3; OrderID=2300`
   d. `CartID=; OrderID=2300`

5. If the browser sends the following two cookies to the Web server, how will the Web server pass them to the requested Windows CGI program?

```
Item=M17
Quantity=2
```

   a. The Web server never passes the cookie information to a Windows CGI program
   b. By adding the line `Cookie=Item=17; Quantity=2` in the CGI section of the CGI profile (`.INI`) file
   c. By adding the line `Cookie=Item=17; Quantity=2` in the Extra Headers section of the CGI profile (`.INI`) file
   d. By adding two lines `Item=17` and `Quantity=2` in the Cookie section of the CGI profile (`.INI`) file

EXERCISE 4

Complexity: Easy

1. Read the original Netscape's cookie specification from the following URL:

```
http://home.netscape.com/newsref/std/cookie_spec.html
```

   Then answer the following questions:

   1. What is the maximum number of cookies (name=value pairs) a browser can send to a CGI program?

   2. What is the maximum size of the name=value pair that you can send through a cookie?

   3. How can a CGI program delete a cookie?

Complexity: Moderate

2. The `CGIOUT.EXE` program sets two cookies when you make the following URL request:

```
http://localhost/cgi-win/wdbic/cgiout/cgiout.exe?cookie.out
```

   List the extra header cookie line that the Web server will create in the CGI profile line in the following subsequent requests:

```
http://localhost/cgi-win/wdbic/cgiout/cgiout.exe?cookie.out
http://localhost/cgi-win/wdbic/cgiout/cgiout.exe?ctypehtm.out
```

USING COOKIES IN A DATA ENTRY WIZARD

Lesson 4 described how a CGI program can make the browser transmit extra information (cookies) along with each subsequent Web request to that program. This lesson explains how the $EVENTENTRY.EXE program uses this concept of cookies to conduct the second phase of the event entry wizard demonstrated in Lesson 4.

Handling the Fourth Input Form of the Event Entry Wizard

When the $EVENTENTRY.EXE program receives the event header information from the fourth input form (see Figure 12-9), the CGI_Main procedure of this program (see Listing 12-1 in Lesson 2) passes control to the HandleForm4 procedure, which is presented in Listing 12-12.

Listing 12-12 The HandleForm4 procedure of the $EVENTENTRY.EXE program

```
Public Sub HandleForm4()
   AddEventToTempTable
   SendForm5
End Sub
```

The HandleForm4 procedure first calls the AddEventToTempTable procedure (see Listing 12-13) to store the event header information in a table named tblTemp_Events residing in the calendar database. The tblTemp_Events table duplicates the structure of the tblEvents table except that its primary key is named TempEventID. Although this table was not part of the original design of the sample calendar database, it was added to that database solely for this purpose.

Listing 12-13 The AddEventToTempTable procedure of the $EVENTENTRY.EXE program

```
Public Sub AddEventToTempTable()

   'Read event header fields
   EventName = GetSmallField("EventName")
   EventTypeID = GetSmallField("EventTypeID")
   EventDescription = GetSmallField("EventDescription")
   'Validate event
   CheckRequiredField EventName, "event name"
   'Get value of the sponsor contact ID hidden field
   SpContactID = GetSmallField("SponsorContactID")
```

```
'Add event to temp table
OpenCalendarDatabase
Set rsTempEvent = dbCalendar.OpenRecordset("tblTemp_Events")
With rsTempEvent
  .AddNew
  !EventName = EventName
  !EventTypeID = CByte(EventTypeID)
  !EventDescription = EmptyToNull(EventDescription)
  !SponsorContactID = CLng(SpContactID)
  .Update
  .Bookmark = .LastModified
End With

End Sub
```

The `AddEventToTempTable` procedure first ensures that the information received contains at least the event name and then creates a new record with this information in the `tblTemp_Events` table. As its final step, this procedure makes this newly created record the current record of the `rsTempEvent` recordset. This way, any other procedure can determine the `TempEventID` assigned to this record by referring to the `TempEventID` field of the current record of this recordset.

After the `AddEventToTempTable` terminates, the `HandleForm4` procedure calls the `SendForm5` procedure to send the fifth input form. The design of the `SendForm5` procedure is shown in Listing 12-14.

Listing 12-14 The `SendForm5` procedure of the $EVENTENTRY.EXE program

```
Public Sub SendForm5()

  Dim CookieLines As String

  'Create the header lines for the cookies
  CookieLines = SetCookie("TempEventID", rsTempEvent!TempEventID) &
SetCookie("EventID", "")
  'Generate the HTML content-type response with the cookie header lines
  Result = HTMLContentTypeWithHeaderLines(CookieLines)
  'Read the template file for the fifth input form
  Result = Result & ReadFile(App.Path & "\Responses\evententry_5.htm")
  'Set the form's target path
  Result = ReplaceString(Result, "**CGI_ExecutablePath**", CGI_ExecutablePath)
  'Display the specified event name on the form and store it in the EventName hidden
field
  Result = ReplaceString(Result, "**EventName**", rsTempEvent!EventName)

End Sub
```

The `SendForm5` procedure first creates a string holding the following two `Set-Cookie` header lines and stores that string in a local variable named `CookieLines`:

```
Set-Cookie: TempEventID=The current event's TempEventID; path=CGI_ExecutablePath
Set-Cookie: EventID=; path=CGI_ExecutablePath
```

The first **Set-Cookie** header line creates a cookie named **TempEventID** and assigns it the **TempEventID** value of the event header record that was added to the **tblTemp_Events** table. The second header line creates a cookie named **EventID** and assigns it a blank value. Both these cookies are targeted to accompany any subsequent requests made to the program during the current browser session (that is, until the user closes the browser). The combination of these two cookies represents that the current event is temporarily stored and is not yet added to the permanent **tblEvents** table. To create these two cookie header lines, the **SendForm5** procedure uses the help of the **SetCookie** function, which is presented in Listing 12-15.

Listing 12-15 The `SetCookie` function of the `$EVENTENTRY.EXE` program

```
Public Function SetCookie(CookieName As String, CookieValue As String) As String

    'Returns a string that set's the cookie for the program's URL path
    SetCookie = "Set-Cookie: " & CookieName & "=" & CookieValue _
      & "; path=" & CGI_ExecutablePath & Chr(13) & Chr(10)

End Function
```

After storing the two cookie header lines in the **CookieLines** variable, the **SendForm5** procedure creates the HTTP response header containing these two lines by passing the **CookieLines** variable to the **HTMLContentTypeWithHeaderLines** function, which is shown in Listing 12-16.

Listing 12-16 The `HTMLContentTypeWithHeaderLines` function of the `$EVENTENTRY.EXE` program

```
Public Function HTMLContentTypeWithHeaderLines(HeaderLines As String)

    'Start the CGI output for an HTML-based response and include the given header lines
    HTMLContentTypeWithHeaderLines = "Content-type: text/html" & Chr(13) & Chr(10) _
      & HeaderLines & Chr(13) & Chr(10)

End Function
```

The remaining portion of the **SendForm5** procedure simply appends the HTML document stored in the **EVENTENTRY_5.HTM** template file after substituting the ****CGI_ExecutablePath**** and ****EventName**** tokens in that file with the appropriate values to generate the fifth input form. Note that this fifth input form does not contain any hidden fields. This is because the two **Cookie** fields provide all the information the program needs to track and handle this event during subsequent requests, as you will see later in the lesson.

Handling the Fifth Input Form of the Event Entry Wizard

When the user provides the name of the city and the number of occurrences of the event in that city through the fifth input form, the $EVENTENTRY.EXE program passes control to the HandleForm5 procedure, which is presented in Listing 12-17.

Listing 12-17 The HandleForm5 procedure of the $EVENTENTRY.EXE program

```
Public Sub HandleForm5()

  CityName = GetSmallField("CityName")
  NumTimes = GetSmallField("NumTimes")
  EventName = GetSmallField("EventName")    'Hidden field
  If Not IsNumeric(NumTimes) Then
    ErrorMessage = "Please specify a numeric value for the number of occurrences."
    Error ERR_BAD_REQUEST
  End If
  OpenCalendarDatabase
  MakeLocationList      'Make an HTML-formatted option list of matching location
  MakeCityList          'Add the city as the only option in the city selection list
  MakeStateList         'Make an option list of the states
  MakeAdditionalDateAndTimeRows  'Create more date and time input fields as required
  SendForm6             'Send the sixth (last) input form

End Sub
```

The HandleForm5 procedure first retrieves and validates the information supplied through the fifth input form. It then calls the MakeLocationList, MakeCityList, and MakeStateList procedures to generate HTML-formatted option lists that will populate the location, city, and state selection lists of the sixth input form. The design of these procedures is shown in Listing 12-18.

Listing 12-18 The MakeLocationList, MakeCityList, and MakeStateList procedure of the $EVENTENTRY.EXE program

```
Public Sub MakeLocationList()

  'Open a recordset containing location records in the input city
  Set qd = dbCalendar.QueryDefs("qryLocations_SelectedCity")
  qd!pCityName = EmptyToNull(CityName)
  Set rs = qd.OpenRecordset()

  'Store the HTML-formatted option list of these locations (location name and state name) in the
  'in the MatchingLocations string variable
  MatchingLocations = ""
  Do Until rs.EOF
    MatchingLocations = MatchingLocations & "<option value=""" & rs!LocationID &
```

continued on next page

continued from previous page

```
"""">"
        MatchingLocations = MatchingLocations & rs!LocationName & " - " _
          & rs!State & "</option>" & Chr$(13) & Chr$(10)       rs.MoveNext
    Loop

End Sub


Public Sub MakeCityList()

  'Makes one HTML-formatted option containing the name of the
  'input city with the option value set to the ID of that city.
  'If the city does not currently exist in the city lookup table then
  'the ID is set to "New-" + name of the new city. The "New" prefix
  'will tell the receving program that the city is a new city and
  'that the text after the hyphen contains the name of the new city.

  If CityName = "" Then
    CityID = ""
  Else
    Set rsCity = dbCalendar.OpenRecordset("tblLocationsCities_lkp", dbOpenDynaset)
    rsCity.FindFirst "Description = '" & CityName & "'"
    If rsCity.NoMatch Then CityID = "New-" & CityName Else CityID = CStr(rsCity!ID)
  End If
  SelectedCity = "<option value=""" & CityID & """>"
  SelectedCity = SelectedCity & CityName & "</option>"

End Sub


Public Sub MakeStateList()

  'Open a recordset containing known states
  Set rsState = dbCalendar.OpenRecordset("qryStates_SortedByName")

  'Store the HTML-formatted option list of these states in the
  'StateList string variable
  StateList = ""
  Do Until rsState.EOF
    StateList = StateList & "<option value=""" & rsState!ID & """>"
    StateList = StateList & rsState!Description & "</option>"
    rsState.MoveNext
  Loop

End Sub
```

Note that the **MakeCityList** procedure creates only one option representing the specified city. If that city exists in the city lookup table, the procedure sets the ID of that city as the option value; otherwise, the option value is set to the city name with the **New-** prefix. (The new city is not added to the city lookup table at this point. It is added once the user submits the sixth input form, as you will see later in the lesson.)

After the location, city, and state option lists have been generated and stored in their designated string variables, the **HandleForm5** procedure calls the **MakeAdditionalDateAndTimeRows** procedure presented in Listing 12-19.

Listing 12-19 The `MakeAdditionalDateAndTimeRows` procedure of the `$EVENTENTRY.EXE` program

```
Public Sub MakeAdditionalDateAndTimeRows()

  'Creates 2nd, 3rd, 4th, and additional input rows for date and time
  'based on the value of the NumTimes variable and stores the
  'resulting string in the NewDateAndTimeRows variable

  Dim NL As String    'New line characters
  Dim S As String      'Temporary string

  NL = Chr(13) & Chr(10)

  S = ""
  For i = 2 To CByte(NumTimes)
    S = S & "<tr>" & NL
    S = S & "<th><strong>" & i & "</strong></th>" & NL
    S = S & "<td align=""center""><input type=""text""" & NL
    S = S & "size=""12"" maxlength=""12"" name=""EventDate_" & i & """></td>" & NL
    S = S & "<td align=""center""><input type=""text""" & NL
    S = S & "size=""10"" maxlength=""10"" name=""StartTime_" & i & """></td>" & NL
    S = S & "<td align=""center""><input type=""text""" & NL
    S = S & "size=""10"" maxlength=""10"" name=""EndTime_" & i & """></td>" & NL
    S = S & "</tr>" & NL
  Next
  NewDateAndTimeRows = S

End Sub
```

The `MakeAdditionalDateAndTimeRows` procedure creates the HTML code need-ed for displaying one less than the number of date and time rows specified by the user in the first input form. Why one less? Because the template file for the sixth input form (`EVENTENTRY_6.HTM`) already contains the first date and time row and has a token (dis-guised within an HTML comment) for adding additional rows. (We handled the creation of the date and time rows in this roundabout way so that the `EVENTENTRY_6.HTM` template file looks complete and error free when displayed directly through an HTML editor.)

Finally, the `HandleForm5` procedure passes control to the `SendForm6` procedure to generate the sixth input form. The design of the `SendForm6` procedure is shown in Listing 12-20.

Listing 12-20 The `SendForm6` procedure of the `$EVENTENTRY.EXE` program

```
Public Sub SendForm6()

  Result = HTMLContentType()
  Result = Result & ReadFile(App.Path & "\Responses\evententry_6.htm")
  Result = ReplaceString(Result, "**CGI_ExecutablePath**", CGI_ExecutablePath)
```

continued on next page

continued from previous page

```
    Result = ReplaceString(Result, "**EventName**", EventName)
    Result = ReplaceString(Result, "<option>**MatchingLocations**</option>",
MatchingLocations)
    Result = ReplaceString(Result, "<option>**SelectedCity**</option>", SelectedCity)
    Result = ReplaceString(Result, "<option>**StateList**</option>", StateList)
    'Specify the value of the NumDateAndTimeRows hidden field
    Result = ReplaceString(Result, "**NumDateAndTimeRows**", CByte(NumTimes))
    Result = ReplaceString(Result, "<!-- **AdditionalDateAndTimeRows** -->",
NewDateAndTimeRows)

End Sub
```

Note that the **SendForm6** procedure does not set any cookies. So when the user submits the sixth input form, the browser simply transmits the cookies that were set by the **SendForm5** procedure.

Handling the Sixth Input Form of the Event Entry Wizard

When the user specifies the location, date, and time information through the sixth input form, the form request is handled by the **HandleForm6** procedure of the **$EVENTENTRY.EXE** program. The design of this procedure is shown in Listing 12-21.

Listing 12-21 The **HandleForm6** procedure of the **$EVENTENTRY.EXE** program

```
Public Sub HandleForm6()

    AddEventInfoToDatabase
    FormatEventForOutput
    SendResponse7

End Sub
```

The **HandleForm6** procedure first calls the **AddEventInfoToDatabase** procedure, which inspects the value of the incoming cookies to determine what event relation information has to be stored into the database. The design of the **AddEventInfoToDatabase** is presented in Listing 12-22.

Listing 12-22 The **AddEventInfoToDatabase** procedure of the **$EVENTENTRY.EXE** program

```
Public Sub AddEventInfoToDatabase()

    AddEvent_ReadFormData
    AddEvent_ValidateFormData
    OpenCalendarDatabase
    DBEngine(0).BeginTrans
    If LocationID = "New" Then AddNewLocation
    EventID = NullToEmpty(GetCookieField("EventID"))
    TempEventID = NullToEmpty(GetCookieField("TempEventID"))
    If IsNull(EventID) Or IsNull(TempEventID) Then
```

```
        'At least one expected cookie did not come with this request
        ErrorMessage = "Unable to determine cookie information. Please start over."
        Error ERR_BAD_REQUEST
    End If
    If TempEventID <> "" Then AddNewEvent
    AddDateAndTimeRecords
    DBEngine(0).CommitTrans

End Sub
```

The `AddEventInfoToDatabase` procedure first retrieves and validates the location and timing information supplied through the sixth input form. Next, it starts a transaction and checks if the user specified a new location, in which case it adds the new location by calling the `AddNewLocation` procedure. The `AddNewLocation` procedure (not shown here), which also automatically handles any new city or state value, is coded based on the design of the `LOCATIONENTRY.EXE` program discussed in Chapter 11, Lesson 3.

After dealing with the location information, the `HandleForm6` procedure tries to retrieve the values of the `EventID` and the `TempEventID` cookies using the `GetCookieField` function. The `GetCookieField` function is a powerful general purpose function that returns the value of the specified cookie. Its design is shown in Listing 12-23; as you can see, it uses two more general purpose functions named `GetExtraHeaderField` and `GetParameter` to complete its task.

Listing 12-23 The `GetCookieField`, `GetExtraHeaderField`, and `GetParameter` functions of the `$EVENTENTRY.EXE` program

```
Public Function GetCookieField(FieldName As String) As Variant

    'Returns the value of the specified cookie field.
    'Returns Null if the specified field not found in the incoming cookie

    Dim i As Integer                'Loop index
    Dim Cookie As String            'The complete cookie string
    Dim CookiePair As String        'name=value pair of the cookie
    Dim CookieName As String        'name portion of the name=value pair
    Dim CookieField As String       'value portion of the name=value pair
    Dim FN As String                'FieldName argument converted to uppercase

    Cookie = GetExtraHeaderField("Cookie")
    GetCookieField = Null
    If Not IsNull(Cookie) Then
        FN = UCase(FieldName)
        i = 1
        Do Until False                              'Start looping
            CookiePair = GetParameter(Cookie, i, ";") 'Get ith name=value pair from the⇐
cookie string
            If IsNull(CookiePair) Then Exit Do         'If no more pairs left to inspect,⇐
then exit loop
            'Otherwise, get the name portion of the pair and convert it to uppercase
            CookieName = UCase(Trim(GetParameter(CookiePair, 1, "=")))
```
continued on next page

continued from previous page

```
        If CookieName = FN Then   'If name portion same as FieldName
          'then return the value portion of the pair
          GetCookieField = GetParameter(CookiePair, 2, "=")
          Exit Do
        Else
          'else, set index for the next pair
          i = i + 1
        End If
      Loop
    End If

End Function


Public Function GetExtraHeaderField(Key As String) As Variant

  'Returns the value of the specified extra header field.
  'Returns Null if the specified header field is not found.

  Dim i As Integer        'Index variable

  GetExtraHeaderField = Null
  'Search the CGI_NumExtraHeaders array
  For i = 0 To (CGI_NumExtraHeaders - 1)
    If CGI_ExtraHeaders(i).Key = Key Then
      GetExtraHeaderField = Trim(CGI_ExtraHeaders(i).value)
      Exit For              ' ** DONE **
    End If
  Next i

End Function


Function GetParameter(ParameterString As String, ParameterNumber As Integer, Delimiter⇐
As String)

' Gets the Nth parameter value from the given Parameter string
'
' Inputs
' _____
' ParameterString: String from which the parameter has to be extracted
' ParameterNumber: Tells which parameter to extract
' Delimiter: Character used to separate the parameters
'
' Example
' _____
' GetParameter("This+is+a+string",2,"+") returns "is".
'
' Notes
' _____
' Returns Null if ParameterString is empty or if no matching
' parameter is found
```

```
Dim StartPos  As Long     'Starting position of the sought parameter
Dim EndPos As Long        'Ending position of the sought parameter
Dim i As Integer          'Index variable

'Check for empty parameter string
If ParameterString = "" Then
  GetParameter = Null
  Exit Function
End If
'Get the starting position of the sought parameter by
'jumping over the delimiters
StartPos = 1              'Initialize
For i = 2 To ParameterNumber
  StartPos = InStr(StartPos, ParameterString, Delimiter) + 1
  If StartPos = 1 Then  'If number of delimiters are not enough found
    StartPos = 0          'then indicate that the matching parameter
    Exit For              'does not exist
  End If
Next
If StartPos = 0 Then      'If no matching parameter exists
  GetParameter = Null     'then return Null
  Exit Function           'and exit
End If
'Otherwise, return the parameter value
'First, get the ending position of this parameter
EndPos = InStr(StartPos, ParameterString, Delimiter)
If EndPos = 0 Then 'If its the last parameter
  'then return the string portion from start to the end of the parameter string
  GetParameter = Mid(ParameterString, StartPos)
Else
  'else, return the string portion between startpos and endpos
  GetParameter = Mid(ParameterString, StartPos, EndPos - StartPos)
End If

End Function
```

After storing the two cookie values into the EventID and TempEventID variables, the HandleForm6 procedure inspects the value of the TempEventID variable to determine if the event header information has to be copied from the temporary event table (tblTemp_Events) to the main event table (tblEvents). The event is copied if TempEventID contains the ID of the temporary event record; the AddNewEvent procedure shown in Listing 12-24 takes care of this copying task. If TempEventID happens to be empty, then the HandleForm6 procedure assumes that the event header has already been added to the tblEvents table (during a previous request) and the EventID of that event is available through the EventID cookie. In this case, the procedure simply proceeds with adding the date and time information.

Listing 12-24 The `AddNewEvent` procedure of the `$EVENTENTRY.EXE` program

```
Public Sub AddNewEvent()

    'Select the event from the temp table
    Set rsTempEvent = dbCalendar.OpenRecordset("tblTemp_Events", dbOpenDynaset)
    rsTempEvent.FindFirst "TempEventID = " & TempEventID
    'Get SponsorID from the sponsor contact ID
    Set rsSpContact = dbCalendar.OpenRecordset("tblSponsorsContacts", dbOpenDynaset)
    rsSpContact.FindFirst "SponsorContactID = " & rsTempEvent!SponsorContactID
    SponsorID = CStr(rsSpContact!SponsorID)
    'Security check point
    AuthenticateUser
    'Add event to the main event table
    Set rsEvent = dbCalendar.OpenRecordset("tblEvents")
    With rsEvent
      .AddNew
      !EventName = rsTempEvent!EventName
      !EventTypeID = rsTempEvent!EventTypeID
      !EventDescription = rsTempEvent!EventDescription
      !SponsorContactID = rsTempEvent!SponsorContactID
      UpdateRecord rsEvent
      .Bookmark = .LastModified
      EventID = CStr(!EventID)
    End With

End Sub
```

The `AddNewEvent` procedure locates the temporary event record based on the incoming `TempEventID`, but before it copies that record from the temporary table to the main table, it performs a security check similar to the one described in Lesson 2. As the last step, this procedure stores the `EventID` of the added event record into the `EventID` variable to indicate that the new event is now a part of the main event table. This way the `AddEventInfoToDatabase` procedure can proceed with the `AddDateAndTimeRecords` (shown in Listing 12-25) with the correct assumptions.

Listing 12-25 The `AddDateAndTimeRecords` procedure of the `$EVENTENTRY.EXE` program

```
Public Sub AddDateAndTimeRecords()

    'This procedure assumes that the LocationID of the current location
    'is available in the LocationID variable, that the data has already
    'been validated, and the number of date and time rows are indicated
    'by the NumDateAndTimeRows variable

    Set rsEventLocation = dbCalendar.OpenRecordset("tblEventsLocations")
    For i = 1 To NumDateAndTimeRows
      'Check if current date and time row is to be processed
      If EventDate(i) <> "" Then
        'Add this row to the database
        With rsEventLocation
```

```
        .AddNew
        !EventID = CLng(EventID)
        !LocationID = CLng(LocationID)
        !EventDate = CVDate(EventDate(i))
        !StartTime = CVDate(StartTime(i))
        If EndTime(i) <> "" Then !EndTime = CVDate(EndTime(i))
        UpdateRecord rsEventLocation
      End With
    End If
  Next

End Sub
```

When the **AddEventInfoToDatabase** procedure is successful in storing the appropriate event-related information in the database, it commits the transaction. The control again returns to the **HandleForm6** procedure, which calls the **FormatEventForOutput** procedure to create a string containing the HTML code that displays the current event, as shown in Figure 12-14. (The string is stored in a string variable named **FormattedEvent**.) The code of the **FormatEventForOutput** procedure (not shown here) is designed based on the event-formatting procedures described in Chapter 10, Lesson 5.

After the current event has been formatted based on the information stored in the database, the **HandleForm6** procedure calls the **SendResponse7** procedure, which is presented in Listing 12-26.

Listing 12-26 The SendResponse7 procedure of the $EVENTENTRY.EXE program

```
Public Sub SendResponse7()

  Dim CookieLines As String

  CookieLines = SetCookie("TempEventID", "") & SetCookie("EventID", EventID)
  Result = HTMLContentTypeWithHeaderLines(CookieLines)
  Result = Result & ReadFile(App.Path & "\Responses\response_7.htm")
  Result = ReplaceString(Result, "**CGI_ExecutablePath**", CGI_ExecutablePath)
  Result = ReplaceString(Result, "**ShowEvent**", FormattedEvent)

End Sub
```

As its first step, the **SendResponse7** procedure creates the cookie header lines that set the value **TempEventID** cookie to an empty string and set the value of the **EventID** cookie to the **EventID** assigned to the current event. This combination ensures that even when a user submits additional information about this event through an existing form (using the Back button method), the **HandleForm6** procedure will be able to figure out that the event header is already stored in the main **tblEvents** table while processing those requests. Only when the user goes back to the fourth input form to specify the header information for another event will the **TempEventID** cookie get a numeric ID value and the **EventID** cookie will be reset to an empty string. Review the explanation of the **HandleForm4** and the **SendForm4** procedures presented earlier in this lesson to verify this claim.

Lesson Summary

This lesson explained how the **$EVENTENTRY.EXE** program constructs and processes the input forms used in conducting the second phase of the event entry wizard. The event header record received from the fourth input form is first stored in a database table named **tblTemp_Events**; the **TempEventID** value that is assigned to that record is passed as a cookie along with the fifth input form. Another cookie named **EventID** is also passed back with a blank value to override any previous value the browser may have sent for this cookie.

The fifth input form asks for the city name and the number of occurrences of the new event in that city and helps the **$EVENTENTRY.EXE** program construct the sixth input form, which collects the event's location, date, and time information. When the user submits valid data through the sixth input form, the **$EVENTENTRY.EXE** program first determines the current storage state of the event header information by inspecting the value of the **TempEventID** cookie. A nonblank value of **TempEventID** indicates that the event header information has to be copied from the temporary event table (**tblTemp_Events**) to the main event table (**tblEvents**) before the program can store the location and date information.

After appropriately storing each event-related component, the **$EVENTENTRY.EXE** program formats and displays the complete information of that event in its response and changes the values of the **TempEventID** and **EventID** cookies. The **TempEventID** cookie is set to a blank value and the **EventID** cookie is set to the ID assigned to the event header record when it was added to the **tblEvents** table. With these new values, the **$EVENTENTRY.EXE** program can easily detect where the event header is currently stored when the user enters another location and timing information for this event using the previously generated input forms.

This lesson concludes our discussion of how the event entry wizard can be implemented to conduct data entry tasks on the Web. In the next lesson, we will show how you can extend this wizard to edit and delete existing tasks.

1. At what points does the **$EVENTENTRY.EXE** program send cookies back to the browser?
   a. In response to the fourth input form
   b. In response to the fifth input form
   c. In response to the sixth input form
   d. All of the above

2. Which of the following combinations of the **TempEventID** and **EventID** cookies does the **$EVENTENTRY.EXE** program expect to receive from the browser?
   a. Both **TempEventID** and **EventID** have a blank value.
   b. **TempEventID** has a nonblank value and **EventID** has a blank value.
   c. **TempEventID** has a blank value and **EventID** has a nonblank value.
   d. Both **TempEventID** and **EventID** have a nonblank value.

3. Let's say that the user specifies `Omaha` for the city name in the fifth input form of the event entry wizard and this city does not exist in the city lookup table. How will `$EVENTENTRY.EXE` set the option tag for the `CityID` selection list of the sixth input form?
   a. `<option value="New">Omaha</option>`
   b. `<option value="Omaha">Omaha</option>`
   c. `<option value="Omaha">(New City)</option>`
   d. `<option value="New-Omaha">Omaha</option>`

4. What markup code in the `EVENTENTRY_6.HTM` template file is used as a place-holder for the additional date and time records?
   a. `AdditionalDateAndTimeRows`
   b. `**AdditionalDateAndTimeRows**`
   c. `<!-- **AdditionalDateAndTimeRows** -->`
   d. `<!-- **NewDateAndTimeRows** -->`

5. What will the expression `GetCookieField("TempEventID")` return, assuming that the browser sends the following two cookies with the request

`TempEventID=; EventID=17`

   a. `Null`
   b. An empty string
   c. A run-time error
   d. None of the above

EXERCISE 5

Complexity: Easy
1. Let's say a user wants to enter a lot of events for a specific sponsor and contact but not all during the same session; the user expresses a desire to not have to go through the sponsor and contact selection process of the event entry wizard each time. What shortcuts can you suggest to that user without modifying the `$EVENT-ENTRY.EXE` program in any way?

Complexity: Advanced
2. Currently, when you add a new sponsor through the event entry wizard and then enter a new event for this sponsor, the browser asks you to reenter the user name and password information for this sponsor after you submit the sixth input form. Explain why this happens and then modify the `$EVENTENTRY.EXE` program to prevent this from happening if the user enters a new sponsor and new events for that sponsor during the same session. (Hint: Use the cookie technique to indicate if the current sponsor is a newly added sponsor.)

EDITING AND DELETING DATA OVER THE WEB

Until now we have concentrated on how to allow users to add new information to a multiple table relational database using the HTML-based Web interface. However, a true Web database application cannot be considered complete until it facilitates the maintainence of existing database information. The *data maintenance task*, which refers to both editing and deleting existing data, can be looked at as a two-step process:

1. Selecting the data that requries maintenance

2. Making the necessary changes to that data

In addition, you need to consider all the usual factors such as security, a multiuser environment, and the stateless Web model when handling these steps.

Facilitating online maintenance of data is not difficult if you have implemented a data entry process based on the wizard approach, because many of the wizard's existing screens and procedures can be reused to conduct the data-maintenance-related tasks. In this lesson, we shall demonstrate this technique through a small example in which we show how the event entry wizard can be extended to allow users to edit and delete their sponsor information (stored in the sponsor table). Refer to the design of the fully functional Web calendar application (described in the Installation section of the "Introduction") to see how this example can be extended for supporting online maintenance of contact and event information.

Exploring the Web-Based Sponsor Maintenance Process of the Calendar Database

The **$EVENTENTRY3.EXE** program (residing in the **C:\WEBSITE\CGI-WIN\WDBIC\ EVENTENTRY3** directory) is an extended version of the original event entry wizard that allows you to edit or delete a sponsor in addition to supporting the regular event entry process. Let's run this program to see how it carries out this additional functionality:

1. Start this program by entering the following URL from your browser:

   `http://localhost/cgi-win/wdbic/Evententry3/$evententry3.exe`

   The program returns the first input form, asking for the first few characters of the sponsor name. (See Figure 12-4 in Lesson 2)

2. Enter the characters Gr and then press the Next button.

   The program returns a slightly modified version of the second input form, as shown in Figure 12-16. This input form contains three radio buttons that indicate the types of action you can perform on the sponsor selected.

3. For this demonstration, select Grampian Corporation from the sponsor selection list, select the radio option labeled Edit Sponsor, and then press the Next button.

   The browser asks for the user name and password information.

4. Enter Quality for the user name and benchmark for the password.

   The $EVENTENTRY.EXE program returns the sponsor edit form displaying the current information about this sponsor in the sponsor input fields (see Figure 12-17).

5. Change the sponsor type to Scientific, change the user name to Oil, and then press the Save Sponsor button.

   The $EVENTENTRY.EXE program returns a confirmation message indicating that the sponsor information has been successfully changed (see Figure 12-18).

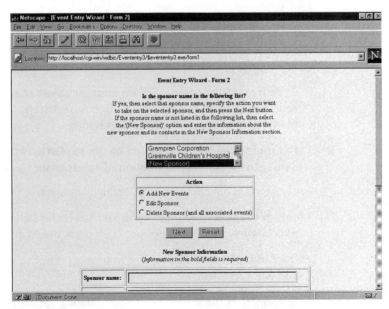

Figure 12-16
The second input form returned by the $EVENTENTRY3.EXE program

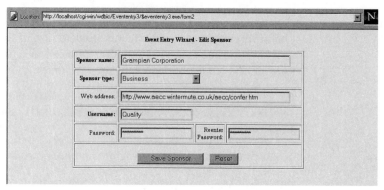

Figure 12-17
The sponsor edit form returned by the $EVENTENTRY3.EXE program

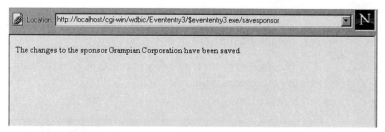

Figure 12-18
Response to submitting the sponsor edit form

6. To verify that the sponsor information has been changed as claimed, close your browser and open it again. Then repeat steps 1 through 4 but specify Oil instead of Quality for the user name.

The sponsor edit form returned by the $EVENTENTRY.EXE program should display the modified information of this sponsor.

Now let's look at how this program conducts the sponsor deletion process.

1. Return to the second input form and select the Delete Sponsor (and all associated events) radio option. Then press the Next button.

The program returns a message indicating that the sponsor deletion operation was successful.

2. To verify that the sponsor has been deleted, return to the second input form and try to edit or add a new event for this sponsor.

The program will respond with an error message indicating that the selected sponsor no longer exists in the calendar database.

Examining How the $EVENTENTRY3.EXE Program Handles the Sponsor Editing and Deletion Process

When the user submits the second input form, the CGI_Main procedure of the $EVENTENTRY3.EXE program passes control to the HandleForm2 procedure (just like the original $EVENTENTRY.EXE program). However, the HandleForm2 procedure of $EVEN-TENTRY3.EXE has been modified to perform different tasks based on the action selected in the second input form. The design of this HandleForm2 procedure is shown in Listing 12-28.

Listing 12-28 The HandleForm2 procedure of the $EVENTENTRY3.EXE program

```
Public Sub HandleForm2()

  'Get the option selected in the sponsor selection list
  SponsorID = GetSmallField("SponsorID")
  If SponsorID = "New" Then  'If new sponsor option is selected
    AddNewSponsor            'then add the new sponsor and its contacts to database
    If ContactCount = 1 Then 'If only one contact was specified for this new sponsor
      SendForm4              'then proceed directly to input form 4
      Exit Sub              'and exit
    End If
  Else
    'An existing sponsor was selected so ask for and verify
    'username and password information by calling the following procedure
    AuthenticateUser         'Signals error if unable to authenticate user
  End If
  'If here, then the user has passed authentication
  'so, handle things according to the selected action
  Action = GetSmallField("Action")
  Select Case Action
    Case "AddNewEvents"
      SendSponsorContactForm
    Case "EditSponsor"
      SendSponsorEditForm
    Case "DeleteSponsor"
      DeleteSelectedSponsor
    Case Else
      ErrorMessage = "Invalid action: " & Action
      Error ERR_BAD_REQUEST
  End Select

End Sub
```

Whenever you select an existing sponsor from the second input form (irrespective of what action you specify), the HandleForm2 procedure performs a security check. This ensures that only those users who know the correct user name and password information of the selected sponsor can add a new event for that sponsor or maintain that sponsor's information.

After completing the security check, the **HandleForm2** procedure examines the value of the incoming **Action** field (the selected option in the radio button group) and passes control to the appropriate procedure designed for handling the specified action. The **SendSponsorContactForm** procedure sends the third input form of the event entry wizard just as the original **$EVENTENTRY.EXE** program does. **SendSponsorEditForm** (described in the next section) constructs the sponsor edit form shown in Figure 12-17 and the **DeleteSelectedSponsor** procedure (shown in Listing 12-29) applies the **Delete** method of the recordset to delete the record of the selected sponsor. The Cascade Delete referential integrity option set for **tblSponsors**, **tblSponsorContacts**, **tblEvents**, and **tblEventsLocations** causes all the contact and event records related to the selected sponsor to be automatically deleted.

Listing 12-29 The DeleteSelectedSponsor procedure of the $EVENTENTRY3.EXE program

```
Public Sub DeleteSelectedSponsor()
  'Deletes the selected sponsor

  'Note: The AuthenticateUser procedure has already set the record of
  'the selected sponsor as the current record of the rsSponsor recordset

  'Save the sponsor name for the confirmation message
  SponsorName = rsSponsor!SponsorName
  'Delete sponsor record
  rsSponsor.Delete
  'Send confirmation message
  Result = HTMLContentType()
  Result = Result & "The sponsor " & SponsorName & " and all its events have been
deleted."

End Sub
```

The SendSponsorEditForm *Procedure of the* $EVENTENTRY3.EXE *Program*

The design of the **SendSponsorEditForm** is shown in Listing 12-30.

Listing 12-30 The SendSponsorEditForm procedure of the $EVENTENTRY3.EXE program

```
Public Sub SendSponsorEditForm()

  'Note: The AuthenticateUser procedure has already set the record of
  'the selected sponsor as the current record of the rsSponsor recordset

  Dim OptionValueToSelect As String
```

```
   Result = HTMLContentType()   'Start with the content type line
   Result = Result & ReadFile(App.Path & "\Responses\sponsoredit.htm")
   'Set the form's destination path
   Result = ReplaceString(Result, "**CGI_ExecutablePath**", CGI_ExecutablePath)
   'Set the value of the SponsorID hidden field
   Result = ReplaceString(Result, "**SponsorID**", SponsorID)
   'Set current values of the Sponsor record
   Result = ReplaceString(Result, "**SponsorName**", rsSponsor!SponsorName)
   'Make the current sponsor type of this sponsor as the selected option
   OptionValueToSelect = "value=""" & rsSponsor!SponsorTypeID & """"
   Result = ReplaceString(Result, OptionValueToSelect, "selected " &⇐
OptionValueToSelect)
   Result = ReplaceString(Result, "**WebAddress**",⇐
NullToEmpty(HyperLinkPart(rsSponsor!WebAddress, 2)))
   Result = ReplaceString(Result, "**UserName**", rsSponsor!UserName)
   Result = ReplaceString(Result, "**Password**", NullToEmpty(rsSponsor!Password))
```

```
End Sub
```

SendSponsorEditForm uses the SPONSOREDIT.HTM template file to create the sponsor edit form. This template file contains different markup codes to act as the default values for the text-type sponsor-related input fields; SendSponsorEditForm dynamically replaces these codes with the current information of the selected sponsor. The Sponsor-type input field, which is a selection list, is handled a little differently.

The SPONSOREDIT.HTM template file contains the options for the available sponsor types for the sponsor type field. SendSponsorEditForm simply makes the option representing the selected sponsor's sponsor type the selected option by substituting the value="*ID*" text of that option with the text selected value="*ID*". So if the selected sponsor belongs to the Business category, then the SendSponsorEditForm procedure changes the following HTML text for the Business option:

```
<option value="2">Business</option>
```

to the following text with the help of the ReplaceString function:

```
<option selected value="2">Business</option>
```

Note that this substitution approach works for input forms that contain only one selection list control.

The HandleSponsorEditForm *Procedure of the* $EVENTENTRY3.EXE *Program*

When the user submits the sponsor edit form, the CGI_Main procedure of the $EVENTENTRY3.EXE program passes control to the HandleSponsorEditForm procedure, which is presented in Listing 12-31.

Listing 12-31 The `HandleSponsorEditForm` procedure of the `$EVENTENTRY3.EXE` program

```
Public Sub HandleSponsorEditForm()

    ReadSponsorData
    ValidateSponsorData
    ProcessSponsorData
    'Get the value of the hidden SponsorID field
    SponsorID = GetSmallField("SponsorID")
    'Retrieve the sponsor record of this sponsor through the rsSponsor recordset
    SelectSponsorRecord
    'Edit this sponsor's record based on the new information
    With rsSponsor
      .Edit
      'Assign values to the fields
      !SponsorName = SponsorName
      !SponsorTypeID = CByte(SponsorTypeID)
      !WebAddress = EmptyToNull(WebAddress)
      !UserName = UserName
      !Password = EmptyToNull(Password)
      'Save the record
      .Update
    End With
    'Send confirmation message
    Result = HTMLContentType()
    Result = Result & "The changes to the sponsor " & SponsorName & " have been saved."

End Sub
```

The `HandleSponsorEditForm` procedure reads the values of the sponsor input fields and performs the standard sponsor-related data-validation and postprocessing tasks. Next, it calls the `SelectSponsorRecord` (shown in Listing 12-32) to set the record of the edited sponsor (whose `SponsorID` came through the `SponsorID` hidden field of the sponsor edit form) as the current record of the `rsSponsor` recordset. The `HandleSponsorEditForm` procedure then uses the `Edit` and `Update` methods of the `rsSponsor` recordset to save the new values in this sponsor's record. Note that the `SponsorID` field of the sponsor record is left untouched. If the update operation is successful, the `HandleSponsorEditForm` generates an appropriate confirmation message that the program can then return to the user.

Listing 12-32 The `SelectSponsorRecord` procedure of the `$EVENTENTRY3.EXE` program

```
Public Sub SelectSponsorRecord()

    'Select the sponsor record
    OpenCalendarDatabase
    Set rsSponsor = dbCalendar.OpenRecordset("tblSponsors", dbOpenDynaset)
    rsSponsor.FindFirst "SponsorID = " & SponsorID

End Sub
```

Lesson Summary

This lesson described how the event entry wizard could be extended to facilitate the maintenance of sponsor information over the Web. An additional radio option group named **Action** was added to the second input form of the event entry wizard. This option group presented the following three choices for the sponsor selected in the sponsor selection list of the second input form:

● Add New Events

● Edit Sponsor

● Delete Sponsor (and all associated events)

The Add New Events action simply acts as a gateway for the regular data entry process of the event entry wizard. The Edit Sponsor action generates another input form that contains all the sponsor-related input fields with the current sponsor information presented as default values. The modified sponsor information submitted through this form was accepted as a replacement for the original information once it met all the data validation criteria.

The Delete Sponsor action caused the record of the selected sponsor to be deleted from the **tblSponsors** table of the calendar database. The Cascade Delete referential integrity option set between **tblSponsors** and all the related tables automatically propagated the deletion of the contact and event information associated with the deleted sponsor.

In all the above actions, users were first authenticated to ensure that that they were making changes to their data only. The implementation of the Edit and Delete actions was explained by examining the relevant portions of the **$EVENTENTRY3.EXE** program.

 **QUIZ 6**

1. What steps does the **$EVENTENTRY3.EXE** program take to implement the process of editing an existing sponsor?
   a. Select the sponsor.
   b. Authenticate the user.
   c. Provide a sponsor input form displaying the current information about the selected sponsor in its input fields.
   d. Ask for a confirmation when the user submits the modified information about the selected sponsor.

2. How does the **$EVENTENTRY3.EXE** program ensure that the browser supplies the **SponsorID** of the selected sponsor when the user submits the sponsor edit form?
   a. By setting the cookie named **SponsorID**
   b. By embedding **SponsorID** as a hidden field in the sponsor edit form

c. By listing **SponsorID** in the query string portion of the form's URL

d. None of the above

3. How does the **$EVENTENTRY3.EXE** program replace the original sponsor information with the new information supplied through the sponsor edit form?

a. By deleting the original sponsor record and then adding another sponsor record with the new information using the **Delete** and **AddNew** methods of the sponsor recordset

b. By replacing the field values of the original sponsor record with the new values using the **Edit** method of the sponsor recordset

c. By replacing the field values of the original sponsor record with the new values using an Update Action query

d. None of the above

4. Records from which of the following tables may be deleted if you delete an existing sponsor:

a. **tblSponsorsContacts**

b. **tblEvents**

c. **tblLocations**

d. **tblEventsLocations**

5. Let's say you change the user name of a sponsor through the sponsor edit form (and submit the form), then return to that form using the browser's Back button. Enter another user name value and then resubmit that form. How will the **$EVENTENTRY3.EXE** program react to this resubmission?

a. It will again update the **Username** field of that sponsor record.

b. It will return a message indicating that the user cannot resubmit the same sponsor edit form.

c. It will ignore the resubmitted data.

d. It will ask for the user name and password combination and update the sponsor record only if you provide the user name and password specified during the first submission of the sponsor edit form.

EXERCISE 6

Complexity: Moderate

1. The **$EVENTENTRY3.EXE** program performs an important data maintenance task when you request its services using the following URL:

```
http://localhost/cgi-win/wdbic/Evententry3/$evententry3.exe/maintain
```

Identify the nature of this data maintenance task and how it is implemented.

Complexity: Advanced

2. Enhance the **$EVENTENTRY3.EXE** program so that it allows a user to maintain the contact information (edit, add, or delete contacts) of a selected

sponsor. As an additional requirement, the program should not allow the deletion of a contact if that contact is the only contact of the selected sponsor.

CHAPTER SUMMARY

This chapter demonstrated the implementation of the event entry wizard, the Web-based interface for populating and maintaining the calendar database. Various issues relating to the design of the wizard, the generation of dynamic input forms, and user security were explained. Hidden fields and persistent cookies have an important role in the implementation of the event entry wizard, as shown in this chapter. Specifically, the following points were covered in this chapter:

- Implementing a data entry wizard is more difficult than using a single Web form for accepting all the input at the same time.

- The event entry wizard is designed using a modular approach and performs two main tasks of getting the sponsor and contact information and getting events for the selected sponsor contact.

- The separation point was chosen after determining when it would be appropriate to store the provided information in the calendar database permanently without disturbing the database business rules.

- The event entry wizard handles the security issue by ensuring that users enter a correct user name and password combination for the selected sponsor before adding any new information.

- The issue of bandwidth friendliness is handled by making sponsor selection a two-step process.

- The technique of using the inputs of one form to generate another form dynamically helps avoid the limitation on the number of records a user can enter using a single form.

- A dynamically generated form is an HTML document comprising a sequence of static and dynamic sections.

- In the template file approach, special markup codes are embedded as place markers for the dynamic sections of the form in the static version of the HTML document that is to be published dynamically. The CGI program reads this text file and replaces each markup code with the appropriate dynamic content.

- The principles of self-contained and adaptive Web applications make the event entry wizard path independent and allow the creation and running of multiple versions of this application at the same time by putting each version in a different directory.

● Because of the sessionless model of the Web, security checks should be done after each form submission or whenever you want to ensure that requests are coming from the same user.

● One way to carry out this security check is to use the browser's Username and Password dialog box, which the wizard uses to gather user authentication information. The browser automatically passes the user name and password combination with every subsequent request a user makes during a session.

● Hidden fields are a more suitable way to propagate information from one form to the next when the flow of information occurs only in one direction.

● Persistent cookies are a general mechanism that server-side connections (such as CGI programs) can use to both store and retrieve information on the client side of the connection.

● The difference between persistent cookies and the server's authentication mechanism is that the CGI program sets the cookie, whereas the Web user provides the authentication information.

● The name=value parameter of the Set-Cookie header field is a sequence of characters, excluding semicolon, commas, and white space, for which special coding such as URL-style %XX encoding is recommended.

● The expires attribute specifies a date string that defines the valid lifetime of a cookie.

● The domain attribute specifies the Internet domain name of the host that must be specified while making the request to send a cookie.

● The path attribute specifies the subset of URLs in a domain for which a cookie is valid.

● A cookie marked Secure will be transmitted only if the communications channel with the host is a secure one.

● By sending multiple Set-Cookie header lines, a CGI program can set multiple cookies in a single response.

● The value of an existing cookie can be overwritten only if the CGI program sends another cookie with the same name and path attributes.

● The event header information is temporarily stored in a table named tblTemp_Events residing in the calendar database. This table duplicates the structure of the tblEvents table but has TempEventID as its primary key.

- A combination of two cookies named `TempEventID` and `EventID` is used to conduct the second phase of the event entry wizard.

- Implementing the process of data maintenance over the Web is made simpler once you implement the data entry process using the linked form (wizard) approach.

Until now, we have been handling all the form-processing tasks at the server-end (through our CGI programs). The Web browser simply played the role of accepting and passing user data to the server and did not participate in any data processing. One big advantage of this approach is that our Web application can work with almost all types of Web browsers available on the market.

However, popular Web browsers such as Netscape and Internet Explorer now include powerful client-side scripting languages, such as JavaScript and VBScript, that allow you to process data at the client-end. The main advantage of client-side processing is that you can catch data-entry errors before the data is passed to the server, thereby reducing the network traffic and the load on the Web server. The next chapter describes how these JavaScript and VBScript scripting languages work and how they can be utilized to enhance your Web application without losing the versatility of your Web application.

CHAPTER 13

USING CLIENT-SIDE SCRIPTING LANGUAGES: JAVASCRIPT AND VBSCRIPT

This chapter describes how to use JavaScript and VBScript client-side scripting languages for enhancing a Web database application in terms of both performance and flexibility. Although this chapter explains many important constructs and features of these two languages, it is not designed to act as a comprehensive reference. Rather, our objective is to illustrate how client-side scripts can supplement your existing Windows-CGI–based Web database applications and give you a jump start on creating these scripts with the help of practical examples such as SQL criteria generation and form validation. In particular, you will learn about:

- The browser object hierarchy
- Properties, methods, and events associated with the `Window`, `Document`, `History`, `Form`, and different types of input control objects

⬤ Generating SQL criteria at the client end using JavaScript

⬤ Performing client-side form validation using JavaScript

⬤ Performing client-side form validation using VBScript

⬤ Differences between JavaScript and VBScript

LESSON 1

THE BROWSER OBJECT MODEL

So far, the design of the Web database applications has followed the most basic form of the client-server model, where the client (the browser) simply presents the information and accepts user input while the CGI programs at the server end handle all the data processing and response generation tasks. The main advantage of following this *thin-client fat-server* model is that it acts as the lowest common denominator for developing Web database applications and works with almost any browser-server combination available.

However, recent versions of popular browsers such as Netscape and Internet Explorer include support for client-side scripting, whereby you can embed code within the HTML document to enhance the basic functionality of the browser. The ability to incorporate browser scripts within a Web application opens a whole new world of ideas and techniques you can use to improve your application. We will look at two frequently used ideas (data preprocessing and data validation) based on client-side scripting later in the chapter.

JavaScript and VBScript are two scripting languages currently available for writing browser-side code; JavaScript is the most widely supported language. Although these two languages are syntactically quite different (JavaScript is derived from the C language, whereas VBScript is derived from Visual Basic), they both act as an extension of a common browser object model. The *browser object model* treats the browser as a hierarchy of objects (just as the DAO model covered in Chapter 9, "Accessing Database Records from Visual Basic: Data-Access Objects," treats a database environment as a hierarchy of database-related objects).

In this and the next lesson, we shall present an overview of this browser object model (as originally formulated by Netscape) and detail the object components that you are most likely to use in a Web database application. For a comprehensive and in-depth coverage of these topics, please refer to the following books published by Waite Group Press:

⬤ *JavaScript Primer Plus* by Gabriel Torok, Jeffrey Payne, and Matt Weisfeld

⬤ *JavaScript How-To* by George Pickering, Shelley Powers, and Ron Johnson

● *VBScript Super Bible* by Jinjer L. Simon

● *VBScript Interactive Course* by Noel Jerke, Michael Hatmaker, and Jonny Anderson

The Browser Object Hierarchy

The hierarchy of browser objects begins with the `Window` object, as shown in Figure 13-1.

You will notice that the hierarichal structure of browser objects reflects the hierarchical structure of an HTML page. When you run the browser, it creates and destroys instances of these objects depending on the user activity.

Referring to the Properties and Methods of the Browser Objects

Like any programming object, each browser object supports a set of properties and methods. Furthermore, certain objects can also generate specific events, as described later in this lesson.

The generic format for referencing an object's property is

`object.propertyName`

whereas the generic format for referencing an object's method is

`object.methodName()`

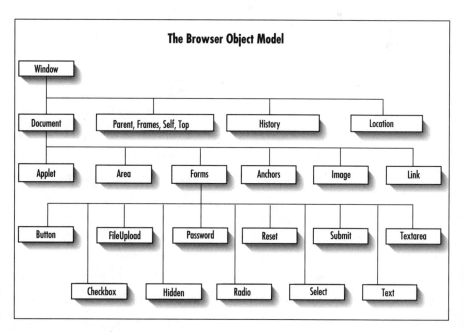

Figure 13-1
The hierarchy of browser objects

To refer to a particular browser object, you must start with the `Window` object, then add a period, followed by the object at the next level, then another period, and so on. For example, the following syntax refers to a checkbox object named `CheckBox1` listed within the form named `Form1` of the document currently loaded in the browser's window:

```
window.document.Form1.CheckBox1
```

To refer to the value property or the click method of this checkbox, use the following expressions:

```
window.document.Form1.CheckBox1.value
window.document.Form1.CheckBox1.click()
```

The `Window` object is assumed by default and you are not required to specify it.

Reference Is Case Sensitive

The object name, property name, and method name are case sensitive. Thus `document.Form1.`*`Checkbox1`* and `document.Form1.`*`checkbox1`* refer to two different checkboxes on the same form.

Next, we present a quick overview of the properties, methods, and events associated with the `Window`, `Document`, `Location`, and `History` objects based on the browser object model originally formulated for the Netscape browser.

Although Microsoft's Internet Explorer follows a similar object model, it does not support all the properties and methods of the Netscape model. Refer to the following URL to see if Microsoft's object model supports a particular property or method:

```
http://www.microsoft.com/workshop/prog/sdk/docs/scriptom/
```

The `Window` Object

The `Window` object represents the top level in the hierarchy of objects. The `Window` object has methods and properties that apply to the entire window as well as objects for each child window that may be contained in a frame. It is the parent object for the `Document`, `Location`, and `History` objects.

Properties of the `Window` Object

Below is a list of the properties of the `Window` object.

- `defaultStatus`: This is a string value containing the default value displayed in the status bar.

- `frames`: This is an array of objects of all frames defined in a window.

- `length`: This is an integer value indicating the number of frames in a parent window.

- `name`: This is a string value containing the name of the window or frame.

- `self`: This is an alternate name to refer to the current window.

- `status`: This can be used to display a message in the status bar by assigning a string value to this property.

The `self` and `window` properties are synonyms for the current window, and you can optionally use them to refer to the current window. For example, you can close the current window by calling either `window.close()` or `self.close()`.

Methods of the `Window` *Object*

Below is a list of the methods of the `Window` object.

- `alert (message)`: Displays the message that is passed in an Alert box.

- `blur`: Removes focus from the window.

- `confirm (message)`: Displays the message that is passed with the OK and Cancel buttons. Depending on the value chosen by the user, it returns `True` or `False`.

- `focus`: Returns focus to the window specified.

- `open("URL", "windowName", ["windowFeatures"])`: Opens a URL in a window specified by `name`. If a window specified in `name` does not exist, then a new window is created with that name. `WindowFeatures` is a list of optional parameters such as `height`, `width`, `menubar`, and `scrollbars` that can be specified for the new window.

- `prompt(message, response)`: Displays a message in a dialog box with a text entry field containing the default value specified in `response`. The user's response in the text field is returned as a string value when the user hits the OK button.

Events Associated with the `Window` *Object*

Following is a list of events associated with the `Window` object.

- `onBlur`: Triggers when focus is removed from a window.

- `onError`: Triggers when a JavaScript error occurs while loading a document. This can be used to capture the rather cryptic JavaScript error messages and replacing them with your own, more user-friendly, messages. Setting the value of this event to `Null` prevents the JavaScript messages from being displayed to a user.

- `onFocus`: Triggers when a window receives focus.

- `onLoad`: Triggers when the window or a frame finishes loading a document.

- `onUnload`: Occurs when you exit a document.

The Document Object

The Document object contains properties and methods based on the content of the document. These include the title, anchors, links to other pages, forms, images, background color, and applets.

Properties of the Document Object

Following is a list of the properties of the Document object.

- anchor: An Anchor object is the place in a document that is the target of a hyperlink. This property is typically used to specify a target URL within a very large document, whereas the links themselves are displayed in another frame in the form of a menu. An anchor property is an array of objects corresponding to named anchors in source order.

- applet: This is an array reflecting all the applets in a document in source order.

- Area: This is a type of link object that is used to define an area of an image as an image map. When the user clicks the area on the image map, the area's hypertext reference is loaded into its target window.

- bgColor: This is a string specifying the color of the document background. The colors are designated by specifying the RGB value of the color in triplet hex notation.

- cookie: This is a string value of a cookie, which is a small piece of information stored by the browser. (Chapter 12, Lesson 4, covered the concept of cookies in detail.)

- domain: Specifies the domain name of the server that served a document.

- lastModified: This is a string representing the date that a document was last modified.

- referrer: Specifies the URL of the document that calls the current document when a user clicks on a link.

- title: This is a string containing the title of a document.

- URL: This is a string specifying the complete URL of the document.

Methods of the Document Object

Following are the methods of the Document object.

- write(expression1, .. expression_n): This method is used to write one or more HTML expressions to a document in the specified window. Expression1 through *Expression_n* are any JavaScript expressions or the properties of existing objects.

● writeln(*expression1,* .. *expression_n*): This method writes one or more HTML expressions to a document and follows them with a new line character.

The Location **Object**

The **Location** object has methods and properties that provide information on the current location or URL that the browser is pointing to. Each property of the **Location** object represents a part of the URL.

Properties of the Location *Object*

Following is a list of the properties of the **Location** object.

● hash: This is a string value containing the anchor name in the URL.

● host: This is a string value that represents the host and domain name of the network host. This is usually a numeric IP address.

● hostname: This is a string value containing the domain name from the URL.

● href: This is a string value that contains the entire URL.

● pathname: This is a string value containing the path portion of the URL.

● port: This is a string value containing the port number from the URL.

● protocol: This is a string value representing the beginning of the URL up to and including the colon, but without the slashes.

● search: This is a string value containing any query information passed to the server-side GET call. The search string includes the question mark (?) and contains variable and value pairs with each pair separated by an ampersand (&). Note that this property applies to http URLs only.

Methods of the Location *Object*

Following are the methods of the **Location** object.

● reload: Forces a reload of the current document.

● replace (url): Loads the URL specified over the current entry in the history list. This prevents the user from reloading the previous document in the history list using the Back button.

The History **Object**

The History object has methods and properties that provide locations or URLs that the client has previously requested. The information is stored in a history list array and is accessible through the browser's Go menu. Each entry in the history list array is a string containing a URL that the client has visited in source order.

Properties of the History *Object*

Following is a list of the properties of the History object.

- current: This is a string containing the URL of the document that the browser is currently pointing to.

- length: This is a string containing an integer value for the number of objects in the history list array.

- next: This is a string containing the URL of the next entry in the history list.

- previous: This is a string containing the URL of the previous entry in the history list.

Methods of the History *Object*

Following is a list of the methods of the History object.

- back: Loads the document specified by the previous URL from the history list.

- forward: Loads the document specified by the next URL in the history list.

- go (location): Loads the document specified by the URL in the location argument from the history list. The location argument can be a string that represents the complete or partial URL in the history list or it can be a positive or negative integer representing the relative location of the URL in the history list.

Experimenting with the Window, Document, *and* Location *Objects*

The EXAMPLE1.HTM file residing in the C:\WEBSITE\HTDOCS\WDBIC\CHAP13\ LESSON1 directory is an HTML document that demonstrates the occurrence of the onLoad event and uses a little bit of JavaScript code to display the values of some of the properties of the Document and Location objects. The contents of the EXAMPLE1.HTM file are presented in Listing 13-1.

Listing 13-1 The contents of the `EXAMPLE1.HTM` file residing in the `C:\WEBSITE\HTDOCS\WDBIC\CHAP13\LESSON1` directory

```
<HTML>
<HEAD>
<TITLE>Browser Object Model Example 1</TITLE>
</HEAD>
<BODY onLoad="alert('Document Loaded!')">
<H2>Browser Object Model Example 1</H2>
<SCRIPT LANGUAGE="JavaScript">
document.writeln("Title: " + document.title + "<BR>");
document.writeln("Background color: " + document.bgColor + "<BR>");
document.writeln("Hostname: " + location.hostname + "<BR>");
document.writeln("Pathname: " + location.pathname + "<BR>");
</SCRIPT>
</BODY>
</HTML>
```

We will cover the details of writing the JavaScript code in Lesson 4. For now, start your WebSite server and load this file in your browser by requesting the following URL:

`http://localhost/wdbic/chap13/lesson1/example1.htm`

The browser should display the specified property values and generate a message box notifying the occurrence of the load event, as shown in Figure 13-2.

Lesson Summary

This lesson explained how the browser object model, JavaScript, and VBScript fit together and presented an overview of the **Window**, **Document**, **Location**, and **History** objects.

The browser object model represents the browser window and the loaded documents as a hierarchical set of objects that you can access and manipulate through scripting languages such as JavaScript and VBScript. To refer to a particular object, you must use a period-delimited object chain that always starts from the top of the object hierarchy (although the elimination of the **Window** object from this chain is permitted). When creating this chain, remember that the object, property, and method names are case sensitive and not all browsers support every property and method of the original browser object model formulated for the Netscape browser.

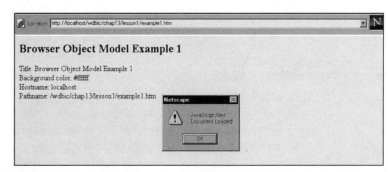

Figure 13-2
Browser displaying the `EXAMPLE1.HTM` file

We will continue our discussion of the browser object model in the next lesson, where we will focus on all the form-related objects.

QUIZ 1

1. What is the main advantage of using the thin-client fat-server model for creating a Web application?
   a. Flexibility
   b. Portability
   c. Performance
   d. Widespread applicability

2. Which of the following expressions refer to the value of the **host** property of the **Location** object?
   a. `window.location.host`
   b. `document.location.host`
   c. `Location.Host`
   d. `location.host`

3. What expressions can you use to simulate the action of pressing the browser's Back button?
   a. `history.back`
   b. `history.back()`
   c. `window.history.forward(-1)`
   d. `window.history.go(-1)`

4. How can you determine the complete URL of the current document?
   a. Using the `pathname` property of the `Location` object
   b. Using the `href` property of the `Document` object
   c. Using the `href` property of the `Location` object
   d. Using the `URL` property of the `Document` object

5. Which event is triggered when you load a document?
   a. `onBlur`
   b. `onLoad`
   c. `onFocus`
   d. `onUnload`

EXERCISE 1

Complexity: Easy

1. List three properties or methods of Netscape's browser object model that are not supported by Microsoft's browser object model. (Hint: Read the documentation of Microsoft's browser object model from the URL given in this lesson.)

Complexity: Easy

2. Create an HTML document named **EXAMPLE2.HTM** in the **C:\WEBSITE\ HTDOCS\WDBIC\CHAP13\LAB1** directory that lists the following information about itself:

● The last modification date

● The entire document URL

● The length of the URL history

LESSON 2

THE FORM-RELATED BROWSER OBJECTS

The previous lesson introduced you to the browser object model hierarchy and reviewed the properties, methods, and events associated with the upper-level objects such as **Document** and **Location**. In this lesson, we will examine the objects representing an HTML form and its input controls. As mentioned in Lesson 1, a comprehensive explanation of all the browser objects can be the subject of a book in itself. Familiarity with the form-related objects is sufficient to begin writing useful code for Web database applications, as you will see later in this chapter.

The Form **Object**

The **Form** object represents an HTML form and is one of the most commonly used objects in an interactive Web application using client-side scripting. It allows you to gather user input, validate or manipulate that input, and communicate the results back to the user, all using only client-side processing.

A separate instance of the **Form** object is created for each form in a document. Forms can be referred to by name or can be referred through the **forms[ ]** array that is created and maintained by the browser. You can define a form using standard HTML syntax, as shown in the following example:

```
<FORM>
    NAME="formName"
    ACTION="URL"
    METHOD=GET | POST
    ENCTYPE="encodingType"
    TARGET="windowName"]
    [onReset="userCode"]
    [onSubmit="userCode"]
</FORM>
```

Each attribute of the <FORM> tag becomes the property of the corresponding Form object; you can designate event handlers for two form-related events, onReset and onSubmit.

Properties of the Form Object

Following is a list of the properties of the Form object.

- name: This is a string containing the value of the NAME attribute of the HTML form tag that is used to specify the name of the form.

- target: This is a string containing the name of the window targeted by a form submission. This string is used to specify the name of the window that the form responses go to. When you submit a form with a target attribute, server responses are displayed in the specified window instead of the window that contains the form. If the specified window does not exist, then a new window is launched.

- action: This is a string containing the value of the ACTION attribute of the HTML form tag. The action property is a string that is used to specify the destination URL of a server for submitting the form data.

- method(get/post): This is used to specify how information is sent to the server specified by the action property.

- enctype: This is a string containing the MIME type used for encoding the form contents sent to the server. You can access this value using the encoding property.

- elements: This is an array containing an entry for each input control in the form.

- length: The browser maintains an array of Form objects. The length property returns the length of the forms[ ] array.

Methods of the Form Object

Following are the methods of the Form object.

- reset: Simulates a mouse click on the Reset button of the form.

- submit: Simulates a mouse click on the Submit button of the form.

Event Handlers of the Form Object

Following are the event handlers of the Form object.

- onReset: A Reset event occurs when a user clicks on the Reset button in a form. Navigator executes the JavaScript code associated with the Reset button.

● onSubmit: A Submit event occurs when a user clicks on the Submit button on a form to post the form data to the server.

Form Elements

In addition to the form properties described above, a form has several child objects, or input controls, that are used to construct the form. Each of these controls has its own properties and methods that make it very useful in interacting with the user. The basic syntax for creating each input control was described in Chapter 1, "Gathering User-Data: HTML Forms and Queries." However, the browser object model extends this syntax by allowing you to specify event handlers with their HTML tags. The following sections present a brief description, properties, methods, and associated event handlers of each type of input control object.

The Button Object

The Button object represents a normal button that does not act as a Submit or Reset button.

Properties of the Button Object

Following is a list of the properties of the Button object.

● type: This is a string specifying the type of form element.

● name: Specifies the name of the Button object to be created. You can use this name when indexing the elements array

● value: Specifies the label to display on the button. You can access this value using the value property.

Event Handlers and Methods of the Button Object

Following is a list of the event handlers of the Button object.

● onBlur: A blur event occurs when an object, such as a window or a frame, or a form element loses focus. In this case, when the button loses focus, the associated code is executed. The blur event can result either from a call by the blur() method or from the user clicking the mouse on another object or tabbing with the keyboard.

● onFocus: The onFocus event occurs when a Form object, window, or frame receives input focus. The focus event can result from a focus() method or from the user clicking the mouse on an object or tabbing with the keyboard. Note that selecting within a field results in a select event, not a focus event.

● onClick: The onClick event occurs when an object is clicked on the form. The associated JavaScript code is executed by the event handler when an onClick event occurs. The click() method is associated with the onClick event.

For checkboxes, links, radio buttons, Reset buttons, and Submit buttons, the onClick event handler can return False to the calling function to cancel the action normally associated with a click event. Returning False in an onClick event handler for a button has no effect.

The Reset Button

The Reset button is a special instance of the Button object that is used to reset the elements on a form to their default values. You can define a Reset button using the same syntax as used for a Button object except to change the type to reset. Although all the properties and events of a button are available with the Reset button, remember that the Reset button's onClick event handler cannot prevent a form from being reset; once the button has been clicked, you cannot cancel the Reset event.

The Submit Button

A Submit button is a form element that allows you to submit the contents of the form to the URL specified by the form's action property. Just like with the Reset button, the Submit button's onClick event handler cannot prevent a form from being submitted once it has been triggered.

You can define a Submit button using the same syntax as that for a button, except change the type to submit. All the properties and events of a button are available with the Submit button.

Checkbox

A checkbox is a toggle switch that lets the user select or unselect a value by setting the checkbox on or off. Checkboxes are used to allow a user to select multiple elements from a list of choices.

Properties of the Checkbox Object

In addition to the type, name, and value properties, which are similar to those described for a button, a Checkbox object has the following properties:

● checked: Returns True or False depending on the current state of the checkbox. You can also specify that the checkbox be displayed as checked or unchecked by using this property.

● defaultChecked: Returns True or False depending on the default status of the checked property.

Event Handlers and Methods of the Checkbox *Object*

The Checkbox object supports the onBlur, onClick, and onFocus event handlers, which are the same in behavior as the ones described for the Button object. The click() method simulates the clicking of the checkbox by the user and causes the checkbox's onClick event handler to be executed.

File Upload

A file upload field in a form allows the user to specify a file to be submitted with the form. A file upload object has the type and name properties associated with it. The type property returns the string value file, whereas the name property indicates the name of the file upload object. This name is different from the name of the file to be uploaded.

Hidden

A Hidden field object is used for passing information in the form of name=value pairs to the sever when a form submits. (See Chapter 12, "Creating a Data Entry Wizard: Advanced Data Entry and Maintenance," Lesson 3.)

The Hidden object has three properties: type, name, and value. The value property is used to set the initial value of the Hidden object. VALUE="textValue" specifies the initial value of the Hidden object. There are no methods or event handlers associated with the Hidden object.

Password

Password is another unique type of text entry field in which the text entered by the user is displayed as astersiks (*).

Properties of the Password *Object*

In addition to the usual type, name, and value properties, the Password object has another property called defaultValue, which refers to the VALUE attribute of the <INPUT> tag that defines the password control.

Event Handlers and Methods of the Password *Object*

In addition to onBlur and onChange, the Password object supports the following two event handlers:

● onChange: Triggers after the user enters new text in the password field.

● onSelect: Triggers when the user selects (highlights) the text in the password field or when the Password object's select() method is called through code.

Radio Controls

Radio controls are toggle switches that can be combined together to form an option group in which only one button can be selected by a user at a time. The following example defines an option group of radio buttons named `justForKicks`:

```
<INPUT TYPE ="radio" NAME = "justForKicks" VALUE="1" CHECKED >Option 1<BR>
<INPUT TYPE ="radio" NAME = "justForKicks" VALUE="2" >Option 2<BR>
<INPUT TYPE ="radio" NAME = "justForKicks" VALUE="3" >Option 3<BR>
```

Multiple radio control objects are maintained as an array with index starting at 0. You could use `justForKicks[0]` to refer to the first radio button in this group. You could also use the array's `length` property (`justForKicks.length`) to return the number of radio buttons participating in the option group.

In addition to the `type` (radio), `name`, and `value` properties, the `Radio control` object offers the `checked` property that was described above in the context of a `Checkbox` object. Radio buttons support the `onBlur`, `onClick`, and `onFocus` event handlers and the associated methods.

Select **and** Options **Array**

The `Select` object respresents a selection list that allows the user to select one or more options from a drop-down or scrollable list of items. This object contains an `options` array, each entry of which represents one of the select list options defined using the `<OPTION>` tag within the `<SELECT>...</SELECT>` tag pair. Each entry in the `options` array is an object with its own properties, although these `Option` objects do not have their own methods or event handlers.

Properties of the Select *Object*

Following is a list of the properties of the `Select` object.

- `length`: Refers to the SIZE attribute of the `<SELECT>` tag that defines the select list.

- `name`: Refers to the NAME attribute of the `<SELECT>` tag.

- `options[0..n]`: This is an array in which each entry represents one of the options defined with the `<OPTION>` tag. The properties of each option object are listed in the next section.

- `selectedIndex`: Contains the position of the currently selected option. If multiple options are selected, it contains the position of the first selected option. This property is most useful for selection lists defined without the MULTIPLE attribute.

- `type`: Refers to the type of the `select` object; the value is `select-one` for single selection lists and `select-multiple` for multiple selection lists.

Options *Array Properties*

Following is a list of the **options** array properties.

- **defaultSelected**: Indicates whether (True or False) this option item is selected by default (whether the SELECTED atribute was used in its <OPTION> tag).

- **index**: Returns the index of the **option** object in the **options** array. The first <OPTION> tag is at index 0, the second is at index 1, and so on.

- **length**: Returns the number of entries in the **options** array.

- **selected**: Indicates whether (True or False) the option is currently selected.

- **text**: Contains the text that follows the <OPTION> tag.

- **value**: Refers to the VALUE attribute of the <OPTION> tag that defines the select list option.

Event Handlers and Methods of the Select *Object*

The **Select** object supports the **onBlur**, **onChange**, and **onFocus** event handlers and their associated **blur()** and **focus()** methods.

Text

The **Text** object allows a user to enter a single line of text data in the field. The properties, methods, and event handlers of the **Text** object are the same as the ones available for the **Password** object.

Textarea

The **Textarea** object allows the user to enter multiline input on an HTML form and the event handlers. The associated methods and properties for this object are the same as those available for the **Text** object.

Experimenting with the Form and Text Objects

The **EXAMPLE1.HTM** file residing in the **C:\WEBSITE\HTDOCS\WDBIC\CHAP13\LESSON2** directory is an HTML document that demonstrates some **Form** and **Text** object related properties and events. The contents of this HTML file are presented in Listing 13-2.

Listing 13-2 The contents of the EXAMPLE1.HTM file residing in the C:\WEBSITE\HTDOCS\WDBIC\CHAP13\LESSON2 directory

```
<HTML>
<HEAD>
<TITLE>Form and Text Object Example</TITLE>
</HEAD>
<BODY>
<H2>Form and Text Object Example</H2>
<FORM NAME="Form1" ACTION="/cgi-win/cgitest32.exe/form" METHOD="POST"
  onSubmit="alert('Form Submit Event!')">

  Text1: <INPUT TYPE="text" NAME="Text1" VALUE="Default text"
            onFocus="alert('Text 1 Focus')">
  <BR><BR><INPUT TYPE="Submit" NAME="Send" VALUE="Submit"><BR>

</FORM>

<SCRIPT LANGUAGE="JavaScript">
document.writeln("Form's name: " + document.Form1.name + "<BR><BR>");
document.writeln("<B>Text box properties:</B>" + "<BR>");
document.writeln("Type: " + document.Form1.Text1.type + "<BR>");
document.writeln("Name: " + document.Form1.Text1.name + "<BR>");
document.writeln("Default value: " + document.Form1.Text1.defaultValue + "<BR>");
document.Form1.Text1.value = "New text";  //Setting a property
</SCRIPT>

</BODY>
</HTML>
```

Start your WebSite server and load this **EXAMPLE1.HTM** file in your Web browser using the following URL:

```
http://localhost/wdbic/chap13/lesson2/example1.htm
```

The document should contain information about the form's name and the properties related to the text box control, as shown in Figure 13-3.

Figure 13-3
Browser displaying
the form and text
box properties

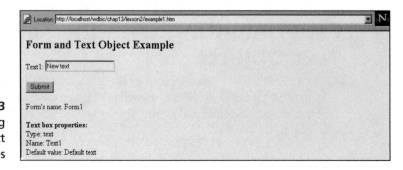

Note that the `Text1` input field contains the text `New text` instead of the default value `Default text` that was set in its `<INPUT>` tag. This effect is achieved by setting `Text1`'s value property to `New text` using JavaScript code while the document was being loaded.

Click into the `Text1` input field. The browser should show an alert message notifying the occurrence of the `focus` event. Press OK to remove the alert message and then press the Submit button. This time the browser should notify you about the occurrence of the form's `Submit` event. We will demonstrate a practical application of these events and various form-related objects later in the chapter.

Lesson Summary

This lesson described the properties, methods, and event handlers of the browser objects representing an HTML form and its different types of input controls. You specify an event handler of a form-related object within the HTML tag used to create that object. The properties and methods of these objects can be accessed and manipulated through a scripting language, as demonstrated in this lesson.

Now that you have gained some familiarity with the different types of browser objects, we will switch our focus to the JavaScript language in the next three lessons. However, we will not follow the traditional approach of first covering the language syntax and then giving examples of how to use that syntax. Instead, we will immediately show how to apply JavaScript code to enhance a Web application and then explain the syntax as and when needed.

1. The `Name` and `Type` attributes are available in
   a. All the browser objects
   b. All types of input control objects
   c. All `Window` objects
   d. Not available in any browser object

2. What does the `elements` array hold?
   a. References of all the `Form` objects in the HTML document
   b. References of all the input control objects in a form
   c. References of all the radio buttons in an option group
   d. None of the above

3. How can you automatically place the mouse cursor in a specific input control?
   a. Using the `focus()` method of the `Form` object
   b. Using the `focus()` method of that input control
   c. Using the `focus()` method of the adjacent input control
   d. By setting an event handler for the `onFocus` event of that input control

4. Which of the following input control objects support the **checked** property?
   a. Submit button
   b. Radio control
   c. Checkbox
   d. Selection list

5. Which of the following statements are true?
   a. Each entry of the options array refers to an object.
   b. The browser object model gives you access to the text that follows the **<OPTION>** tag.
   c. Multiple radio control objects are maintained as an array with index starting at 1.
   d. You can set an object property through JavaScript only after the browser completely loads the document.

Complexity: Easy
1. Modify the **EXAMPLE1.HTM** file presented in this lesson so that the browser automatically sets focus to the **Text1** input field once it loads this file.

Complexity: Easy
2. Create a form containing the **justForKicks** radio control group presented in this lesson and then use JavaScript to display the values associated with each option. Store this HTML document in a file named **EXAMPLE2.HTM** in the **C:\WEBSITE\HTDOCS\WDBIC\CHAP13\LAB2** directory.

USING JAVASCRIPT IN A WEB APPLICATION

In Chapter 10, Lesson 6, we described how to implement a field-based search application for the calendar database to locate the events of interest over the Web quickly. Like any Web-based operation, this application consisted of a front-end interface and a back-end program. The front-end interface comprised an HTML search form (**SEARCH.HTM**) that collected the search parameters from the user. The back-end search program (**SEARCH.EXE**) performed the search and returned an HTML-formatted response containing the details of all the matching events. To perform the search, the **SEARCH.EXE** program created a recordset from an SQL statement that it constructed dynamically based on the search parameters received through the front end.

Although having the **SEARCH.EXE** program handle all the search-related tasks helps keep the design of the front end simple, this approach has a couple of drawbacks:

● The server machine has to bear the entire request-processing load.

● The **SEARCH.EXE** program has to be modified and recompiled every time you want to add new search parameters or change the interpretation of the existing search parameters.

Although the first drawback is quite obvious, the second drawback can best be explained with a small example. Refer to the event search form (**SEARCH.HTM**) shown in Figure 10-21 (in Chapter 10, Lesson 6). This search form has only one input field for the search keyword, which the **SEARCH.EXE** program uses to search both the **EventName** and **EventDescription** fields of the calendar database. For performance reasons, say you want the supplied keyword searched only in the **EventName** field. Currently, the only way to make this change is to modify the **GenerateSQLCriteria** function of the **SEARCH.EXE** program (see Listing 10-15) and then recompile the program.

In this lesson, we shall describe how you can reduce the effect of the above drawbacks by having the browser construct the SQL criteria from the given search parameters (using JavaScript) and letting the back-end search program directly use those criteria to perform the search. This way, not only does the browser share the request-processing load but you also have the flexibility to modify the SQL criteria without having to change or recompile the **SEARCH.EXE** program.

A good example of how you can practically use this flexibility is to give users an option of two search forms: basic and advanced. The basic search form could be designed for novice users and contain a few search fields such as start date and event type. The advanced search form could provide several search fields with different search options to cater to the needs of users with specific search requirements.

Preparing an HTML Document for JavaScript Code

To design a JavaScript-enabled HTML document, the easiest way to start is by first creating a regular HTML document that depicts the desired layout and contains most of the essential elements. In this case, the original event search form (the **SEARCH.HTM** file residing in the **C:\WEBSITE\HTDOCS\CHAP10\LESSON6** directory) is a good starting point. It already contains the necessary input fields for accepting the search parameters. However, the objective is to have the browser pass the SQL criteria string constructed from these search parameters to the back-end search program. To do that, you will use a hidden field named **SQLCriteria**. Then, using JavaScript, you can have the browser set the value of this field to the appropriate criteria string just before the user submits the form request.

Follow the steps given below to add the `SQLCriteria` hidden field to the event search form:

1. Copy the `SEARCH.HTM` file from the `C:\WEBSITE\HTDOCS\CHAP10\LESSON6` directory to the `C:\WEBSITE\HTDOCS\CHAP13` directory.

2. Open the `C:\WEBSITE\HTDOCS\CHAP13\SEARCH.HTM` file in a text or HTML editor. You will notice that this HTML file contains the following `<FORM>` line:

   ```
   <form action="/cgi-win/wdbic/search/search.exe" method="POST">
   ```

3. Insert the following line after the above `<FORM>` line to add the `SQLCriteria` hidden field:

   ```
   <input type="hidden" name="SQLCriteria" value="(None)">
   ```

Note that the initial value of this hidden field is set to `"(None)"`. The JavaScript code that you will add later in this lesson will modify this value. However, if the back-end program receives this initial value, then the program can safely assume that the browser did not execute the JavaScript code. This can happen for a couple of reasons:

● The browser does not support JavaScript.

● The browser's JavaScript option was disabled. (For example, in Netscape 3.0, you can do that by selecting Options, Network Preferences, and then Languages.)

Now that you have established a channel for passing the browser-constructed SQL criteria string, you need to set up a mechanism to trigger the JavaScript code when the user submits the form. This can be done by setting a function (in this case the `GenerateSQLCriteria()` function) to act as an event handler for the form's `Submit` event. So modify the `<FORM>` line of the search form as follows:

```
<form action="/cgi-win/cgitest32.exe/form" method="POST"⇐
onSubmit="GenerateSQLCriteria()">
```

Adding a Wrapper for the JavaScript Code

The `GenerateSQLCriteria()` function that you have designated as the event handler for the event search form's `Submit` event must be defined within the HTML document. Because you want to write this function in JavaScript, its code must be embedded within the `<script>...</script>` tag pair, as shown below:

```
<script language="JavaScript">
...
</script>
```

It is possible that the JavaScript code embedded within this tag pair may be read by old non-JavaScript–aware browsers, which will simply ignore the **<script>...</script>** tags and display the code within them as regular HTML text. Hence, it is always a good practice to embed the JavaScript code within an HTML comment, as shown below:

```
<script language="JavaScript">
<!-- //Hide code from non-Javascript browsers

//Javascript code goes here

// 'Ignore the HTML comment-end marker -->
</script>
```

When encountering the above code, the non-JavaScript browsers will simply ignore everything within the **<!-- and -->** tag pair. The JavaScript-enabled browsers are designed to ignore the **<!--** tag but parse the JavaScript code within the **<script>...</script>** tag pair. The **//** text before the **-->** tag represents a JavaScript comment that makes the JavaScript-enabled browsers ignore the **-->** text when parsing the JavaScript code.

The next question you may ask is "Where should the JavaScript code be placed within the HTML document?" The answer is that it does not matter as long as all the references made to the HTML elements within the code are known to the browser before it executes the code. In the case of the event search form, you can embed the above JavaScript code wrapper anywhere before the **<FORM>** line.

Adding the JavaScript Code

After setting up the JavaScript code wrapper, you can start writing the code itself within that wrapper. The code may consist of the definition of JavaScript functions or direct JavaScript statements. The browser will not execute the code within the JavaScript function until the function is called. However, the browser executes all the direct statements within the code as it loads the document. In the case of the event search form, you are interested in creating the **GenerateSQLCriteria** function, which will be responsible for constructing the SQL criteria string and storing it in the **SQLCriteria** hidden field.

Listing 13-3 shows how you can design the **GenerateSQLCriteria** function that emulates the SQL criteria construction process of the **SEARCH.EXE** program described in Chapter 10, Lesson 6. Note that the design of this function is simplified by using other smaller functions, which are listed before this function.

Listing 13-3 The **GenerateSQLCriteria** and other related functions within the JavaScript wrapper

```
<script language="JavaScript">
<!-- //Hide from non-JavaScript browsers

function ReplaceQuotes(inputstr){
  /* Replaces each single quote with two single quotes
  */
```

continued on next page

continued from previous page

```
        var s1 = inputstr;
        var s2 = "";
        var inplen = inputstr.length;

        for (var i=0; i<inplen; i++){
          var c = s1.charAt(i);
          s2 = s2 + c;
          if (c=="'") s2 = s2+c;
        }
        return s2;
}


function GetSelectedOption(selectlist){
    /* Returns the first selected option object from the given
       selection list
    */
    return selectlist.options[selectlist.selectedIndex];
}


function MakeMultiListCriteria(c, selectlist){
    /* Adds the multilist criteria in the form of "AND IN(x1,x2,...)"
       expression based on the given selectlist to the current
       criteria string c.
    */

    //Check if the All option is selected
    if (selectlist.options[0].selected)
      return c;  //All option is selected, so make no change to the current criteria

    var idlist = "";  //Initialize
    //Now go through each option of the selection list
    for (var i = 1; i < selectlist.length; i++){  //start the for loop
      if (selectlist.options[i].selected)  //If the current option is selected
        //then add its value to idlist
        idlist = idlist + "," + selectlist.options[i].value;
    }  //end of for loop

    //Remove the beginning comma from idlist
    idlist = idlist.substring(1,idlist.length);
    //Append idlist to the current criteria and return the result
    return c + " AND (" + selectlist.name + " IN (" + idlist + "))";
}


function GenerateSQLCriteria(){

    var c = "";  //Initialize the criteria to an empty string
    //Set the first form of this document as the default object
    with (document.forms[0]){

      //Handle EventTypeID input field
      var F = GetSelectedOption(EventTypeID).value;
      if (F != "-1")
        c = c + "(EventTypeID = " + F + ")";
```

```
//Handle Keyword input field
F = Keyword.value
if (F != ""){
  F = ReplaceQuotes(F);
  c = c + " AND ((EventName Like '*" + F + "*') OR (EventDescription Like '*" +⇐
F + "*'))"
}

//Handle StartDate input field
F = StartDate.value;
if (F != ""){
  c = c + " AND (EventDate >= #" + F +  "#)"
}

//Handle EndDate input field
F = EndDate.value
if (F != ""){
  c = c + " AND (EventDate <= #" + F +  "#)"
}

//Handle multi-select lists
c = MakeMultiListCriteria(c, CityID)
c = MakeMultiListCriteria(c, StateID)
c = MakeMultiListCriteria(c, CountryID)

//Remove the beginning " AND ", if present from the criteria string
if (c.substring(0,5) == " AND ")
  c = c.substring(5,c.length)

//Set the criteria string c as the value of the SQLCriteria hidden field
SQLCriteria.value = c

//Display the SQL criteria before submitting the form, helpful for debugging
alert("Criteria: " + SQLCriteria.value);

} //The scopr of the With block ends here
} //End of function, after which the browser would submit the form

// --></script>
```

At first glance, the code presented in Listing 13-3 may appear cryptic if you are a Visual Basic programmer with little exposure to the C language. (This is a normal reaction anytime someone sees code written in an unfamiliar language.) However, because JavaScript is the first and the most widely used client-side scripting language, it is worthwhile to learn this language if you are planning to design Web applications for the global community.

We will explain how this JavaScript code works in the next lesson. At this point, you can either type the code presented in Listing 13-3 in your SEARCH.HTM file or refer to the sample SEARCH.HTM file that we have provided in the C:\WEBSITE\ HTDOCS\WDBIC\CHAP13\LESSON3 directory for your convenience.

Testing the JavaScript Code

After you have added the JavaScript code to your HTML document, you can test it by loading the document within the browser, commencing the appropriate event to trigger the code (if necessary), and observing the effect. Furthermore, if the JavaScript code is responsible for sending specific data to the back-end program (as in the case of the search example), then you can test that functionality by making CGITEST32.EXE (a Windows CGI test utility described in Chapter 1, "Gathering User-Data: HTML Forms and Queries") the request destination.

To test the JavaScript code presented in Listing 13-3, use the event search form provided in the SEARCHTEST.HTM file residing in the C:\WEBSITE\HTDOCS\ WDBIC\CHAP13\LESSON3 directory. This file mimics the JavaScript-aware SEARCH.HTM form, except that it sends the data to the CGITEST32.EXE utility, as indicated by its following <FORM> line:

```
<form action="/cgi-win/cgitest32.exe/form" method="POST"⇐
onsubmit="GenerateSQLCriteria()">
```

1. Start your WebSite server if it is not already running.

2. Load the following URL within a JavaScript-enabled Web browser such as Netscape 3.0 (or a higher version) or Internet Explorer 3.0 (or a higher version):

   ```
   http://localhost/wdbic/chap13/lesson3/searchtest.htm
   ```

   The browser should display the event search form like any regular HTML form.

3. Enter the following search parameters and then press the Search button:

   ```
   Event type: Workshops, Conferences, and Seminars
   Event name or description contains text: home
                         Start date: 1/25/97
                          Cities: Houston, Knoxville
   ```

   The browser should display a message box containing the SQL criteria string it constructed from the above search parameters, as shown in Figure 13-4.

4. Press the OK button.

   The CGI32TEST.EXE program responds by returning the name=value pairs it received from the browser, as shown in Figure 13-5.

Note that the SQLCriteria (hidden) field contains the SQL criteria string created through the JavaScript code. At this point, try some other test cases before proceeding to the next section.

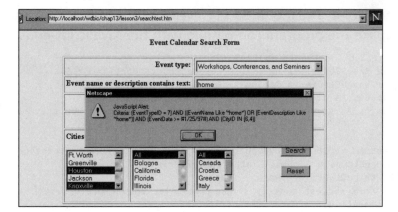

Figure 13-4
Browser displaying the SQL criteria string it constructed from the given search parameters

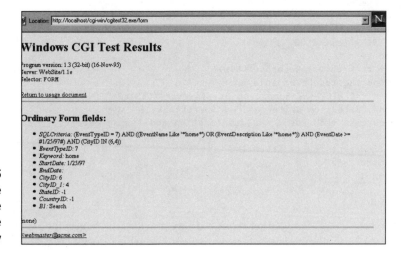

Figure 13-5
The name-value pairs sent by the browser to the CGITEST32.EXE utility

Modifying the Back-End Program to Handle Requests from the JavaScript-Enabled Front End

Now that you have tested the JavaScript-enabled event search form, it is time to put it into production. However, before you do that, you need to make the back-end **SEARCH.EXE** program recognize the SQL criteria string constructed and sent by the browser and use that criteria string to conduct the search. Listing 13-4 shows how you can modify the **ListEvents** procedure of the original **SEARCH.EXE** program to achieve this objective. Note that when the request comes from a non-JavaScript–enabled browser, the modified **SEARCH.EXE** program reverts to its original functionality (by calling its own **GenerateSQLCriteria** function to create the SQL criteria string).

Listing 13-4 The modified `ListEvents` procedure of the `SEARCH.EXE` program to make the program compatible with the JavaScript-enabled front end

```
Public Sub ListEvents(db As Database)
   Dim BaseSQL As String       ' Record source portion of SQL
   Dim WhereClause As String  ' Criteria portion of SQL
   Dim SQL As String           ' Complete SQL statement
   Dim rs As Recordset         ' Recordset based on the SQL statement


   BaseSQL = "SELECT qryEvents_Locations.* From qryEvents_Locations"
   WhereClause = GetSmallField("SQLCriteria")
   If WhereClause = "(None)" Then
     'form request sent by a non-javascript compatible browser
     WhereClause = GenerateSQLCriteria()
   End If
   If WhereClause <> "" Then
     SQL = BaseSQL & " WHERE " & WhereClause & ";"
   Else
     SQL = BaseSQL & ";"
   End If
   Set rs = db.OpenRecordset(SQL)
   'Send the result of this query
   Send "<CENTER><H2>Sponsored Events</H2></CENTER>"
   Send "Selection Criteria: " & WhereClause & "<P>"
   'Now List each event and its location and timing details
   Do Until rs.EOF
     ShowEvent rs, rs![EventID]
     Send "<P>"
   Loop

End Sub
```

For your reference, we have provided the project for the `SEARCH.EXE` program with the modified `ListEvents` procedure in the `C:\WEBSITE\CGI-WIN\WDBIC\SEARCH3` directory. The `SEARCH.HTM` file provided in the `C:\WEBSITE\HTDOCS\WDBIC\CHAP13\LESSON3` directory has its `<FORM>` tag directed toward this modified `SEARCH.EXE` program. Load the event search form represented by the `SEARCH.HTM` file by requesting the following URL within your browser and then run through the sample test presented in the previous section:

`http://localhost/wdbic/chap13/lesson3/search.htm`

This time, the browser should display the actual events matching the search criteria.

Lesson Summary

This lesson described the basic steps involved in creating and testing a JavaScript-enabled Web operation using the example of the Web-based event search application. The process can be summarized as follows.

Start by creating a regular HTML document and adding the necessary HTML elements and event handlers to interact with the JavaScript code. Next, add the JavaScript wrapper text that considers the possibility of an HTML document being loaded by both the JavaScript and non-JavaScript browsers. Then insert the JavaScript code within this wrapper text and test your code by loading the document within your browser and triggering the appropriate events. Verify the data sent through this JavaScript-enabled front end by using a CGI testing utility such as `CGITEST32.EXE`. Finally, design your back-end program to adapt to both the JavaScript- and non-JavaScript–based requests and then retest the front-end interface with this back-end program.

In the next lesson, we shall examine the JavaScript code presented in Listing 13-3 and cover the syntax of several important JavaScript constructs.

Quiz 3

1. How does JavaScript help enhance the event search application?
   a. The browser shares the responsibility of creating the SQL search criteria.
   b. You get more flexibility on how the criteria is constructed.
   c. The browser takes the responsibility of formatting the search result.
   d. All of the above.

2. How does the browser pass the prefabricated SQL criteria string to the `SEARCH.EXE` program in the event search example presented in this lesson?
   a. Through a `Textarea` field
   b. Through a hidden field
   c. Through a cookie
   d. None of the above

3. How do you make a JavaScript-based HTML document work with non-JavaScript browsers?
   a. By enclosing the `<script>...</script>` section in an HTML comment
   b. By enclosing the JavaScript code listed between the `<script>...</script>` tag pair in an HTML comment
   c. By starting the JavaScript code with a JavaScript comment line
   d. None of the above

4. Where should you place the following JavaScript code within the HTML document for it to work correctly?

   ```
   <script LANGUAGE="Javascript">
   document.frmFeedback.text1.value = "";
   </script>
   ```

   a. Anywhere in the HTML document
   b. Before the HTML text that defines the form `frmFeedback`
   c. After the form `frmFeedback` has been completely defined
   d. None of the above

5. Which of the following statements are true?
    a. You can have only one **\<SCRIPT>...\</SCRIPT>** section within an HTML document.
    b. The JavaScript syntax is derived from the C language.
    c. In JavaScript, two backslash characters (\\) signify the beginning of a comment.
    d. The (modified) **SEARCH.EXE** program ignores the rest of the form input fields once it determines that the **SQLCriteria** field already contains an SQL criteria string.

Complexity: Easy

1. Modify the **SEARCHTEST.HTM** file so that the **GenerateSQLCriteria()** function is called through the **onClick** event handler of the Submit button instead of the **onSubmit** event handler of the search form. Do you notice any difference in how the browser behaves when you submit the form?

Complexity: Easy

2. Add the following JavaScript statement just before the **\</SCRIPT>** line of the **SEARCHTEST.HTM** file:

```
document.forms[0].EventTypeID.focus();
```

This statement tells the browser to set focus to the **EventTypeID** selection list.

Load the **SEARCHTEST.HTM** file in your browser. The browser should respond with an error message. Why does the browser complain? How can you rectify the error and still set the initial focus to the **EventTypeID** field?

GENERATING SQL CRITERIA THROUGH JAVASCRIPT

This lesson explains the design of each JavaScript function presented in Listing 13-3 and describes the general syntax of each JavaScript construct used in these functions. Although we realize that the constructs covered in this lesson are just a subset of what JavaScript supports, they should be sufficient for you to begin writing useful code in JavaScript and experimenting with other JavaScript features.

The `GenerateSQLCriteria` Function

As explained in Lesson 3, `GenerateSQLCriteria` is the designated handler for the form's `Submit` event. This means that the browser executes this function whenever the form is submitted (either interactively by the user or through code). Note that we call `GenerateSQLCriteria` a function and not a procedure, even though from the comments in Listing 13-3 it does not appear to return any value. This is because in JavaScript every subroutine (whether it explicitly returns a value or not) is represented as a function, which must be defined using the following format:

```
functionname(){

//** Function code goes here

}
```

Declaring and Initializing a Variable

The `GenerateSQLCriteria` function starts by initializing a variable named `c` to an empty string. Variable `c` is a temporary variable that will be used to hold the current state of the SQL criteria string. Note that the initialization and the declaration process of this variable are done on the same line. Moreover, `c` is not attached to any specific data type. This *typeless* variable declaration approach is typical in JavaScript because the browser dynamically determines the type of a variable (`string` type in the case of variable `c`) from the value that you assign to that variable.

The `with` Block

After initializing variable `c` to an empty string, the `GenerateSQLCriteria` function sets the first form of the current document (`document.forms[0]`) as the default object through the `with` block. (Note that if this form had a name, then we could have also referred to this form using the syntax `document.formname`.)

Within the `with` block (whose scope is defined by the `{` and `}` character pair), you can refer to all the objects and properties of this first form by simply entering their names (without the `document.forms[0]` prefix).

Passing and Receiving Objects Between Functions

After establishing the default object through the `with` construct, `GenerateSQLCriteria` begins the SQL construction process. As the first step of this construction process, it passes the `EventTypeID` selection list object to the `GetSelectedOption` function to retrieve the object representing the first selected option of the `EventTypeID` selection list (using the `selectedIndex` property described in Lesson 2). This first selected option is also the only selected option because `EventTypeID` is defined as a single selection list.

Note that the `GetSelectedOption` function receives a selection list object and returns an `Option` object. As explained in Lesson 2, this `Option` object supports a `value` property, which returns the text you set for the `VALUE` attribute of that option when defining your form. Hence, the `GenerateSQLCriteria` function refers to this property to store the selected option value in a variable named `F`.

The if Statement

After setting variable `F` to the selected `EventTypeID` option value, the `GenerateSQLCriteria` function uses the `if` statement to check if that value is something other than −1. A −1 value indicates that the user selected the All option from the `EventTypeID` selection list, in which case the `GenerateSQLCriteria` function does not include `EventTypeID` in the SQL criteria string and proceeds to process the next form criteria input field. On the other hand, if the All option was not selected, then the `GenerateSQLCriteria` function appends the criteria string "`EventTypeID = `*`option-value`*" to variable `c`.

The syntax of the `if` statement in JavaScript is as follows:

```
if (condition)
   //Statement if condition is true
else
   //Statement if condition is false
```

Note that the `else` clause is optional and if you want multiple statements within an `if` or `else` block, then you need to enclose those statements within a `{` and `}` character pair, as shown below:

```
if (condition){
   //Statement 1
   //Statement 2
}
else{
   //Statement 1
   //Statement 2
}
```

The *condition* within the `if` statement must evaluate to `True (1)` or `False (0)`. Table 13-1 lists all the comparison operators you can use to create a conditional expression.

Table 13-1 Conditional operators in JavaScript

Operator	Stands for
==	Equal to
!=	Not equal to
<	Less than
<=	Less than or equal to
>	Greater than
>=	Greater than or equal to

Java's Built-In Objects

The format of the JavaScript code used for creating the SQL criteria string from other input fields is syntactically not much different than the code used for the `EventTypeID` field, so we will not go into its explanation any further. (Besides, the attached comments guide you through the overall logic flow, and the `ReplaceQuotes` and `MakeMultiListCriteria` functions called from this code are explained in the following sections.)

The result of the `GenerateSQLCriteria` function is that by the time it is done processing the last input field (`CountryID`), the variable `c` contains the resulting SQL criteria string. However, this criteria string can begin with the text `" AND "` in certain cases (where the All option was selected for `EventTypeID`). The `GenerateSQLCriteria` function detects such cases and removes the beginning `" AND "` text from the criteria string. For that, it applies the `substring` method to the `string` value stored in variable `c`.

The `substring` method, which works like the `MID` function of Visual Basic, takes two arguments (`index1` and `index2`) and returns the substring specified by the two indexes. The returned substring begins with the character at the position given by the lesser of the two indexes and ends with the character at the position just before the greater of the two indexes.

In JavaScript, a `string` value is treated as an object and the `substring` method is one of the many methods available for a `String` object. Refer to any of the JavaScript books mentioned in Lesson 1 for an explanation of all the methods available for the `String` object.

The `ReplaceQuotes` Function

The `ReplaceQuotes` function (see Listing 13-3) is called by the `GenerateSQLCriteria` function to ensure that each single quote within the `search keyword` input field is replaced by two single quotes. As explained in Chapter 10, Lesson 6, making this replacement is essential to keeping the SQL criteria string syntactically correct.

The logic of the `ReplaceQuotes` function is quite simple. It uses a `for` loop to go through each character of the keyword string (accessed using the `charAt` method of that string) and appends that character to another string (which initially starts as an empty string). Anytime this function finds a single-quote character during a loop, it appends another quote character in addition to the original quote character. The resulting string is then returned to the calling function using the `return` statement.

In JavaScript, the `for` loop is constructed as follows:

```
for (initialization statement; termination condition; continuation statement){

//code within the loop

}
```

The *initialization statement* contains code that is executed prior to the beginning of the loop. It usually includes initializing (and sometimes even declaring) the loop control variable.

The *termination condition* is a logical expression (`True` or `False` type) that is tested before every loop iteration. The statements within the loop are executed while this condition is `True`. Once the condition is `False`, the loop exits and the statement just after the loop construct is executed.

The *continuation statement* contains the code that is executed after each loop iteration. This code is generally used to assign a new value to the loop control variable. The `continuation` statement in the `for` loop of the `ReplaceQuotes` function (`i++`) is a shortcut for `i=i+1` and is often used for incrementing a numeric variable.

The `MakeMultiListCriteria` **Function**

The `MakeMultiListCriteria` function accepts the current criteria string and a multiselection list (`CityID`, `StateID`, or `CountryID`) as its two parameters, appends the multilist SQL criteria expression (involving the `IN` operator) to the current criteria (if the All option is not selected), and then returns the resulting criteria string.

To create the multilist SQL criteria, the `MakeMultiListCriteria` function starts with an empty string variable named `idlist`. It then goes through the selected property of each option of the multiselection list using a `for` loop to decide if that option's value should be appended to the `idlist` variable. The `MakeMultiListCriteria` function uses the `length` property of the selection list to determine the loop's `termination` condition. Once the loop ends, the function removes the starting comma character (that is added during the loop) from `idlist` and concatenates an `IN` criteria expression based on this `idlist` to the current SQL criteria string. The resulting criteria string is then returned to the calling `GenerateSQLCriteria` function.

Lesson Summary

This lesson explained the `with`, `if`, `for`, and other JavaScript constructs used in the JavaScript code presented in Listing 13-3. A key point to remember is that reserved words and variable names in JavaScript are case sensitive. For example, you cannot use `If` to create an `if` statement. In the next lesson, we shall look at how to use JavaScript to validate form input, another popular technique of using JavaScript to enhance a Web database application.

1. Which of the following statements are true about JavaScript variables?
   a. A variable is declared using the `var` keyword.
   b. A variable can be declared and initialized on the same line.
   c. A variable must be specifically associated with a particular data type.
   d. All of the above.

2. How can you extract the first character from a string variable named `strText` in JavaScript?
   a. `strText[0]`
   b. `srtText.charAt(0)`
   c. `charAt(strText,1)`
   d. `strText.substring(0,1)`

3. What operator do you use in JavaScript to compare if one value equals another value?
   a. `=`
   b. `==`
   c. `!=`
   d. None of the above

4. Which character pair do you use to specify a group of statements as one block?
   a. `(` and `)`
   b. `{` and `}`
   c. `/*` and `*/`
   d. `[` and `]`

5. How many times will the following loop run?

```
var numloops=10;
for (var i=10;i<=numloops;i++){
//code in the loop
}
```

   a. Zero
   b. Once
   c. Twice
   d. Three times

EXERCISE 4

Complexity: Easy
1. Modify the JavaScript-enabled `SEARCH.HTM` form so that the search keyword is used to search only the `EventName` field.

Complexity: Advanced
2. Modify the JavaScript code of the `SEARCH.HTM` form so that it sends a descriptive version of the search criteria containing the displayed text of the selected options instead of their numeric IDs through the hidden field named `SQLCriteriaDescription`. For example, if the user specifies a start date of `11/1/97` and selects `Houston` and `Knoxville` from the city selection list, then the `SQLCriteriaDescription` field should contain the text `Start date = 11/1/97 and City in (Houston,Knoxville)` as the criteria description.

Next, modify the **SEARCH.EXE** program so that it lists the descriptive search criteria in its response for a request sent by a JavaScript-enabled browser and lists the regular SQL criteria for a request sent by a non-JavaScript–enabled browser. Place the modified **SEARCH.EXE** program and its project files in the **C:\WEBSITE\CGI-WIN\WDBIC\SEARCH4** directory.

FORM VALIDATION AND FIELD NAVIGATION THROUGH JAVASCRIPT

As you already know, the input controls provided by HTML do not support any inherent mechanism to validate the input data or act differently based on that data. Consequently, you have to carry out all the data validation and processing tasks within your back-end CGI program, which means that every time a user enters invalid data, he or she must wait for the server's response to find out that the submitted data is unacceptable.

Clearly, the notification of data input errors using this request-response cycle over a network connection is an expensive operation (in terms of response time as well as the use of Web server resources). Fortunately, you can minimize the occurrence of such cycles by creating client-side scripts that make the browser validate the input data before it sends that data to the Web server. In this lesson, we illustrate how you can use JavaScript to perform browser-based data input validation by taking the example of the sponsor entry form (the second input form) of the event entry wizard descibed in Chapter 12, "Creating a Data Entry Wizard: Advanced Data Entry and Maintenance."

Demonstrating How JavaScript Can Be Used to Perform the Data Validation Process at the Browser End

The **C:\WEBSITE\CGI-WIN\WDBIC\EVENTENTRY4** directory contains an enhanced version of the event entry wizard that uses JavaScript to validate the new sponsor information and to automate screen navigation tasks (such as simulating the browser's Back button operations). To demonstrate these new features, let's add a new sponsor (GR Enterprises) through this wizard:

1. Start the WebSite server if it is not already running.

2. Start the event entry wizard by loading the following URL in your browser:

   `http://localhost/cgi-win/wdbic/evententry4/$evententry4.exe`

   The `$EVENTENTRY4.EXE` program returns the wizard's first input form. (Refer to Figure 12-4 in Chapter 12, Lesson 2.)

3. Enter `GR` in the input text box of this first input form and then press the Next button.

   The `$EVENTENTRY4.EXE` program returns the second input form, as shown in Figure 13-6. Note that the focus is already set to the Sponsor Selection list box.

4. Keeping the sponsor selection as `(New Sponsor)`, click on the Next button underneath the sponsor selection list.

   Instead of submitting the form, the browser takes you to the `sponsor name` input field.

5. Fill in the new sponsor information as shown below and then press the Next button.

   ```
       Sponsor name: GR Enterprises
       Sponsor type: Business
        Web address: http://www.grenterprises.com
           Username: gre
           Password: cubs
    Verify password: cubs
   ```

   This time, the browser asks you to specify at least one contact for this new sponsor, as shown in Figure 13-7.

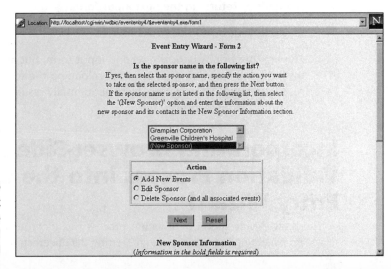

Figure 13-6
The second input form of the JavaScript-based event entry wizard

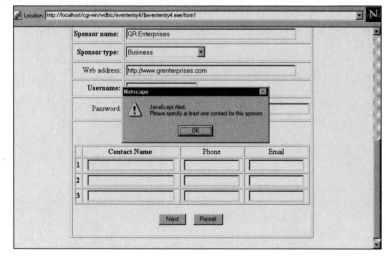

Figure 13-7
The browser notifying about the one contact requirement for the new sponsor

6. Press OK to remove the message box, enter the following contact information in the first contact row, and then press the Next button:

```
Contact name: Gordon Rich
       Email: grich.aol.com
```

The browser now notifies you that the email address is invalid and puts the cursor to the email address input field of the first contact row.

7. Change the email address to grich@aol.com and press the Next button once again.

This time the browser submits the form and the $EVENTENTRY4.EXE program responds by returning the next input form.

8. Click the Back button of your browser.

The browser brings back the second input form, but all form fields are reset, thereby providing an effect of reloading the form. This automatic reset also helps prevent users from accidentally resubmitting previously submitted sponsor information.

Incorporating Browser-Side Data Validation Process into the Event Entry Wizard

The browser-side sponsor validation process was incorporated to the event entry wizard by adding JavaScript code and setting the document load (onLoad) and form submit (**onSubmit**) event handlers in the **EVENTENTRY_2.HTM** response template file residing in the **C:\WEBSITE\CGI-WIN\WDBIC\EVENTENTRY4\RESPONSES** directory. The **$EVENTENTRY4.EXE** program is an identical copy of the **$EVENTENTRY3.EXE** program you studied in Chapter 12, Lesson 6. The reason why the addition of JavaScript code did not require any changes to be made to the **$EVENTENTRY3.EXE** program will be explained at the end of this lesson.

The JavaScript-related portion of the **EVENTENTRY_2.HTM** template file is shown in Listing 13-5.

Listing 13-5 The JavaScript-related portion of the **EVENTENTRY_2.HTM** template file

```
<body bgcolor="#FFFFFF"
  onLoad="document.forms[0].reset();document.forms[0].SponsorID.focus()">

<script language="JavaScript"><!--
//hide from non-Javascript browsers

//* BEGIN GENERAL PURPOSE FUNCTIONS *//

function GetSelectedOption(selectlist){
  /* Returns the first selected option object from the given
     selection list
  */
  return selectlist.options[selectlist.selectedIndex];
}

function ValidateEmail(EmailField){
  var EmailAddress = EmailField.value;
  if (EmailAddress.indexOf('@')==-1){
    alert("Please enter a valid E-mail Address");
    EmailField.focus();
    return false;
  }
  return true;
}

function CheckRequired(field){
  if (field.value == ""){
    alert("Please specify " + field.name);
    field.focus();
    return false;
  }
  return true;
}

//* END GENERAL PURPOSE FUNCTIONS *//

function GetSponsorIDValue(){
  return GetSelectedOption(document.forms[0].SponsorID).value;
```

continued on next page

continued from previous page

```
    }

    function SetNextControl(){
      if (GetSponsorIDValue() == "New")
        document.forms[0].SponsorName.focus();
    }

    function ValidateSponsor(){
      with (document.forms[0]){
        if (GetSponsorIDValue() == "New"){
          //Validate sponsor fields
          if (!CheckRequired(SponsorName)) return false;
          if (!CheckRequired(UserName)) return false;
          if (Password.value != VerifyPassword.value){
            alert("Password verification failed!");
            Password.focus();
            return false;
          }

          // Validate contacts
          var contactcount = 0;
          for (var i=0; i<3; i++){
            var indexContactName1 = 12;  // index of the first contact name field
            /* Now get the contact, phone, and email fields for the ith row based
               on the array index of the first contact name field */
            var ContactName_i = elements[indexContactName1 + i*3];
            var Phone_i = elements[indexContactName1 + i*3 +1];
            var Email_i = elements[indexContactName1 + i*3 + 2];
            if (ContactName_i.value != ""){
              if (Email_i.value != "")
                if (!ValidateEmail(Email_i)) return false;
              // Valid contact found so increment contact count
              contactcount++;
            }
          }
          // Ensure that at least one valid contact has been entered
          if (contactcount == 0){
            alert("Please specify at least one contact for this sponsor.")
            ContactName_1.focus();
            return false;
          }
        }
      }
    }


    //done hiding from non-Javascript browsers
    // --></script>

    <p align="center"><strong>Event Entry Wizard - Form 2</strong></p>

    <form action="**CGI_ExecutablePath**/form2" method="POST"
    name="Event Entry Form 2" onSubmit="return ValidateSponsor()">
```

```
<div align="center"><center><table border="0">
      <tr>
            <td align="center"><strong>Is the sponsor name in the
            following list?<br>
            </strong>If yes, then select that sponsor name,
            specify the action you want<br>
            to take on the selected sponsor, and then press the
            Next button.<br>
            If the sponsor name is not listed in the following
            list, then select<br>
            the '(New Sponsor)' option and enter the information
            about the <br>
            new sponsor and its contacts in the New Sponsor
            Information section.<br>
            <br>
            <select name="SponsorID" size="3"
            onBlur="SetNextControl()">
                  <option>**MatchingSponsors**</option>
                  <option selected value="New">(New Sponsor)</option>
            </select><br>

<!-- The rest of the form -->
```

Using the Load *and* Blur *Events*

As you saw earlier in the demonstration, when the **$EVENTENTRY4.EXE** program returns the second input form, the focus is automatically set to the Sponsor Selection list box. Furthermore, when you leave this list box while the **(New Sponsor)** option is selected, the browser automatically moves the focus to the **sponsor name** input field. This effect is achieved by the combination of the **Load** and **Blur** event handlers.

The **Load** event occurs right after the browser loads the input form. Its event handler is specified within the **<BODY...>** tag, as shown below:

```
<BODY onload="EventHandler">
```

In the case of the second input form (see Listing 13-2), the event handler for the **Load** event is set as follows:

```
<body bgcolor="#FFFFFF"
  onload="document.forms[0].reset();document.forms[0].SponsorID.focus()">
```

Here, the event handler calls the JavaScript statements directly rather than calling a JavaScript function containing these statements. (This is a quick way of embedding JavaScript instructions within the HTML document.)

The first statement, **document.forms[0].reset()**, executes the **reset()** method of the input form, which instructs the browser to reset all the input fields whenever the form is loaded into the display window. The second statement, **document.forms[0].SponsorID.focus()**, instructs the browser to set focus to the Sponsor Selection list box (**SponsorID**) control. This list box control has an event handler (the **SetNextControl** function) set for its **Blur** event, as shown below:

```
<select name="SponsorID" size="3" onblur="SetNextControl()">
```

The `Blur` event occurs when you leave the `SponsorID` list control; then the browser executes the `SetNextControl` function. This function simply moves the focus to the sponsor name input field if the `SponsorID` list control contains `(New Sponsor)` as the selected option.

Submitting a Request Only When Input Data Is Valid

A main requirement of the browser-side validation process is that the browser should submit the form request only when the input data meets all validity criteria. If any data component is deemed invalid, then the browser should not send the request and should generate an appropriate error message. To accomplish this task, the event handler for the form's `Submit` event is made to produce a `True` or `False` return value, which is returned to the browser as shown below:

```
<form ... onSubmit="return EventHandler">
```

The browser then submits the form request only when it receives a `True` value from the designated event handler.

In the case of the second input form (see Listing 13-5), the event handler for the form's `Submit` event is set as follows:

```
<form action="**CGI_ExecutablePath**/form2" method="POST"
    name="Event Entry Form 2" onsubmit="return ValidateSponsor()">
```

The `ValidateSponsor` function proceeds with the validity checks only if the user selects the `(New Sponsor)` option in the sponsor selection list. Its code closely follows the new sponsor validation logic used in the `MULTIENTRY3.EXE` program (refer to Chapter 11, "Populating Tables: Web-Based Data Entry," Lesson 6), except that whenever it detects invalid data, it returns a `False` value instead of generating an error. (Unlike Visual Basic, JavaScript does not support all the exception-handling features used in the `MULTIENTRY3.EXE` program.)

Another point to observe in the implementation of the `ValidateSponsor` function is how it uses the `elements` array of the `Form` object to refer to the contact-related input fields within a `for` loop. The browser automatically stores references to the input fields of a form within that `Form` object's (zero-based) `elements` array. In this case, the `contact name` input field of the first contact row happens to be the 13th form field and can be referenced through the `elements` array as follows:

```
document.forms[0].elements[12]
```

All the contact-related input fields can then be accessed based on the index position relative to the index position of this contact name field.

Can Browser-Side Validation Replace Server-Side Validation?

Although conducting data validation on the browser-side does help prevent invalid data from reaching the Web server, it cannot be considered a complete replacement for data validation performed on the server end. The reason is simple. Even though you may put a lot of effort in the browser-side validation process, there is no guarantee that the back end will always receive valid data. One case where this can happen is when a user submits the form through a browser that does not support client-side scripting.

Another case is where part of the data validation process may require the use of data that exists at the back end (for example, checking for duplicate sponsor names), or sometimes the browser-side scripting language may not provide sufficient means for verifying data correctness. For example, validating dates in JavaScript requires a lot of code (see the article, "JavaScript Date Object Techniques" by Danny Goodman at `http://developer.netscape.com/news/viewsource/goodman_dateobject.html`), whereas it can be done with one function call (`IsDate`) in the back-end VB-based Windows CGI program.

The browser-side and server-side validation processes are best thought of as supplemental error-checking techniques that have their own place and role in a Web application.

Lesson Summary

This lesson described an example of how to use JavaScript code to validate user input on the client-side before passing the data to a database program on the server side. This technique helps reduce network traffic and takes some of the load off the server, thereby increasing the overall performance of a Web application.

Form input validation through JavaScript is conducted by creating a JavaScript function that performs data-validity tests and returns a `True` or `False` value depending on if the input meets or fails data validity criteria. This function is then set as the event handler for the form's `Submit` event using the following syntax:

```
<FORM ... onSubmit="return functionname()">
```

The `return` keyword before *functionname* passes the function's return value to the browser, which then submits the form only when that value is `True`.

In addition to form validation, this lesson also showed how you can programmatically reset a form using the form's `reset()` method and navigate through its input controls using each control's `focus()` method. Finally, note that client-side data validation cannot be treated as an alternative to server-side data validation, especially if you are planning to run the application in an environment in which you do not have control over what browsers the users may use.

However, if you are developing your application for an intranet (where it is feasible to require every user to use a specific browser), then you can consider using VBScript for your scripting needs. VBScript is lot easier to work than JavaScript because VBScript uses the familiar Visual Basic syntax. The next lesson presents evidence of this claim when we repeat our client-side search criteria generation and form validation example using VBScript.

QUIZ 5

1. What are the advantages of performing data validation at the client end?
   a. Reduces network traffic
   b. Easy to program
   c. Decreases the load on the Web server
   d. All of the above

2. How do you specify the event handler for the `Submit` event when you want the browser to submit a form conditionally?
   a. `<FORM... onSubmit="functionname()">`
   b. `<FORM... return onSubmit="functionname()">`
   c. `<FORM... onSubmit=return "functionname()">`
   d. `<FORM... onSubmit="return functionname()">`

3. What does the `CheckRequired` JavaScript function do when it encounters an empty field?
   a. Signals an error.
   b. Makes the browser display an error message.
   c. Sets the focus to the empty field.
   d. Returns a `False` value to the calling function.

4. Which of the following expressions will return the value of the `contact name` input field of the first row?
   a. `document.forms[0].elements[12].value`
   b. `document.forms[0]("ContactName_1").value`
   c. `document.forms[0].ContactName_1.value`
   d. `document.forms[0].12.value`

5. What is the best option for validating data in a Web database application that is be used in an open Web environment?
   a. Use client-side scripting.
   b. Validate data at the server end.
   c. Use both client-side and server-side scripting.
   d. Do not perform any data validation.

EXERCISE 5

Complexity: Moderate

1. The JavaScript input validation code presented in this lesson (Listing 13-5) does not check for one data validation criterion pertaining to the new sponsor information. List this missing validation criterion and modify the `EVENTENTRY_2.HTM` file to add this criterion to the data validation process.

Complexity: Moderate

2. Enhance the event entry wizard (`$EVENTENTRY4.EXE`) so that it applies the client-side scripting approach using JavaScript to validate the new sponsor contact information specified through the third input form (generated from the `EVENTENTRY_3.HTM` file). Hint: You need to add JavaScript-based validation code to the `EVENTENTRY_3.HTM` template file.

USING VBSCRIPT

VBScript is a client-side scripting language that you can use in place of JavaScript. It supports the browser object model described in Lesson 1 and recognizes most properties and methods of those objects. Its VB-based syntax (which you are already familiar with) may be the biggest reason why you may prefer VBScript to JavaScript. Unfortunately, VBScript is not as widely supported as JavaScript is.

As of the writing of this book, VBScript is natively supported only by Microsoft's Internet Explorer browser. (Netscape currently supports VBScript only as a plug-in option, and that option is not automatically installed when you install Netscape.) Due to this limited support of VBScript, you can use VBScript when developing a Web database application in an intranet environment, where you know your user base and can force users to use Internet Explorer.

This lesson shows how you can implement the client-side form-validation example (described in Lessons 4 and 5) using VBScript. Interestingly, you will notice that even though VBScript follows the Visual Basic syntax, it has several limitations. First and foremost, it does not support all the features found in regular Visual Basic. Second, VBScript is still in an evolutionary stage. Some odds and ends (one of which we describe in this lesson) appear to be inconsistent with the documentation provided by Microsoft. But in spite of these limiting factors, VBScript is a strong contender for implementing client-side scripts in a controlled intranet environment.

Validating Form Input Using VBScript

The event entry wizard (`$EVENTENTRY5.EXE`) residing in the `C:\WEBSITE\ CGI-WIN\WDBIC\EVENTENTRY5` directory uses VBScript to validate the new sponsor information that it collects through the second input form. Run this wizard by loading the following URL in Internet Explorer (version 3.0 or higher) and then follow the demonstration example described in Lesson 4:

```
http://localhost/cgi-win/wdbic/evententry5/$evententry5.exe
```

For the most part, you will notice that this wizard functions similar to the JavaScript-based wizard (`$EVENTENTRY4.EXE`). As you may have already guessed, the only difference between these two wizard versions is in the design of their

EVENTENTRY_2.HTM template file. So, let's examine how the EVENTENTRY_2.HTM template file of this VBScript-based wizard is constructed (see Listing 13-6).

Listing 13-6 The VBScript-related portion of the EVENTENTRY_2.HTM template file of the $EVENTENTRY5.EXE event entry wizard

```
<!DOCTYPE HTML PUBLIC "-//IETF//DTD HTML//EN">
<html>

<head>
<meta http-equiv="Content-Type"
content="text/html; charset=iso-8859-1">
<meta name="GENERATOR" content="Microsoft FrontPage 2.0">
<title>Event Entry Wizard - Form 2</title>
</head>

<body bgcolor="#FFFFFF" language="VBScript" onLoad="Init">
<script language="VBScript">

Sub Init
   'Called after the browser loads the document

   document.Form2.reset()               'Reset the document
   document.Form2.SponsorID.focus()     'Set initial focus to the Sponsor selection list

End Sub

Function GetSponsorID()

   Dim SponsorList     'Reference to the SponsorID selection list

   Set SponsorList = document.Form2.SponsorID     'Use SET to point to an object
   GetSponsorID = SponsorList.options(SponsorList.selectedIndex).value

End Function

Function SetNextControl()

   If GetSponsorID() = "New" Then
     document.Form2.SponsorName.focus()
   End If

End Function

Sub CheckRequiredField(FieldValue, FieldCaption)

   If FieldValue = "" Then    'Empty field
     'Signal an error
     Err.Raise 30000, "RequiredField", "Please specify " & FieldCaption
   End If

End Sub
```

```vbscript
Sub ValidateContactFields()

  Dim IndexContactName1    'Index position of the first contact
  Dim i                    'Loop index
  Dim ContactCount         'Number of valid contacts
  Dim ContactName_i        'ith ContactName field value
  Dim Phone_i              'ith Phone field value
  Dim Email_i              'ith Email field value
  Dim ErrorMessage         'Error message string
  Dim F                    'Shortcut to the Form object

  'Initialize
  Set F = document.Form2
  IndexContactName1 = 12
  ContactCount = 0
  'Loop through each contact row
  For i = 0 To 2
    ContactName_i = F.elements(IndexContactName1 + i * 3).value
    If  ContactName_i <> "" Then
      'Validate Phone and Email fields of the ith row
      Phone_i = F.elements(IndexContactName1 + i * 3 + 1).value
      Email_i = F.elements(IndexContactName1 + i * 3 + 2).value
      If Phone_i = "" And Email_i = "" Then
        CheckRequiredField Phone_i, "phone or email for contact " & i+1
      End If
      'Check if email-address is valid
      If Email_i <> "" Then
        If InStr(Email_i, "@") = 0 Then
          ErrorMessage = "Please specify a valid internet email address for contact⇐
" & i+1  & "."
          Err.Raise 30000, "ValidateContact", ErrorMessage
        End If
      End If
      ContactCount = ContactCount + 1
    End If
  Next
  'Check if any valid contacts found
  If ContactCount = 0 Then
    ErrorMessage = "Please specify at least one contact for this sponsor."
    Err.Raise 30000, "ValidateContact", ErrorMessage
  End If

End Sub

Sub ValidateNewSponsor()

  Dim F

  If GetSponsorID() <> "New" Then Exit Sub
  Set F = document.Form2
  'Validate sponsor data
  CheckRequiredField F.Sponsorname.value, "Sponsor name"
```

continued on next page

continued from previous page

```
        CheckRequiredField F.Username.value, "Username"
        If F.Password.value <> F.VerifyPassword.value Then
          Err.Raise 30000, "ValidateSponsorData","The password could not be verified."
        End If
        'Validate Contacts
        ValidateContactFields

    End Sub


    Function Form2_OnSubmit()

      On Error Resume Next        'Trap errors generated by any of the following statements
      ValidateNewSponsor          'Returns error if any invalid data found
      If Err <> 0 Then            'If error was raised
        MsgBox Err.Description     'then show error
        Form2_OnSubmit = False    'stop the form from getting submitted
      End If

    End Function

    </script>


    <p align="center"><strong>Event Entry Wizard - Form 2</strong></p>

    <form action="**CGI_ExecutablePath**/form2" method="POST" name="Form2">
        <div align="center"><center><table border="0">
           <tr>
               <td align="center"><strong>Is the sponsor name in the
               following list?<br>
               </strong>If yes, then select that sponsor name,
               specify the action you want<br>
               to take on the selected sponsor, and then press the
               Next button.<br>
               If the sponsor name is not listed in the following
               list, then select<br>
               the '(New Sponsor)' option and enter the information
               about the <br>
               new sponsor and its contacts in the New Sponsor
               Information section.<br>
               <br>
               <select name="SponsorID" size="3" language="VBScript"⇐
    onBlur="SetNextControl()">
                   <option>**MatchingSponsors**</option>
                   <option selected value="New">(New Sponsor)</option>
               </select><br>

    <!-- The rest of the form -->
```

Notifying the Use of VBScript to the Browser

Internet Explorer supports both VBScript and JavaScript (or *Jscript*, as Microsoft calls it). Furthermore, you can embed both JavaScript and VBScript code in the same HTML document So it is your responsibility to tell the browser what scripting language you are referring to when you list a language-specific entity in your HTML document. You provide this information through the **LANGUAGE** attribute. For example, observe the **<BODY>** tag in Listing 13-6. It is set as follows:

```
<body bgcolor="#FFFFFF" language="VBScript" onLoad="Init">
```

Note how its **LANGUAGE** attribute is set to **VBScript**. This notifies the browser to execute the **Init VBScript** procedure instead of the **Init JavaScript** function, which brings up another important difference between JavaScript and VBScript. Whereas JavaScript supports the use of functions only, VBScript supports the use of both functions (subroutines that return a value) and procedures (subroutines that do not return any value). The lack of parentheses after a subroutine name tells the browser that you are calling a VBScript procedure.

Another place you use the **LANGUAGE** attribute is with the **<SCRIPT>** tag. This tells the browser that all the code within the **<SCRIPT>...</SCRIPT>** tag pair is written in the syntax of the specified language.

Referring to the Properties and Methods of the Browser Objects

As you saw in the previous section, you can set an event handler of a browser object to a VBScript procedure or function (in this case the **Init** procedure for the **Load** event) in a manner similar to how you link an event handler to a JavaScript function.

The **Init** procedure simply calls the **reset** method of the **Window** object and the **focus** method of the **SponsorID selection list** object using VBScript. Notice that the syntax used for calling these methods is identical to the syntax you used in JavaScript to achieve the same effect. The only difference in this regard is that VBScript requires each statement to be on a different line, whereas in JavaScript you can put two statements on the same line by separating them with a semicolon. (This is also the reason why you cannot have more that one statement directly attached to an event handler in VBScript.)

The Alternative Method of Specifying an Event Handler in VBScript

Observe the **<FORM...>** line in Listing 13-6. It does not contain any event handler for the **Submit** event (as in the case of the JavaScript-based example). So how does the browser know what code to execute for validating input data when the user submits the form? The answer lies in the use of special procedure names for specifying event handlers.

Notice that a function named `Form2_OnSubmit` is defined in Listing 13-6. This is no ordinary function. Because we have named our input form `Form2`, the VBScript engine of the browser automatically treats the `Form2_OnSubmit` function as the event handler for this form's `Submit` event. The return value of this function determines if the browser actually submits the data to the server.

We did try to use the original approach of specifying `onSubmit = "return ValidateSponsor()"` in the `<FORM>` tag itself, but found out that the VBScript engine (version 2.0) does not like this syntax, even though the Microsoft documentation (`http://www.microsoft.com/workshop/prog/sdk/docs/scriptom/omscr006.htm`) says that this approach should work.

Error Handling in VBScript

Validating form input in the VBScript example is conducted using the error-generation and error-detection approach, which is similar to the approach we have been following in all our server-side Windows CGI programs. VBScript allows you to trap any run-time error using the `On Error Resume Next` statement. Furthermore, you can signal runtime errors through code in VBScript (a feature not available in JavaScript) using its `Err` object's `Raise` method, which immediately reverts control to the calling procedure that is trapping the error.

In our example, the error trap is set by the `Form2_onSubmit` function, which calls the `ValidateNewSponsor` function to conduct the data validation. The `ValidateNewSponsor` procedure and all subprocedures called by this procedure (`CheckRequiredField` and `ValidateContactFields`) are designed to signal a run-time error (using an arbitrary error number, `30000`) anytime they detect a case of invalid data. This way, when the execution returns to the `Form2_onSubmit` function, it simply inspects the `Err` object to see if a run-time error has occurred. If an error has occurred, then this function generates a message box containing the error description (supplied by the procedure that raised the error signal) and terminates by returning a `False` value.

You can trap errors in VBScript only using the `On Error Resume Next` statement. VBScript does not support the `On Error Goto` statement (although some books on VBScript claim that it does).

Subtle Differences Between JavaScript and VBScript

While we are on the subject of implementation variations between JavaScript- and VBScript-based form-validation processes, we can point out some other subtle distinctions that you need to be aware of:

● **Case sensitivity:** Unlike JavaScript, VBScript is not case sensitive. `Document` and `document` in VBScript refer to the same `document` object.

● Array element reference: In JavaScript, you use square brackets to refer to an array element (for example, `document.forms[0].SponsorID.options[2]`). In VBScript, you use parentheses instead of square brackets (for example, `document.forms(0).SponsorID.options(2)`).

● Setting a default object: In JavaScript, you use the `with` statement to specify a default object (for example, `with (document.form[0])`). VBScript does not support an equivalent of this `with` keyword. However, you can use a variable to point to the default object using the `set` keyword and then refer to the descendent objects through that variable. (For example, the `Set F = document.forms(0)` and `Spname = F.Sponsorname.value` statement combination would assign the value of the `Sponsorname` input field to the `Spname` variable.)

Lesson Summary

This lesson described how you can use the VBScript scripting language to implement the client-side form-validation process, while pointing out its key features and its subtle differences from JavaScript. VBScript, which is essentially a subset of regular Visual Basic, is currently not as widely supported as JavaScript, although this scenario may change. Until then, you may find VBScript a strong alternative to JavaScript in intranet-oriented Web database applications. In that case, you may also consider the ActiveX technology (not covered in this book), which gives you a lot more options for scaling up your browser's capabilities. Finally, we want to reiterate that this lesson covered only some relevant portions of VBScript; you should refer to the following URL for a comprehensive reference:

`http://www.microsoft.com/vbscript`

1. Which of the following constructs are supported in VBScript?
   a. Function
   b. Procedure
   c. The `with` block
   d. All of the above

2. VBScript is similar to JavaScript in what ways?
   a. Both are client-side scripting languages.
   b. Both are natively supported by popular browsers such as Netscape Navigator and Internet Explorer.
   c. Both use the same syntax for referring to a property or method of a browser object.
   d. Both are case-sensitive languages.

3. What error-trapping and error-handling features does VBScript support?
   a. You can signal an error using the **Raise** method of the **Err** object.
   b. You can trap an error using the **On Error Resume Next** statement.
   c. You can specify an error-handling section using the **On Error Goto** statement.
   d. All of the above.

4. Which of the following VBScript expressions return the value of the first option of the **SponsorID** selection list?
   a. `document.Form2.SponsorID(0).value`
   b. `document.Form2.SponsorID.options[0].value`
   c. `document.Form2.SponsorID.options(0).value`
   d. `document.forms(0).SponsorID.options(0).value`

5. How can you set an event handler for the **Focus** event of a text box named **CompanyName** in VBScript?
   a. By adding **"onFocus=*functionname()*"** to the **<INPUT>** tag that creates the **Companyname** text box.
   b. By creating a procedure or function named **Companyname_Focus**.
   c. By creating a procedure or function named **Companyname_onFocus**.
   d. All of the above.

EXERCISE 6

Complexity: Moderate

1. Enhance the event entry wizard (**$EVENTENTRY5.EXE**) so that it applies the client-side scripting approach using VBScript to validate the new sponsor contact information specified through the third input form (generated from the **EVENTENTRY_3.HTM** file). Hint: You only need to add VBScript-based validation code to the **EVENTENTRY_3.HTM** template file.

Complexity: Advanced

2. Create a new version of the **SEARCH.HTM** file (in the **C:\WEBSITE\HTDOCS\ WDBIC\CHAP13\LAB6** directory) that is functionally equivalent to the **SEARCH.HTM** file described in Lesson 3 but uses VBScript instead of JavaScript to send the client-generated SQL criteria to the server.

CHAPTER SUMMARY

This chapter described how to create active HTML pages using JavaScript and VBScript client-side scripting languages. Both languages treat the browser and the loaded HTML documents as a group of objects forming a hierarchy that starts with the **Window** object. The browser objects are created and destroyed automatically as and when the browser loads and unloads the document.

Each browser object supports a set of properties and methods and may respond to certain events. Using JavaScript and VBScript, you work with these preexisting objects by accessing and manipulating their properties, executing their methods, and setting their event handlers as needed. (Note that JavaScript and VBScript also provide some of their own objects and even let you create new objects.)

To familiarize you with the syntax of JavaScript and VBScript, this chapter presented two practical examples of applying client-side scripts to enhance different aspects of the event calendar application. The first example demonstrated the use of JavaScript to construct the SQL criteria at the browser end and to have the server-side CGI program directly use that criteria string to perform the search. The second example demonstrated how to make the browser validate the form input using either JavaScript or VBScript and sending only valid data to the server.

Here is a recap of the salient points covered in this chapter:

- JavaScript and VBScript are two client-side scripting languages that support an almost similar browser object model.

- JavaScript is based on the C language and is a case-sensitive language, whereas VBScript is a subset of Visual Basic and is not case sensitive.

- The generic format for referencing an object's property is by using the syntax `object.propertyName` and `object.methodName`, where the `object` is referred to by using a period-delimited object chain that always starts from the `Window` object.

- You can eliminate the `Window` object from the object chain. So `window.document.forms[0]` and `document.forms[0]` refer to the same `Form` object.

- All event-handlers of the `Window` object are specified in the `<BODY>` tag.

- The `onLoad` event handler is executed after the browser is done loading the document.

- The `onSubmit` event handler of a `Form` object is executed when the user submits the form.

- In JavaScript, you can use the syntax `onSubmit = "return functionName()"` in the `<FORM>` tag to make the browser submit a form based on the value returned by the handling function. In VBScript, you achieve a similar effect by creating a function named *formName*_onSubmit.

- The input controls of a `Form` object can be accessed by their name or through that form's elements array.

- The options of a selection list control can be accessed through the `options` array of that `List` object.

● The client-side scripting option should be considered a supplement for and not a replacement of the server-side processing for Internet-oriented Web database applications.

So, where do you go from here? Needless to say, what we have covered in this book is just the tip of the iceberg. You can explore several options at this point. You can apply the concepts and techniques discussed in this book to create other types of Web database applications. Or you can look at how other Web servers support the Web database interface. For example, Microsoft's Web Server (IIS) advocates the use of ActiveX technology for Web database applications.

Several Web database integration products are available, such as ColdFusion and dbWeb, that let you publish and maintain databases without requiring much coding effort. Now that you understand what is involved in a Web database application, you can examine the features supported by these products more carefully to see if they can help decrease Web application development time.

If performance is your main concern or if your Web application requires large databases, then consider migrating to a client-server type of database environment using Access databases as a prototype for your application.

Whatever you decide, remember that new technologies and techniques are introduced every day, so don't be afraid of learning and be prepared for fun and adventure in Web database land.

APPENDIX A

QUIZ AND EXERCISE ANSWERS

This appendix contains answers to the quiz questions. The answers to the lab exercises are provided in the HTML-formatted file named `LABANSWERS.HTM` in the root directory of the accompanying CD-ROM.

CHAPTER 1: GATHERING USER-DATA: HTML FORMS AND QUERIES

Lesson 1: *The Web Comunication Model*

1. a, c
2. d

The request method is not part of a URL. The Web client attaches the request method to the URL when constructing the HTTP request.

3. a

HTTP is a stateless protocol, which means that all Web transactions are conducted independent of each other and no data is automatically passed from one Web transaction to another.

4. a, b
5. c

Lesson 2: *Using the Extra Path and Query String for Passing Data*

1. b, c
2. c

The extra path is the string of all the characters occurring between the name of the executable program and the **?** character of a URL, which in this case would evaluate as **/form**.

3. c

The Web server translates the extra path information to a physical directory path based on its current configuration and provides that directory information to the CGI program. The CGI program will not get this directory information if you try to pass the extra path characters through the query string portion of the URL.

4. b

The query string is the portion of a URL that is listed after the question mark (**?**) character.

5. b, d

Option a is an invalid URL because it contains a space. Option c is an invalid URL because it does not have a location path.

Lesson 3: *Adding a User Interface*

1. b
2. a, b, d

You cannot embed an HTML form within another HTML form.

3. b, c, d

4. d

5. d

Lesson 4: *Text Controls*

1. b
2. a, b, c
3. a
4. a, c
5. c

Lesson 5: *Radio Controls, Checkboxes, and Selection Lists*

1. b
2. b, c, d
3. a
4. a, b
5. c

In a multiple selection list, a name=value pair is sent for each selected item.

Lesson 6: *Form Submission Techniques and Data Encoding Schemes*

1. a, c
2. d
3. c

Two pairs represent the x and y coordinates of the point at which the image was clicked.

4. b, c, d

The URL encoding scheme does not encrypt data, it simply encodes it.

5. b, c

Option a is incorrect because the multipart encoding scheme does not perform any data compression. Option d is incorrect because conceptually both encoding schemes allow you to send any amount of data.

CHAPTER 2: HANDLING USER REQUESTS: STATIC AND DYNAMIC RESPONSE

Lesson 1: *Role of the Web Server*

1. a
2. b, c
3. b
4. a, c
5. d

The server looks for the largest path in the document mapping that completely matches the beginning segment of the given URL. In this case, this largest path is `/icons/` and the server thus returns the document `C:\WEBSITE\ICONS\BOOK.GIF`. Note that the path `/icons/book/` in the document mapping does not completely match the beginning portion of the given URL (because of the trailing `/` in that path).

Lesson 2: *MIME Types, Content Mapping, and CGI Mapping*

1. a, b
2. c, d

Option a is incorrect because it starts with `html`, which is not one of the main MIME types. Option b is incorrect because the MIME subtype begins with a `y-` prefix, which is not standard practice.

3. b
4. a, c
5. b, d

There is no CGI mapping for the current URL path, so the server treats it as a regular URL path and goes with the information provided in the document mapping. The content mapping for the `.bat` extension causes the server to send the `application/x-script-batch` MIME type for the `Content-type` header field.

Lesson 3: *The Standard CGI*

1. b, c
2. c, d
3. c
4. c, d
5. a

Lesson 4: *The Windows Common Gateway Interface*

1. a, b
2. a, b, c, d
3. b
4. c
5. d

Because the `Cookie` header field is not one of the standard CGI fields, the Windows CGI specification requires the Web server to place it in the [Extra Headers] section of the CGI profile file.

Lesson 5: *Windows CGI and Form Data*

1. a, c

Option a is correct because under Windows CGI the Web server automatically appends `_1` as a suffix for the second name=value pair to make the name portion unique. Option c is correct because the original data itself contains the `_1` suffix for the second name=value pair.

2. b
3. c, d
4. d
5. c

Lesson 6: *CGI Response*

1. d
2. b, c, d
3. d
4. c

Using the Location header, all you need is one line:

```
Location: <URL path to the GIF image>
```

5. a, c

CHAPTER 3: ORGANIZING DATA: TABLES AND RELATIONSHIPS

Lesson 1: *The Importance of Data Organization*

1. a, c

Both the insurance planner and the astrology-based future predictions system would require some expert knowledge to function.

2. c
3. c
4. a, b, c
5. a, b, d

Lesson 2: What Is a Relational Database?

1. a, c, d
2. c, d
3. c

Because there is no rule saying that a driver's license number has to be a numeric value and it is not used in any computation, the safest bet is to use `VARCHAR` as its data type.

4. a
5. d

Lesson 3: *Table Relationships*

1. c
2. b
3. c
4. a, d
5. c, d

Lesson 4: *Normalizing Tables*

1. b, c
2. c, d
3. b, c

Note that the first normal form also helps achieve data consistency.

4. b
5. b

Lesson 5: *Data Validation and Field Properties*

1. a, d
2. c, d
3. b
4. a

Note that option b is also correct, if the start time needs to be validated as being less than the end time.

5. a

Lesson 6: *Security and Multiuser Issues*

1. a
2. a, d
3. b
4. b, d
5. a, b

CHAPTER 4: CONSTRUCTING A RELATIONAL DATABASE: THE MICROSOFT ACCESS WAY

Lesson 1: *What Is Microsoft Access?*

1. b, c

Access is a multiuser file-based RDBMS that can also access data from another database server.

2. a

Because all raw data has to be transferred from the file server to the client to be processed by the client, the speed of the client, the server, and the network all play an important role.

3. d
4. a, c
5. c

Lesson 2: *Data Types and Field Properties in Microsoft Access*

1. a

A new database is empty.

2. a, b

`Name` is generally less than 255 characters; `AuthorID`, being a primary key, is a good candidate for an `AutoNumber` or `Long Integer` number; and `Bibliography` should be `Memo`.

3. a, c

Access allows hyperlinks to PowerPoint and other Office documents. You can also use the OLE data type.

4. d

`Date/Time` data types have only one field size.

5. a

Input mask allows you validate data against a pattern, although it works only at the user-interface level.

Lesson 3: *Creating Tables in Access*

1. b

Access automatically sets the `Index` property to `Yes(No Duplicates)` for a field defined as a primary key.

2. a
3. a, c

You cannot use the `Default Value` property because any default value can be overwritten with a `Null` value.

4. c, d

You cannot refer to another field in the `Validation rule` property of a field.

5. c

`AutoIncrement` requires 32 bits storage and we don't plan to have too many (less than 20 if possible) sponsor types.

Lesson 4: *Defining Indexes, Relationships, and Referential Integrity in Access*

1. d
2. c, d
3. b
4. b, c
5. b

Lesson 5: *Adding, Editing, and Deleting Records Through Access*

1. a, d

The parent tables must contain link data before you add records to the child table to meet the referential integrity requirements.

2. b, c, d

Access automatically tries to save the current edited record if you move to another record or close the table. You can force it to save the record anytime by pressing SHIFT-ENTER.

3. a, c

An AutoNumber field can have gaps in the numeric sequence and can be linked to only a Long Integer–sized foreign key.

4. d

If no display text is specified, Access automatically inserts the address as the display text. Further, if the address URL does not contain a protocol, Access automatically adds the `http://` prefix to the address portion.

5. d

Lesson 6: *Importing and Attaching Data*

1. b, c
2. a, b

Maintaining the Referential Integrity option is part of specifying the relationship and cannot be changed during data import.

3. b, d

You cannot manipulate the table design of the external source, just the data in a linked source. For certain types of links, you cannot even change data.

4. d
5. d

CHAPTER 5: SORTING AND SEARCHING: SIMPLE SELECT QUERIES

Lesson 1: *What Is an Access Query?*

1. d
2. c, d
3. d
4. a, c

Access saves the SQL statement it creates for the query.

5. a, c, d

Access generates the SQL from the visual design, and the JET engine executes that SQL.

Lesson 2: *Creating Calculated Fields*

1. a, b, c

Option d is incorrect because the field name precedes the field expression in a calculated field.

2. c

The expression says add one month from the current date; because the current date is the last day of January 1996, Access returns the last day of February 1996.

3. b, d

The `Email` field must be enclosed within square brackets and you can use the `IsNull` function either directly, as shown in option b, or indirectly with the `IIF` function, as shown in option d.

4. d

5. b

`"A"+Null = Null` and `Null & "B" = "B"` so⇐ `("A" + Null)& "B" = "B"`

Lesson 3: *Sorting Data*

1. b, c
2. c
3. d

Text fields are sorted alphabetically, not chronologically.

4. b
5. b, d

Option c is incorrect because indexing on the secondary sort field does not help improve the sort performance; indexing on the primary sort field does help, though.

Lesson 4: *Filtering Data*

1. a, b, d

You can use the `IN` operator, as `IN(Value)`; use the `Between...And` operator, as in `Between Value and Value`; and use the = operator, as in `=Value`.

2. b

`Not In (CountryIDofCanada, CountryIDofUSA)` would work best in this case.

3. b, d

Access allows both `Is Not Null` and `Not Is Null` syntaxes for selecting records with non-`Null` data in the specific field.

4. c, d

Interchanging the limits in the `Between...And` expression does not make any difference, and you can use more than one built-in function in the same criteria expression.

5 c

You can include functions as values for the `IN` expression. The correct expression for option a is `>= "test"` and for option b it is either `NOT BETWEEN 1.AND 2` or `NOT BETWEEN "1" AND "2"`, depending on the data type of the criteria field.

Lesson 5: *Pattern Matching and Multifield Criteria*

1. a

`#` stands for any digit. Any other character, including the `#` character, is considered unmatched.

2. c
3. d

`!` stands for `NOT` in a `Like` expression.

4. b, c, d
5. b, d

Option a is incorrect because you cannot have text criteria for a number or currency field. Option b is valid because comparing a `long integer` field against a real value is allowed. Option c is invalid because the `Year` function returns a number and not a date. Option d is correct because you can enclose a text value in single quotes.

Lesson 6: *Parameter Queries*

1. a

You cannot change the criteria or the table source in a Parameter query, just specify parameters.

2. b, c, d

`[StateID]` in option a refers to the `StateID` field and is not a parameter.

3. b
4. a, b

You cannot use parameters to specify sort order, and you can change the parameters in query design.

5. c

CHAPTER 6: COMBINING TABLES AND GROUPING DATA: JOINS AND TOTAL QUERIES

Lesson 1: *Inner and Outer Joins*

1. b

A join exists between two tables using compatible fields from each table.

2. a, b

Because the EventTypeID field is required, both option a and option b will produce the same result. Option c will not work because it will produce additional records for event types that are not used by any event record.

3. a, b
4. b

An inner join between two tables forming a one-to-many relationship with referential integrity will always return records whose number is the same as the number of records in the many table.

5. d

Lesson 2: *Sorting and Filtering in Multiple Table Queries*

1. b
2. c
3. d

The inner join of Table A and Table B produces 40 records. Criteria B limits these to 15 records. Although Criteria A may limit these 15 records further, it is possible that the 10 records of Table

A filtered by Criteria A may match all 15 filtered records of Table B, hence producing all 15 records in the query result.

4. a, b
5. b, c

Lesson 3: *Grouping and Aggregating Data*

1. b

Only summary information is listed in a Total query.

2. a, b, d
3. b, c

The Group By function does not ignore records with a Null value in the field being grouped.

4. c
5. a

Lesson 4: *Advanced Data Analysis*

1. a, c
2. d
3. b, c

The precriteria in option b or the postcriteria in option c will both get the desired result.

4. b
5. a, c

Lesson 5: *Nested Queries*

1. b
2. c
3. c

The asterisk field represents all fields, so the new field will automatically appear in the result of Query B if it contains the asterisk field in its Field row.

4. c, d
5. a, b

For option b, Access allows you to nest queries at more than one level. For option c, some Nested queries are very hard and in some cases not possible to replace using regular queries. For option d, you can edit the data directly from a dependent query in some cases.

Lesson 6: *Subqueries, Union Queries, and Query Performance Issues*

1. b, c
2. a
3. c, d

For option a, you can unite more than two data sources in a Union query. For option b, only the last `SELECT` statement must end with a semicolon.

4. d
5. b, c, d

Because the Show checkbox of the calculated field is off, the calculated field can be removed. Specifying a `Is Not Null` criterion against Field A produces the same result as the current filter criterion of this query. Because now the criterion is directly applied against Field A, indexing this field will improve performance.

CHAPTER 7: DESIGNING QUERIES TO MAINTAIN DATA: ACTION QUERIES

Lesson 1: *Update Queries*

1. b, c

Update means adding or removing information from one or more table fields.

2. a, c

Option b is incorrect because Access does not display a message box when running a Select query.

3. b, c
4. b

You can update fields of only one table but you can use fields from multiple tables to build an `update` expression. Option c is incorrect because

Access ignores the fields whose Update cell is empty.

5. d

Lesson 2: *Delete Queries*

1. a, b, c
2. c
3. d

A Delete query tries to delete as many records as it can without disturbing the Referential Integrity options set between the related tables.

4. b, c
5. b

Lesson 3: *Make-Table Queries*

1. b, c
2. c
3. a, b, c

Any query that produces data can be used as the source of a Make-Table query.

4. a, d
5. c

Lesson 4: *Append Queries*

1. c
2. d
3. a, c

You can't use the asterisk field if any of the source and destination field names do not match.

4. b, c
5. a, c, d

Lesson 5: *Combining Action Queries and Temporary Tables to Perform a Task*

1. a, b
2. c

In most cases, the order in which you run your queries is critical. Option b is also correct under some circumstances.

3. a, b

Converting the Update query into an Append or Make-Table query by itself won't do much good.

4. d

Because the two tables are linked on their primary key, Access treats that link as a one-to-one relationship and allows you to delete records from either table.

5. c

Because it's a temporary table and an Append query only appends data, in most cases you need to ensure that the table is empty.

Lesson 6: *Importing Data Into Multiple Related Tables*

1. c
2. a, c

Table B, the many table, would not generally have the common field as one of its fields.

3. a, b, c
4. c
5. a, b

You cannot tell Access to supply unique values to an `ID` field that is not set as an `AutoNumber` type.

CHAPTER 8: CREATING WINDOWS CGI APPLICATIONS: THE VISUAL BASIC FRAMEWORK

Lesson 1: *What Is a Windows CGI Program?*

1. b, c
2. a
3. c
4. a, d
5. b

Lesson 2: *Creating Your First Windows CGI Program*

1. a, b
2. a, b

Option c is incorrect because the `NEWAPP.VBP` project template does not contain any program-specific code.

3. a, b
4. c
5. d

The HTML output of the modified program is functionally the same as the original, so nothing would change from the user's perspective.

Lesson 3: *The `Main` Procedure*

1. b, c, d
2. b

The `ErrorHandler` procedure overwrites the CGI output file with the error message and passes control back to the `Main` procedure, which terminates the program.

3. b
4. b
5. c

Lesson 4: *Accessing the CGI Environment Variables*

1. c
2. b
3. b, d
4. b

Most browsers do not send any parameters that are separated by a space in the URL, so the `DAY.EXE` program only gets the value `05` in its `CGI_QueryString variable`, which constitutes an invalid date.

5. c

In the first run, the PASS.EXE program asks the browser to prompt for the user name and password. Only in the second run will it be able to authenticate the user; this process may have to repeat until the user provides the proper combination.

Lesson 5: *Accessing Accept Type and Extra Header Data*

1. c
2. d

Remember, the CGI_AcceptTypes is a zero-based array; CGI_AcceptTypes(2) refers to the third element.

3. c
4. c, d

Both FindExtraHeader("cookie") and CGI_ExtraHeaders(2).Value will return the string "username=abc". So, extracting the 10th, 11th, and 12th character from this resulting string with the MID$ function will return "abc". Note that FindExtraHeader("username") will return an empty string.

5. a, c, d

The matching method used by FindExtraHeader is case sensitive.

Lesson 6: *Handling Form Data*

1. a, b
2. c
3. d
4. a, c

Option d is incorrect because CGI_FileTuples(0).File would be C:\WEBSITE\CGI-TEMP\9EWS.002.

5. d

CHAPTER 9: ACCESSING DATABASE RECORDS FROM VISUAL BASIC: DATA ACCESS OBJECTS

Lesson 1: *The Data Access Object (DAO) Model*

1. b, c

Name is just another object property, not a distinct element.

2. d
3. a, c

Option b is incorrect because VB provides no such variable to refer to the default workspace. Option d is incorrect because Admin is the value of the Username property of the default workspace.

4. b, d

Option b would generate an error because Password is not a property of a Workspace object. Option d would generate an error because the workspace has not yet been appended to the Workspaces collection.

5. b

Only the default workspace is part of the Workspaces collection, because the new workspace was appended to that collection.

Lesson 2: *Opening a Database*

1. b
2. c, d

Option c will return an error because pws does not refer to any existing Workspace object yet. Option d will return an error because there is no database object that initially resides in the Databases collection of the default workspace.

3. a, b

Option c is incorrect because by default a database is opened with full read/write privileges.

4. d

Three **Database** objects were created, even though two of them represent the same database.

5. c

Lesson 3: *The* Recordset *Object*

1. a

By default, a recordset based on a single table is created as a table-type recordset.

2. b

3. b, d

Option a is incorrect because **dbDynasetType** is not a valid constant. Option c is incorrect because the **dbDenyWrite** option denies other users write access to the records represented by your recordset.

4. b, d

5. c

Lesson 4: *Navigating Through a Recordset*

1. c, d

2. c, d

3. b

Because the **rs.MoveNext** statement is missing, the recordset will never reach its end and the code will keep executing until **i** reaches its maximum allowable value and an overflow error is generated.

4. c

The **Caption** property of the **WebAddress** field was set to **Web URL** in the design of the **tblSponsors** table.

5. c

Lesson 5: *Creating Recordsets Based on a Parameter Query*

1. c

2. b, c

Option a will not work because the query name contains a hyphen character.

3. b, c

4. c

The **StartDate = Left$(CGI_QueryString, DelimiterPos - 1)** line in the **CGI_Main** procedure of **EVENT1.EXE** will generate a run-time error.

5. b

The **CVDate** function recognizes the format of the specified date parameters and translates them to the appropriate date values, so the program works normally.

Lesson 6: *Troubleshooting Windows CGI Programming Errors*

1. b, c

Line 1 is syntactically correct, so the compiler assumes **ws** to be a variant type variable. However, a variant type cannot be used to represent object types, so lines 5 and 6 will generate a compilation error because they expect **ws** to be declared as a workspace. Line 6 will not generate an error because of the missing **Set** keyword because the **Set** keyword is not required. Line 3 will cause an error to flag because no line with that label is present in the procedure.

2. b, c

Line 4 will not generate any error because you are assigning **wsCount** to the number of **Workspace** objects currently in the **Workspaces** collection.

3. d

4. a, b

5. c

CHAPTER 10: PRESENTING INFORMATION: WEB DATABASE PUBLISHING

Lesson 1: *Web Database Publishing Approaches*

1. a, b

Information from all the tables may not be needed by the user; putting it all together on one page would make the page very large. Options c and d are incorrect because combining tables is possible and relatively easy using Access queries.

2. a, b, c

The drill-down technique establishes cross-links between data organized in a hierarchical manner. Each link generates a new page that contains information related to that link only.

3. b

The field-based search will allow you to specify criteria on the EventDate field and the related Country field of each event occurrence.)

4. a, c

The search feature works best if the database is densely populated. If the database is scarcely populated, then the search result will often turn out to be empty. Also, if the scope of the data is not known in advance, as in what words have been used for the sponsor type in the calendar database, then making good search criteria becomes difficult.

5. d

You could create static pages for events that occurred in the past months and dynamic pages for events that will occur in the coming months.

Lesson 2: *Static Publishing Using Access*

1. a, b

Option c is incorrect because the wizard does not create a template file, it just uses it.

2. d

3. a, c

Option b is incorrect because the Web wizard does give you the option to specify more than one template file per session.

4. c

5. c

The Web publishing wizard converts

 to

 in the publication, which the browser translates back to

.

Lesson 3: *Dynamic Browsing and Creating Page Breaks*

1. c

If the starting record position exceeds the position of the last recordset, the For loop of the ShowRecordsSubset procedure will terminate without listing any record but will not generate any error. The condition in the ShowNextSubsetLink will also prevent it from presenting the Next hyperlink.

2. b

3. d

4. a, b

5. b, d

Option a is incorrect because qryEvents_Upcoming always returns all the upcoming events. Option c is incorrect because the fixed-size date range does not guarantee that there will be a fixed number of records in each date range.

Lesson 4: *Drill-Down Browsing*

1. c

2. d

3. d

Because the list being requested belongs to Level 2, the extra path must be sponsors and the query string must be the sponsortypeID, which in this case is 2.

4. b, c

5. b, d

Lesson 5: *Grouping and Formatting Data Pages*

1. c

You can avoid repeating the same information by grouping the common part into a Header section and then listing the part that changes in a Detail section.

2. b

The HyperlinkPart function is not supported in VB. So if you open a recordset in VB using any query containing this function, VB will generate a run-time error.

3. a, c

The ShowEvent procedure requires that all the event occurrence records associated with an event appear contiguously. This is because it starts with the first occurrence record of the event and processes all the subsequent records with the same EventID as the first one.

4. a, b

N2S is a quick function to convert Null values to   and comes handy when presenting fields that may contain Null values through an HTML table.

5. b

The ShowLocationAndDate procedure of DRILL.EXE lists all the locations and the corresponding dates of a given event.

Lesson 6: *SQL-Based Searching*

1. c, d

Parameter queries work only when you have the same criteria fields but different criteria values.

2. b

If the event search form is submitted in its default, the SEARCH.EXE program returns all events.

3. d

Options a and b are incorrect because the SEARCH.EXE program does not use the Between...And operator for the date range criteria. Option c is incorrect because the SEARCH.EXE program uses the IN operator for the CountryID field.

4. a

If the ALL option is selected, the SEARCH.EXE program ignores all other options.

5. b, d

Option b encloses the search text in a pair of single quotes, hence each single quote within the text has to be represented by two single quotes. Option d encloses the search text in a pair of double quotes, hence each double quote within the text has to be represented by two double quotes.

CHAPTER 11: POPULATING TABLES: WEB-BASED DATA ENTRY

Lesson 1: *Single Table Data Entry*

1. a, c

Option b is incorrect: An HTML data entry form should not contain input controls for system-maintained fields. Option d is incorrect because the goal of an entry form is to be intuitive to the user irrespective of the page size needed to create that layout.

2. b

The SPENTRY.EXE program terminates with a Sponsor name must be specified error message the moment it detects that the no value was entered for the sponsor name field.

3. a

Because the SponsorName field can accept duplicate values, the program will add two records of the same sponsor, giving each record a different SponsorID value.

4. a, b

Option c is incorrect because you still need the VerifyPassword field to ensure that the user entered the correct password.

5. b, d

WebAddress and Password are optional fields and their Allow Zero Length property is set to No, which means that they can accept Null values but not empty strings.

Lesson 2: *Developing Front Ends Involving Lookup Values*

1. b, d

The static lookup tables promote the use of HTML forms that can be statically generated and do not require special programming.

2. a, c

Option b is incorrect because the use of dynamic lookup tables can negatively affect the overall performance. Option d is incorrect because some lookup tables cannot be left static for the application to work intuitively and provide maximum flexibility.

3. b

The Back button generally does not cause a browser to request a new form, so you will see the original form in the state before it was submitted.

4. b, d

The SendLocationEntryForm procedure of the program uses the LOCATIONENTRY_1.HTM and LOCATIONENTRY_3.HTM external files.

5. b

Small countries such as Monaco and Singapore are not broken into cities, which is why the CityID field of the location table is not required, and users need a blank option to describe a location in these countries.

Lesson 3: *Maintaining Dynamic Lookup Tables*

1. a, c, d

Option b is incorrect because the LOCATIONENTRY.EXE program accepts new cities.

2. b
3. a

Because the CityID input field holds the ID value of the city selected from the selection list, the program does not even bother to check for a new city.

4. b, c

Because the new city already exists, the FindFirst method sets the current position of the recordset to point to the matching record and indicates that a match has been found by setting the NoMatch property to False.

5. b

Two copies of the LOCATIONENTRY.EXE program will be executed concurrently and both will try to add the new city name to the city lookup table. One of these copies will be successful on the first try, whereas the other copy's first try will generate an error. But in the second try, this other copy will find the city record saved by the first copy and use its ID to save the location record.

Lesson 4: *Multiple Table Data Entry Using One Form*

1. a, d
2. b, d
3. d

HTML imposes a constraint that the number of controls you want on a form must be fixed at design time, which limits the number of records you can enter at a time through that form.

4. d

5. a, c

Using one form for multiple table data entry allows the back-end program to receive and process all the data at once.

Lesson 5: *Processing Single-Form-Based Multiple Table Data Entry Requests*

1. b

To determine the sponsor of an event, you have to go through the sponsor contact table.

2. c

The program requires that at least one contact be specified for the new sponsor and every valid contact have a contact name. Because no contact name was listed, the program returns an error.

3. d

4. a, d

Option b is incorrect because the `MULTIENTRY1.EXE` program requires either one or two valid contacts for the new sponsor. Option c is incorrect because the `MULTIENTRY1.EXE` program accepts a valid contact specified in second row even if the first row is left blank.

5. a, c

The `ValidateData` procedure counts only the number of valid contacts and uses that count to ensure that at least one valid contact came with the Web request.

Lesson 6: *Transaction Processing*

1. c, d

Options a and b can be done in one database operation, but options c and d cannot, so c and d could benefit from transaction processing.

2. b

3. a, c

Option b is incorrect because each database operation is validated at the time the operation is executed. Option d is incorrect because transactions should be as small as possible so as to free up the locks they establish on the updated tables.

4. a

The `GenerateResponse` procedure is called after the transaction in which the sponsor and contact information is saved. The `rollback` method called by the `HandleError` procedure would not have any effect.

5. b, c

CHAPTER 12: CREATING A DATA ENTRY WIZARD: ADVANCED DATA ENTRY AND MAINTENANCE

Lesson 1: *Designing a Data Entry Wizard*

1. a, b

Option c is incorrect because the main objective of any data entry wizard is to accept user input through a series of simple and small forms.

2. b, c

3. b

4. c

5. c

The event entry wizard stores the event header after it receives one record of the location and the associated timings for that event.

Lesson 2: *Generating Dynamic Input Forms*

1. b, c

2. c

Options a and b are incorrect because the `$EVENTENTRY.EXE` program allows any text to be set as the markup code.

3.a, c

Option b is incorrect because a true self-contained application is completely independent of any hard-coded paths, whether these paths are used by the front end to refer to the back end or by the back end to refer to external files.

4. d

The `ReplaceString` function that the `$EVENTENTRY.EXE` program uses to perform markup code replacements is designed to replace all occurrences of a specified string with the replacement string.

5. c

The Parameter query, `qrySponsors_Matching`, is designed to return all the sponsor records if the `pSponsorName` parameter is set to an empty string.

Lesson 3: *Adding User Security and Maintaining State Using Hidden Fields*

1. a, b

Because the requests are generated using the HTML forms that anyone can create using a text editor, and because all Web requests are independent due to the sessionless nature of the Web, there is no way of knowing that the requests are coming from the same user; hence, multiple security checks have to be performed.

2. a, b

Option c is incorrect because the use of the browser's authentication dialog box increases the number of CGI requests.

3. a

The event entry wizard performs user authentication only when you select an existing sponsor.

4. a

The third input form contains the `SponsorID` as its hidden field.

5. b

The fourth input form contains the `SponsorContactID` hidden field. The `SponsorID` is not passed as a hidden field because it can be determined from the contact record corresponding to the `SponsorContactID` hidden field.

Lesson 4: *Persistent Cookies*

1. b, c

Option a is incorrect because `Set-Hidden field` is not a valid HTTP header field. Option b is correct because the CGI program cannot change a hidden field in the input form that's already been sent. However, the program can send another copy of that input form (option c) and supply a different value for the hidden field, but only if the user makes another request for that input form.

2. a, c, d

Option b is incorrect because the browser supplies the authentication information with each subsequent request made to the CGI program.

3. c

Cookies are set and transmitted without Web users ever being aware of it.

4. b

The `CartID` cookie has expired, so the browser will send only the `OrderID` cookie.

5. c

Lesson 5: *Using Cookies in a Data Entry Wizard*

1. a, c

Option b is incorrect because the `$EVENTENTRY.EXE` program does not set or modify any cookies on receiving the fifth input form.

2. b, c

The $EVENTENTRY.EXE program never sets the TempEventID and EventID cookies so that they both have either a blank or a nonblank value at the same time.

3. d

The $EVENTENTRY.EXE program handles a new city by setting the city option value to the city name with the New- prefix.

4. c
5. b

The GetCookieField function returns a Null value only when it does not find any name=value cookie pair matching the specified cookie name.

Lesson 6: *Editing and Deleting Data Over the Web*

1. a, b, c

Option d is incorrect because the $EVENTENTRY3. EXE program does not ask for any confirmation once a user submits the modified sponsor information through the sponsor edit form.

2. b
3. c
4. a, b, d

The tblLocations table is not a direct descendant of the tblSponsors table, so the Cascade Delete referential integrity option set between tblSponsors and all its descendant tables (related as a one-to-many chain) will not affect the tblLocations table.

5. a

The HandleSponsorEditForm procedure of the $EVENTENTRY3.EXE program does not perform any security check and would simply update the sponsor record with the resubmitted sponsor data. Note that this could be treated as a potential security flaw in the $EVENTENTRY3.EXE program.

CHAPTER 13: USING CLIENT-SIDE SCRIPTING LANGUAGES: JAVASCRIPT AND VBSCRIPT

Lesson 1: *The Browser Object Model*

1. d

In thin-client fat-server model, a Web browser is expected to play the role of displaying information and accepting user input, features that most browsers currently support.

2. a, d

Option b is incorrect because the Location object is a descendent of the Window object, not the Document object. Option c is incorrect because the words location and host must be lowercase.

3. b, d

Option a is incorrect because you need to specify parentheses with a method name. Option c is incorrect because the forward method does not accept any arguments.

4. c, d

Option a is incorrect because the pathname property contains only the URL path value, not the entire URL information. Option d is incorrect because the Document object does not support the href property.

5. b

Lesson 2: *The Form-Related Browser Objects*

1. a
2. b

The elements array is a property of the Form object and contains an entry for each input control in the form.

3. b

Option a is incorrect because the `Form` object does not support the `focus` method. Option c is incorrect because it would cause the adjacent control to take focus. Option d is incorrect because the event handler is triggered by the focus event; the event handler does not cause the focus event to occur.

4. b, c

5. a, b

Option c is incorrect because the radio control object array is a zero-based array. Option d is incorrect because you can change the property of an input control any time after the browser loads the HTML text that creates that input control.

Lesson 3: *Using JavaScript in a Web Application*

1. a, b

Option c is incorrect because the server still takes the responsibility of formatting the search result in the event search example, although this task can be assigned to the browser through JavaScript.

2. b

3. b

4. c

This JavaScript code is not part of a function, so the browser will execute it while loading the document. Because this code refers to the `value` property of the `Text1` input control, the browser needs to be aware of the form `frmFeedback` and the `Text1` control, hence this code must be placed after the form definition.

5. b, c, d

Option a is incorrect because you can embed multiple `<SCRIPT>...</SCRIPT>` sections in an HTML document.

Lesson 4: *Generating SQL Criteria Through JavaScript*

1. a, b

Option c is incorrect because JavaScript variables change their data type based on the value they store.

2. b, c

The `if` keyword needs to be lowercase.

3. b

`For` loops and functions are JavaScript constructs, not objects.

4. b

5. b

Variable i is initialized to 10 and the loop's continuation criteria is $i <= 10$, so the loop will run once. After that, i will be incremented by 1 and will not meet the continuation criteria, so the loop will terminate.

Lesson 5: *Form Validation and Field Navigation Through JavaScript*

1. a, c

Option b is incorrect because writing client-side programs is not always easy.

2. d

3. b, c, d

4. a, c

Option b is incorrect because you cannot use a string expression in JavaScript to access an input field. You can, however, use the field name directly, as shown in option c. Option d is incorrect because you can access an input field using an index value only through the elements array, as indicated in option a.

5. c

Lesson 6: *Using VBScript*

1. a, b

VBScript does not support the **WITH** construct.

2. a, c

Option b is incorrect because VBScript is natively supported only by Internet Explorer (although this may change with time). Option d is incorrect because only JavaScript is case sensitive.

3. a, b

Option c is incorrect because VBScript does not support the **On Error Goto** statement.

4. c, d

Option a is incorrect because you can get to an option only through the selection list object's **option** array. Option b is incorrect because it uses square brackets to refer to an array element, which is incorrect syntax.

5. a, c

APPENDIX B
INTERNET EXPLORER 3: A FIELD GUIDE

A new day dawned. The sun reached its fingers over the digital outback. The mighty Navigators (*Netscapus navigatorus*)—a species that reproduced like rabbits and ran nearly as fast—covered the landscape. Yonder, on a cliff that seemed to be beyond the horizon, a trembling new creature looked out over the Internet jungle. This strange new creature, calling itself the Explorer (*Microsoftus interneticus explorus*), sniffed around, considering whether it should enter the fragile ecosystem. Netscape gators gnashed their teeth, but the Explorer was not daunted. Explorer was a formidable beast. It became a part of the jungle and thrived. And even though it began as a mere pup, it evolved, and it evolved, and it evolved.

Now the jungle is rife with two intelligent species.

What follows is a guide to domesticating Internet Explorer. You will learn how to care for your Explorer and even how to teach it tricks. Before long, you shall find truth behind the old axiom that the Explorer is man's (and woman's) best friend.

INTRODUCING EXPLORER TO YOUR ECOSYSTEM

Whether you're running a Macintosh, Windows, Windows NT, or Windows 95, installing Explorer is easy. Explorer's own installation program makes setup a breeze, and you need only to select the appropriate file on the CD-ROM to launch this installer. Make sure the CD-ROM included with this book is in the CD-ROM drive; then follow the directions for your operating system.

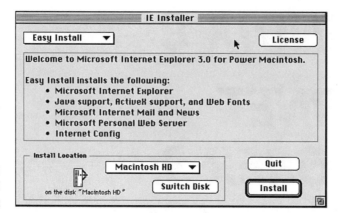

Figure B-1
The Macintosh IE
Installer box

Macintosh Installation Instructions

1. Insert the CD-ROM into your CD drive.

2. You will see a CD icon when the CD is mounted by your Macintosh. Double-click on the CD icon.

3. You will see four folders: 3RDPARTY, ARCHIVES, SOURCE, and EXPLORER. Double-click on the EXPLORER folder.

4. Launch Internet Explorer's installer by double-clicking on IE Installer. A dialog box similar to the one shown in Figure E-1 appears. Follow the onscreen prompts to finish the installation.

Windows 95 Installation

1. Click the Start button in the lower left corner of your screen.

2. Click on the Run... option in the Start menu. A dialog box similar to the one shown in Figure B-2 appears.

3. Using the Run dialog box, type in a pathname and specify the location of the Explorer installation program. IE302M95.EXE is in the CD's \EXPLORER directory, so if your CD-ROM drive is designated as D:, you'd type

```
d:\explorer\ie302m95.exe
```

Figure B-2
The Windows 95
Run dialog box

If your CD-ROM drive has a different designation letter, type in the appropriate drive designation letter in place of D:.

4. After typing the proper pathname, click the OK button to start the Explorer's installation program. Depending upon your system, it may take a moment to load.

5. Once the installation program loads, follow the on-screen prompts to set up Explorer on your computer.

Windows NT 4 Installation

1. Click the Start button in the lower left corner of your screen.

2. Click on the Run... option in the Start menu. A dialog box similar to the one shown in Figure B-3 appears.

3. Using the Run dialog box, type in a pathname and specify the location of the Explorer installation program. IE302MNT.EXE is in the CD's \EXPLORER directory, so if your CD-ROM drive is designated as D:, you'd type

```
d:\explorer\ie302mnt.exe
```

If your CD-ROM drive has a different designation letter, type in the appropriate drive designation letter in place of D:.

4. After typing the proper pathname, click the OK button to start the Explorer's installation program. Depending upon your system, it may take a moment to load.

5. Once the installation program loads, follow the on-screen prompts to set up Explorer on your computer.

Figure B-3
The Windows NT
Run dialog box

Windows 3.1 and Windows NT 3.51 Installation

1. Click on File in the main menu bar in Program Manager.

2. Click on Run... option in the File menu. A dialog box similar to the one shown in Figure B-4 appears.

3. Using the Run dialog box, type in a pathname and specify the location of the Explorer installation program. SETUP.EXE is in the \EXPLORER\WIN31NT3.51 directory. If your CD-ROM drive is designated D:, type:

```
d:\explorer\win31nt3.51\setup.exe
```

   If your CD-ROM drive has a different designation letter, type in the appropriate drive designation letter in place of D:.

4. After typing the proper pathname, click the OK button to start Explorer's installation program. Depending on your system, it may take a moment to load.

5. Once the installation program loads, follow the on-screen prompts to set up Explorer on your computer.

Once you've run the installation, you'll need to restart your system. You can then click on the Internet icon on your desktop. If you've already selected an Internet provider with Windows dial-up networking, you'll be connected. If not, you'll be walked through the dial-in process. You'll need to enter the phone number of your Internet provider, your modem type, and other related information. Ultimately, you'll be taken to Microsoft's home page, where you can register your Explorer and find out about its latest features.

The Explorer is a constantly evolving animal. For the latest updates, plug-ins, and versions, be sure to regularly check out Microsoft's neck of the woods at `http://www.microsoft.com/ie/`.

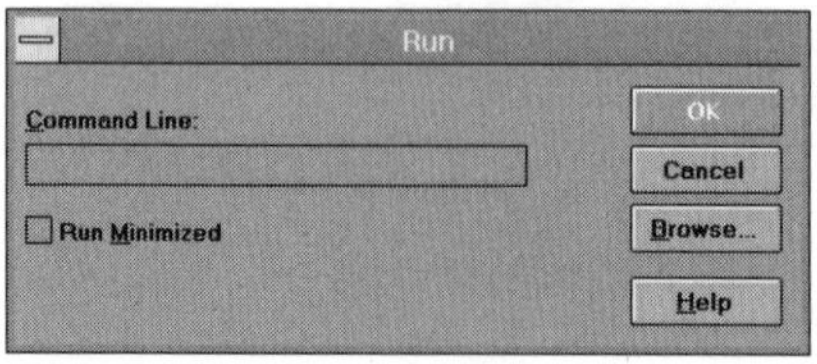

Figure B-4
Windows 3.1 and
Windows NT 3.51
Run dialog box

Explorer Components

Explorer is more than a plain-Jane Web browser. As you work through the installation, you'll be able to choose a variety of components. You can select the following add-ons:

● *Internet Mail*—This is a comprehensive email package. Using simple icons, you can write and read your mail off-line and then log on quickly to send and receive your latest batch of correspondence. See Figure B-5.

● *Internet News*—This is a window that lets you browse through thousands of newsgroups, read through the threads, and post your own messages. The News system is very easy to use. You can easily keep track of your favorite topics and automatically update with the latest news.

● *ActiveMovie*—This feature of Explorer lets you watch all sorts of video clips— MPEG, AVI, and QuickTime formats. It even supports a special streaming version of video that downloads movies as you watch them, letting you view video with little delay. The ActiveMovie system also lets you listen to all popular formats of audio files—AU, WAV, MIDI, MPEG, and AIFF. This makes it easy to add background sound to Web pages.

● *VRML Support*—This feature is a separate module that lets you download and coast through Virtual Reality Modeling Language worlds. This allows you to explore true 3D landscapes and objects.

● *NetMeeting*—This is a full-featured package that lets you hold entire meet- ings over the Internet. You can chat with one person or with dozens. If you have a microphone, you can use the Internet phone feature to hold voice conversations with other people. You can share applications. For example, you and a client can edit the same word processing document together. A whiteboard feature lets you draw on a "digital blackboard" that can be updated live across the Internet.

● *HTML Layout Control*—This tool lets Web page publishers create spiffy versions of HTML pages, the way professional designers would lay out a magazine page or a newspaper. Designers can choose exactly where to place elements within a Web page. You can make objects transparent and layer objects over each other, which helps make a Web page eye-catching yet uncluttered.

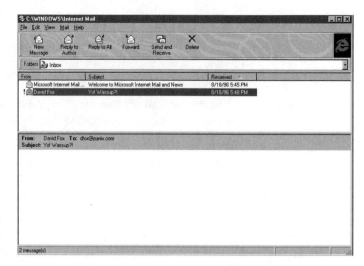

Figure B-5
The Internet Mail
main window

THE NATURE OF THE BEAST

Internet Explorer features very up-to-date HTML. It supports HTML 3.2, including the following:

- *Frames*—These break up the Web page window into several areas. For example, you can keep an unchanging row of navigation controls along the top of the page while constantly updating the bottom. You can use *borderless frames*, which split up the page without making it seem split. A special type of frame known as the *floating frame* lets you view one Web page within another.

- *Cascading Style Sheets*—This allows all your Web sites to have the same general look and feel.

- *Tables*—You can create or view all sorts of fancy tables, with or without graphics, borders, and columns.

- *Embedded Objects*—Internet Explorer can handle Java applets, ActiveX controls, and even Netscape plug-ins. These objects are discussed later, in the "Symbiotic Partners" section of this appendix.

- *Fonts*—Explorer supports many fonts, allowing Web pages to have a variety of exciting designs.

From the get-go, Internet Explorer has included a few special bells and whistles. For example, it's easy to create and view marquees across Web pages. This lets you scroll a long, attention-drawing message, similar to a tickertape, that puts a great deal of information in a very small space.

TRAINING THE EXPLORER

By its very nature, the Explorer is a friendly beast. You can access the full range of the Explorer's talents by pushing its buttons. These buttons, which appear in the toolbar at the top of the screen as depicted in Figure B-6, are as follows:

- *Back*—Use this to return to the Web page you've just come from. This will help you retrace your steps as you take Explorer through the Internet maze.

- *Forward*—Use this after you've used the Back button, to jump forward again to the page from which you began.

- *Stop*—If a Web page is taking too long to load, press this button. Any text and graphics will immediately stop downloading.

- *Refresh*—If your Web page is missing some graphics, or if you've previously stopped its loading using the Stop button, you can reload it using Refresh.

- *Home*—This takes you to your pre-set home page. By default, this is Microsoft's main Web page, but you can set your home to any you'd like. See the "Taming the Beast" section.

- *Search*—This takes you to a special page that allows you to search for a Web page, using a number of cool search engines. See the "Hunting Skills" section.

- *Favorites*—This button lets you access a list of your favorite Web sites. See the "Favorite Haunts" section.

- *Print*—This allows you to print out the current Web page, allowing you to keep a perfect hard copy of it.

- *Font*—Find yourself squinting at a Web page? Just click here to zoom in. The font size will grow several degrees. Too big now? Click a few more times and the size will shrink once again.

- *Mail*—This will launch the Internet Mail program, which allows you to send and receive e-mail and to access newsgroups.

Figure B-6
A cosmetic look at
Explorer

PLAYING FETCH

Your Explorer is a devoted friend. It can scamper anywhere within the Internet, bringing back exactly what you desire.

If you know where you want to go, just type the URL into Explorer's Address box at the top of the screen. If you like, you can omit the `http://` prefix. The Web page will be loaded up. You can also search for a page or load up a previously saved page.

You can now click on any hyperlink—an underlined or colored word or picture—to zoom to that associated Web page or Internet resource. Some hyperlinked graphics may not be obvious. Explorer will tell you when you are positioned over a valid hyperlink, because the cursor will change into a pointing finger. Continue following these links as long as you like. It's not uncommon to start researching knitting needles and end up reading about porcupines.

If you're an aspiring Web page writer, you might want to take a peek at the HTML source code to see how that page was created. Just select View|Source.

HUNTING SKILLS

If you want to find Web pages dealing with a specific category, the Explorer makes it easy to find them. Click the Search button. The Search screen will appear, as in Figure B-7. You can search for more than Web pages. With Explorer, it's easy to find

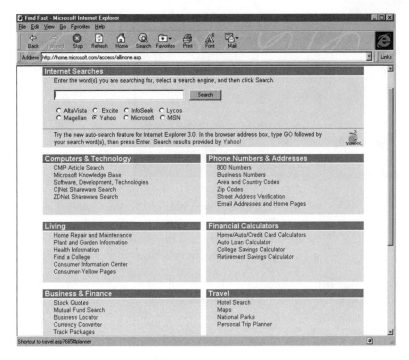

Figure B-7
The Search screen

● Phone numbers, ZIP codes, and addresses

● Information on a number of topics—health, home, education, consumer affairs, finance, weather, sports, travel, and so on

● References—maps, a dictionary, a thesaurus, quotations, and an encyclopedia

● On-line books, newspapers, and magazines

You can also quickly hunt for any idea, word, or category. Simply type GO in the Address box at the top of the screen, followed by the word or phrase you want to search for.

FAVORITE HAUNTS

It's easy to keep track of the Web pages you visit most. When you want to save a page for future reference, simply click the Favorites button or choose the Favorites menu item. Select the Add To Favorites option. The current Web page will now be added to the list of favorites, which appears each time you click on the Favorites button or menu.

After a while, your list of favorites will get long and cluttered. It's simple to keep track of huge lists of favorites—just put them into separate folders. Organize your favorites, as shown in Figure B-8, by selecting Favorites|Organize Favorites.

Figure B-8
Organizing the
Favorites list

To create a new folder, click on the New Folder icon (the folder with the little glint on it) at the top of the window. Now drag and drop your Web page bookmarks into the appropriate folders. You can also move, rename, or delete a folder by selecting it and using the corresponding buttons at the bottom of the screen.

You can even include or attach a favorite Web document within an email message, the way you would attach any other file.

On Windows systems, the Favorites list is actually a folder within your Windows directory. This reflects a Microsoft trend—treating the entire World Wide Web as just another folder to explore on your desktop. Eventually, you'll be able to drag and drop documents across the Internet as easily as you would within your own hard drive.

MEMORY

Internet Explorer keeps track of every Web page you visit. This is kept in a vast History list. You can view the entire History list, in chronological order, by clicking the View History button. Just click on any page you'd like to revisit.

The History list is cleared every 20 days—you can set this value within the Navigation properties sheets.

TAMING THE BEAST

Now that you and your Explorer are getting acquainted, why not tame it so that it acts and looks exactly like you want? Select View|Options and pick a tab at the top of the window to customize the following properties:

● *General*—The general properties sheet is illustrated in Figure B-9. Since multimedia content (such as sounds, movies, and graphics) takes longer to load in Web pages, you can choose not to load certain media types. You can also easily customize the color of the text and hyperlinks. Finally, you can decide how little or how much information appears in your toolbar.

Note You can change the size and position of your toolbar simply by clicking on its borders and dragging it to a desired location.

● *Connection*—You can adjust your connections settings, as shown in Figure B-10, by clicking on this tab. This lets you choose your Internet provider. If you're connecting to the Internet through a network firewall, you can also set your proxy server information here.

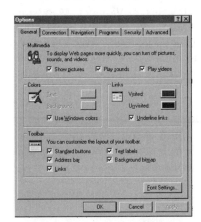

Figure B-9
The General
properties sheet

Figure B-10
The Connection
property sheet

● *Navigation*—You can customize which page you'd like to use as your starting home page. Just enter its URL in the Address box here.

● *Programs*—This allows you to set which programs you'd like to use for e-mail and for Usenet news. By default, you can use Microsoft's Internet Mail and Internet News, which are included with Explorer. You can also tell Explorer how to handle various types of files by selecting the File Types button. It allows you to designate which program or plug-in should be launched whenever Explorer comes across various unfamiliar file formats.

● *Security*—You are able to customize how securely documents will be handled by Explorer. If you want to keep your computer extremely safe, you may tell Explorer not to download possible security risks such as ActiveX controls, Java applets, or other plug-ins. Another nice feature is a Content Advisor. Click on Settings; the Content Advisor window will appear as in Figure B-11. You may now decide which Web pages to skip based on Adult Language, Nudity, Sex, or Violence. Many questionable Web pages are written with certain tags so that the pages can be weeded out by people who don't want to see them. This is a great option to use if your kids surf the Internet, or if your sensibilities are offended. To turn ratings on, click on the Enable Ratings button. You can also lock this window with a password.

● *Advanced*—This properties sheet lets you customize when Internet Explorer will issue warnings. This is useful if you deal with sensitive information and want to know which Web pages are secure and which are not. You can also set a number of other advanced Java and Security options here.

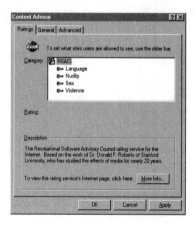

Figure B-11
The Content
Advisor window

SYMBIOTIC PARTNERS

Explorer includes many of the latest Web technologies. These make your Web pages sing, dance, and even act as entire applications. The line between what a computer can do in general and what a computer can do over the Internet is thinning.

ActiveX

Microsoft's proprietary ActiveX technology lets you drop controls into your Web pages. Controls are software components such as specialized buttons, input forms, graphics viewers, sound players, and so forth.

When you load a page with an ActiveX control, Explorer will check if you already have that control on your system. If not, you'll be asked whether you'd like to download it. You'll be told whether the control has been authenticated by Microsoft. If the control is secure, it'll automatically be downloaded and installed for you. The resulting Web page may look more like a software program than a Web page. Don't be surprised to find all new types of buttons, such as the up and down arrow controls in Figure B-12.

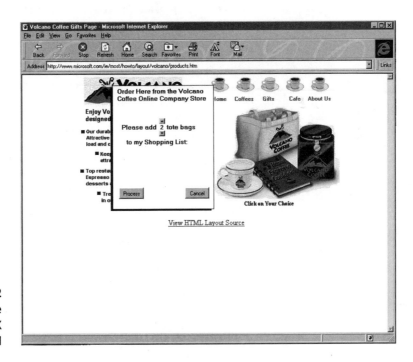

Figure B-12
Loading a page with an ActiveX control

Scripts

Internet Explorer allows Web page writers to add different types of scripts right into the source code of the Web page itself. This means you can get instantaneous feedback and control of the Web browser, ActiveX controls, Java applets, and other plug-ins. This makes interactivity fast and easy. Internet Explorer supports Visual Basic, Scripting Edition and JavaScript languages.

Java

Finally, Explorer fully supports the popular Java language. Java is a programming language that lets you write full applications that run directly within your Web browser. Java is great for writing games, graphics demonstrations, databases, spreadsheets, and much more.

Total Mastery

Now that you are fully in control of Explorer, you can learn, work, and have fun using it with the greatest of ease. Wandering through the Internet faster than ever, you are ready to investigate new paths of adventure with your trusty, obedient Explorer guiding you every step of the way.

INDEX

Symbols

A

C

W-Z

MARQUETTE
UNIVERSITY™

*Get Continuing Education Units
from Marquette University.*

You did all the work, now get the credit!

Marquette University is offering Continuing Education Units for Interactive Courses. You can use these credits to validate your skills for a new job or a promotion at your current job. Your company may even reimburse you if you get units and your course may be tax deductible.

The procedure is easy. When you complete an Interactive Course with a score of 70% or higher, a special certificate screen automatically pops up. Click the Continuing Education Units link. Print the registration form, fill it in, and send it to Marquette with your payment ($100 per course). Go to the next page, and click the link to send your passing grade and student information to Marquette.

In a very short time, you will receive a special Marquette certification test in the mail. Complete the test and return it to Marquette for grading. If you get a passing grade, you'll receive full units for the course.

So, work hard and get the real benefits from all that you have learned by applying for Continuing Education Units from Marquette University.

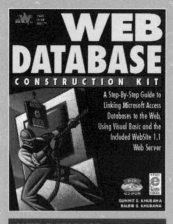

Message from the
Publisher

WELCOME TO OUR NERVOUS SYSTEM

Some people say that the World Wide Web is a graphical extension of the information superhighway, just a network of humans and machines sending each other long lists of the equivalent of digital junk mail.

I think it is much more than that. To me, the Web is nothing less than the nervous system of the entire planet—not just a collection of computer brains connected together, but more like a billion silicon neurons entangled and recirculating electro-chemical signals of information and data, each contributing to the birth of another CPU and another Web site.

Think of each person's hard disk connected at once to every other hard disk on earth, driven by human navigators searching like Columbus for the New World. Seen this way the Web is more of a super entity, a growing, living thing, controlled by the universal human will to expand, to be more. Yet, unlike a purposeful business plan with rigid rules, the Web expands in a nonlinear, unpredictable, creative way that echoes natural evolution.

We created our Web site not just to extend the reach of our computer book products but to be part of this synaptic neural network, to experience, like a nerve in the body, the flow of ideas and then to pass those ideas up the food chain of the mind. Your mind. Even more, we wanted to pump some of our own creative juices into this rich wine of technology.

TASTE OUR DIGITAL WINE

And so we ask you to taste our wine by visiting the body of our business. Begin by understanding the metaphor we have created for our Web site—a universal learning center, situated in outer space in the form of a space station. A place where you can journey to study any topic from the convenience of your own screen. Right now we are focusing on computer topics, but the stars are the limit on the Web.

If you are interested in discussing this Web site or finding out more about the Waite Group, please send me email with your comments, and I will be happy to respond. Being a programmer myself, I love to talk about technology and find out what our readers are looking for.

Sincerely,

Mitchell Waite

Mitchell Waite, C.E.O. and Publisher

200 Tamal Plaza
Corte Madera, CA 94925
415-924-2575
415-924-2576 fax

Website:
http://www.waite.com/waite

CREATING THE HIGHEST QUALITY COMPUTER BOOKS IN THE INDUSTRY

Waite Group Press

Come Visit
WAITE.COM
Waite Group Press
World Wide Web Site

Now find all the latest information on Waite Group books at our new Web site, **http://www.waite.com/waite.** You'll find an online catalog where you can examine and order any title, review upcoming books, and send email to our authors and editors. Our FTP site has all you need to update your book: the latest program listings, errata sheets, most recent versions of Fractint, POV Ray, Polyray, DMorph, and all the programs featured in our books. So download, talk to us, ask questions, on **http://www.waite.com/waite.**

The New Arrivals Room has all our new books listed by month. Just click for a description, Index, Table of Contents, and links to authors.

The Backlist Room has all our books listed alphabetically.

The People Room is where you'll interact with Waite Group employees.

Links to Cyberspace get you in touch with other computer book publishers and other interesting Web sites.

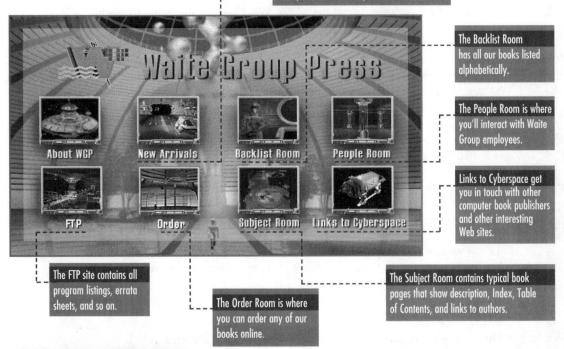

The FTP site contains all program listings, errata sheets, and so on.

The Order Room is where you can order any of our books online.

The Subject Room contains typical book pages that show description, Index, Table of Contents, and links to authors.

World Wide Web:

COME SURF OUR TURF—THE WAITE GROUP WEB

http://www.waite.com/waite
Gopher: gopher.waite.com
FTP: ftp.waite.com

This is a legal agreement between you, the end user and purchaser, and The Waite Group®, Inc., and the authors of the programs contained in the disc. By opening the sealed disc package, you are agreeing to be bound by the terms of this Agreement. If you do not agree with the terms of this Agreement, promptly return the unopened disc package and the accompanying items (including the related book and other written material) to the place you obtained them for a refund.

SOFTWARE LICENSE

1. The Waite Group, Inc. grants you the right to use one copy of the enclosed software programs (the programs) on a single computer system (whether a single CPU, part of a licensed network, or a terminal connected to a single CPU). Each concurrent user of the program must have exclusive use of the related Waite Group, Inc. written materials.

2. The program, including the copyrights in each program, is owned by the respective author, and the copyright in the entire work is owned by The Waite Group, Inc., and they are therefore protected under the copyright laws of the United States and other nations, under international treaties. You may make only one copy of the disc containing the programs exclusively for backup or archival purposes, or you may transfer the programs to one hard disk drive, using the original for backup or archival purposes. You may make no other copies of the programs, and you may make no copies of all or any part of the related Waite Group, Inc. written materials.

3. You may not rent or lease the programs, but you may transfer ownership of the programs and related written materials (including any and all updates and earlier versions) if you keep no copies of either, and if you make sure the transferee agrees to the terms of this license.

4. You may not decompile, reverse engineer, disassemble, copy, create a derivative work, or otherwise use the programs except as stated in this Agreement.

GOVERNING LAW

This Agreement is governed by the laws of the State of California.

LIMITED WARRANTY

The following warranties shall be effective for 90 days from the date of purchase: (i) The Waite Group, Inc. warrants the enclosed disc to be free of defects in materials and workmanship under normal use; and (ii) The Waite Group, Inc. warrants that the programs, unless modified by the purchaser, will substantially perform the functions described in the documentation provided by The Waite Group, Inc. when operated on the designated hardware and operating system. The Waite Group, Inc. does not warrant that the programs will meet purchaser's requirements or that operation of a program will be uninterrupted or error-free. The program warranty does not cover any program that has been altered or changed in any way by anyone other than The Waite Group, Inc. The Waite Group, Inc. is not responsible for problems caused by changes in the operating characteristics of computer hardware or computer operating systems that are made after the release of the programs, nor for problems in the interaction of the programs with each other or other software.

THESE WARRANTIES ARE EXCLUSIVE AND IN LIEU OF ALL OTHER WARRANTIES OF MERCHANTABILITY OR FITNESS FOR A PARTICULAR PURPOSE OR OF ANY OTHER WARRANTY, WHETHER EXPRESS OR IMPLIED.

EXCLUSIVE REMEDY

The Waite Group, Inc. will replace any defective disc without charge if the defective disc is returned to The Waite Group, Inc. within 90 days from date of purchase.

This is the Purchaser's sole and exclusive remedy for any breach of warranty or claim for contract, tort, or damages.

LIMITATION OF LIABILITY

THE WAITE GROUP, INC. AND THE AUTHORS OF THE PROGRAMS SHALL NOT IN ANY CASE BE LIABLE FOR SPECIAL, INCIDENTAL, CONSEQUENTIAL, INDIRECT, OR OTHER SIMILAR DAMAGES ARISING FROM ANY BREACH OF THESE WARRANTIES EVEN IF THE WAITE GROUP, INC. OR ITS AGENT HAS BEEN ADVISED OF THE POSSIBILITY OF SUCH DAMAGES.

THE LIABILITY FOR DAMAGES OF THE WAITE GROUP, INC. AND THE AUTHORS OF THE PROGRAMS UNDER THIS AGREEMENT SHALL IN NO EVENT EXCEED THE PURCHASE PRICE PAID.

COMPLETE AGREEMENT

This Agreement constitutes the complete agreement between The Waite Group, Inc. and the authors of the programs, and you, the purchaser.

Some states do not allow the exclusion or limitation of implied warranties or liability for incidental or consequential damages, so the above exclusions or limitations may not apply to you. This limited warranty gives you specific legal rights; you may have others, which vary from state to state.

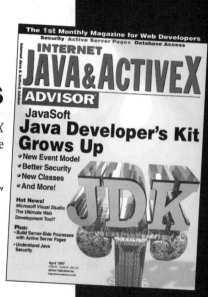

MACMILLAN COMPUTER PUBLISHING USA

A V I A C O M C O M P A N Y

Technical ---- Support:

If you cannot get the CD/Disk to install properly, or you need
assistance with a particular situation in the book, please feel
free to check out the Knowledge Base on our Web site at
http://www.superlibrary.com/general/support. We have
answers to our most Frequently Asked Questions listed there.
If you do not find your specific question answered, please
contact Macmillan Technical Support at **(317) 581-3833**.
We can also be reached by email at **support@mcp.com**.

SATISFACTION REPORT CARD

Please fill out this card if you wish to know of future updates to
Visual Basic Web Database Interactive Course, or to receive our catalog.

First Name: _____ **Last Name:** _____

Street Address: _____

City: _____ **State:** _____ **Zip:** _____

Email Address _____

Daytime Telephone: (   ) _____

Date product was acquired: Month _____ **Day** _____ **Year** _____ **Your Occupation:** _____

Overall, how would you rate *Visual Basic Web Database Interactive Course?*

☐ Excellent   ☐ Very Good   ☐ Good
☐ Fair   ☐ Below Average   ☐ Poor

What did you like MOST about this book? _____
_____
_____

What did you like LEAST about this book? _____
_____
_____

Please describe any problems you may have encountered with installing or using the disc: _____
_____

How did you use this book (problem-solver, tutorial, reference...)?
_____

What is your level of computer expertise?
☐ New   ☐ Dabbler   ☐ Hacker
☐ Power User   ☐ Programmer   ☐ Experienced Professional

What computer languages are you familiar with? _____
_____

Please describe your computer hardware:
Computer _____ Hard disk _____
5.25" disk drives _____ 3.5" disk drives _____
Video card _____ Monitor _____
Printer _____ Peripherals _____
Sound Board _____ CD-ROM _____

Where did you buy this book?
☐ Bookstore (name): _____
☐ Discount store (name): _____
☐ Computer store (name): _____
☐ Catalog (name): _____
☐ Direct from WGP   ☐ Other _____

What price did you pay for this book? _____

What influenced your purchase of this book?
☐ Recommendation   ☐ Advertisement
☐ Magazine review   ☐ Store display
☐ Mailing   ☐ Book's format
☐ Reputation of Waite Group Press   ☐ Other

How many computer books do you buy each year? _____

How many other Waite Group books do you own? _____

What is your favorite Waite Group book? _____
_____

Is there any program or subject you would like to see Waite Group Press cover in a similar approach? _____
_____

Additional comments? _____
_____
_____

Please send to: **Waite Group Press™**
200 Tamal Plaza
Corte Madera, CA 94925

☐ **Check here for a free Waite Group catalog**

STOP!

BEFORE YOU OPEN THE DISK OR CD-ROM PACKAGE ON THE FACING PAGE, CAREFULLY READ THE LICENSE AGREEMENT.

Opening this package indicates that you agree to abide by the license agreement found in the back of this book. If you do not agree with it, promptly return the unopened disk package (including the related book) to the place you obtained them for a refund.